BYZANTIUM BETWEEN THE OTTOMANS
AND THE LATINS

This is the first detailed analysis of Byzantine political attitudes towards the Ottomans and western Europeans during the critical last century of Byzantium. The book covers three major regions of the Byzantine Empire – Thessalonike, Constantinople, and the Morea – where the political orientations of aristocrats, merchants, the urban populace, peasants, and members of ecclesiastical and monastic circles are examined against the background of social and economic conditions. Through its particular focus on the political and religious dispositions of individuals, families, and social groups, the book offers an original view of late Byzantine politics and society which is not found in conventional narratives. Drawing on a wide range of Byzantine, western, and Ottoman sources, it authoritatively illustrates how late Byzantium was drawn into an Ottoman system in spite of the westward-looking orientation of the majority of its ruling elite.

NEVRA NECIPOĞLU is Professor of History at Boğaziçi University, Istanbul. She has written numerous journal articles on late Byzantine society, economy, and politics, and edited *Byzantine Constantinople: Monuments, Topography and Everyday Life* (2001).

BYZANTIUM BETWEEN THE OTTOMANS AND THE LATINS

Politics and Society in the Late Empire

NEVRA NECIPOĞLU

CAMBRIDGE
UNIVERSITY PRESS

CAMBRIDGE UNIVERSITY PRESS
Cambridge, New York, Melbourne, Madrid, Cape Town,
Singapore, São Paulo, Delhi, Tokyo, Mexico City

Cambridge University Press
The Edinburgh Building, Cambridge CB2 8RU, UK

Published in the United States of America by Cambridge University Press, New York

www.cambridge.org
Information on this title: www.cambridge.org/9781107403888

First published 2009
First paperback edition 2011

A catalogue record for this publication is available from the British Library

Library of Congress Cataloguing in Publication Data
Necipoğlu, Nevra.
Byzantium between the Ottomans and the Latins : politics and society in the
late empire / Nevra Necipoğlu.
p.   cm.
Includes bibliographical references and index.
ISBN 978-0-521-87738-1 (hardback)
1. Byzantine Empire – Politics and government – 1081–1453.   2. Political culture – Byzantine Empire.
3. Byzantine Empire – Social conditions.   4. Turkey – History – Ottoman Empire, 1288–1918.
5. East and West.   6. Byzantine Empire – Relations – Turkey.   7. Byzantine Empire – Relations –
Europe, Western.   8. Thessalonike (Greece) – History.   9. Istanbul (Turkey) – History.
10. Peloponnesus (Greece) – History.   I. Title.
DF631.N43   2008
949.5′04 – dc22   2008052116

ISBN 978-0-521-87738-1 Hardback
ISBN 978-1-107-40388-8 Paperback

To my parents, Ülkü and Hikmet Necipoğlu,
and
in loving memory of Angeliki Laiou

Contents

Maps

Acknowledgements

This book grew out of my doctoral dissertation submitted to the History Department of Harvard University in 1990. In the course both of the evolution of the dissertation and of its transformation into a book, I benefited from the guidance and support of numerous individuals and institutions.

My deepest gratitude goes to Angeliki E. Laiou – an exemplary teacher, thesis supervisor, colleague, and friend – who has been an endless source of inspiration and wisdom through all these years. Without her encouragement and continued interest, this project might have taken even longer to complete the transformation from thesis to book. The late Nicolas Oikonomidès deserves particular mention for the many invaluable suggestions as well as the enthusiastic support he provided up until his much regretted death in May 2000. To Ihor Ševčenko, who introduced me to the intricacies and mysteries of Byzantine Greek, I extend my very special thanks for his instruction, encouragement, and genuine interest in my work. Along the way, I was fortunate to have stimulating discussions with and to receive invaluable guidance, comments, references, offprints, or, during moments of despair, much needed personal support and encouragement from a number of friends and colleagues, among whom I warmly acknowledge Michel Balard, Irène Beldiceanu-Steinherr, Faruk Birtek, the late Robert Browning, Melek Delilbaşı, Marie Theres Fögen, Thierry Ganchou, Selahattin Hakman, Halil İnalcık, Mahnaz Ispahani, David Jacoby, Cemal Kafadar, Michel Kaplan, the late Alexander Kazhdan, Klaus-Peter Matschke, Cécile Morrisson, Gülru Necipoğlu, Soli Özel, Yeşim Sayar, Kostis Smyrlis, Alice-Mary Talbot, Betül Tanbay, and Elizabeth Zachariadou. I am also grateful to my colleagues at the History Department of Boğaziçi University, as well as to my graduate students, who contributed to the completion of this book through their moral support and enthusiasm in things Byzantine. Furthermore, I wish to thank Elif Çakın for her help in drawing the maps. Finally, I would like to express my lifelong indebtedness to my parents

Ülkü and Hikmet Necipoğlu, for they were the ones who sparked both my general interest in history and my particular curiosity for the Byzantine past of Istanbul on the occasion of our memorable visits to the Hagia Sophia and other historic sites of the city in my childhood days.

Material support for this work was provided by generous grants from a number of institutions. The Department of History and the Graduate School of Arts and Sciences of Harvard University supplied grants throughout the writing of the dissertation. A Junior Fellowship at Dumbarton Oaks during 1986–7 afforded me the first opportunity to engage in full-time research directed towards my topic. Much subsequent groundwork was laid once again at the same institution, where I spent the academic year 1993–4 as a Fellow in Byzantine Studies. I hereby would like to extend my thanks to all the members of the Dumbarton Oaks community, in particular to Irene Vaslef and Mark Zapatka of the Byzantine Library, who created a warm and friendly atmosphere that was most conducive to productive work on both occasions. Owing to the initiative and encouragement of Nuşin Asgari, I also spent a profitable month at Oxford as a Martin Harrison Memorial Fellow in the summer of 1995, which enabled me not only to utilize the abundant resources of the Bodleian Library, but to enjoy as well the hospitality of Mrs. Elizabeth Harrison. Further work on the book was undertaken during leave as a visiting professor at the University of Paris I in the spring of 2002. I am grateful to Michel Kaplan for his kind invitation and to the staff members of the Byzantine libraries of the Sorbonne, Collège de France, and Centre National de la Recherche Scientifique for their assistance.

Some of the material in this book has been discussed or has appeared in different versions in the following publications: "Ottoman merchants in Constantinople during the first half of the fifteenth century," *Byzantine and Modern Greek Studies* 16 (1992), 158–69; "Economic conditions in Constantinople during the siege of Bayezid I (1394–1402)," in *Constantinople and its Hinterland*, ed. C. Mango and G. Dagron (Aldershot, 1995), pp. 157–67; "Constantinopolitan merchants and the question of their attitudes towards Italians and Ottomans in the late Palaiologan period," in *Polypleuros nous: Miscellanea für Peter Schreiner zu seinem 60. Geburtstag*, ed. C. Scholz and G. Makris (Munich and Leipzig, 2000), pp. 251–63; "The aristocracy in late Byzantine Thessalonike: a case study of the city's *archontes* (late 14th and early 15th centuries)," *Dumbarton Oaks Papers* 57 (2003), 133–51; "Social and economic conditions in Constantinople during Mehmed II's siege," in *1453. Η άλωση της Κωνσταντινούπολης και η μετάβαση από τους μεσαιωνικούς στους νεώτερους χρόνους*, ed. T. Kioussopoulou (Iraklion, 2005), pp. 75–86.

Note on transliteration

In general, I have employed a Greek transliteration of Byzantine proper names and technical terms. However, some common first names have been rendered in their modern English form: for example, John, not Ioannes, and Constantine, not Konstantinos. By the same principle, for well-known place names I have generally preferred the use of conventional modern English spelling: for example, Constantinople, Athens, and Coron. For proper names and technical vocabulary pertaining to the Ottomans, on the other hand, modern Turkish orthography has been used.

Abbreviations

Anagnostes–Tsaras 　　　Ἰωάννου Ἀναγνώστου Διήγησις περὶ τῆς
　　　　　　　　　　　　τελευταίας ἁλώσεως τῆς Θεσσαλονίκης, ed.
　　　　　　　　　　　　J. Tsaras (Thessalonike, 1958)

Aşıkpaşazade–Atsız 　　　*Tevârîh-i Âl-i Osmân*, in *Osmanlı Tarihleri*, ed.
　　　　　　　　　　　　N. Atsız, vol. 1 (Istanbul, 1949)

Aşıkpaşazade–Giese 　　　*Die altosmanische Chronik des 'Āşıḳpaşazāde*,
　　　　　　　　　　　　ed. F. Giese (Leipzig, 1929)

ASLSP 　　　　　　　　*Atti della Società Ligure di Storia Patria*

B 　　　　　　　　　　*Byzantion*

Badoer 　　　　　　　　*Il libro dei conti di Giacomo Badoer
　　　　　　　　　　　　(Costantinopoli 1436–1440)*, ed. V. Dorini and
　　　　　　　　　　　　T. Bertelè (Rome, 1956)

Badoer: Indici 　　　　　*Il libro dei conti di Giacomo Badoer
　　　　　　　　　　　　(Costantinopoli 1436–1440). Complemento e
　　　　　　　　　　　　indici*, a cura di G. Bertelè (Padua, 2002)

BF 　　　　　　　　　　*Byzantinische Forschungen*

BMFD 　　　　　　　　*Byzantine Monastic Foundation Documents*,
　　　　　　　　　　　　ed. J. Thomas and A. C. Hero, 5 vols.
　　　　　　　　　　　　(Washington, DC, 2000)

BMGS 　　　　　　　　*Byzantine and Modern Greek Studies*

BS 　　　　　　　　　　*Byzantinoslavica*

ByzSt 　　　　　　　　*Byzantine Studies/Études Byzantines*

BZ 　　　　　　　　　　*Byzantinische Zeitschrift*

Chalkok.–Darkó 　　　　*Laonici Chalcocandylae Historiarum
　　　　　　　　　　　　Demonstrationes*, ed. E. Darkó, 2 vols.
　　　　　　　　　　　　(Budapest, 1922–7)

Chilandar 　　　　　　　*Actes de Chilandar*, vol. 1: *Des origines à 1319*,
　　　　　　　　　　　　ed. M. Živojinović, V. Kravari, and Ch. Giros
　　　　　　　　　　　　(Paris, 1998)

Chilandar (P)	*Actes de Chilandar*, vol. I: *Actes grecs*, ed. L. Petit, *Vizantijskij vremennik* 17 (1911; repr. Amsterdam, 1975)
Darrouzès, *Reg.*	J. Darrouzès, *Les regestes des actes du patriarcat de Constantinople*, vol. I: *Les actes des patriarches*, fasc. 6: *Les regestes de 1377 à 1410* (Paris, 1979)
Dionysiou	*Actes de Dionysiou*, ed. N. Oikonomidès (Paris, 1968)
Docheiariou	*Actes de Docheiariou*, ed. N. Oikonomidès (Paris, 1984)
Dölger, *Reg.*, vol. v	F. Dölger, *Regesten der Kaiserurkunden des oströmischen Reiches*, vol. v: *1341–1453* (Munich and Berlin, 1965)
DOP	*Dumbarton Oaks Papers*
Doukas–Grecu	*Ducas, Istoria Turco-Bizantină (1341–1462)*, ed. V. Grecu (Bucharest, 1958)
EEBΣ	Ἐπετηρὶς Ἑταιρείας Βυζαντινῶν Σπουδῶν
EHB	*The Economic History of Byzantium: From the Seventh through the Fifteenth Century*, ed. A. E. Laiou, 3 vols. (Washington, DC, 2002)
EI	*The Encyclopaedia of Islam*
EI²	*The Encyclopaedia of Islam*, 2nd edn.
Esphigménou	*Actes d'Esphigménou*, ed. J. Lefort (Paris, 1973)
Iorga, *Notes*	N. Iorga, *Notes et extraits pour servir à l'histoire des Croisades au XVe siècle*, 4 vols. (Paris, 1899–1915)
Isidore–Christophorides	Ἰσιδώρου Γλαβᾶ Ἀρχιεπισκόπου Θεσσαλονίκης ὁμιλίες, ed. B. Ch. Christophorides, 2 vols. (Thessalonike, 1992–6)
Isidore–Lampros	"Ἰσιδώρου μητροπολίτου Θεσσαλονίκης, Ὀκτὼ ἐπιστολαὶ ἀνέκδοτοι," ed. Sp. Lampros, Νέος Ἑλληνομνήμων 9 (1912), 343–414
Isidore–Laourdas	Ἰσιδώρου Ἀρχιεπισκόπου Θεσσαλονίκης, Ὁμιλίαι εἰς τὰς ἑορτὰς τοῦ Ἁγίου Δημητρίου, ed. B. Laourdas (Thessalonike, 1954)
Iviron	*Actes d'Iviron*, vols. III–IV, ed. J. Lefort, N. Oikonomidès, D. Papachryssanthou, and

	V. Kravari, with the collaboration of H. Métrévéli (Paris, 1994–5)
JÖB	*Jahrbuch der Österreichischen Byzantinistik*
Kalekas–Loenertz	*Correspondance de Manuel Calécas*, ed. R.-J. Loenertz (Vatican City, 1950)
Kritob.–Reinsch	*Critobuli Imbriotae Historiae*, ed. D. R. Reinsch (Berlin and New York, 1983)
Kydones–Loenertz	*Démétrius Cydonès Correspondance*, ed. R.-J. Loenertz, 2 vols. (Vatican City, 1956–60)
Lavra	*Actes de Lavra*, vols. II–IV, ed. P. Lemerle, A. Guillou, N. Svoronos, and D. Papachryssanthou (Paris, 1977–82)
Manuel II, Fun. Or.	*Manuel II Palaeologus, Funeral Oration on his Brother Theodore. Introduction, Text, Translation and Notes*, ed. J. Chrysostomides (Thessalonike, 1985)
MM	F. Miklosich and J. Müller, *Acta et diplomata graeca medii aevi sacra et profana*, 6 vols. (Vienna, 1860–90)
MP	J. Chrysostomides (ed.), *Monumenta Peloponnesiaca. Documents for the History of the Peloponnese in the 14th and 15th Centuries* (Camberley, 1995)
NE	Νέος Ἑλληνομνήμων
OCP	*Orientalia christiana periodica*
ODB	*The Oxford Dictionary of Byzantium*, gen. ed. A. P. Kazhdan, 3 vols. (New York and Oxford, 1991)
PG	*Patrologia cursus completus. Series graeca*, ed. J.-P. Migne, 161 vols. (Paris, 1857–66)
PLP	*Prosopographisches Lexikon der Palaiologenzeit*, ed. E. Trapp *et al.* (Vienna, 1976–94)
PP	Παλαιολόγεια καὶ Πελοποννησιακά, ed. Sp. Lampros, 4 vols. (Athens, 1912–30; repr. 1972)
REB	*Revue des Études Byzantines*
RESEE	*Revue des Études Sud-Est Européennes*
RIS	*Rerum italicarum scriptores*, ed. L. A. Muratori, new edn.
ROL	*Revue de l'Orient Latin*

Saint-Pantéléèmôn	*Actes de Saint-Pantéléèmôn*, ed. P. Lemerle, G. Dagron, and S. Ćirković (Paris, 1982)
Sathas, *Documents*	C. N. Sathas, *Documents inédits relatifs à l'histoire de la Grèce au Moyen Âge*, 9 vols. (Paris and Venice, 1880–90)
Schatzkammer	F. Dölger, *Aus den Schatzkammern des Heiligen Berges* (Munich, 1948)
Sphrantzes–Grecu	*Georgios Sphrantzes, Memorii, 1401–1477*, ed. V. Grecu (Bucharest, 1966)
StVen	*Studi veneziani*
SüdostF	*Südost-Forschungen*
Symeon–Balfour	*Politico-Historical Works of Symeon Archbishop of Thessalonica (1416/17 to 1429)*, ed. D. Balfour (Vienna, 1979)
Symeon–Phountoules	Συμεὼν ἀρχιεπισκόπου Θεσσαλονίκης. Τὰ λειτουργικὰ συγγράμματα, vol. ι: Εὐχαὶ καὶ ὕμνοι, ed. I. M. Phountoules (Thessalonike, 1968)
Thiriet, *Assemblées*	F. Thiriet, *Délibérations des assemblées vénitiennes concernant la Romanie*, vol. ιι: *1364–1463* (Paris and The Hague, 1971)
Thiriet, *Régestes*	F. Thiriet, *Régestes des délibérations du Sénat de Venise concernant la Romanie*, 3 vols. (Paris and The Hague, 1958–61)
TM	*Travaux et Mémoires*
Vatopédi	*Actes de Vatopédi*, vol. ιι, ed. J. Lefort, V. Kravari, Ch. Giros, and K. Smyrlis (Paris, 2006)
VV	*Vizantijskij vremennik*
WZKM	*Wiener Zeitschrift für die Kunde des Morgenlandes*
Xénophon	*Actes de Xénophon*, ed. D. Papachryssanthou (Paris, 1986)
Xéropotamou	*Actes de Xéropotamou*, ed. J. Bompaire (Paris, 1964)
Zographou	*Actes de Zographou*, ed. W. Regel, E. Kurtz, and B. Korablev, *VV* 13 (1907)
ZRVI	*Zbornik radova Vizantološkog Instituta*

Map 1 The Byzantine world in the fourteenth–fifteenth
centuries

0   50   100   150   200   250 km

0   50   100   150 miles

Tana

Sea of Azov

CRIMEA

Kaffa

Symbolon
(Cembalo)

LACHIA

River Danube

B l a c k   S e a

Nikopolis
GARIA
Trnovo

Varna

Mesembria

River Maritsa

Amastris

Trebizond

Edirne
(Adrianople)
Černomen
Didymoteichon
THRACE

Rhaidestos (Rodosto)
Herakleia
Selymbria
CONSTANTINOPLE
Pera (Galata)
Scutari (Üsküdar)

Panidos
Thasos   Ainos
Tzympe
Imbros   Gallipoli (Gelibolu)
Lemnos   Abydos
Tenedos

Yarhisar
Göynük
Daraklı Yenicesi
Bursa

Bithynia

Ankara

ANATOLIA

Kotyaeion
(Kütahya)

River Euphrates

Lesbos
Skyros
Chios

Nea Phokaia
Phokaia

Philadelphia

Aegean Sea

Ephesus   Aydın

Naxos

Rhodes

CYPRUS

Candia

CRETE

S e a

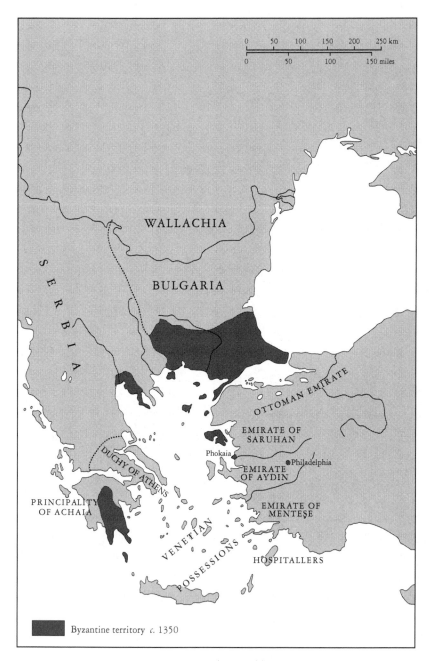

0   50   100   150   200   250 km
0   50   100   150 miles

Byzantine territory *c.* 1350

Map 2 Byzantium and its neighbors, *c.* 1350

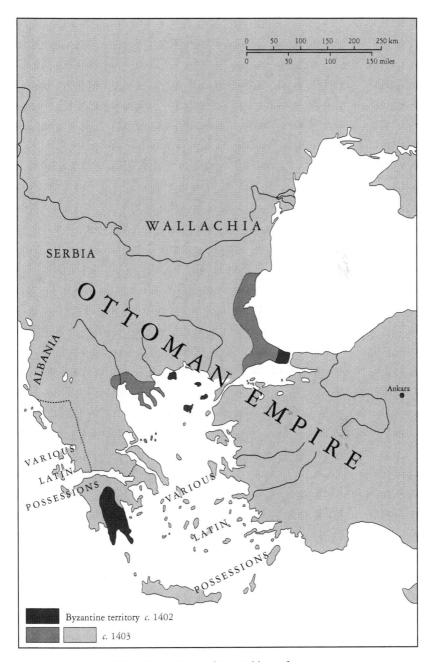

Map 3 Byzantium and its neighbors after 1402

PART I

Introduction and political setting

CHAPTER I

The topic and the sources

This book is a study of the political attitudes that emerged among different segments of Byzantine society in response to the Ottoman expansion. Its principal aims are, first, to categorize these attitudes with regard to specific groupings among the urban and rural populations of the Byzantine Empire (e.g. the aristocracy, merchants, lower classes, ecclesiastical and monastic circles) and, secondly, to explore the underlying social and economic factors, besides the more apparent political and religious ones, that played a role in the formation of political attitudes. In an atmosphere of extreme political and military instability marked by a number of civil wars and foreign invasions during the fourteenth and fifteenth centuries, people from different segments of Byzantine society in different regions of the empire sought by various means to secure their best interests in the face of the rapidly expanding Ottoman Empire. How they reacted to the Ottoman advance, the kinds of solutions they sought, the preferences they developed with respect to foreign alliances, and the local factors that played a role in regional variations are complex issues that merit careful investigation. In themselves, the options that were available as far as foreign political orientations are concerned were perhaps limited, consisting of either a cooperation with the Latin West against the Ottomans, or an accommodation with the Ottomans, or, in rejection of both, the maintenance of an opposition to the Ottomans by means of the empire's own resources and capacities.[1] What is, however, more complex and of greater interest for the purposes of

---

[1] During the first half of the fourteenth century, a cooperation with the Orthodox Balkan states against the Ottomans was another option that some Byzantines had tried, but it was no longer operative in the period covered by the present work. See D. A. Zakythinos, "Démétrius Cydonès et l'entente balkanique au XIVe siècle," in Zakythinos, *La Grèce et les Balkans* (Athens, 1947), pp. 44–56; J. W. Barker, "The question of ethnic antagonisms among Balkan states of the fourteenth century," in *Peace and War in Byzantium. Essays in Honor of George T. Dennis, S.J.*, ed. T. S. Miller and J. Nesbitt (Washington, DC, 1995), pp. 165–77; E. Malamut, "Les discours de Démétrius Cydonès comme témoignage de l'idéologie byzantine vis-à-vis des peuples de l'Europe orientale dans les années 1360–1372," in *Byzantium and East Central Europe*, ed. G. Prinzing and M. Salamon (= *Byzantina et Slavica Cracoviensia*, vol. III) (Cracow, 2001), pp. 203–19.

this study is the links that can be established between specific individuals or groups, their political dispositions, and their socioeconomic interests. Through a multilayered comparison of the views embraced by different groups within a given urban or rural environment and those embraced by members of the same group across different regions of the empire, the aim is to present political attitudes in all their complexity and ambivalence.

From what has been said above, it ought to be clear that this is not a study of late Byzantine politics as such. It has not been my intention to investigate the institutions and structures through which political choices were negotiated and implemented in the late Byzantine world. My main objective is to explore Byzantine attitudes towards the Ottomans and western Europeans, focusing on the political and religious views of individuals, families, and social groups, which previously have not been investigated adequately. Thus the reader should not be surprised to find that certain aspects of the political history of late Byzantium which seemed to have little relevance for an analysis of political attitudes have been overlooked in this book. It might have been worthwhile, for instance, to concentrate on the political process itself, which would have required an in-depth analysis of the role of the emperor, the imperial family, the aristocracy, the populace, and the clergy and monks in the politics of the late Byzantine Empire, as well as a discussion of the structure of the aristocratic family and how it affected Palaiologan imperial politics. But such themes would take us well beyond the parameters of the present study and constitute the subject matter of an entirely different book.

For the sake of convenience the attitudes corresponding to the three options enumerated above could be labeled as pro-Latin/anti-Ottoman, pro-Ottoman/anti-Latin, and anti-Latin/anti-Ottoman. But such labels, when used without qualification, conceal the nuances and variations involved in the formation of political attitudes. In the present work, the terms "pro-Ottoman," "pro-Latin," "anti-Ottoman," and "anti-Latin" are used most of the time to designate people who actively supported or opposed the Ottomans or the Latins. An effort is made to avoid these terms as much as possible in cases when the Byzantines showed an inclination to favor one or the other foreign group out of other considerations, such as in order to put an end to a siege or war, or so as to overcome hunger, famine, and/or poverty. It is preferable to speak in these cases of conciliatory attitudes or of attitudes of accommodation, and to try to outline the specific circumstances that led people to adopt particular political positions. Another term whose meaning and use require some explanation in advance is the word "Latin." In Byzantine texts the word appears both as a collective designation for adherents to the Roman Catholic faith, and as a term describing people from specific political entities in the West, such as the Venetians, the Genoese, or the Navarrese. In this study the term is used in the latter sense primarily – that is, in reference to western European powers, and especially, but not exclusively, in reference to Italians, with whom many Byzantines had close economic and political contacts in the Palaiologan period. Following Byzantine practice, however, it is sometimes used in a predominantly religious sense as a synonym for "Catholic" as well. In either case, the context in which the term "Latin" appears reveals the sense in which it is being used if its specific meaning has not been pointed out.

Reduced politically, administratively, and economically, the Byzantine Empire in the late Palaiologan period had neither sufficient strength nor the means to resist the Ottomans on its own and consequently needed the assistance of foreign allies. In addition to the military pressure of the Ottomans, the weak and decentralized empire of the Palaiologoi faced the economic pressure of the Italian maritime states, which controlled much of its trade at this time. Furthermore, the appeals of the Byzantine state to the West for a joint military venture against the Ottomans were by necessity often addressed to the pope, who alone had sufficient influence and authority to unite and mobilize the diverse powers of Christian Europe towards such an enterprise. Yet on each occasion the Byzantines appealed to the papacy, they encountered the recurring response that the centuries-old schism that separated the Roman Catholic and Greek Orthodox Churches had to be healed first, through the return of the latter to the former's fold. Such, then, was the dual challenge that Byzantium faced from the Ottoman and Latin worlds during the late Palaiologan period.

In terms of chronology, this study covers the pivotal period from the early 1370s, when Byzantium became a tributary vassal of the Ottomans, to 1460, the year in which Mistra and the so-called Despotate of the Morea fell to the forces of Mehmed the Conqueror. Geographically, it focuses on three major areas of the Byzantine Empire: Thessalonike, Constantinople, and the Morea.[2] Some general problems are addressed throughout the book with the purpose of establishing links between political attitudes and socioeconomic factors. These include, first, the impact of Byzantine–Ottoman military conflicts on economic and social life in the two cities mentioned above, and their influence on the political orientation of different segments of the urban population. Secondly, within the context of

---

[2] For the reasons underlying the exclusion of Trebizond from this work, see below, ch. 2, note 55.

rural areas encompassing the environs of Thessalonike and the province of Morea in the Peloponnese, the social and economic consequences of the loss of major productive Byzantine territories to the Ottomans are considered, with special emphasis on the political behavior of the landed aristocracy. The position of the members of ecclesiastical and monastic circles with regard to the Ottomans and the Latins constitutes another theme that is embedded in each individual treatment of the geographic regions named above.

These broad issues provide the framework for the specific questions which are explored in particular chapters. Chapter 2 is intended to set the historical background through a discussion of major political developments of the Palaiologan era, including some of the long-term consequences of the Fourth Crusade, the expansion of the Ottomans in Byzantine territories and their methods of conquest, as well as the official Byzantine policy towards the Ottomans, the western powers, and the papacy. In Part II, which is devoted to Thessalonike and its surrounding countryside, chapter 3 begins by presenting a general outline of the city's social structure, historical events, and the political attitudes of its inhabitants from 1382 to 1430. Chapters 4 and 5 supplement this overview with individual analyses of the social and economic conditions during three different administrations – Byzantine, Ottoman, and Venetian – under which the Thessalonians lived in the course of this period. With Part III we turn to Constantinople, the imperial capital. Chapter 6 examines the dissensions and rivalries within the Byzantine court, both among members of the ruling dynasty and among civil dignitaries, which opened the way for a considerable degree of Ottoman interference in the internal affairs of Byzantium during the late fourteenth and early fifteenth centuries. Chapter 7 deals with the first Ottoman siege of Constantinople by Bayezid I, treating it as a case study for the specific economic adjustments, social tensions, and political responses to which a direct military threat from the Ottomans gave rise in the imperial city. In chapter 8 the dispositions of various individuals or social groups in Constantinople vis-à-vis the Ottomans, the Latins, and the question of Church union are set forth and analyzed within the context of the political, economic, and social developments of the last fifty years preceding the city's fall to the Ottomans in 1453. The final two chapters of the book, constituting Part IV, focus on the Despotate of the Morea. They pick up some of the themes addressed in connection with the countryside of Thessalonike and provide a comparative basis for highlighting the local factors that played a role in the attitudes embraced by the empire's rural populations within the realm of foreign politics.

This book is intended to close a gap in Byzantine studies, given that no comprehensive work has yet been undertaken on the political orientations of individuals or groups in Byzantine society during the period in question, even though several monographs are available on the political history of the late Byzantine Empire and its diplomatic relations with foreign states. There exist some specialized studies concerned with various aspects of the relations of Byzantium with the Ottomans and/or the Latins which take into account the political preferences of individuals or social groups, but the scope of these works is limited either chronologically, or geographically, or both. Such, for instance, is George T. Dennis' excellent monograph on the independent regime of Manuel II in Thessalonike from 1382 to 1387.³ Klaus-Peter Matschke's inspiring book on the battle of Ankara and its aftermath, too, covers a relatively short period between 1402 and 1422. Moreover, within the general framework of Byzantine–Ottoman relations, this particular period which coincides with the Ottoman interregnum is quite unrepresentative, being marked by intense political instability and internal dissension unprecedented at any other point in Ottoman history.⁴ Perhaps the study that comes closest to part of the subject matter of the present book is an article by Michel Balivet entitled "Le personnage du 'turcophile' dans les sources byzantines antérieures au Concile de Florence (1370–1430)," which, as its title indicates, is restricted to evidence from Byzantine sources, does not go beyond the Council of Florence, and is constrained in scope and range.⁵ By contrast, the same author's more recent book on the contacts and exchanges between the Byzantine and Turkish worlds, which spans the eleventh to the nineteenth centuries, offers a global view yet lacks for obvious reasons a detailed and systematic treatment of the vast period under consideration.⁶ As for Speros Vryonis' monumental book on the Turkification and Islamization of medieval Anatolia, this study focuses on a region that had by and large fallen out of the hands of the Byzantine Empire in the period treated by the present work.⁷ Finally, much

³ G. T. Dennis, *The Reign of Manuel II Palaeologus in Thessalonica, 1382–1387* (Rome, 1960).
⁴ K.-P. Matschke, *Die Schlacht bei Ankara und das Schicksal von Byzanz; Studien zur spätbyzantinischen Geschichte zwischen 1402 und 1422* (Weimar, 1981). For Matschke's articles that are relevant to the present topic, see the Bibliography.
⁵ *Travaux et Recherches en Turquie* 2 (1984), 111–29. This article and the same author's other essays on various aspects of Byzantine–Ottoman relations have been collected and reprinted in M. Balivet, *Byzantins et Ottomans: relations, interaction, succession* (Istanbul, 1999).
⁶ M. Balivet, *Romanie byzantine et pays de Rûm turc: histoire d'un espace d'imbrication gréco-turque* (Istanbul, 1994).
⁷ Sp. Vryonis, Jr., *The Decline of Medieval Hellenism in Asia Minor and the Process of Islamization from the Eleventh through the Fifteenth Century* (Berkeley and Los Angeles, 1971). For Vryonis' articles that are of relevance to our subject matter, see the Bibliography.

relevant material on Byzantine–Ottoman relations can be found scattered throughout the voluminous works of Halil İnalcık, as illustrated by the abundance of references to his studies in my footnotes.[8]

Concerning Byzantine–Latin relations, on the other hand, research over the last few decades has made important strides, particularly with regard to the social and economic aspects of the topic. This book, in fact, owes a great deal to the pioneering works of Michel Balard, Nicolas Oikonomidès, and Angeliki E. Laiou which have laid the groundwork for demonstrating the commercial interests that linked part of the Byzantine aristocracy to the Italians in the Palaiologan period.[9]

In approaching a subject such as the present one, much depends on the kinds of primary sources used and their possible biases, and, in this particular case, on their position regarding the Ottomans and the Latins. It is, therefore, necessary to proceed with a discussion of the sources and the political attitudes they themselves stand for in order to be able to assess the reliability of the information they provide on the political attitudes of others. Among Byzantine sources, narrative histories ought to be mentioned first. For the period following 1370 there are the fifteenth-century histories of George Sphrantzes, Doukas, Laonikos Chalkokondyles, and Kritoboulos of Imbros, all written after the fall of Constantinople. Sphrantzes' work covers the period from 1401, the year of his birth, to 1477, and is written in the form of annalistic memoirs. Sphrantzes was a court official who served the last three emperors of Byzantium and held administrative functions both in the imperial capital and in the Despotate of the Morea. He went on several diplomatic missions and embassies to the Ottomans, the king of Georgia, Trebizond, the Morea, and Cyprus. He also lived through the Ottoman conquest, first, of Constantinople and, then, of the Morea, after which he fled to the Venetian island of Corfu. Hence, Sphrantzes was a well-informed historian as well as an active participant in the events about which he wrote.[10] During the conquest of Constantinople, Sphrantzes and

[8] See the Bibliography.

[9] See especially M. Balard, *La Romanie génoise (XIIe–début du XVe siècle)*, 2 vols. (Rome and Genoa, 1978); N. Oikonomidès, *Hommes d'affaires grecs et latins à Constantinople (XIIIe–XVe siècles)* (Montreal and Paris, 1979); A. E. Laiou-Thomadakis, "The Byzantine economy in the Mediterranean trade system, thirteenth–fifteenth centuries," *DOP* 34–5 (1982), 177–222; A. E. Laiou-Thomadakis, "The Greek merchant of the Palaeologan period: a collective portrait," Πρακτικά τῆς Ἀκαδημίας Ἀθηνῶν 57 (1982), 96–132. For the current state of scholarship on this subject, see now K.-P. Matschke, "Commerce, trade, markets, and money: thirteenth–fifteenth centuries," in *EHB*, vol. II, pp. 771–806, esp. 789–99.

[10] On Sphrantzes, see R.-J. Loenertz, "Autour du Chronicon Maius attribué à Georges Phrantzès," in *Miscellanea Giovanni Mercati*, vol. III (Vatican, 1946), pp. 273–311; G. Moravcsik, *Byzantinoturcica. Die byzantinischen Quellen der Geschichte der Türkvölker*, 2nd edn., vol. I (Berlin, 1958; repr. Leiden,

his family were taken captive by the Ottomans, but soon thereafter he was ransomed and a year later secured the ransom of his wife as well. Yet his children, whom Mehmed II bought for himself, remained under Ottoman domination. His son John, accused of plotting to assassinate the Sultan, was executed at the end of 1453, while his daughter Thamar died of an infectious disease in Mehmed II's harem in 1455.[11] The hardships Sphrantzes and his family suffered at the hands of the Ottomans, his flight, twice, from Ottoman-occupied places, and his eventual settlement in Venetian Corfu indicate that he had no sympathy at all for the Ottomans. In addition to signs of his pro-western inclinations, Sphrantzes is also known, just on the eve of the fall of Constantinople, to have favored the implementation of the Union of Florence and the appointment of Cardinal Isidore of Kiev as patriarch of Constantinople, "in the hope that various advantages would come from him."[12] Yet later, with the benefit of hindsight, he pointed to the Union of Florence as the major cause for the capture of the Byzantine capital and held this opinion at the time when he was composing his chronicle.[13]

Doukas, on the other hand, who lived most of his life in the service of the Genoese, first in New Phokaia, then on the island of Lesbos, not only fostered pro-Latin feelings but was also a staunch advocate of the union of Churches, which he viewed as the only policy capable of saving the Byzantine Empire. He, therefore, blamed the activities of the anti-unionists in Constantinople for the failure of the city before the Ottoman armies in 1453.[14] It is of interest to note that Doukas' grandfather, Michael Doukas, had been a partisan of John VI Kantakouzenos in the civil war of 1341–7 and, following his imprisonment by John VI's opponents, had fled from Constantinople and sought refuge in Ephesus with Isa Beg, the Turkish emir of Aydın. Doukas claims that his grandfather remained thereafter in the service of the Aydınoğlu dynasty, foreseeing that the Turks would soon take control over the European territories of the Byzantine Empire, just as they had conquered Asia Minor.[15] Yet, while the historian inherited his grandfather's dislike of the Palaiologos dynasty of Byzantium,[16] he chose a different course by orienting himself not towards the Turks but rather

---

1983), pp. 282–8; V. Grecu, "Georgios Sphrantzes. Leben und Werk. Makarios Melissenos und sein Werk," *BS* 26 (1965), 62–73.
[11] Sphrantzes–Grecu, pp. 98, 104, 106.   [12] Ibid., p. 100.   [13] Ibid., p. 58.
[14] Doukas–Grecu, pp. 315–19, 323–5, 327–9, 365. On Doukas, see W. Miller, "The historians Doukas and Phrantzes," *Journal of Hellenic Studies* 46 (1926), 63–71; V. Grecu, "Pour une meilleure connaissance de l'historien Doukas," in *Mémorial Louis Petit* (Paris, 1948), pp. 128–41; Moravcsik, *Byzantinoturcica*, vol. I, pp. 247–51.
[15] Doukas–Grecu, pp. 41–7.   [16] Ibid., pp. 49, 73.

towards the Latins, and entering the service of the Genoese in their eastern Mediterranean possessions. Despite his firm pro-Latin stance, Doukas tries to be objective in his narrative, which goes down to the year 1462, finding fault at times with the Genoese, at times with the Venetians, but particularly in his account of the union controversy he cannot conceal his partiality and biases.

While Sphrantzes and Doukas took as the theme of their histories the fall of the Byzantine Empire, the Athenian aristocrat Laonikos Chalkokondyles centered his work, covering the period 1298–1463, around the theme of the Ottomans and their rise to power. However, as far as Chalkokondyles' political preferences are concerned, he can be described as neither pro-Ottoman nor pro-Latin. When composing his history during the 1480s, he still cherished the hope that the day might come when the Byzantine people would be reunited within a state ruled by a Greek emperor.[17] Chalkokondyles, who spent the years 1435–60 at the court of the Despots in Mistra, provides a detailed firsthand account of events in the Peloponnese. For the rest, his narrative, though useful, is filled with chronological inaccuracies and requires the aid of other sources.

Kritoboulos of Imbros, another aristocratic author, differs from the three historians discussed above in terms of both his political standing and the scope of his work, which is a partial account of the reign of Mehmed II covering the years from 1451 to 1467. In 1453 Kritoboulos, through embassies to the Sultan and to Hamza Beg, the governor of Gallipoli (Gelibolu) and admiral of the Ottoman fleet, arranged for the peaceful surrender of the islands of Imbros, Lemnos, and Thasos in order to prevent their capture by force. Shortly thereafter, Kritoboulos' submission to the Sultan was rewarded by his assignment to Imbros as governor, a post he held until the island's capture by the Venetians in 1466.[18] He then fled to Ottoman Istanbul, where he wrote his history of Mehmed II, whom he regarded as "the supreme autocrat, emperor of emperors . . . lord of land and sea by the will of God."[19] In short, Kritoboulos was a representative of the group

---

[17] Chalkok.–Darkó, vol. 1, p. 2. On Chalkokondyles, see W. Miller, "The last Athenian historian: Laonikos Chalkokondyles," *Journal of Hellenic Studies* 42 (1922), 36–49; Moravcsik, *Byzantinoturcica*, vol. 1, pp. 391–7; A. Wifstrand, *Laonikos Chalkokondyles, der letzte Athener. Ein Vortrag* (Lund, 1972); N. Nicoloudis, *Laonikos Chalkokondyles, A Translation and Commentary of the "Demonstrations of Histories" (Books I–III)* (Athens, 1996), pp. 41–86; J. Harris, "Laonikos Chalkokondyles and the rise of the Ottoman Turks," *BMGS* 27 (2003), 153–70.

[18] Kritob.–Reinsch, pp. 85–6, 107. On Kritoboulos, see V. Grecu, "Kritobulos aus Imbros," *BS* 18 (1957), 1–17; Moravcsik, *Byzantinoturcica*, vol. 1, pp. 432–5; G. Emrich, "Michael Kritobulos, der byzantinische Geschichtsschreiber Mehmeds II.," *Materialia Turcica* 1 (1975), 35–43.

[19] Kritob.–Reinsch, p. 3: "αὐτοκράτορι μεγίστῳ, βασιλεῖ βασιλέων Μεχεμέτει . . . κυρίῳ γῆς καὶ θαλάσσης θεοῦ θελήματι."

in Byzantium that opted for an accommodation and understanding with the Ottomans in the face of the political realities of the time, and that recognized Sultan Mehmed II as the legitimate successor of the Christian Byzantine emperors.

Besides the works of these four major historians, shorter works by Byzantine eyewitnesses to particular events have survived, such as an anonymous account of Bayezid I's blockade of Constantinople (1394–1402),[20] John Kananos' description of the siege of the capital by Murad II in 1422,[21] or John Anagnostes' account of the capture of Thessalonike by the same Sultan in 1430.[22] Since the last source is used extensively in the chapters on Thessalonike, its author merits a few words here. From what he writes, it appears that Anagnostes, a native Thessalonian, was not particularly fond of the Venetians who ruled his city during 1423–30 and seems to have shared the opinion of those who wished to surrender to Murad II's forces without resistance.[23] In the course of the city's conquest, Anagnostes fell captive to the Ottomans but soon afterwards regained his freedom along with many others by means of the money which the Serbian Despot George Branković offered for their ransom. The author then returned to the Ottoman-occupied city, even though he was to regret this later when, around 1432–3, Murad II began to institute a set of new policies, including the confiscation of religious and secular buildings, that hurt the interests of the Greek community in Thessalonike.[24] Finally, together with the more concise historical works used in this study, the Byzantine short chronicles ought to be mentioned as well, since one often finds in these brief and chronologically accurate notices invaluable information that is unattested elsewhere.[25]

Among the most important contemporary literary sources written by Byzantines are the works of Demetrios Kydones. The leading intellectual and statesman of his time, Kydones came from an aristocratic family of Thessalonike and started his political career as a partisan of John VI Kantakouzenos in the civil war of 1341–7. Following the latter's abdication in 1354, he entered the service of John V Palaiologos and held the post

[20] P. Gautier, "Un récit inédit sur le siège de Constantinople par les Turcs (1394–1402)," *REB* 23 (1965), 100–17.

[21] Giovanni Cananos, *L'assedio di Costantinopoli. Introduzione, testo critico, traduzione, note e lessico*, ed. E. Pinto (Messina, 1977).

[22] Anagnostes–Tsaras. For an evaluation of this work, see Sp. Vryonis, Jr., "The Ottoman conquest of Thessaloniki in 1430," in *Continuity and Change in Late Byzantine and Early Ottoman Society*, ed. A. Bryer and H. Lowry (Birmingham and Washington, DC, 1986), pp. 281–304.

[23] Anagnostes–Tsaras, pp. 6–8.   [24] Ibid., pp. 56, 64–6.

[25] P. Schreiner (ed.), *Die byzantinischen Kleinchroniken*, 3 vols. (Vienna, 1975–9).

of *mesazon* for the next thirty years during which he maintained a tight friendship with the Emperor's son Manuel II, to whom he was initially assigned as tutor. Kydones, who from a religious, intellectual, and political standpoint identified strongly with the world of Latin Christendom, converted to the Catholic faith around 1357. In 1369 he accompanied John V to Rome and was closely involved with the Emperor's own conversion to Catholicism, which was in accordance with Kydones' belief that only a policy of rapprochement, political as well as theological, with the papacy and western European powers could save the empire from the Ottoman threat.[26] Concerning the Latins and Rome, he wrote, "from the beginning we were both citizens of, as it were, one city, the Church, and we lived under the same laws and customs, and we obeyed the same rulers. Later on – I don't know what happened – we separated from one another."[27] Indeed, Kydones spent almost all his professional life trying to bring this separation to an end. He also appealed to the Venetian Senate for citizenship, which he was granted in 1391.[28] Kydones' writings, which include several hundreds of letters addressed between 1346 and 1391 to almost all the prominent figures of the period,[29] "Apologies" documenting the evolution of his religious convictions,[30] and speeches exhorting the Byzantines to unite with the Latins or other Christians against the Ottomans,[31] are invaluable sources that portray different aspects of the political climate of the Byzantine Empire in the second half of the fourteenth century. The correspondence of Manuel Kalekas (d. 1410), who was a pupil of Kydones, as well as a Catholic convert and a supporter of ecclesiastical union like his teacher, is of importance, too, in this respect.[32] Another contemporary of Manuel Kalekas who lived into the late 1430s and wrote letters, poems,

---

[26] On Demetrios Kydones, see R.-J. Loenertz, "Démétrius Cydonès. I: De la naissance à l'année 1373," *OCP* 36 (1970), 47–72 and "Démétrius Cydonès. II: De 1373 à 1375," *OCP* 37 (1971), 5–39; F. Tinnefeld (trans.), *Demetrios Kydones, Briefe*, vol. I/1 (Stuttgart, 1981), pp. 4–52; F. Kianka, "Demetrius Cydones (c.1324 – c.1397): intellectual and diplomatic relations between Byzantium and the West in the fourteenth century," unpublished PhD thesis, Fordham University (1981); F. Kianka, "Byzantine–Papal diplomacy: the role of Demetrius Cydones," *The International History Review* 7 (1985), 175–213; F. Kianka, "Demetrios Kydones and Italy," *DOP* 49 (1995), 99–110.

[27] Demetrios Kydones, "Apologie della propria fede: I. Ai Greci Ortodossi," ed. G. Mercati, in *Notizie di Procoro e Demetrio Cidone, Manuele Caleca e Teodoro Meliteniota ed altri appunti per la storia della teologia e della letteratura bizantina del secolo XIV* (Vatican City, 1931), p. 401, lines 39–45; trans. by F. Kianka, "The *Apology* of Demetrius Cydones: a fourteenth-century autobiographical source," *ByzSt* 7/1 (1980), 70, n. 82.

[28] Kydones–Loenertz, vol. II, pp. 452–3 (Appendix E.1); cf. R.-J. Loenertz, "Démétrius Cydonès, citoyen de Venise," *Echos d'Orient* 37 (1938), 125–6.

[29] Kydones–Loenertz, vols. I–II.   [30] Mercati (ed.), *Notizie*, pp. 359–435.

[31] "Oratio pro subsidio Latinorum" and "Oratio de non reddenda Callipoli," both in *PG* 154, cols. 961–1008, 1009–36; cf. Malamut, "Les discours de Démétrius Cydonès," pp. 203–19.

[32] See Kalekas–Loenertz.

and other short works was John Chortasmenos.[33] He served as a scribe in
the patriarchate of Constantinople and was a champion of Orthodoxy, in
contrast to both Kydones and Kalekas. The monk Joseph Bryennios, too,
was an ardent supporter of Orthodoxy, whose writings, like those of his
contemporary Chortasmenos, are of particular interest not only as reflections of the anti-unionist position, but also on account of the information
they bear on social conditions in the late Byzantine capital.[34]

The writings of Emperor Manuel II Palaiologos occupy a significant
place among the literary sources of the late fourteenth and early fifteenth
centuries. Since Manuel II's views and policies regarding the foreign political and religious orientation of the Byzantine state are discussed in detail
throughout the book, they will not be dealt with here. Suffice it to say
that his letters and the funeral oration which he composed for his brother
Theodore I (d. 1407) are rich in historical information, the latter specifically on the Morea, while his "Discourse of Counsel to the Thessalonians"
is a short but important text that reveals the political tendencies of the
citizens of Thessalonike in the 1380s.[35]

About Thessalonike another group of literary sources exist that are of
a different nature than those discussed so far. These are the homilies of
the metropolitans Isidore Glabas (1380–96) and Symeon (1416/17–29).[36]
The aristocratic origin and high rank of nearly all the aforementioned
authors may have already prompted suspicions about whether the attitudes
reflected in their writings were held by Byzantine society at large or whether
these represent the views of a limited circle of intellectuals who had little
understanding of or interest in the beliefs held by the common people of
Byzantium. Evidence from homiletic literature provides a partial remedy to
this fundamental problem since the preachings of the clergy were directed
at the entire society and can therefore be expected to be more representative

---

[33] *Johannes Chortasmenos (ca.1370–ca.1436/37). Briefe, Gedichte und kleine Schriften; Einleitung, Regesten,
Prosopographie, Text*, ed. H. Hunger (Vienna, 1969).

[34] Ἰωσὴφ μοναχοῦ τοῦ Βρυεννίου τὰ εὑρεθέντα, vols. I–II, ed. E. Boulgares (Leipzig, 1768);
vol. III: Τὰ παραλειπόμενα, ed. T. Mandakases (Leipzig, 1784). On Bryennios, see N. B. Tomadakes,
Σύλλαβος Βυζαντινῶν μελετῶν καὶ κειμένων (Athens, 1961), pp. 489–611; Kalekas–Loenertz,
pp. 95–105.

[35] *The Letters of Manuel II Palaeologus*, ed. and trans. G. T. Dennis (Washington, DC, 1977); *Manuel
II, Fun. Or.*; " Ὁ 'συμβουλευτικὸς πρὸς τοὺς Θεσσαλονικεῖς' τοῦ Μανουὴλ Παλαιολόγου," ed.
B. Laourdas, *Μακεδονικά* 3 (1955), 290–307.

[36] Isidore–Christophorides, vols. I–II; Isidore–Laourdas; "Ἰσιδώρου Ἀρχιεπισκόπου Θεσσαλονίκης
ὁμιλία περὶ τῆς ἁρπαγῆς τῶν παίδων καὶ περὶ τῆς μελλούσης κρίσεως," ed. B. Laourdas,
Ἑλληνικά 4 (1953), 389–98; Symeon–Balfour. It should be noted that the published homilies of
the metropolitan Gabriel (1397–1416/17) are of a predominantly religious character and not so rich
in historical information: "Γαβριὴλ Θεσσαλονίκης ὁμιλίαι," ed. B. Laourdas, Ἀθηνᾶ 57 (1953),
141–78.

of the attitudes that prevailed among people of lower social rank. As to the particular politico-religious outlook of Isidore Glabas and Symeon, they both were proponents of an anti-Ottoman/anti-Latin position, even though Isidore, who witnessed the subjection of Thessalonike to Ottoman domination, adopted in the end a conciliatory attitude towards the Turks, while Symeon eventually came to accept the city's transfer to Venetian rule as an act that prevented its betrayal to the Ottomans.[37]

From the last decades of Byzantium, a large number of rhetorical, theological, and epistolary works by Byzantine authors have survived which shed some light on the question of political attitudes in Constantinople and in the Morea. The issue that preoccupied many intellectuals at this time was the controversial union concluded at the Council of Florence in 1439. Among works dealing with this issue, those by the anti-unionist leaders George-Gennadios Scholarios and John Eugenikos are very useful.[38] We also have a somewhat apologetic account of the Council of Florence and its aftermath by Sylvester Syropoulos, the grand ecclesiarch of Saint Sophia in Constantinople, who accepted the Union at Florence, but upon returning to the capital renounced his act along with many others, including Scholarios.[39] On the opposite side, the writings of the partisans of union, most notably of Bessarion and Isidore of Kiev, who both became cardinals in the Roman Catholic Church, serve as a counterbalance to the anti-unionists' views.[40] Concerning the Morea, on the other hand, a letter by Cardinal Bessarion to the Despot Constantine Palaiologos and two advisory addresses by the eminent humanist and philosopher George Gemistos Plethon to Emperor Manuel II and to the Despot Theodore II are of particular interest.[41] In these addresses Plethon proposes a reorganization of the Morean state as a solution to its social, economic, and political

[37] For details on the politico-religious stance of Isidore Glabas and Symeon of Thessalonike, see Part II below. For a recent survey of the metropolitans of Thessalonike in the Palaiologan period, see G. T. Dennis, "The late Byzantine metropolitans of Thessalonike," *DOP* 57 (2003), 255–64.

[38] *Œuvres complètes de Georges (Gennadios) Scholarios*, ed. L. Petit, H. A. Sideridès, and M. Jugie, 8 vols. (Paris, 1928–36) (hereafter Scholarios, *Œuvres*); John Eugenikos, in *PP*, vol. I, pp. 47–218, 271–322.

[39] *Les "Mémoires" du Grand Ecclésiarque de l'Église de Constantinople Sylvestre Syropoulos sur le concile de Florence (1438–1439)*, ed. and trans. V. Laurent (Paris, 1971) (hereafter Syropoulos, *"Mémoires"*). For an evaluation of Syropoulos' reliability, see J. Gill, "The 'Acta' and the Memoirs of Syropoulos as history," *OCP* 14 (1948), 303–55.

[40] Texts published in *PP*, vols. I–IV.

[41] Bessarion, "Κωνσταντίνῳ δεσπότῃ τῷ Παλαιολόγῳ χαίρειν," in *PP*, vol. IV, pp. 32–45; Plethon, "Εἰς Μανουὴλ Παλαιολόγον περὶ τῶν ἐν Πελοποννήσῳ πραγμάτων," in *PP*, vol. III, pp. 246–65 and "Συμβουλευτικὸς πρὸς τὸν δεσπότην Θεόδωρον περὶ τῆς Πελοποννήσου," in *PP*, vol. IV, pp. 113–35. For an analysis of these texts, see below, ch. 10, pp. 273ff.

problems, upholding as a priority the salvation of the Greek race and of the empire by its own resources.[42]

Official documents constitute another major category of Byzantine source material in addition to the literary sources already discussed. Among these, the acts of the patriarchal tribunal of Constantinople,[43] despite their essentially ecclesiastical character, offer important information directly related to the effects of the Ottoman expansion and to certain aspects of Byzantine–Ottoman–Italian social and economic relations. Most of this information bears primarily on Constantinople but is not always restricted to it since cases from the provinces were also brought to the patriarchal court from time to time. A second important group of Byzantine documents, concerned principally with socioeconomic conditions in rural areas, originate from the archives of Mount Athos.[44]

The western sources for the period can also be broken down into two groups as literary and documentary. The first group includes accounts of travelers who visited the Byzantine Empire (e.g. Johann Schiltberger, Clavijo, Cristoforo Buondelmonti, Pero Tafur, Bertrandon de la Broquière),[45] as well as eyewitness reports about particular events, most notably the accounts of the fall of Constantinople by the Venetian surgeon Nicolò Barbaro, the Florentine merchant Jacopo Tedaldi, or Leonardo of Chios, the Latin archbishop of Mytilene.[46] While these narrative sources occasionally provide useful material, the second category of western sources, archival and diplomatic documents, have consistently been of utmost significance, both in terms of giving general information about the relations of Italian

---

[42] On this last point, see especially *PP*, vol. IV, p. 130.

[43] MM, vol. II: *Acta patriarchatus Constantinopolitani, MCCCXV–MCCCCII* (Vienna, 1862). For the acts dated between 1315 and 1363, the new critical edition with German translation should be consulted: *Das Register des Patriarchats von Konstantinopel*, vol. I, ed. H. Hunger and O. Kresten; vol. II, ed. H. Hunger, O. Kresten, E. Kislinger, and C. Cupane; vol. III, ed. J. Koder, M. Hinterberger, and O. Kresten (Vienna, 1981, 1995, 2001).

[44] *Actes de l'Athos*, vols. I–VI, in *VV* (1873–1913); *Archives de l'Athos*, vols. I–XXII (Paris, 1937–2006).

[45] *The Bondage and Travels of Johann Schiltberger, 1396–1427*, trans. J. B. Telfer (London, 1879); Clavijo, *Embassy to Tamerlane, 1403–1406*, trans. G. Le Strange (New York and London, 1928); Buondelmonti, *Description des îles de l'Archipel*, ed. and trans. E. Legrand (Paris, 1897); Pero Tafur, *Travels and Adventures, 1435–1439*, trans. M. Letts (London, 1926); *Le voyage d'Outremer de Bertrandon de la Broquière*, ed. Ch. Schefer (Paris, 1892; repr. 1972). On western travel accounts of this period, see M. Angold, "The decline of Byzantium seen through the eyes of western travellers," in *Travel in the Byzantine World*, ed. R. Macrides (Aldershot, 2002), pp. 213–32.

[46] Nicolò Barbaro, *Giornale dell'assedio di Costantinopoli 1453*, ed. E. Cornet (Vienna, 1856); Jacopo Tedaldi, "Informazioni," in *Thesaurus novus anecdotorum*, ed. E. Martène and U. Durand, vol. I (Paris, 1717; repr. New York, 1968), cols. 1819–26; Leonardo of Chios, "Historia Constantinopolitanae urbis a Mahumete II captae per modum epistolae," in *PG* 159, cols. 923–44. For these and other contemporary western accounts of the siege and fall of Constantinople, see also A. Pertusi (ed.), *La caduta di Costantinopoli*, vol. I: *Le testimonianze dei contemporanei* (Verona, 1976).

maritime republics with Byzantium and the Ottomans, and in terms of presenting concrete data on specific individuals. The latter include the deliberations of the Venetian Senate and other assemblies, summaries of which have been published by F. Thiriet; various documents from Venice and Genoa edited by K. N. Sathas, N. Iorga and others; or documents drawn up by Genoese notaries in Pera.[47] In addition, the account book kept by the Venetian merchant Giacomo Badoer, who was based in Constantinople during 1436–40, is an invaluable document that displays the commercial ties of many Byzantine aristocrats with Italians and the activities of a group of Ottoman merchants in the Byzantine capital.[48]

Finally, there are a number of Ottoman sources that contain some details unavailable elsewhere and, thus, supplement the information gathered from Byzantine and western sources. Unfortunately, prior to the mid fifteenth century the Ottoman source material is relatively scarce.[49] This is especially true for archival documents, only a small number of which predate the fall of Constantinople. As for the literary historical sources, almost nothing survives from the fourteenth century. Yet, of utmost importance is the work of the dervish-chronicler Aşıkpaşazade (b. 1392/3?), which, though compiled during the last quarter of the fifteenth century, draws heavily upon an authentic fourteenth-century narrative (the *menakıbname* of Yahşi Fakih) as well as other early Ottoman historical traditions, while for the account of events after 1422 its author relies mostly upon his personal experiences and contacts.[50] The chronicle of Neşri, written a little later

---

[47] Thiriet, *Régestes*; Thiriet, *Assemblées*; Sathas, *Documents*; Iorga, *Notes*; G. G. Musso, *Navigazione e commercio genovese con il Levante nei documenti dell'Archivio di Stato di Genova (secc. XIV–XV)* (Rome, 1975); M. Balard, "Péra au XIVe siècle. Documents notariés des archives de Gênes," in *Les Italiens à Byzance. Édition et présentation de documents*, ed. M. Balard, A. E. Laiou, and C. Otten-Froux (Paris, 1987), pp. 9–78; A. Roccatagliata, *Notai genovesi in Oltremare. Atti rogati a Pera e Mitilene*, vol. I: *Pera, 1408–1490* (Genoa, 1982); L. T. Belgrano, "Prima serie di documenti riguardanti la colonia di Pera," *ASLSP* 13 (1877), 97–336 and "Seconda serie di documenti riguardanti la colonia di Pera," *ASLSP* 17 (1884), 932–1003.

[48] *Badoer*. A useful complementary volume containing analytical indexes prepared by T. Bertelè, completed and revised by his son G. Bertelè, along with a list of errata, glossary of difficult terms, etc. is now available: see *Badoer: Indici*.

[49] For studies on early Ottoman historiography, see H. İnalcık, "The rise of Ottoman historiography" and V. L. Ménage, "The beginnings of Ottoman historiography," both in *Historians of the Middle East*, ed. B. Lewis and P. M. Holt (London, 1962), pp. 152–67 and 168–79; C. Kafadar, *Between Two Worlds: The Construction of the Ottoman State* (Berkeley, Los Angeles, and London, 1995), pp. 90–117.

[50] Aşıkpaşazade–Giese; Aşıkpaşazade–Atsız. On this chronicle and its author, in addition to the works cited in the previous note, see V. L. Ménage, "The Menāqib of Yakhshī Faqīh," *Bulletin of the School of Oriental and African Studies* 26 (1963), 50–4; H. İnalcık, "How to read 'Āshık Pasha-zāde's History," in *Studies in Ottoman History in Honour of Professor V. L. Ménage*, ed. C. Heywood and C. Imber (Istanbul, 1994), pp. 139–56; E. Zachariadou, "Histoires et légendes des premiers ottomans," *Turcica* 27 (1995), 45–89. It should be noted that, as interrelated texts which share much material

towards the end of the fifteenth century, follows Aşıkpaşazade to a large extent, but incorporates different sets of early Ottoman traditions as well, thus offering a certain amount of original and unique information.[51] There also exists an anonymous text, probably by an eyewitness, celebrating Murad II's victory over the crusaders at Varna in 1444, which is a significant and reliable source that complements the contemporary Christian sources on the events of 1443–4.[52] The history of Mehmed the Conqueror by Tursun Beg, a high government official who served the Sultan and who was presumably present at the siege of Constantinople, is of particular interest for us because of its detailed account of the city's conquest.[53] Another contemporary source of Mehmed II's reign, the verse chronicle of Enveri, also contains some useful details about the siege and conquest of Constantinople.[54] The Ottoman sources utilized in this study have been helpful above all for checking the accuracy of Byzantine and western accounts of certain events and for filling some important gaps in the information provided by Greek and Latin sources; however, one should hardly expect to find in them specific references to the political attitudes of particular individuals or groups within Byzantine society.[55]

in common with Aşıkpaşazade, the chronicle of Uruç and the anonymous chronicles do not bear additional information relevant to the present study.

[51] Mehmed Neşrî, *Kitâb-ı Cihân-nümâ – Neşrî Târihi*, ed. F. R. Unat and M. A. Köymen, 2 vols. (Ankara, 1949–57). On this chronicle, see V. L. Ménage, *Neshrī's History of the Ottomans: The Sources and Development of the Text* (London, 1964).

[52] *Gazavât-ı Sultân Murâd b. Mehemmed Hân. İzladi ve Varna Savaşları (1443–1444) Üzerine Anonim Gazavâtnâme*, ed. H. İnalcık and M. Oğuz (Ankara, 1978). An English translation of this text is now available in C. Imber, *The Crusade of Varna, 1443–45* (Aldershot, 2006), pp. 41–106.

[53] Tursun Bey, *Târîh-i Ebü'l-Feth*, ed. A. M. Tulum (Istanbul, 1977). For a facsimile edition and summary English translation of this text, see H. İnalcık and R. Murphey, *The History of Mehmed the Conqueror by Tursun Beg* (Minneapolis and Chicago, 1978). On Tursun, see also H. İnalcık, "Tursun Beg, historian of Mehmed the Conqueror's time," *WZKM* 69 (1977), 55–71. For doubts concerning his participation at the siege, see now N. Vatin, "Tursun Beg assista-t-il au siège de Constantinople en 1453 ?," *WZKM* 91 (2001), 317–29.

[54] *Fatih Devri Kaynaklarından Düstûrnâme-i Enverî: Osmanlı Tarihi Kısmı (1299–1466)*, ed. N. Öztürk (Istanbul, 2003).

[55] A notable exception is an unpublished Ottoman survey book (*tahrir defteri*) for Istanbul and Galata dated December 1455. Despite the fact that parts of the document are inextant, the survey is expected to reveal the names of a large proportion of Byzantines who chose to become Ottoman subjects and remained in Constantinople after 1453 or returned there following a short period of flight. Professor İnalcık is preparing an edition of this crucial document for publication. For a detailed analysis of its sections covering Galata, see H. İnalcık, "Ottoman Galata, 1453–1553," in *Première rencontre internationale sur l'Empire Ottoman et la Turquie moderne*, ed. E. Eldem (Istanbul and Paris, 1991), pp. 31–44, 115–16 (Tables I and II); for the sections dealing with Istanbul, see H. İnalcık, "Istanbul," *EI²*, vol. IV, p. 225.

CHAPTER 2

The shrinking empire and the Byzantine dilemma between East and West after the Fourth Crusade

Towards the end of his life Emperor Manuel II (d. 1425) is reported to have remarked, "Today, as troubles accompany us constantly, our empire needs not an emperor (βασιλεύς) but an administrator (οἰκονόμος)."[1] Manuel uttered these words in reference to his son and co-emperor, John VIII, with whom he was in disagreement over the two interrelated, principal foreign policy issues of the time: first, whether to adopt an aggressive or a peaceful stance towards the Ottomans, and, secondly, whether or not to implement the union of the Byzantine Church with the Church of Rome. With regard to the second matter, Manuel's preference was to sustain negotiations with the papacy so as to intimidate the Ottomans, yet without ever allowing the union to materialize. In relation to the Ottomans, he was in favor of maintaining a façade of peace and friendship with them, rather than pursuing an openly aggressive policy. John VIII's views on both matters differed from those of his father, whose policies he found to be excessively passive and conciliatory. On his part the senior emperor, Manuel II, regarded his son as an ambitious ruler with unrealistic visions and ideals that might have been appropriate in the Byzantine Empire's old days of prosperity, but by no means befitting its current circumstances. The two questions of foreign policy which brought the co-emperors into conflict with each other were crucial issues that in essence dominated the political history of the Byzantine Empire throughout the entire last century of its existence. Faced with the constant threat of collapse under the pressure of Ottoman attacks, Byzantium had been reduced at this time to a small-scale state squeezed between the Ottomans and western powers, and with its continuously shrinking boundaries it was an "empire" in name only. Hence Manuel II's call for an "administrator" (*oikonomos*) to manage

---

[1] Sphrantzes–Grecu, XXIII.7, p. 60, lines 1–2, and on what follows, see XXIII.5–7, pp. 58–60; cf. J. W. Barker, *Manuel II Palaeologus (1391–1425). A Study in Late Byzantine Statesmanship* (New Brunswick, NJ, 1969), pp. 382–3, 329–30; 350–4, 390–1.

and coordinate the state affairs on the basis of relatively modest goals, as opposed to an "emperor" (*basileus*) with universalist aspirations.

Around the middle of the fourteenth century, when the Ottomans crossed to Europe and began to establish themselves in the Balkan peninsula, all that was left of the Byzantine Empire besides Constantinople and its environs was the city of Philadelphia in Asia Minor, some territories in Thrace and Macedonia, the city of Thessalonike, a few islands in the Aegean, and part of the Peloponnese. Almost all of Asia Minor, once the empire's backbone for manpower, food resources, and tax revenues, had long been lost to a number of Turkish principalities. A large portion of the Peloponnese was in the hands of various Latin princes and the Republic of Venice, while the Byzantine possessions in the peninsula suffered under the double pressure of foreign incursions and internal strife. In the Balkans the neighboring states of Serbia and Bulgaria, with their constant fighting and attempts to enlarge their boundaries, enhanced the political instability of the area. The empire's remaining territories in Thrace and Macedonia were in a devastated state and depopulated, first, because of plundering raids by Serbian and Turkish forces; secondly, because of a series of dynastic struggles in the first half of the fourteenth century that quickly evolved into major civil wars; and finally because of the Black Death of 1347–8. The disruption of the empire's agricultural base in this way seriously undermined the food supplies and made the Byzantines increasingly dependent on grain transports from Genoese-controlled areas in the Black Sea.[2]

The state finances and economy, too, were in a precarious situation during the Palaiologan period. In the first place, tax revenues from the countryside were severely diminished by the *pronoia* grants of successive emperors to state officials or to their own political supporters, as well as by donations of imperial land to ecclesiastical institutions, both phenomena dating back to the second half of the thirteenth century as far as the Palaiologan period is concerned.[3] Territorial losses to foreign invaders also resulted in progressive cuts in the tax yields. Thus, in the final years of the fourteenth century, as the Byzantine scholar John Chortasmenos observed,

---

[2] For the general political history of the Palaiologan period, see D. M. Nicol, *The Last Centuries of Byzantium, 1261–1453*, 2nd rev. edn. (Cambridge, 1993). For surveys of the rural and the urban economy in the same period, with extensive bibliography, see A. E. Laiou, "The agrarian economy, thirteenth–fifteenth centuries," in *EHB*, vol. I, pp. 311–75; K.-P. Matschke, "The late Byzantine urban economy, thirteenth–fifteenth centuries," in *EHB*, vol. II, pp. 463–95.

[3] G. Ostrogorskij, *Pour l'histoire de la féodalité byzantine* (Brussels, 1954), esp. pp. 83–186; P. Charanis, "The monastic properties and the state in the Byzantine Empire," *DOP* 4 (1948), 99–118. For a review of modern debates on the *pronoia* institution, see A. Kazhdan, "*Pronoia*: the history of a scholarly discussion," in *Intercultural Contacts in the Medieval Mediterranean: Studies in Honour of David Jacoby*, ed. B. Arbel (London, 1996), pp. 133–63.

Constantinople was almost the only place from which the emperor still collected revenues.[4] But here, too, the state treasury was deprived of a large portion of its former revenues owing to the commercial privileges, including complete or partial exemptions from customs duties, that had been granted to Italian merchants, who dominated Byzantium's foreign trade and, to a smaller extent, its domestic trade throughout the Palaiologan period. In this context, the striking gap between the respective figures reported by Gregoras for the mid-fourteenth-century annual customs revenues of Byzantine Constantinople (30,000 *hyperpyra*) and of Genoese Pera (200,000 *hyperpyra*) is indicative, albeit somewhat exaggerated.[5]

Another key weakness of the Byzantine Empire during these years of intense military danger was the state's inability to maintain a strong army and a well-equipped fleet of its own. Soldiers with *pronoia*-holdings did not always fulfill their military obligations as growing numbers of *pronoia* grants, which had originally been handed out only for the lifetime of an individual in return for services performed, became hereditary, most notably from the mid fourteenth century onwards. The state, therefore, came to rely more and more either on private armies of landed magnates when these were available, or on mercenary soldiers who could only be hired in small numbers given the state's limited financial resources and the fact that mercenaries were expensive and required cash payments.[6] Meanwhile, the lack of a proper Byzantine fleet served to increase the empire's already excessive dependence on the maritime cities of Italy, particularly Venice and Genoa, which possessed strong navies.

Furthermore, the civil wars of the first half of the fourteenth century not only helped to speed up the process of political disintegration and economic decay but also played a direct role in facilitating the expansion of the Ottomans as many of the contending parties turned to the latter for military assistance. Although by no means the first contender to have recourse to Turkish aid, John VI Kantakouzenos stands out among the rest on account of the intimate ties he formed consecutively with Umur Beg of Aydın (r. 1334–48) and with the Ottoman ruler Orhan Beg (r. 1324–62).

[4] H. Hunger, "Zeitgeschichte in der Rhetorik des sterbenden Byzanz," *Wiener Archiv für Geschichte des Slawentums und Osteuropas* 3 (1959), 157, n. 22.

[5] *Nicephori Gregorae Byzantina Historia*, vol. II, ed. L. Schopen (Bonn, 1830), pp. 841–2. On the commercial privileges of Italians in this period, see J. Chrysostomides, "Venetian commercial privileges under the Palaeologi," *StVen* 12 (1970), 267–356; M. Balard, "L'organisation des colonies étrangères dans l'Empire byzantin (XIIe–XVe siècle)," in *Hommes et richesses dans l'Empire byzantin*, vol. II, ed. V. Kravari, J. Lefort, and C. Morrisson (Paris, 1991), pp. 261–76. On customs duties in general, see H. Antoniadis-Bibicou, *Recherches sur les douanes à Byzance* (Paris, 1963), pp. 97–155.

[6] N. Oikonomidès, "À propos des armées des premiers Paléologues et des compagnies de soldats," *TM* 8 (1981), 353–71; M. C. Bartusis, *The Late Byzantine Army: Arms and Society, 1204–1453* (Philadelphia, 1992); M. C. Bartusis, "The cost of late Byzantine warfare and defense," *BF* 16 (1991), 75–89.

It is a well-established fact that the Ottomans, whether independently or with the consent of their own government, began to settle permanently on European soil after having come to Thrace as Kantakouzenos' allies in the civil war of 1341–7.[7] Yet while Kantakouzenos was certainly responsible for precipitating this development, it is also true that the events that transpired in the course of the next hundred years, culminating in the Ottoman conquest of the Byzantine capital in 1453 and of the Despotate of the Morea in 1460, ought to be viewed against the background of a combination of factors in which he had little or no part. These factors include some of the long-term consequences of the Fourth Crusade, the policies and methods of conquest employed by the Ottomans, as well as the official course pursued by successive Byzantine governments with regard to the Ottomans, the western powers, and the papacy. What follows is a brief examination of these factors that will serve to highlight the dual challenge Byzantium faced from the Ottoman and Latin worlds during these critical times. It will hence establish the proper background for subsequent chapters in which the political attitudes that prevailed among various segments of Byzantine society vis-à-vis the Ottomans and the Latins are analyzed, in conjunction with contemporary socioeconomic conditions, within the framework of three particular regions of the empire comprising Thessalonike, Constantinople, and the Morea.

It might be appropriate to begin with the Fourth Crusade, which preceded the foundation of the Ottoman state by nearly a century but left deep and long-lasting marks on the consciousness and ideology of the Byzantine people, while at the same time fundamentally affecting the structure of Byzantine society. For instance, a characteristic trait of the Palaiologan period, the political fragmentation and dismemberment of the once unified structure of the Byzantine Empire, is a transformation fostered by the creation of a number of Latin and Greek successor states on the empire's territories at the end of the crusading enterprise.[8] It is true that

[7] On this civil war between John Kantakouzenos and the supporters of John V Palaiologos, see G. Weiss, *Joannes Kantakuzenos – Aristokrat, Staatsmann, Kaiser und Mönch – in der Gesellschaftsentwicklung von Byzanz im 14. Jahrhundert* (Wiesbaden, 1969); K.-P. Matschke, *Fortschritt und Reaktion in Byzanz im 14. Jahrhundert. Konstantinopel in der Bürgerkriegsperiode von 1341 bis 1354* (Berlin, 1971); E. de Vries-van der Velden, *L'élite byzantine devant l'avance Turque à l'époque de la guerre civile de 1341 à 1354* (Amsterdam, 1989); D. M. Nicol, *The Reluctant Emperor: A Biography of John Cantacuzene, Byzantine Emperor and Monk, c. 1295–1383* (Cambridge, 1996), pp. 45–83. For Kantakouzenos' relations with the Turks, see also the references cited in note 1 of ch. 6.

[8] On the Fourth Crusade and its consequences, see now A. Laiou (ed.), *Urbs Capta: The Fourth Crusade and its Consequences. La IVe Croisade et ses conséquences* (Paris, 2005). For the successor states, see the general overviews by D. Jacoby, "The Latin Empire of Constantinople and the Frankish states in Greece" and M. Angold, "Byzantium in exile," both in *The New Cambridge Medieval History*, vol. v, ed. D. Abulafia (Cambridge, 1999), pp. 525–42 and 543–68.

decentralizing and secessionist tendencies existed within the empire prior to 1204,[9] but the Fourth Crusade transformed these somewhat random tendencies into a firmly established pattern with the result that they re-emerged as a standard feature of the restored Byzantine Empire after 1261. Thus, decentralization was accompanied in the course of the Turkish expansion of the Palaiologan period by the creation of more or less autonomous local administrative units supervised by certain individuals or groups who either seized or were granted the rights of government, as in Thessalonike, Byzantine Morea, and other places.[10] This led to the emergence of a multiplicity of centers where foreign policy decisions could be, and were, made independently of and sometimes at variance with the decisions of the central government in Constantinople. While the state theoretically continued to function as a central power in the sphere of foreign policy, in practice the above-mentioned developments created a political atmosphere that was conducive to conflicts and differences of opinion. In the face of Ottoman attacks, when unity was essential for putting up an effective front against the enemy, the Byzantine central government's inability to override the particularism of provincial governors and magnates oftentimes proved to be a severe impediment to defense.

Another consequence of the Fourth Crusade with significant long-term implications was the crystallization of anti-Latin sentiments among the predominantly Greek population of Byzantium. Such sentiments had been in existence already since the eleventh century, but after the disruption and shock of the Latin conquest, Greek antagonism towards Latins – as the Byzantines collectively referred to Catholics of western Europe – intensified.[11] Nevertheless, it is crucial to differentiate between various aspects or forms of anti-Latin feeling because the resentment that existed

[9] N. Oikonomidès, "La décomposition de l'Empire byzantin à la veille de 1204 et les origines de l'Empire de Nicée: à propos de la *Partitio Romaniae*" in *XVe Congrès international d'études byzantines. Rapports et co-rapports* (Athens, 1976), vol. 1.1, pp. 3–28; J.-Cl. Cheynet, "Philadelphie, un quart de siècle de dissidence, 1182–1206," in *Philadelphie et autres études*, ed. H. Ahrweiler (Paris, 1984), pp. 39–54; R. Radić, "Odpacni gospodari i vizantiji krajem XII i prvim dečenijama XIII veka," *ZRVI* 24–5 (1986), 151–283, with English summary at 283–90; J.-Cl. Cheynet, *Pouvoir et contestations à Byzance (963–1210)* (Paris, 1990), esp. pp. 446–73.

[10] E. A. Zachariadou, "Ἐφήμερες ἀπόπειρες γιὰ αὐτοδιοίκηση στὶς Ἑλληνικὲς πόλεις κατὰ τὸν ΙΔ´ καὶ ΙΕ´ αἰῶνα," *Ἀριάδνη* 5 (1989), 345–51; N. Oikonomidès, "Pour une typologie des villes 'séparées' sous les Paléologues," in *Geschichte und Kultur der Palaiologenzeit*, ed. W. Seibt (Vienna, 1996), pp. 169–75.

[11] H. Ahrweiler, *L'idéologie politique de l'Empire byzantin* (Paris, 1975), pp. 75–87, 103–28; Oikonomidès, *Hommes d'affaires*, pp. 23–33. For the background to the use of the term *Latinoi* as a generic appellation for western Europeans, see A. Kazhdan, "Latins and Franks in Byzantium: perception and reality from the eleventh to the twelfth century," in *The Crusades from the Perspective of Byzantium and the Muslim World*, ed. A. E. Laiou and R. P. Mottahedeh (Washington, DC, 2001), pp. 83–100.

between Byzantines and Latins in the Palaiologan period was not merely religious in scope.[12] In the writings of contemporary Byzantines the word "Latin" often carries different connotations, depending on whether it is used as a generic term denoting Catholics as a whole, or in reference to constituents of distinct political entities such as, for instance, the Venetians, the Genoese, or the Navarrese. As Barlaam of Calabria explained to Pope Benedict XII in 1339, "it is not so much difference in dogma that alienates the hearts of the Greeks from you, as the hatred that has entered their souls against the Latins, because of the many great evils that at different times the Greeks have suffered at the hands of Latins and are still suffering every day."[13] Barlaam's allusion is to the frictions in social relations that emerged after 1204 in Latin-occupied areas where the Greek population was forced to submit to the political, economic, and ecclesiastical domination of the Latins. Despite strong regional variations, in many places the Latins not only interfered with the religious freedom of native Greeks but also dispossessed the Greek Church and the majority of local aristocrats of their lands and imposed their own feudal principles in the countryside, which resulted in an overall debasement of the social and economic status of the rural populations.[14]

Moreover, the restoration of the Byzantine Empire in 1261 did not diminish the Italian economic dominance in the recovered territories. To the contrary, whereas Venice by virtue of having been the only participant from Italy in the Fourth Crusade enjoyed an almost unique and unchallenged economic role in the eastern Mediterranean during 1204–61, thereafter the commercial activities of Italians intensified with the penetration first by the Genoese and subsequently by others who, alongside the Venetians, received extensive trading privileges from Palaiologan emperors. The stereotypical image of Latins as people who occupied themselves only with war, trade, and tavernkeeping, which seems to have prevailed among Byzantines in the second half of the fourteenth century if not

---

[12] On the religious antagonism between Byzantines and Latins and its social and cultural subcontext, see T. M. Kolbaba, *The Byzantine Lists: Errors of the Latins* (Urbana and Chicago, 2000) and T. M. Kolbaba, "Byzantine perceptions of Latin religious 'errors': themes and changes from 850 to 1350," in *Crusades*, ed. Laiou and Mottahedeh, pp. 117–43.

[13] *Acta Benedicti XII, 1334–1342*, ed. A. L. Tăutu, Fontes 3, vol. VIII (Vatican City, 1958), doc. 43; trans. by J. Gill, *Byzantium and the Papacy, 1198–1400* (New Brunswick, NJ, 1979), pp. 197–8.

[14] See F. Thiriet, *La Romanie vénitienne au Moyen Âge* (Paris, 1975), pp. 105–39, 287–302; P. Topping, "Co-existence of Greeks and Latins in Frankish Morea and Venetian Crete" and D. Jacoby, "Les états latins en Romanie: phénomènes sociaux et économiques (1204–1350 environ)," both in *XVe Congrès international d'études byzantines. Rapports et co-rapports*, vol. 1.3 (Athens, 1976); and the collection of essays in *Latins and Greeks in the Eastern Mediterranean after 1204*, ed. B. Arbel, B. Hamilton, and D. Jacoby (London, 1989).

earlier,[15] is undoubtedly a direct manifestation of the continued strong commercial presence of Italians within the restored Byzantine Empire.

But the same forces that resulted in the strengthening of prejudices and the development of tensions between Greeks and Latins also brought the two groups into daily contact with each other. Thus, side by side with instances of overt hostility, cases of close communication and cooperation began to evolve, particularly within the economic sphere. In important trade centers such as Constantinople and Thessalonike certain Byzantine merchants who established commercial relations with their Italian counterparts benefited from the infiltration of the foreign element into their own domain of activity during the Palaiologan period, even though they were henceforth pushed to a position subordinate to Italian interests.[16] While an undercurrent of hostility and alienation continued to color the ideological outlook of the majority of Byzantines towards the Latin world, practical considerations and economic motives simultaneously led some among them to cooperation and association with specific groups of Latins who exercised a particular social, economic, and, in some places, political influence in the realm of Byzantine affairs. It is against this background of contradictory attitudes towards the "Latins" that we can now proceed to an observation of the relations of the Byzantines with the Ottomans.

Founded at the turn of the fourteenth century in Bithynia, in northwestern Asia Minor, the Ottoman state was at its origins a small frontier principality of *gazi* warriors, who engaged in raiding expeditions driven by the spirit of *gaza*, an ideology of war that incorporated, along with religious motivation aiming at the expansion of the power of Islam, other factors such as the search for booty or pasture and political opportunism.[17] At the

---

[15] Demetrios Kydones, "Apologie della propria fede: I. Ai Greci Ortodossi," ed. Mercati, in *Notizie*, pp. 364–5, esp. lines 77–84: "οἱ γὰρ ἡμέτεροι . . . πάντας ἀνθρώπους εἰς Ἕλληνας καὶ βαρβάρους διχοτομοῦντες . . . οἷς καὶ Λατίνους συναριθμοῦντες οὐδὲν περὶ αὐτῶν ἀνθρώπινον ὑπελάμβανον, ἀλλ᾽ αὐτοῖς . . . ὅπλα μόνον καί τινας ἐμπορείας ἀγεννεῖς τε καπηλείας ἀπέρριπτον."

[16] K.-P. Matschke, "Zum Charakter des byzantinischen Schwarzmeerhandels im 13. bis 15. Jahrhundert," *Wissenschaftliche Zeitschrift der Karl-Marx-Universität Leipzig, Gesellschafts- und sprachwiss. Reihe* 19/3 (1970), 447–58; Oikonomidès, *Hommes d'affaires*; Laiou-Thomadakis, "Byzantine economy," 177–222; Laiou-Thomadakis, "Greek merchant," 96–132; N. Necipoğlu, "Byzantines and Italians in fifteenth-century Constantinople: commercial cooperation and conflict," *New Perspectives on Turkey* 12 (spring 1995), 129–43; Matschke, "Commerce, trade, markets, and money," pp. 771–806. For examples of cooperation between Greek and Italian merchants in Latin-dominated areas, particularly in Venetian Crete and Genoese Pera, see A. E. Laiou, "Observations on the results of the Fourth Crusade: Greeks and Latins in port and market," *Medievalia et humanistica*, n.s. 12 (1984), 51–7.

[17] On the role of the ideology of *gaza* in the early phase of the Ottoman expansion, see the classic work of P. Wittek, *The Rise of the Ottoman Empire* (London, 1938); cf. H. İnalcık, *The Ottoman Empire: The Classical Age 1300–1600* (New York and Washington, 1973), pp. 5–8; H. İnalcık, "The question of

outset, there was perhaps little to distinguish the Ottoman state from the other *gazi* principalities of Turkish origin that were scattered throughout former Byzantine Asia Minor. Within half a century of their foundation, however, the Ottomans gained a crucial advantage over the rest of these principalities by acquiring their first footholds on European soil through their interference in civil wars at Byzantium. Their occupation of Tzympe in 1352 was followed in 1354 by the capture of the strategic port of Gallipoli, both situated on the European shore of the Dardanelles.[18] The acquisition of Gallipoli in particular secured the Ottomans passage from Anatolia to Europe and opened the way for their systematic advances and settlement in the Balkan peninsula. During the following decade they extended their conquests to Didymoteichon and Adrianople, the chief Byzantine cities of Thrace. Thereafter, they rapidly overran most of what remained of Byzantine territory, capturing in the 1380s important cities such as Christoupolis (Kavalla), Serres, Thessalonike, and Berroia, and beginning to make inroads further south into Thessaly and into the Morea. By the time of John V's death in 1391, in addition to the lands they had conquered from the Byzantines, the Ottomans had subjugated Bulgaria and most of Serbia and extended their northern frontier to the Danube. In Anatolia, on the other hand, their annexation of the Turkish maritime principalities of Saruhan, Aydın, and Menteşe during 1389–90 transformed the Ottomans into a threatening sea power.[19] As far as the security of the Byzantine Empire was concerned, the presence of the Ottomans in the Balkan peninsula and their growing naval power endangered not only the empire's outlying provinces but Constantinople itself, which henceforth had to contend with Ottoman pressures coming from east and west, by land and by sea. It was on the basis of this advantageous position that in 1394 Sultan Bayezid I (r. 1389–1402) conceived of the first concrete Ottoman plan to conquer the Byzantine capital.

the emergence of the Ottoman state," *International Journal of Turkish Studies* 2/2 (1981–2), 71–9. For a new assessment of modern scholarship on the rise of the Ottoman Empire and the role of warriors who claimed to champion the *gaza* spirit, see Kafadar, *Between Two Worlds*, with full bibliography. For a different perspective, rejecting outright the role of *gaza* and attributing the early Ottoman conquests singularly to "the greed and ambition of a predatory confederacy," see now H. W. Lowry, *The Nature of the Early Ottoman State* (New York, 2003).

[18] N. Oikonomidès, "From soldiers of fortune to gazi warriors: the Tzympe affair," in *Studies in Ottoman History in Honour of Professor V. L. Ménage*, ed. C. Heywood and C. Imber (Istanbul, 1994), pp. 239–47; H. İnalcık, "The Ottoman Turks and the Crusades, 1329–1451," in *A History of the Crusades*, gen. ed. K. M. Setton, vol. VI: *The Impact of the Crusades on Europe*, ed. H. W. Hazard and N. P. Zacour (Madison, 1989), pp. 229–35; H. İnalcık, "Gelibolu," *EI²*, vol. II, pp. 983–7. For the politico-military history of the early Ottoman state, in addition to the works cited in the previous note, see C. Imber, *The Ottoman Empire, 1300–1481* (Istanbul, 1990).

[19] İnalcık, "Ottoman Turks and the Crusades," pp. 239–40.

The early Ottoman conquests in the Balkans generally conformed to a similar pattern whereby, in the first stage, the native population of the countryside was driven into the region's more secure fortified towns by the incessant raids of the *gazis*. Once the Ottoman forces gained control of the surrounding country, their next step was to apply pressure on the fortified towns themselves. At this stage, however, the Ottomans did not immediately resort to open warfare but, in accordance with Islamic principles, offered the inhabitants the option of surrendering on terms. Islamic law ruled that the inhabitants of a place taken by war could legitimately be enslaved, thereby being forced to undergo the loss of their personal freedom and property. By contrast, those who accepted Ottoman (or any other Islamic state's) sovereignty by surrendering were granted the safety of their lives and movable property, together with their religious freedom, on the sole conditions of obedience and payment of a special tax called *harac* or *cizye*. In either case, though, whether capture by force or surrender was the means of subjugation, all lands reverted to the possession of the Ottoman state. The underlying principle of this policy was that the ultimate goal of *cihad* (and of its lesser category *gaza*), namely the expansion of the abode of Islam (*darülislam*), could be fulfilled by securing a non-Muslim community's submission to the authority of an Islamic state and hence did not necessitate religious conversion or direct conquest under all circumstances. Applying this policy extensively and liberally, the Ottomans used it with success to draw into their fold many Christians of the Byzantine Empire and of other Balkan states by peaceful means rather than by war.[20] The first Ottoman occupation of Thessalonike in 1387, to be discussed thoroughly in Part II, took place more or less in this manner with the surrender of the city's inhabitants, though after exposure to a four-year-long siege.

By extension, the Ottomans made use of the same principle in their treatment of states that accepted the sovereignty of the Ottoman ruler. These states were relegated to the status of vassalage and were expected to provide an annual tribute and military forces for participation in Ottoman campaigns. As long as they remained loyal and performed these obligations,

---

[20] H. İnalcık, "Ottoman methods of conquest," *Studia Islamica* 2 (1953), 103–29; E. A. Zachariadou, "More on the Turkish methods of conquest," *Eighth Annual Byzantine Studies Conference, Abstracts of Papers* (Chicago, 1982), p. 20; M. Delilbaşı, "Selanik ve Yanya'da Osmanlı egemenliğinin kurulması," *Belleten* 51 (1987), 75–106; V. Panaite, *The Ottoman Law of War and Peace. The Ottoman Empire and Tribute Payers* (Boulder, 2000). See also "Dar al-ᶜahd" and "Dar al-sulh," in *EI²*, vol. ɪɪ, pp. 116, 131; M. Khadduri, *War and Peace in the Law of Islam* (Baltimore, 1955); J. T. Johnson and J. Kelsay (eds.), *Just War and Jihad: Historical and Theoretical Perspectives on War and Peace in Western and Islamic Traditions* (New York, 1991). On the difference between *gaza* and *cihad*, see Kafadar, *Between Two Worlds*, pp. 79–80.

their vassal status relieved them, at least in theory, from Ottoman attacks and allowed them to maintain their political and ecclesiastical autonomy. To the Ottomans, on the other hand, the system provided extra revenues, auxiliary forces, and control over territories which they had not conquered yet. It will be seen shortly that all three major Balkan states – Serbia, Bulgaria, and the Byzantine Empire – had become Ottoman vassals by the early 1370s.

In the conquered regions, too, the Ottomans pursued a conciliatory policy towards the native Christians. A significant feature of this policy was the readiness of the Ottomans to preserve the status particularly of landowning aristocrats and military elites by incorporating them into the fabric of the Ottoman state through the grant of military fiefs known as *timars*. Thus, it was possible for former *pronoia*-holders to become *timar*-holders under the Ottoman system, which essentially allowed them to maintain their social status along with their Christian faith. In newly conquered areas the Ottomans made effective use of this policy as a mechanism for winning the loyalty of the local populations.[21]

While the Ottomans were rapidly extending their dominion over Byzantine territories to the west of Constantinople by such means, how did the Byzantine emperors respond to the changing international political situation in the course of the second half of the fourteenth century? In 1354, several months after the Ottoman occupation of Gallipoli, a council of state was held in Constantinople by the co-emperors John VI Kantakouzenos (r. 1347–54) and John V Palaiologos (r. 1341/54–91) to determine the policy to be pursued for the recovery of Gallipoli and the removal of the Ottomans from Thrace. John VI, at whose instigation the Ottomans had entered Thrace in large numbers during 1346–52 and who had given a daughter in marriage to the Ottoman ruler Orhan, was known to be the promoter and advocate of a policy of coexistence with the Turks. On this occasion, judging that the economic and military resources of the empire, particularly in the absence of a fleet, were insufficient to undertake armed action against the Ottomans, and recognizing furthermore the dangers inherent in fighting them on Byzantine soil, he suggested settling the matter through diplomacy and negotiation, by means of which he believed Orhan might be persuaded to withdraw his men from Thrace. "Once we have thus

---

[21] İnalcık, "Ottoman methods of conquest"; İnalcık, "Stefan Dušan'dan Osmanlı İmparatorluğuna, XV. asırda Rumeli'de hıristiyan sipahiler ve menşeleri," in *Fatih Devri Üzerinde Tetkikler ve Vesikalar* (Ankara, 1954), pp. 137–84. On the Ottoman *timar* system in general, see Ö. L. Barkan, "Tımar," *İslam Ansiklopedisi*, vol. XII (Istanbul, 1972–3), pp. 286–333; N. Beldiceanu, *Le timar dans l'État ottoman (début XIVe–début XVIe siècle)* (Wiesbaden, 1980).

driven them beyond our frontiers," he argued in a speech recorded in his own history, "it will be easier to make war upon them, provided always that we have the ships to control the sea." The majority of the senators and leading officials, however, were in favor of immediate, direct military action and disagreed with John VI. The latter abdicated a few days later and his coexistence policy with the Turks was abandoned, at least for the time being.[22]

When John V Palaiologos, who had apparently refrained from expressing an opinion at the above-mentioned meeting, became sole emperor upon John VI's abdication, he at once resolved to take action against the Ottomans. He knew as well as John VI that the empire's resources were not adequate for this task but was not reluctant to turn to western powers for help. He immediately initiated negotiations with the papacy, striving for nothing less than a crusade for the elimination of the Ottoman threat.[23] As late as 1366, however, nothing on the scale of a crusade had yet materialized except for a relatively small expedition led by John V's cousin, Count Amadeo VI of Savoy. Amadeo's forces recaptured Gallipoli from the Ottomans in 1366. But by this time the Ottomans had already pushed their way well into Thrace, and about ten years later they would manage to take Gallipoli once again.[24] In 1366 John V, hoping to engage Hungary as well in his struggle against the Ottomans, took the unprecedented step of going in person to Buda to ask King Louis the Great (r. 1342–82) for military assistance.[25] John's next major move in his quest to inspire the western Christian world to action on behalf of his empire was his trip to Rome, where he converted to the Catholic faith in 1369, taking care, however, not to commit his subjects to a union with the Roman Church.[26]

---

[22] *Ioannis Cantacuzeni Eximperatoris Historiarum libri IV*, vol. III, ed. B. G. Niebuhr (Bonn, 1832), pp. 295–300. On this meeting and its aftermath, together with translated passages from John VI's speech, see Nicol, *Last Centuries*, pp. 244–6; Nicol, *Reluctant Emperor*, pp. 130–1.

[23] O. Halecki, *Un Empereur de Byzance à Rome. Vingt ans de travail pour l'union des églises et pour la défense de l'Empire d'Orient, 1355–1375* (Warsaw, 1930; repr. London, 1972), pp. 31–59; Nicol, *Last Centuries*, pp. 256–61. See also R. Radić, *Vreme Jovana V Paleologa (1332–1391)* (Belgrade, 1993), pp. 248ff., with English summary at 465–90.

[24] For Amadeo's expedition, see K. M. Setton, *The Papacy and the Levant (1204–1571)*, vol. I (Philadelphia, 1976), pp. 285–326, with references to the sources and previous secondary literature. On the final Ottoman capture of Gallipoli *c.* 1377, see below, ch. 6, p. 123.

[25] Halecki, *Un Empereur*, pp. 111–37; P. Wirth, "Die Haltung Kaiser Johannes V. bei den Verhandlungen mit König Ludwig von Ungarn zu Buda im Jahre 1366," *BZ* 56 (1963), 271–2; F. Pall, "Encore une fois sur le voyage diplomatique de Jean V Paléologue en 1365–66," *RESEE* 9 (1971), 535–40; J. Gill, "John V Palaeologus at the court of Louis I of Hungary (1366)," *BS* 38 (1977), 31–8.

[26] Halecki, *Un Empereur*, pp. 188–236; Dölger, *Reg.*, vol. V, nos. 3120, 3122, 3126. On the strictly personal nature of John V's conversion, see also Nicol, *Last Centuries*, pp. 270–1; Radić, *Vreme Jovana V*, p. 346. For Byzantine–Papal negotiations preceding John V's conversion, see J. Meyendorff, "Projets de concile oecuménique en 1367: un dialogue inédit entre Jean Cantacuzène et le légat Paul," *DOP* 14 (1960), 147–77; see also Kianka, "Byzantine–Papal diplomacy," 175–94.

None of John V's appeals to European powers produced any concrete results. To make matters worse, on his way back to Constantinople the Emperor was detained at Venice for unpaid debts, and he did not return home until about the end of 1371.[27] In the meantime, on September 26, 1371, Ottoman forces won an overwhelming victory against the Serbians at Černomen on the Maritsa river. The Ottoman victory, which coincided with John V's disillusionment with prospects of help from the Catholic world, seems to have led him towards reconsidering the foreign policy he had pursued for nearly twenty years. Shortly afterwards, he decided to seek peace with the Ottomans and bound himself to be a tribute-paying vassal of Murad I (r. 1362–89), following the example of the Serbian princes who survived the Maritsa disaster and became Ottoman vassals.[28] Bulgarian princes, too, pursued the same course of vassalage to the Ottomans at this time.

The reduction of Byzantium to the status of an Ottoman vassal in the early 1370s marked a turning point not only in the reign of John V but, from a broader perspective, within the whole history of the Palaiologan period. Compared, for instance, with John VI Kantakouzenos' former policy of coexistence with the Ottomans, the policy of peace and reconciliation to which John V reverted after 1371 belongs to an entirely different category. For Kantakouzenos not just vassalage but any status implying inferiority or subordination to the Ottomans had been out of the question. Kantakouzenos had set up his alliance with Orhan in such a way that by giving the latter a daughter he had made himself the Ottoman ruler's father-in-law, which denoted a relationship of superiority within the hierarchical framework of Byzantine imperial ideology. Moreover, the main purpose of Kantakouzenos' alliance with Orhan was to have recourse to Ottoman troops, whereas by contrast John V was bound to provide Orhan's son and successor, Murad I, with armed forces in fulfillment of his vassalage obligations. Thus, having set out to rid Byzantium of the Ottoman menace, John V ended up by reducing his state to the rank of an Ottoman vassal.

The agreement between John V and Murad I was interrupted for some years in the midst of a civil war at Constantinople in which the Ottoman ruler initially interfered on the side of his ally John V, but then transferred his support to the Emperor's son and rival, Andronikos IV, during

---

[27] On John V's detention at Venice and its aftermath, see D. M. Nicol, *Byzantium and Venice: A Study in Diplomatic and Cultural Relations* (Cambridge, 1988), pp. 304–9 and the works cited on p. 308, n. 1.

[28] G. Ostrogorski, "Byzance, état tributaire de l'Empire turc," *ZRVI* 5 (1958), 49–58.

1376–9.[29] Once this crisis was settled and Murad I joined his old ally in 1379, the former agreement between them was renewed, and John V resumed paying tribute and providing military assistance. Byzantine loyalty and subservience to the Ottomans were reaffirmed a few years later, in the Byzantine–Genoese treaty of November 2, 1382.[30] Thereafter, to the end of his life in 1391, John V maintained the policy of appeasement and conciliation with the Ottomans.

As a result of the developments described above, at the time of his death in 1389 Murad I was able to bequeath to his son and successor, Bayezid I, an "empire" consisting of vassal principalities in the Balkans and Anatolia. A new stage in Byzantine–Ottoman relations was initiated by Bayezid I, who shortly after his accession embarked upon a systematic policy of imposing direct control over these vassal states, first in Asia Minor, then in the Balkans.[31] The earliest signs of Bayezid's new policy were witnessed in the Balkans in 1393, with the transformation of Bulgaria into a directly administered Ottoman province in retaliation for John Šišman of Bulgaria's cooperation with Sigismund of Hungary in the plans for an anti-Ottoman expedition. Bulgaria thus lost its vassal status alongside the political and ecclesiastical autonomy this status provided. The same policy was applied in 1394 to Thessalonike and its surrounding regions, which Bayezid placed under his direct rule, thereby depriving the city of the relatively independent, semi-autonomous status it had enjoyed since its surrender in 1387.[32] During the winter of 1393–4 Bayezid also summoned his

[29] For a full discussion of the Ottoman interference in Byzantine civil wars of the late fourteenth and early fifteenth centuries, including this episode, see below, ch. 6.

[30] Belgrano, "Prima serie," no. 26, pp. 133–40; Dölger, *Reg.*, vol. v, no. 3177. Cf. Dennis, *Reign of Manuel II*, pp. 50–1.

[31] H. İnalcık, "Bāyazīd I," *EI²*, vol. i, pp. 1117–19; İnalcık, "Ottoman Turks and the Crusades," pp. 248–54.

[32] A considerable amount of controversy exists over Bayezid I's transformation of Thessalonike into a directly administered Ottoman territory. Besides the chronological controversy, which is definitively settled in favor of 1394, some scholars have formulated the theory of a "second capture," arguing that the city must have reverted to Byzantine rule at some time between 1387 and the early 1390s so as to induce Bayezid to reconquer it. The problem stems from references to Bayezid's "capture" or "occupation" of Thessalonike, found in the accounts of some Ottoman chroniclers (e.g. Neşri, following the Ahmedi–Ruhi tradition), as well as in that of Doukas. But although Bayezid must have certainly had recourse to a show of arms in imposing his stricter regime on Thessalonike, there are no grounds for supporting the theory of a "second capture" in the absence of direct evidence indicating that the city had returned earlier to Byzantine rule. Rather, Bayezid's treatment of Thessalonike must be seen in the same light as the policy he pursued in the Balkans after 1393, and it represents within the general scheme of Ottoman methods of conquest a regular (i.e. the final) stage. Almost identical is the case of Trnovo, which was formally subjugated to Ottoman domination in 1388 and which Bayezid actually occupied in 1393. See İnalcık, "Ottoman methods of conquest"; and his review of Barker's *Manuel II*, in *Archivum Ottomanicum* 3 (1971), 276–8. See also G. T. Dennis, "The second Turkish capture of Thessalonica. 1391, 1394 or 1430?," *BZ* 57 (1964), 53–61, esp. 53–4

Christian vassals to Serres with the intention of having them reaffirm their vassalage ties to him. Those who were summoned included Manuel II, who had succeeded John V as emperor; Manuel's brother Theodore I, Despot of the Morea; their nephew John VII, who held an appanage centered in Selymbria at this time; the Serbian prince Constantine Dragaš, whose daughter had married Manuel II in 1392; and Stefan Lazarević of Serbia.[33] According to Chalkokondyles, shortly after the dissolution of the Serres meeting and Manuel II's return to Constantinople, Bayezid summoned the Emperor to his presence again. When Manuel ignored the summons twice, the Sultan sent an army to Constantinople, and thus started the first Ottoman siege of the Byzantine capital in the spring of 1394. Yet in reality Manuel's disobedience must have been a mere pretext for Bayezid, whose policy of direct control was ultimately aimed at building a unified empire with a centralized government, stretching from the Danube in the West to the Euphrates in the East. The capture of Constantinople was therefore crucial for the realization of Bayezid's imperial ambitions.[34]

While the siege of Constantinople was going on, other Ottoman armies attended to the occupation of Thessaly and soon brought most of this region under their direct rule. Having reached the borders of the Pelo- ponnese, Ottoman forces then started pressuring the Morea as well. By this time reactions to Bayezid's aggressive policy had begun to escalate in Europe under the initiative of King Sigismund of Hungary, who persuaded the religious and secular leaders of the West to launch a crusade against the Ottomans. However, on September 25, 1396 the crusaders met with a disastrous defeat at Nikopolis, which brought their venture to an end while at the same time confirming Bayezid's control of the Balkans.[35] Freed of

---

(n. 2), with full bibliography on proponents of the "second capture" theory; A. Vakalopulos, "Zur Frage der zweiten Einnahme Thessalonikis durch die Türken, 1391–1394," *BZ* 61 (1968), 285–90. In more recent times, the "second capture" argument has been embraced by T. E. Gregory in his entry on Thessalonike in *ODB*, vol. III, p. 2072: "... the city fell in April 1387. It returned briefly to Byzantine hands but was taken by Bayezid I on 12 April 1394."

[33] For more on this meeting and references to the sources, see below, ch. 9, pp. 242ff. According to İnalcık, who follows K. Hopf and M. Silberschmidt, the meeting took place not in Serres (rendered as Φερραί by Chalkokondyles), but in Verrai (Berroia, Turkish Fere or Kara-Ferye): see his review of Barker's *Manuel II*, in *Archivum Ottomanicum* 3 (1971), 276–7 and, more recently, his "Ottoman Turks and the Crusades," pp. 248–9.

[34] In other words, the Serres meeting was not so much a *cause* of the siege of Constantinople as presented by Chalkokondyles (Chalkok.–Darkó, vol. I, pp. 76–7), but rather these two events, together with the direct occupation of Thessalonike and the campaigns against Thessaly and the Morea mentioned below, all formed part of one whole scheme; namely, the aggressive policy that Bayezid began to pursue in the Balkans in the wake of the settlement of his problems in Anatolia.

[35] On this crusade, see A. S. Atiya, *The Crusade of Nicopolis* (London, 1934); Setton, *The Papacy and the Levant*, vol. I, pp. 341–69. For the impact of the Ottoman victory at Nikopolis on events inside Constantinople, see below, ch. 7, pp. 150–1.

this threat, the Sultan tightened his blockade of Constantinople which was to last until 1402, when an unexpected force, not from the West but from the East, rescued the Byzantines. The lengthy siege came to an abrupt end as Timur's (Tamerlane's) forces defeated and captured Bayezid in the battle of Ankara on July 28, 1402, at a moment when the Constantinopolitans were preparing to surrender their city to the Ottomans.[36] The battle of Ankara thus signalled the failure of Bayezid's imperial designs and ushered in a period of confusion and civil wars among his sons.

In the course of the new phase of Ottoman conquests and expansion inaugurated by Bayezid I, the foreign policy of the Byzantine state was accordingly altered and adapted to meet the changed circumstances. When Manuel II ascended the throne in 1391, Bayezid, who was occupied then with establishing his authority over the Turkish principalities of Anatolia, had not turned his attention yet to the Balkans. At this time Manuel found it expedient to continue John V's policy of peace and accommodation with the Ottomans.[37] Earlier in his career Manuel had followed quite a different course when during the 1380s he led from Thessalonike an openly aggressive movement against the Ottomans in an attempt to re-establish Byzantine authority in Macedonia. As already mentioned and as will be discussed further in chapter 3, this movement turned into an utter failure with the surrender of the Thessalonians to the Ottomans, leaving Manuel with no other choice than to go to Bursa and seek peace with Murad I by promising him allegiance.[38] When Manuel assumed power as emperor, the memory of his failure in Thessalonike was most likely to have given him added incentive to remain faithful to his father's foreign policy and maintain friendly terms with the Ottomans. Hence, only about three months after his accession, Manuel took part in one of Bayezid's Anatolian campaigns in compliance with his duties as vassal. In a letter he wrote to Demetrios Kydones during this campaign, the Emperor justified his conciliatory attitude towards the Ottomans by pointing out that the dangers he faced in Asia Minor were much smaller and less serious than "those we can expect from them if we do not fight along with them."[39]

---

[36] See below, ch. 7, pp. 181–2.

[37] Barker, *Manuel II*, pp. 84–122, esp. 86. For a review and interpretation of the early interactions between the Palaiologoi and Bayezid, see also S. W. Reinert, "The Palaiologoi, Yıldırım Bāyezīd and Constantinople: June 1389–March 1391," in *TO EΛΛHNIKON. Studies in Honor of Speros Vryonis, Jr.*, vol. I, ed. J. S. Langdon *et al.* (New Rochelle, 1993), pp. 289–365.

[38] Kydones–Loenertz, vol. II, nos. 352, 354, 355, 363, 365, 370; Chalkok.–Darkó, vol. I, pp. 42–4, 48. Cf. Dennis, *Reign of Manuel II*, p. 158; Barker, *Manuel II*, pp. 61–4.

[39] Dennis, *Letters of Manuel II*, no. 14, pp. 38–9.

However, following the unfolding of Bayezid's overtly hostile program of forceful unification in the Balkans, and in particular subsequent to the meeting at Serres, Manuel changed his policy once again and abandoned the compliant conduct he had pursued during the first three years of his reign. He made an open demonstration of his new position by refusing to obey Bayezid's summons after the Serres gathering, thereby giving the Sultan a pretext for laying siege to Constantinople. As in John V's initial endeavors to resist the Ottomans, Manuel's anti-Ottoman position immediately converged into a policy of cooperation with western powers. Manuel had some involvement, though minor, in the organization of the Crusade of Nikopolis.[40] But it was in the years after the failure of Nikopolis that the Emperor ventured forth on a full-scale and militant quest for aid from abroad, which reached a climax with his famous journey to Europe at the end of 1399, exactly thirty years after John V's trip to Rome and Venice. Though Manuel's journeys took him beyond Italy, to France and England, where he carried out negotiations with the secular and ecclesiastical leaders of the West, a central and consistent feature of his policy was to avoid by all means committing himself and his empire to the union of the Churches. Despite long years of travels and negotiations, Manuel's policy of resistance to the Ottomans based on expectations of military and financial help from the Latin West proved ineffective. At the time of Bayezid's defeat by Timur in the battle of Ankara, the Emperor was still in Europe, waiting for the Christian powers of the West to take organized action against the Ottomans. Nonetheless, to the end of his rule Manuel II never completely gave up hope on this policy and maintained at least a semblance of it, regardless of the numerous occasions in which the responses and conduct of western powers disappointed him.[41]

With no recourse to western aid, at any rate, the Byzantines were able to gain the upper hand in their relations with the Ottomans during the two decades following the battle of Ankara. At the beginning of 1403 one of Bayezid I's sons and successors, Süleyman Çelebi, restored by treaty a significant portion of territory to the Byzantine Empire, including Thessalonike and Kalamaria with their environs, the Thracian coast from Panidos to Mesembria, the islands of Skiathos, Skopelos, and Skyros, as well as some unidentified places in Anatolia. In addition to these territorial concessions, the treaty of 1403 freed Byzantium from its tribute obligation to the Ottomans and guaranteed the release of all Byzantines held captive by the Turks. Finally, Süleyman promised that his ships would not sail through

---

[40] See Barker, *Manuel II*, pp. 129–33.   [41] Ibid., pp. 120–99.

the Straits without the permission of either the Byzantine emperor or the other Christian co-signatories of the treaty.[42] Noteworthy, moreover, from an ideological point of view is the fact that in the text of the treaty (which has only survived in Italian translation of a Turkish original) Süleyman continuously addresses the emperor as his "father," thus assuming a subordinate position in relation to the Byzantine ruler. The elevation of the emperor's status from vassal to that of "father" is a clear manifestation of the reversal brought about in Byzantine–Ottoman relations after the battle of Ankara.[43]

Throughout the next decade the Byzantine government was able to maintain the ascendancy it gained over the Ottomans in 1402–3, by merely playing the game of diplomacy and exploiting the rivalries among Bayezid's sons. Supported by Manuel II, one of these sons, Mehmed I, ended up being the final victor of the internecine strife and ascended the Ottoman throne as sole ruler in 1413. Relations between the Byzantines and Ottomans remained relatively peaceful during much of the reign of Mehmed I (r. 1413–21), who immediately upon his accession acknowledged the terms of the treaty of 1403 as well as his position as the "obedient son" of the emperor.[44] Conflicts or tensions did arise occasionally, and Manuel II never ceased from his efforts to obtain assistance from the West; yet a semblance of peace and friendship was preserved by both sides.[45]

However, Mehmed I's death in 1421, shortly after the coronation of Manuel II's son John VIII as co-emperor, became the occasion for a crisis within the Byzantine court that, in turn, led to a bigger crisis in Byzantine–Ottoman relations. Having grown accustomed during the interregnum period to interfering in the rivalries for succession to the Ottoman throne, the Byzantine government held a council meeting in 1421 to determine Mehmed I's successor. Manuel II's opinion was not to interfere at all and to accept Mehmed's eldest son and designated successor, Murad II, as sultan. John VIII, on the other hand, suggested supporting a rival

[42] The treaty of 1403, concluded in Gallipoli before Manuel II's return from his European journey, was signed by John VII, who acted as Manuel's regent and co-emperor during the latter's absence. The other co-signatories included Venice, Genoa, the duke of Naxos, and the Hospitallers of Rhodes, who had formed an anti-Turkish league (*liga*) at this time. G. T. Dennis, "The Byzantine–Turkish treaty of 1403," *OCP* 33 (1967), 72–88 (text of the treaty at 77–80); Matschke, *Ankara*, pp. 40–141; E. A. Zachariadou, "Süleyman Çelebi in Rumili and the Ottoman chronicles," *Der Islam* 60/2 (1983), 268–96.

[43] See Matschke, *Ankara*, pp. 51–6. It should be added too that Doukas does not fail to mention the father–son relationship between the Byzantine emperor and Süleyman: Doukas–Grecu, XVIII.2, p. 111.

[44] Doukas–Grecu, XX.1, XXII.5, pp. 133, 157–9.

[45] Barker, *Manuel II*, pp. 287–9, 318–20, 331–54, 389–90.

claimant to the throne, the pretender Mustafa, whom the Byzantines held in their custody at Lemnos since 1416. At the root of these diverging opinions lay in reality a much broader conflict concerning the empire's general international orientation, as the Byzantine court stood divided between those who supported Manuel II's policy of passive resistance to the Ottomans, and those who clustered around the young Emperor John VIII and advocated a more aggressive policy. The latter group, we do not know whether by the strength of their numbers or by their arguments, won the debate. Manuel, who was quite old by this time, did not fight back and left the matter to the care of his son.[46] However, the scheme of John VIII and his supporters backfired when Murad II (r. 1421–44, 1446–51), after immediately capturing and killing Mustafa, retaliated by laying siege to both Constantinople and Thessalonike. Manuel II's words about his son cited at the opening of this chapter were triggered in part by the outcome of the Mustafa affair, which laid bare the dangers associated with the course of action John VIII was prepared to take in contradiction to the policy Manuel had pursued since the battle of Ankara.

Murad II's siege of Constantinople turned out to be short and unsuccessful, but his armies continued to pressure Thessalonike so forcefully that in 1423 the city was ceded to Venice and remained under Venetian domination until 1430, when Murad finally conquered it. In 1423 another Ottoman army attacked the Morea and caused great destruction in the peninsula. Towards the end of the same year, in response to the growing Ottoman danger, John VIII decided to explore the possibility of western aid and traveled to Venice, Milan, and Hungary, without, however, achieving much and merely adding his name to the list of previous emperors who had made likewise fruitless attempts. Meanwhile, in February 1424, about three months after John VIII's departure from Constantinople and probably without his knowledge,[47] a treaty was concluded between the Byzantine and Ottoman governments which introduced peace, yet through terms that were extremely unfavorable to Byzantium. The price for peace basically amounted to the revocation of the major advantages that Byzantium had acquired by the treaty of 1403: a large portion of the territory that Süleyman had restored to the empire was surrendered to the

---

[46] Sphrantzes–Grecu, VIII.3; Chalkok.–Darkó, vol. II, pp. 1–3. Cf. Barker, *Manuel II*, pp. 340–59. The pretender Mustafa claimed to be a son of Bayezid I.

[47] Despite his failing health, Manuel II (d. 1425) presumably took advantage of John VIII's absence to initiate peace talks with the Ottomans at this time. John's brother and regent, the future emperor Constantine XI, may have been involved in the arrangements too, even though on the basis of what is known about Manuel's foreign policy it is more likely that the initiative came from the latter.

Ottomans, and, more significantly, after about twenty years of freedom from the burden of tribute, the Byzantine emperor was once again reduced to the status of a tribute-paying Ottoman vassal.[48]

The question of Church union, it may be recalled, was the second bone of contention between Manuel II and John VIII. As the union of the Churches was inextricably linked with the question of western aid to Byzantium, each emperor who turned to the Latin West for military and financial assistance against the Ottomans had to confront it. John V had sought a solution to the problem through his personal conversion. Manuel II, for his part, perpetuated the negotiations for union, yet by making its implementation strictly conditional upon military assistance, he could avoid it so long as this prerequisite did not materialize.[49] John VIII, too, used the inducement of union to get help from the West, but he deviated from the pattern set by his predecessors by actually agreeing to the union at the Council of Florence in 1439, whereas both John V and Manuel II, for all their differences, had been extremely cautious about not committing their subjects to such an act.[50] The Union of Florence, accepted on papal terms and implying therefore the Byzantine Church's subordination to the Church of Rome, was bitterly resented by the populace of Constantinople, who simply regarded it as the betrayal of their Orthodox faith.[51] For the next thirteen years until the city's fall to the Ottomans, the inhabitants of Constantinople were torn by controversy over this issue. And while conflicts between the unionists and anti-unionists dominated the city's political atmosphere and consumed the energies of both the citizens and

[48] Byzantium's territorial losses in 1424 included the cities and towns on the Black Sea coast (except some fortresses such as Mesembria and Derkoi), Zeitounion, and the lands along the Strymon: Doukas–Grecu, XXIX.1, p. 245. Compare these losses with Byzantium's territorial gains in the decade following the battle of Ankara: Doukas–Grecu, XVIII.2, pp. 111–13 (treaty with Süleyman, 1403), XX.1, p. 133 (treaty with Mehmed I, 1413); Dennis, "Byzantine–Turkish treaty of 1403," 78. The amount of the tribute demanded by the Ottomans in 1424 was 300,000 aspers according to Doukas, or 100,000 ducats according to a contemporary Venetian document from Coron reproduced in Marino Sanuto, *Vite dei duchi di Venezia*, ed. L. A. Muratori, *RIS*, 22 (Milan, 1733), col. 975B. It should be noted that while Constantinople was free from the tribute obligation throughout 1403–24, in Thessalonike payment of tribute may have been resumed around 1411: see below, ch. 4, p. 64 and note 38; ch. 5, note 6. Cf. Dölger, *Reg.*, vol. v, nos. 3412–14.

[49] Barker, *Manuel II*, pp. 321–31, 391; J. Gill, *The Council of Florence* (Cambridge, 1959; repr. with corrigenda: New York, 1982), pp. 20–39. For Manuel II's earliest projects for union during his regime in Thessalonike, see below, ch. 3, pp. 46, 52.

[50] Even though the union was concluded at the end of the Council of Ferrara–Florence (1438–9), John VIII initiated negotiations with the papacy much earlier, in 1430, during the same year as Thessalonike fell to the Ottomans. See Gill, *Council of Florence*, pp. 42–3.

[51] J.-L. van Dieten, "Der Streit in Byzanz um die Rezeption der Unio Florentina," *Ostkirchliche Studien* 39 (1990), 160–80.

their rulers, the Ottomans, who were themselves experiencing factional politics, continued to make their headway in Christian lands.

In November 1444 Ottoman forces inflicted a devastating defeat on a crusading army at Varna, in Bulgaria. The Christian army that Murad II crushed on this occasion was the long-delayed prize for which John VIII had concluded the Union of Florence five years earlier. The failure of the Crusade of Varna demonstrated to the Byzantines that their submission to the Latin Church had been in vain, thereby strengthening the position of the anti-unionists, while at the same time leading to despair many of those who had put their trust in Latin help for the salvation of Constantinople. As for John VIII, there was little he could do after Varna apart from trying to placate the Sultan with gifts and congratulations.[52] But Murad II was hard to placate at this stage, and in 1446 he struck back by invading Thessaly and the Morea. The Sultan's armies exposed the Despotate of the Morea to the most severe attack it had met from the Ottomans to that day, and the province was subsequently reduced to a tributary status.[53]

Thereafter rapid deterioration set in at Byzantium. Inside Constantinople, the Union of Florence was so unpopular that John VIII's successor, Constantine XI (r. 1448–53), avoided imposing it on his subjects (that is, till the very eve of the city's fall) even though he considered himself officially bound by it in the international arena. While pursuing a consciously ambiguous policy towards the Union, Constantine made the usual appeals to western powers – Venice, Genoa, Florence, Ragusa, Hungary, Aragon, and the papacy – for assistance against the Ottomans. Despite his many pleas, which were accompanied by extra inducements such as the offer of Lemnos to King Alfonso V of Aragon and Naples, or of Mesembria to John Hunyadi of Hungary, Constantine XI had no success in arousing the westerners to his plight.[54] At the time when Murad II passed away (1451), leaving

[52] O. Halecki, *The Crusade of Varna. A Discussion of Controversial Problems* (New York, 1943); F. Babinger, "Von Amurath zu Amurath. Vor- und Nachspiel der Schlacht bei Varna (1444)," *Oriens* 3/2 (1950), 233–44; Setton, *The Papacy and the Levant*, vol. II, pp. 82–107; A. Hohlweg, "Der Kreuzzug des Jahres 1444," in *Die Türkei in Europa*, ed. K.-D. Grothusen (Göttingen, 1979), pp. 20–37; M. Chasin, "The Crusade of Varna," in *A History of the Crusades*, gen. ed. K. M. Setton, vol. VI: *The Impact of the Crusades in Europe*, ed. H. W. Hazard and N. P. Zacour (Madison, 1989), pp. 276–310; Imber (trans.), *Crusade of Varna*, pp. 1–39 (Introduction).

[53] D. A. Zakythinos, *Le Despotat grec de Morée*, rev. edn. by C. Maltezou (London, 1975), vol. I, pp. 204–40; see below, ch. 10, pp. 272–3.

[54] The most recent contribution to this subject is E. Malamut, "Les ambassades du dernier empereur de Byzance," in *Mélanges Gilbert Dagron* (= *TM* 14) (Paris, 2002), pp. 429–48. In addition to the sources and earlier studies cited in this article, see M. Carroll, "Constantine XI Palaeologus: some problems of image," in *Maistor. Classical, Byzantine and Renaissance Studies for Robert Browning*, ed. A. Moffatt (Canberra, 1984), pp. 329–30 (n. 2), 338–43; D. M. Nicol, *The Immortal Emperor*.

the throne to his son Mehmed II (r. 1444–6, 1451–81), who shared the imperial ambitions of Bayezid I, it seemed as though Constantinople had little to
rely upon besides the legendary strength of its walls. Conquering the Byzantine capital on May 29, 1453, Mehmed II realized his great-grandfather
Bayezid's premature and unfulfilled goal of building a universal empire
with Constantinople at its center. Seven years later, Mehmed II subjugated
the Morea as well, thus putting an end to the last vestige of the Byzantine
Empire.[55]

The Life and Legend of Constantine Palaiologos, Last Emperor of the Romans (Cambridge, 1992),
    pp. 16–17, 41, 48–51, 55–63.

[55] Although in a broad sense the Empire of Trebizond, which Mehmed II conquered in 1461, might be
    considered the last outpost of Byzantium, technically speaking it had not been part of the Byzantine
    Empire since its establishment as an independent, separatist state just on the eve of the Fourth
    Crusade. Moreover, it was remote and had little bearing on events in Constantinople and the rest
    of the empire. Therefore, the discussion of Trebizond falls outside the scope of the present book.

Thessalonike

INTRODUCTION TO PART II

Thessalonike, the "second city" of the Byzantine Empire and the major administrative, economic, and cultural center of medieval Macedonia, was the scene of almost uninterrupted military struggles and climactic political events between 1382 and 1430, which once resulted in the city's complete independence from Constantinople under Greek rule, and no fewer than three times in its subjection to foreign domination. In 1382 Manuel II Palaiologos, deprived recently of his right of succession to the imperial throne at the conclusion of a civil war in Constantinople, left the Byzantine capital with some followers and established himself in Thessalonike as Emperor.[1] Acting independently of John V's government in Constantinople, Manuel started from his new base a vigorous campaign against the Ottomans with the aim of recovering the regions of Macedonia and Thessaly that had been conquered by them. In spite of some minor victories initially, at the end of four years under Ottoman siege the Thessalonians pressured Manuel to give up the struggle, and following his departure from the city they surrendered to the Ottomans in the spring of 1387. For the next sixteen years Thessalonike remained under Ottoman domination, until its restoration to Byzantium by the Byzantine–Ottoman treaty of 1403 signed in the wake of the battle of Ankara. The city was then ceded to John VII Palaiologos (d. 1408), who ruled there semi-independently as "Emperor of all Thessaly"[2] to the end of his life. After him, from 1408 to 1423, Manuel II's third son Andronikos (under the tutorship of Demetrios Laskaris Leontares during his minority) managed the affairs of the city, holding the title "Despot" (*despotes*). Throughout this period, the

---

[1] Manuel II was not a foreigner to Thessalonike, where he had ruled as Despot during 1369–73. On the civil war of 1379–81, which ended with the re-designation of Manuel's brother and nephew, Andronikos IV and John VII, as successors of John V, see below, ch. 6, pp. 126–30.

[2] John VII's title is reported only by Doukas: Doukas–Grecu, p. 113.

Ottomans made several attempts to capture Thessalonike. The financial and military resources, supplies, and strength of the city were so reduced by these persistent attacks that the Despot Andronikos, unable to obtain help from Constantinople, was in the end compelled to hand it over to Venice. During the seven years of their administration the Venetians made many peace advances to the Ottomans, all of which failed. Nor did they succeed in protecting and provisioning Thessalonike adequately. On March 29, 1430, the city finally fell to the forces of Sultan Murad II.[3]

With this complex background permeated by constant political fluctuations in the mere space of half a century, Thessalonike stands out as a remarkably appropriate and interesting setting for an analysis of political attitudes. Moreover, the city's particularly volatile internal history punctuated by a series of social upheavals provides an ideal opportunity for studying the Thessalonians' attitudes within their proper sociopolitical and socioeconomic context. The aim of the chapters in Part II is to enhance our perception of Thessalonike's internal history as well as its relations with Constantinople, the Latins, and the Ottomans during the period in question, by on the one hand examining the effects of Ottoman pressures in terms of the different political attitudes that emerged there, and on the other hand exposing and analyzing the socioeconomic adjustments and internal tensions that accompanied these turbulent years of siege, military struggle, and political change.

[3] On these events, see A. Vakalopoulos, *History of Thessaloniki* (Thessaloniki, 1972), pp. 62–75; Dennis, *Reign of Manuel II*; Dennis, "Byzantine–Turkish treaty of 1403," 72–88; J. Tsaras, "La fin d'Andronic Paléologue dernier Despote de Thessalonique," *RESEE* 3 (1965), 419–32; P. Lemerle, "La domination vénitienne à Thessalonique," *Miscellanea Giovanni Galbiati*, vol. III (Milan, 1951), pp. 219–25; D. Jacoby, "Thessalonique de la domination de Byzance à celle de Venise. Continuité, adaptation ou rupture?," *Mélanges Gilbert Dagron* (= *TM* 14) (Paris, 2002), pp. 303–18; M. Delilbaşı, "Selânik'in Venedik idaresine geçmesi ve Osmanlı–Venedik savaşı," *Belleten* 40 (1976), 573–88; Delilbaşı, "Selânik ve Yanya'da Osmanlı egemenliği," 75–92; Vryonis, "Ottoman conquest of Thessaloniki," pp. 281–321; J. Tsaras, *Η τελευταία άλωση της Θεσσαλονίκης (1430)* (Thessalonike, 1985).

CHAPTER 3

Social organization, historical developments, and political attitudes in Thessalonike: an overview (1382–1430)

In the early fourteenth century the social structure of Thessalonike incorporated, like most other Byzantine cities of the time, three distinct layers. The top layer comprised the landed aristocracy, both lay and ecclesiastical; below them were the *mesoi*, a "middle class" consisting of rich merchants, small landholders, minor functionaries, the small clergy, and those exercising independent professions; at the very bottom were the poor, to whose ranks belonged small artisans, manual laborers, and small cultivators.[1] However, around the middle of the same century, following the loss of their landed possessions in Macedonia and Thrace successively to Serbian and Ottoman conquerors, members of the landholding aristocracy, who by tradition had always disdained trade and commerce, began to engage in commercial activities. When the fundamental distinction that separated aristocrats from rich middle-class merchants was removed in this manner, the term designating the middle class (οἱ μέσοι) also disappeared from the sources. Consequently, in a society which became more and more characterized by commercial interests, the principal distinction that remained effective was that between the rich (including merchants, bankers, landowners) and the poor, who suffered from deep economic and social problems.[2]

---

[1] On the social structure of late Byzantine cities and these three groups, see now K.-P. Matschke and F. Tinnefeld, *Die Gesellschaft im späten Byzanz: Gruppen, Strukturen und Lebensformen* (Cologne, Weimar, and Vienna, 2001), with extensive bibliography. For Thessalonike in particular, though considerably dated, see O. Tafrali, *Thessalonique au quatorzième siècle* (Paris, 1913; repr. Thessalonike, 1993), pp. 19–34; P. Charanis, "Internal strife in Byzantium during the fourteenth century," *B* 15 (1941), 212–13.

[2] Oikonomidès, *Hommes d'affaires*, pp. 114–23; Matschke and Tinnefeld, *Gesellschaft*, pp. 154–7, 166–72. In the fourteenth and fifteenth centuries the social structure of Thessalonike also incorporated members of guild-like organizations or corporations such as those of the sailors, perfume producers, builders, and salt miners: see *Iviron*, vol. III, nos. 78, 84 (= *Schatzkammer*, nos. III, 112); *Chilandar* (P), nos. 84, 85; *Zographou*, no. 25; *Docheiariou*, no. 50; *Dionysiou*, no. 14; H. Hunger and K. Vogel, *Ein byzantinisches Rechenbuch des 15. Jahrhunderts* (Vienna, 1963), no. 31. On the social structure of Thessalonike around the beginning of the fifteenth century, see Matschke, *Ankara*, pp. 144–75.

While the Ottoman invasions certainly played a decisive role in accelerating this sharp social and economic differentiation in Thessalonike, it must be pointed out that an atmosphere of civil discord prevailed in the city prior to and independently of the Ottoman threat, as demonstrated by the developments of the first half of the fourteenth century which culminated in the so-called Zealot movement.[3] The increased grievances of the lower classes in connection with the oppressive practices of the rich were already evident in the earlier part of the fourteenth century. Sources of this period are filled with references to the burdens imposed upon the poor by speculators, moneylenders, storekeepers, and even by certain ecclesiastics who practiced usury.[4] The city's governors, in their inability to force the rich to pay taxes, often turned to the poor to make up for their declining revenues. Soldiers who were dissatisfied with their pay also found in the poor a suitable target for molestation. Because of the corruption of judges, moreover, it was almost impossible for people belonging to the lower classes to obtain justice at the law courts.[5]

Such wrongs and the resulting social tensions seem to have spread so fast that the city's archbishop Gregory Palamas, in a letter he sent to his flock from Asia Minor at the time of his captivity among the Ottomans (1354–5), found it necessary to urge those "who love money and injustice" to practice temperance and equity.[6] But the Thessalonians do not appear to have taken heed of Palamas' words, for his successors, the archbishops Isidore Glabas and Symeon, continued in later years to complain about offenses and injustices committed for the sake of material gain by both the rich and the poor; the transgression of laws; malpractices of officials; and conflicts between the rich and the poor, between the "powerful" and the "powerless," or between the rulers and their subjects.[7] Despite the strong moral tone

---

[3] On the Zealot movement, see most recently K.-P. Matschke, "Thessalonike und die Zeloten. Bemerkungen zu einem Schlüsselereignis der spätbyzantinischen Stadt- und Reichsgeschichte," *BS* 55 (1994), 19–43. For a survey of the extensive literature on the subject, see also J. W. Barker, "Late Byzantine Thessalonike: a second city's challenges and responses," *DOP* 57 (2003), 29–33 (Appendix 2).

[4] These can be found in the writings of Nicholas Kabasilas, Alexios Makrembolites, Nikephoros Choumnos, Thomas Magistros, Gregory Palamas, *et alii*. See Tafrali, *Thessalonique*, pp. 104–6, 111–16. For a recent discussion of these authors' negative attitudes towards usury as responses to contemporary realities in fourteenth-century Thessalonike, see A. E. Laiou, "Economic concerns and attitudes of the intellectuals of Thessalonike," *DOP* 57 (2003), 210–23.

[5] Tafrali, *Thessalonique*, pp. 63–5, 105, 108–9.

[6] A. Philippidis-Braat, "La captivité de Palamas chez les Turcs, dossier et commentaire," *TM* 7 (1979), 164.

[7] See, for example, Isidore–Christophorides, vol. II, Homilies 19, 21, 22, esp. pp. 299–300, 329–30, 344–7; Isidore–Christophorides, vol. I, Homily 28, pp. 45–9 (= "Συμβολὴ εἰς τὴν ἱστορίαν τῆς Θεσσαλονίκης. Δύο ἀνέκδοτοι ὁμιλίαι Ἰσιδώρου ἀρχιεπισκόπου Θεσσαλονίκης," ed. C. N.

and rhetorical character of these pronouncements which typically embody literary *topoi* and exaggeration, the marked increase in their frequency throughout the second half of the fourteenth and the beginning of the fifteenth century suggests, nonetheless, that the new conditions and hardships brought about by Ottoman attacks intensified the already existing socioeconomic tensions within Thessalonike and produced opportunities for certain groups of people who took advantage of the circumstances. On the other hand, the lack of unity and social cohesion among the inhabitants weakened their resistance to the Ottomans. Contemporary observers such as Demetrios Kydones, Isidore Glabas, Symeon of Thessalonike, and John Anagnostes all present the internal divisions of Thessalonian society as the major cause for the city's failure before the enemy.[8] Making a biblical allusion, Symeon of Thessalonike notes, "'Every kingdom divided against itself is brought to desolation'; and this is what happened."[9]

The political orientation of Thessalonike in relation to Constantinople also played a role in determining the outcome of military conflicts with the Ottomans. In 1382, when Manuel II established himself in Thessalonike and waged war against the Ottomans, he stood in open violation of the imperial policy of peace and reconciliation that was being pursued then by John V's government at Constantinople. Consequently, rather than receiving approval and assistance from the capital, Manuel's anti-Ottoman campaign aroused tensions between the two cities, as indicated by John V's punitive measures against the Constantinopolitans who were suspected of intending to join Manuel in Thessalonike.[10]

But if the frictions in this particular case were due to the exceptional circumstances provoked by Manuel II, who had seized the government of Thessalonike by force, generally speaking the opposition between the two cities and their conflicting foreign policies stemmed from the actions of Thessalonike's local governors (ἄρχοντες), who displayed a firm desire to dissociate themselves from central authority. This incentive for independence from Constantinople had already been expressed in the course of the civil war between John VI and John V, and by the movement of the

---

Tsirpanlis, Θεολογία 42 [1971], 567–70), Homily 31, pp. 85–95; Isidore–Laourdas; Symeon–Balfour; Symeon–Phountoules, nos. 16 and 22.

[8] Kydones–Loenertz, vol. II, nos. 273, 299; Isidore–Christophorides, vol. I, Homily 30, pp. 77–8, 79–80, 82; Isidore–Laourdas, pp. 32, 56–7; Isidore–Lampros, pp. 349–50, 385; Symeon–Balfour, pp. 47, 53, 55–6; Anagnostes–Tsaras, pp. 8–12.

[9] Symeon–Balfour, p. 53, lines 32–3.

[10] Kydones–Loenertz, vol. II, nos. 247 and 264. On John V's policy of peace and reconciliation with the Ottomans, see above, ch. 2, pp. 29–30.

Zealots.[11] Its persistence through the fifteenth century is suggested by the archbishop Symeon, who alludes to the opposition of the Thessalonian *archontes* against the palace courtiers at Constantinople, adding that the latter in turn were opposed to the burghers (οἱ ἀστοί) of Thessalonike.[12] Moreover, on the occasion of Thessalonike's restoration to the Byzantine Empire in 1403, it is reported that Demetrios Laskaris Leontares, who went there as Emperor John VII's envoy to receive the city from the Ottomans, met with resistance and intrigues (ἐπιβουλαί) on the part of the citizens.[13] Likewise, in 1408, when Emperor Manuel II traveled to Thessalonike to install his young son Andronikos as Despot and Demetrios Laskaris Leontares as the latter's regent, there was another disturbance (ταραχή) in the city.[14] The disorders of 1403 and 1408 are most likely to have been expressions of Thessalonike's insubordination to Constantinople since they both coincide with the appointment to the city of people closely linked to the imperial government.[15] Symeon, who has described these events, was strongly against the separatism that existed between the two cities, which he found to be detrimental to the security of Thessalonike. In his account of an Ottoman siege that took place in 1422–3, he wrote:

[A]mbassadors had wrongly been sent out from Thessalonike to the Emir without consulting the Basileus; I myself was averse to this and kept advising that nothing be done without consulting the Basileus, but they would not listen at all to my words; and this became one of the principal reasons why the Thessalonians' city landed in grave danger. The result was that certain imperial agreements with the barbarians, which were ready to be implemented, were left in abeyance.[16]

In addition, the city of Thessalonike possessed special privileges which further distanced it from Constantinople.[17] Although the precise nature and content of these privileges are not all that clear to us, Manuel II certainly recognized their importance in a public speech he delivered in

[11] Separatism seems to have been a consistent feature in Thessalonike's history since earlier times, finding expression from the seventh century onwards in the cult of St. Demetrios, the city's patron saint whom local tradition transformed into a symbol of Thessalonian independence from Constantinople: see R. J. Macrides, "Subversion and loyalty in the cult of St. Demetrios," *BS* 51 (1990), 189–97. On the Thessalonian tendencies of separatism from the capital during the Palaiologan period, see now Barker, "Late Byzantine Thessalonike," 14–23.

[12] Symeon–Balfour, p. 53, lines 30–1: "καὶ κατὰ τῶν ἐν τοῖς βασιλείοις μὲν οἱ προέχοντες τοῦ κοινοῦ, κατ' ἀστῶν δὲ πάλιν ἐκεῖνοι."

[13] Ibid., p. 44.   [14] Ibid., p. 48.   [15] See ibid., pp. 115 (n. 59), 122–3.

[16] Ibid., pp. 57 (text), 161 (trans.). It is not clear what the "imperial agreements" with the Ottomans mentioned at the end of this passage were. As Balfour notes (p. 161, n. 162), the unsuccessful Byzantine embassy of September 1422 that sought peace with Murad II (Dölger, *Reg.*, vol. v, no. 3393) seems too early to be identified with this incident.

[17] See Tafrali, *Thessalonique*, pp. 24, 49, 66–71, 150, 157; G. I. Brătianu, *Privilèges et franchises municipales dans l'Empire byzantin* (Bucharest and Paris, 1936), pp. 108–9, 115–22; Lj. Maksimović, *The*

1383 before the citizens of Thessalonike. Addressing the Thessalonians as the descendants of Philip and Alexander, Manuel emphasized the fact that they were accustomed to greater freedom compared with the inhabitants of other Macedonian and Anatolian cities, and that they were exempt even from the tribute that all free Byzantines had to pay to the emperor.[18] It is noteworthy, moreover, that in 1423 the agreement concerning the transfer of Thessalonike to Venetian rule was concluded with the condition that the privileges and customs of the city's inhabitants were to be respected.[19]

The partial autonomy which the Thessalonians enjoyed, or sought at any rate, constituted part of an empire-wide phenomenon whereby throughout the fourteenth century, with the progressive decline of the power and authority of the Palaiologan state, Byzantine cities steadily achieved a considerable degree of independence.[20] In the course of this process particular urban groups or institutions started taking over the traditional functions of the Byzantine state. The Church, for instance, assumed judicial functions, while the aristocracy took over administrative functions along with the management of the finances and defense of certain towns and cities. Within the context of the struggle against the Ottomans, parallel developments in Thessalonike meant that its inhabitants, as they were alienated from Constantinople, had to manage the war by their own efforts and means. And when they could no longer sustain the military undertaking by themselves, their only remaining alternative was to seek foreign alliances which contributed to the splintering of the population since opinions varied over the question of which foreign power(s) to approach.

The sequence of events during Manuel II's independent regime illustrates well the impact of Thessalonike's isolation from Constantinople on the emergence of a range of policies and corresponding attitudes in the

---

Byzantine Provincial Administration under the Palaiologoi (Amsterdam, 1988), pp. 248–57; E. Patlagean, "L'immunité des Thessaloniciens," in *EYΨYXIA. Mélanges offerts à Hélène Ahrweiler* (Paris, 1998), vol. II, pp. 591–601.

[18] "Συμβουλευτικός," ed. Laourdas, 296–8. For some practical applications of the fiscal privilege to which Manuel II refers, all dating from the first half of the fourteenth century, see Patlagean, "L'immunité," p. 592. On the interest in Philip and Alexander in Palaiologan Byzantium, see A. Karathanassis, "Philip and Alexander of Macedon in the literature of the Palaiologan era," in *Byzantine Macedonia: Identity, Image and History*, ed. J. Burke and R. Scott (Melbourne, 2000), pp. 111–15.

[19] Sathas, *Documents*, vol. I, no. 86, pp. 133, 135–8. See also K. D. Mertzios, Μνημεῖα μακεδονικῆς ἱστορίας (Thessalonike, 1947), p. 72.

[20] Zachariadou, "Ἐφήμερες ἀπόπειρες γιὰ αὐτοδιοίκηση," 345–51; Oikonomidès, "Pour une typologie des villes 'séparées'," pp. 169–75. For earlier signs of the trend towards urban autonomy, see A. P. Kazhdan and A. W. Epstein, *Change in Byzantine Culture in the Eleventh and Twelfth Centuries* (Berkeley, Los Angeles, and London, 1985), pp. 52–3; P. Magdalino, *The Empire of Manuel I Komnenos, 1143–1180* (Cambridge, 1993), pp. 150–60.

city. When his initial successes against the enemy troops came to a halt, Manuel, who had openly violated the official imperial policy of peace by his anti-Ottoman campaign, could not seek help from Constantinople. Thus, in 1384 he entered an alliance with Nerio Acciaiuoli, the Florentine Lord of Corinth, and his own brother Theodore I Palaiologos, the Despot of the Morea. Acquiring no concrete benefit from this alliance, he then initiated negotiations with Pope Urban VI and also sought military and financial assistance from Venice. But these subsequent attempts at obtaining western help failed as well.[21] Interestingly, the Senate of Venice turned down Manuel's requests so as to endanger neither its political relations with the Byzantine imperial government, nor the commercial privileges Venetian merchants enjoyed in Ottoman territories.[22] Inside the city, on the other hand, Manuel's negotiations with the papacy had the effect of alienating certain groups, particularly the clergy and the hesychast monks, who were opposed to the union of their Church with the Church of Rome.[23] At the same time, a number of people who advocated the capitulation of the city to the Ottomans began to raise their voices. As early as 1383, in his "Discourse of Counsel to the Thessalonians," Manuel had already reproached certain citizens who did not want to fight against the Ottomans, but preferred instead to submit to them and pay them tribute.[24] In 1383 or 1384 Demetrios Kydones also wrote with great concern that he had heard about some Thessalonians who "do not hesitate to proclaim freely that to try to free our native land from the Turks is clearly to war against God."[25] By 1387 the segment of the population in favor of an accommodation with the Ottomans, which presumably expanded in the meantime, forced Manuel out of the city and then surrendered to the enemy. In his "Epistolary Discourse" to Nicholas Kabasilas written shortly afterwards, Manuel bitterly complained that the Thessalonians, on whose behalf he risked his life, had

---

[21] For Manuel II's dealings with western powers, see Kydones–Loenertz, vol. II, nos. 302–6, 308–11, 313–16, 318, 322, 327, 334, 335; *MP*, no. 28, pp. 60–1. Cf. Dennis, *Reign of Manuel II*, pp. 114–26, 136–50; Barker, *Manuel II*, pp. 54–6.

[22] Dennis, *Reign of Manuel II*, pp. 125–6. For the negotiations of the Venetian Senate with the Turks concerning commercial privileges during 1384, see Thiriet, *Régestes*, vol. I, nos. 667, 672, 677, 678. On the good relations between Murad I and Venice, see also E. A. Zachariadou, *Trade and Crusade; Venetian Crete and the Emirates of Menteshe and Aydın (1300–1415)* (Venice, 1983), p. 74 and n. 328; E. A. Zachariadou, "Marginalia on the history of Epirus and Albania (1380–1418)," *WZKM* 78 (1988), 201–2. Although the Ottomans had been allied to the Genoese since 1352 and maintained close commercial relations with them, Murad I simultaneously welcomed the diplomatic approaches of the Venetians so as to neutralize the two rival Italian powers: see İnalcık, "Ottoman Turks and the Crusades," p. 245.

[23] Kydones–Loenertz, vol. II, no. 302, lines 34–40.   [24] "Συμβουλευτικός," ed. Laourdas, p. 298.

[25] Kydones–Loenertz, vol. II, no. 324, lines 39–42.

treacherously fought on the side of the enemy.[26] It is evident that as the Ottoman siege persisted for several years and meanwhile no help came to Thessalonike from Constantinople, from the Morea, or from any of the western powers to which Manuel made overtures, more and more inhabitants joined the ranks of those who were from the beginning in favor of an accommodation with the enemy.

After the restoration of Thessalonike to Byzantine rule in 1403, the city seems to have enjoyed a period of relative peace and prosperity owing to the internal problems of the Ottomans in the aftermath of the battle of Ankara.[27] However, as soon as the Ottomans recovered their strength and resumed their attacks, beginning with Musa's siege of 1411–13, Thessalonike turned into a scene of conflicts between those in favor of fighting against the Turks with western assistance and those inclining towards an accommodation with them.[28] These conflicts reached a climax during another siege launched in 1422–3 by the forces of Murad II. Symeon's account of these years makes it clear that once again Thessalonike's isolation from Constantinople and the unavailability of assistance from the imperial government played a crucial role in the outcome of events. Pointing to the fact that the Despot Andronikos (r. 1408–23) had no one to call on for help against the Ottomans, Symeon states that the Emperors in Constantinople (Manuel II and John VIII) "had their own preoccupation with the capital city."[29] He then reports that he himself and the Despot both petitioned Manuel II several times, requesting people with military skills and financial resources to be sent to the city's aid. In response to their repeated pleas, the Emperor eventually dispatched an unidentified military commander to Thessalonike. But the latter brought with him neither financial help nor, it seems, any ammunition. Instead he proposed the use of local resources for the city's defense needs, suggesting the establishment of a common fund "to which each member of the Senate and of the citizen body (ἕκαστος τῶν τε τῆς συγκλήτου καὶ πολιτείας) would contribute out of his own assets." This proposal met with opposition from all sides. Some wealthy Thessalonians responded by taking flight. The common people began to riot in favor of surrender when the news spread in the city that the Ottomans had approached the above-mentioned military commander for

---

[26] Dennis, *Letters of Manuel II*, p. 187.

[27] See below, ch. 4, pp. 62–3. See also Doukas–Grecu, XVIII.2, p. 113.

[28] See Symeon–Balfour, pp. 47–59 (text) and 119–72 (commentary).

[29] Ibid., p. 56. The "preoccupation" mentioned by Symeon refers no doubt to Murad II's siege of Constantinople (1422) which, like the simultaneous blockade of Thessalonike, was an act of retaliation for John VIII's support of the pretender Mustafa: see above, ch. 2, pp. 34–5; and below, ch. 8, pp. 187–9.

a peace settlement, provided that he would drive the Despot Andronikos out of Thessalonike. Some rich and influential men, on the other hand, tried to convince the Despot to make an alliance with Venice. In the end, Andronikos gave in to the pressure of the latter group, and Thessalonike was ceded to the Venetians who took over its provisioning and defense.[30] Concerning the same event, Doukas states somewhat more briefly that the Thessalonians, subjected to daily Ottoman attacks, starving from a shortage of provisions, and expecting no assistance from Constantinople, which "was suffering her own calamities and was unable to send help," dispatched ambassadors to Venice.[31]

The city's transfer was presumably arranged without consulting the authorities at Constantinople since the Venetians, after accepting Andronikos' offer, took the additional step of announcing the decision to the imperial government in order to ensure its approval. The Venetians were prepared in fact to call off their agreement with the Despot, should the Byzantine Emperor not consent to it.[32] But the Emperor did apparently give his consent, for, according to the Chronicle of Morosini, on the day of the city's takeover (September 13, 1423) the Venetian galleys that entered the harbor of Thessalonike were accompanied by a Byzantine imperial galley.[33]

It is evident from Symeon's description of Murad II's blockade and subsequent events that, in the absence of help from Constantinople, the inhabitants of Thessalonike were left with two choices: either to surrender to the Ottomans as in 1387, or to submit to Venetian authority.[34] Even

---

[30] Symeon–Balfour, p. 57; cf. pp. 161–3.   [31] Doukas–Grecu, XXIX.4, p. 247.

[32] Sathas, *Documents*, vol. I, nos. 86 (July 7, 1423) and 89 (July 27, 1423), pp. 133–9, 141–50; Thiriet, *Régestes*, vol. II, nos. 1892 and 1898.

[33] Lemerle, "Domination vénitienne," p. 222. In a Venetian document dated April 2–4, 1425, we find another confirmation of Manuel II's consent: see Setton, *The Papacy and the Levant*, vol. II, p. 21, n. 66. For the date of the Venetian takeover, see Schreiner, *Kleinchroniken*, vol. II, pp. 423–4.

[34] The Chronicle of Morosini, too, presents these as the two options, both of which had been pursued: ". . . quelo imperio eser in debel condition e queli da Salonichi aver mandado a dir al Signor turco de volerseli dar con questi pati: diser loro apareclarli de darli le do parte de soa intrada, e de la terza viver per loro e de remagnir in bona paxe, e in quanto no queli manderia al Rezimento de Negroponte, che queli se daria puo (puoi) a la dogal Signoria de Viniexia . . ." Quoted in F. Thiriet, "Les Chroniques vénitiennes de la Marcienne et leur importance pour l'histoire de la Romanie gréco-vénitienne," *Mélanges d'Archéologie et d'Histoire* 66 (1954), 278, n. 1. The question arises as to whether the negotiations between the Thessalonians and the Sultan mentioned by Morosini can be identified with those described by Symeon (Symeon–Balfour, p. 57, lines 31–4) between the Ottomans and the military commander from Constantinople. The terms given by the two sources are different; however, Morosini's focus is on the terms offered by the Thessalonians (⅓:⅔ division of the city's income between the Greeks and the Turks respectively), whereas Symeon states the terms offered by the Ottomans (lifting of the siege in return for the Despot's removal from the city). On the other hand, Morosini shows the Thessalonians as approaching the Ottomans, while Symeon presents the Ottomans as making overtures to the Byzantine general. Another possibility is to identify

Symeon, who was nearly as much opposed to the Latins as he was to the Turks, declared that Thessalonike, by being handed over to Venice, "escaped being betrayed to the infidel."[35] Hence in 1423, by contrast to the situation in 1387, the political attitude that won the day in Thessalonike was pro-Latin, and specifically pro-Venetian. This attitude was embraced primarily by people who supported the cause of war against the Ottomans and wielded substantial power and influence over the governance of the city. Their opinion thus prevailed over that of the common people who were agitating in favor of surrender to the Ottomans. In addition, there was another group inside Thessalonike that shared pro-Latin sympathies but, not truly believing in the cause of war, chose to depart from the city. Their flight to Venetian territories is attested as of 1411.[36]

Yet, as the above-mentioned riots of 1423 in favor of surrender indicate, the option of an accommodation and reconciliation with the Ottomans continued to be popular among certain segments of the population, particularly among the lower classes, in the course of the years that followed the restoration of Thessalonike to Byzantine rule. In fact, a group of citizens who actively supported this position were instrumental in sending embassies to negotiate with the Ottomans during the sieges of Musa (1411–13) and of Murad II (1422–3).[37] It is also reported that many inhabitants fled from Thessalonike at this time to join the Ottomans.[38]

During the period of the Venetian domination, the popularity of an accommodationist policy with regard to the Ottomans appears to have grown considerably, spreading across to other sectors of Thessalonian society besides the lower classes. Doukas informs us that the Venetian authorities in Thessalonike seized large numbers of native aristocrats who were suspected of cooperating with the enemy and deported them to Negroponte, Crete, and Venice.[39] Doukas' testimony is confirmed by a group of Venetian documents that report the arrest and exile of four Thessalonians to Crete on the grounds of their suspected association with the Ottomans at the onset of the Venetian regime. The arrested Thessalonians, whose

the Thessalonian embassy to the Ottomans in Morosini's account with a similar embassy, again depicted by Symeon (p. 57, lines 4–5), that was sent out from Thessalonike before the arrival of the Constantinopolitan general, in fact, even before Andronikos and Symeon asked Manuel II for assistance. For different views on the reliability of Morosini, see Thiriet, "Chroniques vénitiennes," 272–9 and Tsaras, "Fin d'Andronic," 421–5.

[35] Symeon–Balfour, p. 59, lines 7–8.
[36] N. Iorga, "Notes et extraits pour servir à l'histoire des Croisades au XVe siècle," *ROL* 4 (1896), 554–5, 573–4; Thiriet, *Régestes*, vol. II, nos. 1592 and 1635; Mertzios, Μνημεῖα, pp. 81–2; Symeon–Balfour, pp. 47, 57, 59.
[37] Symeon–Balfour, pp. 49, 55–7.   [38] Ibid., p. 59.   [39] Doukas–Grecu, XXIX.4, pp. 247–9.

leader was a man called Platyskalites,[40] presumably had close ties with Murad II since in 1424 their release was proposed to the Sultan in exchange for the Venetian ambassador Nicolò Giorgi (Zorzi), who was held captive by the Ottomans. This plan never materialized and the four Thessalonians remained in exile until 1430, at which time only two of them were still alive. Throughout this period the Venetians kept them under strict surveillance and deported them successively from Crete to Venice and then to Padua in order to eliminate their chances of scheming with the local inhabitants of any one place. The two remaining Thessalonians were finally set free in or after May 1430, as the Senate of Venice, no longer threatened by them subsequent to the fall of Thessalonike, decided that the cost of detaining them in prison was henceforth superfluous.[41]

We possess further evidence of the widening appeal of a conciliatory attitude towards the Ottomans in the course of the Venetian regime. During an Ottoman attack that took place in 1425 or 1426, it is reported that many Thessalonians, including people who had been appointed to guard the city walls, fled to the enemy.[42] Shortly before the final assault on Thessalonike, on the other hand, as the eyewitness Anagnostes observed, "the majority were annoyed because it was not possible for them to surrender the city to the Turks."[43] According to Anagnostes, Murad II, who twice sent a group of Christian officers in his army to persuade the Thessalonians to rise up against their Venetian governors, expected indeed to take the city without bloodshed, through the cooperation of its inhabitants.[44] The Venetians, too, suspected a favorable attitude towards the Ottomans on the part of the Thessalonians and placed among them troops of "*Tzetarioi*" – described by Anagnostes as robbers gathered by the Venetians from various places and employed as guards – who were given orders to kill those who might be contemplating surrender.[45] After the city's conquest, moreover, some Thessalonians blamed the archbishop Symeon (although he had died about six months earlier) for what happened, presumably because of his determined opposition to the Turks and the pains he had taken to prevent the city's capitulation to the enemy.[46] The diffusion of this

[40] For more on Platyskalites and his family connections, see below, ch. 4, pp. 69, 75 and notes 59, 78.
[41] Sathas, *Documents*, vol. I, nos. 104, 108 (June 28, 1424); Iorga, "Notes et extraits," *ROL* 5 (1897), 169 (June 25, 1424), 354–7 (May 2–8, 1427); *ROL* 6 (1898), 53 (May 15, 1429); H. Noiret, *Documents inédits pour servir à l'histoire de la domination vénitienne en Crète de 1380 à 1485* (Paris, 1892), p. 328; Mertzios, Μνημεῖα, pp. 58–9 (July 7, 1425); Thiriet, *Régestes*, vol. II, nos. 1943, 2115 (Nov. 27, 1428), 2135, 2197 (May 11, 1430).
[42] Symeon–Balfour, p. 60.   [43] Anagnostes–Tsaras, p. 12, lines 5–7.   [44] Ibid., pp. 16–18, 20.
[45] Ibid., pp. 20 (lines 1–9), 24 (lines 9–12).   [46] Ibid., pp. 20–4.

conciliatory attitude towards the Ottomans among various elements of the population, which by 1429–30 was recognized both by the Ottomans and the Venetians, must be attributed in part to the Thessalonians' discontent with the Venetian regime and to the failure of the Venetians to bring the war with the Ottomans to an end.[47]

Another factor that drew many to support submission to Ottoman rule is to be sought in the policies and methods of conquest applied by the Ottomans in the course of their expansion in Byzantine territories. A quick glance at the evidence presented above concerning the "pro-Ottoman" Thessalonians reveals that all their activities coincide with times during which the city was either blockaded by Ottoman forces or was under threat of an attack. Such was the case, for instance, during the sieges of 1383–7, 1411–13, and 1422–3, as well as throughout the period from 1423 to 1430, when the Ottomans, aggravated by the Venetian takeover, noticeably increased their assaults upon the city.[48] The primary goal of the "pro-Ottoman" activists in all these instances was to ensure the peaceful surrender of Thessalonike to the Ottoman armies stationed outside its walls. In other words, their pro-Ottomanism manifested itself first and foremost as a favorable attitude towards surrender. This was due to the well-dispersed knowledge that the Ottomans, acting in accordance with the principles of Islamic law as pointed out earlier, offered their Christian enemies the option of surrendering with certain guarantees and rights as an alternative to capture by force.[49] Consequently, during periods of intense military threat in particular, many Thessalonians showed a determined preference for the peaceful occupation of their city by the Ottomans in order to avoid enslavement. In 1383 Manuel II, observing this tendency among the citizens of Thessalonike, had written of the need to persuade them that "it is nobler and far less shameful to suffer willingly the lot of slaves for the sake of their own freedom than, after having become slaves in heart, to try to gain the rights of free men."[50] Manuel's failure to persuade the Thessalonians became clear when they surrendered to

---

[47] For the tensions between native Thessalonians and Venetian authorities during 1423–30, see below, ch. 5, pp. 105ff. Some later chronicles mention that Thessalonike was betrayed to the Ottomans in 1430: see Vryonis, "Ottoman conquest of Thessaloniki," pp. 287, 309–10. Given that none of the contemporary sources provide such evidence, this must be a later distortion stemming from the knowledge of the presence of a strong group in the city that favored and worked for its surrender to the Ottomans.

[48] Doukas–Grecu, XXIX.4, p. 247.

[49] See above, ch. 2, pp. 26–7, 30–1 (note 32) for a discussion of the Ottoman methods of conquest.

[50] Dennis, *Letters of Manuel II*, no. 4, pp. 12–13. For a similar pronouncement by Manuel II to Thessalonians during the same year, see "Συμβουλευτικός," ed. Laourdas, p. 298.

the Ottoman forces in 1387. Approximately four decades later, under the Venetian regime, it seemed almost as if history was about to repeat itself in Thessalonike. As pointed out above, the Thessalonians were deterred from surrendering in 1430 only because of the strong pressure the Venetian authorities applied on them. According to Anagnostes, it was as a result of this, and "not because of the disobedience and resistance of those within," that Murad II declared war on the city and took it by force.[51]

In addition to the people with pro-Venetian sympathies and those who on the contrary favored an accommodation with the Ottomans, there was yet a third group in Thessalonike consisting of individuals who objected to any rapprochement with either the Latins or the Ottomans. The leading members of this group were the hesychast monks. During the siege of 1383–7, for instance, they challenged Manuel II, when he appealed to the pope for military assistance and promised in return to bring about the union of the Church of Thessalonike with the Roman Church. The pro-Latin Demetrios Kydones, who was naturally critical of these hesychasts, portrays them contemptuously as people "who think that they can serve God only by hunger, pallor, and [sitting in] a corner, and who make ignorance the symbol of virtue."[52] Among those who reacted to Manuel II's project for union, alongside the hesychast monks Kydones specifically names a certain Pothos, who may perhaps be identified with Manuel Pothos. The latter was the recipient of a flattering letter from Joseph Bryennios, whose anti-unionist sentiments are well known.[53] Possibly as early as 1391 Manuel Pothos resided in Constantinople, and in 1401 he received a letter from Paris written by the Emperor Manuel II. At this time Constantinople was besieged by Bayezid I, and the Emperor encouraged Manuel Pothos to continue doing his best for the protection of the capital against the Ottomans.[54] If the proposed identification of Manuel Pothos with the anti-unionist Pothos in Thessalonike is correct, then the Emperor's letter of 1401 suggests that an anti-Ottoman outlook accompanied and complemented his stance against the Catholics of western Europe.

---

[51] Anagnostes–Tsaras, p. 24, lines 9–14.

[52] Kydones–Loenertz, vol. II, no. 302, lines 34–40. On Manuel's embassy of 1385 to Pope Urban VI and the conclusion of an ecclesiastical union in 1386, see Dennis, *Reign of Manuel II*, pp. 136–50.

[53] "Ἐκ τῆς βυζαντινῆς Ἐπιστολογραφίας. Ἰωσὴφ μοναχοῦ τοῦ Βρυεννίου Ἐπιστολαὶ Λ΄ καὶ αἱ πρὸς αὐτὸν Γ," ed. N. B. Tomadakes, *EEBΣ* 46 (1983–6), no. 13, pp. 323–4 (= Ἰωσὴφ μοναχοῦ τοῦ Βρυεννίου, vol. III: *Τὰ παραλειπόμενα*, ed. T. Mandakases [Leipzig, 1784], pp. 159–60). See also *PLP*, nos. 23433 and 23450, where a possible identity between the two men is suggested; cf. Dennis, *Letters of Manuel II*, p. li.

[54] Dennis, *Letters of Manuel II*, no. 42, pp. 110–13. See also nos. 17 (to Pothos, κριτής; date:1391) and 35 (to Manuel Pothos; date:1397–8?).

Perhaps the most fervent and outspoken advocate of an anti-Ottoman/anti-Latin position in the period following the restoration of Thessalonike to Byzantine rule was the city's archbishop Symeon (1416/17–29). In his opinion, the best policy for the Thessalonians to pursue was to put their trust in "our Orthodox masters" and to remain loyal and obedient to the central government at Constantinople. "In my converse and my advice," he wrote, "I have been ceaselessly standing up for our own interest throughout, and urging that we should remain with our own people and show endurance and stand our ground and trust in God."[55] But, as Symeon himself admitted, those who upheld this position were clearly in the minority during the first quarter of the fifteenth century.[56] Moreover, they do not appear to have come forth with any practical program of their own capable of guaranteeing the security of Thessalonike against enemy attacks. Symeon, for example, unrealistically hoped that obedience to Constantinople would ensure help from that quarter, when he was well aware that the emperors there had "their own preoccupations." It is equally dubious whether the hesychast monks who opposed Manuel II's project for union with the papacy ever formulated an alternative policy for resistance to the Ottomans. The most they seem to have done was to accept the status quo once the Ottomans came to power, just as Symeon himself bowed to the authority of the Venetians despite his initial opposition to them. The monk Gabriel, for instance, reflecting around 1384 that Thessalonike stood no chance before the Ottomans and fearing captivity, fled to Constantinople in the company of several other monks, but he moved back to Thessalonike after the establishment of Ottoman rule and in 1397 became the city's archbishop. In this role Gabriel paid at least two visits to the Ottoman court in order to secure concessions and kindly treatment for his flock.[57] Likewise, the archbishop Isidore Glabas (1380–4, 1386–96), who fled from Thessalonike to the capital at approximately the same time as Gabriel, thought it best to send a letter to his see after the city's capitulation to the Ottomans, urging the inhabitants to be obedient to their new masters in the interest of keeping Orthodoxy "unstained."[58] Isidore, too,

[55] Symeon–Balfour, pp. 55 (text), 157 (trans.); see also pp. 57, 63, 73 (lines 34–5): "... τὸ μένειν ὑμᾶς μετὰ τῶν εὐσεβῶν ἡμῶν αὐθεντῶν."

[56] Ibid., pp. 55–6.

[57] Kydones–Loenertz, vol. II, no. 324; L. Syndika-Laourda (ed.), "Ἐγκώμιον εἰς τὸν ἀρχιεπίσκοπον Θεσσαλονίκης Γαβριήλ," *Μακεδονικά* 4 (1955–60), 352–70, esp. 362–7. Gabriel's *enkomion*, published by Syndika-Laourda as anonymous, has been attributed by Loenertz and, more recently, by Argyriou to Makarios Makres: see the new edition of the text in *Μακαρίου τοῦ Μακρῆ συγγράμματα*, ed. A. Argyriou (Thessalonike, 1996), pp. 101–20, esp. 111–17.

[58] Isidore–Lampros, pp. 389–90.

eventually returned to Ottoman-ruled Thessalonike, where he continued to serve as archbishop until his death. He is known also to have traveled to Asia Minor in order to negotiate with the Ottomans on behalf of his flock, thus setting an example to his successor Gabriel.[59]

To recapitulate, it has been observed that the most consistent feature in the political history of Thessalonike between 1382 and 1430 was the pressure that the Ottomans exerted on the city, which to a large extent determined its political atmosphere during these years. In response to the Ottoman threat, the citizens of Thessalonike became divided, first, over the issue of whether to support the cause of war or peace. The people who believed in the cause of war were further divided into two main groups: those in favor of an alliance with western, primarily Italian, powers (pro-Latin/anti-Ottoman) and those insisting that the Thessalonians, regardless of their past failures, continue to fight on their own (anti-Latin/anti-Ottoman). It must be emphasized, however, that the respective attitudes of these two groups towards the Latins were determined by different sets of criteria. The champions of the anti-Latin/anti-Ottoman position, consisting primarily of members of Thessalonike's ecclesiastical hierarchy, were compelled in their anti-Latinism by purely religious convictions and regarded all "Latins" as Catholics without differentiating between them. For the advocates of the pro-Latin/anti-Ottoman position, including, for instance, the people who convinced the Despot Andronikos to call in the Venetians in 1423, "Latins" were constituents of distinct political entities, cooperation with whom was expected to provide concrete public and personal advantages in the economic, political, and military realms. As for the Thessalonians who supported the policy of peace, these were generally inclined towards an accommodation with the Ottomans, the majority among them being driven by the urge to see the hostilities with the Ottomans reach an end rather than yearning or working directly for the establishment of Ottoman sovereignty in the city. The discontentment with the Venetian regime of 1423–30 seems to have added a strong anti-Latin component to the ideology of those who were well-disposed towards an accommodation with the Ottomans, this being a feature that was perhaps not so strongly pronounced earlier, particularly in the period 1383–7. Finally, another group distinguished by its pro-Latin sympathies, but refusing to undergo the

---

[59] Isidore's trip "to Asia" is mentioned in the monody of Constantine Ibankos on his death, published in E. Legrand, *Lettres de l'empereur Manuel Paléologue* (Paris, 1893), p. 107. A reference to Isidore's "long journeys" is also found in his eulogy, composed by Symeon of Thessalonike, in the Synodikon of Orthodoxy, J. Gouillard (ed.), "Le synodikon de l'Orthodoxie, édition et commentaire," *TM* 2 (1967), 114–15. Cf. Isidore–Laourdas, pp. 56–7.

hardships imposed by the ongoing struggle against the Ottomans, consisted of people who fled from Thessalonike and sought new homes in Italian territories.

The question that must be considered next is what were the specific circumstances and factors that played a role in the formation of the various political attitudes delineated above. With this purpose, the following two chapters investigate the social and economic conditions that prevailed in Thessalonike in the late fourteenth and early fifteenth centuries, considering separately the periods during which the city was under Byzantine, Ottoman, and Venetian domination.

CHAPTER 4

Byzantine Thessalonike
(1382–1387 and 1403–1423)

In the late fourteenth and early fifteenth centuries Thessalonike was no longer the thriving city it used to be in the earlier part of the Palaiologan period. Subjected from the 1380s onwards to continuous Ottoman assaults and sieges, it was completely cut off by land. Because of the insecurity of the surrounding countryside, the fields outside the city walls remained untilled. Commercial activity was disrupted due to the city's isolation from its hinterland. As early as 1384 or 1385 Demetrios Kydones wrote that the suburbs of Thessalonike were devastated and that its once flourishing market was reduced to misery.[1] This picture of economic decline is confirmed by archaeological evidence, which has revealed no sign of any major construction activity inside the city or in the surrounding countryside after 1380.[2] In the subsequent generation Symeon described how Mehmed I interfered with the food supplies in 1417/18 and also lamented the breakdown of business within the city and the destruction of the lands outside during the siege of 1422–3.[3] The city gates seem to have remained closed throughout the duration of the Ottoman threat.[4] The only regular access that Thessalonians had to the outside world was by sea, and it was by this means that the provisioning of the city was maintained during these critical times. Nevertheless, contemporary references to exhausted food

---

[1] Kydones–Loenertz, vol. II, no. 299, lines 13–16. This may be compared with Kydones' description of the city as a lively commercial center in the 1340s: J. W. Barker, "The 'Monody' of Demetrios Kydones on the Zealot rising of 1345 in Thessaloniki," in *Essays in Memory of Basil Laourdas* (Thessalonike, 1975), p. 292. The description of Thessalonike found in the anonymous *vita* of Makarios Makres (d. 1431), who was born in this city *c.* 1383 and lived there until *c.* 1401, is not useful for our purposes since it is a purely eulogistic sketch with no precise information about the actual conditions during the years Makres spent in it: see the text published in *Macaire Makrès et la polémique contre l'Islam*, ed. A. Argyriou (Vatican City, 1986), pp. 186–9.

[2] Ch. Bakirtzis, "The urban continuity and size of late Byzantine Thessalonike," *DOP* 57 (2003), 35–64, esp. 38–9.

[3] Symeon–Balfour, pp. 50, 55.

[4] Kydones–Loenertz, vol. II, no. 299; Iorga, "Notes et extraits," *ROL* 5 (1897), 318; Mertzios, Μνημεῖα, pp. 56–7.

reserves, to lack of necessities, and to outbreaks of famine indicate that the provisions brought in by sea were by no means sufficient.[5] Besides these difficulties the major problem of financing the war with the Ottomans made things worse. Under such severe conditions, almost all the inhabitants of Thessalonike were adversely affected: landowning aristocrats were deprived of their possessions; merchants were hindered from commercial activity; and the lower classes were forced to endure increased poverty and distress.

The losses of the aristocracy occurred both directly, through conquests and confiscations carried out by the Ottomans, and indirectly, as a result of the incessant warfare which devastated the countryside and hindered cultivation, thereby compelling many landowners to alienate their inoperative and unprofitable estates. For example, a Thessalonian by the name of Constantine Prinkips, who owned some property in the region, had come to lose all his possessions by the time of his death (probably during the siege of 1383–7) with the sole exception of a vineyard which was entirely ruined and deserted because of the ongoing war with the Turks.[6] Another revealing case is that of Manuel Deblitzenos, member of a landowning Thessalonian family of military background, who had a hereditary estate in Hermeleia, in Chalkidike, which had been confiscated at the time of the Serbian occupation.[7] Although Manuel recovered his estate when the Serbian domination came to an end, shortly afterwards (*c.* 1376) he decided to give it to the monastery of Docheiariou on Mount Athos in exchange for three *adelphata* (annual pensions for life, mostly in kind, sold or granted by monasteries to individuals).[8] The *adelphata* were supposed to be delivered to Manuel throughout his lifetime and, after his death, to a second person designated by him. However, the monastery failed to render to Manuel the promised amount and the agreement was cancelled, to be renewed though once again around 1381 with the same terms and conditions. Considering that an annuity of three *adelphata* appears low, already from the outset,

[5] Dennis, *Letters of Manuel II*, no. 4; Symeon–Balfour, pp. 49–50, 56, 59.

[6] MM, vol. II, no. 471 (July 1394), pp. 221–3.

[7] On this family, see N. Oikonomidès, "The properties of the Deblitzenoi in the fourteenth and fifteenth centuries," in *Charanis Studies; Essays in Honor of Peter Charanis*, ed. A. E. Laiou-Thomadakis (New Brunswick, NJ, 1980), pp. 176–98. The documents pertaining to the Deblitzenoi have been subsequently published by the same author in *Docheiariou*, nos. 10 (*c.* 1307), 26 (Oct. 1349), 47 (Oct. 1381), 48 (*c.* 1381), 49 (Aug. 1384), 50 (Jan. 1389), 51 (Oct. 1404), 57 (Dec. 1419), 58 (Dec. 1419).

[8] For two recent discussions of the institution of the *adelphaton*, with references to earlier works on the subject, see A. Laiou, "Economic activities of Vatopedi in the fourteenth century," in Ιερά Μονή Βατοπεδίου. Ιστορία και Τέχνη (Athens, 1999), pp. 66–72; K. Smyrlis, *La fortune des grands monastères byzantins (fin du Xe–milieu du XIVe siècle)* (Paris, 2006), pp. 138–45.

relative to the value of the property which Manuel ceded to Docheiariou,[9] the contract's renewal five years later with no readjustment is puzzling. Hence we are led to speculate that on both occasions Manuel was induced to give away his property to the monastery owing to the economic constraints he faced because of the combined effects of Serbian and Ottoman invasions on his estate; namely, destruction of fields, shortage of cultivators, and lack of potential buyers.[10] Under such precarious circumstances, and despite Docheiariou's failure to fulfill its obligation at the time of the initial agreement, it is conceivable that Manuel opted for receiving from the monastery fixed quantities of foodstuffs, for the duration of his life and that of one of his inheritors successively, as a less risky and more profitable alternative to venturing the cultivation of the estate himself. One may well imagine what might have become of the estate in the latter case, considering that a vineyard under his management that formed part of his wife's dowry, who also came from a rich landowning family (the Angeloi), was abandoned and no longer productive in 1384.[11]

During the same year, Manuel Deblitzenos died while fighting against the Ottomans in the battle of Chortaïtes. His widow, Maria, who tried subsequently to settle her dowry and inheritance rights, faced certain problems as the Ottoman blockade hindered the assessment of the couple's

[9] The high value of Deblitzenos' estate is implied in *Docheiariou*, no. 48, lines 12–13: "τὸ ὅλον κτῆμα μου . . . πολλοῦ ἄξιον ὄν . . ." Given also the fact that the estate's annual tax revenue amounted to 100 *hyperpyra* back in 1349 (*Docheiariou*, no. 26), its value, notwithstanding the loss of productivity and depreciation it suffered in the meantime under Serbian occupation, must have exceeded by far the standard price of 300 *hyperpyra* required to purchase three *adelphata* in the second half of the fourteenth century. Moreover, even the quantities of food per *adelphaton* which Docheiariou promised to deliver in this case are lower on average than those registered in other *adelphaton* contracts of the same period: see Oikonomidès, "Properties of the Deblitzenoi," pp. 184–5. However, a plausible explanation for why Docheiariou kept the annuities low may be that it was obliged to dispense these for a rather long period (to two consecutive individuals for life, as opposed to one only), as proposed by Laiou, "Economic activities of Vatopedi," pp. 67–8. Manuel's three *adelphata* comprised 24 *tagaria adelphatarika* (= 3 *kartai*) of wheat, 4 *tagaria* of dried vegetables, 16 *tagaria* of wheat in replacement for wine, 2 *tetartia* of olive oil, and 50 *litrai* of cheese, which would roughly correspond to a monetary value of 9 *hyperpyra* per *adelphaton* according to a calculation by Laiou, "Economic activities of Vatopedi," pp. 71–2 (Appendix). For the measures mentioned here, see Laiou, pp. 71–2; E. Schilbach, *Byzantinische Metrologie* (Munich, 1970); *Docheiariou*, p. 255; Smyrlis, *La fortune des grands monastères*, pp. 144–5 and n. 351, who, however, considers the total amount of food mentioned in our document to be the equivalent of two *adelphata* rather than three (see Table 9).

[10] Oikonomidès, "Properties of the Deblitzenoi," pp. 184–6. Documents dealing with the effects of Serbian invasions on the Byzantine countryside in general and on the aristocracy in particular reveal striking parallels to the effects of Turkish invasions: see *Docheiariou*, nos. 42, 43; *Xéropotamou*, no. 26; etc.

[11] *Docheiariou*, no. 49, p. 263.

remaining possessions outside Thessalonike.[12] Throughout the blockade it seems unlikely that Maria received any revenues from her holdings in the outlying region; nor does she appear to have been able to receive from the monastery of Docheiariou the three *adelphata* to which she became entitled after her husband's death.[13] At any rate, both she and her daughter lived through the period of the first Ottoman domination in Thessalonike and saw the city's restoration to Byzantium in 1403. As late as 1419 Manuel's daughter, born of parents who both belonged to large landholding families and married furthermore to a prominent man (the *archon* Bartholomaios Komes), was evidently still reduced in economic terms and pressed by financial difficulties, as she claimed property rights, without any legal basis, over the estate in Hermeleia held by the monastery of Docheiariou.[14]

In the period following the return of Thessalonike to the Byzantine Empire, there were other Thessalonians with wealthy family backgrounds who, like Manuel Deblitzenos' daughter, were hard-pressed and impoverished. For example, a woman called Maria Hagioreitisa, finding herself unable to look after her hereditary church (*kellydrion*) of Forty Martyrs within the city, donated it to the monastery of Dionysiou in 1420. Although the property was exempt from taxation, Maria could not keep it in good condition since she had been reduced to poverty by the troubles and misfortunes of the times. Her search for someone well-off who might be willing to take charge of the church bore no result "in the oppressive atmosphere of the imminent storm." At the end, it was not an individual but the monastery of Dionysiou that came forth with the economic backing to fulfill Maria's expectations.[15]

In the countryside of Thessalonike, too, property transfers to monasteries often turned out to be the best solution for landowners who did not have the financial means to maintain their lands or to restore them to a productive state. Shortly before April 1409 the monastery of Lavra acquired through exchange a domain in the village of Hagia Maria near Thessalonike which had been in the possession of various members of an aristocratic family since at least 1304. As late as 1404 the domain seems to have been

---

[12] For the time being, a legal commission established her rights without conducting a proper assessment, which was postponed until the return of peace: *Docheiariou*, nos. 49 and 58, esp. pp. 264 (lines 41–3), 295 (lines 14–19).

[13] It seems that Docheiariou started paying Maria's *adelphata* only after the surrender of Thessalonike to the Ottomans, as suggested by the agreement concluded between the two parties in January 1389: *Docheiariou*, no. 50. Maria was recognized by this agreement as the second and final beneficiary of the *adelphata*, in accordance with the original arrangement made by her late husband.

[14] *Docheiariou*, nos. 57 and 58.   [15] *Dionysiou*, no. 19.

in fairly good condition, for at that time it became the object of a dispute between Kale Thalassene, who held the property as her dowry, and her brother Demetrios Skampavles, who was scheming to take possession of half of it. But in 1409 the village of Hagia Maria is qualified as a *palaiochorion*, which may well be the reason behind the domain's transfer to Lavra.[16] Shortly before January 1420 Lavra also gained possession of an escheated landholding (ἐξαλειμματικὴ ὑπόστασις) near Thessalonike from a woman called Zerbalo.[17] The recurrence of such property transfers from individuals to Athonite monasteries demonstrates that, in the midst of the instability and uncertainty created by the Ottoman expansion, well-established monastic foundations managed to maintain their economic power, unlike the Thessalonian landowning aristocracy, and, indeed, derived economic benefits from the misfortunes of many lay landowners.[18] As will be discussed more fully in the next chapter, the greater strength and reliability of Athonite monasteries as financial institutions, combined with their conciliatory attitude towards the Ottomans, were instrumental in saving them from the fate suffered by the majority of aristocrats.

On a political level, some members of the Thessalonian aristocracy responded to their economic plight by adopting anti-Turkish sentiments. It will be recalled, for instance, that Manuel Deblitzenos, whose economic difficulties we observed above, lost his life fighting in battle against the Ottomans. It might also be postulated that among Manuel II's anti-Turkish supporters who flocked out of Constantinople during 1382–3 some were native Thessalonians who had lost their landholdings in the region to the Ottomans. The news of Manuel's initial military successes may well have stimulated such dispossessed aristocrats with the prospects of recovering their property. Unfortunately, only a few of the people who followed Manuel to Thessalonike can be identified by name, which renders it difficult to prove this point. Among them a certain Rhadenos, who served Manuel II as counselor during 1382/3–7, is known to have been a native Thessalonian even though he was residing in the capital at the time of

---

[16] *Lavra*, vol. II, no. 98 (1304); *Lavra*, vol. III, Appendix XII (1341) and nos. 156 (1404), 161 (1409). The document (no. 161) does not specify what the domain was exchanged for (e.g. a sum of money, or *adelphata*, or another piece of land?).

[17] *Lavra*, vol. III, no. 165. See M. C. Bartusis, "*Exaleimma*: escheat in Byzantium," *DOP* 40 (1986), 55–81.

[18] One must, however, take into account the biases of documentation deriving from monastic archives where property transactions between individuals are unlikely to be recorded. Nonetheless, in the well-documented cases between individuals and monasteries, the preponderance of transfers from the former to the latter is indicative.

Manuel's departure. He either accompanied Manuel or joined him afterwards, but in any case he was in Thessalonike by the summer or fall of
1383, at which time he received a letter from Demetrios Kydones.[19] It is
plausible, of course, that Rhadenos had chosen to return to his native city
and attach himself to Manuel II out of purely patriotic sentiments. Besides,
we know nothing about his immediate family's landed possessions in or
around Thessalonike. His father was a wealthy merchant, and he had two
brothers, both of whom were engaged in their father's business affairs while
Rhadenos himself went in pursuit of literary and intellectual interests, at
least for a time.[20] Yet, in the early fourteenth century the Rhadenos family
of Thessalonike included military magnates who were great landowners in
Chalkidike.[21] Until the final Ottoman conquest of 1430, members of this
prominent Thessalonian family took up a leading role in the city's political
affairs and in the struggles against the Ottomans.[22] Secondly, John Asanes,
who was suspected of planning to join Manuel II in Thessalonike (but did
not actually go there), has a family name also encountered in the fourteenth
century among landowners in the region, even though we have no direct
evidence concerning John's personal connections with Thessalonike.[23] The
same can be said for Theodore Kantakouzenos, the only other person
known by name who followed Manuel II to Thessalonike, leaving his wife
and children behind in Constantinople.[24] Theodore's signature appears on
a document concerning the donation of land near Serres to the monastery of
Philotheou in December 1376.[25] Among people bearing his family name,
a John Kantakouzenos is attested in 1414 as one of the witnesses who
signed an act of the governor (κεφαλή) of Thessalonike.[26] In addition,
a Theodore Palaiologos Kantakouzenos, an inhabitant of Constantinople
who had acquired the status of a Venetian, is known to have gone to

---

[19] Kydones–Loenertz, vol. II, nos. 248, 202. See G. T. Dennis, "Rhadenos of Thessalonica, correspondent of Demetrius Cydones," Βυζαντινά 13 (1985), 261–72; F. Tinnefeld, "Freundschaft und
ΠΑΙΔΕΙΑ: Die Korrespondenz des Demetrios Kydones mit Rhadenos (1375–1387/8)," *B* 55 (1985),
210–44.

[20] Kydones–Loenertz, vol. II, nos. 177, 169. It has been argued that Rhadenos himself engaged in
trade too; however, the evidence for this is not conclusive: see Matschke and Tinnefeld, *Gesellschaft*,
pp. 195 (n. 183), 202–4.

[21] *PLP*, nos. 23987 and 23992.   [22] See below, pp. 79ff., and Appendices I and II.

[23] *PLP*, no. 1497. For suspicions concerning John Asanes' desire to go to Thessalonike, see Kydones–
Loenertz, vol. II, no. 264, lines 79–82. For members of the Asanes family connected with Thessalonike
in the fourteenth century, see *Xéropotamou*, no. 26 (1349) and *Esphigménou*, no. 18 (1365). Cf. E.
Trapp, "Beiträge zur Genealogie der Asanen in Byzanz," *JÖB* 25 (1976), 163–77.

[24] Kydones–Loenertz, vol. II, nos. 250, 254. Cf. *PLP*, no. 10965.

[25] V. Kravari, "Nouveaux documents du monastère de Philothéou," *TM* 10 (1987), 323 (no. 6).

[26] *Docheiariou*, no. 54 (Feb. 1414). Cf. *PLP*, no. 92318.

Thessalonike for a short visit at the beginning of the fifteenth century.[27]
So, all together, this is as much evidence as we can gather regarding the
Thessalonian connections of Manuel II's supporters from Constantino-
ple who joined him, or wanted to join him, in his campaign against the
Ottomans.

The difficulties met by the landowning aristocracy of Thessalonike constitute only one aspect of the desolation that in effect extended to the
entire agricultural economy of the region in the two periods with which
we are concerned. There is but one exception to this. The sole indications
of relative peace and prosperity are attested in the first decade and a half of
the fifteenth century, during a period which more or less coincides with the
internal problems of the Ottomans in the aftermath of the battle of Ankara.
A letter written by Manuel II between 1404 and 1408 and Symeon's account
of the rule of John VII (1403–8) both depict Thessalonike as a flourishing
city following its restoration to Byzantine authority.[28] Venetian documents
mention cotton exports from Thessalonike to Venice throughout 1405–12,
while no evidence has come to light for comparable exports at any other
time in the two periods when the Byzantines held the city.[29] In 1404 several
gardens just outside the city which belonged to the monastery of Iveron
were leased to members of the Argyropoulos family. Whereas the gardens
seem to have fallen into decay in the course of the first Ottoman domination or even earlier, the Argyropouloi managed them successfully after
1404 and raised their productivity. In 1421 the monks of Iveron, no longer
wanting all the profits to accrue to the Argyropouloi, took the gardens
back from them.[30] Similarly, sometime before 1415, a man called Dadas,
who leased from the monastery of Xenophon five adjacent grocery shops
and three houses situated in the Asomatoi quarter of Thessalonike, transformed them all into one large wine shop, from which he derived an annual
income of at least 30 *hyperpyra* against the rent of 3 *hyperpyra* that he had

[27] Hunger, *Chortasmenos*, nos. 36, 38, 53, and pp. 104–7. Cf. D. M. Nicol, *The Byzantine Family of Kantakouzenos (ca. 1100–1460)* (Washington, DC, 1968), pp. 165–6; D. M. Nicol, "The Byzantine family of Kantakouzenos. Some addenda and corrigenda," *DOP* 27 (1973), 312–13; *PLP*, no. 10966.
[28] Dennis, *Letters of Manuel II*, no. 45, lines 168–75, 218–25; Symeon–Balfour, p. 48, lines 1–15.
[29] Sathas, *Documents*, vol. II, nos. 357, 364, 395, 460, 472, 520, 533, pp. 131, 135, 161, 220, 226, 257, 267; Thiriet, *Régestes*, vol. II, nos. 1193, 1204, 1340, 1440. On Thessalonian cotton, see K.-P. Matschke, "Tuchproduktion und Tuchproduzenten in Thessalonike und in anderen Städten und Regionen des späten Byzanz," Βυζαντιακά 9 (1989), 68–9. For an implicit reference to the export of silk and kermes from Thessalonike to Venice in 1407, see Sathas, *Documents*, vol. II, no. 410; cf. D. Jacoby, "Foreigners and the urban economy in Thessalonike, ca. 1150–ca. 1450," *DOP* 57 (2003), 108, n. 156.
[30] *Iviron*, vol. IV, nos. 97 and 98 (= *Schatzkammer*, nos. 102 and 24). On this case, see Matschke, *Ankara*, pp. 159–75.

agreed to pay to the monastery. As late as 1419 the wine shop still brought Dadas' family a good income, so the monastery took action to cancel the contract.[31]

Yet, apart from these last two examples, which may in all likelihood be unique cases of individual entrepreneurship,[32] most of the evidence we possess suggests that conditions in Thessalonike and its environs had already begun to deteriorate following the resumption of hostilities with the Ottomans around 1411. Along with reports of famine conditions in the narrative sources, we find in the Athonite documents an increasing number of references to abandoned villages, which must be attributed to the incessant raids of the Ottomans in the area.[33] A case that illustrates the negative impact of Ottoman military operations on the countryside concerns the abandoned village of Mariskin on the Kassandreia peninsula, which John VII granted to the monastery of Dionysiou in 1408. A decade later the village was still not restored to full-scale cultivation, despite the fiscal exemptions it enjoyed in the meantime. The grant to the monastery had been made with the stipulation that a tower was to be built there for the protection of the village and its inhabitants. But the presence of Ottoman troops in the region hindered both the construction of the tower and the cultivation of the land. At last, it was through the financial support of the Despot Andronikos, who took a special interest in Mariskin between 1417 and 1420, that a tower was built, new cultivators were installed, and necessary equipment was purchased, thus providing for the return of the village to agricultural production.[34]

As revealed by the foregoing discussion, one of the most pressing problems that affected the agricultural economy of the region was the difficulty

---

[31] *Xénophon*, no. 32.

[32] See K.-P. Matschke, "Bemerkungen zu M. J. Sjuzjumovs 'Jungem Unternehmeradel' in spätbyzantinischer Zeit," *Antičnaja drevnost'i srednie veka* 26 (Barnaul "Den," 1992), 237–50; A. Kazhdan, "The Italian and late Byzantine city," *DOP* 49 (1995), 17–20; cf. Matschke and Tinnefeld, *Gesellschaft*, pp. 130, 192.

[33] Symeon–Balfour, pp. 49–50, 56, 59; *Dionysiou*, nos. 10, 11, 13; *Docheiariou*, no. 53; *Lavra*, vol. III, nos. 161, 165; *Saint-Pantéléèmôn*, no. 18; etc. Besides references to abandoned villages, a comparison between fourteenth- and fifteenth-century *praktika* points to a general demographic decline in Macedonia: see N. Oikonomidès, "Ottoman influence on late Byzantine fiscal practice," *SüdostF* 45 (1986), 16, n. 65. On the population of Macedonia in the fourteenth–fifteenth centuries, see also J. Lefort, "Population et peuplement en Macédoine orientale, IXe–XVe siècle," in *Hommes et richesses dans l'Empire byzantin*, vol. II, ed. V. Kravari, J. Lefort, and C. Morrisson (Paris, 1991), pp. 75–82, who, however, argues for a demographic decline in the second half of the fourteenth century, followed by a rise from the beginning of the fifteenth century onwards.

[34] *Dionysiou*, nos. 10, 13, 16, 17, 18, 20. On the economic importance of Kassandreia for the food supplies of Thessalonike, which explains Andronikos' special interest in reviving Mariskin, see Mertzios, Μνημεῖα, p. 48.

of finding people to work on the land. Although the insecurity and instability directly resulting from Ottoman attacks was a major factor in creating this problem, malpractices or arbitrary exactions by fiscal agents of the Byzantine government in Thessalonike must have contributed to it also. For example, in 1418 the monastery of Docheiariou took action against three censors who extorted undue charges from one of its domains in Chalkidike. The new charges were cancelled when the censors admitted that they had made a "mistake."[35] In some ways, too, the fiscal policy pursued by the Byzantine government in the years following the restoration of Thessalonike to Byzantine rule seems to have created difficulties for the rural population. In 1409 the monks of Esphigmenou complained about the heavy burdens which fiscal agents inflicted upon the peasants who worked on their holdings at Rentina and Kassandreia. The monks were particularly worried that the peasants, suffering from impoverishment under these burdens, might attempt to flee the monastic domains.[36] We know that in Chalkidike the taxes that peasants had to pay in money (the *telos/harac*) climbed up sharply during the early fifteenth century, registering an increase of five to seven times in comparison with the equivalent fourteenth-century taxes. Although the other payments peasants were liable for (i.e. taxes in kind and rent) declined simultaneously, nonetheless, paying a much higher proportion of their taxes in money must have hurt many peasants.[37] Finally, it should be added that Musa Çelebi's demand in 1411 for the resumption of the annual *harac* payment to the Ottomans may have compelled the Byzantine government to institute extra taxes, thereby causing further distress among the peasantry.[38]

While such conditions prevailed in the countryside during the two periods of Byzantine rule, merchants inside Thessalonike suffered from the disruption of their commercial activities, except perhaps in the brief interval after 1403 when cotton exports to Venice are attested, as noted above.[39] The presence of Ottomans and the city's isolation from its hinterland had already rendered overland trade impossible for some time. Although the sea continued to serve as an accessible alternate route, maritime trade was

---

[35] *Docheiariou*, no. 56. For a similar case in which censors have made a "mistake," see Γρηγόριος ὁ Παλαμᾶς 3 (1919), 335.

[36] *Esphigménou*, no. 31.

[37] See Oikonomidès, "Ottoman influence," 18–24; *Docheiariou*, nos. 53, 56, and pp. 273–6, 288–9; *Dionysiou*, no. 18; *Lavra*, vol. III, nos. 161, 165. It may be noted in this context that Plethon objected to the collection of most taxes in money in early fifteenth-century Morea and suggested that all taxes be rendered in kind: see below, ch. 10, p. 274 and note 73.

[38] Concerning Musa's demand and its date, see Matschke, *Ankara*, pp. 70–5.

[39] See above, p. 62 and note 29.

not very safe either. In 1407 a proposal was brought before the Senate of Venice concerning the protection of private Venetian ships that carried merchandise from Negroponte to Thessalonike. It was reported that merchant ships which customarily traveled unarmed frequently fell victim to the Turks sailing in these waters, who seized the defenseless ships and dispatched them to "Turchia" together with the men and merchandise on them. Therefore, in order to reduce the hazards of their journey to Thessalonike, the merchants active in the region requested from the Senate to be escorted henceforth by the Venetian galleys stationed at Negroponte.[40] Another indicator of the insecurity of maritime trade can be found in the extremely high interest rates charged for sea loans in Thessalonike in the early fifteenth century. Faced with the challenge of a 20 percent interest rate, which came to replace the customary 12 percent rate, many Thessalonian merchants must have accumulated large debts, unless, of course, they had sufficient funds to engage in moneylending themselves.[41]

In 1418 the Senate of Venice instructed its *bailo* in Constantinople to demand from Manuel II, on behalf of two Venetian creditors called Giorgio Valaresso and Demetrio Filomati, the payment of outstanding debts incurred by certain unidentified Thessalonians who may well have been merchants.[42] Such a demand from the Emperor concerning the debts of private individuals seems unusual and can be explained, in part, if one assumes that the sums borrowed were very high and that the creditors were persons of some influence. In the present context, it is the second Venetian creditor, Demetrio Filomati, who deserves particular attention from us, given that he bears a Greek name (Philomates) which reveals his Greek origin. In a recent article D. Jacoby has argued that Demetrio was the son of a Greek who had apparently emigrated from Candia to Venice sometime before 1400 and had acquired full Venetian citizenship.[43] As a

---

[40] Sathas, *Documents*, vol. II, no. 410, pp. 175–6; Thiriet, *Régestes*, vol. II, no. 1265 (June 14, 1407). For an earlier measure dating back to 1359 and involving the transportation of Venetian merchandise from Negroponte to Thessalonike on board the Euboea galley for protection against Turkish pirates, which seems to have fallen into disuse sometime between 1374 and 1407, see Jacoby, "Foreigners and the urban economy," 106–7.

[41] Under the Venetian regime (1423–30) the interest rate was reduced to 15 percent, but in response to a request made by the Thessalonians in 1425 the Senate of Venice allowed the 20 percent rate to be applied to sums borrowed prior to this new regulation: Mertzios, Μνημεῖα, pp. 55–6. On sea loans of the Palaiologan period in general, see Oikonomides, *Hommes d'affaires*, pp. 59–60; G. Makris, *Studien zur spätbyzantinischen Schiffahrt* (Genoa, 1988), pp. 272–5.

[42] Iorga, "Notes et extraits," *ROL* 4 (1896), 595–6 (July 21, 1418); Thiriet, *Régestes*, vol. II, no. 1705. For further connections of Giorgio Valaresso with Thessalonike on the eve of and during the Venetian regime, see Jacoby, "Foreigners and the urban economy," 110.

[43] Jacoby, "Foreigners and the urban economy," 109–10 and n. 162. Emphasizing their status as full Venetian citizens, Jacoby points out that the members of the Filomati/Philomates family in question

second generation Venetian citizen of Greek descent, Demetrio seems to have pursued close business links with Byzantium and was particularly active in the affairs of Thessalonike. He also had a brother, Giorgio Filomati, who occupied the post of the Venetian consul in Thessalonike. For some unknown reason the *bailo* of Constantinople removed Giorgio from this office in 1418, but at his brother's request he was reinstated in 1419. On this occasion the Senate of Venice referred to Giorgio as *"militem, civem et fidelem nostrum."*[44] When the latter died in a shipwreck near Negroponte in 1422, Demetrio replaced him as consul until the establishment of Venetian rule in Thessalonike the following year.[45] Demetrio Filomati is next encountered in 1430 in Venice, where a charge was brought against him for having Orthodox religious services performed in his house.[46] We thus learn that his Venetian citizenship did not affect his religious standing and that he remained attached to the Orthodox rite even though for economic and political reasons he and his family had chosen to place themselves under the dominion of Venice. In 1431 Demetrio went back to Thessalonike, once again as consul, when the Venetian Senate decided to re-establish the office in the Ottoman-ruled city and appointed him, at his own request, to his former post.[47]

Demetrio Filomati's wealth, suggested by his ability to loan money to Thessalonians who were evidently having financial problems, gives a hint of the economic benefits likely to derive from the acquisition of Venetian citizenship, which, however, was not very easy for Greeks to obtain at this time. Almost as advantageous and easier to acquire was the status of a naturalized Venetian granted to foreigners residing in non-Venetian territories, but it is hard to assess whether there were many Thessalonians who opted for

here were not naturalized Venetians as formerly stated in his "Les Vénitiens naturalisés dans l'Empire byzantin: un aspect de l'expansion de Venise en Romanie du XIIIe au milieu du XVe siècle," *TM* 8 (1981), 225–6.

[44] Iorga, "Notes et extraits," *ROL* 4 (1896), 602 (Jan. 15, 1419); Thiriet, *Régestes*, vol. II, no. 1725. For the Venetian consulate in Thessalonike, see below, p. 67 and note 51.

[45] Iorga, "Notes et extraits," *ROL* 5 (1897), 128 (Dec. 10, 1422); Thiriet, *Régestes*, vol. II, no. 1863. According to Jacoby, the ship on which Giorgio lost his life belonged to the Filomati brothers themselves, whose commercial interests were concomitant with their official function in Thessalonike: Jacoby, "Foreigners and the urban economy," 110 and n. 166.

[46] Thiriet, *Assemblées*, vol. II, no. 1326 (Feb. 15, 1430). The Greek community in Venice was forbidden from celebrating the Orthodox liturgy anywhere in the city prior to the second half of the fifteenth century: see N. G. Moschonas, "I Greci a Venezia e la loro posizione religiosa nel XVe secolo," *'O Ἐρανιστής* 5/27–8 (1967), 105–37; G. Fedalto, *Ricerche storiche sulla posizione giuridiche ed ecclesiastica dei Greci a Venezia nei secoli XV e XVI* (Florence, 1967).

[47] Thiriet, *Régestes*, vol. III, no. 2225 (Feb. 3, 1431).

naturalization in the period that concerns us.[48] It is plausible, on the other hand, that some Thessalonian merchants who either could not or did not want to obtain this status sought financial gains through private arrangements with Italians. We can be almost certain, for instance, that several of them tried to bypass the payment of customs duties (the *kommerkion*) to the Byzantine state by offering the *kommerkion*-exempt Venetian merchants bribes to carry their merchandise into the city. In 1418 Manuel II complained to the Senate of Venice about this practice which seriously undermined the Byzantine economy. Although the Emperor articulated his complaint with reference to Byzantine merchants in general, without specifically mentioning the Thessalonians, the document which reports it contains sections that deal directly with Thessalonike. It is, therefore, quite likely that the statement about the evasion of customs duties by "Greeks" was directed not only against Constantinopolitan merchants but against Thessalonians as well.[49]

Yet, apart from certain individuals who may have enjoyed benefits through their association with Italians, on the whole the presence of Italian merchants in Thessalonike was not very favorable to the interests of the native commercial classes. In the early fifteenth century, the city contained a fairly sizable population of Venetian merchants, as suggested by the instructions sent from Venice to the *bailo* of Constantinople in 1419, ordering him to abolish the new charges he had imposed on the Venetian merchants and merchandise of Thessalonike.[50] From the late thirteenth century, in fact, a Venetian consul was stationed in Thessalonike to look after the interests of the Republic's merchants who conducted business there.[51] Genoese merchants are also attested in the city during this period, though it must be admitted that they were less in evidence than the Venetians. Their numbers certainly had to have been large enough to warrant

[48] On the distinction between full citizenship and naturalization, see Jacoby, "Vénitiens naturalisés," 217–35. For a probable case of naturalization in early fifteenth-century Thessalonike, see Jacoby, "Foreigners and the urban economy," 108; cf. Matschke, *Ankara*, p. 63, for a different interpretation.

[49] Iorga, "Notes et extraits," *ROL* 4 (1896), 595–6 (July 21, 1418); Thiriet, *Régestes*, vol. II, no. 1705; Chrysostomides, "Venetian commercial privileges," 354–5 (no. 19).

[50] Thiriet, *Régestes*, vol. II, no. 1725 (Jan. 15, 1419). On Venetian traders and their operations in late Byzantine Thessalonike, see now Jacoby, "Foreigners and the urban economy," 96–111.

[51] For the latest discussion on the Venetian consul at Thessalonike, see Jacoby, "Foreigners and the urban economy," 98–103, 106–7, 109–10; cf. F. Thiriet, "Les Vénitiens à Thessalonique dans la première moitié du XIVe siècle," *B* 22 (1953), 323–32; Nicol, *Byzantium and Venice*, pp. 199–200, 239–40. See also P. Schreiner, "Eine venezianische Kolonie in Philadelpheia (Lydien)," *Quellen und Forschungen aus italienischen Archiven und Bibliotheken* 57 (1977), 339–46. It has been argued that the document published here by Schreiner, which mentions a Venetian consul, pertains to Thessalonike rather than to Philadelphia: Oikonomidès, *Hommes d'affaires*, p. 126, n. 296.

the installation of a Genoese consul in the city as early as 1305; however, from the mid fourteenth century onwards sources only occasionally mention their activities in Thessalonike.[52] Hence, a document dating from 1412 refers to two men from Genoa who had bought slaves in Thessalonike in or shortly before 1410. Although they are not explicitly identified as merchants, one of them traveled to Chios in May or June 1410, no doubt for trading purposes, while the other one, who appears to have been his agent, remained in Thessalonike and handled the former's affairs, including a dispute over the ownership of a runaway female slave.[53] Even under the Venetian regime, Genoese merchants continued to be active in Thessalonike despite the strong commercial rivalry between the two Italian republics. This is revealed by a document dated 1425, which mentions the exemption enjoyed by Genoese (and Venetian) traders from commercial taxes on the goods they imported into the city.[54] Had the activities of foreign merchants in Thessalonike been restricted to international trade, their presence would not have necessarily posed so big a threat to the native merchants. However, conflicts were inevitable whenever the Italians, through their interference in the city's retail trade, began to compete against and impede the activities of Thessalonian merchants.[55] During the period of the Venetian domination, for example, Thessalonians demanded from the Senate of Venice the recognition of a former privilege which granted to Greeks the exclusive right to sell cloth at retail within the city.[56] Clearly, the native merchants were striving to protect their retail activities from the intervention of the Venetians. It is very likely that such intervention occurred earlier, too, while Thessalonike was still under Byzantine authority, considering that there was a fairly large community of Italian merchants active inside the city then.

In their attempt to safeguard their commercial interests, another group of Thessalonian merchants seem to have entered into deals with the

---

[52] On the volume and nature of Genoese presence and trading in Thessalonike, see now Jacoby, "Foreigners and the urban economy," 114–16; cf. Balard, *Romanie génoise*, vol. I, p. 164; M. Balard, "The Genoese in the Aegean (1204–1566)," in *Latins and Greeks*, ed. Arbel, Hamilton, and Jacoby, pp. 159–60.

[53] Musso, *Navigazione*, no. 24 (Aug. 27, 1412), pp. 266–8.

[54] Mertzios, Μνημεῖα, p. 55; see below, ch. 5, p. 107 and note 82. Presumably because of the great dearth of provisions and other necessities during the Venetian domination, the authorities must have ignored the traditional rivalry with Genoese merchants and encouraged them to import needed goods into Thessalonike.

[55] For an elaboration of this idea within the framework of Byzantine trade at large, see Laiou-Thomadakis, "Byzantine economy" and "Greek merchant."

[56] Mertzios, Μνημεῖα, pp. 57–8; Thiriet, *Régestes*, vol. II, no. 1995. On the cloth merchants of Thessalonike, see Matschke, "Tuchproduktion," 66–7.

Ottomans, thus following a course different from their counterparts who established contacts with the Italians. During the years 1404–23 the Ottoman *akçe* circulated quite regularly inside Thessalonike.[57] Of course, this by itself does not prove the existence of commercial relations between Thessalonians and Ottomans. For one thing, the circulation of Ottoman coins may merely represent a spill-over effect from the time of the first Ottoman domination (1387–1403). Besides, by about 1400 the *akçe* functioned as an international currency even in countries beyond the Danube.[58] Nonetheless, we do possess further clues pointing to the existence of trade relations between the two groups. For instance, a certain Platyskalites, who was arrested during the period of Venetian rule because of his suspect alliance with the Ottomans, bears the name of a Thessalonian family involved in banking and trade in the early fifteenth century.[59] Platyskalites' political orientation may well have been linked to his business interests; however, in the absence of direct evidence concerning his actual occupation, this can only be stated as a hypothesis. Similarly, on the eve of the city's handover to Venice, the "prominent men" (οἱ δοκοῦντες) whom the archbishop Symeon explicitly reproached for wanting to surrender Thessalonike to the Ottomans because of their material interests might have incorporated Greek merchants for whom coming to terms with the enemy would have ensured access to the city's hinterland and the resumption of disrupted commercial activities.[60]

While some Thessalonian merchants formed beneficial connections with the Italians and some possibly with the Ottomans, others tried to resolve their financial and economic problems by turning to profiteering. Yet the commercial classes were by no means the only ones who engaged in illegal means of making money; both Isidore Glabas and Symeon state that almost everyone in Thessalonike, regardless of rank, committed offenses for the

---

[57] T. Bertelè, *Numismatique byzantine, suivie de deux études inédites sur les monnaies des Paléologues*, ed. C. Morrisson (Wetteren, 1978), pp. 88–9; Oikonomidès, "Ottoman influence," 17. For a practical example, see *Iviron*, vol. IV, no. 97.

[58] See M. Berindei, "L'Empire ottoman et la 'route Moldave' avant la conquête de Chilia et de Cetatea-albă (1484)," *Journal of Turkish Studies* 10 (1986) (= *Raiyyet Rüsûmu. Essays presented to Halil İnalcık on his Seventieth Birthday*), 47–71.

[59] For documents on the arrest and exile of Platyskalites together with three other Thessalonians, see above, ch. 3, note 41. In two of these documents, the name is curiously rendered as "Cazicaliti": Sathas, *Documents*, vol. I, nos. 104 and 108, pp. 168, 170. For the involvement of the Platyskalites family in trade and banking, see S. Kugéas, "Notizbuch eines Beamten der Metropolis in Thessalonike aus dem Anfang des XV. Jahrhunderts," *BZ* 23 (1914), 153 (§ 86). See also A. E. Vacalopoulos, "Συμβολὴ στὴν ἱστορία τῆς Θεσσαλονίκης ἐπὶ Βενετοκρατίας (1423–1430)" and M. Th. Laskaris, "Θεσσαλονίκη καὶ Τάνα," in *Τόμος Κωνσταντίνου Ἀρμενοπούλου* (Thessalonike, 1952), pp. 135–6 and 334–5; Mertzios, *Μνημεῖα*, p. 45; Symeon–Balfour, pp. 274–7.

[60] Symeon–Balfour, pp. 55–6.

sake of material gains.[61] Isidore describes how certain wealthy citizens habitually exploited the poor, both inside the city and in its countryside. Not only did they demand extremely high interest rates from needy people who were obliged to borrow money, but when poor peasants could not repay their debts, their rich neighbors did not hesitate to take over the little plots of land which constituted the small peasants' livelihood.[62] According to Symeon, the local governors (*archontes*) of the city, overtaken by greed and love of money, misused the authority of their position to snatch away the belongings of the lower classes. In this manner they set such a bad example that some among the poor too, imitating the *archontes*, tried to seize each other's possessions.[63] Such abuses seem to have been very common in Thessalonike during both periods of Byzantine rule, when the hardships and privations due to the war with the Ottomans created opportunities which some people did not fail to take advantage of. The wealthy upper classes, however, having greater means for exploitation than the vulnerable poor, were more active in this sphere. For this reason, back in 1372, when Demetrios Kydones advised the *megas primikerios* Demetrios Phakrases to make use of the local *dynatoi* in the defense of Thessalonike against a Turkish attack, he specifically told him to warn the notables "that the present situation is not an occasion for grasping at some advantage, nor should they further provoke those who are desperate."[64]

---

[61] Isidore–Christophorides, vol. II, Homily 19, pp. 299–300 and Homily 22, pp. 344–7; Isidore–Christophorides, vol. I, Homily 30, pp. 77, 82; Symeon–Balfour, p. 47; Symeon–Phountoules, no. 22.

[62] Isidore–Christophorides, vol. II, Homily 21, pp. 329–30 and Homily 22, pp. 345–7; Isidore–Laourdas, Homily I, p. 29.

[63] Symeon–Balfour, p. 47. It must be granted that in virtually all periods and provinces of the Byzantine Empire examples can be found of abuses and oppression exercised by the *archontes* over the lower classes. The problem assumed the aspect of a conventional and proverbial theme, finding one of its best expressions in the Byzantine saying, "Even the most miserable of the *archontes* will bully the people under him," transmitted by Eustathios of Thessalonike in the twelfth century: see M. Angold, "Archons and dynasts: local aristocracies and the cities of the later Byzantine Empire," in *The Byzantine Aristocracy, IX to XIII Centuries*, ed. M. Angold (Oxford, 1984), p. 249 and n. 67. Whether or not such conventional statements reflect existing practices can be questioned of course. But given the fact that the problem is not only brought up in purely theoretical, moralistic, and theological contexts, but is also confirmed in notarial documents as well as other legal sources, it seems reasonable to accept its presence as a real issue in Byzantine society. It remains crucial, however, to evaluate the existing references in the light of the particular historical and social conditions in which they occurred. On this subject, see H. Saradi, "The twelfth-century canon law commentaries on the ἀρχοντικὴ δυναστεία: ecclesiastical theory vs. juridical practice," in *Byzantium in the 12th Century; Canon Law, State and Society*, ed. N. Oikonomidès (Athens, 1991), pp. 375–404; H. Saradi, "On the 'archontike' and 'ekklesiastike dynasteia' and 'prostasia' in Byzantium with particular attention to the legal sources: a study in social history of Byzantium," *B* 64 (1994), 69–117, 314–51.

[64] Kydones–Loenertz, vol. I, no. 77, lines 27–31; cf. Dennis, *Reign of Manuel II*, pp. 55–6. For Demetrios Phakrases, see *PLP*, no. 29576.

Compared with the problems and hardships which the landowning aristocrats, merchants, and bankers of Thessalonike faced, the city's lower classes seem to be the social group that suffered the most during both 1382–7 and 1403–23. Contemporary sources frequently mention the poor and describe their deplorable state. One of the most striking examples of the extreme poverty of the lower classes and their resulting unwillingness to fight against the Turks is found in a letter written by Manuel II in 1383:

They are almost all Iroses, and it is easy to count those who do not go to bed hungry. Indeed, we need either the wealth of Croesus or an eloquence above average to be able to persuade them to bear poverty in good repute rather than desire a blameworthy wealth. They have to be convinced, moreover, that it is nobler and far less shameful to suffer willingly the lot of slaves for the sake of their own freedom than, after having become slaves in heart, to try to gain the rights of free men.[65]

Later, Symeon also wrote about widespread poverty, misery, and suffering in Thessalonike in an encyclical he composed in 1422, and he urged the citizens living under such conditions to endure and not to deviate from Orthodoxy.[66] According to the testimony of Symeon, at this time there was a strong opposition among the lower classes to the policy of resistance pursued against the Ottomans by members of the city's governing body. This opposition was spurred by two interrelated considerations on the part of the lower classes. First of all, the resistance policy which prolonged the years of warfare had only helped to intensify their hardships; secondly, it was supported and executed by the ruling elite who, in the opinion of the lower classes, were merely considering their own interests and not those of the masses:

Now on top of this the majority were shouting against and bitterly reproaching those in authority and me myself, accusing us of not striving to serve the welfare of the population as a whole. They actually declared that they were bent on handing the latter over to the infidel.[67]

The lower classes were further aggravated because the *archontes* and some wealthy Thessalonians who supported the cause of war made no financial contributions towards defense needs. Their reluctance could not have resulted from their lack of means for in the early fifteenth century the *archontes* of Thessalonike were criticized for living wantonly and hoarding their wealth, while burying money was commonly practiced by wealthy

---

[65] Dennis, *Letters of Manuel II*, no. 4, pp. 12–13. [66] Symeon–Balfour, p. 74.
[67] Ibid., pp. 55–6 (text), 157 (trans.).

citizens during the blockade of 1383–7.[68] According to Isidore Glabas, one of the prerequisites for winning the struggle against the Ottomans in the 1380s was to convince those with financial resources to contribute to military expenditures.[69] It is also evident that the aforementioned Constantinopolitan general, who proposed in 1423 the setting up of a common fund for defense purposes through contributions by Thessalonians out of their personal assets, had as his main target the upper classes who could afford to pay the necessary sums. But it was precisely these people who, in apprehension of a forceful exaction of their money, opposed the general's proposal. The reaction of the lower classes to the conduct exhibited by the rich was to protest and riot in favor of surrender to the Ottomans.[70] Their outrage, provoked in the first place by the unwillingness of the rich to contribute to the war cause, may well have been accompanied and enhanced by the fear that the civil authorities might turn to the populace to make up for the resources that could not be procured from the well-to-do. Such a policy seems to have been applied in 1383, when under comparable circumstances a new tax may have been imposed even on the poor citizens of Thessalonike because of the inadequacy of other sources of revenue.[71]

Symeon reports that some of the inhabitants who objected to the Constantinopolitan general's proposal had recourse to flight. There are other indications pointing to the fact that the urge to escape fiscal burdens associated with war expenses was often a determining factor in the flight of many Thessalonians. In 1415 Manuel II requested from Venice the return of Byzantine subjects from Thessalonike, Constantinople, and the Morea who had fled to Venetian territories. In the surviving reply of the Venetian Senate to the Emperor, it is explicitly stated that the refugees from the Morea had run away in order to circumvent the charges imposed on them for financing the reconstruction of the Hexamilion, undertaken for protection against Ottoman attacks. As far as the refugees from Thessalonike and Constantinople are concerned, we know only that they had fled to the Venetians at the time of the sieges of their respective cities by the Ottoman prince Musa. But it seems reasonable to conjecture that the incentive to avoid fiscal burdens played a role in their flight too.[72] About a year and a

---

[68] Ibid., p. 47; Isidore–Christophorides, vol. II, Homily 19, p. 301 and Homily 21, p. 333; cf. Homily 4, p. 68.

[69] Isidore–Christophorides, vol. I, Homily 33, p. 120 and Homily 37, p. 187.

[70] Symeon–Balfour, p. 57. See above, ch. 3, pp. 47–8.

[71] This is suggested by Isidore Glabas' allusion to officials laying hands on the belongings of the poor in a homily that was probably delivered in September 1383: Isidore–Christophorides, vol. II, Homily 19, p. 300, lines 1–2.

[72] Iorga, "Notes et extraits," *ROL* 4 (1896), 554–5 (Sept. 23, 1415); Thiriet, *Régestes*, vol. II, no. 1592.

half after the Emperor's call, there were still some Thessalonians in Negroponte who had not returned to their native city despite the fact that almost
four years had elapsed since the termination of Musa's siege.[73] They probably remained on the Venetian island because shortly after Musa, in 1416,
Mehmed I started threatening the environs of Thessalonike.[74] As long as
Ottoman pressures persisted, the fear of being forced to supply money
towards defense needs, coupled with anxiety over the unstable military situation, no doubt deterred these refugees from returning to Thessalonike.

At some time between 1417 and 1420 a group of Christian captives and
conscripts who deserted the Ottoman army and took refuge in Thessalonike
prompted another crisis. When Mehmed I demanded as compensation
either ransom money or the return of the fugitives, the inhabitants decided
to deliver them to the Ottoman ruler, against the protests of only a number
of religious people led by the archbishop Symeon.[75] Besides the fear of
Mehmed I, a fundamental factor that led the Thessalonians to this decision
must have been the urge to escape paying the ransom fee. Given the
other cases which confirm the unwillingness of the rich to make financial
sacrifices, it is not difficult to conceive why the community as a whole,
with the exception of a few religious persons, resigned itself to handing in
the captives.

A portrait of Thessalonian society which likewise gives the impression
of the existence of an upper class that remained indifferent to the demands
brought on by the war with the Ottomans and continued to spend money
in pursuit of a wanton, carefree, and luxurious lifestyle can be found in a
fifteenth-century text attributed to John Argyropoulos. The text in question is an invective against a certain Katablattas, who was a native of Serres
but spent the years between about 1403 and 1430 in Thessalonike, having
fled there from Bursa after a period of service in the Ottoman army as a
foot soldier.[76] Katablattas became a school instructor in Thessalonike and
also served as a scribe in the city's tribunal. He had close ties with people
from the uppermost levels of Thessalonian society, including members of

---

[73] Iorga, "Notes et extraits," *ROL* 4 (1896), 573–4 (Jan. 12, 1417); Thiriet, *Régestes*, vol. II, no. 1635.
[74] See B. Krekić, *Dubrovnik (Raguse) et le Levant au Moyen Age* (Paris, 1961), no. 630 (Dec. 25, 1416).
On Mehmed I's campaign, see also M. Balivet, "L'expédition de Mehmed Ier contre Thessalonique:
convergences et contradictions des sources byzantines et turques," *Comité International d'Études
Pré-Ottomanes et Ottomanes: VIth Symposium, Cambridge, 1–4 July 1984* (Istanbul, Paris, and Leiden,
1987), pp. 31–7.
[75] Symeon–Balfour, p. 51.
[76] "La Comédie de Katablattas. Invective byzantine du XVe s.," ed. P. Canivet and N. Oikonomidès,
Δίπτυχα 3 (1982–3), 5–97. For the identification of the author and the dates given above, see
ibid., 9, 15–21. The portion of the text that corresponds to Katablattas' years in Thessalonike is on
pp. 35–51.

the ruling class. He frequently visited the palace of the Despot Andronikos, had contacts with the senators, gave public speeches, and seems to have enjoyed a certain degree of influence with Andronikos as suggested by the request of a woman who asked him to write a letter to the Despot on her behalf. The text's depiction of the social gatherings (e.g. banquets, weddings, hunting parties) attended by Katablattas, elaborately focusing on all the singing, dancing, drinking, and eating that took place on these occasions, corresponds closely with the wanton lifestyle attributed by other contemporary sources to the milieu in which Katablattas was active. Therefore, while it is important to keep in mind that the work at hand is an invective and that some of the accusations found in it against Katablattas may be false or exaggerated, there is no reason to reject the authenticity of the general image of Thessalonian upper-class society it conveys.

Viewed all together, then, the evidence presented above suggests that in spite of the hardships and unfavorable conditions that affected all social groups within Thessalonike, there remained a small fraction of the population consisting of people at the top who had in their possession a considerable amount of money. A question worth asking is where this money came from. Traditionally the Byzantine aristocracy, despite the fact that it always constituted an essentially urban group, drew its wealth predominantly from land. We have seen, however, that in Thessalonike and its environs, as elsewhere in the empire, the landowning aristocracy suffered major property losses and became impoverished in the course of the fourteenth and fifteenth centuries as a result of civil wars and the successive invasions of Serbians and Ottomans. Thus it is not in land, but elsewhere, that we must seek the source of the money that accumulated in the hands of those who refused to channel it towards the defense needs of Thessalonike.

The answer to our question seems to lie in long-distance commercial activity and banking. While the military, political, and economic circumstances that posed considerable obstacles to trade have been outlined above, it has also been demonstrated that some Thessalonian merchants were able to create conditions favorable to themselves and to perpetuate their commercial enterprises. Sources every now and then give glimpses of the trade connections of certain Thessalonians with foreign markets during this period. For instance, Andreas Argyropoulos, who bears the name of the distinguished Thessalonian family already mentioned in connection with a dispute over a group of gardens belonging to the monastery of Iveron, was involved in the fur trade of Wallachia in the early fifteenth century.[77] Secondly, a moneychanger (*katallaktes*) called Platyskalites, whose sister was married to another moneychanger by the family name of Chalazas (an archontic family of Thessalonike), had a stepbrother, Michael Metriotes, who made a journey to Tana at the end of the fourteenth century.[78] In view of the commercial importance of Tana, Michael Metriotes' trip there is quite likely to have been for trading purposes. We have more conclusive evidence, on the other hand, concerning the international enterprises of two other Thessalonians, John Rhosotas and Theodore Katharos, whose realm of activity encompassed Venice, Dubrovnik, and Novo Brdo. In 1424–5 Theodore Katharos can be traced in Dubrovnik, where he was acting as John Rhosotas' business agent. At an earlier date Theodore had made a deal in Venice with a Ragusan merchant, to whom he entrusted a certain amount of money and merchandise. The Ragusan was then arrested and died in prison at Venice. Hence in Dubrovnik Theodore was mainly occupied with trying to recover the money the deceased merchant owed him which, as he claimed, amounted to slightly over 3,875 ducats. It seems that Theodore did not possess sufficient proof, and in the end he lost about one-third of this money.[79] During his visit to Dubrovnik, he may have been involved in other enterprises too, as suggested by a document of 1424 which mentions a *Teodorus Grecus* who exported cloth from there to Serbia.[80]

It is not clear whether Theodore acted alone or once again as John Rhosotas' agent in the last-mentioned enterprise. Yet several sources demonstrate that a certain *Caloiani Rusota*, who may be identified with John Rhosotas of Thessalonike, held a prominent place at the Serbian court in the 1420s and 1430s, where he actively engaged in business and banking, providing loans particularly to Ragusan merchants who were dealing in Serbia. He served

---

[77] MM, vol. II, no. 564, pp. 374–5. The Polos Argyros, mentioned in the fifteenth-century satire of Mazaris, who returned rich from Wallachia, has been identified with Andreas Argyropoulos: Laiou-Thomadakis, "Byzantine economy," 201–2, n. 97; cf. *PLP*, no. 1255. Yet it is by no means certain whether Andreas belonged to the Thessalonian branch of the Argyropouloi; we possess no evidence concerning his place of origin or residence. Several other members of the family – Argyropoulos Mamoli; John Melachrinos, son of George Argyropoulos; Constantine and Demetrios Argyropoulos – are mentioned among the "nobles and small nobles" of Thessalonike who were in the pay of Venice and received salary raises during the period of the Venetian domination (in 1425), but nothing is known of their occupations: see below, Appendix II, nos. 24, 30, 31, 58.

[78] Kugéas, "Notizbuch," 153 (§ 86); cf. Laskaris, "Θεσσαλονίκη καὶ Τάνα," pp. 331–40. For *archontes* among the Chalazas family of Thessalonike in the fourteenth century, see *Iviron*, vol. III, no. 78 (= *Schatzkammer*, no. III); *Docheiariou*, no. 50; cf. Appendix I below.

[79] Krekić, *Dubrovnik*, nos. 686, 688, 690, 691, 697, 699, 702, 708, 709, 718, 721.

[80] Ibid., no. 695.

furthermore as customs officer at Novo Brdo until his death in 1438.[81] If these two men are identical as suggested, this raises of course the question of when John Rhosotas left Thessalonike, to which a precise answer cannot be given. It is possible, though not so significant from our point of view, that Rhosotas may have already established himself in Serbia while Theodore Katharos was acting on his behalf in Dubrovnik.[82] Supposing this were the case, it is of far greater significance for present purposes that Rhosotas did not totally disengage himself from his native city and delegated the management of part of his affairs to a fellow Thessalonian. In any event, without his prior international enterprises and foreign contacts, his rise to prominence at the Serbian court would have been quite unlikely. It is also noteworthy that the aforementioned fifteenth-century invective attributed to John Argyropoulos has brought to light a certain Rhosotas who gave a big party in Thessalonike on the occasion of his daughter's wedding, sometime between 1403 and 1430.[83] Whether this last piece of evidence concerns our John Rhosotas or, as seems more likely, one of his kinsmen in Thessalonike, it lends in either case further support to my hypothesis that links the financial resources and sumptuous lifestyle of the city's social elite in these critical times to profits from long-distance trade and banking.

Since the civil discords in Thessalonike and the lack of unity among the citizens constituted according to Kydones, Isidore, Symeon, and Anagnostes the major cause for the failure of the city before the Ottomans, it is essential at this point to return to the hostilities between the lower classes and the *archontes* which were briefly mentioned earlier and to subject them to a careful analysis. Symeon is our best source of information on this subject for the period 1403–23. Like most of his contemporaries, Symeon has a tendency to attribute the misfortunes of the Thessalonians and their helplessness before the Ottomans in stereotypical fashion to their sinful behavior, depravity, and need for repentance. However, underneath his moralistic tone, it is possible to detect traces of concrete information on social conditions in the city during these years. In a long passage, after

---

[81] Ibid., nos. 808 and 810; M. Spremić, "La Serbie entre les Turcs, les Grecs, et les Latins au XVe siècle," *BF* 11 (1987), 438, n. 16; K.-P. Matschke, "Zum Anteil der Byzantiner an der Bergbauentwicklung und an den Bergbauerträgen Südosteuropas im 14. und 15. Jahrhundert," *BZ* 84–5 (1991–2), 57–67.

[82] Matschke suggests, for instance, that Rhosotas' move to Serbia may have coincided with the first period of Ottoman domination in Thessalonike: "Zum Anteil der Byzantiner an der Bergbauentwicklung," 62–3.

[83] "Comédie de Katablattas," ed. Canivet and Oikonomidès, 49. Note that in one of his letters Isidore Glabas names a certain Rhosotas, along with a Tzymisches and a Klematikos, among the notables of Thessalonike: Isidore–Lampros, Letter 6, pp. 380–1. Cf. *PLP*, no. 24579.

reproaching the wrongdoings and ingratitude of the citizens towards God, Symeon writes:

The *archontes* live wantonly, hoard their wealth, and exalt themselves above their subjects, freely performing injustices, not only offering nothing to God, but also stealing away from God. They believe this to be their power, and they consider the poor citizens and their subordinates as scarcely human. But the poor, too, imitating those in authority, arm themselves against each other and live rapaciously and greedily.[84]

Then follows a description of various religious offenses, committed both by the rulers and the subjects, on account of which God has punished them by their present misfortunes. But the common people, not realizing this according to Symeon, blame the *archontes* for all their troubles and are prepared to rise up in rebellion against them, expecting that "they might thus live freely and uncontrolled." This account, marked by Symeon's critical and disapproving attitude towards the *archontes*, whom he holds responsible for the reprehensible actions of the common people as well, reveals to what extent the latter felt oppressed in the early fifteenth century by the conduct of the civil authorities and were consequently inclined to give up – indeed some of them did, as Symeon acknowledges – their own masters (δεσπόται) of the same faith and race in favor of either Ottoman or Venetian sovereignty.[85]

    A similar atmosphere of social discontent was witnessed in Thessalonike earlier in 1393, when the hostility of the common people towards the *archontes* had reached such an intensity that the latter, anticipating the outbreak of a popular movement against their rule, wanted to resign.[86] In this case, too, the overriding grievance of the populace was that they were being oppressed by their political leaders. At this date Thessalonike was under Ottoman rule. However, as the city was granted a semi-autonomous status following its surrender to the Ottomans in 1387, the administrative functions had remained in the hands of native Greek officials who were obliged to pay regular visits to the Ottoman court. The social conflicts of 1393 depicted by Isidore Glabas are, therefore, relevant to the present discussion.

    A notable feature of Isidore's account is his favorable and positive attitude towards the *archontes*, which sharply contrasts with Symeon's account composed about three decades later. Although at an earlier date Isidore had voiced complaints against certain municipal governors who declined

[84] Symeon–Balfour, p. 47, lines 9–14.   [85] Ibid., p. 47, lines 14–38.
[86] Isidore–Laourdas, Homilies IV and V, see esp. pp. 64–5.

to give assistance to poor and wronged citizens or else executed orders for the secularization of ecclesiastical property,[87] in principle he considered it proper, useful, and necessary for all Thessalonians to revere, to love, and to give support to the *archontes*.[88] Fearing that the disagreements between the people and the governors in 1393 might lead to some form of political change, he composed two homilies, one to instruct the citizens to put an end to their disturbances, and the other to persuade the *archontes* not to resign from their posts.[89] He argued that the *archontes* deserved respect for all the tasks and troubles they shouldered on behalf of the people: they were the ones who acted as mediators between the Thessalonians and the Ottomans, who bore the latter's insults and maltreatment, who left their families behind, traveled through dangerous lands on embassies to the Ottoman court, and thus enabled the inhabitants to continue to live in peace.[90] Drawing a comparison between those who govern the state and the common people who work with their hands (i.e. craftsmen, artisans, and peasants), Isidore suggested that the latter were unfit to take part in the administration of the city since they did not have the benefit of education that distinguished the ruling elite from themselves.[91] He advised the *archontes* – whom he qualified as "the distinguished," "the honorable," "the few select" citizens – to act as befitted their own class and to ignore the complaints of the people as incoherent utterings.[92]

The divergence between Symeon's and Isidore's views need not, however, be taken as evidence that the *archontes* in power during the last decade of the fourteenth century differed fundamentally from the ones who held office in the early decades of the fifteenth century, at least in terms of their treatment of and attitude towards the common people. From the distinction Isidore draws between those who were created by God as fit for governing and those who knew how to use different tools yet had no education, it is clear that he is not talking about the actual *archontes* in office in 1393, but that he is referring in abstract and idealized terms to a traditional ruling class to which the *archontes* belonged. Symeon, on the other hand, who is more precise compared with Isidore, seems to be pointing a direct finger at the specific *archontes* of his own day. In any case, since the tensions between the people and their governors appear in the

[87] Ibid., Homily I, p. 29 and Homily II, pp. 38–9; Isidore–Christophorides, vol. II, Homily 19, p. 300 and Homily 22, p. 345; Isidore–Christophorides, vol. I, Homily 28, pp. 46–9 (= Isidore–Tsirpanlis, 568–70) and Homily 30, pp. 82–4.

[88] Isidore–Laourdas, Homily II, p. 39, lines 15–18.

[89] Ibid., Homilies IV and V, respectively.   [90] Ibid., Homily IV, pp. 57–8.

[91] Ibid., Homily V, pp. 61, 63.   [92] Ibid., Homily V, pp. 63–4, 61.

writings of both, there is no reason for supposing that there was a change in the social conditions existing within Thessalonike. Isidore feared, however, that such a change might take place and, therefore, focusing on the positive attributes of the *archontes* as a class, praised and defended them. Symeon, not interested in the theoretical attributes of a superior ruling class, seems to have looked at the actual state of affairs and reported his observations in a more or less realistic and critical manner, openly revealing his bitterness towards both the *archontes* and the common people who imitated them.

But who precisely were the *archontes* who became the object of so much discussion and controversy? Given the key role they played in the political and social life of late Byzantine Thessalonike, it is unfortunate that they remain by and large unidentified in the writings of Isidore and Symeon, who always refer to them collectively, without naming any particular individuals.[93] However, with the use of prosopographic data compiled mainly from fourteenth- and fifteenth-century Athonite documents, it has been possible to uncover the identities of some fifty *archontes* of Thessalonike.[94] Thanks to this additional body of concrete evidence, we can form a more precise idea of the *archontes* than our literary sources would permit and gain further insights particularly about the social and economic characteristics of this group, which may, in turn, enhance our understanding of the sociopolitical conflicts discussed above. As can be seen from the list presented in Appendix I, many of the *archontes* belonged to well-known aristocratic families of Thessalonike, including the Angeloi, Deblitzenoi, Kasandrenoi, Melachrinoi, Metochitai, Rhadenoi, Spartenoi, Tarchaneiotai, and Choniatai. In addition, certain family names show continuity over time: for example Kokalas (*c.* 1320 and 1336), Kyprianos (1348–61 and 1414), Metochites (1373–6 and 1421), Prinkips (1407–9 and 1421), and possibly Komes (1366 and 1404–19). Some other cases of recurring family names, yet without any indication of continuity over time, may be noted as well: Nicholas and Petros Prebezianos (1366), George and Andronikos Doukas Tzykandyles (1373–81 and *c.* 1381, respectively), John Rhadenos and Stephanos Doukas Rhadenos (1415–21). Occasionally kinship ties can be traced between *archontes* who bear different family names, as in the case of the brothers-in-law Manuel Phaxenos and Theodore Doukas Spartenos (1341), or that of Manuel Deblitzenos (1381) and his son-in-law Bartholomaios Komes (1404–19). It is not certain, but Symeon Choniates (1361–6)

---

[93] See note 83 above for an exception.
[94] See Appendix I below, with references to the documents. For some earlier observations on the *archontes* of Thessalonike, see Tafrali, *Thessalonique*, pp. 22–3, 75–80; B. T. Gorjanov, *Pozdnevizantijskij feodalizm* (Moscow, 1962), pp. 86–7, 252–3, 269–71, 349.

may have been the grandfather of George Angelos (1381), and the latter, in turn, Manuel Deblitzenos' brother-in-law.[95] On the basis of these observations, we can thus conclude that a series of interrelated local families yielded successive generations of *archontes*, forming what appears to have been a tightly linked, more or less homogeneous social group.

More than half of the *archontes* listed in Appendix I are qualified in the documents as *oikeioi* and/or *douloi*, sometimes of the emperor, sometimes of the Despot of Thessalonike, and sometimes of both. While there is nothing unusual about the application of these honorific epithets to civil dignitaries, which was standard procedure in the Palaiologan period, being an *oikeios* or *doulos* was nonetheless a mark of distinction and undoubtedly enhanced the *archontes'* sense of belonging to the elite of their society.[96] Noteworthy also is the fact that the last seven individuals who appear in Appendix I were all members of the Senate of Thessalonike in 1421. The presence of Senate members among the *archontes* of Thessalonike is confirmed in another Athonite document dating from 1414, which makes reference to two ἄρχοντες τῆς συγκλήτου, but unfortunately does not disclose their names.[97] Besides people of civilian status, moreover, we can also detect some individuals of military status in the list: for example one *megas primikerios* (Demetrios Phakrases, 1366), one *megas droungarios* (Demetrios Glabas [Komes?], 1366), one *megas chartoularios* (Laskaris Metochites, 1373–6), and one *kastrophylax* (Demetrios Talapas, c. 1381). Manuel Deblitzenos, too, belonged to a family of soldiers and was himself a military man.[98]

The documentary sources, in addition to allowing us to identify a substantial number of *archontes* and their social profile, also provide data with regard to the economic character of this group. It is not clear from the documents what kinds of material compensation they received for holding government offices, yet the prosopographic survey suggests that the bulk of their income derived from other sources of revenue. Some *archontes* or their extended families were landowners in possession of large- to medium-sized holdings in the surrounding countryside, primarily in Chalkidike.[99]

---

[95] See Oikonomidès, "Properties of the Deblitzenoi," p. 195, n. 27; *Docheiariou*, p. 260.

[96] On these epithets, see J. Verpeaux, "Les oikeioi. Notes d'histoire institutionnelle et sociale," *REB* 23 (1965), 89–99; *ODB*, vol. i, p. 659; vol. iii, p. 1515.

[97] *Docheiariou*, no. 54, line 11.

[98] On the military character of this family, see Oikonomidès, "Properties of the Deblitzenoi," pp. 177–8.

[99] E.g. the *archontes* Manuel Phaxenos, Theodore Doukas Spartenos, Manuel Tarchaneiotes, and Manuel Deblitzenos cited in Appendix I below, as well as various members of the archontic families of Kokalas (*PLP*, nos. 14090, 14094), Stavrakios (*PLP*, nos. 26702, 26703), Maroules (*PLP*, no. 17156), Kasandrenos (*PLP*, nos. 11312, 11313), Angelos (*PLP*, nos. 91030, 91031), Gazes (*PLP*, no. 3444), Melachrinos (*PLP*, no. 17633), and Rhadenos (*PLP*, nos. 23987, 23992).

In addition, some possessed urban properties (such as houses, shops, or workshops) inside Thessalonike.[100] Some *archontes* were connected, on the other hand, with the guild-like associations of Thessalonike:[101] Theodore Brachnos (1320) was *exarchos ton myrepson*, while Theodore Chalazas (1314–26) was simply *myrepsos*. The latter, moreover, bears the name of a family among whose members moneychangers (*katallaktai*) are attested in the early fifteenth century, thus suggesting that some *archontes* may have been engaged in business and banking.[102] Incidentally, Rhadenos, who served Manuel II as counselor during 1382/3–7, was the son of a wealthy merchant and had two brothers who engaged in business, even though we possess only clues, but no conclusive evidence, to his personal involvement in business affairs.[103] On the other hand, it seems most likely that the *archon* Nicholas Prebezianos (1366) engaged in trade himself, for a mid-fourteenth-century account book originating from Thessalonike gives evidence of a businessman (cloth merchant?) by the name of *kyr* Nicholas Prebezianos.[104] It should be noted that the author of this account book, a landowning merchant who was the nephew of the latter, is identified through his brother's name as a Kasandrenos[105] and might have possibly belonged to the same branch of this well-known Thessalonian family from which stemmed the *archon* Manuel Kasandrenos (1381). Kasandrenos' business circle in the 1350s included at least two other individuals who may also have been connected with archontic families: one Tzykandyles, who traded in various commodities including wheat, barley, caviar, fish, and different items of clothing,[106] and one George Gazes, who traveled to Serres with wheat he acquired from Kasandrenos.[107] Finally, Demetrios Laskaris Leontares, who

---

[100] Manuel Deblitzenos owned several houses and small shops in the city: *Docheiariou*, no. 49, pp. 263–4. A certain Maroules who owned some properties in the Omphalos quarter of Thessalonike may perhaps be identified with the *archon* John Maroules: ibid., p. 263; cf. *PLP*, nos. 17143 and 17153. House-owners are also attested among members of the archontic families of Allelouias (*PLP*, no. 674), Melachrinos (*PLP*, no. 17627), etc.

[101] See ch. 3, note 2 on these associations.

[102] Kugéas, "Notizbuch," 153 (§ 86); see p. 75 above. The involvement of Thessalonian *archontes* in business and banking, suggested here, runs parallel to the phenomenon discussed by K.-P. Matschke, "Notes on the economic establishment and social order of the late Byzantine *kephalai*," *BF* 19 (1993), 139–43, where the author presents evidence for the connection between provincial municipal administration and commercial/financial enterprise in the Palaiologan period.

[103] See above, pp. 60–1 and notes 19, 20. For a female pawnbroker belonging to the Rhadenos family in early fifteenth-century Thessalonike, see Kugéas, "Notizbuch," 144 (§ 9).

[104] P. Schreiner, *Texte zur spätbyzantinischen Finanz- und Wirtschaftsgeschichte in Handschriften der Biblioteca Vaticana* (Vatican City, 1991), p. 85 (§§ 61, 63); cf. *PLP*, nos. 23700 and 23702. See also Schreiner, *Texte*, p. 84 (§ 53), for Nicholas' brother, *kyr* Manoles Prebezianos, who traded in cloth (from Serres).

[105] Schreiner, *Texte*, pp. 82 (§ 4), 86f.; cf. pp. 81, 98. For a discussion of this text and the individuals in question here, see also Matschke and Tinnefeld, *Gesellschaft*, pp. 166–72.

[106] Schreiner, *Texte*, pp. 83, 84, 87, 88 (§§ 26, 45, 50, 100, 125, 136).   [107] Ibid., p. 84 (§ 48).

as a non-native of Thessalonike cannot strictly be considered among the city's traditional ruling families, but who was nonetheless very active in its government between 1403 and 1416, may have had important commercial dealings in Pera and perhaps bribed two Genoese officials in 1402.[108]

The names of some of these *archontes* themselves or of their family members reappear in a Venetian document of 1425, dating from the period of the Venetian domination in Thessalonike. This document lists fifty-nine Thessalonians, described as *gentilomeni e gentilomeni piçoli*, whose names are reproduced in Appendix II.[109] They were granted raises in the monthly salaries they received from Venice for the services they rendered in the defense of Thessalonike. Among them, *Calojani/Jani Radino*, one of the three ambassadors sent to Venice in 1425 to request these raises and to make other demands, can be identified with the *apographeus* John Rhadenos (1415–21). In all likelihood, he also participated in a second embassy dispatched to Venice for similar purposes in 1429.[110] Included in the Venetian payroll of 1425, we also find one *Georgio Radino*, who was presumably someone related to John Rhadenos. Secondly, *Thomas Grusulora/Chrussulora*, another ambassador present at Venice in 1425, is no doubt the same person as the senatorial *archon* Thomas Chrysoloras (1421). Thirdly, *Ducha Melacrino* may be identified with John Douk(a)s Melachrinos (1415) in Appendix I. Four additional members of the Melachrinos family appear as well in the Venetian document of 1425. One of them, moreover, is reported to be the son of George Argyropoulos, member of a prominent Thessalonian family with three further representatives in the same source. Other familiar archontic patronymics that recur in the Venetian document of 1425 include Hyaleas,[111] Laskaris, Tarchaneiotes, Angelos, and possibly Gazes as well as Pezos. The cross-references between the names listed in Appendices

---

[108] Laiou-Thomadakis, "Byzantine economy," 220 and n. 26; Balard, *Romanie génoise*, vol. II, p. 758; Hunger, *Chortasmenos*, pp. 127–9.

[109] Facsimile reproduction of the document in Mertzios, Μνημεῖα, following p. 48 (ASV, SM, reg. 55, fos. 139ff.); cf. pp. 49–52.

[110] The document concerning the Thessalonian embassy of 1429 to Venice has also been reproduced in facsimile by Mertzios, Μνημεῖα, following p. 73 (ASV, SM, reg. 57, fos. 129ff.); cf. pp. 85–6. It states only that John Rhadenos (*Zuan Radino*) was in Venice at this time. His name is brought up in connection with a request for financial assistance he made on behalf of his son-in-law, one Doukas Lathras (*Ducha Lathra*), who had recently come to Thessalonike after some years of residence under Turkish domination in or near Kastoria, where he possessed many castles and villages. Incidentally Doukas Lathras had a mother and a brother who both lived in Venetian Corfu, yet he and some other relatives of his chose to station themselves in Thessalonike, likewise under the protection of Venice. Because Lathras was highly skilled in military matters and had won great fame for his valor, the Venetian Senate granted him in 1429 a monthly salary of 300 *aspra*, the equivalent of approximately 21 *hyperpyra* (cf. Bertelè, *Numismatique byzantine*, pp. 88–9).

[111] This name appears in the document three times as "Jalca" (nos. 2, 9, 16 in Appendix II below), which must be a misreading for Jalea, i.e. Hyaleas, on the part of the Venetian scribe, who probably copied the names from a list. Cf. Jacoby, "Thessalonique," 308, n. 29. It is also feasible that "Falca"

I and II thus indicate that a significant proportion of the Greek "nobles and small nobles" to whom the Venetians paid salaries for their participation in the defense of Thessalonike against the Ottomans came from the same families, and in some cases were the very same individuals, as those who served as *archontes* prior to the Venetian takeover. This confirms, then, a statement made by Symeon that in 1423 the Despot Andronikos had agreed to the cession of Thessalonike to Venice, acting in response to the counsel of "those who shared governmental functions with him" and "the very magnates of our body politic" – in other words, the *archontes*.[112]

In conclusion, this survey of Byzantine Thessalonike has revealed that almost all the inhabitants of the city from the common people to members of the highest levels of society were negatively affected by the persistent Ottoman sieges and attacks. Consequently some people fled from the city, while the majority who stayed behind became divided over their political preferences as they sought different ways to relieve their hardships. Despite occasional overlaps in the views of people belonging to different strata of Thessalonian society, the political divisions generally followed the social divisions of the city's population. The poorer people, on the whole, opted for the peace that could be achieved by means of surrender to the Ottomans. By contrast, the *archontes* and most members of the Thessalonian aristocracy with whom the common people were in social conflict took an aggressive stance towards the Ottomans, and during the period of Venetian rule many of them fought against the Ottomans in the service and pay of Venice. It is conceivable that the widespread misery which affected nearly everyone helped to some extent to reduce the acute social and economic differentiation characteristic of Thessalonike's social structure. Nevertheless, the same circumstances simultaneously created opportunities for certain groups or individuals who either found ways of profiting from other people's hardships or else succeeded in multiplying their assets through investments in foreign commercial markets. Hence, the impoverishment of the majority of Thessalonians existed side by side with the enrichment of a small minority. This lay at the root of the internal dissensions of the period which, in turn, played a role in determining the city's fate before the enemy.

and "Milca" (nos. 8 and 15, respectively, in Appendix II below) represent further corruptions of "Jalca" caused by the scribe's carelessness and unfamiliarity with Greek names.

[112] Symeon–Balfour, p. 55, lines 20–1: "... οἱ σὺν ἐκείνῳ δὲ τῆς ἀρχοντικῆς μοίρας ... καὶ αὐτοὶ δὲ οἱ τῆς πολιτείας ἡμῶν πρῶτοι ..." For an analogous identification of the Greek *archontes* of the Morea as *gentiles hombres, gentil homme grec,* or *nobiles* in the different versions of the Chronicle of the Morea, see D. Jacoby, "Les archontes grecs et la féodalité en Morée franque," *TM* 2 (1967), 468, n. 240.

CHAPTER 5

Thessalonike under foreign rule

THE FIRST OTTOMAN DOMINATION (1387–1403)

Following the surrender of Thessalonike in April 1387, the Ottoman forces that entered the city no doubt caused a certain amount of commotion and disarray, arousing alarm and apprehension among some of the citizens at least.[1] Yet, as the immediate turmoil and upheaval subsided, things seem to have returned to a normal state. According to an *enkomion* of the city's future archbishop Gabriel (1397–1416/17) which some scholars attribute to Makarios Makres, the Ottomans treated the inhabitants of Thessalonike in an unexpectedly kind and gentle manner during the early 1390s. While Gabriel's encomiast formulaically ascribes this to the continued protection of the city by Saint Demetrios rather than to the policy and actions of the Ottomans themselves, he indicates nonetheless that the Ottoman domination was not as severe as some Thessalonians had expected.[2] It is also clear from Isidore Glabas' two homilies of 1393 (discussed above, chapter 4) that Ottoman rule did not lead to profound changes in the administrative and social structure of Thessalonike. The city maintained a semi-autonomous status, and the task of administration remained in the hands of the local

---

[1] Symeon of Thessalonike, writing about four decades after the events of 1387, states that the Ottomans, despite "their foul oaths," seized many churches and monasteries, insulted and mistreated the citizens, took some as captives, and subjected the rest to taxation. He also adds that a large number of Christians perished, some physically, others spiritually (i.e. by converting to Islam), while some managed to flee from the city in order to escape the exactions of the Turks. Yet Symeon notes as well that those who were not so concerned with spiritual matters did not object to the city's capture by the Ottomans: Symeon–Balfour, pp. 42–3. As the editor of this text has pointed out, Symeon's account of 1387, particularly what he writes concerning the seizure of churches and monasteries, is highly exaggerated and overstated. Such a large-scale Islamization of Christian buildings is not mentioned in any other source (the only reported cases being those of the monasteries of Prodromos and Saint Athanasios), and it is evident that Symeon's underlying objective was "to paint the Turkish occupation of 1387–1403 as a disastrous period to which no right-minded person could possibly wish to return by again capitulating to the 'godless'." See Balfour's comments on pp. 113 (n. 48), 251–3.

[2] Μακαρίου τοῦ Μακρῆ συγγράμματα, ed. Argyriou, pp. 112–13 (= Syndika-Laourda, "Ἐγκώμιον εἰς Γαβριήλ," 363).

Greek magistrates. Consequently, some of the social tensions and civil discords from the Byzantine period, in particular the conflicts between the common people and the *archontes*, were perpetuated through the years of the first Ottoman domination.[3]

Isidore informs us that the common people of Thessalonike, who were on the verge of rising up in rebellion against the *archontes* in 1393, grumbled in particular because of a payment they were obliged to present to their rulers.[4] Although in the present context this reference to a payment might bring to mind the customary tribute (*harac*) which the Ottomans demanded from their non-Muslim subjects, the text states explicitly that the money in question was distributed to the *archontes*. Considering, however, that the latter had always been paid from sums collected among the citizens,[5] the reason for the disgruntlement of the populace calls for further investigation. Despite Isidore's vague language, the fact that he describes the hardships endured by the *archontes* during their embassies to the Ottoman court just before he mentions the disputed payment suggests that he may be referring to a new charge imposed upon the citizens for financing these trips and perhaps also for compensating the *archontes* for their extra services in dealing with the Turkish authorities. Although Isidore thinks that the money demanded was negligible and that everyone including the *archontes* themselves had to pay it, the common people who threatened the rule of the *archontes* for this reason evidently found it far too burdensome, especially in addition to the *harac* which they must have been paying to the Ottomans.[6]

---

[3] See above, ch. 4, pp. 77–9.   [4] Isidore–Laourdas, Homily IV, pp. 58–9; Homily V, p. 64.

[5] Tafrali, *Thessalonique*, p. 77 and n. 6.

[6] Cf. ibid., pp. 78–9. It is almost certain that Thessalonians were subject to *harac* at this time. One of the clauses of the Byzantine–Ottoman treaty of 1403 states that all former tribute paid to the Turks was to be received thereafter by the Byzantine emperor: Dennis, "Byzantine–Turkish treaty of 1403," 78. Manuel II's prostagma to Boullotes (Sept. 1404) confirms that the emperor was to receive ⅓ of the *harac* "as it was received at the time of Emir Bayezid Beg": Γρηγόριος ὁ Παλαμᾶς 2 (1918), 451–2. Symeon of Thessalonike seems to suggest, moreover, that the Ottomans immediately following their entry into the city in 1387 subjected the Thessalonians to *harac*: see note 1 above. Cf. Ostrogorski, "État tributaire," 49–58; N. Oikonomidès, "Le haradj dans l'Empire byzantin du XVe siècle," *Actes du Ier Congrès International des Études Balkaniques et Sud-Est Européennes*, vol. III (Sofia, 1969), pp. 682–3. Unfortunately, we possess no numerical data on the tribute liability of Thessalonians during the first Ottoman domination. Later in the fifteenth century (*c.* 1411–23), an annual sum of 100,000 aspers may have been yielded to the Ottomans as *harac* for Thessalonike, but this is a controversial issue: see M. Spremić, "Harač soluna u XV veku," *ZRVI* 10 (1967), 187–95; Matschke, *Ankara*, pp. 65, 70–5. To get an idea of how the *harac* obligation might have further afflicted destitute Thessalonians in 1393, see Kydones–Loenertz, vol. II, no. 442 (date: 1391), where it is stated that even the poor in Constantinople would have to be taxed as a new measure to meet the heavy tribute demanded by the Ottomans.

Thus the lower classes who had surrendered to the enemy, expecting their condition to improve through the establishment of external peace, were disappointed in some ways. Nonetheless, Ottoman rule did provide certain benefits and privileges to the city's inhabitants. In his two sermons delivered in 1393 Isidore points out that the Sultan (i.e. Bayezid I, who had ascended the Ottoman throne during the second year after Thessalonike's surrender) granted to the city considerable "gifts," greater than any which the Thessalonians could have hoped for.[7] The encomiast of Isidore's successor, Gabriel, notes that from 1397 onwards, through the efforts of their new archbishop, the citizens of Thessalonike continued to receive "great gifts" from Bayezid I that brought about "a more endurable slavery."[8] Anagnostes, too, refers to "grand gifts" bestowed upon the Thessalonians by the generosity of Bayezid I.[9] Unfortunately, none of the sources specify what these "gifts" were. Yet indirect evidence is available on the policy pursued by the Ottomans in some other incidents of surrender later in the fifteenth century, from which inferences may be drawn with regard to Thessalonike. For instance, the terms of conditional surrender (*amanname*) offered in 1430 to the city of Ioannina by Sinan Paşa, the Ottoman *beylerbeyi* of Rumeli, were as follows: "I swear to you ... that you shall have no fear, either from enslavement, or from the taking of your children, or from the destruction of the churches, nor shall we build any mosques, but the bells of your churches shall ring as has been the custom."[10] On the other hand, the concessions granted to the Genoese colony at Galata (Pera), which surrendered to Sultan Mehmed II in 1453, included the following items: "... let them retain their possessions ... their wives, children and prisoners at their own disposal ... They shall pay neither *commercium* nor *kharadj* ... They shall be permitted to retain their churches and ... never will I on any account carry off their children or any young man for the Janissary corps."[11] The question is, of course, which of these concessions

---

[7] Isidore–Laourdas, Homilies IV and V, pp. 55–65, esp. 56–7.

[8] *Μακαρίου τοῦ Μακρῆ συγγράμματα*, ed. Argyriou, pp. 115–17 (= Syndika-Laourda, "Ἐγκώμιον εἰς Γαβριήλ," 366–7).

[9] Anagnostes–Tsaras, p. 60.

[10] Sp. Vryonis, Jr., "Isidore Glabas and the Turkish *devshirme*," *Speculum* 31/3 (1956), 440. Text in Sp. Lampros, "Ἡ ἑλληνικὴ ὡς ἐπίσημος γλῶσσα τῶν σουλτάνων," *NE* 5 (1908), 62–4 (= MM, vol. III, pp. 282–3; with the wrong date 1431). For a similar *amanname* sent to the citizens of Ioannina during the same year (1430) by Sultan Murad II, see K. Amantos, "Ἡ ἀναγνώρισις ὑπὸ τῶν μωαμεθανῶν θρησκευτικῶν καὶ πολιτικῶν δικαιωμάτων τῶν χριστιανῶν καὶ ὁ ὁρισμὸς τοῦ Σινὰν Πασᾶ," *Ἠπειρωτικὰ Χρονικά* 5 (1930), 207–8 (= Lampros, *NE* 5 [1908], 57–61). Cf. Delilbaşı, "Selânik ve Yanya'da Osmanlı egemenliği," 94–8.

[11] Vryonis, "Glabas and the *devshirme*," 440–1. Text in E. Dalleggio d'Alessio, "Le texte grec du traité conclu par les Génois de Galata avec Mehmet II le 1er Juin 1453," *Ἑλληνικά* 11 (1939), 119–23.

were applied to the citizens of Thessalonike in the context of the "gifts" they received following their surrender in 1387 or later, during the early part of the reign of Bayezid I (r. 1389–1402). As far as the payment of *harac* is concerned, the Thessalonians do not seem to have been exempt from it at least during part, if not all, of Bayezid's reign.[12] Similarly, the exemption from the collection of child-tribute (*devşirme*) may have been a "gift" that was perhaps in effect from 1387 to 1394/5, but certainly not afterwards, since during the winter of 1395 Isidore Glabas delivered his well-known sermon entitled "Homily Concerning the Seizure of the Children by the Decree of the Emir."[13] Thus, on the positive side we are essentially left with the recognition of religious freedom, as well as the grant of a number of political and economic privileges which will be discussed below. It was certainly in order to maintain Orthodoxy and to secure such privileges that Isidore, shortly after the surrender of the city, advised the Thessalonians to be obedient to their new masters, the Ottomans, "in all temporal things." Isidore insisted that henceforth the Greek community ought to dedicate all its efforts to preserving Orthodoxy unstained and prevent the "flawless religion" from being betrayed.[14]

With regard to political privileges, the relegation of administrative functions to local Greek magistrates and the semi-autonomous status accorded to Thessalonike in the early years of the first Ottoman domination have already been mentioned. It is possible, albeit difficult to prove, that the Ottomans, besides granting such collective privileges, also promised political favors to particular individuals shortly before or around the time of the city's surrender. Admittedly, all our evidence for this is indirect, occurring either in the context of Thessalonike at a later date or in the context of Constantinople. Symeon, writing about a popular agitation for surrender to the Ottomans that broke out in Thessalonike in the early 1420s, informs us that the lower classes were supported by some "prominent men" (οἱ δοκοῦντες) who were seeking, besides material interests, political power under Ottoman authority: "Their concern was . . . to lack none of the things which . . . turn men into magnates and put them in authority and

---

[12] See note 6 above.

[13] "Ἰσιδώρου ὁμιλία περὶ τῆς ἁρπαγῆς τῶν παίδων," ed. Laourdas, 389–98. For a discussion and partial translation of this interesting text, see Vryonis, "Glabas and the *devshirme*," 433–43. A full English translation is now available by A. C. Hero, "The first Byzantine eyewitness account of the Ottoman institution of *devşirme*: the homily of Isidore of Thessalonike concerning the 'Seizure of the Children'," in *TO ΕΛΛΗΝΙΚΟΝ. Studies in Honor of Speros Vryonis, Jr.*, vol. 1, ed. J. S. Langdon *et al.* (New Rochelle, 1993), pp. 135–43. The whole tenor of Isidore's homily, delivered on February 28, 1395, suggests that the collection of child-tribute was a new and recent practice in Thessalonike, rather than one applied since the commencement of the Ottoman regime in 1387.

[14] Isidore–Lampros, Letter 8, pp. 389–90.

provide them with a horse and a cloak."[15] Symeon supplies us also with a concrete example that does not involve a Thessalonian but is nonetheless revealing because of the light it sheds on the ways in which the Ottomans instilled hopes and expectations in the minds of the Byzantines. This is the case of the aforementioned general who arrived from Constantinople to provide assistance to Thessalonike in 1422/3:

> The envoys of the enemy approached the city and made a show of willingness to come to terms. They had a conversation with the general, in which, as is the immemorial custom of the godless, they led him astray; he should remain in the city, said they, and thus a peace settlement would be made with him, but the Despot should depart, otherwise they would go on blockading the city.[16]

Symeon does not explicitly state it, but in the course of their negotiations with the Byzantine general the Ottomans may well have promised him the governorship of Thessalonike. We know of two parallel incidents that have been reported in the context of Constantinople and that closely resemble the present one. They concern Theologos Korax and Loukas Notaras, both of whom were allegedly promised the governorship of Constantinople on condition that they would cooperate with the Ottomans and help to induce the city's surrender, the former during Murad II's siege of 1422, the latter during that of Mehmed II in 1453.[17] Whether the stories about the last two men, based essentially on rumors, were true or false should not concern us here, since what is significant for present purposes is the fact that such rumors circulated widely among the Byzantines and were considered credible by many, suggesting that the Ottomans did frequently attempt to entice Byzantine subjects with promises of high official posts within their administrative apparatus. As for the above-mentioned general, if he had indeed been "led astray" by the Ottomans as Symeon declares, before he could accomplish his designs Thessalonike was handed over to the Venetians. But back in 1387, when the Ottomans became the rulers of the city, they may have actually granted positions of authority to certain Thessalonians with whom they had made prior arrangements.

Some individuals also received economic benefits that took the form of either property grants or, at the very least, the right to retain their possessions. During the siege of 1383–7 the Ottoman commander, Hayreddin Paşa, bestowed on Makarios Bryennios one half of the village of Achinos in the Strymon region which used to belong to the Thessalonian monastery of Akapniou. In 1393 the other half of the same village was held by Demetrios

---

[15] Symeon–Balfour, p. 56; cf. pp. 157–8. [16] Ibid., pp. 57 (text), 163 (trans.).
[17] Doukas–Grecu, pp. 229–35, 379.

Bryennios Laskaris. According to the Athonite document which registers this information, Demetrios did not have hereditary rights of ownership over the land; it had been granted to him by the Ottoman Sultan (Murad I or Bayezid I) as *pronoia* – this last term having been employed in the Greek text as the equivalent of the Turkish *tımar*, a military fief.[18] The fact that the village of Achinos used to be the property of a Thessalonian monastery and that members of the Laskaris family are attested in Thessalonike might lead one to suppose that the beneficiaries of these grants were citizens of Thessalonike. Yet prosopographic evidence concerning the Bryennios–Laskaris family suggests rather that the two individuals named above were aristocrats from Serres, which is quite likely since Hayreddin Paşa was in charge of the military operations at Serres too.[19] Again in the region of Serres, a certain Palaiologos, who was also related to the Laskaris family, is known to have received the village of Verzani in reward for entering the service of Bayezid I. The village was granted him in full ownership (i.e. as *mülk*), so he had the right to bequeath it to his descendants. In 1464–5 Verzani was still in the possession of his family, having first passed on to his son Demetrios, then to his grandson.[20] Although none of these grants are directly related to Thessalonike, they are mentioned here as models representative of Ottoman practice. Our assumption is that the Ottomans would have repeated in Thessalonike the same policy that they used in Serres, which they captured in 1383, only a few years before the capitulation of Thessalonike. It is known, moreover, from Ottoman documents that the *tımar* system was applied both at Chalkidike and in the Strymon region soon after the conquest of these areas from the Byzantine Empire. The earliest Ottoman official register (*tahrir defteri*) including villages from

---

[18] *Esphigménou*, no. 30 (Feb. 1393) and *Chilandar* (P), no. 160 (Dec. 1392). On the *tımar* system, especially *tımar* grants to Christians, apart from the works cited above in ch. 2, note 21, see H. İnalcık (ed.), *Hicrî 835 Tarihli Sûret-i Defter-i Sancak-i Arvanid* (Ankara, 1954; repr. 1987); M. Delilbaşı and M. Arıkan (eds.), *Hicrî 859 Tarihli Sûret-i Defter-i Sancak-ı Tırhala*, 2 vols. (Ankara, 2001).

[19] For a Demetrios Laskaris, who is cited among the "nobles and small nobles" of Thessalonike in 1425, see Appendix II below. On the Bryennios-Laskaris family and its connections with Serres, see Lefort's prosopographical notes in *Esphigménou*, pp. 172–3.

[20] In the fifteenth-century Ottoman register where this information is recorded, the grandson is called "Palolog," son of "Dimitri," son/descendant of "Laskari": see N. Beldiceanu and I. Beldiceanu-Steinherr, "Un Paléologue inconnu de la région de Serres," *B* 41 (1971), 5–17. The first recipient of Verzani from Bayezid I may perhaps be identified with a Constantine Laskaris Palaiologos, *doulos* of the Emperor, who offered the village of Bresnitza near Strumitza to the monastery of Chilandar in 1374: *Chilandar* (P), no. 155. For a *doulos* Constantine Laskaris, who was in dispute with the monastery of Lavra in 1377 over some property in the region of Serres, see *Lavra*, vol. III, no. 148. Later, a Matthew Palaiologos Laskaris, senator and *oikeios* of Manuel II, was sent as ambassador to Murad II to negotiate for peace before the Sultan's siege of Constantinople (1422): Sphrantzes–Grecu, X.1, p. 14. Cf. *PLP*, nos. 14543, 14539, 14552.

Chalkidike mentions endowments (*vakıf*s) from the time of Bayezid I and cavalrymen (*sipahi*s) with decrees (*berat*s) of Mehmed I.[21] All this evidence points to the establishment of the first *tımar*s in the region of Thessalonike during the reign of Bayezid I, which is in agreement with the statements by Isidore, Gabriel's encomiast, and Anagnostes that this ruler bestowed certain "gifts" upon the Thessalonians. The grants made to the two aristocrats from Serres, attested in Byzantine documents from the archives of Mount Athos, are therefore important additions to the evidence preserved in Ottoman documents. They supplement other known concrete cases of the application of the *tımar* system to Christians as an Ottoman policy for integrating and guaranteeing the loyalty of the local aristocracy in newly conquered regions, treated exhaustively in İnalcık's studies.[22]

A different case which illustrates, directly this time, the grant by the Ottomans of economic privileges to private individuals in Thessalonike concerns Alexios Angelos Philanthropenos, the Caesar of Thessaly, and his small convent (the *monydrion* of Saint Photis) situated inside Thessalonike. In 1389 Alexios, who held hereditary rights of possession over this convent through imperial acts, donated it to the Thessalonian monastery of Nea Mone. It is reported that earlier he had made certain arrangements with the Ottomans ("Muslims") concerning the *monydrion* as well as other immovables he owned. The exact nature of Alexios' arrangements with the Ottomans is by no means clear. What is certain, however, is that it was on account of these arrangements that he was able to retain his possessions in Thessalonike after the city came under Ottoman domination and that he had the freedom to do whatever he pleased with them.[23]

The people who were able to hold on to their lands under Ottoman rule as well as those who were offered new grants benefited further from the novel conditions brought about as a result of the surrender of Thessalonike.

---

[21] V. Dimitriades, "Ottoman Chalkidiki: an area in transition," in *Continuity and Change in Late Byzantine and Early Ottoman Society*, ed. A. Bryer and H. Lowry (Birmingham and Washington, DC, 1986), pp. 39–50, esp. 44; V. Dimitriades, "Φορολογικὲς κατηγορίες τῶν Χωριῶν τῆς Θεσσαλονίκης κατὰ τὴν Τουρκοκρατία," *Μακεδονικά* 20 (1980), 375–462.

[22] See note 18 above.

[23] *Lavra*, vol. III, no. 151 (Dec. 1389), lines 7–8: "ἀλλὰ δὴ καὶ ἐν ταῖς καταστάσεσι ἃς ἐποίησα μετα τῶν Μουσουλμάνων προσένεξα καὶ αὐτὸ εἰς πᾶσαν ἐλευθερίαν μετὰ καὶ τῶν ἑτέρων ἡμῶν κτημάτων." For a plausible interpretation of this passage, see the commentary to the document on p. 120; cf. V. Laurent, "Une nouvelle fondation monastique des Choumnos: la *Néa Moni* de Thessalonique," *REB* 13 (1955), 123. It should be noted that one of the descendants of Alexios Angelos Philanthropenos, possibly his great-grandson, was Mahmud Paşa, who served as grand vizier under Mehmed II, suggesting that the family may have maintained its connections with the Ottomans through several generations: see Th. Stavrides, *The Sultan of Vezirs. The Life and Times of the Ottoman Grand Vezir Mahmud Pasha Angelović (1453–1474)* (Leiden, Boston, and Cologne, 2001), pp. 75–8; cf. *PLP*, nos. 29750, 29771.

Some signs of economic improvement are noted in the area in the years following 1387, as the termination of the siege and the establishment of peace eliminated some of the major obstacles to agricultural production. For example, Constantine Prinkips' vineyard mentioned earlier, which had been destroyed and deserted because of the military conflicts with the Ottomans, was restored by his son George, who spent some money on it during the first years of the Ottoman domination. Between 1387 and 1394 George Prinkips also managed to pay the debts of his deceased father.[24]

By contrast, some Thessalonian property owners suffered losses under Ottoman rule. A piece of land situated at Portarea, in the region of Kalamaria, which belonged to George Anatavlas was confiscated by the Ottomans, who then gave it to one of their Muslim subjects. Shortly afterwards, the monks from the Athonite monastery of Esphigmenou, which happened to own an estate adjacent to the confiscated land, became determined to annex the neighboring property to their monastery. Appealing jointly to the Ottoman Sultan and to Ali Paşa, they managed, "after much effort and expenditure," to solicit the land. When George Anatavlas found out about his property's appropriation by the monastery, he took action to contest his rights over it. In 1388 an agreement was reached between him and the monks, according to which Anatavlas ceded his land to the monastery in return for two *diakoniai* (term designating the annual payment in kind due, in this case, for two *adelphata*), one for himself and one for his son Theodore, to be delivered during their lifetime. The contract ended with a clause guaranteeing that the property transfer was to remain valid even if the situation in the region should turn in favor of the Byzantine Empire.[25] In other words, even if Thessalonike and its environs were to be regained from the Ottomans, George Anatavlas and his son were bound to recognize their agreement with Esphigmenou and could not renounce its validity on the grounds that the property ought no longer to be legally subject to the confiscation carried out by the Ottoman authorities. It is clear that the monks of Esphigmenou, striving to perpetuate their profitable arrangement under all circumstances, added the latter clause to the contract so

---

[24] MM, vol. II, no. 471 (July 1394), pp. 221–3; see above, ch. 4, p. 57.

[25] *Esphigménou*, no. 29 (Feb. 1388). See N. Oikonomidès, "Monastères et moines lors de la conquête ottomane," *SüdostF* 35 (1976), 4, n. 11 for an alternative dating of this document to the year 1403. The two *diakoniai* each consisted of 12 *tagaria* of wheat, 24 *metra* of wine, 6 *metra* of olive oil, 2 *tagaria* of dry vegetables, and 30 *litrai* of cheese, which may be compared with Manuel Deblitzenos' *adelphata* itemized above, in note 9 of ch. 4. The food items listed in Anatavlas' agreement roughly correspond to a monetary value of 20 *hyperpyra* per *adelphaton* according to Laiou, "Economic activities of Vatopedi," pp. 71–2. On the *diakonia*, see Smyrlis, *La fortune des grands monastères*, p. 139.

that in the possible event of a restoration of the region to Byzantine rule there could be no question of a return to pre-conquest conditions insofar as Anatavlas' property was concerned.

Another Thessalonian family which lost its lands during this period was that of the Deblitzenoi. When the Ottomans took over Thessalonike in 1387, they occupied (κατείχοντο) most of Manuel Deblitzenos' estates, comprising at least 3,500 *modioi* of arable land, which were in the possession of his widow Maria at this time.[26] But the family's former estate in Hermeleia, which Manuel Deblitzenos had ceded to the monastery of Docheiariou in return for three *adelphata*, remained undisturbed in the hands of the monastery throughout the period of the Ottoman domination.[27]

The two examples cited above comply with the privileged status that Athonite monasteries as well as some other rural monasteries in the Balkans are known to have enjoyed under Ottoman rule, which allowed them to maintain their economic prosperity, thus differentiating their fate from that of lay landowners such as George Anatavlas or the Deblitzenoi.[28] Yet a close look at the experiences of the monasteries within Thessalonike during the first Ottoman domination reveals that such a privileged status and its economic repercussions do not universally apply to the urban monastic foundations of Byzantium. Notwithstanding the fact that the Ottomans did in principle respect the religious freedom of the Thessalonians and allowed the vast majority of their religious institutions to continue functioning throughout 1387–1403, relatively few monasteries inside the city seem to have been able to maintain their economic prosperity and to flourish like their rural counterparts.[29] So, side by side with certain monasteries that

---

[26] *Docheiariou*, no. 58, lines 19–21. The estates which the Ottomans occupied presumably included 500 *modioi* of land situated in the region of Galikos, 1,000 *modioi* at Kolytaina, and 2,000 *modioi* at Omprastos: ibid., no. 49, lines 38–9.

[27] See above, ch. 4, pp. 57–9.

[28] See Oikonomidès, "Monastères," 1–10; Oikonomidès, "Properties of the Deblitzenoi," pp. 176–98; E. A. Zachariadou, "Early Ottoman documents of the Prodromos Monastery (Serres)," *SüdostF* 28 (1969), 1–12; Delilbaşı and Arıkan (eds.), *Defter-i Sancak-ı Tırhala*, vol. I, p. 73; vol. II, p. 124a (privileges and exemptions enjoyed by the monks of "Kalabakkaya," i.e. Meteora, from the time of Bayezid I to that of Mehmed II). For later developments, see also H. W. Lowry, "A note on the population and status of the Athonite monasteries under Ottoman rule (ca. 1520)," *WZKM* 73 (1981), 114–35; H. W. Lowry, "The fate of Byzantine monastic properties under the Ottomans: examples from Mount Athos, Limnos and Trabzon," *BF* 16 (1990), 275–311; N. Beldiceanu, "Margarid: un timar monastique," *REB* 33 (1975), 227–55.

[29] The discrepancy between the experiences of urban and rural monasteries in Byzantium has been noted by some scholars, but none have examined the particular case of Thessalonike in detail. See A. Bryer, "The late Byzantine monastery in town and countryside," in *The Church in Town and Countryside*, ed. D. Baker (Oxford, 1979), pp. 233–4, where the author notes that under Turkish pressure and conquest "rural monasteries had a six times better chance of survival than urban ones."

received special favors and beneficial treatment in Ottoman Thessalonike, we find many more that experienced major difficulties and went into decline.[30]

After assuming the rule of the city in 1387, the Ottomans are reported to have seized the monasteries of Prodromos and Saint Athanasios.[31] Whereas almost nothing is known about the actual circumstances under which they were seized, we possess more substantial information with regard to the monastery of Akapniou, which was one of the first in the city to suffer at the hands of the Ottomans. We have already seen that during the siege of 1383–7 the Ottoman commander Hayreddin Paşa confiscated one half of the village of Achinos, which belonged to Akapniou, and bestowed it on an aristocrat, presumably from Serres.[32] Subsequent to Thessalonike's surrender, Akapniou tried to reclaim its property and succeeded in getting it back from its new owner. Yet, because of the economic difficulties it was undergoing then, the monastery could not retain the property in its possession for very long. Impoverished and heavily indebted, sometime before the beginning of 1393 its monks appealed to the archbishop Isidore and obtained permission to sell it. Lefort, in his commentary to one of the two documents concerning this matter, has convincingly argued that Akapniou's debts at the time must have been due to the tribute (*harac*) demanded by the Ottomans, for it was only in the case of liabilities

Oikonomidès, in "Monastères," 4, points out, though without explicitly making a case for a rural–urban dichotomy, that the ability of Athonite monasteries to remain in possession of their lands in the post-conquest period "ne fut pas nécessairement le cas de tous les monastères en dehors de l'Athos" and gives reference to confiscations suffered by two monasteries within Thessalonike. A similar situation existed in the province of Trebizond, where during the early years of Ottoman rule "urban monasteries appear to have lost all their properties, while the major rural foundations such as Vazelon, Soumela and the Peristera did not": see H. Lowry, "Privilege and property in Ottoman Maçuka in the opening decades of the *Tourkokratia*: 1461–1553," in *Continuity and Change*, ed. Bryer and Lowry, pp. 119–27 (p. 122 for the quoted statement); Lowry, "Fate of Byzantine monastic properties," 278–9.

[30] In this context, the testimony of the Russian pilgrim Ignatius of Smolensk, regarding the ten "wondrous" monasteries (Blatadon, Peribleptos–Kyr Isaak, Latomou, Akapniou, Nea Mone, Philokalou, Prodromos, Pantodynamos, Gorgoepekoos, and the *metocheion* of Chortiates) which he visited in Thessalonike in 1405, only two years after the city's restoration to Byzantine rule, must be approached with caution. As the evidence presented below demonstrates, many monasteries, including some of those qualified by Ignatius as "wondrous," underwent major difficulties during the first Ottoman domination. To what extent they would have recovered by 1405 is hence open to question. See B. de Khitrowo, *Itinéraires russes en Orient* (Geneva, 1889; repr. Osnabrück, 1966), p. 147. Cf. M. L. Rautman, "Ignatius of Smolensk and the late Byzantine monasteries of Thessaloniki," *REB* 49 (1991), 143–69, with extensive bibliography.

[31] MM, vol. II, nos. 660 (July 1401), 661 (July 1401), pp. 518–24; Anagnostes–Tsaras, p. 56. On these monasteries, see R. Janin, *Les églises et les monastères des grands centres byzantins* (Paris, 1975), pp. 406, 345–6; on Prodromos, see also Rautman, "Ignatius," 159–60.

[32] *Esphigménou*, no. 30 (Feb. 1393); see pp. 88–9 above. On the monastery of Akapniou, see Janin, *Églises et monastères*, pp. 347–9; Rautman, "Ignatius," 151–2.

to the fisc that Byzantine religious foundations were legally allowed to alienate property with the consent of an archbishop.[33] Thus, we observe here two distinct ways in which a Thessalonian monastery was negatively affected by the Ottoman expansion in Macedonia, first by becoming subject to confiscation before the city's conquest and afterwards by the economic strains resulting from the monetary impositions of the conquerors. It is also striking, in terms of the contrast between the conditions of urban and rural monasteries underlined above, that for the right to purchase the property which Akapniou was compelled to sell, three Athonite monasteries – Koutloumousiou, Chilandar, and Esphigmenou – vigorously contested with each other, the last acquiring it in the end.

If, on the other hand, Akapniou managed temporarily to regain possession of its holdings in Achinos after 1387, during the same period the Ottomans seized from the monastery another piece of land situated in the village of Kollydros and gave it to the Nea Mone of Thessalonike.[34] What we have here is a perfect illustration of the differential treatment accorded by the Ottomans to certain monasteries within the city that won their favor somehow. Further inquiry into the affairs of the Nea Mone brings to light other incidents that bear hints of its dealings with the Ottomans. These concern, if not always directly the monastery itself, at least certain individuals who were associated with it. It might be recalled, for example, that in 1389 Alexios Angelos Philanthropenos donated a small convent to the Nea Mone after having made arrangements with the Ottomans.[35] Incidentally, back in 1384 Alexios had already made another donation to the same monastery. The property in question then was his *kastron* of Kollydros.[36] In view of the fact that the land which the Ottomans took away from Akapniou and gave to the Nea Mone was situated inside the village of Kollydros, it may be postulated that the monks of Nea Mone, aspiring to have control over the entire terrain, approached the Ottoman authorities

[33] *Esphigménou*, pp. 173–4.
[34] MM, vol. II, nos. 453 (Jan. 1394), 454 (Jan. 1394), 660 (July 1401), pp. 200–3, 518–20. On the Nea Mone, see Laurent, "Une nouvelle fondation," 109–27; Janin, *Églises et monastères*, pp. 398–9; Rautman, "Ignatius," 153–7. It should be pointed out that caution must be used in dealing with references to grants and confiscations since they do not always necessarily indicate real awards or losses for monasteries. For example, among the Ottoman documents of the Blatadon monastery in Thessalonike, a *ferman* dated 1446 records the bestowal of 20 units of imperial land and exemptions from certain taxes. A later *ferman* dated 1513 reveals, however, that these lands and tax immunities had originally been given to Blatadon by Murad II in exchange for other lands of the monastery which this Sultan had confiscated: I. Vasdravelles, Ἱστορικὰ Ἀρχεῖα Μακεδονίας, vol. III: Ἀρχεῖον Μονῆς Βλαττάδων, 1466–1839 (Thessalonike, 1955), pp. 1–2; Vryonis, "Ottoman conquest of Thessaloniki," p. 313.
[35] See p. 90 above and note 23.   [36] *Lavra*, vol. III, no. 150 (Jan. 1384).

after 1387 and negotiated with them the appropriation of the plot of land in the same village belonging to a rival Thessalonian monastery.

One more detail to be noted in connection with the associations between the Nea Mone and the Ottomans is that during the years following the second capture of Thessalonike (1430) the monastery is seen holding business relations with a Turk to whom it leased a linseed oil press it possessed in the interior of the city.[37] Thus, on account of its good relations with the Turks, the Nea Mone, founded around the third quarter of the fourteenth century,[38] prospered during the period of Ottoman domination and survived the final conquest of Thessalonike. In the interval between the two Ottoman dominations, on the other hand, the monastery seems to have temporarily suffered from a diminution in the revenues it received from one of its properties (an αὐλή) within the city, which further demonstrates how much its prosperity was connected with the advantages it enjoyed under Ottoman rule.[39] By contrast, the much older Akapniou (founded *c.* 1018), which is described in early fourteenth-century documents as the "revered, great, imperial, and patriarchal monastery" and which seems to have been associated with the Palaiologan dynasty,[40] started undergoing major difficulties already during the Ottoman siege of 1383–7 and steadily declined thereafter, even though it too survived the final conquest of the city in 1430.

It is hence evident that, despite exceptional cases like the Nea Mone, Thessalonian monasteries generally suffered in varying ways and degrees, sometimes directly at the hands of the Ottomans as we have already seen, and sometimes indirectly as a result of the confusion and uncertainty that accompanied the establishment of the Ottoman regime. Even the city's highest ranking religious leader, its archbishop, was not entirely averse to grasping some advantage from the new circumstances created after the arrival of the Ottomans, as the following example will demonstrate. In 1401 the archbishop Gabriel of Thessalonike received a letter from the patriarch of Constantinople, who openly accused him of having unjustly appropriated a fishery (βιβάριον) that belonged to the Prodromos monastery. This monastery, it may be recalled, had been seized by the Ottomans in or shortly after 1387. Thereupon its monks had taken refuge in the

---

[37] Ibid., no. 168. But the monastery canceled its lease with the Turk in 1432 and signed a new contract with a Greek called Constantine Manklabites, who seems to have offered more advantageous terms.

[38] For the date of foundation, see Laurent, "Une nouvelle fondation," 115.

[39] *Lavra*, vol. III, no. 163 (March 1415).

[40] *Xénophon*, no. 20 (1324), line 24; *Chilandar*, vol. I, no. 38 (1318), line 7. Cf. Th. Papazotos, "The identification of the Church of 'Profitis Elias' in Thessaloniki," *DOP* 45 (1991), 124–5.

monastery of Akapniou, and according to Gabriel they had consequently lost their rights over the remaining properties annexed to the Prodromos. The patriarch, however, rebuked Gabriel for having taken away from these unfortunate monks that which even the Muslim conquerors had spared them and ordered him to correct his wrongdoing at once by returning the fishery to its rightful owners.[41] Interestingly, before becoming archbishop in 1397, Gabriel had served as the superior of the Nea Mone and was indeed the very person who had received in the name of this monastery the plot of land situated in the village of Kollydros which the Ottomans had seized from Akapniou.[42]

About the same time in 1401 Gabriel became the subject of yet another criticism from the patriarch of Constantinople for his loose conduct in a particular matter which also serves to illustrate how under Ottoman rule the precarious situation of the monasteries inside Thessalonike presented every so often an opportunity for gain to others. The issue concerned the aforementioned monastery of Saint Athanasios, which the Ottomans had confiscated in or around 1387. Later they decided to dispose of it, and the superior of the Pantokrator (Blatadon) monastery, Theodotos, claimed rights over it, pretending that it used to belong to his monastery even though it had actually been attached to the monastery of Hexazenos. The Ottoman officials, either because they believed him or because they engaged in some kind of a deal with him, gave the small monastery to Theodotos. The latter demolished its cells, turned it into a secular structure, and sold parts of it, including its church, to a Turk. When the patriarch found out about this, he immediately wrote to the archbishop Gabriel, objecting to Theodotos' act on the following grounds: first, the superior of the Pantokrator had usurped another monastery's property; secondly, he had secularized it; and thirdly, he had sold it to a non-Christian. The third issue was the most distressing one from the viewpoint of the patriarch, who cited in this connection various canonical regulations prohibiting the alienation of religious property to lay Christians so as to emphasize how much more inadmissible the sale of such property to a non-Christian was. He then instructed Gabriel to redeem the monastery of Saint Athanasios from the Turk by returning the money the latter had paid Theodotos for it. The property was subsequently to be restored to the monastery

---

[41] MM, vol. II, no. 660 (July 1401), pp. 518–20.

[42] On Gabriel and his ties with the Nea Mone, see B. Laourdas, "Ὁ Γαβριὴλ Θεσσαλονίκης. Βιογραφικά," Ἀθηνᾶ 66 (1952), 199–214; V. Laurent, "Le métropolite de Thessalonique Gabriel (1397–1416/19) et le Couvent de la Νέα Μονή," Ἑλληνικά 13 (1954), 241–55; Laurent, "Une nouvelle fondation," 109–27.

of Hexazenos and Theodotos deposed.[43] Here, as also in the case of the Nea Mone, we observe first of all that certain monasteries in Thessalonike conducted economic exchanges (e.g. sale or lease of property) with the Turks which seem to have been overlooked and tolerated by the city's ecclesiastical authorities. Secondly, the case at hand is a clear manifestation of the attempt made by the administrator of a monastery to turn to his institution's advantage the confusion and displacement brought about by the change of regime in the city which in effect hurt the interests of other monasteries. Under such unstable circumstances, even those monasteries that managed to negotiate with and win the favor of the Ottomans may not have felt fully secure or firmly grounded in their privileged status. Was it a mere coincidence, for instance, that in 1392 the monks of the Nea Mone took the initiative all of a sudden to have an act drawn up to confirm an unrecorded donation that had been made to their monastery some sixteen years earlier? They probably feared that the Nea Mone, too, might after all become the victim of a confiscation.[44]

Yet, on the whole, monks knew that it was possible to negotiate with the Ottomans, and many tried their chances with them. Prior to the establishment of Ottoman rule, the monks of Thessalonike were frequently criticized by the ecclesiastical authorities because of the moral decline that prevailed among them. The archbishop Isidore continuously accused them for their insubordination to their superiors, their increasing avarice for material possessions, and their involvement in worldly affairs, particularly in political matters.[45] Isidore was especially critical of monks who collaborated with the civil authorities in the secularization of Church property, aiming thereby to attain high offices in the Church. He also reproached some monks who left the monastic habit in order to become involved in political affairs.[46] Against this background that reveals how deeply monks were entrenched in worldly matters and how they constantly strove to

---

[43] MM, vol. II, no. 661 (July 1401), pp. 520–4. On the Pantokrator monastery, also known as the monastery of Blatadon, see Janin, *Églises et monastères*, pp. 356–8, 416–17; Rautman, "Ignatius," 147–8; on Hexazenos, see P. Magdalino, "Some additions and corrections to the list of Byzantine churches and monasteries of Thessalonica," *REB* 35 (1977), 280–1. The later tradition that the monks of Blatadon betrayed Thessalonike to the Ottomans in 1430 by advising Murad II to cut off the city's water supply is generally rejected. On this, see G. A. Stogioglou, Ἡ ἐν Θεσσαλονίκῃ πατρι-αρχικὴ μονὴ τῶν Βλατάδων (Thessalonike, 1971), pp. 162–73; cf. above ch. 3, note 47 and below, p. 114.

[44] *Lavra*, vol. III, no. 153 (Oct. 1392), line 19: "Νῦν δὲ χρείας γενομένης ποιῶ τὸ παρὸν ἀφιερωτήριον γράμμα . . ."

[45] Isidore–Christophorides, vol. II, Homily 16, pp. 254–5, Homily 19, p. 300, Homily 22, pp. 344–5; Isidore–Christophorides, vol. I, Homily 33, pp. 126–7, Homily 37, p. 186; Isidore–Laourdas, Homily II, pp. 38–9.

[46] Isidore–Laourdas, Homily II, p. 42.

secure their material interests, the emergence of a conciliatory and accommodationist attitude towards the Ottomans among monastic circles during 1387–1403 is not as surprising as it may seem at first sight. Thus, once the Ottomans came to power, the monastic circles of Thessalonike who had been among the foremost champions of an anti-Latin/anti-Ottoman position not only accepted the status quo and showed obedience to their new masters, as observed above in chapter 3, but even went one step further and tried to make the best out of the new circumstances through bargains and negotiations with them, as we see in the present context.

Before concluding this survey of the first Ottoman domination of Thessalonike, my final task will be to assess the impact of sixteen years of Ottoman rule on various aspects of life in the city. First, as regards administrative matters, some traces of Ottoman practices – or rather Byzantino-Ottoman practices, to take into account the possibility of earlier reciprocal influences – are attested in the city after its restoration to Byzantine authority in 1403. Previous scholarship has confirmed that the Byzantine government preserved certain traits of the fiscal policy exercised by the Ottomans during their administration of Thessalonike to the extent that even the Turkish terminology survived occasionally and passed into Byzantine usage.[47] One of the clauses in the Byzantine–Ottoman treaty of 1403 that warranted the return of Thessalonike and its environs to Byzantium stipulated that the tribute (*harac*) which the Greek community used to pay to the sultan was henceforth to be remitted to the emperor.[48] Thus, between 1404 and 1409, the term *harac* is encountered in Byzantine documents from Mount Athos in its Greek form χαράτζιν. These documents demonstrate that the tribute and other taxes which the Ottomans collected formerly from the villages of Athonite monasteries in the region of Thessalonike were now being shared between the monasteries and the Despot of Thessalonike in a $^2/_3$:$^1/_3$ ratio.[49] On the other hand, the *kephalatikion*, normally a special tax payable to the governor (*kephale*) of a district, appears in the region of Thessalonike at the beginning of the fifteenth century as a regular tax (of one *nomisma* per peasant household) often shared between the state and monasteries. According to Oikonomidès this transformation of a special tax into a regular tax, which was probably accompanied by a

---

[47] On what follows, see Oikonomidès, "Ottoman influence," 1–24; Oikonomidès, "Le haradj," pp. 681–8; Ostrogorski, "État tributaire," 49–58.

[48] Dennis, "Byzantine–Turkish treaty of 1403," 78.

[49] See *Docheiariou*, no. 52 (original: Jan. 1409, copy: Nov. 1414); *Lavra*, vol. III, no. 161 (April 1409); and the other references cited in Oikonomidès, "Le haradj," pp. 682–7. In other regions of the empire these taxes were divided between monasteries and the emperor. After 1415 a new ratio of $^1/_2$:$^1/_2$ is attested: see *Docheiariou*, no. 56 (Dec. 1418).

shift in the use of the term *kephalatikion* to designate thereafter a capitation tax matching in meaning the Turkish *baş haracı*, must be attributed to Ottoman influence.[50]

Another Ottoman residue in fiscal practices may be observed in connection with certain novelties in the style and content of early fifteenth-century Byzantine tax registers (*praktika*) from the region of Thessalonike. Compared with earlier *praktika* from the same region or with contemporary ones from other regions of the Byzantine Empire, the fifteenth-century Thessalonian documents are somewhat abbreviated and much less informative. They simply list the names of heads of households, their fiscal status, and their total tax liability, leaving out the names of remaining household members as well as the enumeration of the taxpayers' movables and immovables. As these peculiar features happen to be characteristics found in early Ottoman registers (*tahrir defters*), attention has been called to a likely Ottoman influence in the emergence of this new type of "laconic" *praktika* in the region following its restoration to Byzantine rule.[51]

Apart from administrative practices that bear the stamp of Ottoman influence, perhaps an even more significant factor to consider in determining the impact of sixteen years of Ottoman rule is the extent to which the Turkish element penetrated social and economic life both inside Thessalonike and in its surrounding countryside. As far as the countryside is concerned, early Ottoman chronicles reveal that many villages which had become depopulated in the course of the Ottoman invasions were inhabited afterwards by Turks. Some of these Turks were the very people who took part in the conquest of Macedonia at the end of the fourteenth century, and some were *Yürüks* (Türkmen pastoralist nomads) who were forcibly deported from western Anatolia (Saruhan) by Murad I and by Bayezid I in two successive waves during the 1380s and 1390s. The Ottomans settled

[50] *Docheiariou*, no. 53 (May 1409); *Lavra*, vol. III, nos. 161 (April 1409), 165 (Jan. 1420). See the commentary by Oikonomidès in *Docheiariou*, pp. 275–6 and his "Ottoman influence," 6–7.

[51] *Docheiariou*, no. 53 (May 1409); *Lavra*, vol. III, nos. 161 (April 1409), 165 (Jan. 1420). See the commentary by Oikonomidès in *Docheiariou*, p. 274 and his "Ottoman influence," 10–13. Two of these three documents were prepared by the *apographeis* Paul Gazes and George Prinkips, who were both in Thessalonike during the period of Ottoman domination and are thus likely to have familiarized themselves with Ottoman practices: see Oikonomidès, "Le haradj," p. 685, n. 20 and Oikonomidès, "Ottoman influence," 13, n. 50. On *tahrir defters*, see Ö. L. Barkan, "Essai sur les données statistiques des registres de recensement dans l'Empire Ottoman aux XVe et XVIe siècles," *Journal of Economic and Social History of the Orient* I (1957), 9–36; H. W. Lowry, "The Ottoman *tahrir defterleri* as a source for social and economic history: pitfalls and limitations," in Lowry, *Studies in Defterology. Ottoman Society in the Fifteenth and Sixteenth Centuries* (Istanbul, 1992), pp. 3–18.

the *Yürük*s in a semi-circle around Thessalonike, intending thereby to repopulate the region with Turkish/Muslim inhabitants, partly as a protective measure against potential attempts upon the newly captured city.[52] In addition, during the reign of Bayezid I a number of villages were given as *tımar* to people in the Sultan's service or were made into *vakıf*s (pious foundations).[53] Consequently, the demographic composition of the area underwent some changes during the years of Ottoman rule with the settlement of a group of Turkish newcomers, many of whom were involved in agricultural production and animal husbandry.[54]

The question is, of course, what happened to these Turkish settlers in the aftermath of the region's restoration to Byzantium? According to the Byzantine–Ottoman treaty of 1403, Bayezid I's son Süleyman Çelebi agreed to have all his subjects removed from the territories that were returned to Byzantium, with the exception of those who had bought lands there prior to 1403. What this meant in effect was that all lands held by Ottoman subjects by virtue of *tımar* grants had to be abandoned, while those lands that had been acquired through purchase were to remain in the hands of their Turkish owners who possessed them as *mülk*, with full rights of proprietorship, under Ottoman law.[55] We may, therefore, assume

---

[52] Aşıkpaşazade–Giese, pp. 56, 66–7 (= Aşıkpaşazade–Atsız, pp. 133, 141). See M. T. Gökbilgin, *Rumeli'de Yürükler, Tatarlar ve Evlâd-ı Fâtihân* (Istanbul, 1957), pp. 13–16; Dimitriades, "Ottoman Chalkidiki," p. 43; H. İnalcık, "The Yürüks: their origins, expansion and economic role," in İnalcık, *The Middle East and the Balkans under the Ottoman Empire. Essays on Economy and Society* (Bloomington, 1993), p. 106. On the Ottoman policy of deportations or forced resettlement (*sürgün*), see Ö. L. Barkan, "Osmanlı İmparatorluğunda bir iskân ve kolonizasyon metodu olarak sürgünler," *İstanbul Üniversitesi İktisat Fakültesi Mecmuası* 11 (1949–50), 524–69; 13 (1951–2), 56–79; 15 (1953–4), 209–37; N. Beldiceanu and I. Beldiceanu-Steinherr, "Colonisation et déportation dans l'État ottoman (XIVe–début XVIe siècle)," in *Coloniser au Moyen Âge*, ed. M. Balard and A. Ducellier (Paris, 1995), pp. 172–7.

[53] Dimitriades, "Ottoman Chalkidiki," p. 44; Dimitriades, "Φορολογικὲς κατηγορίες," 377–401. On the Ottomans' use of the *vakıf* institution as a method for repopulation and colonization, see Ö. L. Barkan, "Osmanlı İmparatorluğunda bir iskân ve kolonizasyon metodu olarak vakıflar ve temlikler," *Vakıflar Dergisi* 2 (1942), 279–386.

[54] A possible ramification of this phenomenon outlasting the re-establishment of Byzantine authority in the area may be seen in the occurrence of peasant names such as Theodore Tourko<poulos> or Rhousos, the son of Tourkitzes, in nearby villages at the beginning of the fifteenth century: see *Lavra*, vol. III, no. 161 (April 1409), lines 24, 29–30. However, it is also plausible that the first one of these peasants was an offspring of the so-called "Tourkopouloi," a special military contingent in the Byzantine army made up of Christianized Turks, whose presence in the region is known as of the late eleventh century: see A. G. C. Savvides, "Late Byzantine and western historiographers on Turkish mercenaries in Greek and Latin armies: the Turcoples/Tourkopouloi," in *The Making of Byzantine History. Studies Dedicated to Donald M. Nicol*, ed. R. Beaton and C. Roueché (London, 1993), pp. 122–36.

[55] Dennis, "Byzantine–Turkish treaty of 1403," 78: "*et in quelle contrade tuti queli Turchi che habia possession io li die cazar via de la et in questi luogi tuti queli si Griesi como Turchi che habia comprado alguna cossa per la soa moneda che li sia soy.*" For an excellent interpretation of this clause in terms

that at least some Turks who had become property owners during the Ottoman regime stayed there after 1403 and continued their activities under the successive regimes of the Byzantines and the Venetians. Hence, when Murad II wanted to repopulate Thessalonike during the years following its conquest in 1430, he was able to find Turkish families living in nearby villages and towns, whom he resettled inside the city. The most detailed information on this subject is provided by the eyewitness Anagnostes, who reports that the Sultan forcibly deported a thousand Turks from Gianitsa (Vardar Yenicesi), which was one day's journey to the west of Thessalonike and "had many Turkish inhabitants."[56] Anagnostes' report is confirmed by the Ottoman chroniclers Aşıkpaşazade and Neşri, as well as by Doukas.[57]

The above-mentioned clause in the Byzantine–Ottoman treaty that recognized the validity of the property transactions of Turks and Greeks dating from the period of the Ottoman domination applied, moreover, not only to the rural population but also to the urban dwellers of Thessalonike. Indeed, during the years between the two Ottoman dominations the city appears to have contained a Turkish community that was populous enough to necessitate the installation of a Muslim judge (kadi) there. Hence, by an agreement concluded between the Despot of Thessalonike and the Ottoman Sultan, the Turks in Thessalonike had secured the right to be judged by their own kadi, who was allowed to take up permanent residence inside the city. When the Venetians took over the administration of Thessalonike, they tried to do away with this Muslim official, whose existence they no doubt regarded as an impediment to their own judicial authority.[58]

of Ottoman and Roman legal principles regarding land-property, see Oikonomidès, "Ottoman influence," 3–4.

[56] Anagnostes–Tsaras, p. 62.

[57] Aşıkpaşazade–Giese, p. 106 (= Aşıkpaşazade–Atsız, p. 173); Neşrî, *Kitâb-ı Cihan-nümâ*, vol. ıı, pp. 610–13; Doukas–Grecu, XXIX.5, p. 251. The descendants of some of these deportees can be found in the Ottoman *tahrir defter* of 1478, the earliest extant cadastral survey which covers the city of Selanik. They constitute approximately 40 percent of the city's Muslim population at this time, or about 17 percent of its entire population, as shown by H. W. Lowry, "Portrait of a city: the population and topography of Ottoman Selânik (Thessaloniki) in the year 1478," Δίπτυχα 2 (1980–1), 286–7, 292. It seems highly unlikely that all of the Muslim households listed in this survey were descended from the settlers whom Murad II deported from Vardar Yenicesi, as suggested by Beldiceanu and Beldiceanu-Steinherr, "Colonisation et déportation," p. 174.

[58] Iorga, "Notes et extraits," *ROL* 5 (1897), 194 (April 2, 1425). According to Iorga (ibid., 194, n. 2), followed by Matschke, *Ankara*, p. 63, the Despot who accepted the stationing of an Ottoman kadi in Thessalonike before 1423 was Andronikos. Matschke has presumed, moreover, that the agreement was concluded during the reign of Mehmed I (r. 1413–21). Recently Jacoby has argued (overlooking, however, Matschke's remarks regarding the kadi of Thessalonike) that the agreement was most likely to have been concluded between the Despot John VII and Süleyman sometime shortly after 1403, and "in any event... before 1409, when Suleyman's political position and ability to bargain were weakened": Jacoby, "Foreigners and the urban economy," 121 and n. 253. Yet Jacoby's dating may be

However, in two provisional treaties dating from 1426 and 1427, Venice acquiesced to the appointment of a kadi with authority over financial disputes among the Turks themselves, all other cases being required to go under the jurisdiction of the Venetian tribunal.[59] All this evidence points, then, to the continued presence of a not negligible Turkish community within Thessalonike which was active in commercial affairs during the last three decades preceding the city's definitive conquest by the Ottomans.[60]

According to K.-P. Matschke, the impact of Byzantium's territorial gains in the aftermath of the battle of Ankara could not have been consequential as long as the infiltration of the Turkish element, both into Byzantine cities and into the countryside, remained unchecked. Matschke has argued that a crucial factor in this respect was the insufficiency of Byzantium's own food supplies, which rendered it increasingly dependent on Turkish wheat, influenced the political orientation of certain individuals, and determined the direction and outcome of political events.[61] The discussion above has revealed that, although the *timar*-holders who had settled in the countryside of Thessalonike were forced to leave in 1403, Ottoman property owners and merchants maintained some role in the city's social and economic affairs after the re-establishment of Byzantine authority. As far as the food supplies were concerned, in 1423 the administrators of Byzantine Thessalonike, finding themselves unable to provision the city adequately during an Ottoman siege, and troubled furthermore by internal dissensions, decided to try the option of western help. The city was thus ceded to the Venetians, who took charge over its provisioning and protection against the Ottomans.[62]

questioned, given especially that Süleyman was from the beginning never strong enough in terms of his political position vis-à-vis Byzantium to wield any bargaining power. Indeed, the only clause favorable to the Ottomans that he was able to have inserted into the Byzantine–Ottoman treaty of 1403 concerned the ownership rights of Turks who had legally purchased property in or around Thessalonike, which must be attributed not so much to his bargaining ability as to the binding force of legal contracts. At any rate, it seems more plausible that the agreement concerning the kadi of Thessalonike was reached sometime after the turbulent years of the Ottoman interregnum (1402–13), during the reign of either Mehmed I or Murad II, when Despot Andronikos governed the city.

[59] Iorga, "Notes et extraits," *ROL* 5 (1897), 317–18 (April 20, 1426); Sathas, *Documents*, vol. 1, p. 184 (July 24, 1427).

[60] For a Turkish slave trader who was in Thessalonike in 1410, see Musso, *Navigazione*, no. 24, p. 267. On the Turkish presence in Thessalonike between the two periods of Ottoman domination, see also Matschke, *Ankara*, p. 63; Jacoby, "Foreigners and the urban economy," 119–23.

[61] Matschke, *Ankara*, pp. 56–64, 125–39.

[62] The role played by the shortage of food in Thessalonike's handover to Venice can be inferred from the immediate efforts of the Venetians to procure provisions. The very large number of documents concerning the city's provisioning during 1423–30 is indicative of the perpetuation of this problem throughout the Venetian regime: Thiriet, *Régestes*, vol. II, nos. 1914, 1923, 1950, 1957, 1964, 1967, 1973,

THE VENETIAN DOMINATION (1423–1430)

The transfer of Thessalonike to Venice in 1423 inevitably involved a compromise between financial and military needs on the one hand and religious concerns on the other, since the Venetians expected not only to exercise civil authority, but also to have control over the city's ecclesiastical jurisdiction.[63] According to Symeon, the Thessalonians who favored the Venetian takeover declared that they desired community life to enjoy peace and prosperity through the aid of Venice, even at the cost of their submission to the Latin Church. In response to the archbishop's argument that what was best for the community above all was to hold on to the principles of Orthodoxy, they pointed out the situation of the Greeks living on Venetian islands, saying: "Just as there they are without bishops, but are Christians, so shall we be."[64]

As the majority of the pro-Venetians were of this opinion, it was through the personal insistence of Symeon, who managed to overrule the opposition of the civil officials in charge of the city's transfer, that a clause guaranteeing the independence of the Orthodox Church of Thessalonike was added at the last minute to the terms of agreement with Venice.[65] However, at some time between 1425 and 1429, if not earlier, the Venetians began to disregard the ecclesiastical rights of the Orthodox community, as revealed by a series of complaints and requests concerning religious issues that were articulated by the Greek ambassadors sent from Thessalonike to Venice in the summer of 1429. The ambassadors demanded, first of all, that their archbishop be allowed to retain the customary rights (*le suo uxançe antige*) he had had before the arrival of the Venetians, including the right to exercise judicial powers and to execute his decisions without hindrance. Evidently, the Venetians, despite what they had promised in 1423, were interfering with the judicial authority of the Orthodox archbishop – just as they tried

1995, 2012, 2015, 2033, 2035, 2058, 2064, 2077, 2078, 2081, 2085, 2113, 2129, 2130, 2149, 2183; Thiriet, *Assemblées*, vol. II, nos. 1276, 1284, 1294, 1299, 1306; Iorga, "Notes et extraits," *ROL* 5 (1897), 178, 182, 314–15, 322, 343, 353, 360; Sathas, *Documents*, vol. III, pp. 259, 281–2, 315, 331, 371. Cf. Vryonis, "Ottoman conquest of Thessaloniki," p. 307. On the critical condition of food supplies immediately before the Venetian takeover, see also Symeon–Balfour, pp. 56–7, 59. The Senate of Venice offered special privileges to merchants who brought grain to the city: Thiriet, *Régestes*, vol. II, no. 2033; Iorga, "Notes et extraits," *ROL* 5 (1897), 353. Giorgio Valaresso (on whom see above, ch. 4, p. 65 and note 42) as well as Giacomo Badoer (whose business activities in Constantinople, well known from his account book, will be discussed in Part III below) were among people who transported grain to Thessalonike at this time: Thiriet, *Régestes*, vol. II, nos. 1967 and 2113, respectively.

[63] On the Venetian regime in Thessalonike, see now Jacoby, "Thessalonique," pp. 303–18, with references to earlier works.

[64] Symeon–Balfour, pp. 58 (text), 169 (trans.).

[65] Ibid., pp. 58–9; Sathas, *Documents*, vol. I, no. 86 (July 7, 1423), pp. 135–6, 137–8.

to ostracize the Ottoman kadi – in an attempt to eliminate all possible
limitations to their own power of jurisdiction. Two specific requests of the
Thessalonians with regard to this issue were, first, that cases initiated in
their episcopal court not be taken to another court – which in this context can be none other than the Venetian tribunal – and, secondly, that
Orthodox priests and monks not be judged or imprisoned by the secular
authorities (i.e. Venetian officials). Thus we understand that the Venetians
not only diverted civil law cases away from the Greek ecclesiastical court
to their own secular court but even tried to limit the archbishop's judicial authority in the ecclesiastical sphere by forcing lawsuits involving the
Greek clergy to be handled by the Venetian tribunal. In 1429 the Thessalonian ambassadors further demanded that Church property be inviolable;
that the churches and monasteries of Thessalonike be held and administered by the Greeks themselves and have free access to their land and sea
revenues; and that Orthodox rituals and ceremonies be conducted without interruption or molestation. Concerning the church of Saint Sophia
in particular, the Thessalonians requested that this church be allowed to
maintain its franchises and continue to function as a place of asylum for
convicted people. A special complaint concerned the irreverent treatment
of the churches and monasteries, particularly those close to the city walls,
which had been set aside as places of encampment for Venetian soldiers,
who allegedly performed blasphemous acts such as bringing prostitutes
into them. Finally, the Venetians were asked to compensate the monastery
of Blatadon for the use of one of its houses which they had assigned to the
captain of Thessalonike, one of the two highest Venetian officials present
in the city, without paying any rent. The Senate of Venice accepted all these
demands with one exception, denying the archbishop the right to exercise
jurisdiction over laymen.[66]

As Symeon makes clear in his discussion of the arguments and conflicts
that preceded the city's transfer to Venice, these issues were of interest
only to a small minority with religious concerns, whereas the pro-Venetian

[66] Mertzios, Μνημεῖα, pp. 76–8, 79, 84–5 (2nd Thessalonian Embassy to Venice: July 14, 1429, §§ 12, 13, 15, 29), with facsimile of the original document following p. 73. The religious infractions of the Vene-tians have been assigned to a date between 1425 and 1429 because, while many requests formulated during the embassy of 1429 repeat those from an earlier embassy of 1425 (see Mertzios, Μνημεῖα, pp. 46–61 and facsimile following p. 48: 1st Thessalonian Embassy to Venice, July 7, 1425), com-plaints concerning religious issues appear, with one exception (right of asylum at St. Sophia), only in the report of the second embassy. For some earlier efforts of the Venetians to impose their judicial authority, see Thiriet, *Régestes*, vol. II, no. 1962 (Dec. 17, 1424); G. Fedalto, *La chiesa latina in Oriente*, vol. III: *Documenti veneziani* (Verona, 1978), no. 538 (July 17, 1425), p. 206; Mertzios, Μνημεῖα, pp. 59–60 (1st Embassy: § 20). On the restrictive practices of the Venetian regime in matters of jurisdiction, see also Jacoby, "Thessalonique," pp. 311–14.

Thessalonians who had gained the upper hand at that time "habitually sought their own interests and not those of Christ Jesus."[67] Following the Venetian takeover, however, Ottoman attacks upon Thessalonike increased considerably. Murad II viewed the city's cession to Venice as a transgression of the rights which he claimed to hold over it by virtue of its former subjection to Ottoman domination. According to Doukas, the Sultan rejected the Venetians who approached him for a peace settlement with the following words: "This city is my paternal property (πατρικόν μου κτῆμα). My grandfather Bayezid, by the might of his hand, wrested (ἔλαβεν) her from the Romans. Had the Romans prevailed over me, they would have cause to exclaim, 'He is unjust!' But as you are Latins from Italy, why have you trespassed into these parts?"[68] As the Ottoman attacks subsequently became more frequent and threatening, even those Thessalonians who had favored the installation of the Venetians, hoping thereby to attain peace and prosperity, began to wonder whether they had cherished false expectations and grew disappointed with the Venetian regime. Some fled to Italian territories, while others joined the Ottomans.[69] Inside the city, on the other hand, tensions emerged between the native population and the Italian authorities as several neutral or pro-Venetian Thessalonians started wavering in their loyalties, while others who had been opposed to the Venetians from the beginning became even more hostile when confronted with the ongoing Ottoman threat and their deteriorating conditions.

In spite of the assistance Thessalonike received from Venice in the form of money, galleys, military forces, and provisions, the citizens continued to live in great distress. Hunger and poverty progressively reached unbearable levels. In the spring of 1427 the city's administrators requested from the Venetian authorities in Crete extra supplies of wheat, explaining that the shipments they had so far received were inadequate since lately the Thessalonians had been reduced to living solely on bread. A particularly difficult winter had been experienced that year in Thessalonike under conditions of extreme poverty, dearth, and destitution. Thus, in order to prevent the recurrence of similar hardships in the forthcoming winter, the Venetian administrators were trying to stock up sufficient wheat

---

[67] Symeon–Balfour, pp. 58 (text), 170 (trans.).

[68] Doukas–Grecu, XXIX.4, p. 249; trans. by H. J. Magoulias, *Decline and Fall of Byzantium to the Ottoman Turks by Doukas* (Detroit, 1975), pp. 170–1. This passage, along with another one where Doukas claims that Bayezid I seized (εἷλε) Thessalonike in the early 1390s (Doukas–Grecu, XIII.6, pp. 77–9), is among the principal references used in support of the theory of the city's "second capture" in between 1387 and 1430: see above, ch. 2, note 32.

[69] Anagnostes–Tsaras, p. 54; Symeon–Balfour, pp. 59–60.

supplies.[70] The severe conditions laid out in this document are echoed in a passage by Symeon which vividly illustrates how in the course of the Venetian domination the Thessalonians grappled with the shortage of food. The citizens, writes Symeon, "being at their wits' end" because of the lack of proper vegetables and bread, were forced to feed on radishes or other wild plants, while for their bread they used bran produced from crushed linseed, which they mixed with a small amount of barley-flour or occasionally with some wheat-flour.[71]

As early as December 1424 the Senate of Venice, observing the gravity of the situation in Thessalonike, had decided to provide 2,000 measures (*staia*) of wheat per month as alms for the poor.[72] The decision was in all probability not implemented properly, for during their first embassy to Venice in the summer of 1425 the Thessalonians demanded help for their poor fellow citizens who were on the brink of perishing from hunger and were contemplating deserting the city. The ambassadors urged the Venetians that it would be an act of much greater piety on their part to help these destitute people than to send money to the Holy Sepulchre. Thereupon the Senate agreed once again to distribute 2,000 measures (*mensurae*) of free grain each month to the poor in Thessalonike.[73] However, during their second embassy to Venice four years later, the Thessalonians complained that the monthly distribution of grain had not been carried out and, consequently, many citizens, including those guarding the walls, were forced to flee.[74] The flight of guards and soldiers to Turkish lands (*Turchia*) because of hunger and poverty had been brought up at the time of the first embassy, too.[75] Another confirmation of the same phenomenon can be found in Symeon's description of an Ottoman attack that took place in 1425/6:

[A]s food supplies had all disappeared together, the men whom the city Archons had appointed to guard it were gradually fleeing to the godless and telling our enemies how matters stood with us; also many of the townsmen, impelled by famine, had been letting themselves down by night from off the wall by means of ropes and surrendering voluntarily to the infidel, so that the extent of our neediness became known to the enemy.[76]

---

[70] Iorga, "Notes et extraits," *ROL* 5 (1897), 353 (April 23, 1427). See ibid., 343 (Jan. 2, 1427) for another description of famine conditions in Thessalonike earlier during the same year.

[71] Symeon–Balfour, pp. 59, 63–4; cf. pp. 173, 180.

[72] Iorga, "Notes et extraits," *ROL* 5 (1897), 182 (Dec. 30, 1424); Thiriet, *Régestes*, vol. II, no. 1964.

[73] Mertzios, *Μνημεῖα*, pp. 53–4 (1st Embassy: § 6).   [74] Ibid., p. 73 (2nd Embassy: § 3).

[75] Ibid., p. 49 (1st Embassy: §§ 4 and 5).   [76] Symeon–Balfour, pp. 60 (text), 174–5 (trans.).

The guards were particularly prone to taking flight when their rations were not supplied because in return for their services they received from the Venetian government not cash salaries but only wheat.[77] They were so poor that during Murad II's final attack in 1430 most were without weapons, having been forced to sell these in order to sustain themselves.[78] Since this situation severely endangered the city's security, in 1429 the Greek ambassadors recommended to the Senate that the Venetian authorities conduct a census in Thessalonike to determine the needs of the poor guards and other defenders, so that provisions could then be distributed to each according to his needs.[79]

The poor inhabitants of the city, besides suffering from starvation, were pressed down by debts as well as by the taxes imposed on them. One of the requests of the Thessalonians during the embassy of 1425 was that indigent people who could barely afford to buy bread should not be sentenced to imprisonment for their debts until the war with the Ottomans was over.[80] On the other hand, a special request was made on behalf of ten sailors who had fallen captive to the Ottomans but had been set free afterwards in exchange for a Turkish captive called Hacı. Because the released men were extremely poor, the ambassadors asked in the name of the archbishop and all the citizens of Thessalonike that they be held exempt from two taxes, the *pendamerea* and the *decato*, amounting to a sum of 2,800 *aspra* (i.e. the equivalent of 200 *hyperpyra*).[81] Another proposal concerned the taxes on imported goods. The ambassadors urged that the Venetian and Genoese merchants who transported commodities to Thessalonike should be required to pay commercial duties, since it was unjust for the native inhabitants who bought their merchandise to be the only ones held accountable for sales/purchase taxes.[82] In 1425 the Thessalonians also petitioned the Senate, as a future measure to be applied after the opening of the city gates, to suspend temporarily the tithe on the badly destroyed vineyards outside the city that were to be restored to cultivation, signaling one more tax burden the prospects of which seriously alarmed the impoverished

---

[77] Mertzios, Μνημεῖα, p. 53 (1st Embassy: §§ 4 and 5).   [78] Anagnostes–Tsaras, p. 14.
[79] Mertzios, Μνημεῖα, pp. 82–3 (2nd Embassy: § 24).   [80] Ibid., pp. 56–7 (1st Embassy: § 14).
[81] Ibid., p. 60 (1st Embassy: § 21). The boat (*griparia*) on which the ten crew members fell captive to the Ottomans belonged to a Thessalonian called John Potames or Potamios (*Zan Potami*) and was transporting cargo from Negroponte to Thessalonike. For the rate of conversion applied here between *aspra* and *hyperpyra*, see Bertelè, *Numismatique byzantine*, pp. 88–9. On *pendamerea* and *decato*, see Jacoby, "Thessalonique," p. 316 and nn. 79, 81.
[82] Mertzios, Μνημεῖα, p. 55 (1st Embassy: § 10). Cf. Jacoby, "Thessalonique," p. 316.

citizens who engaged in agricultural production.[83] Finally, drawing attention to the situation of the Jewish community of Thessalonike, which had
become impoverished and much smaller because of the departure of many
of its members, the ambassadors asked for a reduction in the communal tax
of 1,000 *hyperpyra* collected annually from the Jews. The Senate reduced
the amount to 800 *hyperpyra* at this time.[84] Four years later the Jewish
community demanded the suspension of this tax altogether, revealing how
much more their situation must have deteriorated.[85]

People from the lower ranks of society or particular groups such as the
Jews were not the only ones afflicted by financial problems during the
period of the Venetian domination. In 1425 some "nobles," "small nobles,"
and soldiers of Thessalonike (*certi gentilomeni e gentilomeni piçoli e stratioti*),
who found that the salaries they received from Venice did not meet their
needs, demanded higher payments. At the onset of the Venetian regime
they had been satisfied with their salaries in the expectation that peace
would shortly be established. However, the perpetuation of the war with
the Ottomans had increased their present needs and necessitated higher
salaries.[86] In 1429 the Thessalonians asked for further raises, but whereas
in 1425 the Senate granted increased salaries to fifty-nine "nobles and small
nobles" and to seventy soldiers, four years later it refused to do so on
the grounds that Venice had already incurred many expenses on behalf
of Thessalonike and did not have any more funds to contribute.[87] The
only exception in 1429 applied to three individuals: Manuel Mazaris, the
skevophylax ("*sacristano*") of the church of Saint Sophia and one of the four
ambassadors at Venice, was granted a salary of 150 *aspra* per month; John
Kardamis, another ambassador, 200 *aspra* per month; and Doukas Lathras,
a military commander who had recently come to Thessalonike after some
years of residence under Turkish domination in the region of Kastoria, 300
aspra per month. None of these three men had previously received any

[83] Mertzios, Μνημεῖα, p. 58 (1st Embassy: § 17). Cf. Jacoby, "Thessalonique," p. 315, with a different interpretation regarding the tax on vineyards.
[84] Mertzios, Μνημεῖα, p. 59 (1st Embassy: § 19). On the Jewish population of late Byzantine Thessalonike and its fate following the Ottoman conquest, see Lowry, "Portrait of a city," 261–4; S. B. Bowman, *The Jews of Byzantium, 1204–1453* (Alabama, 1985), pp. 67–73; Jacoby, "Foreigners and the urban economy," 123–9.
[85] Mertzios, Μνημεῖα, p. 81 (2nd Embassy: § 21).
[86] Ibid., pp. 49–53 (1st Embassy: §§ 4 and 5).
[87] Ibid., p. 74 (2nd Embassy: § 4). According to a statement made by Andrea Suriano in the Venetian Senate on January 3, 1430, Venice had spent on Thessalonike an average sum of more than 60,000 ducats every year; i.e. approximately 420,000 ducats during the entire Venetian regime. Other estimates reported by Italian chroniclers for the seven-year period range from 200,000 to 740,000 ducats: see Setton, *The Papacy and the Levant*, vol. II, pp. 29–30 and nn. 93–4.

payment from Venice. Hence, the Senate agreed to assign salaries to them in view of their current financial difficulties, and, no doubt, also because it could make use of their services.[88] A further sign that by 1429 the situation had grown worse for nearly everyone is that the Thessalonians requested, apart from higher cash salaries, supplementary provisions for the "nobles" and all the defenders of Thessalonike on the payroll of Venice.[89]

During the embassy of 1429 another petition was made in connection with certain impoverished Thessalonians who had left the city prior to the Venetian takeover. The ambassadors pointed out that these people would gladly return home provided only that they had prospects of financial help from Venice. But the Senate's response to this was negative, either on account of the heavy expenses it claimed to have already undertaken, or, possibly, because the people in question were individuals who had fled to the Ottomans in order to be relieved of their economic hardship.[90] In the latter case, the Venetians may have been reluctant to admit into their midst a group of people who were not only poor but whose trustworthiness was highly questionable, despite the fact that a larger population was needed for the city's defense. We have already seen that the Venetian government, disregarding the same need, expelled from Thessalonike a fairly large number of aristocrats who were suspected of cooperating with the Ottomans.[91]

Yet, these exceptional cases aside, the standard Venetian policy was to apply every possible measure to prevent further losses in the already diminished population of Thessalonike.[92] The administration prohibited the inhabitants from leaving the city, and in order to reduce their chances of running away it outlawed all sales, mortgages, and transfers of property, both movable and immovable. In 1429, when the Greek ambassadors protested that the Thessalonians' freedom of movement and their right

---

[88] Mertzios, *Μνημεῖα*, pp. 83–4, 85–6 (2nd Embassy: §§ 26, 27, 30). On Manuel Mazaris and John Kardamis, see *PLP*, nos. 16121 and 11186. On Doukas Lathras, see above, ch. 4, note 110.

[89] Mertzios, *Μνημεῖα*, pp. 82–3 (2nd Embassy: § 24).

[90] Ibid., pp. 81–2 (2nd Embassy: § 22).   [91] See above, ch. 3, pp. 49–50 and notes 39–41.

[92] In the first half of the fourteenth century Thessalonike, described by many contemporaries as a "populous" city, is estimated to have had about 100,000 inhabitants: E. Werner, "Volkstümliche Häretiker oder sozialpolitische Reformer? Probleme der revolutionären Volksbewegung in Thessalonike 1342–1349," *Wissenschaftliche Zeitschrift der Karl-Marx-Universität Leipzig* 8 (1958/9), 53; Charanis, "Internal strife," 211, n. 8. By contrast, during the Venetian regime its population ranged between 20–25,000 and 40,000 according to figures reported by Italian chroniclers: Sathas, *Documents*, vol. IV, p. xx, n. 2; Mertzios, *Μνημεῖα*, pp. 41–4. By 1429–30 the city's population was reduced perhaps to a mere 10,000 or 13,000: Vryonis, "Ottoman conquest of Thessaloniki," p. 320. For further references to the population of late Byzantine Thessalonike, see Bakirtzis, "Urban continuity," 61 and n. 202.

to dispose of their property had been guaranteed to them at the time of the city's handover and demanded that these rights should continue to be respected, they were told that this was impossible in view of the urgent need to safeguard the city against the Ottomans.[93] As a further coercive measure to discourage the citizens from leaving, the Venetians destroyed the houses, trees, and other properties belonging to those who had gone away. Since it is reported that many of the people who abandoned the city hoped to return when the war with the Ottomans would come to an end, the destruction of the possessions they left behind was certainly aimed at deterring others who might be contemplating flight.[94]

Such measures carried out in violation of the rights and privileges guaranteed by the Venetians in 1423 created hard feelings on the part of the Thessalonians.[95] But what perhaps contributed most to the deteriorating relations between the native inhabitants and the Venetian authorities was a series of malpractices perpetrated by the latter. While the Thessalonians protested that the salaries they received from Venice were insufficient to meet even their basic needs, the Venetian paymasters who distributed these salaries to them frequently extracted heavy and arbitrary dues.[96] In 1429 two irregular soldiers (*asapi*) in the service of Venice, Andreas the *protostrator* and Theodore Olbofaci, appealed directly to the Senate to complain about the extra charges they had been held liable for in addition to the *pendamerea*, which was the only tax they were obliged to pay.[97] The Venetian authorities also kept back part of the wages of the laborers who participated in the rebuilding of the walls of Kassandreia.[98] The mounted guards (*cavalieri*) of the duke and of the captain of Thessalonike were likewise infamous for molesting the citizens.[99] Furthermore, besides their negligence over the distribution of wheat reserved as alms for the poor, the Venetians committed abuses with other food supplies that went on the market for sale. Symeon relates that during the Venetian regime a Cretan ship loaded with

---

[93] Mertzios, Μνημεῖα, pp. 72–3 (2nd Embassy: § 1); Sathas, *Documents*, vol. i, pp. 135–6.

[94] Mertzios, Μνημεῖα, pp. 78–9 (2nd Embassy: § 14).

[95] For more examples of the violation of Thessalonians' privileges and local customs, see ibid., pp. 47 (1st Embassy: § 1. Privileges in general); 54, 73 (1st Embassy: §§ 7 and 8, 2nd Embassy: § 2. Privileges concerning the proper functioning of the Council of Twelve); 79 (2nd Embassy: § 16. Local custom requiring separate incarceration of men and women); and pp. 103–4 and note 66 above (ecclesiastical and judicial privileges). See also Tsaras, "Fin d'Andronic," 426–9.

[96] Mertzios, Μνημεῖα, pp. 56, 76 (1st Embassy: § 12, 2nd Embassy: § 11).

[97] Thiriet, *Régestes*, vol. ii, no. 2131 (May 6, 1429). It has been suggested that "Olbofaci" may be the Latin rendering of the Turkish "Ulufeci," a member of one of the divisions in the Ottoman *kapıkulu* cavalry (i.e. slave soldiers of the royal household): see Matschke, *Ankara*, pp. 120–3. On the *pendamerea*, see note 81 above.

[98] Mertzios, Μνημεῖα, pp. 80–1 (2nd Embassy: § 20).   [99] Ibid., p. 56 (1st Embassy: § 13).

wheat sank just outside the harbor of Thessalonike on a stormy day, and that the soaked grain, which was distributed to the poor at a low price, was thereby saved from falling into the hands of speculators.[100] From the instructions sent by the Venetian Senate to Thessalonike at the end of 1424, we learn that the agents of the duke and the captain tried to gain control over the food market, by personally interfering in the sale of meat, bread, and wine, and forcing the prices to go up. The Senate ordered them to put an immediate end to such practices and to let the sale of these commodities be free.[101] However, abuses and profiteering continued as long as the exigencies of the state of war supplied opportunities for exploitation. In 1429, therefore, when the Thessalonian ambassadors in Venice asked for extra wheat supplies, they warned the Senate to take precautions against profiteering and black-market activities by making sure that the wheat would be sold in the city's square, at cost, and only to those who paid for it at its value.[102] The ambassadors also sought authorization from the Senate for the appointment of two officers, chosen from among the Greek citizens, to supervise weights, measures, and prices, and to serve for a maximum period of three months so as to reduce the chances of bribery.[103]

All this evidence confirms and elucidates some vague references to the bad relations between the native Thessalonians and the Venetians found in the narrative sources. Doukas, for example, writes, "Those who remained in the city were maltreated in countless acts of unprovoked violence," while Anagnostes states, "As you know, the city suffered under Latin domination."[104] A church official who fled to Constantinople in April 1425 and arranged for the flight of his family a few months later, too, refers to the "enslavement of the city by the Venetians."[105] Finally, in a funeral oration for the Despot Andronikos, there is another allusion to the Venetian rule in Thessalonike as being equivalent to slavery.[106] As a result, the general atmosphere within the city became so tense and at the same time the military situation so insecure that even the Venetian authorities in Thessalonike were quite discontent with their condition. In 1426 both the

---

[100] Symeon–Balfour, p. 64.　　[101] Thiriet, *Régestes*, vol. II, no. 1962 (Dec. 17, 1424).
[102] Mertzios, Μνημεῖα, p. 75 (2nd Embassy: § 9).　　[103] Ibid., p. 79 (2nd Embassy: § 17).
[104] Doukas–Grecu, XXIX.4, p. 249, lines 6–7; trans. by Magoulias, *Decline and Fall*, p. 170. Anagnostes–Tsaras, p. 6, lines 31–2. Writing in the late fifteenth century, Theodore Spandounes emphasizes, on the other hand, that the type of government set up by the Venetian administrators of Thessalonike differed considerably from what the Greek inhabitants of the city were used to: Theodoro Spandugnino, *De la origine deli imparatori Ottomani*, ed. K. Sathas, in *Documents*, vol. IX (Paris, 1890), p. 149. See also Tsaras, "Fin d'Andronic," 427.
[105] Kugéas, "Notizbuch," 152.
[106] A. Sideras, *24 unedierte byzantinische Grabreden* (Göttingen, 1982), p. 288; cf. A. Sideras, "Neue Quellen zum Leben des Despotes Andronikos Palaiologos," *BZ* 80/1 (1987), 10, n. 49.

duke and the captain of Thessalonike (Bernabò Loredan and Giacomo Dandolo) declared their wish to resign from their posts. For many months, however, no candidates willing to replace them could be found in Venice. Consequently, they were obliged to stay in office until the end of their two-year term.[107] It is clear that by this time the majority of the Republic's civil servants had come to regard Thessalonike as an unattractive and unwelcome post of appointment.

Under such conditions, the inhabitants of Thessalonike became less and less willing to continue the struggle against the Ottomans. It has been seen that already at the time of the negotiations for the city's transfer to Venice, there was a group of people in favor of surrendering to the Ottomans. Within a few years after the establishment of the Venetian regime, greater numbers of Thessalonians, feeling that the Venetians had not fulfilled most of what they had undertaken to do, and suffering from hunger, poverty, mistreatment, and exhaustion, began to show open signs of reluctance to resist the enemy. In a letter sent to Crete in March 1427 the Venetian authorities in Thessalonike drew attention to the refusal of the citizens to participate in defense and combat. They also referred in the same letter to the flight of three captives, by the names of *Palapan* (Balaban), *Chitir* (Hıdır), and *Apochafo* (Apokaukos?), which particularly worried them because these fugitives would soon be informing the Ottomans about the unstable situation inside Thessalonike.[108] Nevertheless, despite three attempts by Murad II to persuade the citizens to surrender and despite the desire of the majority to do so, the Thessalonians fought until the very last minute.[109] According to Anagnostes, this was, first of all, because the inhabitants who remained in the city were so reduced in number that they were not able to act according to their own wish. Secondly, owing to the divisions among the population, they could not come to an agreement and put up a united front in support of surrender. Finally, they were afraid of the Venetians who pressured them to fight, and particularly of the "*Tzetarioi*" who were appointed to watch over them.[110] The combined efforts of the Thessalonians and the Venetians failed, however, and Thessalonike fell to the Ottomans on March 29, 1430.

From the foregoing discussion of political and socioeconomic conditions in Thessalonike under three separate regimes, the following conclusions can be drawn. First, with the exception of the period of the first Ottoman

---

[107] Thiriet, *Assemblées*, vol. II, no. 1302 (Aug. 24, 1426).   [108] Ibid., no. 1306 (March 1427).
[109] Anagnostes–Tsaras, pp. 16–18, 20, 24.   [110] Ibid., pp. 8, 10–12, 24.

domination (1387–1403) when the city was temporarily relieved from military assaults, a desire for peace, with its corollary prosperity, was what the Thessalonians all strove for in unison. However, the means by which people of varying social backgrounds wanted to implement this peace differed. While opinions did undergo alterations corresponding to changing circumstances, the lower classes on the whole, both urban and rural, exhibited the highest degree of consistency. Yearning to bring an end to their economic problems, which the military conflicts with the Ottomans multiplied and intensified, the common people under both the Byzantine and the Venetian administrations regularly insisted on the idea of surrendering to the enemy on terms. Unfortunately, little is known about the lower classes during the period of the first Ottoman domination apart from their uprising of 1393 against the Greek *archontes* who had been left in charge of the local goverment of Thessalonike. But some pieces of evidence pointing towards improvements in the economic conditions of the countryside under the Ottoman regime suggest that the removal of obstacles to agricultural production following the establishment of peace may have served the region's peasantry well.

As to the upper classes whose financial assets, lands, or commercial interests were at stake, the majority of them preferred to see the establishment of peace in Thessalonike through the elimination of the Ottomans rather than through a rapprochement with them. Despite certain political and economic advantages which some high-standing individuals acquired during the first Ottoman domination, most members of the aristocracy suffered material losses and many may have felt their condition to be insecure, if not deteriorating, under the Ottoman regime. Therefore, following the city's restoration to Byzantine rule in 1403, the initiative to resist the Ottomans with the assistance of Venice came from this segment of society. The policy they supported was one that in the short run necessitated the continuation of military struggles in order to bring about a lasting peace. To this end they were even prepared to accept submission to the Latin Church. Afterwards, however, some among them became deeply disillusioned with the Venetian regime because it failed to establish the conditions of peace to which they aspired.

Among ecclesiastical and monastic circles, on the other hand, the only form of peace that was considered acceptable was one that did not endanger the religious freedom of the Thessalonians. In the course of the first Ottoman domination, the citizens witnessed the tolerant attitude of the Muslim authorities with regard to both the teachings and the internal affairs of their Church. Despite the fact that many of the monasteries and small churches within the city experienced a general economic decline, the Ottomans made no large-scale attempt at Islamization throughout this period. By contrast, the Venetians who took over the city's political administration in 1423 applied strict measures to extend their authority to its ecclesiastical jurisdiction as well and interfered with the religious freedom of the Orthodox community, ignoring the guarantees they had offered initially. The striking difference between the religious policies of the Ottomans and the Latins, widely known throughout the Byzantine world, which in fact never forgot the experiences of the Fourth Crusade and its aftermath, was the primary reason why high-ranking ecclesiastics such as the archbishops Isidore and Gabriel, who were fundamentally opposed to both the Latins and the Ottomans, adopted in the end a conciliatory attitude towards the latter when Thessalonike capitulated to Ottoman rule in 1387. Similarly, some monks and monasteries showed signs of accommodation with the Muslim authorities in an attempt to win their favor and to receive benefits from them during the first Ottoman domination. In the decades following the restoration of Thessalonike to Byzantine rule, and particularly during the Venetian administration, the anti-Latin attitude of monastic circles seems to have grown stronger. For instance, the anti-unionist monks of the Blatadon monastery were so firmly opposed to the Venetian regime that according to a later tradition they allegedly betrayed Thessalonike to the Ottomans in 1430 by disclosing to Sultan Murad II a stratagem to conquer the city by way of cutting off its water supply.[111] That this highly dubious tradition is rejected by almost everyone is beside the point. What is more to the point is that the story reflects surviving memories of the generally more favorable attitude of monks towards the Ottomans than towards the Latins. It is after all an authenticated fact that in 1423/4, immediately before or shortly after the cession of Thessalonike to Venice, the monks of Mount Athos, with Despot Andronikos' consent, went to the Ottoman capital Edirne (Adrianople) and gave obeisance to Murad II, presumably because they anticipated that the Venetians would not be as tolerant or as flexible in religious matters as the Ottomans.[112] As for the monasteries within Thessalonike, after the problems which we saw they confronted under the domination of Venice, the city's conquest by the Ottomans in 1430 may have come as a relief to them, especially when Murad II granted them "by letters and by word" the right to maintain their immovables together with their sources of revenue. The Sultan was

---

[111] Chronicle of Hierax (c. 1580), ed. C. N. Sathas, Μεσαιωνικὴ Βιβλιοθήκη, vol. I (Venice, 1872), p. 257. See also note 43 above.

[112] Schreiner, *Kleinchroniken*, vol. I, Chr. 63/4, p. 473; vol. II, pp. 422–3.

to reverse his policy a few years later, but perhaps no one at the time could have foreseen this.[113]

When the Ottoman army entered Thessalonike in 1430, it is reported that money and valuables belonging to wealthy citizens were found hidden underneath church altars or buried in graveyards and in other places.[114] As contemporaries to the events of 1453 would later observe in Constantinople too,[115] there was an affluent minority in Thessalonike which refused to extend its financial resources towards the city's defense needs. It has been seen that this group opted, instead, for assistance from Venice. Next to these people stood the bulk of the population which was impoverished and reduced to misery by the concurrent military and economic hardships of the times. In a letter written towards the end of the fourteenth century, Demetrios Kydones had expressed his fear that the deplorable condition of the poor citizens of Constantinople would eventually lead to civil war.[116] Kydones' prediction concerning the imperial capital turned out to be the fate of Thessalonike, as revealed by the internal dissensions and social conflicts discussed in the present and preceding chapters. The city's survival before the external enemy, thus, became hopelessly linked to and dependent upon foreign help from the West, while internally it remained weak and divided. In many ways, the fate of the "second city" of the Byzantine Empire foreshadowed what was to take place in Constantinople a few decades later. As Doukas observed with the benefit of hindsight, "This was the evil and ill-fated firstfruits of future calamities destined to befall the imperial capital."[117]

---

[113] Anagnostes–Tsaras, pp. 58, 64–6.
[114] Ibid., pp. 44–8. Cf. Aşıkpaşazade–Giese, p. 106 (= Aşıkpaşazade–Atsız, p. 173); Neşrî, *Kitâb-ı Cihan-nümâ*, vol. II, pp. 610–11.
[115] See below, ch. 8, pp. 225ff.   [116] Kydones–Loenertz, vol. II, no. 433 (date: 1391).
[117] Doukas–Grecu, XXIX.5, p. 251; trans. by Magoulias, *Decline and Fall*, p. 172.

Constantinople

INTRODUCTION TO PART III

In the course of the fourteenth and fifteenth centuries Constantinople, which had once been one of the most glorious and populous urban centers of the Mediterranean world, was reduced politically and economically to a rather modest state of existence and was merely able to hold out against the Ottomans for another twenty-three years following the definitive conquest of Thessalonike. Constantinople shared with Thessalonike a more or less identical social structure during this period. In the earlier part of the fourteenth century its population was made up of three distinct social layers: a very rich aristocracy, which drew its wealth primarily from land; a rich "middle" class (the *mesoi*), including merchants, bankers, small property owners, and minor functionaries; and the poor, consisting of small artisans, manual laborers, small cultivators, as well as entirely destitute people at the lowest end of the social spectrum. After the middle of the fourteenth century, however, as more and more people from the first group, having lost their landed possessions to the Serbs and Ottomans, were compelled to channel their economic activities towards trade and banking, the social criteria separating them from rich middle-class merchants became less clearly distinguishable. Thereafter, as in Thessalonike, a bipartite social structure with the rich at one end and the poor at the other became typical in Constantinople.[1]

Yet, by virtue of its role as the capital of the Byzantine Empire and the seat of the imperial government, Constantinople maintained a distinct character from Thessalonike. It was here that the empire's foreign policy decisions were taken and implemented. Consequently, in their proximity to the Byzantine court, the citizens of Constantinople were at once more familiar with and more directly influenced by the actions of the central

---

[1] See Oikonomidès, *Hommes d'affaires*, pp. 114–23; Matschke, *Fortschritt*, pp. 38–62, 74–106; Matschke and Tinnefeld, *Gesellschaft*, pp. 154–66.

government than the Thessalonians. This factor must necessarily be taken into consideration in examining the effects of Ottoman advances in Byzantine territories upon the political attitudes of the citizens of Constantinople.

The following chapter, with its direct focus on the Byzantine court and its relations with the Ottomans during the late fourteenth and early fifteenth centuries, is intended to elucidate this particular aspect of Constantinople. Having once laid out the proper setting, I will proceed in subsequent chapters to examine the political attitudes and socioeconomic conditions that prevailed in the city, first during the siege of Bayezid I, and then in the course of the final fifty years of Byzantine rule there.

CHAPTER 6

The Byzantine court and the Ottomans: conflict and accommodation

A distinguishing feature of Constantinople in its role as the capital of the Byzantine Empire was that it often became the scene of struggles for the imperial throne. Since the civil war of 1341–7 between John VI Kantakouzenos and the partisans of John V Palaiologos, it had become almost customary for claimants to the Byzantine throne to run to the Turks for assistance.[1] But what course was a claimant to follow when the ruling emperor himself happened to be officially allied with the Ottomans? In 1373 while Emperor John V was serving on an Ottoman campaign in Asia Minor in compliance with his recent agreement with Murad I whereby he had become a tributary vassal of the Ottomans, his son and regent, Andronikos IV, and the Sultan's son Savcı Çelebi prepared a joint plot to overthrow their fathers. John V and Murad I responded to this conspiracy by likewise joining forces against their sons. Within a few months the movement was suppressed, and the young princes were captured. After having Savcı blinded and beheaded, Murad I ordered the Emperor to put out the eyes of his own son. John V reluctantly obeyed, but made sure that Andronikos did not lose his sight completely. For the time being, the failed usurpation additionally cost Andronikos his right of succession to the Byzantine throne, which was transferred to his younger brother Manuel (II).[2]

---

[1] On the relations of Kantakouzenos with the Turks, see P. Lemerle, L'émirat d'Aydin, Byzance et l'Occident (Paris, 1957); E. Werner, "Johannes Kantakuzenos, Umur Paša und Orchan," BS 26 (1965), 255–76; Nicol, Family of Kantakouzenos, pp. 35–103; J. Gill, "John VI Cantacuzenus and the Turks," Βυζαντινά 13/1 (1985), 55–76; H. İnalcık, "The rise of the Turcoman maritime principalities in Anatolia, Byzantium, and the Crusades," BF 9 (1985), 179–217; Balivet, Romanie byzantine, pp. 113–22. See also ch. 2 above, pp. 20–1 and note 7.
[2] See R.-J. Loenertz, "La première insurrection d'Andronic IV Paléologue (1373)," Echos d'Orient 38 (1939), 334–45; P. Charanis, "The strife among the Palaeologi and the Ottoman Turks, 1370–1402," B 16 (1942–3), 293–5; F. Dölger, "Zum Aufstand des Andronikos IV. gegen seinen Vater Johannes V. im Mai 1373," REB 19 (1961), 328–32; Barker, Manuel II, pp. 18–23; Nicol, Last Centuries, pp. 277–8; F. Babinger, "Sawdji," EI, vol. VII, p. 192. None of the Ottoman sources that report Savcı's rebellion

In a letter to John V dated to the fall of 1373, Demetrios Kydones noted that many Byzantines went over to the Turks and collaborated with them against the Emperor. After participating in the banquets of the Turks and exchanging presents, they returned to the Byzantine capital without making any effort to conceal themselves. Kydones expressed indignation that these people were neither detained from going over to the Turks, nor indicted for their open association with them.[3] It may well be that Kydones was alluding in his letter to Andronikos IV and his partisans. This, of course, can be stated as no more than a hypothesis in the absence of concrete evidence. Nonetheless, Kydones' letter is instructive because it reveals the freedom of movement and open contact between Byzantine and Ottoman territories that made the coordination of a joint plot like that of Andronikos and Savcı possible.[4] In addition, the letter highlights the awkward situation of the Byzantine government which could apparently take no strict action against its subjects who formed ties with the Ottomans, given that the head of the state, the Emperor himself, had declared official allegiance to the Turkish Sultan. We have evidence, moreover, indicating that the traffic between Byzantine and Ottoman lands did not necessarily flow in a single direction, from the former to the latter, as Kydones' letter might suggest. In 1375 Pope Gregory XI wrote to John V that, "those Turks, after the truce which you have made with them, have entered the city [Constantinople] in no small multitude and there dare to perform many horrible deeds, and we fear that they may deceive your Majesty and occupy the city."[5] Unless the Pope, concerned primarily with the safety of the Byzantine capital, was referring to the presence of Ottoman soldiers rather than ordinary civilians inside Constantinople, we may take his statement as a further demonstration of the contacts between Byzantine and Ottoman subjects that would have been facilitated by John V's peace treaty with Murad I.

In 1376 Andronikos IV escaped from Constantinople, where he was held in confinement together with his wife and son, to the Genoese colony of Pera. It was not difficult for him to obtain the support of the Genoese, whose commercial interests had recently been threatened by John V's

---

mention his cooperation with the Byzantine prince. According to some sources, Andronikos' infant son, the future emperor John VII, was partially blinded at this time too.

[3] Kydones–Loenertz, vol. I, no. 117, p. 156. Cf. Balivet, "Personnage du 'turcophile'," 118, 120.

[4] See also Kydones, "Oratio de admittendo Latinorum subsidio," *PG* 154, col. 1005, discussed below, pp. 124–5.

[5] As quoted in Dennis, *Reign of Manuel II*, p. 36. On Pope Gregory's policies with regard to the Ottomans, see A. Luttrell, "Gregory XI and the Turks: 1370–1378," *OCP* 46 (1980), 391–417.

cession of the island of Tenedos to Venice.[6] The Emperor's rebellious son sought, in addition, the support of the Ottoman ruler Murad I. After his failed attempt to seize the throne three years earlier, Andronikos must have come to realize that his future efforts would be in vain as long as the alliance between John V and Murad I remained in effect. Accordingly, he approached the Sultan and offered him his allegiance and tribute payment in return for the use of Ottoman cavalry forces.[7] Two Venetian sources report that Andronikos also promised his sister to Murad in marriage, one adding that God took her life in order to prevent this "abominable sin."[8]

Although the Venetian chronicler objected to Murad's marriage with Andronikos' sister, it is a well-known fact that such unions had already taken place between the Byzantine and Ottoman ruling houses. The first and most celebrated of these marriages was the one consummated in 1346 between Orhan, Murad I's father, and Theodora, John VI Kantakouzenos' daughter, during the civil war between John V and John VI.[9] Murad was not born of this union, but his mother, too, was a Byzantine, though she was a woman of lower rank.[10] In the late 1350s, moreover, Orhan's youngest son Halil was betrothed to a daughter of John V Palaiologos and Helena Kantakouzene called Eirene. This betrothal was the upshot of a complex affair that began with the capture of Halil by Phokaian pirates,

---

[6] John V had originally promised Tenedos to the Venetians in 1370, but the agreement had not been put into effect. In 1376 John V made a new deal with the Venetians concerning the island's cession to them. See Dölger, *Reg.*, vol. v, no. 3150; F. Thiriet, "Venise et l'occupation de Ténédos au XIVe siècle," *Mélanges d'archéologie et d'histoire* 65 (1953), 219–45; Nicol, *Byzantium and Venice*, pp. 305–7, 312. It seems that Andronikos played a key role in disallowing the island's cession to Venice in 1370, probably acting under the influence of the Genoese: see pp. 125–6 and note 26 below.

[7] Chalkok.–Darkó, vol. i, pp. 55–6; Doukas–Grecu, XII.3, p. 73; Schreiner, *Kleinchroniken*, vol. i, Chr. 9/31, 22/15; vol. ii, pp. 311–12. Chronologically at fault, Chalkokondyles places these events in the reign of Bayezid I (r. 1389–1402). See also P. Charanis, "An important short chronicle of the fourteenth century," *B* 13 (1938), 335–62; Charanis, "Strife," 295–9; Dennis, *Reign of Manuel II*, pp. 28–9, 37–8; Barker, *Manuel II*, pp. 24–9; Nicol, *Last Centuries*, pp. 278–9.

[8] Raffaino Caresini, *Chronica AA. 1343–1388*, ed. E. Pastorello, *RIS*, 12/2 (Bologna, 1923), p. 32; J. Chrysostomides, "Studies on the Chronicle of Caroldo," *OCP* 35 (1969), 143, 168–9.

[9] A. Bryer, "Greek historians on the Turks: the case of the first Byzantine–Ottoman marriage," in *The Writing of History in the Middle Ages; Essays Presented to Richard William Southern*, ed. R. H. C. Davis and J. M. Wallace-Hadrill (Oxford, 1981), pp. 471–93; Nicol, *Reluctant Emperor*, pp. 76–9; M. Izeddin, "Notes sur les mariages princiers en Orient au moyen âge," *Journal asiatique* 257 (1969), 143–5. See also G. E. Rakintzakis, "Orthodox–Muslim mixed marriages, ca. 1297–1453," unpublished MA thesis, University of Birmingham (1975).

[10] She was the daughter of the Byzantine commander (*tekvur*) of Yarhisar in Anatolia, near Bursa. This marriage took place in 1299–1300, that is, before Orhan ascended the throne. Unlike Theodora Kantakouzene, who retained her Orthodox faith, Orhan's former wife (i.e. Murad I's mother) converted to Islam and adopted the name Nilüfer. See Aşıkpaşazade–Giese, p. 19 (= Aşıkpaşazade–Atsız, p. 102); Neşrî, *Kitâb-ı Cihan-nümâ*, vol. i, p. 104. Cf. F. Babinger, "Nilüfer Khatun," *EI*, vol. vi, p. 921 (reprinted in *EI²*, vol. viii, p. 43).

but ultimately it too had some connection, albeit indirect, with Byzantine dynastic conflicts. For it was because Leo Kalothetos, the governor of Phokaia and a devoted partisan of John VI Kantakouzenos, delayed Halil's release through his refusal to obey Emperor John V's orders to this effect, that the latter was compelled to appease Orhan by means of a marriage settlement.[11] Clearly, when Andronikos IV, following the examples of John VI and John V, offered his sister as wife to Murad I, his principal motive must have been to rally the Sultan's support to achieve his dynastic ambition. In addition, Andronikos may have hoped to reinforce the status of his own line within the Palaiologos family, by initiating a marriage alliance that would supersede the former links of the Ottoman house with John V's branch and with the Kantakouzenoi.

Thus allied with the Ottomans and the Genoese, Andronikos attacked Constantinople in the summer of 1376 and seized the throne from his father. Shortly afterwards, John V was put in prison with his other sons, Manuel and Theodore.[12] One of Andronikos' first acts upon assuming power was to reward the Genoese by ceding to them the island of Tenedos. This set the stage for the war of Chioggia (1377–81) between Venice and Genoa, part of which was fought in Byzantine waters and in which the Genoese obliged Andronikos to participate.[13] Thus the new Emperor's alliance with the Genoese culminated in his costly involvement in a war that was in essence of no direct interest to Byzantium. "In the midst of so much misery," wrote Kydones in a letter, "he is preparing arms, munitions, engines of war and ships, and is forced to hire troops, a thing which for him is more difficult than flying."[14] Andronikos also granted the Genoese the right to extend the boundaries of their colony in Pera.[15]

---

[11] A. D. Alderson, *The Structure of the Ottoman Dynasty* (Oxford, 1956), Tables XXII, LXI, pp. 165, 184; Nicol, *Family of Kantakouzenos*, pp. 134–5, n. 4; Izeddin, "Mariages princiers," 145–6; F. Tinnefeld, "Kaiser Ioannes V. Palaiologos und der Gouverneur von Phokaia 1356–1358: ein Beispiel für den Verfall der byzantinischen Zentralgewalt um die Mitte des 14. Jahrhunderts," *Rivista di studi bizantini e slavi* 1 (1981), 259–82; H. İnalcık, "The conquest of Edirne," *Archivum Ottomanicum* 3 (1971), 189–92; de Vries-van der Velden, *Élite byzantine*, pp. 143–5.

[12] Chalkok.–Darkó, vol. I, pp. 56–7; Doukas–Grecu, XII.3, p. 73; Schreiner, *Kleinchroniken*, vol. I, Chr. 7/17, 9/32, 11/5, 12/2, 22/16–17; vol. II, pp. 312–13, 316–17, 613 (Chron. Not. 47); *Manuel II, Fun. Or.*, pp. 100–7; Kydones–Loenertz, vol. II, nos. 167, 222; Caresini, *Chronica*, ed. Pastorello, p. 32; Daniele di Chinazzo, *Cronica de la guerra da Veneciani a Zenovesi*, ed. V. Lazzarini (Venice, 1958), p. 18.

[13] C. Pagano, *Delle imprese e del dominio dei Genovesi nella Grecia* (Genoa, 1846), pp. 307–9; Belgrano, "Prima serie," no. 24, p. 131; Dölger, *Reg.*, vol. V, nos. 3155, 3156. On the war of Chioggia, see F. C. Lane, *Venice: A Maritime Republic* (Baltimore and London, 1973), pp. 189–96, 469; Nicol, *Byzantium and Venice*, pp. 312–17.

[14] Kydones–Loenertz, vol. II, no. 167, p. 38; trans. by Dennis, *Reign of Manuel II*, p. 39. Cf. Charanis, "Strife," 298; Nicol, *Last Centuries*, pp. 279–80.

[15] W. Heyd, *Histoire du commerce du Levant au Moyen Âge*, vol. I (Leipzig, 1885; repr. Amsterdam, 1967), pp. 518–19.

The price that Andronikos had to pay for the assistance he received from the Ottoman Sultan in deposing his father was even higher, especially in view of its long-term consequences. Shortly after his accession to the throne, the young Emperor is known to have visited Murad I's court.[16] It was probably during this visit that Andronikos, in addition to the annual tribute he had promised in advance, made arrangements to surrender Gallipoli to the Sultan as a token of his subservience. Gallipoli, it will be recalled, had been occupied by the Ottomans about two decades earlier, and it was of great strategic importance for their expansion in the European territories of the Byzantine Empire. In 1366, however, the Ottomans had lost the fortress to the forces of Amadeo of Savoy, who restored it to Byzantium. Murad's recovery of Gallipoli, which we know he had been striving for at least since 1371,[17] was therefore a most welcome prize, made all the more valuable since it was achieved through peaceful means simply by manipulating the conflict between John V and Andronikos IV. The Ottomans entered the town *circa* 1377, which remained in their possession permanently thereafter, serving as their principal naval base and a stepping stone for their future conquests in the Balkans.[18] In a letter written in the winter of 1376–7 Kydones summarized the detrimental consequences of this situation for Byzantium:

[T]he old scourge, the Turks, roused to arrogance by the alliance which they concluded with the new Emperor against his father, have become more oppressive for us. Thus they received Gallipoli as compensation for this and seized many other things belonging to us and exacted such an amount of money that nobody could easily count it. Still, they claim that they are not sufficiently paid for their aid. They command everything and we must obey or else be imprisoned. To such a point have they risen in power and we been reduced to slavery.[19]

These, then, were the concessions Andronikos IV made to the Genoese and the Ottomans with whose help he ascended the throne in 1376. But, in addition to his foreign allies, Andronikos also appears to have had a fairly strong following among the inhabitants of Constantinople. There are clear

---

[16] Iacobus Zeno, *Vita Caroli Zeni*, ed. G. Zonta, *RIS*, 19/6 (Bologna, 1940), p. 14; Schreiner, *Kleinchroniken*, vol. I, Chr. 9/34; vol. II, pp. 315–18. See Barker, *Manuel II*, pp. 458–61.

[17] In the summer of 1371 Murad I sent an envoy to Constantinople to negotiate the return of Gallipoli to the Ottomans, whereupon Demetrios Kydones composed his "Oratio de non reddenda Callipoli petente Amurate," *PG* 154, cols. 1009–36. On the controversy over the dating of this speech (1371 vs. 1376 or 1377), see Nicol, *Last Centuries*, p. 273, n. 33; recently, though, Barker, "Question of ethnic antagonisms," p. 171, has joined those who date the oration to 1371. See also Kianka, "Byzantine–Papal diplomacy," 201–2; Malamut, "Les discours de Démétrius Cydonès," pp. 212–15.

[18] İnalcık, "Gelibolu," pp. 983–7. See also ch. 2 above, pp. 25, 27–8.

[19] Kydones–Loenertz, vol. II, no. 167, p. 38; trans. by Dennis, *Reign of Manuel II*, p. 38. Cf. Charanis, "Strife," 297–8; Nicol, *Last Centuries*, pp. 280–1.

indications at any rate that during the decade preceding Andronikos' rise to the throne, part of the capital's population actively opposed the pro-Latin policy pursued by the Emperor John V until about the year 1373 and favored instead a rapprochement with the Ottomans. Although we cannot be sure that these people worked at that time in cooperation with Andronikos, it may not have been by mere coincidence that their anti-Latin/pro-Ottoman activities became manifest during John V's absences from Constantinople when Andronikos had been left as regent in charge of the government. Hence, in 1366, at the time of John V's visit to the court of the Catholic king of Hungary, when Amadeo of Savoy, who had just recovered Gallipoli from the Ottomans, arrived at the Byzantine capital, certain people did not wish to admit the Count into the city. It was in order to overcome their opposition and to urge his fellow citizens to accept the aid of the Latins that Demetrios Kydones delivered an oration.[20] Kydones' speech was effective and Amadeo entered the city on September 2, 1366. Yet the speech reveals how greatly the safety and independence of Constantinople were endangered by the undertakings of a large group of dignitaries (τῶν πολιτευομένων πολλοί) who acted in collusion with the Ottomans so as to bring about the city's surrender to the enemy at this particular juncture when Andronikos happened to be ruling as regent. Kydones relates that these people openly visited the Ottomans, among whom they stayed for specified lengths of time and were rewarded with gifts of sheep, oxen, horses, and money for their collaboration in the betrayal of their country. When they returned to Constantinople, they gave public speeches by which they tried to stir their fellow citizens to hasten to deliver the city to the Ottomans and to accept the latter as their masters.[21] Likewise, when Murad I demanded the return of Gallipoli in the summer of 1371 (while Andronikos was once again acting as regent for John V, who was away this time in Italy), the majority of the capital's population and the members of the Senate spoke out in favor of surrendering the fortress to the Ottomans, according to the testimony of Kydones who composed another oration on this occasion.[22] Given the polemical nature of Kydones' speech and the strength of his anti-Ottoman convictions, it is questionable that those who

---

[20] Kydones, "Oratio de admittendo Latinorum subsidio," *PG* 154, cols. 961–1008. Cf. Nicol, *Last Centuries*, pp. 265–6; Barker, "Question of ethnic antagonisms," pp. 165–6, 172; Malamut, "Les discours de Démétrius Cydonès," pp. 205–12.

[21] Kydones, "Oratio de admittendo Latinorum subsidio," col. 1005. Cf. Balivet, "Personnage du 'turcophile'," 118–19.

[22] Kydones, "Oratio de non reddenda Callipoli," col. 1009: "καὶ τό γε πλεῖστον τῆς πόλεως, καὶ τῶν συμβουλεύειν εἰωθότων, φασὶ δεῖν ἤδη διδόναι." See note 17 above.

favored the surrender of Gallipoli actually formed "the majority."[23] Be that as it may, his statement, together with his earlier oration of 1366 and the aforementioned letter of 1373 to John V, all seem to indicate that plenty of people in Constantinople would have readily welcomed and encouraged Andronikos' cooperation with the Ottomans in his successive attempts to seize the throne from his father.

We know, moreover, from a short chronicle notice that soon after John V returned from Italy (October 28, 1371), he ordered the arrest of several *archontes* in Constantinople who may well have been partisans of Andronikos.[24] Indeed it might not be too far-fetched to link them with the pro-Ottoman activists frequently mentioned in the writings of Kydones since 1366. One *panhypersebastos* Tzamplakon among the arrested *archontes* bears the family name of a former associate of John VI Kantakouzenos,[25] suggesting that certain dignitaries at the Byzantine court who wished to revive the ex-Emperor's policy of coexistence with the Ottomans may have clustered around Andronikos IV, particularly after John V's conversion to the Catholic faith in Rome at the end of 1369 and his subsequent offer of the island of Tenedos to the Venetians in 1370, if not earlier. We may even speculate that those within the Senate who advocated the cession of Gallipoli to Murad I in the summer of 1371 were possibly seeking a direct retaliation for John V's deal with Venice over Tenedos, both places being key points for control of the Dardanelles. In any case Andronikos, perhaps at the instigation of the Genoese, seems to have refused to carry out John's orders with regard to the island's cession in 1370, and he also declined

[23] It should be noted that what has been said here about the possible effects of Kydones' political convictions and polemical style on the information he provides is applicable in general to all of his writings, which tend to give an exaggerated and one-sided picture of the political make-up of the Constantinopolitan population. Apprehensive about the consequences which might result from the activities of his fellow countrymen who were well-disposed towards the Ottomans, Kydones is inclined to emphasize and amplify the role played by these people in Constantinople, whereas the pro-Latin people at the opposite end of the city's political spectrum do not receive similar treatment from him. Therefore, although Kydones' writings are used extensively throughout this chapter, the purpose of which is to document the various forms of cooperation between members of the Byzantine court and the Ottomans, the reader should not be misled about the dimensions of the "pro-Ottoman" phenomenon suggested by the testimony of Kydones, which conceals the existence of a "pro-Latin" phenomenon that was equally, if not more, widespread in Constantinople, as is going to be seen in subsequent chapters.

[24] Schreiner, *Kleinchroniken*, vol. I, Chr. 9/23, p. 94. The likelihood of a connection between the arrested persons and Andronikos has already been suggested by Charanis, "Strife," 291 and Nicol, *Last Centuries*, pp. 275–6. But Schreiner (*Kleinchroniken*, vol. II, p. 302) rejects this on the grounds that the time gap is too great between the arrests (December 5, 1371) and Andronikos' earliest known insurrection of 1373. Yet, as will be shown below, Andronikos' designs against his father most probably predated his first open insurrection, extending back it seems to 1370.

[25] See *PLP*, no. 27752 (the *megas papias* Arsenios Tzamplakon).

lending aid to his father who was detained at Venice when the Tenedos deal fell through.[26] It seems reasonable, therefore, to seek the unstated cause of the above-mentioned arrests in these particular circumstances that emerged in the context of John V's visit to Italy. Unfortunately the names of the other *archontes* who were arrested on December 5, 1371 – John Asanes, Manuel Bryenni(o)s, Glabas, and Agalos – are hardly useful for purposes of clarifying this issue, since almost nothing else is known about them even though they all belong to distinguished Byzantine families.[27] In short, on the basis of the evidence presented above, all that can be said with certainty is that there was an anti-western faction in Constantinople that sought, as early as 1366, to come to terms with the Ottomans rather than fight against them with Latin aid in accordance with the current policy of John V. Whether this faction ever became linked to Andronikos IV is impossible to prove definitively, but there are strong signs suggesting that by the time of John V's trip to Italy (1369–71), if not before, Andronikos had already taken up leadership of this group that presumably backed him in his subsequent rebellions of 1373 and 1376 in collaboration with the Ottomans.

Yet even with a considerable number of influential followers Andronikos IV could not ensure for himself a long and secure reign, for in those days the success of Byzantine rulers seems to have depended less on the support of their own people than on the support they received from Ottoman sultans. Thus, the young Emperor suffered a major blow in 1379, when Murad I decided to change sides once again and came to the aid of his former ally John V. The latter had just escaped from prison with his two sons and arrived at Murad's court, seeking assistance for the recovery of his throne. At the sight of the Ottoman troops accompanying John V into Constantinople, Andronikos fled, as he had done before, to Pera. He took with him as hostages his maternal grandfather, John VI Kantakouzenos, his mother, the Empress Helena, and two aunts, one of whom was probably Theodora Kantakouzene, the widow of Orhan.[28] The Genoese forces that Andronikos left behind in the capital were soon rendered harmless by

---

[26] R.-J. Loenertz, "Jean V Paléologue à Venise (1370–1371)," *REB* 16 (1958), 217–32; J. Chrysostomides, "John V Palaeologus in Venice (1370–1371) and the Chronicle of Caroldo: a reinterpretation," *OCP* 31 (1965), 76–84; Nicol, *Byzantium and Venice*, pp. 305–8.

[27] Schreiner, *Kleinchroniken*, vol. II, pp. 301–2. Only John Asanes, it has been suggested, may be identified with a θεῖος of Manuel II by the same name who was the recipient of letters from Kydones between 1374/5 and 1389. See Trapp, "Beiträge zur Genealogie der Asanen," 171–5; *PLP*, no. 91371.

[28] Doukas–Grecu, XII.4, p. 73; Chalkok.–Darkó, vol. I, pp. 57–8; Kydones–Loenertz, vol. II, nos. 222, 244; *Manuel II, Fun. Or.*, pp. 110–11; Schreiner, *Kleinchroniken*, vol. I, Chr. 7/19, 12/3, 22/20; vol. II, pp. 320–1. Doukas attributes John V's escape to the help of a certain Angelos Diabolos, who was nicknamed Diabolangelos. According to Kydones (Letter 222), the Empress Helena was

John V's Venetian allies. A western chronicler relates that Venetian help was assured on this occasion through the pressure and insistence of the citizens of Constantinople, *"grandi e picholi,"* who kept cheering *"Viva San Marco"* before the somewhat reluctant captains of the ships that had arrived from Venice to assist John V.[29] Hence, these people belonging to both the upper and the lower classes constituted a group that favored John V and his Venetian allies against Andronikos IV and the latter's Genoese allies. Although Andronikos, too, had followers among the citizens of Constantinople as shown above, at this point John V had regained the support of the Ottomans, which seems to have tipped the scale in his favor. Andronikos meanwhile continued his resistance from Pera, which not only drew Constantinople into a new civil war for the next two years but also sustained the intervention of foreign powers – namely, the Ottomans, the Venetians, and the Genoese – in Byzantine internal affairs.

According to Chalkokondyles, before John V re-established himself in Constantinople, Murad I sent a messenger to the city to consult the inhabitants on whether they would prefer to have himself or John as their emperor. After hearing the opinion of the Constantinopolitans in favor of the latter, Murad allegedly consented to reinstalling him on the throne.[30] Some modern scholars have dismissed this story as belonging to the realm of legend and pro-Ottoman propaganda on the part of Chalkokondyles.[31] Yet, whether fictitious or not, the story is worth drawing attention to, for it reflects the Byzantines' perception of Ottoman sovereignty and influence over the internal affairs of their own state. Chalkokondyles, it must be granted, was writing with hindsight in the second half of the fifteenth century, but a contemporary Genoese document demonstrates that Andronikos IV's Italian allies, at any rate, observed with great apprehension the growing Ottoman influence in Byzantine affairs during the very period with which we are concerned. On March 7, 1382, the Genoese Council of Elders noted that as a result of the civil war between John V and Andronikos, "father as much as sons are rendered subject to the Turk

suspected of having played a role in John V's escape. Cf. Barker, *Manuel II*, pp. 35, 38–9; Nicol, *Family of Kantakouzenos*, pp. 135, 137.

[29] Chinazzo, *Cronica*, ed. Lazzarini, pp. 214–16. See also Caresini, *Chronica*, ed. Pastorello, p. 36; *Vita Caroli Zeni*, ed. Zonta, pp. 22–3; Caroldo quoted by Chrysostomides, in *Manuel II, Fun. Or.*, pp. 108–9, n. 27. Cf. Dennis, *Reign of Manuel II*, pp. 41–2, n. 65. For Pietro Grimani, *bailo* of Constantinople, among John V's Venetian allies in his conflict with Andronikos, see below, ch. 9, p. 244 and note 41.

[30] Chalkok.–Darkó, vol. I, p. 57. Continuing his aforementioned chronological error (see note 7 above), Chalkokondyles relates this story with reference to Bayezid I and Manuel II.

[31] See Schreiner, *Kleinchroniken*, vol. II, p. 321 (n. 97). For those who do not entirely reject the story, see Barker, *Manuel II*, p. 34 (n. 88).

Amorat, and the danger faces the city of Constantinople that it be subjected to the aforesaid Turk Amorat."[32]

As far as the concrete advantages which Murad I derived from his diplomatic maneuver of 1379 are concerned, these must have entailed further concessions on the part of John V with regard to the annual tribute and military service obligations of Byzantium. It should be safe to assume in any case that they would have equaled, if not surpassed, in magnitude Murad I's former gains from Andronikos IV. Chalkokondyles reports that the annual tribute promised to the Sultan in 1379 was 30,000 gold coins.[33] Pseudo-Phrantzes (Makarios Melissenos), on the other hand, claims that the Emperor agreed to pay the same tribute that Andronikos had previously committed himself to, without specifying its amount. He adds in more specific, though questionable, terms that the military forces which the Byzantines were required by the agreement of 1379 to contribute yearly to Ottoman campaigns amounted to twelve thousand foot soldiers and cavalrymen.[34] Unfortunately, we possess no figures concerning the terms of Murad I's former agreements with John V in 1373 or with Andronikos IV in 1376–7 that would have enabled us to conduct a numerical comparison.[35] However, two letters written by Kydones, one in the winter of 1376–7 and the other in 1391, give the general impression that during the time that elapsed between the dates of their composition the tribute levied by the Ottomans increased considerably, creating a very burdensome situation by 1391. In the earlier letter Kydones wrote that the Turks "exacted such an amount of money that nobody could easily count it."[36] In 1391 he noted with increased alarm that the sum of the tribute was so great that all the public revenues combined would not be sufficient to pay it, and that it would be necessary to levy a tax even on the poor citizens.[37] As to

---

[32] J. W. Barker, "Miscellaneous Genoese documents on the Levantine world of the late fourteenth and early fifteenth centuries," *ByzSt* 6 (1979), 55, 57.

[33] Chalkok.–Darkó, vol. I, p. 58.

[34] Pseudo-Phrantzes, *Macarie Melissenos Cronica, 1258–1481*, in *Georgios Sphrantzes, Memorii, 1401– 1477*, ed. V. Grecu (Bucharest, 1966), p. 196. Like Chalkokondyles, Pseudo-Phrantzes identifies the emperor who carried out these negotiations with the Ottomans as Manuel II rather than as John V. For reservations about the figure given by Pseudo-Phrantzes, see Barker, *Manuel II*, p. 34 (n. 89); Bartusis, *Late Byzantine Army*, p. 107 (n. 7).

[35] For a discussion of the evidence concerning Byzantium's tributary obligation to the Ottomans in the late fourteenth and early fifteenth centuries, see Matschke, *Ankara*, pp. 64–75; Ostrogorski, "État tributaire"; O. Iliescu, "Le montant du tribut payé par Byzance à l'Empire Ottoman en 1379 et 1424," *RESEE* 9 (1971), 427–32.

[36] Kydones–Loenertz, vol. II, no. 167, p. 38.

[37] Ibid., no. 442, p. 407. See also no. 443 (date: 1391), p. 410: ". . . ἀηδέστατα δὲ ἄλλως διὰ τὴν βαρβάρων πλεονεξίαν καὶ ὕβριν, καὶ τὸ μηδὲ τοῖς φόροις οὓς ἐκείνοις τελοῦμεν ⌐μηδὲ τὸ πᾶν ἀρκεῖν⌐ τῆς Πόλεως τίμημα, δεῖν δὲ τούτῳ καὶ τὰς ἰδίας τῶν πολιτῶν οὐσίας προσκεῖσθαι . . ."

the requirement of military service, the vehemently anti-Turkish Kydones wrote in 1381 to Manuel II, who was serving on an Ottoman campaign, that for Manuel's sake he had been compelled to pray for the well-being of "the barbarian" (i.e. Murad I).[38] One of the most dramatic consequences of Byzantium's military service obligation occurred in 1390 when Manuel II and John VII, who were called to take part in Bayezid I's expedition against Philadelphia, became instrumental in the loss of this last Byzantine possession in Asia Minor to the Ottomans.[39] The following year Manuel II, who accompanied the Sultan in yet another campaign, wrote to Kydones, "for us it is especially unbearable to have to fight along with those and on behalf of those whose every increase in strength lessens our own strength."[40]

In 1381, after having fought in vain for nearly two years against Andronikos IV and his Genoese allies at Pera, Emperor John V was driven to a compromise. He restored Andronikos, who had been formally disinherited in 1373, and his son John (VII) as successors to the throne. For the time being, Andronikos was given Selymbria, Daneion, Herakleia, Rhaidestos, and Panidos, where he was to rule independently.[41] The grant of this appanage was no doubt partly intended as a measure to guarantee peace through the temporary removal of the unruly Andronikos from the capital. However, it failed to achieve this result. In 1385 Andronikos sent his son to Murad I and requested a fortress from the Ottoman ruler.[42] Shortly

In a third letter (no. 432), likewise dated 1391, Kydones expressed his fear that the rapid spread of poverty within Constantinople might soon be affecting the rich as well, eventually leading to another civil war. It is likely that the circumstances related in this letter were the result, in part, of the heavy tribute demanded by the Ottomans.

[38] Ibid., no. 218, p. 97; no. 220. Cf. Dennis, *Reign of Manuel II*, pp. 47–9.

[39] Chalkok.–Darkó, vol. I, p. 58; cf. Gautier (ed.), "Récit inédit," 104. See H. Ahrweiler, "La région de Philadelphie au XIVe siècle (1290–1390). Dernier bastion de l'Hellénisme en Asie Mineure," *Comptes Rendus de l'Académie des Inscriptions et Belles-Lettres* (1983), 175–97; P. Schreiner, "Zur Geschichte Philadelpheias im 14. Jahrhundert (1293–1390)," *OCP* 35 (1969), 375–431. In Chalkokondyles' chronologically misleading account the discussion of the capture of Philadelphia (Alaşehir) is placed immediately after the events of 1376–9. Thus, what he writes has been taken to imply that the city was perhaps ceded to the Ottomans during the peace settlement of 1379 between John V and Murad I; but as its inhabitants refused to surrender then, Bayezid I took it by force in the fall of 1390. See Barker, *Manuel II*, p. 34 and n. 89, pp. 79–80 and n. 211; Nicol, *Last Centuries*, pp. 281, 292–3. On the other hand, Doukas (ed. Grecu, IV.3, p. 41), Aşıkpaşazade (ed. Giese, pp. 59–60; ed. Atsız, pp. 135–6), and Neşri (*Kitâb-ı Cihan-nümâ*, vol. I, pp. 312–13) report that the Philadelphians surrendered their city to Bayezid. Recently, Reinert, "Palaiologoi," pp. 299–301, 308, 345–7 (n. 57), maintaining that Philadelphia was captured in late 1389 or early 1390 (rather than in the fall of 1390), has concluded that the participation of John VII, and probably of Manuel II also, in Bayezid's expedition against Philadelphia is chronologically untenable.

[40] Dennis, *Letters of Manuel II*, no. 19, pp. 56–7.

[41] MM, vol. II, no. 344 (May 1381), pp. 25–7; Doukas–Grecu, XII.4, p. 73; Kydones–Loenertz, vol. II, nos. 155, 198, 201, 218–20, 222. Cf. Dennis, *Reign of Manuel II*, pp. 42–6.

[42] R.-J. Loenertz, "Fragment d'une lettre de Jean V Paléologue à la commune de Gênes, 1387–1391," *BZ* 51 (1958), 37, lines 7–8.

afterwards, Andronikos captured a fortress in Thrace, near the town of Melitias, from his father's realm of control.[43] It may be not only that these two events were connected with each other, but that the fortresses in question were one and the same. If this is correct, then the somewhat unusual demand of a Byzantine fortress from the Ottoman ruler requires an explanation, which is evidently to be sought in the vassalage relationship of Byzantium to the Ottomans. In other words, it must have been the vassal status of the Byzantine state that inspired Andronikos to appeal to Murad I as the overlord who had the authority to grant him his request. The Sultan's response is not known, yet judging from Andronikos' forceful capture of the fortress it was probably negative. The outcome of this incident was a battle between John V and his son, in which the old Emperor won the final victory, but after severe hardship.[44]

As these events demonstrate, Andronikos IV was not pacified despite the considerable concessions John V offered. It should also be stressed that not only did the settlement of 1381 fall short of bringing peace, but the grant of a whole region to Andronikos led to the further weakening of Byzantium through the division of its few remaining territories. The renewal of Andronikos' succession rights, which had been transferred to his younger brother Manuel on September 25, 1373,[45] contributed also to the breakup of the empire's unity. As we saw earlier (in Part II), Manuel's reaction to the loss of his right to the throne was to transplant himself in Thessalonike, where he set up his independent rule and pursued a foreign policy which contradicted the official imperial policy of peace and reconciliation that was in effect with the Ottomans. In Constantinople, meanwhile, John V, Andronikos IV, and the Genoese of Pera signed a treaty on November 2, 1382, in which they agreed to help each other against all enemies except "Murad Beg and his Turks," thus reconfirming their allegiance and subservience to the Ottomans.[46] In the end, the series of civil wars between John V and Andronikos IV proved to be of utmost advantage to the Ottomans, who successfully manipulated the quarrels within the Byzantine imperial family.

Andronikos IV's death in 1385 may have momentarily relieved John V of the internal troubles that were prompted by his rebellious son for over

---

[43] Ibid., 37, lines 1–3; Schreiner, *Kleinchroniken*, vol. I, Chr. 7/20; vol. II, pp. 330–1. See Dennis, *Reign of Manuel II*, pp. 109–11.

[44] In addition to the sources cited in the previous note, see Kydones–Loenertz, vol. II, nos. 308 (esp. p. 230, lines 23–8), 309 (esp. pp. 233–4, lines 83–9).

[45] Schreiner, *Kleinchroniken*, vol. I, Chr. 9/29; vol. II, pp. 309–10.

[46] See note 30 of ch. 2 above.

a decade. Not long afterwards, however, Andronikos' son John VII, who inherited Selymbria together with neighboring territories in Thrace, turned against the old Emperor and attempted to overthrow him.[47] Following his father's example, John VII allied himself with the Genoese and the Ottomans. His ties with the former did not escape the attention of John V, who complained to the Commune of Genoa, sometime between 1387 and 1391, that since Andronikos' death the inhabitants of Pera had been saluting and acclaiming John VII as though he were emperor. By contrast, they had denied John V the proper honors and customary acclamations as he sailed by Pera, probably on his way back from Thrace, where, as recounted above, in 1385 he had recaptured from Andronikos a fortress near the town of Melitias.[48]

Documents from Genoese archives give evidence that John VII also formed economic relations with his Italian allies. From 1389, if not earlier, he appears to have actively participated in the export of wheat to Genoa from the Thracian territories under his rule.[49] The deterioration of the Byzantine Empire through the separation and division of its lands among contesting members of the imperial family has been pointed out above. John VII's commercial activities constitute a concrete example of the economic consequences of such territorial grants, which weakened the Byzantine state by depriving it of important resources and diminishing its revenues. While in his appanage John VII reaped profits from the export of Thracian wheat to Italy, inside Constantinople John V was driven to confiscate two Venetian ships loaded with grain in 1390. During that year an Ottoman attack was anticipated in the capital, and the Emperor was no doubt trying to reinforce the city's food supplies.[50]

As anticipated, Constantinople suffered an attack in the spring of 1390, but the person leading it was John VII, who succeeded in entering the city and deposing his grandfather within just a few weeks. John VII owed his victory to the strong support he had secured both from foreigners and from Constantinopolitans. Shortly before laying siege to the capital, the young

[47] See Th. Ganchou, "Autour de Jean VII: luttes dynastiques, interventions étrangères et résistance orthodoxe à Byzance (1373–1409)," in *Coloniser au Moyen Âge*, ed. M. Balard and A. Ducellier (Paris, 1995), pp. 367–85, with references to earlier studies on John VII. See also Reinert, "Palaiologoi," pp. 311–27.

[48] Loenertz, "Fragment," 37–8, 40.

[49] Laiou-Thomadakis, "Greek merchant," 108–9; Laiou-Thomadakis, "Byzantine economy," 220 and n. 25.

[50] Chrysostomides, "Venetian commercial privileges," 326–7, 352 (doc. 16); Thiriet, *Régestes*, vol. 1, no. 772. See also Ignatius of Smolensk, in *Russian Travelers to Constantinople in the Fourteenth and Fifteenth Centuries*, ed. and trans. G. P. Majeska (Washington, DC, 1984), pp. 100–1; cf. 410.

pretender had traveled to Genoa in search of help for his cause.[51] Yet, he did not consider the backing of the Genoese adequate, being well aware of the decisive role the Ottomans could play in his success. Consequently, he approached Bayezid I, who had ascended the Ottoman throne in 1389 following the death of Murad I. If John VII had inherited certain tactics from his father, Bayezid, it seems, had learned equally well his own father's diplomatic skills in sustaining the dissensions within the Byzantine imperial family. The Sultan, therefore, agreed to help John VII and contributed to the latter's takeover of Constantinople by sending him troops.[52]

Inside Constantinople, on the other hand, a large segment of the population favored John VII. In fact, John's entry into the city was facilitated by a group of common people, who opened the Charisios Gate through which he let his forces in. Once he was inside the capital, some coercion was used to oblige the inhabitants to recognize him as emperor, but in the end everyone acclaimed him and submitted to his rule.[53] John VII's reign was short-lived (April–September 1390), yet several years after his overthrow, during the early stages of Bayezid's siege of Constantinople – before 1399 at any rate – there was still a faction within the city, made up mainly of common people, that wanted to bring him back to power. According to Doukas, the "vulgar people" who wished to reinstate John VII were opposed to Manuel II, the Emperor occupying the throne since 1391 as successor to John V, on the grounds that he was not concerned with the salvation of the state and wanted to rule tyrannically.[54] In their eyes, John VII, who had been constitutionally invested with the right of succession in 1381,[55] was the legitimate heir to the throne rather than Manuel II, wherefore they viewed the latter as a usurper or a tyrant who was interested more in his own power than in the welfare of the state. John VII himself apparently made use of the same propaganda to win people over to his side, "day and night, shouting to anyone he met . . . that it is he who cares

---

[51] On this trip, see J. W. Barker, "John VII in Genoa: a problem in late Byzantine source confusion," *OCP* 28 (1962), 213–38; and the other references cited in Reinert, "Palaiologoi," p. 336 (n. 3).

[52] Schreiner, *Kleinchroniken*, vol. 1, Chr. 7/21, p. 68; Ignatius of Smolensk, in *Russian Travelers*, ed. Majeska, p. 100.

[53] Ignatius of Smolensk, in *Russian Travelers*, ed. Majeska, pp. 100–3; cf. 409–12.

[54] Doukas–Grecu, XIV.3, p. 83: "δῆμος" (line 18), "χυδαῖος λαός" (line 21). Note that in his account of the civil war between John V and John VI, Doukas uses almost the same words in reference to John VI's opponents in Constantinople: "οἱ τοῦ δήμου χυδαῖοι" (IX.4, p. 63, line 2). For similar accusations concerning Manuel's tyrannical rule in Thessalonike that compelled the inhabitants of that city to surrender to the Ottomans in 1387, see Dennis, *Letters of Manuel II*, no. 67, p. 187; Chalkok.–Darkó, vol. 1, p. 42.

[55] See p. 129 above.

more for the empire, not you [Manuel]."[56] The timing of the agitations of John VII's sympathizers against Manuel is also significant since they coincided with the siege of Constantinople by Bayezid, who had lent aid to John VII in 1390, posing as the defender of his legitimacy. Indeed, during the siege the Ottoman ruler used the same pretext once more and offered peace terms to the city that were conditional upon John VII's restoration to the throne.[57] Manuel's refusal to accept these terms, which prolonged the siege and prevented the establishment of peace with the Ottomans, was no doubt another major reason underlying the accusations of tyranny leveled against him by the common people who complained of his lack of concern with the salvation of the state.[58]

In addition to the common people, John VII's supporters in Constantinople included inhabitants of high social status. We know that shortly before John VII's entry into the city in April 1390 Emperor John V ordered the arrest of approximately fifty unidentified people who were plotting in favor of his grandson. Some in the group were punished by having their noses slit, and some were blinded.[59] The treatment accorded to these partisans of John VII suggests that they were people presumably of high rank, and not commoners like those who admitted him into the capital. Indeed, when John VII's movement failed and he was driven out of the capital, several *archontes* from Constantinople who favored him followed him to Selymbria. Komnenos Branas, who was married to the Emperor's "aunt" Anna Palaiologina, was one of them.[60] This couple had five children – three

---

[56] *Manuel Palaiologos, Dialogue with the Empress-Mother on Marriage*, ed. and trans. A. Angelou (Vienna, 1991), pp. 114–15.

[57] Doukas–Grecu, XIV.2, p. 83.

[58] It may well be that Manuel had these accusations in mind, as he incorporated into his *Dialogue on Marriage* – which he composed around this time, but extensively revised later on – the following passage that essentially aims to justify his resistance to Bayezid and to rectify his own image as "emperor" against, presumably, the current charges of tyranny: "I have never offended him [Bayezid]: it is just that I did not wish to do and did not give in to doing for him actions offensive in the eyes of those who want to live in piety, and in my own eyes, too, having such a sense of what is proper. An individual's duty is, I think, to choose to die, if the need arises, together with his people of the same race and faith; but a ruler's and an emperor's duty is to accept any risk in order to save his people, and to regard dying a light burden, whenever freedom is at stake and whenever the risk concerns . . . Faith." *Dialogue on Marriage*, ed. and trans. Angelou, pp. 98–9. Although the passage itself contains no explicit reference to Bayezid's siege of Constantinople, the link is suggested by the fact that it is immediately followed by an account of John VII's cooperation with Bayezid during the siege.

[59] Ignatius of Smolensk, in *Russian Travelers*, ed. Majeska, pp. 100–1.

[60] MM, vol. II, nos. 537 (Jan. 1400), 595 (Aug. 1400). See *PLP*, nos. 3177 and 21346. The *PLP* entry on Komnenos Branas mentions neither his move to Selymbria nor his affiliation with John VII. The entry on Anna Palaiologina, on the other hand, identifies the emperor whose aunt (θεία) she was as Manuel II. But it appears from the context of the patriarchal act of August 1400 where her relationship to the imperial family is asserted (MM, vol. II, no. 595) that the emperor in question is

sons who were all familiars (*oikeioi*) of John VII, and two daughters, one of whom was married to an *oikeios* Astras, who is almost certainly to be identified with Michael (Synadenos) Astras, the Emperor's (John VII?) "son-in-law."[61] The other daughter married an *oikeios* of the Emperor as well, by the name of Philip Tzykandyles. The dowry of the latter couple was in part provided by John VII and his mother, the Empress Maria.[62] Komnenos Branas died in Selymbria in the service of John VII before 1399. At the end of the same year, following the reconciliation of John VII with Manuel II, Branas' widow, Anna Palaiologina, returned to Constantinople together with the *archontes* in the young Emperor's retinue.[63] Here, then, is an example of an entire family of high-ranking individuals who had strong personal and political ties with John VII and remained unremittingly loyal to him even after he was ousted from power. Another likely partisan seems to be Manuel Taroneites, who left the capital "because of the troubles" (i.e. the civil war of John VII) but went back to the city shortly before the summer of 1400, at a time which coincides with the reconciliation between John VII and Manuel II.[64]

The aristocrats whom John VII used as agents in his aforementioned commercial deals with Genoa must be cited among his upper-class supporters, too, since they chose to work for John VII despite the latter's tense relations with the Emperor in Constantinople. Some of these people came from the capital's most distinguished families, as, for example, Manuel Kabasilas, George Goudeles, and Nicholas Notaras.[65] In recent decades, historians have uncovered the close economic and political ties of these

---

more likely to have been John VII, who was Emperor-regent in Constantinople at this time. For an *archon* Komnenos Branas, *doulos* of Emperor Andronikos IV in December 1376, who may perhaps be identical with John VII's partisan of the same name, see Kravari, "Philothéou," 323 (no. 6) and *PLP*, no. 93272.

[61] On Michael (Synadenos) Astras, see MM, vol. II, nos. 580 (June 1400), 533 (Nov. 1399). See also ch. 7 below, p. 161; *PLP*, no. 1599; Darrouzès, *Reg.*, pp. 341, 348, 381; cf. Kravari, "Philothéou," 318–19. Clearly, Michael Astras' qualification as the Emperor's γαμβρός, like all such qualifications denoting a relationship to the Byzantine ruler, should not be understood in a literal sense.

[62] MM, vol. II, no. 537, pp. 329–30. For the identification of the Emperor and Empress with John VII and his mother, see Darrouzès, *Reg.*, pp. 347–8. It is noteworthy that Philip Tzykandyles had formerly been a trusted servant of John V; he was present at Rome on the occasion of the Emperor's conversion to the Catholic faith in 1369, and in 1374 he acted as John V's envoy to the pope. When he attached himself to John VII remains uncertain, but it was he who prepared the Latin version of the treaty signed between the Venetians and John VII in June 1390. See Ganchou, "Autour de Jean VII," pp. 370–1 and nn. 26, 27.

[63] MM, vol. II, no. 537, p. 330. For another reference to the *archontes* who returned from Selymbria to the capital in the company of John VII and his mother following the reconciliation with Manuel II, see ibid., no. 556, p. 360.

[64] Ibid., no. 583 (June–July 1400), p. 404; cf. Darrouzès, *Reg.*, pp. 382–3.

[65] Barker, "John VII in Genoa," 236–7; Musso, *Navigazione*, no. 7, pp. 243–5; Balard, *Romanie génoise*, vol. II, p. 758.

three men and of their descendants with Italians.[66] It is now known that they not only engaged in business activities with Italy but also acquired Genoese or Venetian status, and in some cases they became naturalized citizens of both states, like Nicholas Notaras. Consequently, it has been suggested that the old interpretation of late fourteenth-century Byzantine civil wars "as mere internal squabbles of the imperial family, supported and fomented by Venice and Genoa, who acted for their own purposes" is no longer fully acceptable. On the basis of the new evidence revealing the material advantages that some members of the imperial family and certain aristocratic individuals derived from their association with Italians, it is now essential to recognize the role played by the economic interests of this group in the civil wars of the period.[67]

Among religious circles, too, John VII had some adherents who belonged to both the lower and the upper classes. In May 1390 the priests Andrew Rhadarites and Michael Sgouropoulos, who were accused of treachery against the emperor and the state, were forgiven by the patriarchal court of Constantinople, when they promised to be faithful to the emperor thereafter.[68] Since John VII had deposed his grandfather and established himself on the throne in April 1390, it appears at first that the emperor in question, unnamed in the patriarchal act of May 1390, was John VII, and that the two priests had conspired against him. It is known, however, that about three months after his accession to power, John VII installed a new patriarch. This was Makarios, whom Andronikos IV had elected as patriarch back in 1377, and who was removed from this post as soon as Andronikos fell from power.[69] The restoration of Makarios was probably John VII's response to the opposition he faced from the current patriarch Antonios, who was loyal to John V. It may, therefore, be concluded that the emperor mentioned in Patriarch Antonios' act was indeed John V, and that the priests charged with treason were partisans of John VII.

---

[66] Balard, *Romanie génoise*, vol. II, p. 758; Oikonomidès, *Hommes d'affaires*, pp. 20–1 and n. 4, 68, 120–2; Laiou-Thomadakis, "Byzantine economy," 199–201, 220–2; Laiou-Thomadakis, "Greek merchant," 108–9; K.-P. Matschke, "The Notaras family and its Italian connections," *DOP* 49 (1995), 62–72; K.-P. Matschke, "Personengeschichte, Familiengeschichte, Sozialgeschichte: Die Notaras im späten Byzanz," in *Oriente e Occidente tra Medioevo ed Età Moderna. Studi in onore di Geo Pistarino a cura di Laura Balletto* (Genoa, 1997), vol. II, pp. 797–812; Th. Ganchou, "Le rachat des Notaras après la chute de Constantinople ou les relations 'étrangères' de l'élite byzantine au XVe siècle," in *Migrations et diasporas méditerranéennes (Xe–XVIe siècles)*, ed. M. Balard and A. Ducellier (Paris, 2002), pp. 149–229, esp. 158ff. See also Barker, "John VII in Genoa," 229–31 (n. 3).
[67] Laiou-Thomadakis, "Greek merchant," 109.
[68] MM, vol. II, no. 416, pp. 140–1. See also nos. 547 and 554 for later activities of Michael Sgouropoulos.
[69] Ibid., p. 142; no. 417 (Aug. 1390); pp. 142–7. Cf. Darrouzès, *Reg.*, pp. 4–6, 12–13, 163–4, 166–9.

Shortly after John VII lost the throne Antonios was reinstated as patriarch and resumed his hunt for the religious supporters of the deposed Emperor. In April 1391 the patriarch pardoned two priests, the *orphanotrophos* George Kallistos and John Sigeros, who swore in writing that they would no longer refrain from commemorating the Emperors – John V, recently deceased, and Manuel II.[70] It has been pointed out that the misspelled and awkwardly drawn signatures of these two priests betray their low level of culture and education.[71] Hence, they must be included among the lower-class supporters of John VII. On the other hand, John Adeniates, who was involved in a plot against Manuel II about the time of John VII's expulsion from Constantinople (September 17, 1390), belonged to the imperial clergy and was of higher social standing. A patriarchal act drawn up against Adeniates in 1393 reports that he associated himself with a group of "lawless" and "wicked" men with whom he conspired against the Emperor and against the imperial capital. When their intrigues were uncovered, Adeniates, fearing that he might be denounced by some of his accomplices who had been caught and questioned, took flight to Pera. Despite the patriarch's call for his return to Constantinople and the advice of other members of the clergy that he try to seek Manuel II's pardon, Adeniates remained in Pera for about three years, in the course of which he continued his activities against the Emperor, denouncing the Church and the patriarch as well.[72] Given John VII's close ties with the Genoese, Pera was clearly the most obvious place for Adeniates to flee to for refuge. In fact, many people had flocked to Pera and formed a small clique there following John VII's fall from power. In 1391 Demetrios Kydones wrote a letter to Maximos Chrysoberges, who had recently become a Catholic and entered a Dominican monastery in Pera. Kydones stated in his letter that he wished to visit Chrysoberges, but was afraid of encountering in the Genoese colony "people from the other side."[73] Since Kydones always remained loyal to John V and Manuel II in the course of the civil wars of the late fourteenth century, he could have only meant by this expression the partisans of John VII who had established themselves in Pera and who no doubt shared with John VII a favorable disposition towards the Genoese.

Unfortunately, not as much information is available on the attitude of John VII's supporters towards his other foreign allies – the Ottomans. We possess no parallel examples of specific individuals among John VII's partisans, like the pro-Latin aristocrats or the high-ranking priest cited above,

---

[70] MM, vol. II, no. 420. I, p. 151.   [71] Darrouzès, *Reg.*, no. 2885, p. 176.

[72] MM, vol. II, no. 440 (Sept. 1393), pp. 172–4. Cf. Darrouzès, *Reg.*, pp. 204–5.

[73] Kydones–Loenertz, vol. II, no. 443, p. 411, line 74. Cf. Kalekas–Loenertz, p. 58.

whose political tendencies towards the Turks are known. We have, however, the eyewitness account of the Russian pilgrim Ignatius of Smolensk, who reports that the Ottoman soldiers accompanying John VII in 1390 were not allowed to enter Constantinople by the common people who opened the gates of the city to the young pretender.[74] This may have been a precaution resulting from the former experiences of the capital's population with Ottoman soldiers. It will be recalled, for example, that in his letter to John V quoted earlier, Pope Gregory XI had shown deep concern over the activities of Turks who entered Constantinople in large numbers between 1372/3 and 1375.[75] A Venetian document dating from April 9, 1390 reveals, moreover, that at the time of John VII's attack the takeover of the Byzantine capital by Bayezid I was foreseen as a strong possibility in Italy.[76] There may have been similar suspicions in Constantinople, which would further explain the hesitation of the Greek population to admit into their midst the soldiers sent to John VII's aid by the Ottoman ruler.

Despite all the support that John VII had procured, his reign nonetheless lasted merely five months. After two unsuccessful attempts together with "Frankish" forces, Manuel II finally chased John VII out of Constantinople on September 17, 1390, following another attack carried out with the help of the Hospitallers of Rhodes.[77] John V was thus restored, while his ousted grandson seems to have first fled to Pera[78] and then returned to his old residence in Selymbria.[79] Bayezid I, in the meantime, continued his efforts to weaken Byzantium. Turning his attention to the Byzantine capital, he ordered John V to tear down a recently refortified castle by the Golden Gate of Constantinople. At this time Manuel II was with Bayezid I, fulfilling the military obligation of Byzantium to the Ottomans. Since Bayezid threatened to imprison and blind Manuel, John V had no alternative except to obey the order.[80]

This was the last confrontation John V had with the Ottomans. Shortly thereafter he died (February 1391) and was succeeded by Manuel II, who managed to escape from Bayezid I's camp and installed himself on the throne before John VII could take any action. Even on this occasion,

---

[74] Ignatius of Smolensk, in *Russian Travelers*, ed. Majeska, pp. 100–1.

[75] See p. 120 and note 5 above.   [76] Thiriet, *Régestes*, vol. I, no. 772.

[77] Ignatius of Smolensk, in *Russian Travelers*, ed. Majeska, pp. 102–3, cf. 412–14; Schreiner, *Kleinchroniken*, vol. I, Chr. 7/21–2, 10/6. Cf. Reinert, "Palaiologoi," pp. 315–27.

[78] Iorga, *Notes*, vol. I, p. 50 (Sept. 21, 1390): "... *in ratione diverssarum expensarum, casu visitacionii domini Calojane.*"

[79] Barker, "John VII in Genoa," 223; Barker, *Manuel II*, pp. 78, 112 and n. 33.

[80] Ignatius of Smolensk, in *Russian Travelers*, ed. Majeska, pp. 102–5; Doukas–Grecu, XIII.3–4, pp. 75–7; Schreiner, *Kleinchroniken*, vol. I, Chr. 7/23. Cf. Barker, *Manuel II*, pp. 80, 467–8; Reinert, "Palaiologoi," pp. 303, 331–2, 342 (n. 41).

however, the Ottoman ruler was able to handle the situation in such a way as to derive some advantage out of it. From Bayezid's point of view, Manuel had defied him not just by secretly fleeing from his camp, but also by establishing himself as emperor on his own initiative, without consulting or waiting for the opinion of his overlord, the Sultan. Bayezid's strategy was to forgive Manuel's defiance and to recognize him as emperor in return for certain concessions. Thus, demanding obedience, subservience, and the fulfillment of the usual terms and conditions of vassalage, Bayezid additionally requested from Manuel the installation of a Muslim judge (kadi) inside Constantinople to settle the disputes involving the Ottoman merchants there.[81] Earlier the Sultan had perhaps already negotiated with John V for authorization to have a Muslim judicial functionary in the Byzantine capital, because two entries in the account book of the Genoese commune in Pera record expenditures in connection with the reception and transportation of a kadi in October 1390.[82] The repeated request in 1391 suggests, however, that either the practice was discontinued, or, what is more likely, the earlier arrangement had only permitted occasional visits by an Ottoman kadi rather than the permanent residence of one inside Constantinople. In 1391 Bayezid may have also demanded the establishment of a Turkish quarter, containing a mosque, within the city.[83] In the words that Doukas has put in his mouth, the Sultan then threatened Manuel,

---

[81] Doukas–Grecu, XIII.5, p. 77. Cf. Barker, *Manuel II*, pp. 82–6. It should be noted that in 1993 Reinert rejected Doukas' story of Manuel's secret flight from Bursa, suggesting instead that Manuel left for Constantinople with the full knowledge and consent of Bayezid, who favored his accession, and that the installation of a kadi may have already been negotiated between the two men prior to Manuel's departure: Reinert, "Palaiologoi," pp. 332–3, 363 (n. 168). More recently, however, Reinert has proposed a different reconstruction of events surrounding the establishment of the Ottoman kadi in Constantinople, which implicitly rules out the latter part of his earlier hypothesis, as he now dates to 1393/4 Bayezid's demand from Manuel regarding the kadi: S. W. Reinert, "The Muslim presence in Constantinople, 9th–15th centuries: some preliminary observations," in *Studies on the Internal Diaspora of the Byzantine Empire*, ed. H. Ahrweiler and A. E. Laiou (Washington, DC, 1998), pp. 144–7. For further controversy over the dating of the actual implementation of Bayezid's demand, see note 88 below.

[82] Iorga, *Notes*, vol. I, pp. 42 (October 20, 1390), 43 (October 28, 1390).

[83] There is considerable chronological confusion in the sources over these issues. While Doukas places Bayezid's demand for the installation of a kadi in the immediate aftermath of Manuel's accession to the throne (1391), Ottoman sources maintain that this and Bayezid's additional demands were made following the battle of Nikopolis (1396). According to Aşıkpaşazade (ed. Giese, pp. 61–2; ed. Atsız, p. 137), who provides the most detailed account, immediately after his victory at Nikopolis, Bayezid arrived before Constantinople with his army and demanded the city's surrender but then made peace when the Byzantine government agreed to the construction of a mosque (*mahalle mescidi*) and the installation of a kadi inside the city, in addition to the payment of an annual tribute of 10,000 gold pieces (*flori*). Thereupon Bayezid had the inhabitants of the fortresses of Göynük and Darakçı Yenicesi settled in Constantinople within the special quarter assigned to the Ottomans. After the battle of Ankara, the Byzantine Emperor expelled the Ottoman settlers and demolished their mosque. On the other hand, an entry in the *Annales ecclesiastici*, ed. O. Raynaldus and

saying, "If you do not wish to do and grant all that I command you, then shut the gates of the City and reign within. Everything outside the City is mine."[84]

Manuel's direct reply to Bayezid is not known. Judging from the course of events, however, it is almost certain that he conceded to the Sultan's demands. Only about three months after his accession Manuel was back in Asia Minor, fighting in another campaign of Bayezid.[85] Hence, as far as the military obligations of vassalage were concerned, the Emperor obediently fulfilled them as in the time of John V. The same must have been true of the tributary liability of Manuel's government. In order to pay the money demanded by the Sultan in 1391, the Emperor seems to have contemplated imposing extra taxes on the citizens of Constantinople, including even the untaxed poor, or perhaps resorting to confiscation of private property.[86] As to the installation of a kadi in Constantinople, some references in Genoese expense accounts for Pera reveal that it was undertaken before the end of 1391.[87] For Bayezid this was a matter of such importance that during Manuel's trip to western Europe (1399–1403), when John VII was temporarily placed on the throne, the Sultan made certain that the pre-existing agreement to house a kadi inside the Byzantine capital would be observed by John.[88] Bayezid's efforts to protect the rights of his subjects who were trading in Constantinople are indicative of the not negligible number of Ottoman Muslim merchants engaged in commercial relations with Byzantium at the end of the fourteenth century. For the Sultan this was not merely a tool to serve as a symbolic demonstration of his political supremacy over the Byzantine state but a measure founded upon the economic realities of his day. At this time, Bayezid also repeated to

---

C. Baronius, vol. XXVI (Bar-le-Duc, 1878), p. 540, no. 7, reports under the year 1393 Bayezid's demand for an Ottoman quarter, a mosque, and an annual tribute of 10,000 gold pieces.

[84] Doukas–Grecu, XIII.5, p. 77; trans. by Magoulias, *Decline and Fall*, p. 83. See also Kydones–Loenertz, vol. II, no. 442 (date: 1391), p. 407: "... τῶν μὲν βαρβάρων ἔξωθεν πάντα προειληφότων ..."

[85] Dennis, *Letters of Manuel II*, nos. 14–21, pp. 36–63. See also Barker, *Manuel II*, pp. 86–99, and for the date of Manuel's departure (June 8, 1391), p. 87, nn. 3–4.

[86] Kydones–Loenertz, vol. II, no. 442, p. 407 and no. 443, p. 410; see p. 128 and note 37 above. Cf. Matschke, *Ankara*, p. 69.

[87] Iorga, *Notes*, vol. I, pp. 47 (Oct. 16, 1391), 52 (Oct. 17, 1391); Belgrano, "Prima serie," no. 38 (May 24, 1392), pp. 171–2.

[88] Doukas–Grecu, XV.1, p. 87. Contrary to my interpretation, F. Dölger, "Johannes VII., Kaiser der Rhomäer 1390–1408," *BZ* 31 (1931), 31 and Barker, *Manuel II*, p. 86 (n. 2) have taken Doukas' statement as evidence that Bayezid's demand for the establishment of a kadi was not fulfilled by Manuel II in 1391, and that it was John VII who first carried it out after 1399. Reinert, too, has lately argued that Manuel rejected Bayezid's demand (made, according to this author, in 1393/4), which was put into effect only in 1399 by John VII: Reinert, "Muslim presence in Constantinople," pp. 144–7. See now Jacoby, "Foreigners and the urban economy," 121, n. 255, for a convincing rejection of Barker's and Reinert's view on this matter.

John VII his claim to all the territories outside the walls of Constantinople. According to Doukas, "John reigned only within the City."[89]

During the period between John V's death and the above-mentioned arrangement of 1399, John VII persisted in his dynastic ambitions and directed his attacks against Manuel II. In 1391 Kydones, describing the conflict between John VII and Manuel II, drew attention to how it strengthened the position of the Ottomans with respect to Byzantium:

[T]he old evil which caused the general ruin still rages. I mean the dissension between the emperors over the shadow of power. For this they are forced to serve the barbarian; it is the only way of being able to breathe. For everybody admits that to whomever of the two the barbarian gives his support that one will prevail in the future. Therefore the emperors by necessity become his slaves before the citizens and live according to his injunctions.[90]

Kydones' words demonstrate that Bayezid I, who twice – in 1391 and 1399 – made the assertion that Byzantine emperors ruled only within the walls of Constantinople, was not deluded by false visions of his power and influence.

Until his death in 1408 John VII remained a sporadic source of friction and controversy for Manuel II and for the Byzantine Empire at large. If, however, John VII's death brought to an end the recurrent problems generated since the early 1370s by this branch of the imperial family, there were still other dynastic crises awaiting the Palaiologoi. Following the temporary reversal in Byzantine–Ottoman diplomatic relations prompted by Bayezid's defeat at the battle of Ankara (1402), which empowered the Byzantine government to have its share in exploiting the rivalries between the deceased Sultan's many sons,[91] the Ottomans, having resolved their problems by the second quarter of the fifteenth century, started once again to take advantage of the internal squabbles that plagued the Byzantine court. As in the period prior to the battle of Ankara, the rivals in these conflicts often sought the aid of the Ottomans, thereby further endangering the strength and stability of the Byzantine state. In his funeral oration for the Emperor John VIII (d. 1448), Demetrios Katadoukinos alluded to plots against the ruler organized by his own brothers, who received help both from the Turks ("impious barbarians") and from members of the Byzantine elite (*archontes*).[92] The successive attempts by one of these brothers, Demetrios Palaiologos, the future Despot of the Morea, at cooperation

---

[89] Doukas–Grecu, XV.1, p. 87.
[90] Kydones–Loenertz, vol. II, no. 442, p. 407; trans. by Charanis, "Strife," 308–9.
[91] See above, ch. 2, pp. 33–4.   [92] "Comédie de Katablattas," ed. Canivet and Oikonomidès, 85.

with the Ottomans are well documented. In 1423 Demetrios is known to have fled to Pera, from where, according to one source (Sphrantzes), he intended to go over to the Turks.[93] At the time of the Council of Ferrara–Florence (1438–9), John VIII was reluctant to leave Demetrios at home and brought him along to Italy, suspecting that in his absence Demetrios might betray Constantinople, presumably to the Ottomans.[94] In 1442 Demetrios, disappointed by John VIII's choice of his other brother Constantine as successor to the throne and simultaneously denied certain territories which had been promised him, went over to Murad II from his appanage centered on Mesembria. Procuring an army from the Sultan, he led an unsuccessful attack against Constantinople which lasted three and a half months (April 23–August 6).[95] The deep distrust that the Palaiologos brothers cherished for each other, no doubt originating from conduct such as that of Demetrios, is revealed in a passage by Sphrantzes concerning John VIII's grant of Selymbria to Constantine in 1443. As one of Constantine's most trusted servants, Sphrantzes was appointed on this occasion to govern the town. The chronicler relates that Constantine sent him to Selymbria with specific instructions to guard the town not only against Murad II, but also against Demetrios Palaiologos and against John VIII.[96] According to this account, then, Constantine considered his own brothers to be enemies as threatening as the Ottoman ruler. Kydones, embittered and disheartened by similar circumstances in Constantinople back in 1385, had remarked:

To the foreign wars there has now been added civil strife, which formerly spread destruction everywhere and which the fault of all of us has now pushed to a point beyond repair. Nature is disregarded; family ties are merely a name; the one means of life is to betray one's own race and fellow citizens.[97]

Not much had changed more than half a century later. While the Ottomans were consolidating their power during these critical years, the chronic recurrence of civil wars in Constantinople proved to be fatal for Byzantium,

---

[93] Sphrantzes–Grecu, XII.2, p. 16; Schreiner, *Kleinchroniken*, vol. I, Chr. 13/8–9; vol. II, pp. 420–1; Syropoulos, *"Mémoires,"* II.11, p. 112. Demetrios was accompanied by Hilario Doria and the latter's son-in-law George Izaoul. But instead of going over to the Turks, Demetrios set out for Hungary a few days later.

[94] Schreiner, *Kleinchroniken*, vol. I, Chr. 22/43. Cf. Syropoulos, *"Mémoires,"* III.30, pp. 190–1, n. 5.

[95] Sphrantzes–Grecu, XXV.1,3, p. 64; Chalkok.–Darkó, vol. II, p. 80; Schreiner, *Kleinchroniken*, vol. I, Chr. 29/11, 62/10; vol. II, p. 461. Cf. Scholarios, *Œuvres*, vol. III, p. 118 [= *PP*, vol. II, p. 53]; Thiriet, *Régestes*, vol. III, nos. 2583, 2584. For further examples of Demetrios' cooperation with the Ottomans after he became Despot of the Morea in 1449, see below, ch. 10, pp. 278f.

[96] Sphrantzes–Grecu, XXV.6, p. 66.

[97] Kydones–Loenertz, vol. II, no. 309, lines 83–7; trans. by Dennis, *Reign of Manuel II*, p. 111.

particularly as the practice of calling upon the Turks for assistance was transformed into an almost routine custom by claimants to the throne.[98]

Having observed the cooperation of various members of the Byzantine imperial family with the Ottomans in the course of the dynastic struggles of the late fourteenth and early fifteenth centuries, we may now turn to an examination of the comparable conduct of certain palace officials in Constantinople who had recourse to the Ottomans in their own power struggles during the same period. In 1391 Kydones described this phenomenon as follows:

And within the City the citizens, not only the ordinary, but indeed also those who pass as the most influential in the imperial palace, revolt, quarrel with each other and strive to occupy the highest offices. Each one is eager to devour all by himself, and if he does not succeed, threatens to desert to the enemy and with him besiege his country and his friends.[99]

Kydones wrote these lines in connection with the conflict which broke out that year between Manuel II and John VII, with specific reference to the manipulative behavior of their respective supporters at the imperial court. However, the phenomenon he reports was not restricted to this particular event and persisted in later years, as suggested by the example of Theologos Korax, an official in the service of Manuel II, whose career closely corresponds to Kydones' description above. Because of his knowledge of Turkish, Theologos Korax frequently participated in embassies to the Ottomans as translator. This gave him the opportunity to acquaint himself with high-ranking officials in the Ottoman court, where he developed particularly close ties with Mehmed I's grand vizier Bayezid Paşa, a former Christian of Albanian origin. Theologos also won the trust of Mehmed I and was often admitted to the Sultan's dinner table. No one in the Byzantine court objected to Theologos' intimate relations with the Ottomans since he thereby transmitted information about what was taking place at the court of the Sultan. Indeed, as a result of his successful spying on behalf of the Byzantine Empire, Theologos was promoted from his original post as simple translator to that of imperial ambassador. Gradually, however, rumors began to be heard that Theologos was a traitor and that he had been double-dealing with the Ottomans. Finally, during Murad II's

[98] For a contemporary observation of the chronic nature of Byzantine civil wars, see Kydones–Loenertz, vol. II, no. 308, lines 17–18, where civil strife is likened to "a periodic attack of illness."

[99] Ibid., no. 442, lines 51–6; trans. by Charanis, "Strife," 309. For a similar statement by Manuel II concerning people from the Morea who entered the service of the Ottomans in search of wealth, glory, high posts, and material benefits, see below, ch. 9, p. 243 and note 37. For parallels from Thessalonike, see above, ch. 5, pp. 87f.

siege of Constantinople in 1422, Theologos, whom Manuel II sent to the Sultan to negotiate peace terms, was accused of having instead bargained for the governorship of the city, promising in return to guarantee its surrender to the Ottomans. When Theologos was consequently blinded and put into prison, where he survived only three days, Murad II is said to have become very upset. Upon finding out that one of Theologos' informers was a secretary of Byzantine origin at his own court called Michael Pylles, the Sultan had the latter immediately punished. As Michael Pylles had retained his Christian faith while serving the Sultan, the punishment that was deemed appropriate for him was to force him to choose between conversion to Islam or death. "Then," writes Doukas, "he who, according to his deeds, was a Turk before his apostasy, renounced his faith."[100]

Already during the very first years of the fifteenth century, while Timur was invading Asia Minor, Theologos Korax had given an initial sign of his accommodationist and conciliatory attitude towards the external enemies of Byzantium. At that time, Theologos, who was a local magistrate (ἐκ τῶν ἀρχόντων) in his native city Philadelphia, had proposed to his wealthy colleagues (πλούσιοι ὑπάρχοντες) that they should pay the tribute demanded by Timur in order to save their city. When the money was not found, many Christians died at the hands of Timur's forces, but Theologos seems to have suffered no harm, possibly because of an agreement he had made with the invaders.[101] As a result of this incident Theologos Korax may have developed a bad reputation among the Byzantine aristocracy, which, combined with the jealousies aroused by Manuel II's favorable treatment of him, might account for the rumors and suspicions concerning his later activities in Constantinople. Significantly, however, those who most vehemently opposed him in 1422 were not the aristocrats of the capital, but the Cretan guards defending the city against Murad II's forces.[102] Hence, Theologos' pact with the Sultan may be accepted as a reliable piece of information and need not be viewed as a story based merely on rumors and suspicions. Further evidence is provided, moreover,

---

[100] Doukas–Grecu, XXII.7, XXVIII.1–5, pp. 161–3, 229–35. For the translated statement, see Magoulias, *Decline and Fall*, p. 164. Cf. Balivet, *Romanie byzantine*, pp. 105–8; *PLP*, nos. 92415 and 23895.

[101] Doukas–Grecu, XXII.7, p. 161.

[102] Ibid., XXVIII.4, pp. 233–5. Contrasting the Cretans with Theologos Korax, Doukas describes the former as "the most faithful subjects of the empire, distinguished by their sacred zeal for the holy churches and their relics, and for the City's imperial prestige" (trans. by Magoulias, *Decline and Fall*, p. 162). Note the contrary impressions of Manuel Kalekas concerning the inhabitants of Crete, where he fled during Bayezid's siege of Constantinople: Kalekas–Loenertz, nos. 69 and 70 (1400). For the role of Cretans in the defense of Constantinople in 1453, see M. Manoussakas, "Les derniers défenseurs crétois de Constantinople d'après les documents vénitiens," *Akten des XI. internationalen Byzantinistenkongresses, München 1958* (Munich, 1960), pp. 331–40.

by a Venetian source which mentions the punishment accorded to a rich and powerful Byzantine called Theologos, who was blinded and deprived of his wealth in the hands of Greeks from Crete and Negroponte, following a deal he had made with the Sultan.[103] In 1418, on the other hand, a complaint was sent from Venice to Manuel II concerning the insults, ill-treatment, and physical harm inflicted upon Venetians in Constantinople by a certain Theologos, who may well have been Theologos Korax, and his son.[104] During the same year, in a distant region of the Byzantine Empire, a Greek by the name of "Coracha" (Korax?) attracted the attention of the Venetians for his leadership of Albanian troops, with whom he attacked the possessions of Venice in the Morea.[105] If the identifications proposed above are correct, then these last two references suggest that Theologos Korax and some members of his family steered a political course that was openly anti-Latin, in addition to the conciliatory politics they favored with regard to the Ottomans.

The passage by Kydones quoted above and the stories of Theologos Korax and Michael Pylles all illustrate the relative frequency and ease with which Byzantine officials went over to the Ottomans and made their services available to them during the fourteenth and fifteenth centuries. One explanation for the recurrence of this phenomenon lies in the flexibility and openness of the Ottoman administrative structure into which Byzantines and subjects from other neighboring Christian states were freely admitted. These Christians were not required to give up their religion as long as they were content with smaller posts, as, for instance, Michael Pylles' secretarial job. Rising up to higher positions, however, required conversion to Islam,[106] as in the case of Bayezid Paşa, formerly a Christian from Albania. The latter, who had reached the highest post of grand vizier among the Ottomans, had a brother called Hamza, who also served the Ottomans. Bayezid Paşa and Hamza established, moreover, marriage ties with the

---

[103] Dolfin, III, fol. 859, quoted in Iorga, *Notes*, vol. 1, p. 324, n. 1: "... *uno dicto Theologo, suo baron greco, de mazor del suo Conseio, più ricco; e de prexente, dado in le man di Greci de Candia e de Nigroponte, i fexe cavar gli occhi e tutto el suo haver, el qual, scasiado de fuora, fosse appresentado al signor Turco in suo confusion, per caxon cum lui haveva fatto el trattado.*" Doukas relates that after the blinding and imprisonment of Theologos, his house, filled with many treasures, was confiscated and burnt down: Doukas–Grecu, XXVIII.4, p. 235. The two accounts thus agree on all details except Theologos' death.

[104] Iorga, *Notes*, vol. 1, p. 276; Thiriet, *Régestes*, vol. II, no. 1688 (March 11, 1418). According to this document, Theologos owned a Turkish slave; see Necipoğlu, "Byzantines and Italians in fifteenth-century Constantinople," 133.

[105] Sathas, *Documents*, vol. III, pp. 175–6. Cf. Thiriet, *Régestes*, vol. II, no. 1697 (June 11, 1418).

[106] On this, see H. J. Kissling, "Das Renegatentum in der Glanzzeit des Osmanischen Reiches," *Scientia* 96 (1961), 18–26.

family of another Christian convert of Byzantine origin ('Ρωμαῖον τῷ γένει). This was Halil, the commander of Murad II's eastern forces, who became the brother-in-law of Bayezid and Hamza.[107] On Murad II's accession Bayezid Paşa is said to have given the following speech to a group of high-ranking military and civilian officials in the Ottoman court:

It is not necessary to remind you, men, or to lecture you on how we have been raised from our former humble station to a great destiny with God's sanction through the intercession of the Prophet [Muhammad] . . . Despite the power and dignity of their dominion, the Ottoman rulers wisely and prudently selected the most wretched and rural elements from the nations who do not worship the one God proclaimed by the Prophet and made them God-fearing and victorious officers and illustrious governors. I myself am one of those and so are most of you listening to my words . . . [108]

Although it is questionable that Bayezid Paşa actually uttered these words, the passage is of value because it reflects the upward social mobility that attracted many Byzantine subjects to the service of the Ottomans. But it was not only the "most wretched and rural elements" who were thus motivated; for example, neither Michael Pylles nor Theologos Korax can be considered individuals of low social standing. The former came from one of the "noble" families of Ephesus, while the latter was an *archon* in Philadelphia before he moved to Constantinople and entered the palace.[109] As Kydones indicated in 1391, many high-ranking officials employed in the Byzantine imperial palace turned to the Ottomans because they wished to attain even higher positions.[110] Their further advance in the Byzantine court was often impeded by their fall from favor as a result of palace intrigues and rivalries. The corruption and intrigues of certain imperial officials were the subject of another letter Kydones wrote in 1386 on behalf of his friend Theodore Kaukadenos, who would "not allow anyone to steal or embezzle public funds, as so many have been doing," yet who had lost his government post through the negative influence of "insolent people who seek to increase their own position at the expense of the empire."[111]

---

[107] Doukas–Grecu, XXVIII.12–13, pp. 239–41.

[108] Ibid., XXIII.2, pp. 169–71; trans. by Magoulias, *Decline and Fall*, pp. 130–1. See also Doukas' description of the janissary organization, through which the Ottomans raised Christian "shepherds, goatherds, cowherds, swineherds, farmers' children, and horsekeepers" to unthinkable glory: Doukas–Grecu, XXIII.9, p. 179.

[109] Ibid., XXVIII.5, XXII.7, pp. 235, 161. Likewise, some Thessalonians who sought political office in Ottoman service at the beginning of the fifteenth century were described as "prominent men" (οἱ δοκοῦντες) by Symeon of Thessalonike: see above, ch. 5, pp. 87–8 and note 15.

[110] See p. 142 and note 99 above.

[111] Kydones–Loenertz, vol. ii, no. 357, pp. 300–1. Cf. Dennis, *Letters of Manuel II*, pp. xlvii–xlviii; *PLP*, no. 11561.

The political fluctuations that accompanied the recurrent civil wars of the fourteenth and fifteenth centuries no doubt contributed to this problem. In the course of the civil war between John V and Andronikos IV, for instance, Theodore Potamios observed that a number of people won undeserved honors and wealth in Constantinople, while the majority of qualified citizens were displaced and had to endure hardships.[112] To certain displaced individuals such as these, a career in the Ottoman court may have appeared as an appealing alternative.

The incessant quarrels within the Byzantine court, both among members of the Palaiologos family and among government officials, coupled by the threatening military activities of the Ottomans in the vicinity of Constantinople, had a profound impact on the inhabitants of the imperial capital. In their discontent with the conduct of their rulers, some citizens of Constantinople appear to have considered an accord with the Ottomans as a remedy that might alleviate the extreme instability reigning within the Byzantine capital. During the 1380s Kydones observed that many people in Constantinople openly declared their preference for Ottoman rule and made fun of their compatriots who wished to live freely under Byzantine rule rather than submit to slavery under the Turks.[113] In contrast, those who preferred the Ottomans perceived submitting to the enemy as freedom.[114] What the latter meant by "freedom" can be interpreted, first, within the context of the Ottoman-Islamic law of conquest, as freedom from captivity in return for surrender. This was a freedom of which they would be deprived if Constantinople were to be taken by force, since they would all then be enslaved. In addition, however, their notion of freedom seems to have encompassed the desire for liberation from civil strife and maladministration, as revealed by another letter of Kydones written in 1391. Kydones points out that at this time "slavery" – that is, submission to the Ottomans – was regarded in Constantinople as "the only means capable of removing the internal ills."[115] Part of the city's population, judging that the realization of peace with the Ottomans could lead to the re-establishment of internal peace, spoke out in favor of surrendering to them. This act would

---

[112] G. T. Dennis (ed.), "The Letters of Theodore Potamios," in Dennis, *Byzantium and the Franks*, Study XII, pp. 17–18 (Letter 12, to Kydones, text), 32–3 (translation), 39 (commentary).

[113] Kydones–Loenertz, vol. II, no. 320, lines 10–14 (1383–4). See also no. 332, lines 29–31, for some common people of Thessalonike who wished to submit to the Ottomans in 1386–7, "ὑπὸ δεσπόταις ἄνωθεν ὄντες καὶ τῇ ταλαιπωρίᾳ συνειθισμένοι." It is possible to detect beneath this statement an indirect reference to the discontent of these Thessalonians with their Byzantine rulers. Cf. Balivet, "Personnage du 'turcophile'," 115–18.

[114] Kydones–Loenertz, vol. II, no. 360, lines 32–3 (1386, fall?).

[115] Ibid., no. 442, lines 39–40.

relieve them of the negative consequences of the presence of Ottoman forces outside the walls of Constantinople. These included the destruction and loss of the lands in the surrounding countryside, the disruption of agricultural production on the fields outside the city walls, heavy tribute obligation, and the spread of poverty, which were all factors conducive to intensifying the social tensions within the Byzantine capital.[116]

A patriarchal court register reports that before July 1391 a man called Nicholas Boulgaris went over to the Turks and converted to Islam. He later confessed that he had done this out of grief and distress (ἀπὸ λύπης). He returned to Constantinople in 1391 and, renouncing his newly acquired Muslim faith, reconverted to the Orthodox religion. He also promised to deliver his children to Constantinople so that they would be exposed to Christianity and raised as Christians.[117] Nicholas' wife is not mentioned in the patriarchal act; she may have been dead at this time, or a plausible alternative may be that Nicholas had married a Turkish woman whom he renounced as well when he abjured his Muslim faith. It would have been interesting to know whether his children, whose exposure to Christianity seriously concerned the members of the patriarchal court in Constantinople, were born of a Turkish mother. If, on the other hand, these children had been born in Constantinople before Nicholas fled to the Turks, this, too, would constitute an interesting case, indicating that he took his offspring along with him, or else had them transported shortly after his own flight to Turkish territory. Even though Nicholas afterwards regretted his action and returned to his country, what is of interest for present purposes is the reason underlying his decision to go over to the Turks in the first place. It will be recalled that in September 1390 the revolt of John VII in Constantinople had ended with the restoration of John V, and, following the latter's death in February 1391, Manuel II had ascended the throne. Conflicts soon picked up between Manuel II and John VII, but for a while it seemed as if the civil wars of the previous two decades were over and that internal peace was on the way to being re-established in Constantinople. Although the date of Nicholas Boulgaris' departure from Constantinople is not known, it may be safe to speculate that he had left during this twenty-year period of internal strife. Given that he returned to the capital in 1391 when things were calmer, an implicit reference to his discontent with the civil unrest of the preceding period can be detected in his claim that he had fled to the Turks "out of distress." It is conceivable that Nicholas, aggrieved by the state of affairs in Constantinople and longing for a more peaceful

---

[116] Ibid., nos. 442, 443. [117] MM, vol. II, no. 425, p. 155.

atmosphere, sought refuge with the neighboring Turks. He may therefore be placed among the same group of people whom Kydones reproached in 1383–4 for preferring the "barbarians" to rulers of their own race.[118] At least some of these people turned to the Ottomans in their dissatisfaction with the Byzantine ruling class, whose conduct not only hindered the establishment of peace in Constantinople but was in many ways the source of the civil discord that tormented them.[119]

Nicholas Boulgaris' return to Constantinople in 1391 may have been motivated, as suggested above, by the temporary calm experienced in the wake of the suppression of John VII's revolt. Future events were to indicate, however, that Boulgaris had perhaps not picked the best time to desert the Ottomans. A few years later the Byzantine capital was blockaded by the forces of Bayezid I, and it remained under siege for eight consecutive years between 1394 and 1402. During this period, most inhabitants of the city suffered from hardships and deprivations of varying degrees and kinds, including, above all, hunger and famine, impoverishment, and loss of relatives or friends.[120] We shall proceed in the next chapter with an analysis of the impact of Bayezid's siege on social and economic conditions in Constantinople[121] and then examine the role that these conditions played on the political attitudes of the citizens.

[118] See note 113 above.

[119] During the civil war between John V and John VI (1341–7), Michael Doukas had left Constantinople and sought refuge with the Turkish emir of Aydın in Ephesus for similar reasons. His grandson, the historian Doukas, writes that Michael "τὴν μετοικίαν ὡς πατρίδα ἐνηγκαλίσατο καὶ τὸν ἀλλογενῆ καὶ βάρβαρον ὡς θεόστεπτον ἔσεβε καὶ ἐτίμα, εἰς νοῦν λαμβάνων τὰς ἀτασθαλίας τῶν Ῥωμαίων . . ." (Doukas–Grecu, V.5, p. 47).

[120] See D. Bernicolas-Hatzopoulos, "The first siege of Constantinople by the Ottomans (1394–1402) and its repercussions on the civilian population of the city," *ByzSt* 10/1 (1983), 39–51.

[121] For a partial discussion of selected aspects of this complex topic, see N. Necipoğlu, "Economic conditions in Constantinople during the siege of Bayezid I (1394–1402)," in *Constantinople and its Hinterland*, ed. C. Mango and G. Dagron (Aldershot, 1995), pp. 157–67.

CHAPTER 7

The first challenge: Bayezid I's siege of Constantinople (1394–1402)

Ottoman troops roaming the outskirts of Constantinople had seized almost all the lands surrounding the city by the year 1391, that is, a few years before Bayezid I embarked upon the actual siege operations.[1] During the siege, therefore, the control of these areas, besides depriving the capital's inhabitants of agricultural products grown there, enabled Bayezid to restrict overland movements to and from the city and thus prevent the transportation of food supplies and other necessities from elsewhere. The city's gates seem to have remained closed throughout most of the blockade. In a fairly short speech written to commemorate the termination of the siege Demetrios Chrysoloras makes three allusions to the closed gates of the beleaguered capital, indicating the strong impact that this situation must have had on the citizens.[2] According to an anonymous eyewitness account of the siege, Ottoman ships that patrolled the waters around Constantinople prohibited access to its harbor and limited contact with the outside world by means of the sea as well.[3] Indeed, Bayezid's strategy was to ensure the surrender of the Byzantine capital by pushing its population to starvation in this manner.[4] Almost as soon as the siege started, therefore, scarcity of food became such a serious threat that Manuel II was compelled to turn immediately to Venice for grain supplies. However, the Emperor's

---

[1] In addition to the references cited in note 84 of ch. 6 above, see I. M. Konidares and K. A. Manaphes, "Ἐπιτελεύτιος βούλησις καὶ διδασκαλία τοῦ οἰκουμενικοῦ πατριάρχου Ματθαίου Αʹ (1397–1410)," ΕΕΒΣ 45 (1981–2), 478 (= H. Hunger, "Das Testament des Patriarchen Matthaios I. (1397–1410)," BZ 51 (1958), 299); English trans. in BMFD, vol. IV, p. 1637; cf. Schreiner, Kleinchroniken, vol. I, Chr. 70/8, p. 544.

[2] "Action de grâces de Démétrius Chrysoloras à la Théotocos pour l'anniversaire de la bataille d'Ankara (28 Juillet 1403)," ed. P. Gautier, REB 19 (1961), 352, 354, §§ 9, 14, 15.

[3] Gautier (ed.), "Récit inédit," 106.

[4] Several fifteenth-century sources explicitly mention Bayezid's starving out strategy: Gautier (ed.), "Récit inédit," 106; Doukas–Grecu, XIII.7, p. 79; Chalkok.–Darkó, vol. I, p. 78; Neşrî, Kitâb-ı Cihan-nümâ, vol. I, p. 327. See also E. A. Zachariadou, "Prix et marchés des céréales en Romanie (1343–1405)," Nuova rivista storica 61 (1977), 298–9; Matschke, Ankara, pp. 126–8; Bernicolas-Hatzopoulos, "First siege," 39–40.

149

repeated appeals to the Senate of Venice between 1394 and 1396 received positive responses on three occasions only, once each year. At the end of 1394, the Senate ordered the shipment of 1,500 *modioi* (351 tons) of grain to Constantinople, the following year 7,000–8,000 *staia* (441–504 tons), and an unspecified amount in March 1396.[5] Apart from the relatively small size of these annual shipments, it is not even certain that they ever reached Constantinople past the Ottoman ships that guarded the entrance to the city's harbor.

The Byzantine capital may have experienced some relief from the constraints of the blockade at the time of the Crusade of Nikopolis, which engaged most of Bayezid's armed forces in the Balkans during part of 1396. Nonetheless, immediately following his victory at Nikopolis (September 25, 1396), the Ottoman ruler brought his army back before Constantinople and, tightening his grip on the city, demanded its surrender.[6] Thereafter, until the end of the siege in 1402, all sources reiterate the exhausted state of food reserves and the constant outbreaks of famine, which were accompanied by frequent deaths and numerous cases of flight from the city, sometimes to the Italians, sometimes to the Ottomans.[7]

In a letter written in the fall of 1398 Manuel Kalekas describes how the population of Constantinople was worn out by famine and poverty.[8] About two years earlier Kalekas had moved from the Byzantine capital to Genoese Pera, in part to avoid the siege and its privations, following the example of many other people who had lost hope after Nikopolis and fled from the city, leaving it "deserted like a widow."[9] In 1400 Kalekas again wrote about a famine and lack of necessities that afflicted those who stayed behind in Constantinople. He was on the Venetian island of Crete at this time where, just like in Pera, a fairly sizable group of Constantinopolitan refugees had taken up residence.[10] The historian Chalkokondyles, too, reports the death and flight of large numbers of famine stricken inhabitants, but he draws

---

[5] Thiriet, *Régestes*, vol. i, nos. 868 (Dec. 23, 1394), 892 (Dec. 9, 1395), 901 (March 1, 1396). For the conversion of *modioi* and *staia* to kgs/tons, see J.-Cl. Cheynet, E. Malamut, and C. Morrisson, "Prix et salaires à Byzance (Xe–XVe siècle)," in *Hommes et richesses dans l'Empire byzantin*, vol. ii, ed. V. Kravari, J. Lefort, and C. Morrisson (Paris, 1991), p. 344 (Table 3).

[6] Doukas–Grecu, XIV.i, pp. 81–3; Aşıkpaşazade–Giese, pp. 60–1 (= Aşıkpaşazade–Atsız, pp. 136–7).

[7] The only exception to this grim picture concerning the period 1397–1402 is one instance in 1397 when provisions sent from Trebizond, Amastris, Kaffa, Venice, Mytilene, and some other islands temporarily improved the diet and morale of the underfed Constantinopolitans: see the Latin translation of the Bulgarian Chronicle of 1296–1413 by V. Jagić, in J. Bogdan, "Ein Beitrag zur bulgarischen und serbischen Geschichtsschreibung," *Archiv für slavische Philologie* 13 (1891), 542.

[8] Kalekas–Loenertz, no. 48, p. 235.

[9] Ibid., no. 17, p. 190; see also nos. 23, 42, 48 for other references to flight from Constantinople during 1397–8 because of the Ottoman blockade. On Kalekas' stay in Pera (1396–9), see ibid., pp. 27–31.

[10] Ibid., no. 69. On Kalekas' residence at Crete (1399–1400), see ibid., pp. 31–9.

attention to those who went over to the Ottomans rather than to territories under Genoese or Venetian rule as in the previous examples.[11] Likewise, the aforementioned anonymous eyewitness of the siege notes that many citizens fled to the Ottomans, openly as well as in secret, because of the severity of the famine.[12] According to Doukas, moreover, shortly after the Ottoman victory at Nikopolis the majority of the people began to contemplate surrendering the city to Bayezid as they could no longer endure the famine and shortages, but they changed their minds as soon as they recalled how the Turks had destroyed the cities of Byzantine Asia Minor and subjected their inhabitants to Muslim rule.[13] Nonetheless, Doukas' account of later events reveals that around 1399 the persistence of the siege and famine gave rise to a new wave of agitation among the common people of the capital in favor of surrender.[14]

Concerning the last stages of the siege, sources are even more emphatic about the harsh famine conditions and give graphic descriptions of the consequent flight of citizens in order to deliver themselves to the Ottomans standing guard outside the city walls. In an encyclical composed in the sixth year of the siege, the Patriarch Matthew refers more than once to a severe famine. In the same text the patriarch also relates that he pronounced sentences of excommunication against certain Byzantine ambassadors, whom he suspected of intending to negotiate with Bayezid I the city's surrender.[15] While the patriarch does not explicitly draw any causal links between the famine and the concurrent arrangements for surrender, other sources are more direct in expressing such links. For example, the author of the exploits of the French Marshal Boucicaut recounts how the starving citizens of Constantinople, because they could not bear the outbreak of a serious

---

[11] Chalkok.–Darkó, vol. I, p. 77. Mistaken about the length of the siege, Chalkokondyles writes that it lasted ten years.

[12] Gautier (ed.), "Récit inédit," 106.

[13] Doukas–Grecu, XIV.1, pp. 81–3. For further evidence on the impact of the Ottoman victory at Nikopolis, see Manuel II's letter, written during the month immediately following the battle, where the Emperor implies that certain Byzantines who were impressed by the Ottomans' military superiority were converting to Islam: Dennis, *Letters of Manuel II*, no. 31, pp. 83–5, lines 62–79. Another allusion to the conversion of Byzantines to Islam can be found in Joseph Bryennios' letter to Maximos Chrysoberges, written shortly after the battle of Nikopolis, which suggests moreover that the converts (οἱ πρὸς τὰ τῶν Ἀγαρηνῶν μεταβάλλοντες) engaged in proselytizing activity: "Ἐκ τῆς βυζαντινῆς Ἐπιστολογραφίας," ed. Tomadakes, 309–14 (letter 10) (= Ἰωσὴφ μοναχοῦ τοῦ Βρυεννίου, vol. III: Τὰ παραλειπόμενα, ed. T. Mandakases [Leipzig, 1784], pp. 148–55). The main purpose of Bryennios' letter, however, is to dissuade Maximos Chrysoberges, ὁ ἀπὸ Γραικῶν Ἰταλὸς τῆς τάξεως τῶν Κηρύκων, from his efforts to convert the Orthodox to the Catholic faith. For the date, see R.-J. Loenertz, "Pour la chronologie des oeuvres de Joseph Bryennios," *REB* 7 (1949), 20–2. For later evidence of conversion to Islam in the face of the growing power and military successes of the Ottomans in the 1420s, see below, ch. 8, pp. 199–200 and note 62.

[14] Doukas–Grecu, XIV.4, p. 85.   [15] MM, vol. II, no. 626, pp. 463–4.

famine *circa* 1400, escaped from the city by lowering themselves with ropes down the walls at night and turned themselves in to the Ottomans. Bouci-caut's lieutenant Jean de Chateaumorand, who was in Constantinople from 1399 to 1402, tried to reduce the hunger problem by sending his soldiers on small-scale plundering expeditions into the surrounding countryside whenever circumstances made it possible for them to slip out of and then back into the city without being noticed by the Ottomans.[16] The anony-mous eyewitness to the siege likewise indicates that Constantinople was seized by a terrible famine at the outset of 1400, which caused everyone to lose hope and compelled the majority of the inhabitants to go over to the enemy. Meanwhile a large group of men and women who managed to escape from the city by sea fell captive to the Turks near Abydos and Sestos as they were trying to sail through the Dardanelles.[17] Finally, with reference to the spring–summer of 1402 a short chronicle notice reports that, as everyone inside Constantinople was famished, the populace took flight, while at the same time an embassy set out to deliver the city's keys to the Ottoman Sultan.[18]

The direct economic outcome of food shortages, on the other hand, was a sharp increase in prices, not only of foodstuffs, but also of fields and vineyards within the city. Although we do not possess numerical data con-cerning a wide range of food products, we do nonetheless have information about the most basic item of consumption in every Constantinopolitan's daily diet, namely wheat, on the basis of which we may postulate a general upward trend in food prices during the siege years. From about 1399 to 1402 wheat prices in Constantinople varied between 20 and 31 *hyperpyra* per *modios* (= 234 kg).[19] By contrast, in September–October 1402, only a

[16] *Le livre des fais du bon messire Jehan le Maingre, dit Bouciquaut, mareschal de France et gouverneur de Jennes*, ed. D. Lalande (Geneva, 1985), I.35, pp. 152–3. See also D. A. Zakythinos, *Crise monétaire et crise économique à Byzance du XIIIe au XVe siècle* (Athens, 1948), p. 110, for a reference, in a text written by Christine de Pisan (1364–1431), to the famine in Constantinople at the time of Chateaumorand's stay.

[17] Gautier, "Récit inédit," 106.

[18] Schreiner, *Kleinchroniken*, vol. 1, Chr. 22/28, p. 184. See also the references, without any indication of date, to deaths, flight, and decision to surrender because of famine, which seem most likely to be alluding to circumstances during the last years of the siege, in Kritob.–Reinsch, I.16,10, pp. 32–3; G. Th. Zoras (ed.), Χρονικὸν περὶ τῶν τούρκων σουλτάνων (κατὰ τὸν Βαρβερινὸν Κώδικα 111) (Athens, 1958), p. 35.

[19] These prices are reproduced, with references to the sources, but calculated per *modios thalassios* (= 1/18 *modios*), in Cheynet, Malamut, and Morrisson, "Prix et salaires," p. 360 (Table 9: nos. 70, 74, 77), and also in the updated list now available in C. Morrisson and J.-Cl. Cheynet, "Prices and wages in the Byzantine world," in *EHB*, vol. II, pp. 827–8 (Table 5). The evidence from Doukas (ed. Grecu, p. 85) that a *modios* of wheat cost more than 20 *hyperpyra*, which appears under the year 1390 in both of these tables, should preferably be dated to *c*. 1399. An additional piece of evidence, not listed in either table, indicates without giving a precise date that at the time of the siege one

few months after the termination of the siege, the price of one *modios* of wheat immediately dropped down to 7 or 8 *hyperpyra*, and by 1436 further down to 4–6.25 *hyperpyra*, reaching a level comparable to recorded pre-siege prices of 5 *hyperpyra* (in 1343) and 6.75 *hyperpyra* (in 1366) per *modios*.[20] There were not too many Constantinopolitans who could afford the cost of their daily bread corresponding to the exorbitant siege-time wheat prices, which are roughly three to seven times higher than the attested pre- and post-siege prices. Consequently, the meager supplies were used up mostly by the rich, while part of the remaining population either felt constrained to leave the city or contemplated surrendering to the Ottomans in order to avoid starvation.

There is also some evidence indicating that fields and vineyards in the interior of Constantinople rose in value as the possibility of agricultural production outside the city walls declined, side by side with declining imports. At some time between late 1397 and 1399, a field of 44 *modioi* was sold for 800 *hyperpyra* – that is, slightly over 18 *hyperpyra* per *modios*.[21] In 1401 another field, measuring 8 *mouzouria*, went on sale at a price of 160 *hyperpyra*, or approximately 20 *hyperpyra* per *modios*.[22] Although data permitting a direct comparison of these prices with those before or after the siege are lacking for Constantinople, no field price exceeding 1.5 *hyperpyra* per *modios* is attested in the rest of the empire throughout the fourteenth century, with only one exception in Christoupolis, where a price of 12 *hyperpyra* per *stremma* has been registered for 1365, which is still far below the Constantinopolitan figures quoted above.[23] On the other hand, vineyard prices in Constantinople recorded for the years 1397–1401 range between approximately 30 and 45 *hyperpyra* per *modios*.[24] In this case, too, the absence of any earlier or later price information in relation to the capital's vineyards makes a direct comparison impossible, but available fourteenth-century figures from other parts of the empire, ranging roughly between 7 to 15 *hyperpyra* per *modios* and 3 to 12 *hyperpyra* per *stremma*, are much lower than the prices encountered in Constantinople at the time

mouzourion of wheat cost 100 aspers, but this information is problematic because of the uncertain nature of the units in which the price and volume are expressed: see Schreiner, *Kleinchroniken*, vol. I, Chr. 22/26, p. 184.

[20] In 1366 lower prices of 4 and 4.5 *hyperpyra* per *modios* are attested too, though for rotten and for inferior quality wheat, respectively. For all the pre- and post-siege figures cited here, see Morrisson and Cheynet, "Prices and wages," pp. 826–8 (Table 5).

[21] MM, vol. II, no. 528 (Oct. 1399), p. 304.   [22] Ibid., no. 678 (Nov. 1401), p. 558.

[23] See Morrisson and Cheynet, "Prices and wages," pp. 819–20 (Table 4). For the land in Christoupolis, see Cheynet, Malamut, and Morrisson, "Prix et salaires," p. 346 (Table 4).

[24] MM, vol. II, nos. 550 (Nov. 1397), 569 (April 1400), 678 (Nov. 1401), pp. 349, 383–4, 558.

of the siege.[25] Thus, it may be concluded that productive land inside the besieged city, including vineyards, became more expensive, which in turn must have further contributed to the increase already observed in food prices on the basis of available data on wheat.

Faced with this critical situation, the Byzantine government seems to have taken some measures in order to supply the capital with cheaper grain. A *prostagma* of Manuel II for the monastery of Lavra reveals that until 1405 the Athonite monastery was required to deliver annually a certain amount of wheat to Constantinople from its holdings on the island of Lemnos at the low price of 4 *hyperpyra* per *modios*. On May 25, 1405, the Emperor exempted the monastery from this obligation with the condition that, if a famine were to occur in Constantinople, the "customary" delivery of wheat at the aforementioned price would be resumed. The document does not specify since when this "customary" obligation had been in effect, but it may well have been an emergency measure dating from the time of Bayezid's blockade to guarantee the flow of some grain into Constantinople at prices substantially lower than the current market price, probably for distribution to needy citizens.[26]

Yet, apart from a measure such as this one, the Byzantine government was not in a state to provide much help to the poor citizens of Constantinople, given its depleted treasury and severe financial troubles, which prompted the Emperor at some point during the siege to order the removal of two out of the five golden disks that decorated the church of Hagia Sophia, no doubt to be melted down and struck as coins.[27] There is also evidence that Manuel II tried to raise a loan from Venice at the end of 1395, offering the tunic of Christ and other highly venerated relics as securities.[28] However, the Emperor's offer was turned down by the Venetian authorities, who feared that the exchange of these sacred objects might give rise to a popular agitation in the Byzantine capital.[29] Whether this was a real concern or

---

[25] See Morrisson and Cheynet, "Prices and wages," pp. 832–3 (Table 7); Cheynet, Malamut, and Morrisson, "Prix et salaires," p. 348 (Table 5). Even the price of 25 *hyperpyra* per *modios* attested in Thessalonike in 1396, at a time when the city was under Ottoman rule, is lower than the prices in Constantinople.

[26] *Lavra*, vol. III, no. 157, p. 142. The quantity due was 2 *modioi* of wheat for every *doulikon zeugarion* of land Lavra possessed on Lemnos. Since conditions in Constantinople would not have immediately returned to normal once the siege was over, Lavra's obligation must have been maintained for nearly three more years, thus coming to be regarded as a customary tax in kind. The conditional exemption indicates that as late as May 25, 1405 a famine was still anticipated.

[27] *Bondage and Travels of Schiltberger*, p. 80. Depending on the date of this event, the unidentified Emperor could be either Manuel II or John VII.

[28] Thiriet, *Régestes*, vol. I, no. 892 (Dec. 9, 1395).

[29] Ibid., no. 896 (Feb. 17, 1396); N. Iorga, "Veneţia in Mare Neagră," *Analele Academiei Române, Memoriile secţiunii istorice*, ser. 2, 36 (1913–14), 1115–16; G. T. Dennis, "Official documents of Manuel II Palaeologus," *B* 41 (1971), 46–7.

just a pretext on the part of Venice, the crucial point is that the Emperor never received the loan he asked for. Also indicative of the Byzantine government's financial difficulties is a deliberation of the Senate of Venice on June 30, 1396 regarding the lending of 150 *hyperpyra* to Manuel II for the repairs to the Venetian vice-*bailo*'s residence in Constantinople.[30] The Emperor evidently chose to borrow this sum as he must have had more pressing needs than the maintenance of the Venetian vice-*bailo*'s house to which to allocate his limited government funds within the besieged capital. Indeed, imperial agents tried every means during this period to boost up the state's financial resources. Thus, at some time between 1397 and 1398 Manuel Kalekas complained to Manuel II on behalf of a friend who was deprived of his legal inheritance by the fisc. When a distant relative of this man died, the fisc appropriated all the property of the deceased on the grounds that he had no surviving close relatives. Yet, the fisc was legally entitled in such cases to only one-third of the dead man's property, while his distant relatives had the right to one-third as well, the final third being reserved for donation to pious foundations.[31] The fisc's appropriation of all the possessions of this man in violation of the law can be seen as a sign of the financial straits that the Byzantine government was in at this time. The situation was so serious that even the Patriarch Matthew lent his aid to the government's search for extra funds, writing to the metropolitan of Kiev in 1400 that "giving for the sake of guarding the holy city [Constantinople] is better than works of charity and alms to the poor and ransoming captives; and that he who is doing this will find a better reward before God than him who has raised up a church and a monastery or than him who has dedicated offerings to them."[32]

The circumstances were equally distressing for some small to middle-sized business owners within the food sector of the economy, among them bakers, who were hit very hard not only by the short supply and high cost of grain, but also by the growing scarcity of wood in the city.[33] In October 1400 the baker Manuel Chrysoberges, finding himself reduced to extreme poverty and heavily indebted "because of the constraint and force of the war," decided to sell a house which he had bought for 14 *hyperpyra* three

---

[30] Thiriet, *Régestes*, vol. I, no. 911.

[31] Kalekas–Loenertz, no. 34, pp. 213–16. See *Jus graecoromanum*, ed. I. Zepos and P. Zepos, vol. I (Athens, 1931), p. 534.

[32] MM, vol. II, no. 556, p. 361; trans. by Barker, *Manuel II*, p. 203. In the translation I have rendered the word λειτουργίας not as "liturgies" but as "works of charity," following D. Obolensky, "A Byzantine grand embassy to Russia in 1400," *BMGS* 4 (1978), 131, n. 36. Darrouzès has dated this letter to March 1400: *Reg.*, pp. 360–1.

[33] On the lack of wood for cooking as well as for heating purposes, see Doukas–Grecu, XIII.7, p. 79; MM, vol. II, nos. 571 (May 1400) and 613 (Nov. 1400). Cf. Bernicolas-Hatzopoulos, "First siege," 49–50.

years earlier. He had spent all his dowry goods on the house, and was now left without any means to pay off his outstanding debts or to meet his personal needs.[34] The gradual impoverishment of this baker, who in the course of Bayezid's siege used up all his resources and accumulated debts beyond his means, was undoubtedly related to the state of the grain market and other subsidiary markets that affected his business. Two partners who ran a bakery and decided to dissolve their partnership during the siege must have experienced similar hardships. While one of these partners who had provided the bakery shop and a pack animal managed to retain his possessions, the other who had contributed a sum of 30 *hyperpyra* lost his money.[35]

Wine was another commodity of everyday consumption that was difficult to find in the besieged capital.[36] Consequently, some people who were involved in the wine business encountered financial problems too. Towards the end of 1400 the tavernkeeper Stylianos Chalkeopoulos was summoned before the patriarchal court when two of his creditors filed suit against him. At the very beginning of the siege Stylianos had borrowed from them 300 *hyperpyra*, promising to repay the sum within three years. Yet twice this length of time had gone by, and he still had not paid back his creditors. Although at the end of 1400 he made another promise to repay them within six months, and despite the fact that he owned shops in the Kynegoi quarter with an overall value exceeding 400 *hyperpyra*, this tavernkeeper clearly suffered from a shortage of cash, which may be a sign of the problems that hit the wine business due to the extended blockade.[37]

Besides these small shopkeepers who worked with relatively moderate amounts of capital, some wealthier tradespeople as well, both within and outside the food sector, although they certainly did much better at this time, suffered certain losses or misfortunes. When, for instance, the cloth merchant Koumouses died in about 1397, he left his wife and six surviving sons an inheritance worth 7,030 *hyperpyra*. Yet an inventory of all the movable and immovable property he bequeathed revealed that the fabrics in his shop, appraised at 700 *hyperpyra*, had been either lost or stolen; his

[34] MM, vol. II, no. 609, pp. 441–2. For the date, see Darrouzès, *Reg.*, pp. 401–2. Although the document refers to the purchase and sale (ἠγόρασε, πωλῆσαι) of the house by the baker, strictly speaking the transactions in question involved a lease and its transfer.
[35] MM, vol. II, nos. 631 and 635. These acts have been dated to March–April 1401 by Darrouzès: *Reg.*, pp. 413–14, 419, 422–3. See also MM, vol. II, no. 554 (February–March 1400), for the sale of a bakery for 50 *hyperpyra*.
[36] Doukas–Grecu, XIII.7, XIV.4, pp. 79, 85.
[37] MM, vol. II, no. 617. Darrouzès has dated this act to December 20, 1400: *Reg.*, p. 408. The two creditors were *kyr* Nicholas Makrodoukas, *oikeios* of the Emperor, and *kyr* Loukas Linardos.

vineyard, worth 900 *hyperpyra*, had been destroyed and lay unproductive; he owed the banker Sophianos 100 *hyperpyra*; and a business trip which his eldest son Alexios had taken brought no profit to the family but rather resulted in a further loss of 300 *hyperpyra*. Nonetheless, after adjustments were made that took account of these losses and deficits, Koumouses' inheritors still received the fairly large sum of 5,030 *hyperpyra*, which they divided between themselves.[38] Two other shop owners, Theodore Barzanes and Michael Monembasiotes, also managed to survive despite relatively minor constraints due to the siege. While Barzanes complained in 1397 that the common poverty and misery that prevailed in the city had affected his circumstances negatively, nonetheless his recently deceased wife (the daughter of a certain Kaloeidas) left behind an inheritance of 2,250 *hyperpyra*, which was largely made up of immovables within Constantinople, including a garden, a vineyard, several houses (one of which is described as "newly built"), various workshops worth 200 *hyperpyra*, and a bakery with a value of 110 *hyperpyra*. Entitled to one-third of this inheritance, Barzanes could not have been truly desperate in economic terms.[39] As for Michael Monembasiotes, he was able to keep both a tavern and a soap-manufacturing shop in operation during the siege even though the tavern had undergone a 35 percent depreciation in value by the year 1400.[40]

While the Ottomans were primarily responsible for the shortage of provisions and other economic problems that afflicted the inhabitants of Constantinople in varying degrees, a small group of Byzantines who engaged in profiteering activities further aggravated the conditions inside the capital. Taking advantage of the adverse circumstances, these people pushed prices to levels which only the wealthiest among the citizens could afford to pay. For instance, John Goudeles, a member of one of the capital's prominent aristocratic families, made huge profits by selling wheat at the inflated price of 31 *hyperpyra* per *modios*. In order to acquire this wheat, Goudeles had taken a trip to the island of Chios on his own ship.[41] The risks involved in such a venture are indicated by the contemporary experiences of another Byzantine merchant, Constantine Angelos, who fell captive to the Turks during a business trip from Constantinople to

---

[38] MM, vol. II, no. 566 (April 1400), pp. 377–9. Cf. K.-P. Matschke, "Chonoxio – Cumicissi – Coumouses – Chomusi – Commussi – Chomus," *Antičnaja drevnost'i srednie veka* 10 (Sverdlovsk, 1973), 181–3.

[39] MM, vol. II, nos. 549 and 550 (Oct.–Nov. 1397), pp. 347–52.

[40] Ibid., no. 608 (Oct. 1400), p. 440. The tavern in question had depreciated from 200 *hyperpyra*, its value "in times of plenty," to 130 *hyperpyra* in 1400.

[41] Laiou-Thomadakis, "Byzantine economy," 221; Balard, *Romanie génoise*, vol. II, p. 758; Matschke, *Ankara*, p. 131.

the same island on board an armed ship.[42] Constantine Pegonites, on the other hand, who was desperately in need of money and sailed to Symbolon (Cembalo) in the Crimea intending to make some profit with a sum of 36 *hyperpyra* he borrowed from his mother, returned to Constantinople after having lost all the money and began to demolish the houses he had inherited from his father as a last means of sustaining himself.[43] As mentioned earlier, the trading venture of Alexios Koumouses, who was the son of a Constantinopolitan cloth merchant, likewise came to an end with the loss of 300 *hyperpyra*.[44] Moreover, a certain Petriotes found that he could not bring his merchandise into the capital because of the enemy forces that surrounded the city and disrupted commercial activity.[45] The brother of a man called John Magistros, who was held back outside Constantinople at the outset of 1402 on account of the blockade, may well have been another unfortunate merchant; among objects he offered as security against a loan he had taken before his departure were various fabrics (καμουχᾶς, βλαττία) known to be important commodities in Mediterranean trade.[46]

Merchants were not the only people whose movements in or out of Constantinople were restricted as a result of the Ottoman blockade. A nun called Theodoule Tzouroulene, who had left the capital for an unstated reason presumably before the launching of the siege, claimed that the siege hindered her re-entry into the city for several years. She managed to come back before June 1400, but found that in her absence Kaballarios Kontostephanos, who owned a vineyard next to a church that belonged to her, had overstepped into the boundaries of her property.[47] The heir of a certain Spyridon was even less fortunate than her since he could not come back to the city at all to reclaim his inheritance.[48] Similarly, witnesses from abroad who were needed for the resolution of a court case could not be brought into Constantinople because of the siege.[49] For the same reason, bishops from other cities under the jurisdiction of the Byzantine Church were not able to attend an important synod that was held at the capital during the first half of 1402 to discuss the deposition of Patriarch Matthew.[50]

---

[42] MM, vol. ii, no. 680 (Dec. 1401). [43] Ibid., no. 571 (May 1400).

[44] See p. 157 and note 38 above.

[45] H. Hunger, "Zu den restlichen Inedita des Konstantinopler Patriarchatsregisters im Cod. Vindob. Hist. Gr. 48.," *REB* 24 (1966), no. 3, pp. 61–2. Cf. Darrouzès, *Reg.*, no. 3252 (Jan. 1402), p. 471.

[46] Hunger, "Inedita," no. 2, pp. 59–61. Cf. Darrouzès, *Reg.*, no. 3251 (Jan. 1402), p. 470.

[47] MM, vol. ii, no. 579 (June 1400). [48] Ibid., no. 650 (May 1401).

[49] Ibid., no. 564 (March–April 1400).

[50] G. T. Dennis, "The deposition and restoration of Patriarch Matthew I, 1402–1403," *BF* 2 (1967), 102, n. 7.

By contrast, John Goudeles safely returned from Chios with a certain amount of wheat, which he managed to smuggle into Constantinople through the nearby Genoese port of Pera, after bribing some Italian officials there.[51] None of the risks and costs that Goudeles endured, though, can sufficiently account for the exorbitant price he charged for his grain if it is to be recalled that 31 *hyperpyra* is the maximum recorded wheat price surviving from the period of Bayezid's blockade. Goudeles, who also imported wine,[52] did nonetheless find buyers for his merchandise. Moreover, a number of aristocrats from Constantinople invested their money in his commercial enterprises, hoping to profit from his successes. Among these was a woman, Theodora Palaiologina, who pawned the jewels that formed part of her daughter's dowry in order to invest the money (300 *hyperpyra*) with Goudeles, who was preparing to sail to the Aegean on another business venture.[53] Thus, while many Constantinopolitan merchants experienced considerable losses, as did many small tradesmen such as bakers and tavernkeepers, some of whom were forced to close down their businesses, an aristocratic entrepreneur like John Goudeles, who engaged in overseas trade and had contacts in Italian colonies such as Chios and Pera, could make lots of money from the sale of wheat and, probably, of wine. Indeed, Goudeles' cooperation with the Genoese was not restricted to the occasion in which he is said to have bribed the treasurers of Pera. He had a Genoese partner who came from the famous de Draperiis family of Pera, and several high officials of the colony were directly involved in his grain trade.[54]

[51] Laiou-Thomadakis, "Byzantine economy," 221. See MM, vol. II, no. 675 (Oct. 1401) for another example of Byzantine merchants from Constantinople unloading their merchandise in Pera during the siege. Note that one of the two trading partners involved in this venture was George Goudeles, John's father.

[52] Laiou-Thomadakis, "Byzantine economy," 221.

[53] MM, vol. II, nos. 656 (July 1401), 676 (Nov. 1401); see also no. 580 (June 1400). Theodora could use these jewels because, both her daughter and son-in-law being minors, she was vested with authority to administer the young couple's dowry and to provide for their support. She shared this responsibility on an annual basis with her son-in-law's mother, Theodora Trychadaina. The latter was the mother-in-law of John Goudeles.

[54] Laiou-Thomadakis, "Byzantine economy," 221. Goudeles' Genoese partner was Lodisio de Draperiis. On the latter's family, see M. Balard, "La société pérote aux XIVe–XVe siècles: autour des Demerode et des Draperio," in *Byzantine Constantinople: Monuments, Topography and Everyday Life*, ed. N. Necipoğlu (Leiden, Boston, and Cologne, 2001), pp. 299–311, esp. 304ff.; Th. Ganchou, "Autonomie locale et relations avec les Latins à Byzance au XIVe siècle: Iôannès Limpidarios/Libadarios, Ainos et les Draperio de Péra," in *Chemins d'outre-mer. Études d'histoire sur la Méditerranée médiévale offertes à Michel Balard*, vol. I (Paris, 2004), pp. 353–74. It may be added that John's father, George Goudeles, had formed a business partnership with Manuel Koreses, who belonged to a family that originated from Chios; they, too, used Pera to unload and store merchandise during Bayezid's siege: see note 51 above.

It is also noteworthy that whereas authorities in Constantinople did not, or could not, take any measures against the illegal profiteering activities of Byzantine subjects, Genoese authorities in Pera vigorously tried to dissuade their own subjects from participating in these activities.[55] In 1402 legal action was taken in Pera against the Genoese officials who had been associated with John Goudeles' grain sale and had received bribes or made profits from it. Another Byzantine whose name was brought up in connection with the bribing of officials from Pera was a certain Leondarios, described as the agent of the Byzantine emperor. This emperor is to be identified, almost without doubt, as John VII, who took over the government of Byzantium during Manuel II's trip to the West (1399–1403), and whose earlier commercial enterprises in Genoa have been discussed in chapter 6.[56] The imperial agent Leondarios, on the other hand, may have been either Bryennios Leontares, governor of Selymbria and *oikeios* of John VII, or Demetrios Laskaris Leontares, agent and associate of Manuel II who served as John VII's advisor in Thessalonike after 1403.[57] Like John Goudeles, Leondarios was involved in trade and had dealings with the Genoese of Pera. Rather than acting alone, however, he functioned as John VII's intermediary. In this capacity he cooperated with two Genoese officials who had bought cheaper grain in Pera with the intention of reselling it in Constantinople at prices probably approximating Goudeles' earnings. The emperor, Leondarios, and two Italians are reported to have gained 11,000 *hyperpyra* on one occasion which reveals the scope of their undertakings.[58] Thus, in Constantinople, not only were no measures taken against the profiteering activities of Byzantine merchants during the siege years, but even the emperor himself engaged in such activities in collaboration with Greeks and Italians.

It may be recalled that one of John VII's commercial agents in Genoa in the late 1380s and early 1390s was George Goudeles, who was the father of John Goudeles.[59] George, *mesazon, oikeios* of the Emperor, and member of the Senate, was not only an influential statesman and businessman: he was related to the imperial family through his sister Anna Asanina, who

---

[55] On what follows, see Balard, *Romanie génoise*, vol. II, p. 758; Laiou-Thomadakis, "Byzantine economy," 220–1.

[56] See above, ch. 6, pp. 131, 134–5.

[57] Cf. Matschke, *Ankara*, pp. 130–1; *PLP*, nos. 92519 and 14676.

[58] Iorga, *Notes*, vol. I, p. 66. The two Italians involved in this affair were the *massarii* of Pera, Hector Fieschi and Ottobone Giustiniano. On other occasions, the two men are reported to have received from the Byzantine Emperor 8 *vegetes* of wine, 7 *modioi* of grain, and 7,000 or 10,000 *hyperpyra*: ibid., pp. 66–7.

[59] See above, ch. 6, p. 134 and note 65. On George and John Goudeles, see also *PLP*, nos. 91696 and 91697.

had married a Palaiologos and is described as the Emperor's aunt (θεία) in a document dated March 1400, though at this time relations between the brother and sister were strained because of a property dispute.[60] The same document contains a reference to a close family friend of the Goudelai, one Astras,[61] who also belongs to a family that had strong personal and political ties with John VII. It will be recalled that an *oikeios* Astras, again with an unknown first name, was the son-in-law of yet another θεία of the Emperor called Anna Palaiologina and of Komnenos Branas, who were both devoted partisans of John VII.[62] These two men bearing the last name Astras are very likely to have been the same person, who may in turn be identified with Michael (Synadenos) Astras, described as *oikeios* and "son-in-law" of the Emperor in a patriarchal act dated June 1400.[63] We know, moreover, that through his niece Michael Astras was related in a very roundabout and distant fashion to John Goudeles as well. The brother of John Goudeles' wife was married to the daughter of Theodora Palaiologina, who happened to be the sister-in-law of Astras' niece.[64] No matter how distant such family connections may have been, they did every so often lead to the formation of economic ties between various relatives of married parties. Thus Theodora Palaiologina, as noted earlier, invested part of her daughter's dowry in one of John Goudeles' business ventures abroad.[65]

It is quite obvious that we are dealing here with a small network of aristocratic families who all shared an affiliation with John VII and who were further connected by marriage ties and common economic interests. It was the financial and economic backing they had acquired through investments in foreign commercial markets by virtue of their contacts with the Genoese that gave members of this group the opportunity during Bayezid's siege to engage in profiteering activities at home and expand their fortunes, while most others in Constantinople suffered material losses. Thus, just as in Thessalonike during the period when it was exposed to constant Ottoman

---

[60] MM, vol. II, no. 557 (March 1400), pp. 361–6. For George Goudeles' titles and membership in the Senate, see ibid., nos. 650 (May 1401), 675 (Oct. 1401); Kydones–Loenertz, vol. II, no. 357 (1386?); V. Laurent, "Le trisépiscopat du Patriarche Matthieu Ier (1397–1410)," *REB* 30 (1972), 134.

[61] MM, vol. II, no. 557, p. 362.

[62] Ibid., nos. 537 (Jan. 1400) and 595 (Aug. 1400), pp. 329–33, 422–3. See above, ch. 6, pp. 133–4.

[63] MM, vol. II, no. 580 (June 1400), pp. 399–400; see also note 61 in ch. 6 above. For other sources on Michael Astras, son of the *megas stratopedarches* George Synadenos Astras, see *Vatopédi*, vol. II, no. 125 (1366); Kravari, "Philothéou," no. 6 (1376); *Zographou*, no. 47 (1378); *Chilandar* (P), no. 157 (1378); Kydones–Loenertz, vol. II, no. 422; MM, vol. II, no. 533 (Nov. 1399). For a contrary opinion on the identifications proposed here, see Kravari, "Philothéou," 318–19.

[64] MM, vol. II, nos. 580 (June 1400), 656 (July 1401), 676 (Nov. 1401). Astras' niece, too, bears the name Anna Palaiologina. She had a brother called Alexios Aspietes, and her husband was Petros Palaiologos. She was already deceased in June 1400.

[65] See p. 159 and note 53 above.

attacks, the small fraction of the capital's population that maintained an economically favorable position in the course of Bayezid's siege consisted primarily of aristocratic merchants with Italian connections. One additional advantage that the Constantinopolitans had over the Thessalonians was the existence of the nearby Genoese colony of Pera, which had no counterpart in Thessalonike and served part of the capital's population as a place for trade connections and commercial opportunities as well as a place of refuge during political and military crises.

We have seen thus far that the limitations imposed by Bayezid's military operations, particularly the lack of food and other necessities, almost immediately hurt everyone in Constantinople with the exception of a small network of people belonging to the highest ranks of the aristocracy. Nevertheless, the siege does not appear to have seriously threatened the overall economic situation of the upper classes until several years later. Despite minor difficulties, most aristocratic families possessed means by which they could provide for themselves and survive during the initial phases of the siege. Yet their resources were depleted gradually in the course of the eight years they endured under blockade. It is, therefore, not by mere coincidence that the acts of the patriarchal tribunal of Constantinople which reveal the financial difficulties of the capital's aristocracy all date from the last three or four years of the siege. Most of these acts explicitly attribute the economic problems of the aristocracy to the Ottoman siege, alluding to it by some variant of the more or less conventionalized phrase "the precarious circumstances, need, and poverty of the present time."[66]

In 1400 the three sons of σύρ Perios Lampadenos who were all *oikeioi* of the Emperor – Michael Rhaoul, Gabriel Palaiologos, and John Palaiologos – decided to sell their inherited property, which included a house, a bakery, and a *triklinon*. This property, estimated to have a total value of 330 *hyperpyra*, was on the verge of collapse, and the brothers had outstanding debts. The money from the sale would, therefore, help them pay their debts, while they intended to keep the rest for their subsistence.[67]

---

[66] MM, vol. ii, no. 549 (1397), p. 347: "ὑπὸ τῆς τοῦ καιροῦ ἀνωμαλίας"; no. 565 (1400), p. 376: "τῇ τοῦ καιροῦ ἀνωμαλίᾳ τε καὶ ἐνδείᾳ"; no. 646 (1401), p. 492: "τῇ ἐνδείᾳ καὶ τῇ τοῦ καιροῦ ἀνάγκῃ"; no. 648 (1402), p. 496: "τῇ τοῦ καιροῦ ἀνωμαλίᾳ"; no. 609 (1400), p. 442: "διὰ τὴν ἐκ τῆς μάχης ἀνάγκην καὶ βίαν"; no. 610 (1400), p. 443: "ὑπὸ τῆς τοῦ καιροῦ ἐνδείας πιεζόμενοι"; no. 554 (1400), p. 356: "ὑπὸ τοῦ καιροῦ καὶ τῶν πραγμάτων στενοχωρούμενοι"; no. 560 (1400), p. 370: "διὰ τὴν ἔνδειαν καὶ στέρησιν τῶν πραγμάτων"; no. 658 (1401), p. 514: "διὰ τὴν ἐνταῦθα ἔνδειαν"; etc.

[67] Ibid., no. 554. S. Fassoulakis, *The Byzantine Family of Raoul-Ral(l)es* (Athens, 1973), no. 50, p. 64, suggests that Gabriel and John Palaiologos may have been half-brothers of Michael Rhaoul, from two separate marriages of their father Lampadenos. In that case the sons probably adopted their last names from their mothers, which was a common practice in Byzantium.

In November 1401 another member of the Palaiologos family named Michael was constrained to sell a vineyard in the quarter of Saint Romanos in order to pay his debts and to protect his wife and child from the famine that had overtaken Constantinople at this time.[68] During the same month, Michael, in need of more money, decided to sell farmland as well. On this latter occasion his brother Gabriel intervened, probably fearing the gradual loss of the family's entire landed property through continued sales. In order to keep the farmland in the possession of the family, Gabriel proposed to buy part of it himself. Yet having no ready cash to pay his brother, he asked the patriarch for permission to pawn his wife's jewels against a loan of 150 *hyperpyra*. Since the jewels formed part of his wife's dowry, their economic exploitation for such a purpose was subject to legal restrictions. Nonetheless, the patriarch granted him permission on the grounds that the ownership of a revenue-producing immovable was preferable to the possession of jewels, which Gabriel might anyhow be able to redeem in the future.[69] One can detect in the patriarch's decision a conscious economic concern with putting all available resources in the city to productive use so as to prevent them from lying idle in the midst of the destitution and scarcity brought about by the Ottoman siege.

Another court case, which involved Manuel Bouzenos, *oikeios* of the Emperor, and his wife, Theodora Bouzene Philanthropene, has many elements in common with the two cases discussed above.[70] By the seventh year of the siege, Manuel, who had already sold or mortgaged all his possessions because of war-time constraints, was reduced to extreme need. He had incurred large debts; the famine had brought him, his wife, and his children to the verge of starvation; and he no longer had any means of his own left with which he could sustain his family. Consequently he appealed to the patriarch for permission to sell some houses which constituted part of his wife's dowry. Manuel had already made an agreement with a certain Argyropoulos, who had recently come to Constantinople from abroad and was willing to buy the houses for 270 *hyperpyra*. This Argyropoulos, a member of the wealthy aristocratic family whose Thessalonian branch

---

[68] MM, vol. II, no. 678.

[69] Ibid., no. 679, p. 559. Michael and Gabriel Palaiologos are both identified as *oikeioi* of the Emperor in this act. On the more flexible use of dowries during the Palaiologan period despite their protected nature in Byzantine law, see A. E. Laiou, "The role of women in Byzantine society," *JÖB* 31 (1981), 237–41. See also R. Macrides, "Dowry and inheritance in the late period: some cases from the Patriarchal Register," in *Eherecht und Familiengut in Antike und Mittelalter*, ed. D. Simon (Munich, 1992), pp. 89–98.

[70] MM, vol. II, no. 646. This act has been dated to May 1401 by Darrouzès: *Reg.*, pp. 430–1.

we encountered earlier, may perhaps be identified with Andreas Argyropoulos, who was involved in long-distance trade with Wallachia not long before 1400.[71] Although there is no direct indication that Andreas' business involvement had taken him on a journey abroad, the early fifteenth-century Greek satirist Mazaris mentions a Polos Argyros who had returned from Wallachia with great riches.[72] Thus, it seems very likely that all three men in question were one and the same, and the Argyropoulos who wanted to buy Manuel Bouzenos' houses may have been intending to reinvest part of his profits from a recent trading venture in the real-estate market of Constantinople. The patriarch, after hearing Bouzenos' request and making certain that he had no other resources apart from his wife's dowry, agreed to the sale as the survival of the children and the wife herself depended on it.[73] Yet finding the price of 270 *hyperpyra* too low, he demanded that a higher bidder be sought through an eight-day-long auction. No higher bidders appeared, however, during the prescribed time; meanwhile, Argyropoulos decided not to purchase the houses. In the end, when a civil *archon* called Thomas Kallokyres showed interest in buying them for the same price, the patriarch gave his consent. Bouzenos was authorized to pay his debts with part of the money from the sale and to reserve the rest for the sustenance of his family.

Less than a year earlier, in November 1400, the patriarch granted a certain Nicholas, the minor son of the late Exotrochos, permission to sell a house complex comprising an unidentified number of buildings. The complex, which Nicholas inherited from his father, was all the property he owned. For this reason the patriarch objected to its sale at first but gave in when he saw how the child, who had no means of subsistence, suffered from the famine and cold weather which hit the capital that year. An official appraised the houses at 250 *hyperpyra*, factoring into his calculation the current insecurity and uncertainty of affairs. Despite this low price set on the houses, no one wanted to buy them with the exception of Nicholas' cousin, *kyra* Theodora Baropolitissa, who offered to pay only 240 *hyperpyra*.

[71] See MM, vol. ii, no. 564, pp. 374–5; Darrouzès has dated this act to March–April 1400: *Reg.*, p. 367.

[72] *Mazaris' Journey to Hades, or Interviews with Dead Men about Certain Officials of the Imperial Court*, ed. and trans. by J. N. Barry, M. J. Share, A. Smithies, and L. G. Westerink (Buffalo, NY, 1975), pp. 38, 50–2. Polos Argyros has indeed been identified with Andreas Argyropoulos: Laiou-Thomadakis, "Byzantine economy," 201–2; *PLP*, no. 1255.

[73] For Byzantine law permitting the alienation of the dowry under exceptional circumstances when a family's, especially the children's, survival depended on its sale, see C. Harmenopoulos, *Manuale Legum sive Hexabiblos*, ed. G. E. Heimbach (Leipzig, 1851), IV, 11.1; cf. Laiou, "Role of women," 237.

She bought the property at this price, and the money was entrusted to an elder relative of Nicholas.[74]

The difficulty with which both Nicholas and Manuel Bouzenos found buyers for their clearly underpriced houses demonstrates well the scarcity of individuals who were capable of, or interested in, purchasing property of this sort in Constantinople during the latter stages of the siege. The growing frequency with which owners tried to liquidate their property in the midst of grave financial problems and the concurrent shortage of buyers who came forth were related phenomena, both directly resulting from Bayezid's extended blockade. Meanwhile, as house prices continued to drop, the few people who did make investments in the city's housing market took advantage of the exceptionally low prices. The extent to which the situation was open to abuse, with prices falling far below actual values, is illustrated by a dispute concerning an estate, including a courtyard with several buildings and a vineyard, which Jacob Tarchaneiotes had sold for 100 *hyperpyra* in 1398. Two years later, after Jacob complained that the estate was worth about three times more than the price he had received for it, experts reappraised it at 440 *hyperpyra*. Jacob was accordingly granted an indemnity of 95 *hyperpyra* and 8 *keratia*, a sum reflecting the adjustment made for the devaluation of the Byzantine currency during the two years that had elapsed. In this case, however, it was not an individual who had taken advantage of the situation by purchasing extremely cheap, underpriced property, but the Constantinopolitan monastery of Myrelaion.[75] It should also be underlined that contrary to the decline attested in house prices during the advancing years of the siege, the price of well-protected fields and vineyards within the city walls increased simultaneously, in large part because of the precariousness of the food situation which, as already noted, made property with a productive capacity more precious, and in part because of the devaluation mentioned above.

Two other court cases among the patriarchal acts shed further light on the economic problems of the capital's upper classes during the latter years of the siege. In the face of her husband's financial hardships, in 1399 the wife of Constantine Perdikares renounced her rights over her dowry in order to help her husband with the settlement of a debt. Byzantine law

---

[74] MM, vol. ii, no. 613.

[75] Ibid., no. 553 (Feb. 1400). The patriarchal court calculated the above-mentioned indemnity on the basis of its ruling that Jacob was entitled to an amount equivalent to one-third plus one-third of the third – i.e. 4/9 – of the corrected price (= 195 *hyperpyra* and 8 *keratia*). The final figure was obtained by subtracting from this sum the 100 *hyperpyra* Jacob had received initially. For the monastery of Myrelaion, see C. L. Striker, *The Myrelaion (Bodrum Camii) in Istanbul* (Princeton, 1981).

protected a woman's dowry against claims of her husband's creditors, but Perdikares' wife volunteered to give up this protection. Before the ecclesiastical authorities she promised that if her husband fell into arrears, or if he died without having paid off the entire sum, she would on his behalf provide the money from her dowry. The sum in question was 500 *hyperpyra*, and Perdikares owed it to *kyr* Thomas Kallokyres, the same man who, as seen above, purchased an underpriced house from an impoverished and famine-stricken aristocratic couple.[76] In a parallel case, though involving a much smaller amount, a certain Batatzina offered to give up the legal protection her dowry had over the 20 *hyperpyra* which her husband borrowed from George Goudeles.[77]

One can discern in each one of the cases presented above a common pattern whereby members of the aristocracy, having used up their monetary assets from their savings during the first half of Bayezid's siege, were compelled thereafter to seek new sources of money. Although most aristocrats owned houses, shops, gardens, vineyards, or fields in Constantinople, they did not wish to dispense with their immovables, preferring instead to take loans from individuals who were better off. But with limited investment opportunities in the besieged city, and borrowing most of the time for their daily expenditure rather than for reinvesting, many found themselves contracting ever larger debts. Thus, unable to pay off their debts as the siege progressed, these people were often obliged to give up the properties they had mortgaged at the time of borrowing. If henceforth they still had some remaining properties, they tried to sell these too; otherwise, as a last resort they tended to turn to their wives' dowry. In the majority of the cases we have examined, the aristocrats who were compelled either to sell their immovables or to exchange the dowry property of their wives had accumulated large debts that were long overdue.

Under these circumstances interest rates climbed, which is not surprising given the shortage of cash and the overwhelming demand for it. Whereas in fourteenth-century legal codes annual interest rates normally varied from 6 percent for loans between private individuals, to 8 percent for business loans, to 12 percent for maritime loans,[78] and later in 1437 a rate of 10 percent on a business loan is attested in Constantinople,[79] in the course

---

[76] MM, vol. ii, nos. 536 (Dec. 1399) and 562 (March 1400). For Byzantine law acccording protection to the dowry against debts incurred by the husband, see *Peira*, VI.2, XXII.4, in *Jus graecoromanum*, vol. iv, ed. Zepos and Zepos; cf. Laiou, "Role of women," 238–9.

[77] MM, vol. ii, no. 581 (June 15, 1400).

[78] Harmenopoulos, *Hexabiblos*, ed. Heimbach, III, 7.23; cf. Oikonomidès, *Hommes d'affaires*, pp. 54–5.

[79] *Badoer*, p. 360, lines 21–2.

of Bayezid's siege we find annual rates on non-maritime loans ranging from 15 percent to as high as 26.67 percent.[80] By charging such high interest rates, moneylenders could amass great fortunes despite the large number of defaulters. In fact, a handful of people in Constantinople regularly engaged in moneylending at the time of Bayezid's blockade. These included, besides familiar figures such as Thomas Kallokyres and George Goudeles,[81] a certain Sophianos, who belongs to one of the capital's leading families noted for its involvement in banking,[82] and Jacob Sgouropoulos, who harassed a widow in order to make her pay the arrears of her deceased husband.[83] In their quest to derive profits from the adverse circumstances, these moneylenders added to the burdens and misfortunes of the population, in the same way as did certain merchants who inflated grain prices or the individuals who offered very low prices for houses on sale. Furthermore, the names listed above indicate that the people who engaged in all three kinds of economic activity came from identical social backgrounds (i.e. they belonged invariably to the aristocracy), including sometimes members of the same family, and sometimes the very same individuals themselves. It must have been this group of people, and others like them, that the Patriarch Matthew had in mind when he reproached the citizens of Constantinople in 1401 as "unblushing practitioners of every kind of wickedness, attackers of our brothers in their misfortunes, exasperating their troubles, quick to set upon their portion and to trample down and to devour the poor."[84]

Although the patriarchal court allowed the transfer or mortgage of dowry goods in all the aforementioned cases related to such goods, ecclesiastical authorities were not always lenient about the flexible usage of women's dowries. Side by side with cases in which changes in the ownership of dowry property were tolerated because of the exceptional circumstances induced by the siege, there were many instances when the laws concerning dowries were applied very strictly. This seems to have been the case particularly

---

[80] MM, vol. II, no. 568, p. 380: annual interest of 45 *hyperpyra* for a sum of 300 *hyperpyra* lent *c.* 1396–7; no. 530, p. 313: short-term loan in 1399; the interest of 3 *hyperpyra* per 5 months on a principal of 27 *hyperpyra* yields an annual rate of 26.67 percent. Compare these figures with interest rates charged for sea loans in Thessalonike in the early fifteenth century: see above, ch. 4, p. 65 and note 41.

[81] For Thomas Kallokyres' moneylending activities, see MM, vol. II, nos. 536 (Dec. 1399), 562 (March 1400), 568 (April 1400); for George Goudeles, see ibid., no. 581 (June 1400).

[82] Ibid., no. 566 (April 1400), p. 378. See below, Appendix III and ch. 8, p. 202 for a banker John Sophianos, whose name is attested during the third decade of the fifteenth century in the account book of Badoer. For the banking and business activities of the Sophianos family, see also Oikonomidès, *Hommes d'affaires*, pp. 66–8, 121 and n. 264.

[83] MM, vol. II, no. 547 (Feb. 1400).

[84] Ibid., no. 626, p. 464; trans. by Barker, *Manuel II*, p. 208.

when husbands tried to take advantage of the patriarchal court's noted flexibility and encroached upon their wives' dowries while they still had property of their own. Indeed, the patriarchal court frequently intervened in favor of women for the protection of their dowries when it was suspected that their husbands were misusing them. Thus, when the *archontopoulos* Michael Palaiologos was not able to release from mortgage a vineyard, part of which had been reserved as guarantee for his wife's dowry, the patriarchal court stepped in, objecting to the sale of the part that served as security for the dowry.[85] Women, too, opened cases against their husbands who did not administer their dowry goods properly, as did Eirene Synadene, who brought her husband to court for having used up her entire dowry. The court accepted Eirene's request that a house in the quarter of Psatharia, her husband's sole remaining property, be passed on to her as compensation.[86] In another case, Maria Hagiopetretissa Gabraina, the wife of John Gabras, insisted on the legal protection accorded to the dowry against the demands of a husband's creditors in an attempt to recover her dowry of 702 *hyperpyra* from moneylenders. The court admitted that Maria's claim was valid as long as she had not, in full knowledge of the law, given up her rights over her dowry. In addition, she secured, quite shrewdly, her husband's release from prison, where he was detained because of his debts, by arguing that he would be able to compensate her for any portion of the dowry that remained unrestored and also look after her if he were free.[87]

In 1400 a widow called Eirene Gabraina filed suit against her father-in-law, Michael Monembasiotes, who had withheld her dowry of 300 *hyperpyra* from her since the death of her husband seven years ago. At court Monembasiotes' defender argued that Eirene should have requested her dowry at the time of her husband's death, and that she no longer had any claim to it. Although this was what the law stipulated, the patriarch decided in Eirene's favor. First, he excused her delayed petition on the grounds that women were often ignorant of their legal rights. In addition, he took into consideration the fact that she had four children to look after. Consequently, Monembasiotes was ordered to pay his daughter-in-law altogether 407 *hyperpyra*, which included, besides her dowry, the standard charges payable at the death of a husband. On the basis of contrary evidence, however, the patriarch rejected Eirene's additional demand for a sum of 1,000 *hyperpyra*, which she claimed to be her late husband's maternal inheritance also appropriated by her father-in-law.[88] Given the

---

[85] MM, vol. II, no. 569 (April 1400).   [86] Ibid., no. 577 (June 1400).   [87] Ibid., no. 523 (Dec. 1399).
[88] Ibid., no. 608 (Oct. 1400). The money Monembasiotes had to pay over and above the 300 *hyperpyra* comprised a charge of 7 *hyperpyra* for the nuptial gift (*theoretron*) and a payment of 100 *hyperpyra*

argument about the unfamiliarity of women with laws which the court used to justify the delay in Eirene's petition, one cannot help wondering why and under what circumstances she came to familiarize herself with her legal rights on the seventh year following her husband's death, which coincides with the sixth year of Bayezid's siege. It may well be that Eirene Gabraina, suffering like most members of the capital's aristocracy from a deterioration in her financial situation as the siege progressed, decided to inquire about her remaining resources in 1400 and discovered that her father-in-law had kept her dowry from her. As to her other allegation concerning the misappropriation of her husband's maternal inheritance, unless Monembasiotes lied to the court about having turned it over to his son before his death, or unless he told the truth but Eirene had been uninformed about her husband's retrieval of the inheritance, it reveals her desperation for funds to support herself and her children during these difficult times.

If Michael Monembasiotes exploited his daughter-in-law's limited knowledge pertaining to her legal rights on her dowry, in 1400 a widower called Nicholas Branas tried to take advantage of his son's minority to seize the revenues from a vineyard which the boy inherited from his mother. Branas' intentions were brought to light owing to the intervention of the boy's maternal grandmother, Theodora Palaiologina Dermokaïtissa, who had been looking after the child since the mother's death. A short time earlier Branas had asked to take charge of his son, but according to Dermokaïtissa this was merely a pretext so that he could have access to the boy's maternal inheritance. After demonstrating that Branas had used up all his own wealth, she convinced the patriarchal court that the accused had now turned his eyes on his son's property and risked its loss too. The guardianship of the child and his vineyard was consequently conferred upon the grandmother, but the court stipulated that if the child died, Branas was to inherit all his property.[89] It may not be far-fetched to presume that the Ottoman siege lay behind the economic problems which so overwhelmed this father as to make him focus solely on his present situation, to the neglect of his son's future. Another widower by the name of Theodore Barzanes, who refrained from handing over to his mother-in-law property worth 750 *hyperpyra* which his wife left to her by testament, blamed his act on the misery and confusion of the times.[90]

---

equivalent to one-third of the dowry, which must be the *hypobolon*. On the *hypobolon* and *theoretron*, see *ODB*, vol. ii, p. 965; vol. iii, pp. 2068–9.

[89] MM, vol. ii, no. 592 (Aug. 1400).

[90] Ibid., no. 549 (Oct. 1397), p. 347; see also no. 550 (Nov. 1397).

Finally, a court case from the year 1400 concerning another dowry dispute that was resolved in favor of a wife serves to illustrate precisely how the shortage of cash affected the wealthy upper classes of Constantinople during the latter part of the siege. The dispute in question was over a dowry of 1,000 *hyperpyra* which Manuel Papylas had given to his daughter Eirene when she married Alexios Palaiologos. The latter had already spent the cash part of the dowry, and his father-in-law feared that the remainder would soon perish too because of the continued siege. Papylas, therefore, demanded from his son-in-law the restoration of the entire dowry in the form of immovable goods. The patriarch accepted Papylas' demand and ruled that Alexios Palaiologos should make over to his wife from his own possessions a vineyard, a bakery, and an estate which comprised a courtyard and a church.[91] Alexios, who owned all this property, exceeding 1,000 *hyperpyra* in value, can by no means be considered a needy man. What presumably prompted him to seize his wife's dowry must have been his distinct need for liquid assets, and not an overall lack of resources as in the majority of cases discussed earlier.

Having observed the economic problems endured by some of the aristocratic families of Constantinople, it might be inferred that the city's less distinguished inhabitants with more modest means had to wrestle with even greater difficulties during Bayezid's siege. Fortunately, the acts of the patriarchal court shed light on the financial troubles of the latter group as well. Among them was a certain Manuel Katzas, who borrowed 45 *hyperpyra* from his half-brother John Katzas, who in turn had borrowed the money from a Jew. Manuel needed the money in order to release his mother's house from mortgage and promised to repay his brother within a certain period. Still owing John 27 *hyperpyra* in 1399, Manuel was granted an extra term of four months during which to pay this sum plus the accrued interest. Five months later, however, because Manuel had still not made a single payment to his brother, the patriarch decided that the house would have to be sold. John was to receive the money due to him (30 *hyperpyra*), while the remainder from the sale was to be distributed among the heirs of Manuel's mother.[92]

Another person suffering from impoverishment in 1400 was the monk Methodios, who could no longer pay the annual rent of 3 *hyperpyra* for a small plot of land he had leased for life from the church of Saint Euphemia

91 Ibid., no. 565 (April 1400). See also no. 559 (March 1400), for a related dispute between Alexios' mother, Eirene Palaiologina, and Manuel Papylas.
92 Ibid., no. 530. This act has been dated to October–November 1399 by Darrouzès: *Reg.*, pp. 339–40, 334.

in Constantinople some time ago. The rent was reduced to 1 *hyperpyron* owing to the intervention of the Empress (the mother of John VII) on behalf of Methodios, who must have been a monk of some prominence and distinction to merit this kind of imperial attention.[93] A priest called Phokas, on the other hand, spent 40 *hyperpyra* out of a sum of 50 that was entrusted to his care on behalf of his brother-in-law, John Chrysaphes, who was a minor. After hearing the priest's defense that he used the money because of the extreme poverty and need he had fallen into, the patriarchal court decided that he should be entitled to the protection of the law that granted indigent people four months for the repayment of their debts.[94] It was evidently on the basis of the same law that Manuel Katzas was given four extra months to settle his debt in the case discussed above.

Equally hardpressed by destitution were the two sons of the late priest Pepagomenos, both minors, who wished to mortgage their house and church in 1400. At first they gave the house in mortgage to someone for 22 *hyperpyra*. But when the monks of a neighboring monastery offered 50 *hyperpyra* in exchange for the use of the church and the house together, the boys canceled their former agreement by returning the 22 *hyperpyra* to the said person and made a new deal with the monks. According to the patriarchal act in which these procedures are laid out, Pepagomenos' sons needed the money to pay their debts and to supply themselves with necessities. Yet the terms of their new agreement with the monks that are also registered in the act reveal another crucial factor behind the boys' need for money: they were planning to leave Constantinople and wanted to take with them all they could convert into liquid assets. They hoped, however, to return to the city someday, presumably if the siege were to end and peace were to be restored. This explains why, rather than selling their property, they chose to mortgage it and took care to incorporate into the mortgage contract a set of conditions regarding its redemption in the likely event of their return.[95]

Pepagomenos' sons should be considered lucky because in the course of Bayezid's siege many people fled Constantinople without having had the opportunity to sell or mortgage their property. The creditors of the two boys should be considered lucky as well since it was not uncommon for indebted citizens who ran away from the capital to leave behind unpaid accounts. Such was the manner in which the son-in-law or brother-in-law of a priest

---

[93] MM, vol. II, no. 560. This act has been dated to March 1400 by Darrouzès: *Reg.*, pp. 364–5.
[94] MM, vol. II, no. 587 (July 1400).
[95] Ibid., no. 610 (October 1400). The elder brother bears the last name Chrysoberges, while the younger one is called Pepagomenos like their father; the act omits their first names.

called Zotikos fled while he still owed money to a woman by the name of Athenaïsa. At the outset of 1400 his abandoned house in Constantinople lay in such a ruined state that the only use that could be made of it was by way of demolishing it and selling the construction materials. Since the patriarchal act hints at the possibility of this man's return to Constantinople in case of the establishment of peace with the Ottomans, it might be inferred that he had intentionally retained the house, hoping someday to come back and reoccupy it. It is, on the other hand, also conceivable that he kept the old house not because he desired to do so, but because he had not been able to sell it at the time of his departure.[96] Given the cash shortage noted above and the scarcity of citizens able or willing to invest in real estate, it is not surprising that people who left Constantinople during the siege frequently abandoned their immovables within the city. In the Kynegoi quarter, for instance, an estate belonging to a certain Maurommates remained neglected for several years following the flight of its owner. Then, on a piece of land attached to this estate, the proprietor of the adjacent garden, the *oikeios* Markos Palaiologos Iagaris, started cultivating wheat around 1399 or earlier. In May 1401, on account of Maurommates' prolonged absence, the patriarchal court granted Iagaris permission to continue using his neighbor's land for an annual fee of one *hyperpyron*. In addition, Iagaris was authorized to build a fence around it for protection against robbers who had been menacing the area. In the opinion of the patriarchal court and of Iagaris himself, who undertook the construction of the fence at his own expense, the likelihood of Maurommates' return to Constantinople appears to have notably diminished as many years elapsed after he deserted the city along with his property therein.[97]

If the lack of buyers and the urgency of circumstances compelling people to leave Constantinople were factors that reduced their ability to liquidate their immovables prior to the time of departure, the example of Anna Tornaraia Moschopoulina suggests another possible obstacle, namely the joint ownership of property. Anna had inherited from her father, the priest George Moschopoulos Sisinios, one quarter of a church, the rest of which belonged to her orphaned nephew in June 1400. Anna, who was away from Constantinople at this time, had apparently left the city without having made any arrangement for the transfer of her share of the church. Therefore, at the request of her nephew's guardian the patriarchal court ruled that, in case she died abroad intestate, her part must revert to her

[96] Ibid., no. 543 (January–February 1400).
[97] Ibid., no. 649. This act, dated October 1400 in MM, has been redated May 1401 by Darrouzès, *Reg.*, p. 433.

young relative. Had Anna attempted to sell her share prior to her departure, notwithstanding her limited chances of finding someone willing to purchase one-fourth of a church, one may well imagine the objections she might have faced from the nephew's guardian against the idea of her bringing in an outsider as the co-owner of a joint family property.[98]

All the references to flight that have been considered so far involved either individuals or nuclear families.[99] One patriarchal act discloses, on the other hand, a case of mass desertion from a small residential area in the vicinity of the Hippodrome. The inhabitants of this neighborhood, people with low incomes apparently, used to rent their dwellings from the nearby church of Saint John the Theologian. But because of the Ottoman siege, almost everyone had abandoned the place by July 1402, with the exception of one or two tenants.[100] Granted that the present case happens to be a unique documented incident of mass desertion, it is nonetheless significant for several reasons. First of all, incidents like this one are generally hard to come by among the acts of the patriarchal court because of the very nature of these documents; most cases that were brought to court involved disputes between particular individuals. Moreover, the acts tend to mention details such as the flight of people only incidentally, when they occur in connection with the dispute at hand. Consequently, references to the flight of citizens recorded in the acts not only constitute a small fraction of the actual number of people who must have fled Constantinople during Bayezid's siege, they also pertain primarily to propertied people since they are found in cases involving various forms of ownership disputes, partnership agreements, sale or loan contracts, and the like. Hence our last piece of evidence documenting the flight of an entire community made up of people with modest means who occupied the porticoes they rented from the said church is of utmost interest and value. It suggests that citizens belonging to the lower classes who deeply suffered from the hardships of the siege and who had little or no property to forfeit were as inclined as the rest of the population, if not more so, to leave the capital even though they are rarely visible in the documents. Thus, with the additional help of some other references encountered in the literary sources of the period,[101] we can begin to form a more complete picture of

---

[98] MM, vol. II, no. 576 (June 1400).

[99] See also ibid., no. 658, for the flight of another individual, the priest Gabras, who was the great-uncle of Anna Batatzina Gabraina. He left Constantinople sometime before July 1401, "διὰ τὴν ἐνταῦθα ἔνδειαν."

[100] Ibid., no. 648 (July 1402). Cf. C. Mango, "Le Diipion. Étude historique et topographique," *REB* 8 (1950), 152–61, esp. 157–8; Bernicolas-Hatzopoulos, "First siege," 44.

[101] See pp. 150–2 above.

the impact of flight on the overall population and physical appearance of
Constantinople during the siege years.

There can be little doubt that the steady outpouring of Constantinopolitans proved highly detrimental to the security of the besieged city by
depriving it of defenders and, furthermore, by lowering the morale of
those who stayed behind. The Byzantine government and particularly the
Emperor could not help but react to this situation with utmost disapproval.
For instance, in 1396 Manuel II reproached Demetrios Kydones, who had
recently left Constantinople to go to Italy, with the following words:

[Y]ou who have preferred a foreign land to your own... Do not imagine that
you are fulfilling your obligations toward it by loudly lamenting its fate while you
stay out of range of the arrows. In its time of crisis you must come and share the
dangers and, as much as you can, aid it by deeds if you have any interest in proving
yourself a soldier clear of indictment for desertion.[102]

Yet apart from such words of disapproval, sources give no evidence of the
implementation of consistent official measures aimed at restraining the
flight of the capital's inhabitants during this period. Only one patriarchal
act from the year 1399 reveals the personal efforts of Manuel II to prevent
an *oikeios* in his service from leaving the city. The latter, whose name was
Manuel Palaiologos Rhaoul, had fallen into the grip of poverty in the
course of the Ottoman siege. Between October 1397 and October 1399
he sold a large field to the monastery of Saint Mamas for 800 *hyperpyra*
with the intention of departing from Constantinople together with his
entire household. However, the Emperor found out about his plans and
obstructed them.[103] Manuel Palaiologos Rhaoul thus stayed behind, but it
has been seen that many others succeeded in taking flight. In other words,
although Manuel II may have been able to interfere with the plans of an
aristocrat who worked in his service and was close to him, he could not
effectively counteract the overall problem of flight, which may be attributed
to the absence of strict formal measures in Constantinople at this time,
comparable, for instance, to the unpopular prohibition of property sales
enforced in Thessalonike during the Venetian regime.[104]

---

[102] Dennis, *Letters of Manuel II*, no. 62, pp. 172–3. See also ibid., no. 30, written during the same
year (1396), for Manuel II's reprimanding attitude towards another prominent Byzantine, possibly
Manuel Kalekas, who had just moved from Constantinople to a location under Italian rule.

[103] MM, vol. II, no. 528 (Oct. 1399). On Manuel Palaiologos Rhaoul, see Fassoulakis, *Family of
Raoul-Ral(l)es*, no. 41, pp. 56–7; *PLP*, no. 24134. On the monastery of Saint Mamas, see R. Janin,
*La géographie ecclésiastique de l'Empire byzantin. Première partie: Le siège de Constantinople et le
patriarcat œcuménique*, vol. III: *Les églises et les monastères*, 2nd edn. (Paris, 1969), pp. 314–19.

[104] See above, ch. 5, pp. 109–10.

Following the hindrance of his plans, Manuel Palaiologos Rhaoul, who had sold the aforementioned field only because he intended to leave Constantinople, wanted to get it back from the monastery of Saint Mamas. Rhaoul's desire to retrieve his field, for which he had received a rather good price,[105] is not without significance. Despite some depreciation in the real value of goods, immovable property in Constantinople was still considered a safer form of wealth than liquid assets because whereas cash was steadily losing value, prices were expected to go up as soon as the siege came to an end. This optimism about the termination of the siege, coupled with the expectation of a rise in prices, are both reflected in an act of January 1401 concerning the sale of a house, in which the patriarch pointed to a likely increase in the price of the house in the event that peace should be established with Bayezid.[106] In a legal dispute discussed earlier, we have seen that Manuel Papylas, who brought a case against his son-in-law for having spent the cash part of his daughter's dowry, asked for the money to be restored in the form of immovable goods.[107] While Papylas intended in this manner to protect his daughter's dowry from being squandered again by his son-in-law, he may have been simultaneously striving to avoid its becoming devalued under the impact of current economic pressures. It was probably with the same motive that Manuel Palaiologos Rhaoul tried to regain possession of his field after his plans were altered, instead of keeping the 800 *hyperpyra* he had received for it.

If, on the other hand, the monastery of Saint Mamas was financially strong enough to afford to dispense this substantial sum of money on Rhaoul's field, thanks primarily to its wealthy *ktetor* Nicholas Sophianos,[108] numerous other monasteries and private churches in Constantinople showed signs of economic and physical decay during Bayezid's siege. For example, a church named after a certain Gabraina was in a ruined state until a nun called Theodoule Tzouroulene took over its management and restored it with her own money and with donations from others.[109] In 1397 the nuns of the convent of Theotokos Bebaias Elpidos, "because of the necessity and distress they were suffering from the siege," appealed for the right to use as cash 200 *hyperpyra* out of a donation of 300 *hyperpyra*, which had been endowed specifically for the purchase of property. The convent, founded in the early fourteenth century by a niece of the Emperor Michael VIII Palaiologos, also needed repairs even though it had

---

[105] For an evaluation of field prices within the city during the siege, including Rhaoul's, see pp. 153–4 above.
[106] MM, vol. II, no. 623, p. 461.   [107] Ibid., no. 565 (April 1400); see p. 170 above.
[108] On this person, see *PLP*, no. 26412.   [109] MM, vol. II, no. 579 (June 1400).

been restored merely two years prior to the siege. But owing to the patron-
age of Eugenia Kantakouzene Philanthropene, a great-granddaughter of
the original foundress (Theodora Synadene), who made a donation of 200
hyperpyra in September 1400, its church and bell tower "which were in
danger of collapsing" could be restored.[110] The overseer of the monastery
of Saint Basil, on the other hand, had to borrow 209 *hyperpyra* in order to
undertake much-needed repairs and the cultivation of a vineyard.[111] The
vineyards and fields outside the city walls belonging to the Charsianeites
monastery were totally destroyed and remained barren throughout the
Ottoman blockade, while the tower, presumably protecting the monastic
estates, was burnt down during an enemy attack.[112] Not even the monastery
of Bassos, which was the private property of John VII's mother, could ward
off destruction in the midst of the instability and insecurity that prevailed
within the besieged capital.[113] But most importantly, the church of Saint
Sophia too, according to a letter written by the Patriarch Matthew, lay in
critical condition and suffered from great need because it was deprived of
its external revenues as a result of the persistent siege.[114]

The gardens and vineyards of several other monasteries in the city lay
fallow or produced low yields like those of Saint Basil and Charsianeites.
Among the more enterprising monasteries some sought to remedy this
problem by entrusting their unproductive lands to the care of laymen.
For instance, a garden belonging to the convent of Panagia Pausolype was
given to two brothers bearing the family name Spyridon, who were expected
to transform it into a profit-yielding vineyard within five years. Thereafter,
the wine produced from the output was to be divided equally between the
two parties, while the convent for its part was required to pay the brothers 6
hyperpyra at harvest time each year. In addition, the brothers were granted
the right to transmit the vineyard to their heirs as long as the latter agreed to
abide by the same conditions. Whereas the convent used to earn scarcely

[110] H. Delehaye, *Deux typica byzantins de l'époque des Paléologues* (Brussels, 1921), pp. 102–5; English
    trans. in *BMFD*, vol. IV, pp. 1567–8. For the convent, see Janin, *Géographie ecclésiastique*, vol. III,
    pp. 158–60. For Eugenia Kantakouzene Philanthropene, see Nicol, *Family of Kantakouzenos*, no.
    55, p. 164; *PLP*, no. 10936.
[111] MM, vol. II, no. 653 (June 1401), where the editors wrongly locate the monastery in Caesarea,
    Cappadocia. For the Constantinopolitan monastery, see Janin, *Géographie ecclésiastique*, vol. III,
    pp. 58–60; Syropoulos, *"Mémoires,"* pp. 102, 186.
[112] Konidares and Manaphes, "Ἐπιτελεύτιος βούλησις," 478, 480, 481 (= Hunger, "Testament," 299,
    301); English trans. in *BMFD*, vol. IV, pp. 1637, 1639. For the Charsianeites monastery, see Janin,
    Géographie ecclésiastique, vol. III, pp. 501–2.
[113] MM, vol. II, no. 573 (May 1400). Cf. Darrouzès, *Reg.*, pp. 374–5; Janin, *Géographie ecclésiastique*,
    vol. III, pp. 61–2.
[114] MM, vol. II, no. 629, pp. 469–70. This letter to the metropolitan of Stauroupolis has been dated
    to March–April 1401 by Darrouzès: *Reg.*, pp. 417–18.

20 *hyperpyra* from the entire garden prior to this agreement, in 1401 it received more than 50 *hyperpyra* from only its own share of the vineyard. The fivefold increase in the total income derived from this garden/vineyard, even after the probable effects of inflation and devaluation are taken into account, signals a considerable rise in its productivity, which must be attributed to the successful management of the Spyridones.[115] Towards the end of 1401 or the beginning of 1402 the Peribleptos monastery leased a plot of land to a man called Manuel Katalanos, who agreed to exploit it as a vinery for an annual rent of 20 *hyperpyra*. The lease was to last for the duration of Katalanos' lifetime and was transferable to his heirs afterwards.[116] Here we see a different kind of arrangement made by a monastery which, just like the aforementioned convent of Pausolype, was trying to put one of its unproductive or underproducing lands to a better use. Instead of sharing the profit from the output produced, however, Peribleptos found it preferable to receive a fixed rent payment from its tenant. This may well be due to the unstable conditions created by the Ottoman siege which must have rendered successful managers such as the Spyridon brothers unique and exceptional. During the same year as the latter were noted for having substantially raised the productivity of the garden entrusted to them, the nuns of the convent of Saint Andrew in Krisei filed suit against two laymen to whom they had leased a vineyard on the similar condition that the tenants would work on ameliorating the land for four years and thereafter share with the convent half of the yield. The nuns were dissatisfied with the work done on the vineyard in the course of the first two years and wished to cancel the contract. The experts who were sent to examine the vineyard agreed with the nuns' assessment of the two men's performance, and the lease was accordingly canceled.[117] Yet, even in cases when monastic property was leased out in return for a fixed rental fee in order to avoid such risks as in the previous example, there was no guarantee that the lessee would necessarily deliver the due payment. This is illustrated by the example of George Eudokimos, who refused to pay the annual rent of 28 *hyperpyra* for a garden he leased from the monastery of Magistros, alleging as an excuse what appears to have

[115] MM, vol. II, no. 650 (May 1401). For the convent of Pausolype, see Janin, *Géographie ecclésiastique*, vol. III, p. 217. For a parallel example from Thessalonike illustrating the increase in the productivity of gardens leased by the monastery of Iveron to members of the Argyropoulos family, see ch. 4, p. 62 and note 30. See also Kazhdan, "Italian and late Byzantine city," 17–19.

[116] Hunger, "Inedita," no. 1, pp. 58–9; Darrouzès, *Reg.*, no. 3249, p. 469. For the Peribleptos monastery, see Janin, *Géographie ecclésiastique*, vol. III, pp. 218–22.

[117] MM, vol. II, no. 654 (June 1401). For the convent of Saint Andrew in Krisei, see Janin, *Géographie ecclésiastique*, vol. III, pp. 28–31.

been an extra tax demanded at that time for the repair of the fortifications of Constantinople.[118]

The sale of monastic property to laymen, which was prohibited by canon law except under unusual circumstances, also came to be more commonly practiced during Bayezid's siege, serving as another indicator of the economic problems encountered by the religious foundations of Constantinople at this time. In April 1400 the monastery of Christ Akataleptos, lacking adequate funds to pay an upcoming tax on its vineyards (τὸ βουτζιατικόν), obtained the patriarch's permission to sell a small plot of land to the Emperor's cousin Manuel Philanthropenos for a sum of 32 *hyperpyra*.[119] During the patriarchate of Antonios (1391–7), the Constantinopolitan monastery of Hodegoi was likewise allowed to sell a house to a man called Panopoulos, on the grounds that the sale would be beneficial to the monastery. Interestingly, this house had come to the Hodegoi's possession in 1390 through the donation of a lay couple. It changed hands three times within less than a decade, almost being surrendered to a fourth person, Thomas Kallokyres, who temporarily held it as security against a sum of 300 *hyperpyra* that Panopoulos, the current owner, borrowed from him.[120] In a somewhat different case that involved not a sale but a transfer *ad vitam*, the church of Saint Michael in the Eugenios quarter, being on the verge of collapse, was entrusted to the care of a man called Hodegetrianos. Among other things, Hodegetrianos promised to repair half of the church immediately, to attend to its further improvement, and to hire a full-time priest as soon as the siege ended.[121]

The strains imposed by Bayezid's blockade also appear to have given rise to some instances of misconduct in the utilization of religious property. In January 1401 Eirene Palaiologina made an accusation against her brother, the *oikeios* Andronikos Palaiologos, and her uncle, the monk David Palaiologos, with both of whom she shared the ownership of the church of Amolyntos. Claiming that her relatives wanted to use the church as a storehouse for the grapes they harvested on some adjoining vineyards, she requested from the patriarch the installation of a priest to perform regular services in the church. The patriarch granted her request, thus preventing

---

[118] MM, vol. II, no. 651 (May 1401), p. 501. Cf. Janin, *Géographie ecclésiastique*, vol. III, p. 313.

[119] MM, vol. II, no. 567. Cf. Darrouzès, *Reg.*, p. 370 and Janin, *Géographie ecclésiastique*, vol. III, pp. 504–6. For Manuel Philanthropenos, see *PLP*, no. 29769.

[120] MM, vol. II, no. 568 (April 1400). Cf. A. Failler, "Une donation des époux Sanianoi au monastère des Hodègoi," *REB* 34 (1976), 111–17. For the monastery, see Janin, *Géographie ecclésiastique*, vol. III, pp. 199–207.

[121] MM, vol. II, no. 627. Darrouzès has changed the editors' date (Dec. 1399) to Dec. 1401(?): *Reg.*, p. 464. Cf. Janin, *Géographie ecclésiastique*, vol. III, p. 341; *PLP*, no. 21007.

the transformation of a private religious foundation into an economic one by two aristocrats who were seemingly responding to the material opportunities presented by the wartime economy of shortages.[122] In July 1401, on the other hand, three monks from the Kosmidion monastery signed a promissory note, declaring that they would no longer sell sacred objects belonging to their monastery. It appears that these monks, hardpressed by the misery and poverty that struck nearly everyone in Constantinople, had endeavored to earn some extra income by trafficking in the marbles of the Kosmidion.[123]

The sad state of the smaller churches and monasteries of Constantinople illustrated by the foregoing examples stands in striking contrast to the economic strength and relative prosperity maintained by the monasteries of Mount Athos in the late fourteenth and early fifteenth centuries. A comparison of the well-established Athonite monasteries with the monasteries inside the city of Thessalonike revealed in Part II the rather precarious position of the latter.[124] The present analysis has demonstrated how much more pronounced and visible turned out to be the distinction between larger rural and smaller urban monasteries in a particular crisis situation such as a siege or military attack. Lacking the freedom and independence that allowed the monastic institutions of Mount Athos to bargain and come to terms with the Turkish authorities, most of the monasteries within the walls of Constantinople and Thessalonike crumbled when faced with enemy attacks and could, at best, hope to earn some privileges only after these cities fell to the Ottomans.

To recapitulate, when Emperor Manuel II traveled to the West at the end of 1399 in search of financial and military help, the pressures and hardships induced by Bayezid's protracted siege had become excessive in Constantinople. During the next few years conditions inside the city continued to deteriorate, leaving almost everyone from the common people to members of the highest levels of society impoverished and hopeless.

---

[122] MM, vol. II, no. 621 (Jan. 1401), pp. 457–8. On the church of Amolyntos, see Janin, *Géographie ecclésiastique*, vol. III, p. 157. The church had come down to Eirene and Andronikos from their unnamed maternal grandmother, who was related to the imperial family – the document calls her the Emperor's θεία – and bore the rank of *protovestiaria* (MM, vol. II, no. 621, p. 456). The latter had two children: the monk David Palaiologos and Theodora Palaiologina, the mother of Eirene and Andronikos. Eirene, on the other hand, had a son called Alexios Palaiologos (p. 458), who may perhaps be identified with Manuel Papylas' son-in-law by the same name we have encountered earlier (MM, vol. II, nos. 559 and 565; see above, pp. 170, 175). Cf. *PLP*, nos. 21420, 21422, 21354, 21355.

[123] MM, vol. II, no. 657. On the Kosmidion monastery, see Janin, *Géographie ecclésiastique*, vol. III, pp. 286–9.

[124] See above, ch. 4, pp. 59–60; ch. 5, pp. 92–7.

Dilapidated or demolished houses, unattended monasteries and churches, uncultivated gardens, vineyards, and fields were spread throughout the depopulated city that was daily losing growing numbers of inhabitants to Italian or Ottoman territories. Furthermore, those who remained in the city not only had to struggle with starvation and exhausted revenues but also had to protect themselves from opportunistic people who engaged in profiteering. The latter, consisting of a small group of wealthy merchants and businessmen who managed to continue participating in long-distance trade despite the blockade, endured minimal losses in comparison with the rest of the population. Judging from the exorbitant prices they charged for products they brought into Constantinople, the high interest rates they demanded for loans they handed out, and the investments they made in the city's real-estate market at prices well below actual values, they seem to have more than made up for whatever difficulties their trading ventures abroad might have sustained as a result of the siege.

If, on the other hand, Manuel II's departure for Europe in 1399 had initially aroused among the citizens of Constantinople expectations of western help, hopes were most certainly dwindling a year or two later, as the Emperor continued his tour of European courts without having accomplished much that was deemed satisfactory. Consequently, diverse groups of people who could no longer tolerate being confined inside a city with the social and economic conditions outlined above began to agitate in favor of surrender to Bayezid's forces. As early as about the time of Manuel's departure, the common people had been contemplating surrender, hoping that they would thereby escape starvation and misery.[125] During the years that followed, in addition to numerous citizens who fled from the capital and individually turned themselves in to the Ottoman soldiers standing guard outside the city walls,[126] several embassies were dispatched to the Sultan to propose to him the delivery of Constantinople. Patriarch Matthew reports in an encyclical he composed in 1401 that on three occasions, "a short time ago," ambassadors had been sent out of the city to negotiate with Bayezid. The patriarch claims that on each of these occasions he threatened the envoys with excommunication, lest they should attempt to betray the city to the enemy.[127] During the same year a priest called George Lopadiotes was summoned to the patriarchal court for his unseemly and suspicious acts in the service of certain *archontes*,

[125] Doukas–Grecu, XIV.4, p. 85.
[126] *Livre des fais du Mareschal Bouciquaut*, ed. Lalande, I.35, p. 152; Gautier (ed.), "Récit inédit," 106.
[127] MM, vol. II, no. 626, p. 466.

which included conveying messages for them outside the city, presumably to the Turks.[128] Indeed, stories about secret deals struck between various individuals and the Sultan circulated all through Constantinople, revealing how imminent the city's capitulation to the enemy must have seemed to most people at that time. Patriarch Matthew himself was implicated in an affair of this sort and was accused of having sought from Bayezid a guarantee for his personal safety and for the security of his position should the Sultan happen to take the city.[129] Whether the accusation was based on truth or, as Matthew argued, fabricated by his slanderous enemies, it did nonetheless give rise to widespread suspicion and unrest within Constantinople. Thus, in 1401 the patriarch was compelled to defend himself through a public proclamation addressed to "all the citizens, *archontes*, hieromonks and monks, and the entire Christian people."[130]

Shortly before the battle of Ankara (July 28, 1402) "the inhabitants of Constantinople" sent another embassy to Bayezid, selected from the city's notables. This time, however, because the Ottoman ruler was distracted by the recent challenge of Timur, they expected to be able to secure some concessions from him. The ambassadors were to inform the Sultan that the Constantinopolitans were ready to obey all his orders in the capacity of his vassals only, "since it was not possible for them to betray the city voluntarily at any time."[131] But, adds the same source, Bayezid would not hear of such a bargain, and the embassy ended without even a simple achievement as, for instance, the grant of freedom to the inhabitants to leave Constantinople for a place of their own choice, should Bayezid happen to capture the city.[132] What the anonymous Byzantine author reporting this event does not realize, or does not want to admit, however, is that under the precepts of Islamic law, a concession such as the one he mentions would normally be granted to the inhabitants of a city that surrendered, and not of one that was captured by force. Yet the Constantinopolitans at large seem to have been familiar with the Islamic practice since, following the failure of the above-mentioned embassy, "they were all ready to surrender themselves to the barbarians without battle after the victory [of Bayezid over Timur]."[133] This statement is confirmed by a letter John VII wrote to King Henry IV of England scarcely two months before the battle of Ankara, in which he stressed that the Byzantine capital was on the verge of submitting to Bayezid's men and urged the rulers of the Christian West to hurry to the

---

[128] Ibid., no. 637 (April 1401), p. 484.   [129] Ibid., no. 626, pp. 465–6.
[130] Ibid., pp. 463–7. For the English translation of this text, see Barker, *Manuel II*, pp. 208–11.
[131] Gautier (ed.), "Récit inédit," 108–10.   [132] Ibid., 110.   [133] Ibid., 110.

city's aid.[134] According to the historian Kritoboulos, too, sometime before Bayezid's encounter with Timur, an agreement had been reached between the Ottomans and "the citizens" of Constantinople, in which the latter promised to deliver themselves and their city to the Sultan on a specified day.[135]

There is no evidence indicating to what degree, if at all, the Byzantine government was involved in the preceding arrangements which the sources vaguely attribute to the "citizens" or "inhabitants" of Constantinople. Yet, just on the eve of the battle of Ankara, John VII, perhaps pressured by the determined conduct of the citizen body, is said to have made an agreement with Bayezid, promising to surrender Constantinople to the Ottomans immediately after the Sultan's anticipated victory over Timur.[136] About the same time, with or without the Emperor's knowledge or consent, a group of *archontes* from Constantinople set out for Kotyaeion (Kütahya), in order to deliver the keys of the city to the Sultan. Before they had a chance to complete their mission, however, the news was heard that Timur's forces had defeated the Ottoman army near Ankara and taken Bayezid captive. Delighted at this unforeseen development, the *archontes* bearing the city keys returned home, and Constantinople was thus saved from falling into the hands of the Ottomans.[137]

The Byzantines perceived the delivery of their capital from Bayezid's threat in 1402 as a miracle and ascribed it to divine intervention.[138] Some people, while rejoicing over the interference of the Virgin Mary in their

---

[134] Latin text and English translation in Barker, *Manuel II*, pp. 500–1, 213–14. The letter is dated June 1, 1402.

[135] Kritob.–Reinsch, I.16,10, pp. 32–3. This statement is included in a speech that Kritoboulos has put into Sultan Mehmed II's mouth. Chronologically it is rather confused, describing Timur's appearance in Asia Minor as "shortly after" (μικρὸν ὕστερον) the crusade of Nikopolis (1396). It attributes the citizens' decision to surrender to the severity of hunger and famine.

[136] Clavijo, *Embassy*, trans. Le Strange, p. 52. In accordance with the tradition of Byzantine diplomacy, John VII had simultaneously reached an agreement with Timur as well: see Barker, *Manuel II*, pp. 504–9. The statement by Symeon of Thessalonike that John VII had "promised him [Bayezid] many things and professed himself ready to pay him heavy tribute, do homage in other ways and almost serve him as a slave, if only he would consider making peace and not seek to have the City" seems to reflect earlier attempts of the Emperor to make peace with the Sultan so as not to lose Constantinople: see Symeon–Balfour, pp. 46, 118–19. See also MM, vol. II, nos. 543 (Jan. 1400), 556 (March 1400), pp. 341, 359 for references to certain *apokrisiarioi* who were apparently entrusted with the task of negotiating a peace settlement with the Ottomans: cf. Darrouzès, *Reg.*, nos. 3098, 3112, pp. 352, 361. For another official embassy sent by John VII to Bursa, "*ad matrem Zalapi*," in August 1401, see Iorga, *Notes*, vol. I, pp. 112–13 (document reprinted with translation and commentary in G. T. Dennis, "Three reports from Crete on the situation in Romania, 1401–1402," *StVen* 12 [1970], 244–6, 249–55); Barker, *Manuel II*, p. 212, n. 16.

[137] Schreiner, *Kleinchroniken*, vol. I, Chr. 22/28–30, pp. 184–5.

[138] See, for example, Gautier (ed.), "Action de grâces" and "Récit inédit." Note especially the beginning of the latter's title, "Διήγησις περὶ τοῦ γεγονότος θαύματος παρὰ τῆς ὑπεραγίας Θεοτόκου..."

favor on this occasion, were more concerned with what to do in order to maintain her and God's favorable disposition towards themselves during future calamities. Demetrios Chrysoloras, for instance, was of the opinion that the establishment of social and economic equity was the necessary precondition for continued enjoyment of divine beneficence in Constantinople. In a speech composed for the celebration of the first anniversary of the battle of Ankara, Chrysoloras wrote:

If we offer the proper things to the all-pure one [the Virgin], she will deliver us not only from our present misfortunes, but also from those expected in the future. And how will this happen? If those who possess do not revel in their possessions by themselves, but share them with those who do not possess. For it is wrong that some live in luxury while others perish of hunger, and those who suffer cannot rejoice easily, seeing that some enjoy all pleasures, whereas they themselves have a share in none at all.[139]

Stripped of its religious and moral overtones, Chrysoloras' thanksgiving to the Virgin bears testimony to this Byzantine intellectual's awareness that Constantinople was merely saved from destruction in 1402 by the timely emergence of an external power as a rival to Bayezid, and that in the long run only an internal remedy could ensure the city's and the empire's survival before the Ottomans. The remedy that Chrysoloras recommended was one which would be instrumental in reducing the sharp socioeconomic differentiation that existed among the inhabitants of the capital. Thus Chrysoloras' call for a general redistribution of wealth struck at the root of the major problems that weakened Constantinople in its struggle against Bayezid's forces and compelled many of its citizens to yield to the enemy, namely poverty, hunger, and depopulation caused to a large extent by frequent cases of flight from the city to escape the adverse circumstances.

The Virgin Mary was upheld by Byzantines as the patron saint and protectress of Constantinople, comparable to Thessalonike's St. Demetrios.
[139] "Action de grâces," ed. Gautier, 356, lines 142–8.

CHAPTER 8

From recovery to subjugation: the last fifty years of Byzantine rule in Constantinople (1403–1453)

The last fifty years of Constantinople under Byzantine rule constitute a critical period during which the city's inhabitants survived two Ottoman sieges (in 1411 and 1422) and, before finally succumbing to a third one in 1453, faced the union of their Church with the Church of Rome at the Council of Florence in 1439. The Union of Florence became the source of much controversy in the city and led to divisions among the population. That dissensions persisted among the citizens to the very last moment is indicated by Doukas, who reports that when Mehmed II's forces appeared before the Byzantine capital in 1453 a group of Constantinopolitans exclaimed in despair, "Would that the City were delivered into the hands of the Latins, who call upon Christ and the Mother of God, and not be thrown into the clutches of the infidel," while others contradicted them by declaring, "It would be better to fall into the hands of the Turks than into those of the Franks."[1] Although the union of the Churches was essentially a religious matter, reactions to it were not determined solely by people's religious views. Rather they were expressions of overall attitudes towards the Latins and the Ottomans, which in turn had been shaped by a set of political, social, and economic factors predating the Council of Florence. One of the purposes of this chapter is to examine, in the light of political, social, and economic developments, the attitudes displayed towards foreign powers by the inhabitants of the Byzantine capital during the last half century of its existence, in order to reach a better understanding of how or why people from diverse backgrounds were led towards the opinions they defended with regard to the union of the Churches and of the reasons underlying

---

[1] Doukas–Grecu, XXXVII.10, XXXIX.19, pp. 329 (lines 12–15), 365 (lines 29–30). The famous dictum attributed by Doukas to the grand duke Loukas Notaras is a variant of the latter statement: "Κρειττότερον ἐστιν εἰδέναι ἐν μέσῃ τῇ πόλει φακιόλιον βασιλεῦον Τούρκων ἢ καλύπτραν Λατινικήν" (ibid., p. 329, lines 11–12; see below, p. 216 and note 131). As reported by Marino Sanudo the Younger, a similar slogan – "The zarkula [i.e. the Turkish hat] is preferable to the baretta [i.e. the Venetian hat]" – was current among the Greeks of Corfu: see E. A. Zachariadou, "The neomartyr's message," Δελτίο Κέντρου Μικρασιατικῶν Σπουδῶν 8 (Athens, 1990–1), 53.

the two conflicting views, reported by Doukas, that were pronounced in 1453. The analysis of social and economic conditions during these years will, furthermore, enable us to evaluate to what degree Constantinople had been able to recover from the destructive effects of Bayezid I's siege, and in what state the city was by the time of Mehmed II's siege, which sealed its, and with it the Byzantine Empire's, fate before the Ottomans.

Unfortunately, information regarding political attitudes is not evenly distributed throughout these fifty years. For the period prior to the Council of Florence references to political attitudes are quite rare and incidental. Sources do not tend to disclose the dispositions of individuals or groups towards either the Latins or the Ottomans in a direct and systematic manner until after the Council, when they begin to report with some consistency the reactions that were aroused by the acceptance of the union. While this lopsidedness may be viewed as a problem originating from the nature of the sources, to some extent it may also be a reflection of reality itself because, with the exception of the two brief Ottoman sieges mentioned above, relatively peaceful relations were maintained between Constantinople and the Ottomans during most of the period preceding the Council of Florence, wherefore people may not have been as inclined to vocalize their political sentiments as they did in times of crisis or severe danger. The heavier emphasis placed in parts of this chapter on socioeconomic details, which are helpful in elucidating the different forces that played a role in the formation and evolution of political attitudes, is a direct consequence of this lopsidedness.

On the other hand, the source material on Mehmed II's siege, though abundant, is nonetheless limited in terms of its variety, compared with the material available on Bayezid I's siege. Most importantly, we are deprived of the acts of the patriarchal court of Constantinople (inextant after the initial years of the fifteenth century), which served as a rich mine of documentary evidence embodying precise data on socioeconomic conditions during the first Ottoman siege. Thus, for the reconstruction of social and economic life in Constantinople around the time of the Ottoman conquest, we have to depend mainly on literary sources. Given, however, the shortcomings and inaccuracies of the literary accounts of 1453 with regard to this type of information, the data presented in this chapter on the final years of the Byzantine capital will inevitably differ in nature and detail from the data presented in the previous chapter on Bayezid's siege.[2]

---

[2] For a discussion of the inaccurate nature of the literary accounts of 1453 in a different context, see M. Balard, "Constantinople vue par les témoins du siège de 1453," in *Constantinople and its Hinterland,*

In 1403 Demetrios Chrysoloras stated that the poor in Constantinople became rich after the fateful battle of Ankara.[3] This assertion, which is found in the hyperbolic thanksgiving oration delivered by Chrysoloras on the first anniversary of Bayezid I's defeat in the battle, cannot be accepted in a strictly literal sense. In fact, between 1403 and 1408 Chrysoloras himself received a letter from Manuel II in which the Emperor referred to the lack of private and public funds both in Constantinople and in Thessalonike.[4] Furthermore, the Castilian ambassador Clavijo, who visited Constantinople during the same year in which Chrysoloras composed his oration, described the city's ruined houses, churches, and monasteries, its conspicuously sparse population, and the almost village-like appearance of this once great urban center.[5] In his commemorative speech, then, Chrysoloras was clearly trying to paint a positive and optimistic picture which did not fully correspond to the actual conditions in Constantinople in the immediate aftermath of the battle of Ankara.

However, in the course of the decade that followed the battle, the Byzantine capital did embark upon a period of semi-recovery, largely aided by the civil wars among Bayezid's sons. A letter written by Joseph Bryennios during this period makes references, though in somewhat overstated terms, to "topmost prosperity of affairs," "wealth in all quarters," and "great peace," both external and internal.[6] Patriarch Matthew's testamentary *typikon* for the monastery of Charsianeites dated 1407 reports that "everyone," including the monastery itself, began to restore their devastated lands outside the city following Bayezid's removal, and gives evidence also of repairs undertaken on the monastery's tower, which had suffered damage during the latter's siege.[7] When, therefore, one of the contenders to the Ottoman throne, Musa Çelebi, laid siege to Constantinople in 1411, the citizens were able to withstand the challenge and repel his forces without too much hardship, even though a recent plague had wiped out a large part of the

ed. Mango and Dagron, pp. 169–77. The principal sources have been collected and edited, with Italian translation, in A. Pertusi, *La caduta di Costantinopoli*, 2 vols. (Verona, 1976); A. Pertusi, *Testi inediti e poco noti sulla caduta di Costantinopoli*, edizione postuma a cura di A. Carile (Bologna, 1983).

[3] "Action de grâces," ed. Gautier, 352.

[4] Dennis, *Letters of Manuel II*, no. 44, p. 117. See also ibid., no. 49, p. 141, for a reference to the financial straits of the Byzantine government in 1407–8.

[5] Clavijo, *Embassy*, pp. 87–8. Cf. Angold, "Decline of Byzantium," pp. 220–1.

[6] Τὰ παραλειπόμενα, ed. Mandakases, letter 24, pp. 179–80 (= "Ἐκ τῆς βυζαντινῆς Ἐπιστολογραφίας," ed. Tomadakes, 345). Bryennios' letter can be dated to the period of civil wars among Bayezid's sons (1402–13) since he writes of more than one Ottoman ruler, referring to them in the plural as satraps or tyrants none of whom caused trouble to the emperor.

[7] Konidares and Manaphes, "Ἐπιτελεύτιος βούλησις," 480–1 (= Hunger, "Testament," 301); English trans. in *BMFD*, vol. IV, p. 1639. For the destruction of the monastery's estates and tower during Bayezid's siege, see above, ch. 7, p. 176.

population.[8] A group of Constantinopolitans, nonetheless, fled to Venetian territories where they remained long after the lifting of Musa's siege, which prompted Emperor Manuel II to demand from the Senate of Venice their return in 1415.[9]

A more serious threat to the Byzantine capital came in the summer of 1422 with another Ottoman siege conducted by Murad II. A speech concerning the refortification of Constantinople which Joseph Bryennios delivered probably not long after 1415, subsequent to two speeches on the same subject by the Emperor and the patriarch, suggests that the city's walls may not have been in good condition at the time of Murad II's attack, for Bryennios reproached the wealthy citizens, particularly the *archontes*, for building three-story houses for themselves while the fortifications, which were in dire need of repairs, remained neglected over the past thirty years. Pointing out that the Ottomans could easily ravage the city within a single week given the poor state of the walls, Bryennios urged everyone, rich and poor, to hasten to make contributions towards the reconstruction work.[10] We can only guess what little impact the successive exhortations by the Emperor, the patriarch, and Bryennios must have had since John Kananos, the eyewitness to Murad II's siege, informs us that the victory of the Ottomans seemed so likely in 1422 that it gave rise to great panic and fear inside the city. The inhabitants, whose numbers must have been reduced further by plagues in 1417 and in 1420–1,[11] were terrified at the thought

---

[8] According to a short chronicle notice, the plague resulted in the deaths of ten thousand people: Schreiner, *Kleinchroniken*, vol. I, Chr. 9/41. See also ibid., Chr. 33/25 (Sept. 1409–Aug. 1410); vol. II, pp. 394–5; Iorga, *Notes*, vol. I, pp. 179–80; Thiriet, *Régestes*, vol. II, no. 1362 (Jan. 10, 1410). On Musa's siege, see Chalkok.–Darkó, vol. I, pp. 166–7; Doukas–Grecu, XIX.9, pp. 127–9. Doukas (p. 127, lines 30–2) notes, too, the capital's low population at the time of the siege.

[9] Iorga, *Notes*, vol. I, pp. 238–9; Thiriet, *Régestes*, vol. II, no. 1592 (Sept. 23, 1415).

[10] Ἰωσὴφ μοναχοῦ τοῦ Βρυεννίου τὰ εὑρεθέντα, ed. Boulgares, vol. II, pp. 273–82 (= "Ἰωσὴφ Βρυεννίου Δημηγορία περὶ τοῦ τῆς Πόλεως ἀνακτίσματος (1415 μ.Χ.)," ed. N. B. Tomadakes, *ΕΕΒΣ* 36 [1968], 3–12). The exact date of this speech cannot be determined; however, Bryennios' reference to the rebuilding of the Hexamilion as "recently" (ἔναγχος: Boulgares, p. 280; Tomadakes, 9–10, lines 188–92) points to a time shortly after 1415. On the other hand, the reference to "thirty years" during which the walls remained neglected (Boulgares, p. 280; Tomadakes, 9, lines 180–4) seems to be alluding to the former known repairs undertaken by John V c. 1389–91 (see above, ch. 6, p. 137 and note 80), which would place the date in the environs of 1419–21. At any rate, the speech has to antedate Murad II's siege in 1422 since Bryennios explicitly notes that it is a time of peace and truce with the Ottomans (Boulgares, p. 279; Tomadakes, 9, lines 168–9), apparently during the reign of Mehmed I. Three-story houses (τριώροφα: Boulgares, p. 280; Tomadakes, 9, line 183) were considered a symbol of wealth in Byzantium: see I. Ševčenko (ed.), "Alexios Makrembolites and his 'Dialogue between the Rich and the Poor'," *ZRVI* 6 (1960), 221, n. 10. For a concrete example of this type of construction activity, see John Chortasmenos' poems depicting the palace-like house of Theodore (Palaiologos) Kantakouzenos (d. 1410) in Constantinople, built "a short time ago" (νεωστί). On the house and its owner, see below, pp. 197–8.

[11] For these plagues, see Iorga, *Notes*, vol. I, p. 269; Thiriet, *Régestes*, vol. II, no. 1676 (Sept. 6, 1417); Doukas–Grecu, XX.3, p. 135; Sphrantzes–Grecu, V.2, VIII.1, pp. 8, 12. Note that Bryennios cites a

of falling into captivity. They worried, in particular, about the religious dangers which their community would have to face in the event of the capture of Constantinople by Murad II's forces, namely conversion to Islam, circumcision of children, destruction of churches and their replacement by mosques.[12] Meanwhile, a rumor about the capital's betrayal to the enemy culminated in the execution of the imperial official Theologos Korax, who was alleged to have made a secret pact with the Ottoman Sultan.[13] Nonetheless, the majority of the population, from the professional soldier to the untrained civilian, including monks, ecclesiastics, and women, are reported to have rallied to the city's defense against the Ottomans.[14]

As far as help from the West was concerned during the siege of 1422, on August 26 the Senate of Venice rejected a proposal for a naval operation against the Ottoman fleet near the shore of Constantinople. On the same day the Senate also took the decision to inform the Byzantine Emperor that it could not send any military or financial assistance to the besieged city before the following spring. The Venetian authorities suggested that the Emperor should instead seek such assistance from the Genoese and the Hospitallers of Rhodes, unless, they added, he should be amenable to making peace with Murad II, in which case Venice would gladly offer its services to facilitate a mediation between the two parties.[15] It is clear that Venice, in order to secure its commercial interests in the area, was making efforts to maintain good relations with the Ottoman Sultan, to the detriment of Byzantium. Indeed, following Murad II's accession to the throne in 1421, the Venetian Senate had sent the *bailo* of Constantinople, Benedetto Emo, to the Ottoman court in order to request from the new Sultan trading rights for Venetian merchants in Ottoman territories; the *bailo* was specifically instructed to conceal from the Byzantine Emperor the purpose of his visit to the Sultan.[16] Already at the time of Bayezid I's siege

---

figure of seventy thousand people or more in his speech on the rebuilding of the fortifications: Τὰ εὑρεθέντα, ed. Boulgares, vol. II, p. 280 (= "Δημηγορία," ed. Tomadakes, 9, line 188).

[12] Cananos, *L'assedio di Costantinopoli*, pp. 66–7, § 16. It should be noted that Kananos' account is marked by a heavy emphasis on religious matters. For another example of the fear of circumcision expressed by a Christian from Cyprus, whom the traveler Bertrandon de la Broquière met in Konya in the early 1430s, see *Voyage d'Outremer de B. de la Broquière*, pp. 117–19.

[13] Doukas–Grecu, XXVIII.1–4, pp. 229–35. On Theologos Korax, see above, ch. 6, pp. 142–4.

[14] Cananos, *L'assedio di Costantinopoli*, p. 71, §§ 20, 21.

[15] For these deliberations, see Sathas, *Documents*, vol. I, no. 79, pp. 119–23; Iorga, *Notes*, vol. I, pp. 323–4; Thiriet, *Régestes*, vol. II, nos. 1854, 1855.

[16] Iorga, *Notes*, vol. I, pp. 312–13; Thiriet, *Régestes*, vol. II, no. 1825 (Oct. 10, 1421). The requests of Venice from Murad II included the application in Ottoman territories of the same privileges that Venetian merchants enjoyed in Constantinople, and the right to extract from the Sultan's provinces 10,000 *modioi* of wheat annually. It should be noted that although Thessalonike, the second major city and commercial center of the Byzantine Empire, was under Ottoman attack when Venice agreed

the Venetians had shown their bias in favor of the Ottoman state through their unwillingness to provide military assistance to Byzantium, particularly following the failure of the Crusade of Nikopolis, which confirmed the growing power of the Ottomans. In 1398, for example, the Senate had twice rejected the proposition to send galleys to Constantinople and the Black Sea regions, considering the area too insecure for the commercial activities of Venetian merchants and desiring, moreover, not to aggravate Bayezid.[17] During Musa's siege in 1411 as well Venice had maintained a uniform position. Induced by the need to guard Venetian commercial interests, the Senate had sent an ambassador to the Ottoman ruler with specific instructions to resort to a cooperation with the Byzantine Emperor only if all efforts at concluding a favorable agreement with Musa were to fail.[18] As to the Genoese whom the Venetian Senate recommended to the Byzantine Emperor as a potential source of aid in 1422, ironically, it was on Genoese ships that Murad II and his forces had crossed from Anatolia to Rumelia earlier that year.[19] With its commercial interests in mind, Genoa too, like Venice, had made it a policy since the unsuccessful Crusade of Nikopolis to give priority to maintaining good relations with the Ottomans.[20] Constantinople could not, therefore, count on receiving help from either one of these Italian states.

It was by good fortune, though perhaps not by mere chance, that about three months after the beginning of military operations Murad II abruptly abandoned the siege of Constantinople in order to attend to a threat of civil war from his younger brother Mustafa in Anatolia.[21] The next

---

to take over its administration in 1423, the Venetians had no intention of pursuing an aggressive policy there towards the Ottomans, hoping immediately to establish peace with Murad II: Sathas, *Documents*, vol. I, no. 89 (July 27, 1423); Thiriet, *Régestes*, vol. II, no. 1898.

[17] Thiriet, *Régestes*, vol. I, no. 944 (June 13–22, 1398). Cf. E. Ashtor, *Levant Trade in the Later Middle Ages* (Princeton, 1983), p. 120.

[18] Thiriet, *Régestes*, vol. II, nos. 1419 (May 4, 1411), 1422 (June 4, 1411), 1424 (June 7, 1411); Iorga, *Notes*, vol. I, pp. 196–9. See also Thiriet, *Régestes*, vol. II, no. 1444 (March 7, 1412).

[19] Doukas–Grecu, XXV.8, pp. 209–11; Chalkok.–Darkó, vol. II, pp. 6–7; Sprantzes-Grecu, IX.4, p. 14; Kugéas, "Notizbuch," 151, § 78; Neşrî, *Kitâb-ı Cihan-nümâ*, vol. II, p. 565.

[20] See Barker, "Miscellaneous Genoese documents," 63–70. On Ottoman–Genoese commercial relations in the fourteenth and first half of the fifteenth centuries, see K. Fleet, *European and Islamic Trade in the Early Ottoman State. The Merchants of Genoa and Turkey* (Cambridge, 1999).

[21] Manuel II seems to have played a role in inciting Mustafa against Murad II so as to draw the latter away from the Byzantine capital: Doukas–Grecu, XXVIII.6, pp. 235–7. While some sources (Chalkok.–Darkó, vol. II, p. 12; Kugéas, "Notizbuch," 154, § 88; Neşrî, *Kitâb-ı Cihan-nümâ*, vol. II, p. 573) place Mustafa's uprising after the lifting of the siege and show no connection between the two events, such a connection is confirmed by an Ottoman chronological list, or annals, dated 1444–5: O. Turan (ed.), *İstanbul'un Fethinden Önce Yazılmış Tarihî Takvimler* (Ankara, 1954), p. 23. As in the case of Bayezid's blockade, many Byzantines, including Joseph Bryennios and the chroniclers Kananos and Sphrantzes, believed the deliverance of the city in 1422 to be a result of

time Ottoman forces appeared before the Byzantine capital the year was 1442, and on this occasion Murad II's troops were sent there not for a direct Ottoman assault, but to provide assistance to Demetrios Palaiologos, who had set his eye on the imperial throne of Byzantium.[22] During the intervening period of peace which was initiated by the Byzantine–Ottoman treaty of February 1424, the political and military recovery that had been in progress in Constantinople since the battle of Ankara was gradually attended with some degree of economic recovery as well, even though from the standpoint of international politics the peace treaty of 1424 tipped the scale in favor of the Ottomans and represented a major reversal for the Byzantine state.[23] A relatively minor event passed over in silence by all sources except the history of Chalkokondyles may well reflect the economic repercussions of the greater political and military stability provided by the maintenance of peaceful relations with the Ottomans. This was an armed conflict that broke out in 1434 between Genoa and the Byzantine government over the trade of Pera. Chalkokondyles does not give us the details, but it appears from his account that Emperor John VIII took certain measures at this time to put a check on the commercial role of the neighboring Genoese colony that for a long time had had a ruinous effect on the economy of Constantinople and the state treasury by attracting merchants and merchandise away from the Byzantine capital. Whatever the Emperor's measures were, they aggravated the Genoese and compelled them to take up arms against Constantinople. However, primarily as a result of the capable defense mounted by the Byzantine

divine intervention on the part of either the Virgin or God: Τὰ εὑρεθέντα, ed. Boulgares, vol. II, pp. 405ff., 414ff.; Cananos, *L'assedio di Costantinopoli*, pp. 73–5; Sphrantzes–Grecu, X.2, p. 14. See also Pero Tafur, *Travels and Adventures*, pp. 144–5, for a legendary story Pero Tafur heard in 1438 from the citizens of Constantinople about the protection of the city walls by an angel during an unsuccessful Ottoman siege which may well be that of Murad II.

[22] See above, ch. 6, p. 141 and note 95. Earlier, at the end of 1437 or beginning of 1438, Murad II contemplated attacking Constantinople, though not with the aim of conquest but in order to forestall Emperor John VIII, who had set out for the Council of Ferrara–Florence. This attack did not take place as the Sultan was dissuaded by his grand vizier Halil Paşa: see Sphrantzes–Grecu, XXIII.9–11, p. 60. Note also that Pero Tafur (*Travels and Adventures*, pp. 147–8) reports the march of Murad II to a place in the Black Sea region via the environs of Constantinople at the time of John VIII's absence from the city. According to Tafur's eyewitness account, some skirmishing took place near the city walls on this occasion, which must be a reference to the intended attack mentioned by Sphrantzes. I disagree with both Letts (*Travels and Adventures*, pp. 245–6), who sees Tafur's story as a reference to Murad II's siege of 1422, and A. Vasiliev, "Pero Tafur, a Spanish traveler of the fifteenth century and his visit to Constantinople, Trebizond, and Italy," *B* 7 (1932), 116, who believes it to be a reference to a meeting between Manuel II and Mehmed I that took place near Constantinople in 1421.

[23] On this treaty, see above, ch. 2, pp. 35–6 and note 48.

commander John Leontares,[24] the Genoese were not successful in their armed protest and submitted in the end to John VIII's demands, which included a tribute payment of a thousand gold coins, partly for the repair of damages to shops and warehouses along the Mese.[25] Tensions between Pera and Constantinople were nothing new or unusual as the Genoese colony, situated on the other side of the Golden Horn, across from the Byzantine capital, had been from the time of its foundation in 1267 a rival commercial center that absorbed the trade revenues of the latter. Yet what seems outstanding in 1434 was the Byzantine Emperor's attempt to hamper this development that had nearly resulted in the substitution of Pera for Constantinople as a port of commerce. It is true that former Byzantine emperors had made efforts to draw merchants away from Pera back to Constantinople, but the last-known attempts of this sort date back to the late 1340s.[26] Thereafter, particularly subsequent to the 1380s, the political and economic weakness of the Byzantine state did not permit such attempts. In 1434, on the contrary, we see that John VIII not only revived attempts at control but was also partially successful with them, a success which must be attributed to the political recovery noted above. Soon after the termination of hostilities towards the end of 1434, smooth and regular contacts between Pera and Constantinople appear to have been resumed, as Genoese merchants and businessmen figure prominently in the accounts that Giacomo Badoer kept in Constantinople between 1436 and 1440.[27]

Italian merchants, who had considered the Byzantine capital too insecure a port for their trading activities in the late 1390s,[28] poured into the city in continuously increasing numbers throughout the third decade of the fifteenth century. Bertrandon de la Broquière, who visited Constantinople during 1432–3, wrote that he saw many foreign merchants there – most notably Venetians, as well as Genoese and Catalans.[29] Following the Council of Florence in 1439, the Byzantine Emperor offered Florentine merchants a quarter in Constantinople and granted them commercial privileges

---

[24] This commander has been identified as John Laskaris Leontares (d. 1437), governor of Selymbria and son of Demetrios Laskaris Leontares (d. 1431). See Schreiner, *Kleinchroniken*, vol. II, pp. 449, 445; *PLP*, nos. 14679, 14676.

[25] Chalkok.–Darkó, vol. II, pp. 59–62. See P. Schreiner, "Venezianer und Genuesen während der ersten Hälfte des 15. Jahrhunderts in Konstantinopel (1432–1434)," *StVen* 12 (1970), 364–8.

[26] Laiou, "Observations on the results of the Fourth Crusade," 56 and n. 37.

[27] Seventy (14.7 percent) of Badoer's clients were Genoese: see, M. M. Sitikov, "Konstantinopolj i Venetsianskaja torgovlja v pervoij polovine XV v. po dannym knigi sčetov Džakomo Badoera, Delovye krugi Konstantinopolja," *VV* 30 (1969), 53 (Table 1). Cf. *Badoer: Indici*, pp. 98 ("Peroti"), 127 ("Zenoexi").

[28] See p. 189 and note 17 above.   [29] *Voyage d'Outremer de B. de la Broquière*, pp. 150, 164.

similar to, but less extensive than, those enjoyed by merchants from Venice and Genoa.[30] These grants were undoubtedly accorded to Florentine merchants as a diplomatic gesture in honor of the Union of Florence. Nonetheless, the gesture itself is strongly indicative of the interest the Florentines must have had in participating in the revitalized commerce of the Byzantine capital at this time. The information preserved in the account book of the Venetian merchant Giacomo Badoer further demonstrates that by the second half of the 1430s, if not earlier, Constantinople had become once again the bustling center of international trade it was traditionally reputed to be. A detailed description of the city's central marketplace, written by a Byzantine during the third decade of the fifteenth century, may be seen as a by-product of this economic reawakening which must have given rise to a heightened interest in the commercial life of Constantinople.[31]

The list of transactions Badoer recorded in his account book, covering the period of his residence in Constantinople from 1436 to about 1440, bears testimony not only to the large number of foreign, primarily Italian, merchants who had business affairs there, but also to the exchanges that took place between them and their Byzantine counterparts.[32] The Greek subjects of the Byzantine Empire who appear in the account book – altogether 130 people, excluding the Greeks who are specifically reported to be from the Italian colonies – comprise slightly over 27 percent of Badoer's 477 business associates.[33] Among the recurring Byzantine names, those belonging to members of the leading aristocratic families of Constantinople are prominent, as, for example, the Palaiologoi, the Kantakouzenoi, the Doukai and Doukai Rhadenoi, the Notarades, the Sophianoi, the Goudelai, the Iagareis, the Argyroi, the Laskareis, the Synadenoi, and several others.[34]

---

[30] Dölger, *Reg.*, vol. v, nos. 3487–90; MM, vol. iii, p. 202. In 1439 the customs duty (*kommerkion*) required from Florentines was lowered from 4 percent to 2 percent of the value of merchandise, whereas Venetian and Genoese merchants were paying no *kommerkion* at this time. Byzantine subjects, on the other hand, paid the *kommerkion* at its full rate of 10 percent until the mid fourteenth century, after which it was reduced for them to 2 percent. See Antoniadis-Bibicou, *Recherches sur les douanes*, pp. 97–155; Oikonomidès, *Hommes d'affaires*, pp. 43–5, 52. On the Florentine quarter and other merchant colonies of the Latins in Constantinople, see R. Janin, *Constantinople byzantine: développement urbain et répertoire topographique*, 2nd edn. (Paris, 1964), pp. 245–55; Balard, "L'organisation des colonies," pp. 261–76.

[31] "Comédie de Katablattas," ed. Canivet and Oikonomidès, 55–7. The marketplace, where both large- and small-scale trade took place, was situated along the Golden Horn.

[32] Cf. Šitikov, "Konstantinopolj," 48–62; T. Bertelè, "Il giro d'affari di Giacomo Badoer: precisazioni e deduzioni," in *Akten des XI. internationalen Byzantinistenkongresses, München 1958* (Munich, 1960), pp. 48–57; Oikonomidès, *Hommes d'affaires*, pp. 20, 53–4, 58, 60, 68, 80–2, 120–3; Laiou-Thomadakis, "Byzantine economy," 203–4.

[33] Šitikov, "Konstantinopolj," Table 1, p. 53.

[34] See Appendix III below; cf. *Badoer: Indici*, pp. 79–80 ("Griexi").

The earlier contacts of some of these families (namely, the Goudelai, Notarades, and Palaiologoi) with Italian merchants noted in previous chapters indicate the firm and relatively long-standing nature of their economic ties with Italy.

The impression one gets from Badoer's account book can be misleading, however, if one is to assume that the good relations maintained between the Italians and the capital's aristocratic entrepreneurs were characteristic of or extended to all types of merchants in the city. Thanks to a series of Venetian documents dating from the first half of the fifteenth century, we know about certain hostilities and acts of aggression that were inflicted at this time upon the Venetians in Constantinople by the city's native inhabitants. Without going into individual details, since this subject has already been treated elsewhere, it should be sufficient for present purposes to point out that the majority of the conflicts brought to light by these documents had economically related causes, and that the Byzantines against whom charges of violence were leveled appear to have been small merchants and tradesmen, as well as minor government officials.[35] They were, in other words, people of modest social background who stand in stark contrast to Badoer's aristocratic clients. It seems that they resented the dominant role played by the Venetians in the commercial life of Constantinople which, as we know, was not restricted to international trading activities, but extended to enterprises in the city's retail market as well.[36] Hence, while a group of Byzantine aristocrats were able to reap personal profits from their business association with Italians, the small merchants and retail traders of Constantinople, whose economic interests were threatened by the absorption of foreigners into the city's local exchange market, exhibited strong anti-Italian sentiments.

Viewed from a broader perspective, the situation outlined above, by way of exposing the benefits accruing to an affluent minority under circumstances that proved detrimental to the well-being of a larger segment of the population composed of poorer people, points to the existence of a conflict between private and public interests. Although a phenomenon commonly attested in various societies at different times, this conflict merits emphasis here because its existence at this particular juncture in the history of

[35] For a full analysis of the contents of these documents, see Necipoğlu, "Byzantines and Italians in fifteenth-century Constantinople," 132–6.

[36] The Byzantine government took certain measures in the course of the fourteenth and fifteenth centuries to protect the retail activities of the city's native merchants from the encroachment of Italians; however, such measures were rare and in the long run ineffective: see Necipoğlu, "Byzantines and Italians in fifteenth-century Constantinople," 136–7.

Constantinople had serious consequences in terms of the city's fate before the Ottomans. As a matter of fact, the theme of public versus private interests lay at the core of Joseph Bryennios' aforementioned speech concerning the fortifications of Constantinople. Bryennios constantly reminded his audience that unless they gave priority to the common good and contributed to the restoration of the walls, their insistence on their personal well-being, as exemplified by the building of lavish mansions on the part of the rich, would result in the city's captivity.[37] Another example of the conflict between private and public interests is provided by the well-known efforts of some fifteenth-century Byzantine merchants to evade the payment of customs duties (the *kommerkion*) to the Byzantine state, either by trying to pass as *kommerkion*-exempt Venetians, or by entrusting their merchandise to the latter for the duration of customs controls.[38] In a letter to the Senate of Venice dated May 31, 1418, Emperor Manuel II complained about how the Byzantine treasury, deprived of its customs revenues as a result of these practices, was left in a worse state than that to which the wars with the Ottomans had reduced it.[39] Exaggerated though the Emperor's statement may be, it reveals nonetheless the process whereby a group of fraudulent Byzantine merchants steadily multiplied their wealth by what they held back from the state's public revenues. The result was the personal enrichment of a few individuals without any benefit to the Constantinopolitan economy at large.

It is, therefore, crucial at this point to modify or redefine more precisely the meaning of what was designated in broad terms as "economic recovery" at the outset of this discussion of economic conditions in Constantinople during the second quarter of the fifteenth century.[40] In view of the foregoing observations, economic recovery can be understood to mean neither economic recovery of the whole population, nor the recovery of the entire economy. It denotes, on the contrary, a return to opulence and luxury for some propertied citizens, while large sections of the population continued to live in hardship and deprivation. In this respect, it is significant to draw attention to the fact that the Byzantine aristocrats who did business with Badoer purchased from him substantially more goods than they sold to him, revealing the consumption-oriented nature of their commercial activities which, moreover, created a deficit economy owing to the higher total

---

[37] Τὰ εὑρεθέντα, ed. Boulgares, vol. ΙΙ, pp. 277–9 (= "Δημηγορία," ed. Tomadakes, 6–8).
[38] Thiriet, *Régestes*, vol. ΙΙ, nos. 1544 (July 24, 1414), 1705 (July 21, 1418); Iorga, *Notes*, vol. Ι, pp. 281–2; Chrysostomides, "Venetian commercial privileges," doc. 19, pp. 354–5.
[39] Chrysostomides, "Venetian commercial privileges," 354–5.   [40] See p. 190 above.

value of the imported goods they bought in comparison with the total value of the domestic goods they sold.[41]

Such factors explain why indeed in contemporary sources, along with signs of the prospering economic activities of particular individuals, it is not uncommon to come across references to widespread poverty and general economic decline. For example, the Spanish traveler Pero Tafur, who visited Constantinople twice during 1437–8, observed that "the inhabitants are not well clad, but sad and poor, showing the hardships of their lot."[42] He noted on two occasions that the city was sparsely populated, once adding that there was a shortage of good soldiers.[43] Making several allusions to the city's bygone days of prosperity, he described the imperial palace which "must have been very magnificent, but now it is in such state that both it and the city show well the evils which the people have suffered and still endure."[44] By contrast, he described Pera as a flourishing and prosperous city: "It is a place of much traffic in goods brought from the Black Sea, as well as from the West, and from Syria and Egypt, so that everyone is wealthy."[45] After seeing the thriving commercial market of the Genoese colony, Pero Tafur appears not to have been impressed by what he saw of the trade of Constantinople, so he had not a single word to say about the latter. The things he rather found impressive in Constantinople were historic monuments, which merely bore testimony to the former splendor of a city that was in a veritable state of decline in his day. Having observed all this, he finally could not help likening the Byzantine Emperor to "a Bishop without a See."[46]

It is conceivable that the desolation Pero Tafur witnessed in Constantinople was partly due to an outbreak of plague in the city in 1435.[47] Indeed, Tafur himself, though without suggesting any links, wrote about continuing precautions in Constantinople and Pera for protection against the spread of the disease by ships arriving from the Black Sea region early in 1438.[48] Yet even before the plague of 1435, travelers to Constantinople had observed conditions not unlike those reported by Pero Tafur, so it would be a mistake to ascribe in full to the plague the adversity and

---

[41] The goods Byzantines bought from Badoer in Constantinople represent in value 24.7 percent of all his sales, while the goods they sold to him represent in value only 9.5 percent of all his purchases: Šitikov, "Konstantinopolj," Table 1, p. 53.

[42] Pero Tafur, *Travels and Adventures*, p. 146. On Pero Tafur's visits to Constantinople, see Vasiliev, "Pero Tafur," 91–7, 102–17; Angold, "Decline of Byzantium," pp. 223–5.

[43] Pero Tafur, *Travels and Adventures*, pp. 123, 146.   [44] Ibid., pp. 139, 145–6.

[45] Quoted from the revised translation of Letts's text (p. 149) in Vasiliev, "Pero Tafur," 116–17.

[46] Pero Tafur, *Travels and Adventures*, p. 145.   [47] Thiriet, *Régestes*, vol. III, no. 2402 (Dec. 27, 1435).

[48] Pero Tafur, *Travels and Adventures*, p. 138.

distress registered in his pages. Cristoforo Buondelmonti, who visited the Byzantine capital in 1422, called it the "ill-starred city" and wrote about ruined and deserted structures, part of which had found some use in the hands of the local people who planted with vines the lands upon which they were situated.[49] Bertrandon de la Broquière, who spent time in Constantinople during 1432–3, also described the devastated state of the city and its environs.[50] It is clear, then, that despite the breathing space allowed by the relatively peaceful relations with the Ottomans, little overall progress had been experienced in Constantinople since the time of Clavijo's visit in 1403 mentioned at the beginning of the present chapter.

Moreover, some signs of social disturbances are detected in the city during the first half of the fifteenth century, which may possibly be linked to the detrimental gap separating public and private interests. In a letter written between 1404 and 1416, John Chortasmenos depicts an atmosphere ridden by internal strife and civil unrest. The letter, after praising the *archon* and senator Melissenos as a model politician embodying the four Platonic cardinal virtues (σωφροσύνη, δικαιοσύνη, ἀνδρεία, φρόνησις), congratulates the competence with which he appeased the capital's discontented populace who were threatening the ruling classes. Chortasmenos, who portrays Melissenos as a uniquely virtuous and capable statesman whose conduct should set an example to all others in the Senate of Constantinople, unfortunately does not mention his first name.[51] But he may perhaps be identified with Andronikos Apokaukos Melissenos, likewise a member of the Senate, whose name appears in a number of documents dating between 1397 and 1409.[52] These documents reveal that Andronikos Apokaukos Melissenos was an *oikeios* of Manuel II and an influential statesman with many responsibilities. He participated in a survey of the treasures of the church of Saint Sophia (October 1397); he acted as a witness to the Byzantine–Venetian treaty of May 22, 1406; he was present at a synod that excommunicated the bishops Makarios of Ankara and Matthew of Medeia (August 1409). He possibly made a trip to Bursa in 1401 as John VII's envoy to negotiate peace terms with the Ottomans. The mention of a "Melisino" in the account book of Badoer indicates, furthermore, that

---

49 Buondelmonti, *Description des îles de l'Archipel*, pp. 84, 88; cf. Angold, "Decline of Byzantium," p. 228.
50 *Voyage d'Outremer de B. de la Broquière*, pp. 153, 167–9.
51 *Chortasmenos*, ed. Hunger, letter 51, pp. 207–8; cf. 117–18.
52 MM, vol. II, no. 686, p. 566 (Apokaukos Melissenos); MM, vol. III, p. 153 (Andronikos Apokaukos Melissenos); Laurent, "Trisépiscopat," 134 (Andronikos Melissenos); Iorga, *Notes*, vol. I, pp. 112–13 ("Molissinus"). Cf. PLP, no. 17809.

the family incorporated individuals who engaged in trade and business in association with Italian merchants.[53]

The picture of social unrest conveyed by Chortasmenos' letter finds further confirmation in a nearly contemporaneous letter written by Joseph Bryennios between 1402 and 1413. Bryennios, who informs his addressee about the current state of affairs in Constantinople, notes with pleasure that the city was menaced neither by upheavals on the part of the common people nor by disturbances within the Senate, implying how untypical this novel situation was.[54] Since Bryennios and Chortasmenos provide no details about the specific nature or causes of these popular agitations other than the fact that they threatened the rule of the upper classes, we have to turn for clues to additional pieces of contemporary evidence concerning the conduct and lifestyle of the ruling elite in Constantinople. Some relevant information is available about Theodore (Palaiologos) Kantakouzenos, "uncle" (θεῖος) of the Emperor Manuel II and a colleague of Andronikos Apokaukos Melissenos in the Senate.[55] Chortasmenos has left us descriptions of a palatial house Theodore had built for himself in the finest section of Constantinople (ἐν καλλίστῳ τόπῳ), presumably during the first decade of the fifteenth century. According to these descriptions, very valuable and costly materials, including "the best quality of wood" and "the most splendid kind of marble," were used in the construction of this magnificent pillared house.[56] Like most other members of the capital's wealthy upper class, moreover, Theodore had established strong connections with Italy and on December 27, 1398 had received the civil rights of Venice.[57] In fact, a document dated 1409 which lists the names of some twenty Senate members reveals the magnitude of this latter trend among the capital's ruling elite. At least six of the senators listed in the document of 1409 (Theodore Palaiologos Kantakouzenos, Nicholas Notaras, Nicholas Sophianos, George Goudeles, Demetrios Palaiologos Goudeles,

---

[53] *Badoer*, pp. 405, 610. See Appendix III below.

[54] *Τὰ παραλειπόμενα*, ed. Mandakases, letter 24, pp. 179–80 (= "Ἐκ τῆς βυζαντινῆς Ἐπιστολογραφίας," ed. Tomadakes, 345). For the date of the letter, see note 6 above.

[55] Both men attended the synod in August 1409 that excommunicated Makarios of Ankara and Matthew of Medeia: Laurent, "Trisépiscopat," 133–4. See Appendix IV below; cf. *PLP*, no. 10966.

[56] *Chortasmenos*, ed. Hunger, pp. 190–2, 194–5; cf. 104–9. For a plausible identification of this house with Mermerkule in Istanbul, see U. Peschlow, "Mermerkule – Ein spätbyzantinischer Palast in Konstantinopel," in *Studien zur byzantinischen Kunstgeschichte. Festschrift für Horst Hallensleben zum 65. Geburtstag*, ed. B. Borkopp, B. Schellewald, and L. Theis (Amsterdam, 1995), pp. 93–7; U. Peschlow, "Die befestigte Residenz von Mermerkule. Beobachtungen an einem spätbyzantinischen Bau im Verteidigungssystem von Konstantinopel," *JÖB* 51 (2001), 385–403, esp. 394–7, 401–3.

[57] V. Laurent, "Alliances et filiations des Cantacuzènes au XVe siècle. Le Vaticanus latinus 4789," *REB* 9 (1952), 82, n. 6.

and one of either Demetrios Laskaris Leontares or Manuel Bryennios Leontares) are individuals whose political and economic ties with Italy are known; in addition, at least four belong to families that are noted for their connections with Italy (Philanthropenos, Asanes, Melissenos).[58] As far as Theodore (Palaiologos) Kantakouzenos himself is concerned, the sumptuous life he led in Constantinople may be attributed in part to the financial security and flexibility which his association with the Venetian republic was likely to have provided. The stirrings of the common people to which Chortasmenos and Bryennios allude may well have been directed at men like Theodore who continued to live in a somewhat extravagant fashion despite the exigencies of the time that required restraint from excesses. In this context, it might be pertinent to call attention once again to the accusation Joseph Bryennios leveled, *circa* 1415–21, against the wealthy *archontes* of Constantinople who built three-story houses for themselves instead of contributing money for the restoration of the city walls.[59]

The undertakings of another government official who was active in Constantinople from 1430 onwards furnish additional clues about what might have provoked the disorders among the common people. While this official was neither as highly placed as members of the senatorial class nor a native of Constantinople, he nonetheless served in the city as a judge, frequented the imperial palace, knew Emperor John VIII personally, and had close relations with some of the highest dignitaries in the capital. According to a text written as an invective against him (which, therefore, must be used with caution), this man, besides engaging in numerous legal malpractices, habitually abused the authority of his post to obtain victuals, free of charge, for his personal consumption at the marketplace of Constantinople. Coercing some by threats and others by false promises, he regularly pestered small craftsmen for free or underpriced artisanal products as well. The judge in question, who adopted the name "Katadokeinos" in Constantinople, was none other than Katablattas, who lived in Thessalonike during 1403–30 and served as a scribe in that city's tribunal.[60] Assuming that the accusations made against Katablattas-Katadokeinos are simply exaggerated rather than being altogether false, it is conceivable that such abuses of power by well-placed civil servants played a role, too, in triggering the disturbances among the capital's populace.

---

[58] Laurent, "Trisépiscopat," 133–4. See Appendix IV below.

[59] See pp. 187, 194 and note 10 above.

[60] "Comédie de Katablattas," ed. Canivet and Oikonomidès, 51ff.; see above, ch. 4, pp. 73–4. For earlier examples of government officials abusing their authority to make personal gains and profit, see Matschke, "Commerce, trade, markets, and money," pp. 774–5, 800–1.

The evidence presented so far has served to highlight mainly the attitudes embraced by people from the lower classes towards the Italians or towards upper-class Byzantines, many of whom had close associations with Italians. An incident recounted by Bertrandon de la Broquière reflects, in turn, the disposition of two ordinary citizens of the Byzantine capital towards the Ottomans. In 1432 Bertrandon arrived at Constantinople on a Byzantine boat that transported him from Scutari (Üsküdar), the Ottoman port on the Asian side of the Bosphorus, to Pera. At first the two Greek boatsmen who ferried him across the Bosphorus mistook him for a Turk and treated him with great honor and esteem. However, upon their arrival at Pera, when they discovered that he was a European, they abandoned their respectful attitude, and Bertrandon suspected that they would have used force against him had he not been armed. The Burgundian traveler interpreted the behavior of the boatsmen on religious grounds, attributing it to the hatred which the Byzantines nurtured in general towards "Christians who obey the Church of Rome."[61] Yet this does not necessarily account for the better treatment he received when he was misidentified as a Turk. It will be instructive, therefore, to examine some sources which offer additional insights about the attitudes of the inhabitants of Constantinople towards the Ottomans and which shed light on certain forms of contact, other than military encounters, that helped the Byzantines become better acquainted with the Ottomans in the first half of the fifteenth century.

We have seen already that the political and military stability provided by the Byzantine–Ottoman peace treaty of 1424 had some positive economic consequences in Constantinople. In ideological terms, however, the conditions of this treaty, which included the resumption of tribute payment to the Ottomans in addition to important territorial concessions, were regarded by some Byzantines as a clear demonstration of their submission. Disillusioned by the steady decline of Byzantium before the growing power of the Ottomans, and considering the political and military superiority as well as the prosperity enjoyed by the latter to be signs of the truth of their religion, certain people subsequently chose to convert to Islam, and others were apparently inclined to follow their example, as may be inferred from four successive discourses which Makarios Makres composed around this time. These discourses, Christian apologies addressed to "those who are led astray by the success of the infidels," were intended to strengthen the wavering faith of the citizens and to urge them not to be tempted by

<hr/>

[61] *Voyage d'Outremer de B. de la Broquière*, pp. 148–9. On Bertrandon's attitudes towards Byzantines and Turks, see also Angold, "Decline of Byzantium," pp. 222–5.

the prominence and material well-being of the Ottomans into embracing Islam. They should instead resist the enemy, argued Makarios Makres, and, if necessary, be ready to abandon this world as Christian martyrs rather than abandoning their own faith.[62] Thus, it is clear that in the opinion of at least some people the Ottomans deserved respect and admiration on account of their superior military and political power, which confirmed the superiority of their religion as well. That this was the standard argument of the Ottomans repeated in nearly all contemporary anti-Islamic polemical texts, whether written in the form of fictitious dialogues between Christians and Muslims or recording real discussions encouraged by the Ottomans in their own territory, is beside the point.[63] Makarios Makres' four discourses bear testimony to the crucial fact that the same argument found acceptance among some of the citizens of the Byzantine capital who were driven by the particular historical circumstances of the 1420s towards a favorable assessment of the Ottomans and of their religion. At the end of the fourteenth century, too, the Ottoman victory at Nikopolis had given rise to a similar mood, at which time cases of conversion to Islam are attested on the part of some citizens who came to look upon the Ottomans with great esteem.[64]

The inhabitants of Constantinople were also likely to have been influenced by their personal encounters with the Ottomans in forming their opinions of them. We should, therefore, investigate some sources that document the presence and activities of Ottomans, mostly merchants, in the Byzantine capital during the first half of the fifteenth century. Even though these sources do not incorporate evidence directly bearing on political or religious attitudes, they provide nonetheless pertinent information about contacts occurring at the personal level between Constantinopolitans and Ottomans.

---

[62] "Πρὸς τοὺς σκανδαλιζομένους ἐπὶ τῇ εὐπραγίᾳ τῶν ἀσεβῶν, λόγοι δ´," in *Macaire Makrès*, ed. Argyriou, pp. 239–300; see esp. 239–41, 291, 297–8, 300. On the disputed authorship and dating of these discourses, see ibid., pp. 57–62, 65–9. Argyriou presumes the most likely date of composition to be the fall of 1422; yet the discourses must certainly have been composed sometime after the Byzantine–Ottoman treaty of 1424, given that Makres twice mentions the tribute paid to the Ottomans: ibid., pp. 241, 298.

[63] See, for example, "Ἰωσὴφ τοῦ Βρυεννίου μετά τινος Ἰσμαηλίτου Διάλεξις," ed. A. Argyriou, *EEBΣ* 35 (1966–7), 141–95; A. Philippidis-Braat, "La captivité de Palamas chez les Turcs: dossier et commentaire," *TM* 7 (1979), 109–221; *Manuel II. Palaiologos, Dialoge mit einem "Perser,"* ed. E. Trapp (Vienna, 1966). Cf. Ševčenko, "Decline of Byzantium," 178–81; *Macaire Makrès*, ed. Argyriou, pp. 64–5, 156–68; E. A. Zachariadou, "Religious dialogue between Byzantines and Turks during the Ottoman expansion," in *Religionsgespräche im Mittelalter*, ed. B. Lewis and F. Niewöhner (Wiesbaden, 1992), pp. 289–304.

[64] See above, ch. 7, note 13.

It may be recalled that during the last decade of the fourteenth century a Turkish quarter that contained a mosque had been established within Constantinople. At that time a number of Ottoman merchants were active in Constantinople, and in order to settle their commercial disputes a Muslim judge (kadi) had been installed inside the city at the request of Bayezid I.[65] However, following the battle of Ankara, the Byzantine Emperor expelled the inhabitants of the Turkish quarter and ordered the destruction of their mosque.[66] There is no documented evidence thereafter about the presence of a kadi in Constantinople until 1432, the year when Bertrandon de la Broquière visited the city and noted the existence of an Ottoman official there to whom Turkish traders went for litigation.[67] But Ottoman traders did not cease from going to Constantinople during the intervening period, even though the Ottoman port of Scutari (Üsküdar) on the opposite shore seems to have emerged as an alternative site for commercial exchanges between the Turks and Byzantines at this time. According to Clavijo, who stayed in Constantinople/Pera for five months during the winter of 1403–4, Turkish traders daily crossed to Constantinople and Pera, while Byzantines and Latins from these two cities frequented the weekly market in Scutari.[68] Nearly two decades later, the Russian pilgrim Zosima, who visited the Byzantine capital twice between late 1419 and 1422, also observed that Greeks and Latins from Constantinople and Pera went across the straits to Scutari in order to trade with the Turks.[69] On the other hand, two eyewitnesses reported in 1416 that Turks ('Αγαρηνοί, *Turci*) entered the city in large numbers, one adding that some were there only in transit while some were actual inhabitants.[70] In 1418, moreover, when Manuel II complained to the Senate of Venice about Venetian merchants who were helping his own subjects evade the customs duties (*kommerkion*) they were supposed to pay to the Byzantine state, the Emperor cited among the defrauders, in addition to Greeks and other Byzantine subjects, Turkish merchants.[71] The Emperor curiously referred to the latter as "our Turks," which could

---

[65] See above, ch. 6, pp. 138–9.

[66] Aşıkpaşazade–Giese, pp. 61–2 (= Aşıkpaşazade–Atsız, p. 137).

[67] *Voyage d'Outremer de B. de la Broquière*, p. 165.

[68] For this important statement, which does not appear in the English translation of the text by G. Le Strange, see Ruy Gonzáles de Clavijo, *Embajada a Tamorlán*, ed. F. López Estrada (Madrid, 1999), p. 146.

[69] *Russian Travelers*, ed. Majeska, pp. 190–1.

[70] Statement by the metropolitan of Medeia to the Patriarch Euthymios (1410–16) reported by Syropoulos: *"Mémoires,"* p. 102; and observation by John of Ragusa in E. Cecconi, *Studi storici sul concilio di Firenze*, vol. 1 (Florence, 1869), p. dxi.

[71] Chrysostomides, "Venetian commercial privileges," doc. 19, pp. 354–5; cf. p. 194 above.

either mean that they were Turks who resided in Constantinople, or alternatively they may have been Turks who had continued to live in places
such as Thessalonike, Kalamaria, and the coastal cities of Thrace that the
Ottomans restored to Byzantium after the battle of Ankara, wherefore they
would have been considered Byzantine subjects.

Yet, if we leave aside these earlier occasional references to Turkish visitors and residents of Constantinople, it is during the same decade when
Bertrandon de la Broquière first bore witness to the city's re-established
Ottoman kadi, that is in the 1430s, that we also begin to hear extensively
about the activities of a group of Ottoman merchants within the Byzantine capital. This information has been preserved in the account book of
Badoer, who conducted business with at least twelve Ottoman merchants
in Constantinople between 1436 and 1440.[72] These merchants traded in
wax, raisins, hide, wool, flax, and cloth. The scope of their activities, like
their numbers, was certainly small. But it should be borne in mind that
the source in question singularly lists those people who happened to have
commercial transactions with Badoer. Furthermore it gives little indication
of their possible business affairs with other people in Constantinople. For
instance, only two of the twelve Ottoman merchants cited by Badoer can
be observed holding business relations with Byzantines from Constantinople. And not surprisingly, these were banking transactions that transpired
between the Turks and two renowned Constantinopolitan bankers – John
Sophianos and Nicholas Sarantenos – regarding payments for merchandise
that had been exchanged between Badoer and the Turks.[73]

Outstanding among Badoer's Turkish clients is one by the name of "Ali
Basa," who has been identified as the Ottoman grand vizier Çandarlı Halil
Paşa.[74] Evidence of Halil Paşa's involvement in the trade of Constantinople
is quite consequential as it brings a new dimension to what has long been
known from Ottoman, Byzantine, and Latin narrative sources about his
favorable political disposition towards the Byzantine state. These sources
depict him as the leader of a peace faction at the Ottoman court who

---

[72] These merchants were: *Ali Basa turcho* (*Badoer*, pp. 382, 390, 391); *Choza Ali turcho* (pp. 341, 375);
Amet turco de Lichomidia (pp. 7, 27, 33, 84, 85, 86); *Azi turcho* (p. 394); *Ismael turcho* (pp. 139, 178);
Choza/Chogia Is(s)e/Inse turcho (pp. 178, 236, 375, 382); *Jacsia turcho* (pp. 73, 112); *Chazi Musi turcho*
(pp. 58, 139); *Mustafa turcho* (pp. 375, 382); *Ramadan de Simiso* (pp. 73, 97, 144); *Chazi Rastan turcho*
(pp. 402, 465, 483); *Saliet turcho* (pp. 6, 14, 15, 17, 45, 96, 105). In addition, there are several unnamed
Turks (pp. 96, 137, 139, 187, 382), who may or may not already be among the twelve merchants
listed above. Cf. C. Kafadar, "A death in Venice (1575): Anatolian Muslim merchants trading in the
Serenissima," in *Raiyyet Rüsûmu. Essays presented to Halil İnalcık* (= *Journal of Turkish Studies* 10
(1986)), 193, n. 8; *Badoer: Indici*, p. 118 ("Turco").
[73] *Badoer*, pp. 15, 139. The Turks in question were *Saliet* and *Chazi Musi*.
[74] Kafadar, "A death in Venice," 193–4.

consistently advised both Sultan Murad II and his successor, Mehmed II, against making war on Constantinople. The narrative sources also emphasize Halil's alleged inclination to receive bribes and gifts from Byzantine authorities, drawing connections between this and the policy of peace he advocated.[75] The presence of Halil Paşa's name among the business associates of Badoer casts light on another, previously unknown, facet of the material interests underlying his support of peace with Byzantium; namely, his commercial operations within Constantinople. In this context, it is noteworthy that on the eve of the Council of Ferrara–Florence, during the very same time when Badoer recorded Halil Paşa's activities, the Ottoman vizier had competently dissuaded Murad II from launching an attack against Constantinople, which corroborates the suggested link between Halil's economic interests and his political stance.[76] The conspicuous absence of Turkish traders from Badoer's accounts during 1439–40 lends further support to this argument by conveying how an open breach in Byzantine–Ottoman diplomatic relations, as indeed did occur following the conclusion of the union at Florence in 1439, could result in the loss of commercial opportunities at Constantinople on which certain Ottoman merchants were able to capitalize during times of peaceful relations between the two states.

Another individual who merits notice among the Ottoman subjects with whom Badoer conducted business is a merchant called *Choza/Chogia Is(s)e/Inse turcho*, father of *chir Jacob/Jachop*.[77] Given the fact that Badoer consistently uses the title *chir* (= *kyr*) to designate his Byzantine clients, it seems odd that he should apply this form of address to the son of a merchant who is explicitly stated to be a Turk and who bears the Islamic title *hoca* typically used, along with *hacı*, by Ottoman big merchants.[78]

---

[75] See İnalcık, *Fatih Devri*, pp. 81–3; İ. H. Uzunçarşılı, *Çandarlı Vezir Ailesi* (Ankara, 1974), pp. 56–91. Information on Halil Paşa's pro-Byzantine and pro-peace attitude can be found in the following sources: Aşıkpaşazade–Giese, pp. 131–2 (= Aşıkpaşazade–Atsız, p. 192); Sphrantzes–Grecu, XXIII.9–11, p. 60; Doukas–Grecu, XXXIV.2, XXXV.5, XL.3, pp. 293, 311–13, 377; Kritob.–Reinsch, I.76,1–2, p. 87; Leonardo of Chios in *PG*, 159, col. 937; Tedaldi, "Informazioni," in *Thesaurus*, ed. Martène and Durand, vol. 1, cols. 1821–2; cf. Pseudo-Phrantzes, *Macarie Melissenos*, ed. Grecu, pp. 408–12, 436. Note that Doukas records how Halil came to be labeled among his Ottoman adversaries in Turkish as "καβοὺρ ὀρταγή" (*gavur ortağı*), and provides the correct meaning for the expression as "companion or helper of the Greeks" (p. 313, line 6).
[76] For Halil Paşa's role in calling off the attack Murad II contemplated against Constantinople, see Sphrantzes–Grecu, XXIII.9–11, p. 60, and note 22 above.
[77] *Badoer*, pp. 375, 382, 178, 236.
[78] On the use of these titles by Ottoman merchants, see H. İnalcık, "The hub of the city: the Bedestan of Istanbul," *International Journal of Turkish Studies* 1/1 (1979–80), 8–9 and n. 31; H. İnalcık, "Sources for fifteenth-century Turkish economic and social history," in İnalcık, *Middle East and the Balkans under the Ottoman Empire* (Bloomington, 1993), p. 183.

The hypothesis put forward some years ago, which tried to resolve this discrepancy by suggesting that *Choza/Chogia Is(s)e turcho* must have been a former Byzantine who had become an Ottoman subject and converted to Islam, while his son either remained attached to the Christian faith or, having likewise converted, held on to his Greek title for practical reasons,[79] can no longer be maintained in view of additional evidence that has been brought to light recently. Two Genoese documents dated February 25, 1382 and January 28, 1425 – the former concerning a certain *Coia Isse*, son of *Aurami Camalia*, and the latter a certain *Coaia Ysse de Camalia* – disclose new data that correct the previously held assumptions on the origin and descent of the father and son mentioned by Badoer.[80] It emerges from these documents that the latter were descendants probably of an eastern Christian, Armenian, or Jewish merchant family that had migrated from the Middle East to the Crimea, settling, it seems, first in the Turkish-Tatar city of Surgat and then in the Genoese colony of Kaffa, before making its way finally to Constantinople. While a whole series of questions remain unanswered (including when, if at all, Isa converted to Islam; whether he became an Ottoman subject as suggested by Badoer's identification of him as a "Turk" or whether this identification might have stemmed from his father's links with Surgat; how his son Jacob came to acquire the Greek title *kyr*, etc.), it now seems most unlikely that Isa was of Byzantine-Greek origin.[81]

Yet we do come across Ottoman merchants of Byzantine-Greek origin in Badoer's account book, which contains a number of references to Greeks from Ottoman-ruled areas who frequented Constantinople for trading purposes. These references are indicative not only of the lively commercial traffic between the Byzantine capital and Ottoman lands, but also of the mercantile opportunities that were available to Greeks who lived under Ottoman domination. In fact, the competition created by this increased

---

[79] Kafadar, "A death in Venice," 193, n. 8, followed by N. Necipoğlu, "Ottoman merchants in Constantinople during the first half of the fifteenth century," *BMGS* 16 (1992), 163–4.

[80] K.-P. Matschke, "Some merchant families in Constantinople before, during and after the fall of the City 1453," *Balkan Studies* 38/2 (1997), 220–7; for references to the two Genoese documents, see n. 12 (p. 223) and n. 9 (p. 222), respectively. This article also amends the earlier view put forward by the author himself with regard to the origin of *Coaia Ysse de Camalia* in Matschke, "Tuchproduktion," 65, n. 67.

[81] It should be noted, however, that Matschke has claimed the contrary in a more recent publication, without unfortunately providing evidence: "Chogia Ise . . . seems to have come from a Byzantine aristocratic family that, in the early fourteenth century for reasons not entirely clear, relocated to Kaffa and Surgat on the Crimea. There the family was strongly orientalized and became quite wealthy, eventually returning to Constantinople shortly before the end of the empire." See Matschke, "Commerce, trade, markets, and money," p. 795 and n. 138.

commercial traffic between Byzantium and Ottoman domains threatened
Venice so much that around 1430 the Venetian Senate tried to hinder the
trade of Constantinople with "Turchia" through the interception of boats
that carried merchandise in either direction between the two regions.[82] But
the attempts of Venice were ineffective, as the testimony of Badoer makes
clear. In 1436 *Andrea Rixa* of Adrianople (Edirne),[83] in 1436–7 *Todaro
Xingi* of *Simiso* (Samsun),[84] in 1438 *Chostantino Rosso, Michali Sofiano,*
and *Chostantino Strati* of Rodosto (Tekirdağ)[85] – all Greek inhabitants of
Ottoman towns – were engaged in trade with Constantinople.

Conversely, the activities of certain Byzantine merchants and sailors who
made trips to important commercial centers of the Ottomans are visible in
Badoer as well. Between 1436 and 1438, for example, *chir Filialiti, Michali
Sofo*, and *Vasilicho* transported various kinds of merchandise between Bursa
and Constantinople, while in 1439 the shipmaster *Dimitri Tofilato* delivered salted pork from Thessalonike, which the Ottomans had conquered
about a decade earlier.[86] These last examples complete the full spectrum
of Byzantine–Ottoman commercial relations recorded in Badoer's account
book. The picture that emerges is one of relatively busy trade, overland
and by sea, between the Byzantine capital and Ottoman territories, both in
the Balkans and in Asia Minor. Ottoman merchants, whether of Turkish,
Greek, or other origin, were able to participate in this trade by going in person to Constantinople, while their Byzantine counterparts were admitted
simultaneously into various Ottoman towns.

This picture is confirmed by evidence from other sources, which add
further details to our information. According to an anonymous Ottoman
chronicle of the Crusade of Varna, following Murad II's Anatolian campaign against the Karamanids in 1443, a group of soldiers from the Ottoman
army went to Constantinople with the purpose of selling the animals they
had gathered as booty. Evidently, these were Muslim Tatars who lived in the
European domains of the Ottoman Empire and, on their way back from
Anatolia, made a stop at Constantinople in order to earn some money
with their booty.[87] Here, then, we are faced not with professional Ottoman
merchants like the ones recorded by Badoer, but with a different kind of
trader whose activities were somewhat occasional – the soldier who wanted

[82] Thiriet, *Régestes*, vol. II, no. 2209; Iorga, *Notes*, vol. I, pp. 523–4.
[83] *Badoer*, pp. 74, 75.   [84] Ibid., pp. 89, 334.   [85] Ibid., p. 628.   [86] Ibid., pp. 13, 74, 452, 650.
[87] *Gazavât-ı Sultân Murâd*, p. 7. On the so-called "Tatar soldiers" and their role in the Ottoman army
during the fourteenth and fifteenth centuries, see ibid., pp. 83–5 (nn. 6–7); Konstantin Mihailović,
Memoirs of a Janissary, trans. B. Stolz, commentary and notes by S. Soucek (Ann Arbor, 1975),
pp. 159–61, 232 (nn. 6–8).

to capitalize on his war spoils. Professional merchants, too, participated in Ottoman military campaigns. According to John Kananos, Murad II's forces that besieged Constantinople in 1422 were composed of three categories of people who belonged, respectively, to the military, religious, and commercial classes of Ottoman society.[88] It is conceivable that the trip of the Tatar soldiers to Constantinople recounted by the anonymous Ottoman chronicler was not a unique or isolated incident, and that there may have been similar occasions in which soldiers or merchants who took part in Ottoman campaigns interrupted their homeward journey to find buyers for their booty in the Byzantine capital.

We encounter yet another type of Ottoman merchant in a notarial document from the Genoese archives.[89] This document records a number of disputes that took place in Pera in 1443 between one *Ialabi* and one *Corastefanos*, who had joint business ventures in diverse locations such as Bursa and Chios. Most interestingly for present purposes, the document notes that *Ialabi*, presumably an Ottoman-Muslim merchant by the name of Çelebi,[90] lived at that time in Pera together with his wife and family. If the identification of *Ialabi* as an Ottoman on the basis of his name is correct, then we are in the presence of a rare piece of evidence showing an Ottoman-Muslim merchant settled in Pera with his family, unlike the other merchants we have seen so far who were transitory visitors. Although *Ialabi*'s place of residence was Pera rather than Constantinople, the evidence is valuable because it offers a hint as to the degree of the incorporation of Ottoman merchants into the region's daily social and economic life.

We have another piece of evidence that does not directly concern Constantinople but is important in giving a glimpse of how merchandise changed hands in the general region between Ottoman, Byzantine, and Italian traders. In a letter written from Constantinople at the end of 1438, Fra Bartolomeo di Giano states that large quantities of goods which were in high demand among the Turks, steel in particular, were transported on Italian ships to places such as Adrianople, Gallipoli, and Pera. There the Italians sold these commodities to Greek and Jewish merchants, who in turn sold them to the Turks. As Fra Bartolomeo had been living in

---

[88] Cananos, *L'assedio di Costantinopoli*, p. 60, § 8. Kananos defines the military group as "οἱ στρατιῶται" and "οἱ ἐπιστήμονες εἰς τὰ κούρση καὶ τοὺς πολέμους"; the religious group as "οἱ Τουρκοκαλογέροι," who were under the leadership of a certain "Μηρσαΐτης" (i.e. Emir Seyyid Buhari); and the commercial group as "οἱ σαρλίδες, τουτέστι πραγματεῦται, καταλλάκται, μυροψοὶ καὶ τζαγκάροι." On Emir Seyyid Buhari, see H. Algül and N. Azamat, "Emîr Sultan," *Türkiye Diyanet Vakfı İslâm Ansiklopedisi*, vol. 11 (Istanbul, 1995), pp. 146–8.

[89] Roccatagliata, *Notai genovesi*, vol. 1, no. 13, pp. 69–71.

[90] It is also conceivable, however, that he was a Persian.

Constantinople since 1435, it is likely that he would have had occasion to be an eyewitness of transactions of this kind that took place in Pera.[91]

And last but not least, the widespread use of the Ottoman currency within Constantinople ought to be mentioned as a further indicator of the significant role played by the Ottomans in the trade of the eastern Mediterranean, including the Byzantine capital itself. The frequency of Badoer's references to *asperi turcheschi* and *ducati turcheschi* in his account book gives one a clear sense of the regularity with which the Ottoman currency circulated in the international market of Constantinople during the fifteenth century.[92] In fact, western merchants trading with the Ottomans usually changed their money into *akçe*s at Constantinople, where bankers are known to have charged 1 percent on such transactions in the late 1430s.[93] Thus, it is not surprising that some people among those fleeing the city in 1453 had Ottoman *akçe*s in their possession.[94]

In conclusion, the foregoing discussion has demonstrated the indisputable Ottoman presence in the economic life of the Byzantine capital, particularly during the second quarter of the fifteenth century. If in the immediate confusion following Bayezid I's defeat at the battle of Ankara Byzantine authorities had grasped the opportunity to do away with the Turkish quarter, mosque, and kadi of Constantinople, approximately three decades later circumstances had changed again to allow the re-entry of Ottoman traders into the city.[95] The question that immediately arises is why or how the Ottoman element was able to regain the place it occupied in the economic life of the city prior to the battle of Ankara. It would have been helpful in answering this question to know precisely when this development took place. While the available evidence reveals that the activities of Ottoman merchants in the Byzantine capital became especially intense during the fourth decade of the fifteenth century – whereas between 1403/4 and 1422 the Ottomans appear to have conducted their commercial transactions with Constantinopolitan traders more frequently in their own

---

[91] Fra Bartolomeo di Giano, "Epistola de crudelitate Turcarum," in *PG* 158, col. 1063d. See also col. 1058a, for slave trade through the port of Gallipoli.

[92] *Badoer*, pp. 6, 7, 33, 37, 59, 66, 72, 73, 88, 89, 93–7, 102, 110, 112, 115, 121, 157, 179, 186, 236, 264, 265, 306, 308, 336, 362, 375, 396, 499, 572, 579, etc. Cf. Fleet, *European and Islamic Trade*, pp. 13–21, 142–6 (Appendix 1).

[93] Fleet, *European and Islamic Trade*, p. 17 and n. 27.

[94] A. Roccatagliata, "Con un notaio genovese tra Pera e Chio nel 1453–1454," *RESEE* 17 (1979), 224.

[95] It should be noted that a similar break did not occur in Thessalonike, where the Ottomans maintained some role in social and economic affairs even after the battle of Ankara and the subsequent restoration of the city to Byzantium. This is hardly surprising given that Thessalonike had been subject to nearly sixteen years of direct Ottoman rule between 1387 and 1402/3. See above, ch. 5, pp. 101–2.

town of Scutari – it is impossible to establish a conclusive dating in the absence of sources such as Badoer from the earlier decades of the century. Nevertheless, in the light of contemporary political developments, it could be postulated that in 1424 the re-establishment of Byzantium's status as a tributary vassal of the Ottoman state played a determining role in the revitalization of the activities of Ottoman merchants inside Constantinople. It may well have been following the peace treaty of 1424 that Ottoman merchants effectively re-entered the Constantinopolitan market and assumed the economic role which they are known to have played there during the reign of Bayezid I, when Byzantium had once again been in the position of a tribute-paying vassal state of the Sultan.

It is worth speculating at this point about the possible effects of the presence and activities of Ottomans in Constantinople on the Byzantines' perceptions of and attitudes towards them. While the inhabitants of the capital were no doubt disturbed and threatened on the whole by the growing presence of the enemy in their midst, the conditions established thereby for contact between Byzantines and Ottomans at the personal level must have encouraged nonetheless greater knowledge of the dreaded enemy, their society, and their way of life. Consequently, the conventional negative image of the Ottomans inspired by hostile relations in the political and military sphere may have become somewhat modified in an environment of increased personal contact and day-to-day communication occurring mainly in the realm of economic life. It is conceivable that under such circumstances some of the population of Constantinople, rather than maintaining the stereotypical image of the Turks as "barbarous," "cruel," "godless," "lawless," "licentious," "lustful," "ignorant" people, came to regard the Ottomans and certain aspects of their society in a more favorable and humane light.[96] In this context, the presence of merchants of Byzantine origin among the Ottomans active in Constantinople must have played some role, too, in the development of favorable attitudes, by way of exposing Constantinopolitans to the conditions of their fellow Greeks living under Ottoman domination. Thus, along with the disappointment and dilemma caused by the steady decline of Byzantium before the growing power of

---

[96] For earlier examples of Byzantines' negative image of Turks, see N. Oikonomidès, "The Turks in the Byzantine rhetoric of the twelfth century," in *Decision Making and Change in the Ottoman Empire*, ed. C. E. Farah (Missouri, 1993), pp. 149–55. For a parallel case of development of ambivalent attitudes among Italians, see K. Fleet, "Italian perceptions of the Turks in the fourteenth and fifteenth centuries," *Journal of Mediterranean Studies* 5/2 (1995), 159–72. See now also N. Bisaha, *Creating East and West: Renaissance Humanists and the Ottoman Turks* (Philadelphia, 2004).

the Ottoman state, better knowledge of the Ottomans acquired through personal encounters and experiences may well have given rise to a more positive overall assessment of them. After all, it may not have been by pure coincidence that Makarios Makres composed his four discourses, addressed to the citizens of Constantinople who were becoming increasingly well-disposed towards the Ottomans and their religion shortly after the peace treaty of 1424,[97] which, as suggested above, enabled the penetration of the Ottomans into the commercial market of the Byzantine capital, thus opening the way for greater interaction and communication between the two groups.

In the political history of Constantinople during the first half of the fifteenth century, one of the most momentous events after the Byzantine–Ottoman peace treaty of 1424 was the Council of Ferrara–Florence (1438–9). As pointed out earlier, the conclusion of the union at the end of this Council led to an open breach in Byzantine–Ottoman diplomatic relations which ended the period of external peace that had been in effect since 1424. Even more importantly, inside Constantinople differences of opinion about the union resulted in serious problems that left the city's population divided during the next fourteen years preceding its conquest by the Ottomans. Although neither the numbers nor the relative proportion of the unionists and anti-unionists can be estimated from the sparse statistical evidence, in general the upper classes, especially people grouped around the imperial court, were favorably disposed towards the union, whereas opposition to it came primarily from the lower ranks of society, including monks and nuns, the lesser clergy, and lay folk.[98] As with all generalizations, however, there were exceptions to the rule. For example, Doukas writes about an aristocratic woman who was an adversary of the union. This unidentified woman had come under the sway of an anti-unionist monk called Neophytos, who served as confessor in the palace and in the homes of magnates, suggesting that he may have influenced other people of high social standing as well.[99] Conversely, Leonardo of Chios reports the existence of a few unionist monks in Constantinople in 1453.[100]

Among the upper-class supporters of the union of the Churches, families or individuals who had extended associations with Italy and Italians can

[97] See note 62 above.
[98] For a general treatment of the Union of Florence, see Gill, *Council of Florence.*
[99] Doukas–Grecu, XXXVII.6, p. 325. On Neophytos, see *PLP*, no. 20129 and *PG* 159, cols. 925c, 930b (Leonardo of Chios).
[100] *PG* 159, col. 925b.

be detected. It might be best to begin with the Goudeles family, since we have already seen in the previous chapter the close economic and political ties which two prominent members of this family (George Goudeles and his son John Goudeles) established with the Genoese in the late fourteenth century.[101] We possess evidence, moreover, suggesting that the family maintained its business links with the Italians through the years leading up to the Council of Florence. During 1437–8, for instance, a cloth merchant by the name of "Manoli C(h)utela" (Manuel Goudeles?) figures among the clients of the Venetian merchant Giacomo Badoer, who was stationed then in Constantinople.[102] Supposing that the name "C(h)utela" does indeed stand for Goudeles, then the presence of this name in Badoer's account book signifies, first, that the economic interests of the Goudelai remained tied in with the Italians during the following generation, and, secondly, that at this time, if not earlier, the family's association with the Italians extended beyond the Genoese to include the Venetians as well. Again, during the 1430s a tavernkeeper called Goudeles who was reputed to sell "the finest Cretan wine" is attested in Constantinople. His tavern, which was situated on the Golden Horn in the vicinity of the Plateia Gate, may well be identical with a tavern, also run by a Goudeles, where back in 1390 the Genoese podestà of Pera used to buy his wine.[103] In this case too, then, the family's joint ties with the Genoese and the Venetians (the latter because of the Cretan connection) are disclosed by the evidence at hand. Another relevant detail to add is that two sisters belonging to the Goudeles family, who fell captive to the Ottomans during the conquest of Constantinople, were ransomed a few years later by the Veneto-Genoese brothers, Troilo and Antonio Bocchiardi, via Chios.[104]

Insofar as the family's stance towards the union of the Churches is concerned, we know that in the course of Emperor John VIII's negotiations with the papacy on this matter Nicholas Goudeles was dispatched as imperial ambassador from Constantinople to Russia with the task of urging the grand duke of Moscow to participate in the future Council of

---

[101] See above, ch. 7, pp. 157, 159–61.

[102] *Badoer*, pp. 120, 121, 352, 353, 498. It must be noted that the name Κούτελας and its variants (Κουταλᾶς, Κουτελᾶς, Κουτάλης) are attested in Byzantium, which might cast doubt on the identification of Badoer's "C(h)utela" with Goudeles: see *PLP*, nos. 93900, 13613, 13615–17, 92456.

[103] "Comédie de Katablattas," ed. Canivet and Oikonomidès, 66–9; Sp. Lampros, "'Ο βυζαντιακὸς οἶκος Γουδέλη," *NE* 13 (1916), 216–17.

[104] According to an unpublished Genoese document, the sisters *Erigni* and *Atanasia* Goudelina were ransomed at the end of 1455/beginning of 1456 for the high sum of 640 ducats of Chios, i.e. approximately 533 Venetian ducats: see Ganchou, "Le rachat des Notaras," pp. 222, 226 and n. 311.

Ferrara–Florence, and from Russia he traveled on to Ferrara.[105] Thus, it may be deduced from his active involvement in the preparations for the Council that Nicholas was favorably disposed towards the union, which therefore reveals a consistency between his religio-political stance and the economic interests of his wider family, even though we have no clue as to whether Nicholas himself ever personally engaged in trade.[106] Further information about the political or religious dispositions of other members of the family points in the same direction too. In 1453 we can trace two Goudelai among the aristocrats who took active part in the defense of Constantinople against the Ottomans: the aforementioned Nicholas Goudeles (eparch of Constantinople according to Ubertino Pusculo and Nestor-Iskander) and one Manuel Goudeles (who may perhaps be identical with the cloth merchant in Badoer's account book). Fighting against the Ottomans side by side with Nicholas Goudeles was also his father-in-law, Demetrios Palaiologos, who has recently been fully identified as Demetrios Palaiologos Metochites.[107] The latter, a high-ranking court official and governor of Constantinople who died together with his sons at the time of the city's fall, was one of the imperial legates sent to the Council of Basel in 1433.[108] Another son-in-law of Metochites, John Dishypatos, worked even harder to promote the union of the Churches, going as legate twice to Basel, in 1433 and 1437, then to Ferrara in 1438, and finally to Florence in 1439. John Dishypatos' two brothers, George and Manuel, were likewise deeply involved in the negotiations for union, and later, in 1449 and 1453, Manuel Dishypatos went on embassies to Pope Nicholas V and to King Alfonso V of Aragon in order to demand aid against the Ottomans and to

---

[105] Syropoulos, *"Mémoires,"* pp. 162–4, 296, 596. In 1438, Nicholas Goudeles also attended a Diet in Nuremberg as John VIII's representative: *Acta camerae apostolicae et civitatum Venetiarum, Ferrariae, Florentiae, Ianuae, de Concilio Florentino*, ed. G. Hofmann (Rome, 1950), no. 56; cf. Gill, *Council of Florence*, p. 137; *PLP*, no. 4341.

[106] At Ferrara Nicholas sold his well-bred horses to John VIII and his brother Demetrios Palaiologos, who wished to go on a hunting expedition; yet this would not indicate that he engaged in trade on a regular basis: see Syropoulos, *"Mémoires,"* p. 296.

[107] *Ubertini Pusculi Brixiensis Constantinopoleos Libri IV*, in *Analekten der mittel- und neugriechischen Literatur*, ed. A. Ellissen, vol. III (Leipzig, 1857), pp. 64, 80; Leonardo of Chios, in *PG* 159, col. 935b; Nestor-Iskander, *The Tale of Constantinople (Of its Origins and Capture by the Turks in the Year 1453)*, trans. W. K. Hanak and M. Philippides (New Rochelle, 1998), pp. 58–9, 60–1, 92–3; cf. p. 126 (n. 68); *Belagerung und Eroberung von Constantinopel im Jahre 1453 aus der Chronik von Zorzi Dolfin*, ed. G. M. Thomas (Munich, 1868), p. 21. See Th. Ganchou, "Le mésazon Démétrius Paléologue Cantacuzène, a-t-il figuré parmi les défenseurs du siège de Constantinople (29 mai 1453)?" *REB* 52 (1994), 257ff., esp. 262–3 (for the identification of Demetrios Palaiologos Metochites). For an evaluation of the reliability of the sources cited above, see also Th. Ganchou, "Sur quelques erreurs relatives aux derniers défenseurs grecs de Constantinople en 1453," Θησαυρίσματα 25 (1995), 61–4.

[108] *PLP*, no. 17981.

obtain provisions for Constantinople.[109] Presumably, Demetrios Palaiologos Goudeles, *mesazon*, *oikeios*, and cousin of Manuel II, who signed the Byzantine–Venetian treaties of May 22, 1406, October 30, 1418, and September 30, 1423 may also be counted among members of the Goudeles family with pro-Latin sympathies.[110]

Viewed collectively, then, all this information leads to the conclusion that the Goudeles family and its immediate circle not only upheld strong economic ties with the Italians but also maintained a corresponding political/religious allegiance to the Latin world which was complemented in several cases by a visible opposition to the Ottomans. In other words, the economic interests that drew members of this family to Italian-dominated markets also influenced their religio-political stance, which was typically pro-unionist, pro-Latin, and anti-Ottoman.

Another family that was committed to the cause of union and is also known to have had business connections with Italians is that of Iagaris. Three members of this family whose exact relationship to one another remains unknown – Andronikos and Manuel Palaiologos Iagaris, both senatorial *archontes*, and Markos Palaiologos Iagaris, an *oikeios* of the Emperor who held successively the titles of *protovestiarites*, *protostrator*, and *megas stratopedarches* – were closely involved in the Council of Ferrara–Florence. All three served on embassies that prepared the way for the Council; the first two were present at the Council itself; and afterwards one of them, Andronikos, went on a mission to Italy in connection with the preparations for the Crusade of Varna against the Ottomans.[111] As to the family's economic ties with Italians, the evidence for this comes from the account book of Badoer, who has recorded his transactions with a certain Palaiologos Iagaris and a Manuel Iagaris in entries dated 1436 and 1439.[112] Noteworthy also is the fact that among the survivors of the fall of Constantinople an *archontissa* Euphrosyne Iagarina has been traced in

[109] Ibid., nos. 5537, 5529, 5540; Malamut, "Les ambassades du dernier empereur," 435 (nos. 3–4), 438 (no. 37), 445–6. For an Alexios Dishypatos among the defenders of Constantinople in 1453, see Ubertino Pusculo, ed. Ellissen, p. 64; Zorzi Dolfin, in *Belagerung und Eroberung*, ed. Thomas, p. 21. For a branch of the Dishypatos family that moved to Rome after 1453, see J. Harris, *Greek Emigres in the West, 1400–1520* (Camberley, 1995), p. 179.

[110] MM, vol. III, pp. 153, 162, 172; cf. Dölger, *Reg.*, vol. V, nos. 3310–11, 3373, 3408. For Demetrios Palaiologos Goudeles' relationship to the imperial family, see Laurent, "Trisépiscopat," 131–5, where he is also described as a member of the Senate; cf. *PLP*, no. 4335.

[111] *PLP*, nos. 7808, 92054, 7811. On the eve of the Council of Florence, Andronikos had also been sent as an envoy to the Ottoman court to inform Murad II of John VIII's intention to attend the Council. Earlier, in 1422 and 1429, Markos, too, had served on two unsuccessful embassies to the same Sultan aimed at establishing peace.

[112] *Badoer*, pp. 51, 783, 784, 785. See Appendix III below.

Crete in 1454, from where she tried to arrange the ransom of her captive daughter Philippa, employing the services of Troilo Bocchiardi, the afore-mentioned Italian who was to be instrumental as well in the ransom of two Goudelina sisters.[113] Thus the Iagaris family's official status in the Byzantine court, its marriage ties with the Palaiologoi, its economic activities in association with Italians, and its political stance with regard to the Latins and with regard to the question of ecclesiastical union with Rome all show striking similarities to corresponding traits displayed by members of the Goudeles family.

Even John Goudeles' profiteering activities during Bayezid I's blockade of Constantinople find a parallel in an act of opportunism at the time of Mehmed II's siege attributed to a Manuel Iagaris ("Giagari"), who may perhaps be the same person as the above-mentioned unionist senatorial *archon* and/or the client of Badoer, all bearing the same name. Leonardo of Chios reports that Manuel Iagaris, whom Emperor Constantine XI charged with overseeing the restoration of the walls of Constantinople in 1453, embezzled approximately twenty thousand florins of the money that was entrusted to him and to a certain hieromonk Neophytos of Rhodes for the repairs. The two men, adds Leonardo of Chios, "later left a treasure of seventy thousand hidden in a jar for the Turks."[114] The name of Manuel Iagaris appears on a surviving inscription from the walls of Constantinople, which confirms the truth at least of Leonardo of Chios' testimony regarding his assignment over the maintenance of the fortifications.[115]

George Philanthropenos, an aristocrat of senatorial rank and kinsman of the Patriarch Joseph II, is another prominent unionist who should be included in this discussion. Appointed *mesazon* in 1438, George participated in the Council of Florence, where he played a key role with his efforts to persuade reluctant Byzantine clerics to sign the decree of the union. He was also very wealthy, and on the occasion of his trip to attend the Council

---

[113] Ganchou, "Le rachat des Notaras," pp. 226–7 and n. 312. Philippa's ransom fee was between 10,000 and 12,000 aspers; i.e. between 280 and 330 Venetian ducats.

[114] *PG* 159, col. 936c–d; trans. by J. R. Melville Jones, in *The Siege of Constantinople 1453: Seven Contemporary Accounts* (Amsterdam, 1972), p. 30. Leonardo's final remark might signal a shift in the political stance of some members of the Iagaris family during and after 1453. It is worth noting that the maternal grandfather of two prominent figures of Byzantine descent in Mehmed II's service – namely, the grand vizier Mahmud Paşa and George Amiroutzes – was a certain Iagaris according to two later Greek sources. This man has been tentatively identified as Markos Palaiologos Iagaris. See Stavrides, *Sultan of Vezirs*, pp. 78–81; cf. *PLP*, no. 7807.

[115] A. van Millingen, *Byzantine Constantinople: the Walls of the City* (London, 1899), p. 126; H. Lietzmann, "Die Landmauer von Konstantinopel. Vorbericht über die Aufnahme 1928," *Abhandlungen der preußischen Akademie der Wissenschaften, Philosophisch-historische Klasse* 2 (1929), 26. The inscription is now displayed at the Archaeological Museum of Istanbul.

he deposited with a Venetian called Francesco Venerio money, jewels, and other valuables worth approximately 3,000 gold ducats.[116] George Philanthropenos was certainly not unique in this respect, for it is reported that most of the Byzantine delegates attending the Council sent or brought with them to Italy precious objects which they deposited in Venice.[117] It is noteworthy that George's son Manuel Philanthropenos married the daughter of another unionist aristocrat called Graginos Palaiologos, whom Emperor Constantine XI sent as ambassador to Pope Nicholas V in 1452. Manuel Philanthropenos lost his life during the conquest of Constantinople by Mehmed II, while his wife and three sons fell captive to the Ottomans. In 1457 his brother-in-law Manuel Graginos Palaiologos, who had escaped to Italy and wished to ransom his four relatives, appealed to Pope Callixtus III for permission to use the funds which George Philanthropenos had transferred to Venice two decades earlier.[118] A Manuel Palaiologos listed among the refugees who fled from Constantinople on the ship of the Genoese captain Zorzi Doria in 1453 may indeed be the brother-in-law of Manuel Philanthropenos.[119] He may have survived in Italy as late as 1465, for in a letter written during that year the Italian humanist Francesco Filelfo refers to an *archon* Manuel Palaiologos who was in Milan at that time.[120] Hence, the evidence presented here about the two Philanthropenoi and about the branch of the Palaiologos family to which they were linked by marriage conforms to the pattern laid down in reference to the Goudelai and the Iagareis. They are all representatives of the Byzantine ruling class with visible unionist sympathies and concomitant economic interests oriented towards Italy.

Compared with the foregoing families, the position of the Notarades, in particular that of the celebrated *mesazon* and *megas doux* Loukas Notaras,

---

[116] On George Philanthropenos, see *PLP*, no. 29760. For his role in the Council of Florence, see Syropoulos, *"Mémoires,"* pp. 214, 224, 324, 434–6, 486–92, 498–500, 558, 628, etc. For the funds he transferred to Italy, see the document published in V. Laurent, "Un agent efficace de l'unité de l'église à Florence. Georges Philanthropène," *REB* 17 (1959), 194–5. In this document he is described as *"magnificum militem et baronem imperii Constantinopolitani."*

[117] Syropoulos, *"Mémoires,"* p. 278.

[118] Laurent, "Un agent efficace," 194–5. For a "Philanthropus," presumably Manuel Philanthropenos, who was in charge of defending the Plateia Gate in 1453, see Ubertino Pusculo, ed. Ellissen, p. 64; Zorzi Dolfin, in *Belagerung und Eroberung*, ed. Thomas, p. 21. Cf. Ganchou, "Sur quelques erreurs," 64–5. Suggesting that "Graginos" may be a misspelling for Iagaris, Ganchou has proposed to identify Manuel Philanthropenos' father-in-law as Andronikos Palaiologos Iagaris, mentioned earlier: 65–7.

[119] See Appendix V(A) below. For a Manuel Palaiologos, who guarded the Xyloporta in 1453, see Zorzi Dolfin, in *Belagerung und Eroberung*, ed. Thomas, p. 21.

[120] *Cent-dix lettres grecques de François Filelfe*, ed. E. Legrand (Paris, 1892), no. 68 (July 1465). See Appendix V(C) below.

on the matter of ecclesiastical union is rather ambiguous and difficult to fit into a neat pattern. A distinguished family of court officials and businessmen, the Notarades too had strong ties with Italy and Italians which date back to the late thirteenth and early fourteenth centuries.[121] As far as the immediate relatives of Loukas Notaras are concerned, we have seen earlier that his father, Nicholas Notaras, was a partisan of John VII and acted in the latter's commercial deals with Genoa as imperial agent, side by side with George Goudeles, at the end of the fourteenth century. Like Goudeles, Nicholas had acquired the status of a Genoese (*Ianuensis*), which was later granted to his descendants as well; in addition he was made a citizen (*burgensis*) of Pera.[122] There is also evidence that during the same period Nicholas' father, George Notaras, invested money in the Black Sea trade which was dominated by the Genoese.[123] The family simultaneously established relations with Venice. In 1397 Venetian citizenship *de intus* was granted to Nicholas, and later, in 1416, the same status was offered to his sons.[124] Several members of the Notaras family, including, besides Loukas, the *kommerkiarios* Demetrios, one Isaak, and one Theodore, also figure among the business associates of the Venetian merchant Badoer.[125] Moreover, Nicholas Notaras is known to have deposited large sums of money in Italian banking institutions, both in Venice and in Genoa, as well as in the Black Sea colonies of Kaffa and Tana, which, following his death in 1423, passed on to his son Loukas as inheritance.[126] As is well known, sometime before 1453 Loukas Notaras sent his youngest daughter

---

[121] At this time the family was based in the Morea, where some of its members developed commercial relations with the neighboring Venetians both on the peninsula and on surrounding islands, particularly Crete. The Constantinopolitan branch of the family which we are here concerned with moved to the capital around the middle of the fourteenth century. See Matschke, "Notaras family," 59–62; Matschke, "Personengeschichte," pp. 788–97; Ganchou, "Le rachat des Notaras," p. 159.

[122] See above, ch. 6, pp. 134–5; Barker, "John VII in Genoa," 236; Belgrano, "Prima serie," 207; C. Desimoni, "Della conquista di Costantinopoli per Maometto II nel MCCCCLIII, opuscolo di Adamo di Montaldo," *ASLSP* 10 (1874), 299–300; H. Sieveking, "Aus genueser Rechnungs- und Steuerbüchern. Ein Beitrag zur mittelalterlichen Handels- und Vermögensstatistik," *Sitzungs-berichte der kaiserlichen Akademie der Wissenschaften in Wien, Philosophisch-historische Klasse* 162/2 (1909), 30. Cf. D. Jacoby, "Les Génois dans l'Empire byzantin: citoyens, sujets et protégés (1261–1453)," *La Storia dei Genovesi* 9 (1989), 265.

[123] P. Schreiner, "Bizantini e Genovesi a Caffa. Osservazioni a proposito di un documento latino in un manoscritto greco," *Mitteilungen des bulgarischen Forschungsinstitutes in Österreich* 2/6 (1984), 96–100.

[124] Barker, *Manuel II*, pp. 486–7; Iorga, *Notes*, vol. I, p. 250. Cf. Matschke, "Notaras family," 65, n. 34.

[125] See Appendix III below.

[126] For documentation and discussion of Nicholas and Loukas Notaras' funds in Italian banks, see Ganchou, "Le rachat des Notaras," pp. 160–8, where the author has shown that, contrary to widely held scholarly opinion, Loukas himself did not transfer any money to these institutions but simply inherited the assets originally deposited by his father. The only known exception was a case that involved, for practical reasons, the transfer to Genoa of two years' interest accrued on his deceased

Anna away from Constantinople, although he himself remained in the capital with the rest of his household and lived through the city's siege and conquest by the Ottomans. An account book drawn up in 1470–1 by a Greek merchant and banker residing in Venice reveals that the business affairs and activities of at least two of Loukas Notaras' surviving children in Italy – his aforementioned daughter Anna and his son Jacob, both of whom had settled in Venice by then – continued to revolve around Venetian and Genoese circles.[127]

Yet, despite the family's evident links with Italy, in the particular case of Loukas Notaras, the ambivalence surrounding his views on the union of the churches and his alleged attitudes towards the Latins and the Ottomans seem to contradict the existence of a one-to-one correspondence between his economic and political orientation, comparable to that exhibited by the aforementioned families.[128] It is interesting to note, first of all, that Loukas Notaras chose an outspoken anti-unionist monk, namely Neophytos of Charsianeites, to be the godfather of his children.[129] Secondly, and more importantly, according to Doukas, who describes Notaras as the "accomplice and collaborator" (συνεργὸν καὶ συνίστορα) of the anti-unionist leader George-Gennadios Scholarios,[130] on the eve of the fall of Constantinople the grand duke publicly pronounced his preference for Ottoman rule over Latin domination. Nevertheless, doubts have been cast on the attribution to Notaras of the oft-quoted statement, "It would be better to see the turban of the Turks reigning in the center of the City than the Latin miter," which is reported by no other source besides Doukas.[131]

---

father's accounts in Venice (ibid., pp. 162–3, n. 58). Chalkokondyles, too, refers to Loukas' assets in Italy, without mentioning any specific location: Chalkok.–Darkó, vol. II, p. 166.

[127] Schreiner, *Texte*, pp. 108–13. On the activities of Loukas Notaras' children in Italy, the most authoritative study now is Ganchou, "Le rachat des Notaras," pp. 149–229, w‚ith references and corrections to earlier works on the subject.

[128] See Oikonomidès, *Hommes d'affaires*, pp. 19–21, where the complex and contradictory nature of Notaras' position has also been underlined.

[129] Sphrantzes–Grecu, XXXIII.5, p. 88. Although Sphrantzes gives no indication of Neophytos' position on the union, the latter may almost certainly be identified with his anti-unionist namesake known from the writings of Scholarios, Doukas, and Leonardo of Chios, none of whom, however, state his connection to the monastery of Charsianeites: see above, p. 209 and note 99; Scholarios, *Œuvres*, vol. III, p. 193.

[130] Doukas–Grecu, XXXVII.10, p. 329, line 9. Although Scholarios had formerly been in favor of union and played an active role at the Council of Florence, he subsequently changed his attitude and assumed the leadership of the anti-unionist faction after 1445. On him, see J. Gill, *Personalities of the Council of Florence and Other Essays* (London, 1964), pp. 79–94; C. J. G. Turner, "George Gennadius Scholarius and the Union of Florence," *The Journal of Theological Studies* 18 (1967), 83–103; C. J. G. Turner, "The career of George-Gennadius Scholarius," *B* 39 (1969), 420–55.

[131] Doukas–Grecu, XXXVII.10, p. 329; trans. by Magoulias, *Decline and Fall*, p. 210. See note 1 above. For a recent interpretation of this statement, see D. R. Reinsch, "Lieber den Turban als

Moreover, while pro-unionist sources like Doukas tend to portray him as an adversary of union, Loukas Notaras does not emerge in the writings of his anti-unionist contemporaries as someone who actually shared their views. John Eugenikos, for instance, admonished him for frequenting the residence of the unionist Patriarch Gregory Mammas and warned him against thinking and acting like his "Latin-minded" fellow citizens.[132] In a letter dated 1451–2, George-Gennadios Scholarios described his supposed "accomplice and collaborator" as a person who was inclined to make ecclesiastical concessions to the Latins for the sake of salvation from the Ottomans, without truly believing in the Latin faith.[133] Indeed, such a conciliatory attitude based on political expediency rather than religious conviction seems to represent best Loukas Notaras' outlook on the union of the Churches, at least upto the very moment when the fall of the Byzantine capital to Mehmed II's forces came to be regarded by everyone inside the besieged city as imminent and inevitable. In this respect Notaras does not fundamentally differ from most unionists of the time, of whom only a handful are known to have genuinely embraced Latin religious beliefs. As John Eugenikos pointed out in a letter to Constantine XI in 1449, the majority of the dignitaries around the Emperor supported the union of the Churches out of political interests and did not otherwise hesitate to attend religious services performed by anti-unionist priests.[134] At any rate, Loukas Notaras did fight to the end in defense of Constantinople, and several

was? Bemerkungen zum Dictum des Lukas Notaras," in *ΦΙΛΕΛΛΗΝ. Studies in Honour of Robert Browning*, ed. C. N. Constantinides, N. M. Panagiotakes, E. Jeffreys, and A. D. Angelou (Venice, 1996), pp. 377–89. Here Reinsch does not question whether or not the statement was made by Notaras but argues that it cannot be taken as evidence of his anti-unionism because the term "καλύπτρα Λατινική" refers to "eine lateinische Kaiserkrone," and not to the "miter, or tiara, of the Pope" as is often assumed. For present purposes, this argument serves to highlight the noted ambivalence in Notaras' outlook. I am grateful to D. Jacoby for having brought this article to my attention.

[132] *PP*, vol. I, pp. 137–46, esp. 139, 145; cf. 170–3, 175–6. According to Matschke, "Notaras family," 66–7, Loukas was not opposed to the union in principle, but "would have preferred to negotiate the union of the churches with the council in Basel instead of with the Roman pope" at Ferrara and Florence. For further thoughts on Loukas' position with respect to the "turban and tiara" issue, see K.-P. Matschke, "Griechische Kaufleute im Übergang von der byzantinischen Epoche zur Türkenzeit," in *Bericht über das Kolloquium der Südosteuropa-Kommission, 28.–31. Oktober 1992*, ed. R. Lauer and P. Schreiner (Göttingen, 1996), pp. 80–1. See also Reinsch's article cited in the previous note.

[133] Scholarios, *Œuvres*, vol. IV, p. 496; cf. *PP*, vol. II, pp. 125, 127.

[134] The religious insincerity of the majority of unionists who supported ecclesiastical union primarily for political ends is emphasized by both Byzantine and Latin sources: John Eugenikos, in *PP*, vol. I, pp. 123–5; Scholarios, *Œuvres*, vol. III, pp. 147, 165–6; Doukas–Grecu, XXXVI.2,6, pp. 315, 319; Leonardo of Chios, in *PG* 159, cols. 926, 929–30. According to the last, the only genuine unionists in Constantinople in 1452–3 were, apart from a few unidentified monks and lay theologians, John Argyropoulos, Theophilos Palaiologos, and Theodore Karystinos: cols. 925b, 934d, 941b.

days after Mehmed II's entry into the city he was executed together with some members of his family, even though the Ottoman ruler had allegedly promised him the city's governorship.[135] The continued existence of the Notaras family was to depend thereafter on its members in Italy, who could draw upon Loukas' and his father Nicholas' formerly established contacts and money deposits there.

Opposition to the union of the Churches, on the other hand, seems to have encompassed a stronger religious dimension, for the majority of the anti-unionists belonged to ecclesiastical and monastic circles, and their anti-Latin propaganda, which was directed at an audience primarily of lower-class citizens, carried heavy religious overtones.[136] To the common people, the preservation of their religious identity was of prime importance, removed as they were from the political and economic interests that inclined members of the ruling class to accommodation with the Latin West. As noted earlier, moreover, the presence and activities of the Latins in Constantinople often jeopardized the social and economic well-being of the lower classes. Consequently, some among them came to hold that submission to the Latin Church was an evil far less desirable than subjection to the political domination of the Ottomans, whose religious policy, as witnessed on many occasions elsewhere, guaranteed them the preservation of their Orthodox faith. Such was the opinion of John Eugenikos as well, who wrote to Loukas Notaras that Latinization "is a real captivity worse than any captivity to the barbarians."[137]

Religious tensions grew worse in Constantinople following the failure of the Crusade of Varna against the Ottomans in 1444. This catastrophe, which illustrated the limits to the effectiveness of help from the Latin West, weakened the position of the unionists who had placed high hopes on the Crusade.[138] Some among the anti-unionists did not fail to point as well to the example of Thessalonike, which had found no salvation in the hands of the Venetians during 1423–30.[139] Even John VIII's mother, the Empress Helena, considered giving support to the anti-unionists around

---

[135] Doukas–Grecu, pp. 379–83; cf. Chalkok.–Darkó, vol. II, pp. 165–6. For Loukas' role in obtaining loans for the defense of Constantinople in 1453, see Ganchou, "Le rachat des Notaras," pp. 188–9, 199 n. 205; cf. G. Olgiati, "Notes on the participation of the Genoese in the defence of Constantinople," *Macedonian Studies*, n. s. 6/2 (1989), 50. On controversies regarding the reasons behind Notaras' execution, see E. A. Zachariadou, "Τα λόγια κι ο θάνατος του Λουκά Νοταρά," in *Ροδωνιά. Τιμή στον Μ. Ι. Μανούσακα* (Rethymnon, 1994), vol. I, pp. 136–46.

[136] See Doukas–Grecu, XXXI, XXXVI–XXXVII, pp. 265–71, 315–29; Scholarios, *Œuvres*, vol. III, pp. 165–6; *PP*, vol. II, pp. 120–1.

[137] *PP*, vol. I, p. 142.   [138] On the Crusade of Varna, see above, ch. 2, p. 37 and note 52.

[139] John Eugenikos, in *PP*, vol. I, p. 316.

1445, though she changed her mind afterwards.[140] More enduring, however, was the impact of the Varna disaster on other disillusioned unionists who permanently joined thereafter the ranks of the anti-unionists, Gennadios Scholarios presumably being one of them.[141] When John VIII died in 1448, he was buried without the customary ecclesiastical honors, which is indicative of the great influence exercised by the anti-unionists at this time.[142] The unionist Patriarch Gregory Mammas, who had been elevated to the patriarchal throne in 1445, was so unpopular that John VIII's successor Constantine XI chose not to be crowned by him. Hence, he earned the distinction of being the sole Byzantine ruler who did not undergo an official coronation ceremony in the imperial city.[143] In August 1451 Gregory Mammas finally fled to Rome as a result of intense opposition from the anti-unionists, and Constantinople remained without a patriarch until after the Ottoman conquest, when the anti-unionist leader Gennadios Scholarios assumed this position.[144] Over a year after Mammas' flight, the Byzantine capital became the scene of a new series of agitations and riots on the part of the anti-unionists, when the papal legate Cardinal Isidore, the former bishop of Kiev, arrived in the city on a mission to confirm and re-enact the Union of Florence. Isidore had to wait for about a month and a half before he could accomplish his task of proclaiming the union and celebrating the Latin liturgy in the church of Hagia Sophia. He later wrote to Pope Nicholas V that the entire population of the city was present at the ceremony, which took place on December 12, 1452; yet it is questionable whether the participants included all the anti-unionists, despite the mood of terror and panic that had set in by this time due to the completion of Mehmed II's siege preparations.[145] Under such

---

[140] Ibid., pp. 59, 125.

[141] Sp. Vryonis, Jr., "The Byzantine Patriarchate and Turkish Islam," *BS* 57/1 (1996), 92–5; cf. Turner, "Scholarius and the Union of Florence," 92–7.

[142] Scholarios, *Œuvres*, vol. III, p. 100.

[143] On the question of Constantine XI's coronation, see Nicol, *Immortal Emperor*, pp. 36–40 and M. Kordoses, "The question of Constantine Palaiologos' coronation," in *The Making of Byzantine History. Studies Dedicated to Donald M. Nicol*, ed. R. Beaton and C. Roueché (Aldershot, 1993), pp. 137–41, with further bibliography. For the date of Mammas' accession, see Gill, *Council of Florence*, pp. 365–6 (n. 2).

[144] On Mammas' flight, see Sphrantzes–Grecu, XXXI.12, p. 82. On Scholarios' assumption of the patriarchal throne under Ottoman rule, see V. Laurent, "Les premiers Patriarches de Constantinople sous domination turque (1454–1476)," *REB* 26 (1968), 229–63, esp. 243–5; Turner, "Career of Scholarius," 439–55; A. Papadakis, "Gennadius II and Mehmed the Conqueror," *B* 42 (1972), 88–106; Vryonis, "Byzantine Patriarchate," 82–111. See also H. İnalcık, "The status of the Greek Orthodox Patriarch under the Ottomans," *Turcica* 21–3 (1991), 407–36, with further bibliography.

[145] Isidore of Kiev, in Pertusi (ed.), *Caduta*, vol. I, p. 92; Doukas–Grecu, XXXVI.1–6, pp. 315–19. Cf. S. Runciman, *The Fall of Constantinople 1453* (Cambridge, 1965), pp. 69–72; Nicol, *Immortal Emperor*, pp. 57–61. On Isidore of Kiev, see Gill, *Personalities*, pp. 65–78.

circumstances even Scholarios, who was in the forefront of the conflicts between unionists and anti-unionists during the final years of Byzantine rule in Constantinople, could not help observing the detrimental effects of the increasing dissensions upon the security of the city. As early as 1449 he drew attention in one of his sermons to the internal divisions of the Byzantine capital which rendered it helpless before Ottoman attacks.[146] Writing from Rome in 1451, Theodore Gazes likewise expressed his concern that while the inhabitants of Constantinople were engaged in religious disputes and controversies, the Ottomans were capturing their few remaining cities and enslaving their wives and children.[147]

Such, then, was the internal state of Constantinople when Mehmed II ascended the Ottoman throne in 1451 for the second time and steered all his efforts towards the city's conquest.[148] His first move was to start the construction of a fortress on the European shore of the Bosphorus, opposite the Asiatic fortress his great-grandfather, Bayezid I, had built in preparation for his blockade of the same city. Mehmed's fortress was completed by August 1452, and together the two fortresses gave him effective control over the naval traffic through the Bosphorus. On September 13, 1452, Theodore Agallianos, a patriarchal official in Constantinople, recorded the Sultan's recent activities in the area from the time of the fortress's completion until his return to Adrianople, with vivid descriptions of the physical condition of the environs of the Byzantine capital as well as the moral state of the citizens within. According to Agallianos' report, for three days Mehmed II attacked the regions around the construction site, laying waste to the fields and vineyards there, and capturing some important fortresses such as those of Stoudios and Epibatai. Meanwhile, wrote Agallianos, Constantinople received no military or financial help either from within or from foreign powers; and as the inhabitants watched the enemy attacks they feared far worse was still to come, but they felt already exhausted because of the poverty, destitution, and need that had long been reigning in their midst. Their only remaining hope was that God, who had abandoned the Byzantines because of the "evil" and "falsely named" Union of Florence,

[146] Scholarios, *Œuvres*, vol. I, pp. 161–72; esp. 171, lines 23–5.   [147] *PP*, vol. IV, pp. 46–7.

[148] Among the vast literature on Mehmed II's siege and conquest, see F. Dirimtekin, *İstanbul'un Fethi* (Istanbul, 1949); S. Tansel, *Osmanlı Kaynaklarına Göre Fatih Sultan Mehmed'in Siyasî ve Askerî Faaliyeti* (Ankara, 1953), pp. 1–111; İnalcık, *Fatih Devri*, pp. 109–36; F. Babinger, *Mehmed the Conqueror and his Time*, trans. R. Manheim (Princeton, 1978), pp. 64–128; Runciman, *Fall of Constantinople*; Setton, *The Papacy and the Levant*, vol. II, pp. 108–37; Nicol, *Immortal Emperor*, pp. 54–73; F. Emecen, *İstanbul'un Fethi Olayı ve Meseleleri* (Istanbul, 2003); T. Kioussopoulou (ed.), *1453. Η άλωση της Κωνσταντινούπολης και η μετάβαση από τους μεσαιωνικούς στους νεώτερους χρόνους* (Iraklion, 2005).

might show them his merciful and compassionate nature and come to their rescue.[149] The testimony of Agallianos, despite his partisan position as an acclaimed anti-unionist, is significant because it is an eyewitness report conveying the general mood that prevailed among the inhabitants of Constantinople on the eve of Mehmed II's siege, which formally began seven months later, on April 6, 1453. Within a single passage Agallianos expressed the most crucial problems of the Byzantine capital that made it extremely vulnerable at this time to the enemy attacks: the city contained almost no hinterland and lay in isolation, surrounded by destroyed fields and vineyards; the majority of the citizens suffered from overwhelming poverty and in their fatigue and destitution lost all hope, seeing especially that no help was coming from anywhere; finally, there was a strong current of anti-unionist sentiment, accompanied with a resurgent fatalism amongst the people who applied the age-old notion of "punishment for our sins" to the Union of Florence and concluded that God had abandoned the Byzantines because of the sinful union with the Latin Church.[150]

All sources written thereafter also point to the role played by the city's internal problems on the ineffectiveness of defense against the forces of Mehmed II. In his history of the Sultan's deeds, Kritoboulos echoes Agallianos' words, declaring that the morale of the Constantinopolitans was rather poor even before the siege had actually begun. Among the reasons for this state, Kritoboulos enumerates the isolation of the city that resulted from its having been cut off from the sea; the great scarcity of money, supplies, and defenders; and the visible absence of help from any direction.[151]

The situation seemed desperate at the time not only to those within Constantinople but to observers from abroad as well. There were, in fact, unmistakable signs that at least some western powers were contemplating abandoning the Byzantine capital to its fate, as illustrated by the discussions that took place at a meeting of the Senate of Venice on August 30, 1452. Several senators suggested during this meeting that Venice should not become involved in the defense of Constantinople against Mehmed II.[152] Although this proposition failed to win the support of the majority

---

[149] Schreiner, *Kleinchroniken*, vol. II, pp. 635–6. On the capture of the fortresses of Stoudios and Epibatai (near Selymbria), see also Kritob.–Reinsch, I.17.3, I.32.2, pp. 35–6, 47; Doukas–Grecu, XXXIV.10, pp. 303–5.

[150] This was, of course, the exact opposite of the argument made by both unionist Byzantines and the papacy. For instance, in 1451 Pope Nicholas V wrote to Constantine XI that the failures of the Byzantines before the Ottomans were due to the sin of schism which persisted as the Union of Florence had not been put into effect at Constantinople: G. Hofmann, *Epistolae pontificiae ad Concilium Florentinum spectantes*, vol. III (Rome, 1946), no. 304.

[151] Kritob.–Reinsch, I.18, p. 36.   [152] Thiriet, *Régestes*, vol. III, no. 2896.

within the Senate, it demonstrates nonetheless that the skepticism of Constantinopolitans about the readiness of foreign powers to furnish assistance, which both Agallianos and Kritoboulos reiterate, was not unfounded.

Contemporary sources provide a series of conflicting figures concerning the population of Constantinople in 1453.[153] Among them one in particular, the information given by Sphrantzes on the number of available defenders, which modern scholarship has accepted as the most accurate and reliable piece of evidence, reveals the alarming shortage of manpower that put the security of the city at high risk. Sphrantzes reports that early during the siege Constantine XI ordered a census to be taken of all the people who were capable of fighting, including laymen as well as clergy, together with a count of the weapons they had at their disposal. Individual lists of each neighborhood collected by imperial agents (*demarchoi*) were handed over to Sphrantzes, who calculated the totals from them. The figures that emerged from Sphrantzes' final count were so unnerving that the Emperor decided not to reveal them to anyone: the city contained a mere fighting population of 4,773 Greeks and about 200 foreigners.[154]

Despite the city's considerably diminished population, food supplies were in critical condition all through the siege. Like his predecessor Bayezid I, Mehmed II hoped to achieve the surrender of Constantinople by forcing its inhabitants into starvation.[155] Accordingly, in preparation for the anticipated siege, Constantine XI paid particular attention to supplying the city with provisions. After gathering the wheat reserves and other foodstuffs available within the city itself, he demanded additional provisions

[153] Accordingly modern estimates of the city's population in 1453 range widely from 15,000 to 140,000, but the figure on which scholarly consensus has been established is 40,000–50,000, first suggested by A. M. Schneider, "Die Bevölkerung Konstantinopels im XV. Jahrhundert," *Nachrichten der Akademie der Wissenschaften in Göttingen, Philologisch-historische Klasse* 9 (1949), 233–44, esp. 237; cf. E. Francès, "Constantinople byzantine aux XIVe et XVe siècles. Population, commerce, métiers," *RESEE* 7/2 (1969), 405–12, esp. 406; A. Andréadès, "De la population de Constantinople sous les empereurs byzantins," *Metron* 1/2 (1920), 106. See also D. Jacoby, "La population de Constantinople à l'époque byzantine: un problème de démographie urbaine," *B* 31 (1961), 82. For comparison, at its peak level at the end of the twelfth century the city had a population of 400,000, as shown by Jacoby (p. 107), who has modified the much higher estimates of previous scholars.

[154] Sphrantzes–Grecu, XXXV.6–8, p. 96. Note that in the version of Makarios Melissenos, the number of foreigners has been raised from 200 to 2,000: Pseudo-Phrantzes, *Macarie Melissenos*, ed. Grecu, p. 386. Other contemporary sources give slightly higher yet comparable figures, for which see Bartusis, *Late Byzantine Army*, p. 130 and n. 28. See also M. Klopf, "The army in Constantinople at the accession of Constantine XI," *B* 40 (1970), 385–92.

[155] Chalkok.–Darkó, vol. II, pp. 148–9; Kritob.–Reinsch, I.16.15, p. 34; *Düstûrnâme-i Enverî*, ed. Öztürk, p. 49; cf. İnalcık, *Fatih Devri*, pp. 121–2. On Bayezid I's strategy of starvation, see above, ch. 7, p. 149 and note 4.

to be sent from the islands and from the Despotate of the Morea.[156] In order to encourage the transport of further food supplies and armaments from abroad during the siege the Emperor exempted Genoese merchants from all customs duties on merchandise they were to bring into Constantinople. The exemption was effective in inducing at least three large Genoese ships to sail to the besieged city in April 1453.[157] This last measure marks a notable shift from the economic policy which Constantine XI had pursued towards foreign merchants only a few years prior to the siege. Desperately in need of funds for the depleted imperial treasury, in 1450 the Emperor had imposed new taxes on certain commodities that Venetian merchants imported into Constantinople. As late as June 1451 he still insisted on the new taxes, despite the threat of the displeased Venetians to move their colony from the Byzantine capital to the Ottoman port of Ereğli/Herakleia on the northern shore of the Sea of Marmara.[158] During the same year Constantine also refused a request made by the Republic of Ragusa regarding the complete exemption of its merchants from customs duties in Constantinople, and asserted the Byzantine government's right to a 2 percent tax.[159] Certainly, in 1453 the need for extra revenues to replenish the imperial treasury persisted, but the siege must have given rise to an even more urgent need for food supplies, hence incurring the reversal in Constantine's policy towards foreign merchants and merchandise. Nonetheless, the Emperor's efforts were not all that successful since the Venetian surgeon Nicolò Barbaro, who was present in Constantinople during the siege, noted in his diary on the first days of May 1453 the "growing lack of provisions, particularly of bread, wine and other things necessary to sustain life."[160] Some citizens who are described as "drinkers of human blood" by Leonardo of Chios, the Latin archbishop of Mytilene

---

[156] Kritob.–Reinsch, I.18.9–I.19, p. 37; Doukas–Grecu, XXXIV.11, XXXVI.7, XXXVIII.7, pp. 307, 321, 335.

[157] Barbaro, *Giornale*, ed. Cornet, p. 23. Barbaro reports the arrival of four ships "believed to come from Genoa." However, Leonardo of Chios writes, without mentioning the exemption, that there were three Genoese ships from Chios carrying food, arms, and soldiers, accompanied by a fourth ship belonging to the Byzantine emperor and captained by a certain Phlatanelas (*Flectanella*) that was loaded with grain from Sicily: *PG* 159, col. 931a–c. Cf. Olgiati, "Notes," 53. On grain imports from Sicily to Constantinople in the fifteenth century, see C. Marinescu, "Contribution à l'histoire des relations économiques entre l'Empire byzantin, la Sicile et le royaume de Naples de 1419 à 1453," *Studi bizantini e neoellenici* 5 (1939), 209–19.

[158] Thiriet, *Régestes*, vol. III, nos. 2831 (Aug. 4, 1450), 2834 (Aug. 17, 1450), 2856 (June 11, 1451). Cf. Nicol, *Byzantium and Venice*, pp. 390–1.

[159] Krekić, *Dubrovnik*, p. 60 and nos. 1197, 1216, 1217, 1222. For the background and further details of the negotiations between Constantine XI and Ragusa during 1449–51, see also ibid., nos. 1144, 1174, 1175, 1193, 1195, 1196, 1198, 1199.

[160] Barbaro, *Giornale*, ed. Cornet, pp. 33–4; trans. by J. R. Jones, *Diary of the Siege of Constantinople 1453* (New York, 1969), p. 43.

and another eyewitness to the siege, made things worse by hiding part of the available food and driving the food prices up.[161] Furthermore, there is evidence that certain Italian merchants, such as the Genoese Barnaba Centurione, preferred to sell victuals to the Ottomans rather than to the famished Constantinopolitans.[162] The situation was so severe that soldiers in charge of guarding the city walls frequently abandoned their posts in order to look after their starving family members. Consequently, an order was issued for the distribution of bread to the families of soldiers, "so that people should not have to fear starvation even more than the sword."[163]

Besides the shortage of food which compelled soldiers to shun their military duties, overwhelming poverty also pushed many of them into refusing to fight unless they were paid and predisposed them to desert their posts in search of alternative sources of income. Some looked for new employment, but it is doubtful whether jobs were readily available at the time; others turned to the cultivation of fields and vineyards inside the city, which must have been an opportune enterprise under the prevailing circumstances of hunger and poverty. When reproached for neglecting their military duties, some of the soldiers are reported to have replied, "Of what consequence is military service to us, when our families are in need?"[164] In order to overcome the problem of desertion, Constantine XI, who did not have sufficient money in the imperial treasury to pay the soldiers, resorted to the use of Church treasures. He ordered the sacred vessels to be melted down, and with the coins that were struck from them he paid the guards as well as the sappers and construction workers who were responsible for repairing the damaged sections of the fortifications.[165] A similar problem emerged on another occasion towards the end of the siege, when people were needed to carry to the walls a large quantity of newly built mantlets for the battlements. Since no one wanted to do this job without being paid and there was not adequate cash at hand, the mantlets remained unused in the end.[166] Likewise, the Hungarian engineer and cannon-maker Urban, who was in the employ of Constantine XI, abandoned Constantinople in the summer of 1452 and entered the service of Mehmed II because the Emperor

---

[161] *PG* 159, col. 935d.   [162] Olgiati, "Notes," 54 and n. 21.
[163] Leonardo of Chios, in *PG* 159, 935d; trans. by Jones, *Siege*, p. 29.   [164] *PG* 159, col. 935b–c.
[165] Ibid., col. 934b; cf. Barbaro, *Giornale*, ed. Cornet, p. 66 (additional note by Marco Barbaro). See J. R. Jones, "Literary evidence for the coinage of Constantine XI," *The Numismatic Circular* 75/4 (1967), 97; S. Bendall, "A coin of Constantine XI," *The Numismatic Circular* 82/5 (1974), 188–9; S. Bendall, "The coinage of Constantine XI," *Revue Numismatique*, 6e série, 33 (1991), 139–42.
[166] Barbaro, *Giornale*, ed. Cornet, p. 50.

had not been able to pay him a satisfactory salary, if any at all.[167] Hence, lack of public funds, combined with the indigence of average citizens, served in more than one way as impediments to the proper protection of the Byzantine capital.

The advice that some of the imperial officials offered Constantine XI at a point when he was contemplating instituting new taxes for defense purposes illustrates in an even more revealing manner the overall destitution of the citizen body. The officials emphatically counselled the Emperor against this measure, arguing that it would be undesirable to overburden the already impoverished people by means of extra taxes. Indeed, it was in accordance with their suggestion that Constantine XI finally resorted to the use of Church treasures, as noted above.[168] Gennadios Scholarios, too, in a lament he composed after the city's fall on the subject of the misfortunes of his life, stated that the Byzantine capital was poverty-stricken during its last years, thus conveying, as do other sources, how pervasive indigence was throughout the city at that time.[169]

While the theme of widespread and debilitating poverty recurs in most accounts of the siege of 1453, Latin eyewitnesses to the event also proclaim the existence of a wealthy minority in Constantinople who refused to contribute financially to the city's defense needs. The unwillingness of rich Byzantines to make financial sacrifices is underlined by Nicolò Barbaro in his description of the aforementioned incident concerning the transport of mantlets to the walls. According to Barbaro, when no one agreed to carry the mantlets without payment, the Venetians in Constantinople, who had been involved in their construction, decided to offer a sum of money for their transport, expecting those Byzantines who possessed the means to do likewise. However, this decision aroused the anger of wealthy Byzantines, and as they could not be persuaded to contribute part of the money, the project was altogether abandoned.[170] In his letter addressed to Pope Nicholas V on August 16, 1453, Leonardo of Chios reports that the aristocrats of Constantinople, to whom Constantine XI appealed for financial assistance during the siege, told the Emperor that their resources had been exhausted because of the hardships of the time; yet Leonardo quickly adds that the Ottomans later discovered large amounts of money and

---

[167] Chalkok.–Darkó, vol. II, pp. 151–2; Doukas–Grecu, XXXV.1, pp. 307–9; Leonardo of Chios, in *PG* 159, col. 932a.

[168] Leonardo of Chios, in *PG* 159, col. 934b; Barbaro, *Giornale*, ed. Cornet, p. 66 (additional note by Marco Barbaro).

[169] Scholarios, *Œuvres*, vol. I, p. 287: "ὦ πόλις, εἰ καὶ πένις ἐν τοῖς ὑστάτοις χρόνοις καὶ ἄοικος τῷ πλείονι μέρει καὶ φόβοις καθ' ἡμέραν συζῶσα καὶ γυμνὴ τῆς ᾀδομένης περιουσίας ἐν ἅπασιν..."

[170] Barbaro, *Giornale*, ed. Cornet, p. 50.

valuables in their possession.[171] A note appended to the text of Barbaro's diary on July 18, 1453 repeats this information, providing the following additional details: that an unidentified aristocrat had 30,000 ducats with him at the time when the Ottoman army entered the city, that another unnamed aristocrat of high rank had his daughters deliver to Mehmed II two dishes filled with valuable coins, and that the latter's example was followed by several others who showered the Sultan with gifts of money in order to win his favor.[172] Considering the generally hostile attitude displayed towards the Byzantines by both Barbaro and Leonardo of Chios, we may be rightly inclined to doubt the reliability of their pronouncements on this particular subject. However, the evidence they provide is corroborated by other contemporary sources. According to Doukas, for instance, Ottoman janissaries who broke into the house of an unidentified *protostrator* on May 29, 1453 found there "coffers full of treasures amassed long ago."[173] Likewise, the Ottoman historian Tursun Beg, who was presumably present at the siege, reports that the conquering soldiers discovered plenty of gold, silver, and jewels inside the houses of the rich and at the imperial palace, as well as on the corpses of certain members of the Emperor's entourage.[174] Several contemporary sources note also the abundance of hoarded coins, jewels, and other hidden treasures, both new and old, that came to light during the plundering of the city.[175] A hoard, discovered in Istanbul some years ago and containing 158 late Palaiologan silver coins of which the majority belong to the reign of Constantine XI, must undoubtedly have been buried around the time of the siege.[176] Finally, Italian archival documents make reference to numerous cases of money, jewels, and other movable property entrusted by rich Byzantines to Venetian merchants and citizens of Constantinople, both before and after the city's fall.[177] Thus, all this additional evidence, derived from Ottoman and Byzantine literary sources and supported by Italian documents as well as

---

[171] Leonardo of Chios, in *PG* 159, col. 934a.
[172] Barbaro, *Giornale*, ed. Cornet, p. 66 (additional note by Marco Barbaro).
[173] Doukas–Grecu, XXXIX.16, p. 363. On the probable identity of this *protostrator*, see note 179 below.
[174] Tursun Bey, *Târîh-i Ebü'l-Feth*, ed. Tulum, pp. 59, 62; cf. summary trans. by İnalcık and Murphey, *History of Mehmed the Conqueror by Tursun Beg*, p. 37.
[175] Chalkok.–Darkó, vol. ii, pp. 162–3; Doukas–Grecu, XL.1, p. 375; Barbaro, *Giornale*, ed. Cornet, p. 59 (marginal note by Marco Barbaro); Leonardo of Chios, in *PG* 159, cols. 936c, 942a–b; *Düstûrnâme-i Enverî*, ed. Öztürk, p. 50.
[176] On this hoard, see Bendall, "Coinage of Constantine XI," 134–42.
[177] Ganchou, "Le rachat des Notaras," pp. 171–3. Especially revealing is the passage from a Venetian document dated November 5, 1453, cited p. 173, n. 98: "*Quoniam sicut diversis modis habetur tam ante, quam post casum ammissionis urbis Constantinopolis, multi tam Greci quam alii, tunc ibidem existentes, dederunt et consignaverunt in manibus quamplurium civium et mercatorum nostrorum, multas pecunias, iocalia et alia bona sua . . .*"

by archaeological data, confirms the assertions of our hostile Latin authors with regard to the existence of a wealthy group of Constantinopolitans who feigned poverty in 1453, although it must be granted that the rich, too, had probably suffered a decline in their fortunes.

It would have been useful for our purposes if the authors in question had revealed the identities of some of these rich people, since our ultimate objective is to find out how the latter were able to maintain their wealth (or a relatively large portion of it at least) under the existing circumstances that pushed the majority of their fellow citizens into extreme poverty, rather than to blame them or judge them as the contemporary sources do in their typically moralizing and biased manner. At any rate, the fact must not be overlooked that a wealthy aristocrat such as Loukas Notaras, who is known to have kept part of his paternal fortunes in Italian bank accounts, did after all work hard to obtain loans for the protection of Constantinople in 1453,[178] and he also put his life to risk by participating in the final battle against the Ottomans. Unfortunately, in recounting their stories about the feigned poverty of wealthy Constantinopolitans, the relevant sources speak of them in collective terms, without naming any individuals.[179] Nonetheless, we have seen in other contexts earlier in this chapter, as we have also seen in the context of Bayezid I's siege of Constantinople and in the context of Thessalonike during the late fourteenth and early fifteenth centuries,

---

[178] See note 135 above.

[179] The only case where a clue exists that might help us identify one of these rich people turns out not to be very illuminating. This is Doukas' account of the sacking of the *protostrator's* house which contained coffers full of treasures (see note 173 above). In his narrative Doukas names three people who possessed this title then: John Corvinus Hunyadi of Hungary, Giovanni Longo Giustiniani of Genoa, and a certain Palaiologos, who was killed during the siege together with his two sons (Doukas–Grecu, pp. 271, 331, 383). Of these three, the last is most likely to have been the *protostrator* whose house was sacked; nevertheless, his exact identity is difficult to ascertain. Magoulias (*Decline and Fall*, p. 314, n. 287) has proposed to identify him with Theophilos Palaiologos, a unionist who had adopted the Catholic faith and who lost his life while defending Constantinople in 1453 (see *PLP*, no. 21466 and note 134 above); yet there is no evidence to indicate that Theophilos Palaiologos held the title *protostrator*. Perhaps a more likely candidate is the *protostrator* Kantakouzenos mentioned by Sphrantzes (Sphrantzes–Grecu, p. 90, lines 23–5; cf. p. 80, lines 33), who has been identified as the son of the *mesazon* Demetrios Palaiologos Kantakouzenos (Ganchou, "Le mésazon," 245–72, esp. 253–4, 271–2). However, while much information is available on the father, little is known about the son except that he held the title *protostrator* and was, according to the sixteenth-century *Ekthesis Chronike*, one of the aristocrats Mehmed II executed a few days after his entry into the city (see Nicol, *Family of Kantakouzenos*, nos. 75 and 76, pp. 192–5; *PLP*, no. 10962). The argument of Magoulias that Doukas' rich *protostrator* cannot be the son of Demetrios Palaiologos Kantakouzenos because the former and his two sons were killed in battle according to Doukas, and not executed by the Sultan, is not convincing; in the same passage Doukas also claims that the *megas domestikos* Andronikos Palaiologos Kantakouzenos was killed in the final assault, whereas the *Ekthesis Chronike* and the more reliable Isidore of Kiev confirm that he was among those executed a few days later. Cf. Ganchou, "Sur quelques erreurs," 70–82.

that the small circle of people who were able to maintain an economically favorable position under the growing pressure of Ottoman attacks were members of the Byzantine ruling class who had ties, generally of an economic nature, with Italy and Italians. In the present chapter it has been shown that the majority of those within the capital who opted for the policy of ecclesiastical union with the Latin Church belonged to the same circle as well. Moreover, most survivors of 1453 who managed to flee to Italian-dominated territories were also from the same group of families. Five Palaiologoi, two Kantakouzenoi, two Notarades, and two Laskareis are listed among several others in a document which records the names of Byzantine aristocrats (*gentilhuomini*) who escaped with their families on board a Genoese ship on the day of the city's capture.[180] Documents issued after 1453 which report the presence and activities of Byzantine refugees in Venetian territories also include such names as Kantakouzenos, Laskaris Kananos, Sgouros, Basilikos, Mamonas, Notaras, and Phrankopoulos that are familiar to us from Badoer's account book.[181] Finally, a number of Constantinopolitans mentioned in the letters of Francesco Filelfo as being in various parts of Italy between 1453 and 1473 bear once again the names of families whose long-standing economic relations with Italians have been documented: Asanes, Gabras, Palaiologos, Sgouropoulos, Kananos, and the like.[182] It seems safe, therefore, to conclude that the anonymous group of rich Constantinopolitans to whom the literary sources of 1453 allude owed their continued wealth mainly to the connections they (or their former family members) had established with Italy and Italians. In concurrence with their material interests which were oriented towards Italian commercial markets, these people generally supported the policy of ecclesiastical union with the Latin Church and many of them chose to escape to Latin-dominated areas following their city's fall.[183]

But it is also true that some Byzantines who were likewise well connected with Italians remained in Constantinople after 1453, or returned there following a period of absence. Among those who stayed in the city was a group of merchants who had acquired Venetian status presumably

---

[180] See Appendix V(A) below.

[181] In addition to Appendix V(B) and V(D) below, see Harris, *Greek Emigres in the West*, p. 20 and n. 51 (for Constantine Phrankopoulos, who fled from Constantinople to Negroponte, where he remained until the Ottomans overran the island in 1470, whereupon he went to Rome); compare with Appendix III below.

[182] See Appendix V(C) below.

[183] For further references to Byzantine refugees in various Catholic countries of Europe after 1453, see Harris, *Greek Emigres in the West*; H. Taparel, "Notes sur quelques réfugiés byzantins en Bourgogne après la chute de Constantinople," *Balkan Studies* 28/1 (1987), 51–8.

prior to the Ottoman conquest and who continued under Ottoman rule their trading activities in Italian-dominated areas, particularly in Crete. In 1455 Cretan authorities, who were confused about whether to treat these men as Venetians or as foreigners with regard to customs duties subsequent to the changed political situation, decided to consult the Senate of Venice. The Senate deliberated in response that these "white Venetians" of Constantinople should continue to receive in Crete the same treatment as they did before they became Ottoman subjects.[184] In Ottoman treasury accounts dating from 1476–7, moreover, the names of some wealthy aristocrats of Byzantine origin, including two Palaiologoi, one Chalkokondyles, and one Agallianos, are recorded as tax-farmers for the Ottoman government. These Greek entrepreneurs, who competed with Muslim Turks and Jews for the control of the Istanbul customs zone, had huge amounts of capital at their disposal, as indicated by their successive bids ranging from 11 million *akçe* to a sum close to 20 million *akçe*, or about 400,000 ducats.[185] Another member of the old Byzantine aristocracy, Andronikos Kantakouzenos, is attested also as a tax-farmer in an Ottoman document dated *circa* 1481. This document reveals that Andronikos Kantakouzenos had converted to Islam and assumed the name Mustafa; he is mentioned among a group of tax-farmers who took over the mints of Gallipoli and Adrianople for a sum of 18 million *akçe*, or approximately 360,000 ducats.[186] Like the Kantakouzenoi, Palaiologoi, Chalkokondylai, and Agallianoi, the Rhaoul

---

[184] Noiret, *Domination vénitienne en Crète*, pp. 448–9. Cf. Jacoby, "Vénitiens naturalisés," 230.

[185] H. İnalcık, "Notes on N. Beldiceanu's translation of the *Kanūnnāme*, fonds turc ancien 39, Bibliothèque Nationale, Paris," *Der Islam* 43 (1967), 153–5; H. İnalcık, "Greeks in the Ottoman economy and finances 1453–1500," in *TO EΛΛHNIKON. Studies in Honor of Speros Vryonis, Jr.*, vol. II, ed. J. S. Allen *et al.* (New Rochelle, 1993), pp. 312–13. The treasury accounts list their names as follows: "Manul Palologoz/Palologoz of Istanbul," "Palologoz of Kassandros," "Andriya son of Halkokondil," and "Lefteri son of Galyanos of Trabzon." They had a fifth partner, "Yakub, new Muslim," who seems to have left the group after the initial bid. Note that only Manuel Palaiologos among them is specifically stated to be "of Istanbul." The Istanbul customs zone was the principal customs zone of the Ottoman Empire which included, besides the Ottoman capital, the important commercial ports of Galata, Gallipoli, Old and New Phokaia, Varna, and Mudanya. For a Palaiologos of Istanbul, who farmed out the silver and gold mines in upper Serbia in 1473, acting in partnership with three other Greeks from Serres (Yani Kantakouzenos of Novo Brdo, Yorgi Ivrana, Toma Kantakouzenos), see İnalcık, "Greeks in the Ottoman economy," p. 314. During the same year, a Yani Palaiologos of Istanbul, resident of Galata, is attested among the tax-farmers of the mines of Kratova in the province of Küstendil (p. 314). It is uncertain whether the latter can be identified with his namesake who appears as the owner of several houses in Galata in an Ottoman register of 1519: see İnalcık, "Ottoman Galata," pp. 54–5.

[186] H. Sahillioğlu, "Bir mültezim zimem defterine göre XV. yüzyıl sonunda Osmanlı darphane mukataaları," *İstanbul Üniversitesi İktisat Fakültesi Mecmuası* 23 (1962–3), 188, 192. He is identified as "Andronikos, son of Katakuzino, also known as (*nâm-ı diğer*) Mustafa" and, shortly, as "Mustafa bin Katakuzinos."

family became split as well, with several of its members emigrating to the West, and some remaining in Constantinople after 1453.[187]

These last series of examples are quite revealing as they caution us to be aware of the complexities involved in the formation of the economic and political alliances of individuals or groups which did not always conform to strict patterns. They indicate, on the one hand, that a favorable disposition towards the Ottomans could coexist with one favorable towards the Italians, as we have already seen in the context of the civil wars of Andronikos IV and John VII, who had connections with both the Ottomans and the Genoese. On the other hand, they reflect the ease with which attitudes could fluctuate and loyalties could shift, especially when material interests were at stake. Rather illuminating in this respect are the experiences of one Constantine Quioça, who lost all his wealth at the time of the fall of Constantinople and barely managed to escape with his life to Crete. On the Venetian island he accumulated large debts which he could not repay and subsequently decided to go to Adrianople, in search of new prospects among the Ottomans which he had not apparently been able to find among the Latins.[188] Matschke, who has recognized in the name Quioça a Latinized version of the Islamic title *hoca* – the typical designation for an Ottoman big merchant[189] – suggests that Constantine's relations with the Ottomans may have predated the conquest of Constantinople, facilitating therefore his crossing over to their side in 1455. As future events were to show, those Byzantines who chose to join the side of the conquerors and became Ottoman subjects after 1453 seized the opportunity to supplant the Italians who had overshadowed them in large-scale trade in the bygone days of the Byzantine Empire, despite the material gains that a select group of Byzantine aristocrats had been able to enjoy on account of their business enterprises in association with Italian merchants.[190]

---

[187] N. Iorga, *Byzance après Byzance* (Paris, 1992), pp. 19–20; İnalcık, "Greeks in the Ottoman economy," pp. 312, 314. For a Manuel Rhalles of Constantinople who moved to southern Italy with his family, see Harris, *Greek Emigres in the West*, p. 28. See also R. Croskey, "Byzantine Greeks in late fifteenth- and early sixteenth-century Russia," in *The Byzantine Legacy in Eastern Europe*, ed. L. Clucas (Boulder, 1988), pp. 33–9, for members of the Rhaoul family who emigrated to Russia.

[188] M. Manoussakas, "Les derniers défenseurs crétois de Constantinople d'après les documents vénitiens," in *Akten des XI. internationalen Byzantinistenkongresses*, p. 339; Matschke, "Griechische Kaufleute," p. 81.

[189] See p. 203 and note 78 above.

[190] On the reduced economic role of Italians vis-à-vis the Greek and other non-Muslim subjects of the Ottoman Empire in the fifteenth and sixteenth centuries, see H. İnalcık, "The Ottoman state: economy and society, 1300–1600," in *An Economic and Social History of the Ottoman Empire, 1300–1914*, ed. H. İnalcık and D. Quataert (Cambridge, 1994), pp. 209–16.

At the opening of Part III it was pointed out that the social structure of the Byzantine capital in the late fourteenth and early fifteenth centuries resembled very much the social structure of Thessalonike during the same era. It can now be concluded that the political responses of the Thessalonians to Ottoman pressures were closely paralleled by the attitudes that emerged in Constantinople under similar circumstances, and, as in Thessalonike, the political divisions of the Constantinopolitan population generally followed the social divisions. Although the option of acquiring western help in Thessalonike never became as tightly identified with the issue of the union of the Churches as in Constantinople, when faced with what appeared to be an inevitable choice between Ottoman or Latin domination, the urban populations of the Byzantine Empire reacted in more or less similar ways. On the whole, the aristocracy of the capital, comprising mostly high-ranking individuals in court and government circles, many of whom owed their continued prosperity during this period to the economic ties they established with Italy and Italians, supported an anti-Ottoman policy based on the premise of assistance from the Latin West. Since invariably the prerequisite for this assistance was the union of the Byzantine Church with the Church of Rome, this group was prepared in general to give up its Orthodox faith for the salvation of the capital and the empire. Nonetheless, the pro-Latin/anti-Ottoman position did not become firmly established within the ranks of the capital's upper classes until the time of Bayezid I, whose eight-year-long siege directly exposed them to and made them aware of the magnitude of the Ottoman threat for the first time. As has been shown in chapter 6, up to the final years of the fourteenth century there was a fairly strong group within court circles that upheld accommodationist attitudes towards the Ottomans and leaned towards a policy of coexistence with them. Coexistence, however, no longer seemed feasible after the emergence of Bayezid I with his new and aggressive policy of forceful unification, which he applied both in the Balkans and in Asia Minor. It was thereafter that the pro-Latin/anti-Ottoman attitude gained nearly universal popularity among the aristocracy of Constantinople and culminated in the acceptance of the union at the Council of Florence in 1439.

The majority of the lower classes, on the other hand, were opposed to the Latins for religious as well as for social and economic reasons. But their attitude towards the Ottomans is not always clearly distinguishable. During the period of intense danger and hardship prompted by Bayezid I's blockade, they agitated and demonstrated in favor of surrender to the enemy, hoping thereby to secure the establishment of peace. Again, during

Mehmed II's siege in 1453, part of the capital's common people voiced their preference for Ottoman domination over the domination of the Latins; however, at this time there is no evidence of a widespread or unified movement among the lower classes in favor of surrender. This stands in contrast to the situation that was observed in Thessalonike, where the anti-Latinism of lower-class people was generally accompanied by an attitude favorable to the Ottomans, in particular favorable to surrender. The difference may be attributed to the diverse political experiences of the two cities. In addition to the contrast based on Thessalonike's history of rapid political change and subjection to foreign rule (first of the Ottomans, then of the Venetians), Constantinople during the last fifty years covered in this chapter was not exposed to Ottoman attacks as consistently as Thessalonike, and it enjoyed periods of relative peace during 1403–11 and 1424–39. Therefore, the population of Constantinople may not have been under as much pressure as the Thessalonians to adopt an accommodationist stance vis-à-vis the Ottomans. It is, however, also likely that the situation in the imperial capital, as displayed in contemporary sources, reflects in part the interests of the authors who were absorbed in the union controversy and consequently focused more on the attitudes of people towards the Latins and the religious question, while not paying as much attention to their attitudes towards the Ottomans except at certain critical moments.

Finally, similar observations can be made about the attitudes that took shape within the ecclesiastical and monastic circles of Constantinople. As far as the union of the Churches is concerned, although a number of people from the upper ranks of the ecclesiastical hierarchy lent their support to this cause, the majority of religious groups who were characteristically hostile to the Latins emerged unwilling to sacrifice their theological principles for what they regarded as the transient political advantages that most unionists were seeking. In contrast to the pro-Latin sentiments fostered by the unionists, a conciliatory attitude towards the Ottomans was embraced by the anti-Latin/anti-unionist priests and monks of the capital, one of whom – namely George-Gennadios Scholarios – became the first patriarch of Constantinople under the rule of Mehmed the Conqueror.

PART IV

The Despotate of the Morea

INTRODUCTION TO PART IV

In 1453 those among the survivors of the fall of Constantinople who fled
to the Despotate of the Morea for refuge found themselves in the midst
of a turbulent environment. They discovered upon their arrival that the
rulers of the province, the Despots Thomas and Demetrios Palaiologos,
as well as some of the local magnates, were contemplating escaping to
Italy in order to avoid the Ottoman danger. Indeed it was only after
Sultan Mehmed II made a truce with them that the Despotate's rulers and
magnates decided to remain in their homeland.[1] Shortly afterwards peace
in the peninsula was interrupted by an uprising of the Albanian subjects
of the Despotate. The Albanian revolt, in addition to constraining the
Despots to resort to the Ottomans for military help, led to the further
deterioration of the Peloponnesian countryside which had already been
devastated by earlier Ottoman and other foreign incursions.[2] Yet what
perhaps contributed most to the troubled state of affairs in the Byzantine
Morea was the intense discord between the two Despots, brothers of the
deceased Emperor Constantine XI. From the beginning of his political
career Demetrios Palaiologos had been inclined towards collaborating with
and accommodating the Ottomans, while his younger brother Thomas
persistently favored the intervention of western powers as an alternative
to submitting to Ottoman sovereignty.[3] It is, however, noteworthy that
Byzantine sources, while admitting the role of the divergent political views

[1] Chalkok.–Darkó, vol. II, p. 169. See also Kritob.–Reinsch, I.74,1, p. 85.
[2] Albanians had been living in Byzantine Morea since their settlement there by Theodore I Palaiologos
during the last decade of the fourteenth and first decade of the fifteenth centuries: see Zakythinos,
Despotat, vol. II, pp. 31–2; V. Panayotopoulos, *Πληθυσμός καὶ οἰκισμοὶ τῆς Πελοποννήσου (1305–
1805 αἰῶνας)* (Athens, 1985), pp. 78ff. On the Albanian uprising of 1453–4, see Chalkok.–Darkó,
vol. II, pp. 169–76; Sphrantzes–Grecu, XXXVII, pp. 104–8; Schreiner, *Kleinchroniken*, vol. I, Chr.
33/41, 34/22, 36/20, 40/5; vol. II, pp. 482–3; cf. Spandugnino, *De la origine*, in Sathas, *Documents*,
vol. IX, pp. 156–7.
[3] For details and references to the sources, see above, ch. 6, pp. 140–1, and below, ch. 10, pp. 277ff.

and practices of Thomas and Demetrios, attribute the conflict between the Despot brothers primarily to the instigation of the dissident landlords of the Morea who craved for independence from central authority.[4] This suggests that the situation which the refugees from Constantinople encountered there in 1453 was not simply a result of the particular disagreement between the two Despots; nor was it mainly due to the immediate confusion created by the fall of the Byzantine capital. It seems rather to have been a long-term phenomenon rooted in the internal structure of Moreote society. Therefore, it will be illuminating to examine the social conditions in the Despotate from the time of the establishment of the Palaiologoi there in 1382 down to the conquest of this last Byzantine outpost in Greece by the Ottomans in 1460, paying special attention to the relations of the local landowning aristocracy with the Despots of the Morea. Against this background of the internal circumstances prevailing in the province between 1382 and 1460, it will be much easier to comprehend the political attitudes of the Despotate's inhabitants towards the Ottomans and the Latins, and to follow as well the turns and twists in the foreign policy pursued by the government at Mistra during these years.

4 Kritob.–Reinsch, III.19, p. 141; Sphrantzes–Grecu, XXXIX, pp. 110–16; Chalkok.–Darkó, vol. II, pp. 213–14.

CHAPTER 9

The early years of Palaiologan rule in the Morea (1382–1407)

Ever since the Fourth Crusade, followed by the creation of a number of Frankish principalities and the settlement of Venetians in various parts of the Peloponnese, political instability had become a persistent trait that characterized the region. Some order and prosperity were restored to the Byzantine possessions of the peninsula during the long administration of the Despot Manuel Kantakouzenos (r. 1349–80), who asserted his authority over the insubordinate Greek landlords and made favorable alliances with the neighboring Latin princes and states.[1] Yet the region's volatile political situation remained unchanged as military struggles continued among the different powers competing for control in the peninsula and as frontiers kept shifting accordingly. About the time of Manuel Kantakouzenos' death in 1380, the Frankish principality of Achaia in the North had long been broken up into several small fragments; Corinth was held by the Florentine Nerio Acciaiuoli; the Catalan duchy of Athens across the Gulf of Corinth had come under the protection of the Aragonese; and the Venetians still held onto the port cities of Coron and Modon, as well as some neighboring rural areas in the southern Peloponnese. The years shortly preceding 1380 also saw two groups of newcomers in the Morea, namely the Hospitallers of Rhodes and the companies of Navarrese mercenaries, of whom the latter in particular brought further confusion and disorder to the peninsula. The Hospitallers, who had considered moving their headquarters from Rhodes to the Morea as early as 1356, were invited in 1376 by Joanna of Naples, the princess of Achaia (r. 1373–81), who leased her principality to the order for a period of five years. The Navarrese, on the other hand, came to the Morea in 1378 as hired mercenaries in the pay of the Hospitallers. Shortly afterwards, however, most of the Navarrese took service with Jacques de Baux, claimant to the principality of Achaia in opposition to Joanna of

---

[1] On the rule of Manuel Kantakouzenos, younger son of Emperor John VI, in the Morea, see Zakythinos, *Despotat*, vol. I, pp. 95–113; Nicol, *Family of Kantakouzenos*, pp. 123–8; S. Runciman, *Mistra: Byzantine Capital of the Peloponnese* (London, 1980), pp. 50–7.

Naples. But always in search of lands to conquer for themselves, they soon managed to establish effective control over much of Achaia. Following the death of Jacques de Baux in 1383 they pressed direct claims to the principality, and eventually their commander Pierre Lebourd (Peter Bordo) de Saint Superan acquired the title of Prince of Achaia (*c.* 1396). Stationed firmly in the northern Peloponnese up to the death of Saint Superan in 1402, the Navarrese subjected the Byzantine Morea and the rest of the peninsula to constant raids and plundering expeditions throughout this period.[2]

Such were the general conditions in the Peloponnese when Theodore I Palaiologos (r. 1382/3–1407), son of the Emperor John V, arrived at the province as successor to the ruling house of Kantakouzenos. Awaiting Theodore were also a series of internal problems that were intricately linked with the external conditions outlined above. According to a now lost late fourteenth-century inscription found in Parori, near Mistra, which gives a brief account of Theodore's deeds from 1382 to 1389, the Despot was engaged in a relentless fight against the disobedient landlords of the Byzantine Morea during the first five years of his rule. The local land-lords, described as "lovers of dissension" and "treacherous to authority," made every effort to drive Theodore out of the Peloponnese and even plotted to murder him with the intention of being able to remain without a master (ἀδεσπότως μένειν). In their persistent attempts to undermine the Despot's authority, they called on the help of "Latins," in collaboration with whom they attacked their fellow countrymen, uprooting nearly every-thing and causing great harm and physical destruction. Thus, implies the inscription, the dissidence of the landowning aristocracy proved not only detrimental to the internal affairs of the Despotate but, more dangerously, it precipitated the expansion of Latin power within the province: "For us confusion, but strength for the Latins."[3]

[2] A. Bon, *La Morée franque. Recherches historiques, topographiques et archéologiques sur la principauté d'Achaïe (1205–1430)*, vol. 1 (Paris, 1969), pp. 254ff.; J. Longnon, *L'Empire latin de Constantinople et la principauté de Morée* (Paris, 1949), pp. 334ff.; K. M. Setton, "The Latins in Greece and the Aegean from the Fourth Crusade to the end of the Middle Ages," in *The Cambridge Medieval History*, vol. IV/1 (Cambridge, 1966), pp. 388–430; K. M. Setton, *Catalan Domination of Athens, 1311–1388*, 2nd rev. edn. (London, 1975), pp. 125–48; R.-J. Loenertz, "Hospitaliers et Navarrais en Grèce (1376–1383). Regestes et documents," *OCP* 22 (1956), 319–60; A. Luttrell, "Appunti sulle compagnie navarresi in Grecia, 1375–1404," *Rivista di studi bizantini e slavi* 3 (1983), 113–27.

[3] R.-J. Loenertz, "Res gestae Theodori Ioann. F. Palaeologi. Titulus metricus A.D. 1389," *EEBΣ* 25 (1955), 207–8, vv. 5–35. For a French translation of the text, see R.-J. Loenertz, "Pour l'histoire du Péloponèse au XIVe siècle (1382–1404)," *Études Byzantines* 1 (1943), 159–61. An allusion to the internal dissensions of the Despotate can be found in Kydones' letter to Theodore dated 1383, where the native inhabitants are described as "οἱ Πελοποννήσιοι . . . ἀλλήλοις ἐπιβουλεύειν καὶ πολεμεῖν καὶ ληστεύειν ἀφέντες . . .": Kydones–Loenertz, vol. II, no. 293, lines 32–3; cf. lines 72–3.

These conflicts were in part connected with a dynastic struggle that Theodore I Palaiologos confronted as soon as he set foot on the Morea. In the interim between the death of the Despot Manuel Kantakouzenos in April 1380 and Theodore's arrival during the winter of 1382–3, Manuel's elder brother Matthew Kantakouzenos had temporarily assumed power in the Morea. However, one of Matthew's sons, either John or Demetrios Kantakouzenos, who aspired to taking over the government of the Despotate, rose up in rebellion, first against his father, then against Theodore I.[4] The account of these events which Emperor Manuel II Palaiologos has incorporated into the funeral oration he composed for his brother Theodore sheds further light on some of the information recorded on the Parori inscription. Manuel II writes that Matthew Kantakouzenos' son, in order to achieve his dynastic ambitions, had not only won over to his side a considerable number of local Greek people but had also hired mercenary bands of Turks and Latins with whose help he spread confusion and panic throughout the province.[5] It is known that Turkish mercenaries had been employed in the Morea since the latter half of the thirteenth century.[6] As for the "Latins" mentioned in both the funeral oration and the Parori inscription, evidently these were the Navarrese who had established themselves in the neighboring principality of Achaia at this time, as recounted above. This supposition finds confirmation in a letter written by the Latin archbishop of Argos at the onset of 1385, which reports the seditious acts undertaken against Theodore I by the aristocrats (*barones*) of the Despotate – a reference, no doubt, to the son of Matthew Kantakouzenos and his partisans – who had joined forces with the Navarrese.[7]

The sudden and unexpected death of Matthew's son,[8] the exact date of which remains unknown, served only to eliminate the dynastic aspect of these conflicts, without bringing them to an end. It has already been seen that according to the Parori inscription Theodore I's struggles against the dissident elements within the landowning aristocracy of the Morea continued for five years, until about 1387–8, by which time Matthew's

<hr>

[4] Schreiner, *Kleinchroniken*, vol. I, Chr. 33/11; *Manuel II, Fun. Or.*, pp. 115–19. On these events and the debate over the identification of the rebellious son of Matthew Kantakouzenos as either John or Demetrios, see Loenertz, "Pour l'histoire," 161–6; Nicol, *Family of Kantakouzenos*, pp. 157–9.
[5] *Manuel II, Fun. Or.*, pp. 117–19.
[6] See Zakythinos, *Despotat*, vol. I, p. 39; vol. II, pp. 45 (n. 4), 133 (n. 1).
[7] *MP*, no. 27, p. 58. Note also the reference here to the use of Turkish soldiers by Theodore (lines 53–4) rather than by his opponents. A letter by Kydones, also dated 1385, alludes to Theodore's simultaneous battles against "westerners" (i.e. the Navarrese) and his own subjects: Kydones–Loenertz, vol. II, no. 313, p. 239.
[8] *Manuel II, Fun. Or.*, p. 119.

son was certainly dead. Furthermore, even as late as 1395, during a battle of the Despot's forces against the Navarrese, a group of Greek aristocrats were found fighting on the side of the enemy.[9] Hence, it is clear that the opposition of some of the local aristocracy to Theodore I, as well as their collaboration with the Navarrese, outlasted the dynastic war of the early 1380s initiated by Matthew Kantakouzenos' son, whom the unruly Moreote landlords must have regarded and exploited as a mere instrument to gain further independence from central authority.

In order to counteract his internal and external enemies during the first years of his rule, Theodore I had neither adequate financial means nor military resources available to him because of the civil war in Constantinople between his father John V and his brother Andronikos IV which immediately preceded his arrival in the Morea.[10] This explains why he initially sought to appease the Moreote aristocracy by offering them certain unidentified cities and lands.[11] He also sent several embassies to them in an effort to promote peace and bring to an end the civil discords that permeated the Despotate.[12] Meanwhile, during 1384 he entered a triple alliance with his brother Manuel II, who was engaged then in a war against the Ottomans in Thessalonike, and with the Florentine Nerio Acciaiuoli, who was in conflict with the Navarrese.[13] When this alliance did not prove fruitful for either Theodore or Manuel, the following year the two brothers appealed to Venice for help against their respective enemies, the Navarrese and the Ottomans. Despite Theodore's offer to cede to Venice certain territories in the Morea in return for the Signoria's assistance against the Navarrese, the Senate acted hesitantly and two years later, on July 26, 1387, signed a treaty of good neighborliness with the Navarrese.[14] This was the renewal of a treaty signed in 1382, and in choosing to maintain peaceful relations with the Navarrese the Senate was no doubt moved, among other reasons, by the fear that the Navarrese might otherwise transfer the southern Peloponnesian port of Zonklon (Old Navarino) to the Genoese, which would be highly detrimental to Venetian commercial interests.[15]

---

[9] Ibid., pp. 123–7; Schreiner, *Kleinchroniken*, vol. I, Chr. 33/18 (4 June 1395). Cf. Zakythinos, *Despotat*, vol. I, pp. 155–6; Loenertz, "Pour l'histoire," 173–4.

[10] *Manuel II, Fun. Or.*, p. 113. On this civil war, see ch. 6 above.

[11] Loenertz, "Res gestae," 208, vv. 42–3.

[12] Ibid., p. 208, vv. 47–8. Cf. Kydones–Loenertz, vol. II, no. 313, p. 240, for a reference in a letter dated 1385 to a peace agreement between Theodore and certain rebellious subjects of his.

[13] *MP*, no. 27, p. 58. See ch. 3 above, p. 46.   [14] *MP*, nos. 28, 32, 33, pp. 60–1, 67–78.

[15] For the Veneto-Navarrese treaty of 1382, see ibid., no. 17, pp. 36–9. For Venice's persistent efforts from 1384 onwards to acquire Zonklon from the Navarrese and worries that the Genoese might

Finally, frustrated over the futility of his peaceful approaches and concessions to his aristocratic subjects who persisted in their insubordination and
cooperation with the Navarrese, and unable to obtain any relief from the
foreign powers to whom he had so far made overtures, Theodore I decided
during the fifth year of his rule to call on the help of the Ottomans.[16]
Thus, as confirmed by a Byzantine short chronicle, in 1387 (September)
the Ottoman commander Evrenos Beg marched through the Morea "by the
wish of the Despot."[17] Supported by Evrenos' troops, Theodore launched
a successful offensive against his enemies, both internal and external. Yet,
in an ironic way not foreseen by Theodore, part of his territories which
had been previously occupied by the Navarrese and independence-seeking
Greek aristocrats were seized in the course of this campaign by Evrenos
Beg's soldiers, who apparently refused to restore them to the Despotate.[18]
Consequently, Theodore was compelled to pay a visit to the Ottoman ruler
Murad I, with whom he arranged favorable terms, and thereupon, returning to the Morea, he was able to gain full control over those lands that
were held by the local magnates (δυνάσται) prior to Evrenos' intervention. Shortly after the conclusion of his alliance with Murad I, Theodore
also captured Argos, which Marie d'Enghien Cornaro had recently sold to
Venice.[19] It is noteworthy that at the outset Theodore appealed directly
to Evrenos Beg, without entering formal diplomatic relations with the
Ottoman court. He seems to have opted for an official alliance with Murad I
only when Evrenos and his men turned out to be almost as menacing as
the Navarrese forces and the Greek landlords against whom they had been
called in to fight. Theodore's decision to offer allegiance to Murad I at this
time may also have been influenced by the example of his brother Manuel II,
who adopted a conciliatory policy towards the Sultan subsequent to
the Ottoman capture of Thessalonike (spring 1387).[20] Thereafter, with the
Ottoman ruler on his side, Theodore began to assert his authority over the

---

secure the port, see ibid., nos. 25, 26, 32, 33, 117, 118, 168, 314, pp. 54–6, 68, 73, 77, 225–8, 336–7, 587; Sathas, *Documents*, vol. I, nos. 22, 44, 45, pp. 26–7, 52–62.

[16] Loenertz, "Res gestae," 209, vv. 50–61. The Parori inscription calls the Ottomans "Ἄγαρ ἔγγονοι" and "Ἀγαρηνοί." Already in 1385 Theodore had employed the services of some Turkish mercenaries: see note 7 above.

[17] Schreiner, *Kleinchroniken*, vol. I, Chr. 33/14(CP); vol. II, p. 335.

[18] Loenertz, "Res gestae," 209, vv. 68–75.

[19] Ibid., 209–10, vv. 76–80. For the agreement concerning the sale of Argos (and Nauplia) by Marie d'Enghien, widow of Pietro Cornaro, to Venice on December 12, 1388, see G. M. Thomas and R. Predelli, *Diplomatarium Veneto-Levantinum sive acta et diplomata res Venetas, Graecas atque Levantis illustrantia a 1300–1454*, 2 vols. (Venice, 1880, 1889; repr. 1964), vol. II, no. 126, pp. 211–13; cf. *MP*, no. 45, pp. 97–8. For Theodore's siege and capture of Argos, see *MP*, nos. 46 (Dec. 22, 1388) and 47 (Feb. 18, 1389), pp. 99–105. See also pp. 256–7 below, for the aftermath of the Argos affair.

[20] See Loenertz, "Pour l'histoire," 168–70.

Peloponnese and embarked upon repressive measures against his unruly subjects.

Yet it is crucial to consider here, with the benefit of hindsight, the broader implications of Theodore I's appeal to the Ottomans, which introduced them into the Peloponnese for the first time, properly speaking. During the earlier part of the 1380s the Despotate of the Morea had been spared the large-scale Ottoman incursions that other Byzantine possessions in Thrace and Macedonia were undergoing. Apart from Turkish pirates from the Anatolian emirates who incessantly menaced the coast of the Peloponnese[21] and Turkish mercenaries to whom almost all the regional powers, Greek as well as Latin, had recourse at one time or another, there was as yet no Turkish/Ottoman presence to account for in the peninsula until the advent of Evrenos Beg and his troops in response to Theodore's call. Therefore, while through the assistance of Evrenos Beg the Despot was able to fulfill his immediate goal of forestalling the Navarrese and suppressing his rebellious subjects, at the same time he introduced to the area the Ottomans, who in the long run had the potential to turn into a major threat, and he exposed to them the social conflicts troubling his state.

These dangers became apparent during the reign of Bayezid I, who pursued a more aggressive policy towards the Byzantine Empire than his predecessor Murad I. Early in 1395 the Despotate of the Morea suffered its first massive Ottoman raid, which was led by Theodore I's former ally, Evrenos Beg. Acting in alliance now with the Navarrese, Evrenos conquered the Byzantine fortress of Akova (February 21, 1395),[22] but shortly afterwards withdrew his armies. Then, following Bayezid I's victory at Nikopolis, the Morea became the scene of a new wave of Ottoman attacks between 1397 and 1400.[23] Although these were mainly punitive raids that ended with the withdrawal of the Ottomans after a certain amount of plundering activity, the Despotate nonetheless must have been left in a ravaged state. Data concerning Venetian holdings in the Peloponnese, which likewise suffered from Ottoman attacks during this period, give a hint of what corresponding conditions in the Greek Despotate would have been like. For instance, Ottoman raids in 1395 and 1397 resulted in considerable devastation and depopulation in Argos and its environs, due

---

[21] On Turkish naval operations in the Aegean during the early part of the fourteenth century, see E. A. Zachariadou, "The Catalans of Athens and the beginning of the Turkish expansion in the Aegean area," *Studi medievali*, ser. 3, 21 (1980), 821–38; Inalcık, "Rise of the Turcoman maritime principalities," 179–217.

[22] Schreiner, *Kleinchroniken*, vol. I, Chr. 33/17; vol. II, pp. 355–6.

[23] On these attacks, see Zakythinos, *Despotat*, vol. I, pp. 155–8.

in large part to the enslavement and flight of the peasant population.[24] When the forces of the Ottoman commander Yakub Paşa captured Argos in June 1397, at least fourteen thousand people were taken captive and possibly deported to Anatolia.[25] After the withdrawal of the Ottomans, the Venetian authorities took several measures to repopulate Argos and its territory, so as to guarantee both continued agricultural production and proper protection. Efforts were made to settle foreigners, in particular Albanians, who were given arable land and vineland, with the expectation that the newcomers would contribute to cultivation as well as to defense.[26] In addition, former inhabitants who had fled Argos because of Ottoman attacks were encouraged to return through the offer of lands, vacant houses, and a five-year exemption from all required services and payments except the guarding of the walls (*angaria guarde*).[27] Yet, as late as 1404 the region was still depopulated and filled with uncultivated fields and vineyards, which the Venetian government continued to distribute in an attempt to attract inhabitants, both old and new.[28] Conditions were critical in Coron, Modon, and their territories, too. In 1395 the Venetian Senate ordered part of a grain shipment (1,000 out of 4,000 *staria*) which was supposed to be sent to the island of Negroponte to be set aside for Coron and Modon, where there was a serious shortage of food, due presumably to hostilities on the part of the Ottomans.[29] Ottoman raids, persistent throughout 1401–2, forced the inhabitants to remain within the fortifications, resulting in great destruction in the countryside, the enslavement of peasants, cessation of agricultural production, and widespread poverty. By the summer of 1402 the situation had deteriorated so much that the Maggior Consiglio (Great Council) in Venice decided to send food to the villeins of Coron and Modon, where people were perishing daily from famine as no one dared to step outside the walls either to cultivate the fields or to gather the crops.[30]

[24] Argos, occupied by Theodore I in December 1388 or January 1389, had been returned to Venice in 1394: see below, p. 257 and note 90. For the effects of the Ottoman incursions of 1395 in the plain of Argos, see *MP*, no. 169, p. 339 and no. 171, p. 341 (n. 3).
[25] Fourteen thousand captives reported in the *capitula* presented to the Venetian government by the inhabitants of Argos in 1451: *MP*, no. 197, p. 392. According to Chalkokondyles, on the other hand, the captives numbered thirty thousand and were deported from Argos to Asia Minor, but the historian expresses reservations about the truth of this information: Chalkok.–Darkó, vol. I, p. 92. For the Ottoman capture of Argos, see also Schreiner, *Kleinchroniken*, vol. I, Chr. 33/19; vol. II, pp. 360–1; *MP*, no. 198, pp. 393–5.
[26] *MP*, no. 200 (Sept. 7, 1398), p. 397; cf. ibid., no. 301 (Jan. 30, 1398), p. 567.
[27] Ibid., no. 207 (July 27, 1399), pp. 406–7.
[28] Sathas, *Documents*, vol. II, pp. 123–4 (Dec. 31, 1404); Thiriet, *Régestes*, vol. II, no. 1172.
[29] *MP*, no. 177 (Sept. 10, 1395), p. 351; cf. ibid., no. 171 (Aug. 3, 1395), pp. 341–2.
[30] Ibid., nos. 230 (April 22–4, 1401), 231 (May 6, 1401), 260 (June 18, 1402), 261 (Aug. 31, 1402), pp. 460, 468–9, 506–7.

The following year, a Venetian official in Modon still complained about the restrictions brought about by Ottoman incursions.[31] The negative effects lasted, in fact, much longer, as indicated by a Venetian document of 1407 demonstrating the impoverished state of the *veterani* (elders) of Coron and Modon, who were unable to pay their debts accrued at the time of the above-mentioned hostilities.[32] It is not unlikely that similar economic and demographic conditions prevailed in Theodore I's realm as well, under the impact of Bayezid I's increased pressures.

The situation in the Despotate of the Morea was further complicated at this time by the activities of a group of landowning aristocrats who had turned from a cooperation with the Navarrese against Theodore I, to an accommodation with the Ottomans. Referring to these people as "deserters" or "renegade Christians" (οἱ αὐτομολοῦντες χριστιανοί), Manuel II has outlined their activities during 1393–4 in his funeral oration for his brother.[33] We learn from Manuel's account that they appealed directly to the Ottoman Sultan Bayezid I, asking him to come to their aid in person:

Since all the machinations of those abominable devils against you [the Moreotes] were ineffective, they were faced with a stalemate. For they perceived that the barbarian army in Europe was wholly engaged there and could not easily and frequently march into the Isthmus while at the same time obeying the Satrap's commands. They therefore proposed to Bayezid that he should cross to Thrace from Asia Minor by way of the Hellespont and when he had arrived there should proceed to Macedonia and encamp there. Thence he should then send an embassy to my brother [Theodore I] summoning him to his presence.[34]

The outcome of this incident was the famous meeting at Serres, where the Sultan assembled his Christian vassals, Theodore I and Manuel II included among them, allegedly upon the request of their discontented subjects.[35] Although Manuel does not name any specific individuals in his funeral oration, he provides information concerning the motives and social backgrounds of the Peloponnesians who invited Bayezid to Greece. First, like the rebellious native landlords mentioned in the Parori inscription who acted in collaboration with the Navarrese, these people were stimulated by

[31] Ibid., no. 264 (April 1403), p. 510.   [32] Ibid., no. 284 (Feb. 21, 1407), pp. 537–8.
[33] *Manuel II, Fun. Or.*, pp. 127–35. For the establishment of this dating, see Loenertz, "Pour l'histoire," 173–4, 177–8. See also Barker, *Manuel II*, pp. 113–17 for a discussion of what follows.
[34] *Manuel II, Fun. Or.*, p. 133, lines 13–20. This is a slightly altered version of Chrysostomides' translation (p. 132).
[35] See Barker, *Manuel II*, p. 114, n. 38 for relevant bibliography. See also ch. 2 above, p. 31, note 33, for İnalcık's preference for locating this meeting at Verrai/Berroia (Turkish Fere or Kara-Ferye) rather than at Serres.

an overwhelming desire to be freed from the Despot's control.[36] Moreover, they expected that their association with the Ottomans would bring them certain personal benefits:

For they desire to find that on account of which they originally went over to the enemies of the faith – that is, wealth, glory, and those things which are pleasant in the life here . . . I speak of those who think that they will find a most wonderful post among the impious.[37]

Because of such expectations, continues Manuel II, they not only wished to live with the Ottomans and have them as their overlords, but they even went so far as to proclaim Muhammad a prophet. After prompting Bayezid I to cross to Europe, they next summoned Evrenos Beg to enter the Corinthian Isthmus and made a pledge to supply his army with abundant provisions.[38] Manuel II emphasizes that the Peloponnesians who collaborated with the Ottomans were generally of high social standing:

There were some individuals, neither belonging to the common people nor considered to be of low rank, who joined the enemy. At first they did so secretly in so far as this was possible, for I think they felt ashamed, but later they acted openly . . . They became for us an incurable calamity. I do not know what you would call them: Romans and Christians on account of their race and baptism, or the opposite because of their choice and actions?[39]

In short, these people were members of the aristocracy who, for reasons that will be investigated below, believed that their material well-being would improve under Ottoman domination.

The historian Chalkokondyles reports that one of the individuals who made charges against Theodore I at Serres was a certain Mamonas, the former lord (ἄρχων) of Monemvasia (Epidauros). The grievance that brought this Peloponnesian magnate before Bayezid I was that he had been deprived by the Despot of his independent control of Monemvasia.[40] Thanks to a

---

[36] *Manuel II, Fun. Or.*, p. 127: "... μηδὲν ἐγκαλεῖν ἔχοντας ἢ τὸ μὴ θέλειν ἄρχεσθαι ὑφ' οὗ γε δίκαιον ἦν." Throughout the funeral oration, Manuel frequently takes up the notion of "rightful/just ruler" in connection with Theodore's conflicts with his adversaries: see ibid., pp. 117–19, 159.

[37] Ibid., p. 129, lines 14–30: "Ἐπιθυμοῦσι γὰρ εὑρεῖν ὧν ἕνεχ' ἧκον τὸ κατ' ἀρχὰς εἰς τοὺς τῆς πίστεως ἐχθρούς – πλοῦτόν τε λέγω καὶ δόξαν καὶ ὅσα γε τῷ τῇδε βίῳ τερπνά – . . . λέγω δὲ τούς γε δοκοῦντας παρὰ τοῖς ἀσεβέσι χώραν εὑρηκέναι καλλίστην . . ." Chrysostomides has translated the last phrase of this passage as "those who thought that they would succeed in getting a well defended city from our enemies" (p. 128). As my own translation above shows, I disagree with her rendering of "χώραν καλλίστην" as "a well defended city," which seems to make no sense in the context of the quoted passage.

[38] Ibid., pp. 131, 157–9.

[39] Ibid., p. 161, lines 17–24. This is a slightly altered version of Chrysostomides' translation (p. 160).

[40] Chalkok.–Darkó, vol. 1, pp. 74–5. According to the dubious testimony of Pseudo-Phrantzes (*Macarie Melissenos*, ed. Grecu, p. 198), Mamonas' first name was Paul. Cf. *PLP*, no. 16580. On Mamonas

Venetian document, we know indeed that in 1384 Theodore I had granted Monemvasia (*terram Malvasie*) to Pietro Grimani, the *castellanus* of Coron and Modon. According to this document, the cession of Monemvasia to the Venetian official was intended as a compensation for the services he had rendered formerly, as *bailo* of Constantinople, to Emperors John V and Manuel II and to Theodore himself at the time of Andronikos IV's revolt and the Tenedos affair.[41] While this is the explicit reason stated in the Venetian document, which obviously reflects what was of direct interest to Venice, we may suspect that an underlying motive for Theodore was the prospect of curbing the insubordination of his rebellious subjects by way of this grant. In other words, in transferring Monemvasia from Mamonas' control into Pietro Grimani's hands, the Despot may first have intended to discipline Mamonas and, through the latter's example, other unruly *archontes* of the Morea, and secondly he may have hoped to secure for himself the assistance of Venice in his future conflicts with the Peloponnesian aristocracy.

On March 29, 1384, the Venetian Senate authorized Pietro Grimani to take possession of Monemvasia. Yet, until Mamonas' appeal to Bayezid I almost a decade later, nothing is known about the town or about the presence of Grimani there, except for a short chronicle entry which suggests that Monemvasia, or a large part of it at least, was under the direct control of Theodore I around 1391–2.[42] For present purposes, however, the significant issue here is not so much whether Grimani ever took over Monemvasia or not, but rather the dating of the conflict between Theodore I and Mamonas, which has been traced back to 1384. This date places the origins of Theodore's troubles with Mamonas in chronological agreement with the rest of the evidence discussed above concerning the disobedience of

---

and his conflict with Theodore I over Monemvasia, see also Loenertz, "Pour l'histoire," 172–83; Zakythinos, *Despotat*, vol. I, pp. 127–8, 341–2 (Maltezou's notes); Barker, *Manuel II*, p. 117; H. Kalligas, *Byzantine Monemvasia. The Sources* (Monemvasia, 1990), pp. 147–9, 154–6. As will be seen later in this chapter, Mamonas' appeal to Bayezid I led to a temporary Ottoman occupation of Monemvasia and its environs during 1394: see below, pp. 256–7.

[41] *MP*, no. 22 (March 29, 1384), p. 47. Cf. C. A. Maltezou, Ό Θεσμός τοῦ ἐν Κωνσταντινουπόλει Βενετοῦ βαΐλου (1268–1453) (Athens, 1970), pp. 46–7, 118. On Andronikos IV's revolt and the Tenedos affair, see above, ch. 6, pp. 120ff.

[42] Schreiner, *Kleinchroniken*, vol. I, Chr. 32/28 (Sept. 1391–Aug. 1392); vol. II, pp. 346–8; cf. MM, vol. V, pp. 171–4. For a discussion of the privileges Theodore I granted to Monemvasia at this date, see P. Schreiner, "Παρατηρήσεις διὰ τὰ προνόμια τῆς Μονεμβασίας," *Πρακτικὰ τοῦ Β΄ Διεθνοῦς Συνεδρίου Πελοποννησιακῶν Σπουδῶν*, vol. I (Athens, 1981–2), pp. 161–3; P. Schreiner, "I diritti della città di Malvasia nell'epoca tardobizantina," in *Miscellanea di studi storici*, vol. II (Genoa, 1983), pp. 93–7; Kalligas, *Byzantine Monemvasia*, pp. 149–53. It is noteworthy that in a Venetian document dated July 24, 1394 Mamonas is described as "*dominus Malvasie*": see note 90 below.

Morea's landowning aristocracy during the initial years of the Despot's accession to power.

Indeed, it must have been incidents resembling Mamonas' claim to rights over Monemvasia that forced Theodore I to dispossess other local magnates, too, of territories which they tried to rule independently of his authority. It may be recalled that around 1388–9 Theodore I succeeded in asserting his control over the Peloponnese by seizing the lands which were in the hands of the local dynasts.[43] This information which comes from the Parori inscription is confirmed by Manuel II in two passages of his funeral oration where the Emperor describes how his brother subdued his subjects. According to these passages, Theodore I constrained members of the aristocracy to restore to him all the lands they had appropriated, as well as those they had received as grants from previous rulers of the Morea.[44] It is difficult to assign an exact date to these confiscations since both references occur in sections of the oration where Manuel II does not follow a strictly chronological order. But a *terminus ante quem* can be established with the help of a letter written by Demetrios Kydones in 1391, which alludes to the obedience and submissiveness of the Peloponnesians to Theodore I, without specifically referring to confiscations.[45] On the basis of this dating, then, we may suppose that some of the dispossessed landlords mentioned in the Parori inscription and in the funeral oration figured among the Greeks who sought the Ottoman Sultan's support at the Serres meeting of 1393–4, especially since Manuel II, who was present there, refers to more than one "renegade," unlike the historian Chalkokondyles, who names only Mamonas.

On the Mamonas family, further information can be pieced together from various sources. An official document drawn up in Venice in 1278, which lists complaints about pirates who caused damage to Venetian merchants or to their subjects, names a certain Mamonas ("Mamora") among Greek pirates from Monemvasia.[46] Another Mamonas, again with an unknown first name, is mentioned in a letter of Demetrios Kydones addressed to a George the philosopher sometime between 1363 and 1365.[47]

---

[43] See pp. 239–40 and note 19 above.   [44] *Manuel II, Fun. Or.*, pp. 95–7, 123.

[45] Kydones–Loenertz, vol. II, no. 442, p. 408.

[46] *Urkunden zur älteren Handels- und Staatsgeschichte der Republik Venedig*, ed. G. L. Tafel and G. M. Thomas, vol. III: *1256–1299* (Vienna, 1857), no. 370 (March 1278), pp. 164, 192–3, 280. A certain Andreas ("Andream Malvasium"), Mamonas' partner (*socium*), and Eudaimonoiannes ("Demonozannem") are other Monemvasiot pirates cited in the document. Cf. G. Morgan, "The Venetian claims commission of 1278," *BZ* 69 (1976), 411–38, esp. 425, 430–1.

[47] Kydones–Loenertz, vol. I, no. 32, pp. 63–4; cf. *Demetrios Kydones. Briefe*, trans. F. Tinnefeld, vol. I/2 (Stuttgart, 1982), no. 57, pp. 346–50. Loenertz has dated the letter to "1363–1365?", whereas Tinnefeld dates it to "spring or fall(?) of 1363." See also *PLP*, no. 16577.

At that time, this Mamonas had traveled from the Morea to Constantinople to see the Emperor on some business. Despite the efforts of Kydones, who upon the request of his philosopher friend interceded with John V on behalf of Mamonas, the latter was unable to have audience with the Emperor. This was, explains Kydones, because before him certain slanderers (οἱ πευθῆνες) had said negative things to the Emperor about Mamonas.[48] Although the purpose of Mamonas' visit to John V is not specified, the letter reveals that this Peloponnesian aristocrat had enemies at the imperial court who turned the Emperor against him. It may well be that the tensions between Mamonas and the palace officials at the capital were related to a dispute over territorial and administrative rights, such as the one that brought another member of the Mamonas family before Bayezid I thirty years later; but it is impossible to insist on this point, given our limited information.[49]

More specific details about a Gregory Palaiologos Mamonas, who was married to the sister of George Sphrantzes, are contained in the latter's chronicle.[50] Sphrantzes identifies him as the son of the grand duke Mamonas (μεγάλου δουκὸς τοῦ Μαρωνᾶ), the former lord (αὐθέντη ποτέ) of Monemvasia and its environs. Thus, in all likelihood, Gregory Palaiologos Mamonas was the son of the Mamonas who made charges against Theodore I at Serres. Sphrantzes is the only source to mention the title "grand duke" in connection with the latter, who may well have been granted the title in compensation for his dispossession of Monemvasia.[51] Sphrantzes further relates that during the winter of 1416–17 Gregory Palaiologos Mamonas died of the plague in the Black Sea region, where he held charge as the governor of an unidentified fortress. On the basis of this information, Zakythinos has reasonably raised the question as to whether Gregory might not have been given an administrative post in a different region of the Byzantine Empire in order to be hindered from causing trouble to central authority in the Morea as his father had done.[52] Regarding the time and occasion of the establishment of marriage ties between the Mamonades of Monemvasia and the Palaiologoi,

---

[48] Kydones–Loenertz, vol. I, p. 63.

[49] Zakythinos has assumed that the Mamonas mentioned in Kydones' letter is the same person who appeared before the Ottoman Sultan at Serres: *Despotat*, vol. I, p. 127. But this seems unlikely; cf. *PLP*, no. 16580.

[50] Sphrantzes–Grecu, V.1, pp. 6–8. Cf. *PLP*, no. 16578.

[51] On account of this title, it has been proposed that Mamonas might be identical with the grand duke Manuel, whose death in 1409–10 is reported in a Byzantine short chronicle: Schreiner, *Kleinchroniken*, vol. I, Chr. 33/25; cf. *PLP*, nos. 16580 and 16711. Pseudo-Phrantzes, on the other hand, attributes the first name Paul to Mamonas: see note 40 above.

[52] Zakythinos, *Despotat*, vol. I, p. 187.

nothing further is known except Gregory's full name, which indicates that his mother probably was a Palaiologina.

Whereas we have seen that a member of the Mamonas family from Monemvasia, in his struggle for territorial rights and independence from central authority, had recourse to the Ottomans at the time of Bayezid I, other individuals bearing the same family name appear to have formed connections with Italians in later years. For example, a document dating from 1411 makes reference to a shipowner Mamonas who was an inhabitant of the Venetian port of Coron.[53] About the same time, another Mamonas is attested in the Genoese colony of Kaffa, where he probably engaged in trade.[54] During the late 1430s a broker (*sanser*) Mamonas acted in Constantinople as middle-man between the Venetian merchant Badoer and his Greek clients.[55] We encounter yet another unidentified Mamonas in the account book drawn up in Venice during 1470–1 by a Greek merchant and banker residing in that city.[56] Unfortunately, it cannot be ascertained whether the last three Mamonades were of Peloponnesian origin or not. Supposing however that they were, the evidence at hand suggests that while some among the Mamonades who had been deprived of their landed possessions by the Despot Theodore I associated with the Ottomans during the last decade of the fourteenth century, hoping thereby to regain control of their lost property, others gradually turned from landownership to the pursuit of commercial activities in conjunction with the Venetians and the Genoese.[57]

As to why or how the Moreote aristocrats expected that Bayezid I would help them when they made charges against their Despot at the Serres meeting, the confidence with which they approached the Sultan seems to indicate that they possessed a fairly good knowledge of the conciliatory policy pursued by the Ottomans towards Christians in the Balkans. As already pointed out, the Ottoman expansion in Thrace and Macedonia was partly carried out by peaceful means, through the offer of certain guarantees and privileges to native inhabitants. In accordance with Islamic principles, the Ottomans promised peace, prosperity, and religious freedom

---

[53] Sathas, *Documents*, vol. II, no. 527, p. 262.   [54] Iorga, *Notes*, vol. I, p. 19 (1410/11?).

[55] *Badoer*, pp. 79, 133, 135, 139, 229, 276, 521, 582, 647, 651, 725.

[56] Schreiner, *Texte*, p. 109 (Text 4, § 7). See Appendix V(D) below.

[57] An exception to this observation is Demetrios Mamonas Gregoras, to whom the Despot Constantine Palaiologos granted the village of Prinikon along with other properties situated in Helos during 1444: see below, ch. 10, p. 269 and note 46. It is to be recalled, on the other hand, that a tradition of seamanship existed in the family already in the late thirteenth century, but the naval operations of the pirate Mamonas in 1278 were directed against the Venetians: see p. 245 and note 46 above.

to those who agreed to recognize their sovereignty, thereby winning over a significant portion of the indigenous population, among whom figured the landowning aristocracy.[58] Some practical applications of this policy in the environs of Thessalonike and Serres, mostly dating from the reign of Bayezid I, have been shown and discussed in chapter 5.[59] Similar examples specifically concerning the Morea do not exist since the Ottomans did not establish their effective control over this region until much later. But it may not be too farfetched to assume that Mamonas and other discontented *archontes* of the Morea who had been deprived of their landed property by Theodore I had some knowledge of Bayezid I's concessions to their fellow aristocrats in other regions of the Byzantine Empire. These concessions, including the right to retain former holdings as well as new grants of land (*timar*) in return for military service, may well have incited the dispossessed aristocrats of the Despotate to solicit the aid of Bayezid I in 1393–4.

The *archontes* of the Morea, on account of the dual position they traditionally held as great landlords and as government officials in charge of administrative or military duties, had accumulated considerable power and local influence, which they frequently tried to use against central authority. In the years preceding the Fourth Crusade, for instance, they took full advantage of the weakness of imperial authority to extend their own power over different regions of the Peloponnese.[60] And while some among them suffered a decline in their fortunes at the time of the Frankish conquest of the peninsula, many of them were successful in their attempts to reach an understanding with the conquerors on special terms and conditions which included the recognition of their property rights, religious freedom, and local customs. Interestingly, one of the three *archontes* from Monemvasia who submitted to Prince William II Villehardouin of Achaia in 1248 was a certain Mamonas. In return for their submission, Mamonas and the other two *archontes* – Eudaimonoioannes and Sophianos – were left undisturbed in their possessions and granted *pronoiai* in the neighboring region of Vatika as additional presents.[61] During the second half of the fourteenth century, it was the Ottomans who posed the greatest danger to the western

---

[58] See above, ch. 2, pp. 26f.   [59] See above, pp. 88ff.

[60] See Jacoby, "Les archontes grecs," 465–7; D. Jacoby, "The encounter of two societies: western conquerors and Byzantines in the Peloponnesus after the Fourth Crusade," *The American Historical Review* 78/4 (1973), 882–3.

[61] On all this, in addition to Jacoby's articles in the previous note, see Zakythinos, *Despotat*, vol. II, pp. 192–3; J. Ferluga, "L'aristocratie byzantine en Morée au temps de la conquête latine," *BF* 4 (1972), 76–87; A. Ilieva, *Frankish Morea (1205–1262): Socio-cultural Interaction between the Franks and the Local Population* (Athens, 1991), esp. pp. 171–90. See also D. Jacoby, "The Latin Empire of Constantinople and the Frankish states in Greece," in *The New Cambridge Medieval History*, vol. V: *c.1198–c.1300*, ed. D. Abulafia (Cambridge, 1999), pp. 537–9, with further bibliography.

provinces of the Byzantine Empire. Moreover, since Theodore I's appeal to Evrenos Beg, followed by his submission to Murad I's suzerainty shortly after the surrender of Thessalonike to Hayreddin Paşa's forces in 1387, the Ottomans started interfering directly in the affairs of the Morea. Their conquests in Thessaly, which were well under way by 1394, brought them even closer to the borders of the Morea. It is, therefore, not surprising that some archontic families of the Despotate sought to come to terms with the Ottomans around this time, just as they had done with the Frankish conquerors in the thirteenth century. As before, they found that the new conquerors allowed them to maintain their social and economic status, as well as their religion.

Another case of opposition to Theodore I, which occurred approximately a year after the Serres meeting, is brought to light by a document from the patriarchal registers of Constantinople. This document contains the text of a letter written by Theodore I to Emperor Manuel II shortly before August 23, 1395 for the purpose of denouncing the metropolitan of Patras (Maximos), who had expelled the governor of the fortress of Grevenon and replaced him with another man of his own choice. The expelled governor is identified as "the brother of Phrankopoulos," while the new magnate put in charge of the fortress was the *protostrator* Sarakinopoulos, who, the letter proclaims, was disloyal to the Despot and provoked the people of the Morea to revolt against him. Theodore asked the Emperor to present this case to the patriarch, expecting that the latter would depose the metropolitan. The patriarchal court, however, deeming that this would be an uncanonical procedure, decided to try Maximos in Constantinople before taking any action against him.[62] The result of the trial remains unknown; the only relevant information that is available indicates that in January 1397 a new metropolitan was nominated for Patras.[63] But whether this was as a result of Maximos' deposition, or simply the end of his term or his death cannot be determined without further evidence.

In comparison with the other acts of disobedience to the Despot presented earlier, the most distinguishing feature of this affair is the involvement of an ecclesiastical dignitary. Hence, the civil strife between

[62] MM, vol. II, no. 493, pp. 249–55; Theodore I's letter is quoted on p. 250. See Darrouzès, *Reg.*, nos. 3004–9, pp. 269–74 and also no. 3037, p. 300 (Crit. I), where the accused metropolitan of Patras is identified as Maximos; cf. *PLP*, no. 16803. On Sarakinopoulos, see *PLP*, no. 24855; on the likely identity of "Phrankopoulos," brother of the unnamed governor of Grevenon, see note 69 below.
[63] MM, vol. II, no. 511, p. 275; Darrouzès, *Reg.*, no. 3037, p. 300.

Theodore I and the landed magnates of the Morea was further complicated by the intervention of members of the ecclesiastical hierarchy. Theodore must have found the collaboration of his lay subjects with high-ranking religious officials so threatening that he referred the matter at once to the attention of the Emperor and the patriarch in Constantinople, denouncing the metropolitan of Patras as "a second metropolitan of Athens." The Despot does not explain the meaning of this comparison which, nevertheless, must have been clear to his addressee. He only states vaguely that the metropolitan of Patras, not wanting his co-dignitary in Athens to be unique, followed the example of his deeds and manners, and had him as an associate (σύντροφος).[64] A patriarchal letter addressed to the metropolitan Dorotheos of Athens immediately after Theodore's implication of the two metropolitans is not very illuminating either since it does not name the charges on the basis of which Dorotheos was asked to appear before the ecclesiastic tribunal of Constantinople.[65] A month later the patriarch sent a letter to the Greek clergy of Negroponte, who had been excommunicated by the metropolitan of Athens but refused to obey or to commemorate him because of rumors about his deposition. The patriarch asked the islanders to continue recognizing the metropolitan until the court was to reach a decision concerning the accusations against him, still, however, without stating what these were.[66]

Fortunately, an earlier patriarchal act from the year 1393 sheds some light on this issue. We learn from this act that Dorotheos had been ordained metropolitan of Athens during the patriarchate of Neilos (1380–8), probably *circa* 1388. Once stationed in his see, which was then under the political control of Nerio Acciaiuoli, Dorotheos had successfully stood up against the religious suppression of the Latin authorities for several years, until shortly before March 1393 when he had been constrained to take flight from Athens. Thereupon, the Latin authorities dispatched written accusations to the patriarch of Constantinople, claiming that Dorotheos had gone over to the Turks to seek military support against the Latins and promised to give the Turks holy treasures of the Church if they would help him regain control of his see. Although in the end the patriarchal court acquitted the metropolitan of these charges, this was not because any positive evidence had been found to disprove them, but solely on the basis of the canonical

[64] MM, vol. ii, p. 250.
[65] Ibid., no. 494 (August 1395), p. 256; cf. Darrouzès, *Reg.*, no. 3010, pp. 275–6. On Dorotheos of Athens, see *PLP*, no. 5926, which, however, does not follow Darrouzès, accepting rather the former identification of the unnamed metropolitan of Athens in this act with Makarios.
[66] MM, vol. ii, no. 498 (September 1395), pp. 258–9; cf. Darrouzès, *Reg.*, no. 3013, pp. 278–9.

argument that accusations made against Greek bishops by "heretics and schismatics" (i.e. Latins) could not be considered valid.[67] Yet it is a known fact that during 1393–4 Bayezid I's armies were actively engaged in Thessaly and in 1394 they seized from Nerio the city of Neopatras, which was subject to the ecclesiastical jurisdiction of the Greek metropolitan of Athens. Hence, it is not entirely inconceivable that Dorotheos had actually called on the military assistance of the Ottomans in order to be able to return to Athens and to continue his resistance against the Latin authorities there.[68] Two years later the metropolitan of Patras, who according to Theodore I not only imitated the actions of his colleague at Athens but also had him as an accomplice, may likewise have had recourse to Ottoman forces in overthrowing the rightful governor of Grevenon and replacing him with an adversary of the Despot. A less likely possibility, on the other hand, is that in drawing his comparison between the two metropolitans, Theodore I may have considered Maximos' collaboration with the *protostrator* Sarakinopoulos as an act parallel to Dorotheos' collaboration with the Ottomans on the grounds simply that both were examples of a cooperation between ecclesiastics and laymen, regardless of the separate religions of the respective laymen involved.

Whatever the exact details of this collaboration were, the Grevenon affair must be seen, above all else, as another example of aristocratic resistance to the Despot. Leaving aside the involvement of the metropolitan of Patras, at first sight the key issue appears to be the supplanting of one magnate by another, which could be interpreted as a petty rivalry between two archontic families, rather than a struggle for independence from central authority. However, the description of the supplanter, the *protostrator* Sarakinopoulos, as an opponent of Theodore I who incited the people of the Morea against the Despot places the event within its proper context. Additional evidence concerning the Phrankopouloi, the family of the expelled governor, reveals, moreover, that its members included many high functionaries who were loyal servants of successive Palaiologan Despots. For example, Manuel Phrankopoulos was one of Theodore I's most trusted ambassadors, who concluded a treaty in Modon with representatives of the Venetian government on May 27, 1394 and later during the same year conducted further negotiations with the

[67] MM, vol. II, no. 435 (March 1393), pp. 165–9; cf. Darrouzès, *Reg.*, no. 2921, pp. 199–201.
[68] For the ecclesiastical jurisdiction of Dorotheos of Athens over Neopatras (and Thebes), see MM, vol. II, p. 165, repeated on pp. 167, 168, 169. For Bayezid's capture of Neopatras in 1394, see Setton, "Latins in Greece," p. 423; J. V. A. Fine, *Late Medieval Balkans: A Critical Survey from the Late Twelfth Century to the Ottoman Conquest* (Ann Arbor, 1987), pp. 404, 430.

Venetians.[69] The *protostrator* John Phrankopoulos, founder of the Pantanassa monastery in Mistra, was the chief minister (*katholikos mesazon*) of Theodore II and later, in 1444, *generales* of the Despot Constantine.[70] He is also usually identified with the *protostrator* Phrankopoulos, who is mentioned twice in the chronicle of Sphrantzes without any first name. Sphrantzes relates that prior to 1428 Phrankopoulos used to be the governor of several territories, all in the south-western Peloponnese, including Androusa, Kalamata, Pedema, Mani, Nesi, Spitali, Grembeni, Aetos, Loi, Neokastron, and Archangelos. Following an administrative rearrangement in 1428, when these places were transferred from the Despot Theodore II to the Despot Constantine, Sphrantzes was appointed to take over their control from Phrankopoulos.[71] Sphrantzes later reports that in 1443 the *protostrator* Phrankopoulos went to Constantinople as Theodore II's envoy to negotiate a settlement with Emperor John VIII and Despot Constantine.[72] Another Phrankopoulos, bearing the title *megas stratopedarches*, for whom the Despot of the Morea demanded a safe-conduct grant from the Senate of Venice, is mentioned in a Venetian document dating from 1430.[73] Finally, an unpublished argyrobull of the Despot Demetrios issued in 1456 in favor of the sons of a certain Phrankopoulina (Michael and Demetrios) reveals the heights to which this family had risen in terms of economic power and social prestige during the final years of the Despotate. The two sons, inheritors of large estates from their deceased mother, were granted by this document the right to collect on their domains certain

[69] *MP*, no. 141; pp. 270–1; no. 143, p. 278; no. 158, p. 310; cf. no. 151, p. 297 n. 1; no. 153, p. 301 n. 1; no. 155, p. 305 n. 1. On Manuel Phrankopoulos, see K. Hopf, *Geschichte Griechenlands vom Beginn des Mittelalters bis auf unserer Zeit*, 2 vols., in *Allgemeine Encyklopädie der Wissenschaften und Künste*, ed. J. S. Ersch and J. G. Gruber, vols. LXXXV–LXXXVI (Leipzig, 1867–8), vol. II, p. 70; Zakythinos, *Despotat*, vol. I, pp. 129, 138, 166; vol. II, p. 98; Dennis, *Letters of Manuel II*, pp. xli–xlii. These works strangely ascribe to Manuel the title *protostrator*, for which there seems to be no evidence. They also suggest that he may have acted as the guardian and regent of Theodore II during the latter's minority. Furthermore, Zakythinos, followed by Dennis and *PLP*, all suppose that the above-mentioned governor of Grevenon was the brother of Manuel Phrankopoulos, which is quite likely. Cf. *PLP*, no. 30139, with a discussion also of the title *megas doux*, to which Manuel Phrankopoulos was supposedly promoted in 1429.

[70] G. Millet (ed.), "Les inscriptions byzantines de Mistra," *Bulletin de Correspondance Hellénique* 23 (1899), 137; G. Millet (ed.), "Inscriptions inédites de Mistra," *Bulletin de Correspondance Hellénique* 30 (1906), 462–3; *PP*, vol. IV, p. 18. Cf. Zakythinos, *Despotat*, vol. II, pp. 98, 103, 298 and *PLP*, no. 30100, with further bibliography. As noted in *PLP*, "Mit καθολικὸς μεσάζων u. γενεράλης ist offenbar die gleiche Funktion gemeint."

[71] Sphrantzes–Grecu, XVI.7, p. 26.

[72] Ibid., XXV.7, p. 66. Pseudo-Phrantzes, in yet another one of his typical corruptions, affixes the first name Leo to this Phrankopoulos: *Macarie Melissenos*, ed. Grecu, p. 336.

[73] Sathas, *Documents*, vol. III, no. 953 (Jan. 1, 1430), pp. 366–7; Thiriet, *Régestes*, vol. II, no. 2174. This person is also cited in an undated letter of John Eugenikos to Bessarion written before the Council of Florence: see *PP*, vol. I, p. 165; cf. *PLP*, no. 30090.

revenues and tax incomes formerly received by the state. It is noteworthy that the brothers, who are designated only by their first names and their mother's last name, are identified in the argyrobull as "nephews" of the Despot, which could mean that they were related to the imperial family and may have even borne the paternal name Palaiologos.[74] Viewed all together, these references indicate that from the time of Theodore I onwards the Phrankopouloi of the Morea followed a consistent political course as loyal and devoted officials in the service of the central government.[75] Therefore, Sarakinopoulos' collaboration with the metropolitan of Patras in the removal of "the brother of Phrankopoulos," who must have been placed in charge of Grevenon by Theodore I, was in fact an action directed against the Despot with the aim of seizing the fortress from his control and ruling it independently.

A crucial question that begs an answer is why the local landowning aristocrats of the Morea were so zealous about achieving independence from central authority, when this often required obtaining military assistance from Turks or Latins and in some cases resulted even in the acceptance of Ottoman sovereignty. As pure political ambition does not suffice for a convincing explanation, the answer must be sought elsewhere. Some pieces of evidence suggest that one of the major aspirations of the landowning aristocracy was to acquire freedom from certain obligations to the government at Mistra. In the Parori inscription the Peloponnesians who rebelled against Theodore I at the outset of his rule are designated as people who violated their oaths.[76] Similarly, Manuel II censures the Greek aristocrats who fought alongside Navarrese troops against the forces of the Despotate in 1395 for having disregarded the oaths they had taken.[77] Although neither source specifies what kind of obligations such oaths carried with them, presumably they comprised the performance of military service, which may have been one of the duties the aristocracy was seeking to escape from. There is greater certainty, on the other hand, that freedom from tax payments was an essential concern that stimulated the landowners of the Morea in their opposition to the Despot. The evidence for this again comes from the funeral oration where the Emperor praises

---

[74] E. L. Vranoussi, "'Ένας ἀνέκδοτος ἀργυρόβουλλος ὁρισμὸς τοῦ Δημητρίου Παλαιολόγου καὶ τὰ προβλήματα του," *Βυζαντινά* 10 (1980), 347–59; E. L. Vranoussi, "Notes sur quelques institutions du Péloponnèse byzantin," *Études Balkaniques* 14/4 (1978), 81, 86, 87–8. Cf. *PLP*, no. 30078.

[75] After the fall of Constantinople, however, a change seems to have occurred in the family's political position. The Phrankopouloi figured among the *archontes* of the Morea who submitted to and received immunities from Mehmed II in 1454: MM, vol. III, p. 290; see below, ch. 10, p. 283.

[76] Loenertz, "Res gestae," 207, v. 9.   [77] *Manuel II, Fun. Or.*, pp. 125–7.

Theodore I for having restrained the insolence of his ill-willed subjects (τοὺς δυσμενεῖς θρασυνομένους).[78] Among other things, writes Manuel II, his brother forced them to pay their taxes. This was a remarkable and unexpected achievement which, as the Emperor puts it, would have caused these unruly aristocrats to leap from their beds, had they dreamt of it in their sleep.[79] More than half a century later, according to the testimony of Chalkokondyles, the evasion of taxes by the inhabitants of the Morea played a critical role in the final Ottoman conquest of the peninsula. As the Despots Thomas and Demetrios, incapable of collecting taxes from their subjects, failed to deliver the annual tribute due to the Ottomans, Sultan Mehmed II decided to launch a campaign against the Peloponnese which ended with the subjugation of the Despotate in 1460.[80]

It appears, thus, that the landowning aristocracy of the Morea wanted to maintain its possessions without being liable to the government at Mistra for any responsibilities or obligations. Within this scheme the persistence of external conflicts furnished members of the aristocracy with a better chance of success in their resistance to central authority. Hence, when they sided with the Navarrese or invited Ottoman armies into the Morea, they did not necessarily act in response to a particular political preference for these foreign powers, but rather in order to prevent the establishment of external peace. Manuel II reveals this attitude shared by the landowners of the Morea in a passage of his funeral oration where he describes how they changed their stance once the tide started turning against themselves, probably referring to the events of *circa* 1388–9. According to this passage, following several victories which established Theodore I's authority over the landed magnates, the Despot sent them a written offer of peace, which they accepted with unprecedented joy. Manuel II immediately points out, however, that they did not cherish this peace offer for its own sake. Their acceptance of it was a direct result of the recent blows they had received from Theodore, which led them to abandon their former belief that the absence of peace in the Despotate was of advantage to their prosperity and

---

[78] Ibid., pp. 95–7, 123. For an inscription where the word δυσμενεῖς, rather than simply meaning "enemies," is used in a technical sense to designate the people who rebelled against the rule of Manuel Kantakouzenos, see Millet, "Inscriptions byzantines de Mistra," 145; Zakythinos, *Despotat*, vol. II, p. 221, n. 2.

[79] *Manuel II, Fun. Or.*, p. 123.

[80] Chalkok.–Darkó, vol. II, pp. 176, 202, 227. Kritoboulos, however, writes that the Despots did receive from their subjects taxes for the tribute but were unable to pay the Ottomans, for they squandered the money on their personal expenditures: Kritob.–Reinsch, III.1,2, p. 120. For aristocratic opposition to special taxes demanded for the reconstruction of the Hexamilion in 1415 and its maintenance later on, see ch. 10 below.

well-being.[81] Manuel II once again underlines the connection between the interests of the landed magnates and the persistence of external instability when he observes that the Peloponnesians who appealed to Bayezid I in 1393–4 were able to threaten the possessions of the Despotate by relying on the hostility of the Ottomans and the Navarrese of Achaia.[82] In the midst of the confusion created by the persistent attacks of the Navarrese since the early 1380s and the large-scale raids of the Ottomans as of 1395, these people expected to detach themselves from central control more freely, while at the same time being able to maintain their estates and acquire new ones. Consequently, as has been shown above, one of Theodore I's first measures was to confiscate their property when he temporarily gained the upper hand in his conflicts with them following his submission to Murad I.

In addition to Peloponnesian aristocrats who supported the Despotate's enemies only in order to disrupt peace, there emerged a new group of people during the reign of Bayezid I who seem to have joined the Ottomans, genuinely believing in the security and prosperity they might find in the Sultan's service. Those who, as Manuel II acknowledges in the funeral oration, deserted to the "infidels" at this time were probably responding to the military and political situation in the Despotate, which had become extremely unstable by the year 1395 as a result of joint attacks by the Ottomans and the Navarrese. In the opinion of the Emperor, these Christians were seekers of wealth, glory, or high posts among the Ottomans and, having chosen to live according to "barbarian" custom, they had "damaged their souls rather than their bodies."[83] Although the reference to "damaged/defiled souls" might immediately bring to mind conversion to Islam, it is clear from the context that Manuel II is not talking here about Greeks who denied their religion, but about those who submitted to the Ottomans instead of fighting against them. Indeed, the Emperor was very concerned about the mounting number of Peloponnesians who opted for a peaceful coexistence with the Ottomans under the influence of their conciliatory religious policy towards Christians who recognized their authority. He, therefore, warned his audience that even if the Ottomans did not require conversion to Islam, it would be impossible for Christians who accepted their rule to preserve their religion inviolate, "for those who wish to live with the followers of Muhammad and side with the enemies of the faith against us are fighting against Christ, the source of our faith, and openly waging war against Him."[84] In order to further discourage the

---

[81] *Manuel II, Fun. Or.*, p. 95. See also Kydones–Loenertz, no. 251 (1382–3; to Theodore I), p. 156.
[82] *Manuel II, Fun. Or.*, p. 129.   [83] Ibid., pp. 128–31.
[84] Ibid., p. 131; trans. by Chrysostomides (p. 130).

Moreotes who might be thinking of joining the enemy, the Emperor also elaborated on the strong distrust which the Ottomans felt towards the Greeks who went over to their side.[85] These details suggest, therefore, that a pro-Ottoman group still existed among the inhabitants of the Despotate at the time of the composition of the funeral oration upon Theodore I's death in 1407. For these people the security they expected to find under the Ottoman administrative system, which appeared stronger and more stable than that of the Despotate, along with the religious freedom that the Ottomans guaranteed, seems to have mattered more than the desire for independence from central authority or relief from tax payments which induced so many aristocrats to rebellion against Theodore I.

In order to gain a better insight into the unstable and insecure situation that prevailed in the Despotate during and after the last decade of the fourteenth century, we must turn now to the end of the Serres meeting and examine the problems which thence occupied Theodore I. Following the dissolution of the gathering at Serres, Bayezid I detained Theodore, who was forced to accompany the Sultan on a campaign through Macedonia and Thessaly. In return for the Despot's release, Bayezid demanded the fortress of Monemvasia together with its surrounding countryside, no doubt inspired by the controversy Mamonas had created over this place. Monemvasia was then ceded to the Ottomans "as vain ransom," in the words of Manuel II, because immediately thereafter the Sultan requested other important cities, including Argos, "as if they were some inheritances."[86] Since Theodore I had gone to the Ottoman court and paid allegiance to Murad I *circa* 1388, it seems clear that the latter's son and successor, Bayezid I, regarded the territories ruled by the vassal Despot as his own heritage. Bayezid's claims on Argos, in particular, must have been based on the fact that it was after recognizing the overlordship of Murad I and presumably aided by Ottoman troops that in December 1388 or January 1389 Theodore had occupied the city, which the Venetians had recently bought from Marie d'Enghien.[87] At any rate, Theodore soon managed to leave Bayezid's camp with his entire retinue, and he returned to the Morea in time to prevent the cession of Argos to the Sultan. Although shortly afterwards Monemvasia and its environs were to be recovered from Bayezid as well, these events nevertheless demonstrate the extent to which

[85] Ibid., p. 131.

[86] Ibid., pp. 141–5. Cf. Loenertz, "Pour l'histoire," 176–7, 181–3; Barker, *Manuel II*, pp. 118–19.

[87] For Theodore's occupation of Argos, see p. 239 and note 19 above. See also Loenertz, "Pour l'histoire," 169–70; Zakythinos, *Despotat*, vol. I, p. 133; Schreiner, *Kleinchroniken*, vol. I, Chr. 32/27; vol. II, p. 337. Cf. A. Luttrell, "The Latins of Argos and Nauplia: 1311–1394," *Papers of the British School at Rome*, n.s. 21 (1966), 34–55.

the Ottomans were able to manipulate and profit from the disputes between the Despot and the archontic families of the Morea.[88]

Theodore I's first measure upon the termination of his good relations with the Ottomans that lasted from 1387/8 to 1393/4 was to seek the friendship and support of the Venetians, with whom he had been on bad terms since his occupation of Argos.[89] Following the conclusion of a peace treaty on May 27, 1394, the Venetian Senate agreed during the month of July to provide naval help to the Despot for the recapture of Monemvasia from Bayezid I. However, the price that Theodore had to pay for this new alliance with Venice was the cession to the Republic of Kiverion and Thermesion, as well as the much-disputed city and countryside of Argos, which he had only recently saved from falling into Ottoman hands.[90]

Another case that illustrates the weak and insecure position of Theodore I during this period is the sale first of Corinth and later of the entire Despotate to the Hospitallers of Rhodes. Theodore had come into the possession of Corinth sometime between September/October 1395 and January 1396, when he bought the city from Carlo Tocco after a period of armed conflict. However, finding himself unable to rebuild the fortifications across the Corinthian Isthmus and defend the region properly, he decided to sell the city even though hardly a year had elapsed since his purchase. Upon the refusal of the Venetians, who were dissuaded from assuming the protection of the area because of the recent failure of the Crusade of Nikopolis, Corinth was bought in 1397 by the Knights of St. John in Rhodes.[91] According to Emperor Manuel II, who, in conjunction with the Empress-mother Helena, gave his consent and approval to his brother's deed, the sale of Corinth was inevitable in view of the contemporary political situation:

We are not so wretched, spineless or stupid as to prefer those strangers to ourselves. But it was inevitable that either the city would be conquered by the besiegers, that is the Turks, or that it must be given to those who were able to save it from

[88] *Manuel II, Fun. Or.*, pp. 145–59.
[89] For Theodore's strained relations with Venice over the question of Argos throughout 1389–94, see in particular *MP*, nos. 47, 49, 51, 54, 58, 62, 78, 79, 84, 86, 92, 97, 103, 110, 112, 114, 130.
[90] Treaty of May 27, 1394 published in *MP*, no. 141, pp. 269–75; the terms concerning the cession of Argos and other places on pp. 272ff. For Venetian help in the recapture of Monemvasia ("*omnia loca illius Mamone, domini Malvasie, que in partibus illis erant in manibus Turchorum*"), see ibid., no. 145 (July 24, 1394), p. 283. A few months before the treaty, the inhabitants of Monemvasia had offered to cede their town to Venice so as to prevent Bayezid I's takeover to which Theodore I had agreed, but this proposal had been rejected by the Venetian Senate: see ibid., no. 135 (March 5, 1394), p. 259.
[91] J. Chrysostomides, "Corinth 1394–1397: some new facts," Βυζαντινά 7 (1975), 83–110; C. A. Maltezou, "Οἱ ἱστορικὲς περιπέτειες τῆς Κορίνθου στὰ τέλη τοῦ ΙΔ´ αἰώνα," Σύμμεικτα 3 (1979), 29–51; Loenertz, "Pour l'histoire," 186–9. For relevant Venetian documents, see *MP*, index (Corinth).

impending peril. Since we were unable to save it ourselves, it appeared to us that of available possibilities the Hospitallers were best.[92]

At this time Theodore I's problems with the insubordination of his subjects still continued to trouble him. In their report to the Doge of Venice dated April 1, 1397, the *castellani* of Coron and Modon observed that the Despot was despised by all his subjects, and particularly by his "barons."[93] There were, moreover, strong suspicions concerning the surrender of the Peloponnese to the Ottomans by inhabitants who "prefer to enslave themselves rather than be destroyed as a result of the war."[94] Things finally reached a sharp climax when Theodore I, pressured by a new wave of Ottoman attacks during 1399–1400 and lacking sufficient resources, decided to sell the entire Despotate to the Hospitallers. On that occasion, the population of Mistra revealed its resentment towards the domination of the Latin knights by rising up in open rebellion against them and insisting on their expulsion from the capital and the rest of the Despotate.[95] In his funeral oration Manuel II argues that from the beginning his brother had not intended the cession of the Morea to the Hospitallers to be permanent, skillfully scheming to make the Peloponnesians realize through its threat the meaning of subjugation to a foreign power and, thus, stir up in their hearts the zeal they lacked against the Turks.[96] Yet this apologetic argument, further colored by hindsight, cannot be taken seriously. It was owing to the emergence of Timur and the eventual defeat of Bayezid I in the battle of Ankara that the Despotate was spared for the time being from falling into the hands of either the Ottomans or the Latins. By the summer of 1404 Theodore I had redeemed his territories from the Hospitallers,[97] but social problems continued to plague the internal affairs of the Morea until his death in 1407 and well beyond it.

---

[92] *Manuel II, Fun. Or.*, p. 167; trans. by Chrysostomides (p. 166). See also ibid., pp. 193, 195–7, 199–201.

[93] *MP*, no. 193, p. 387; cf. Maltezou, "Οἱ ἱστορικὲς περιπέτειες," 47–8.

[94] *Manuel II, Fun. Or.*, p. 173, lines 9–28; trans. by Chrysostomides (p. 172). See also ibid., p. 191.

[95] *MP*, no. 213 (Feb. 21, 1400), pp. 415–16; *Manuel II, Fun. Or.*, pp. 175–211; Chalkok.–Darkó, vol. I, pp. 91–2. According to Chalkokondyles, the inhabitants of Mistra were stirred up by their archbishop in their opposition to the Hospitallers. Cf. Loenertz, "Pour l'histoire," 189–96. It should be noted that shortly before and during the negotiations for the Despotate's sale to the Hospitallers, Theodore also considered for a while abandoning the Morea and taking refuge in Venice, together with his family and retinue, because of the severity of the Ottoman danger: see *MP*, nos. 211 (Dec. 30, 1399) and 214 (Feb. 27, 1400), pp. 411, 417–18.

[96] *Manuel II, Fun. Or.*, p. 203.

[97] On the retrocession of the Despotate, see ibid., pp. 23, 208 (n. 130), 210–11 (n. 131); *MP*, nos. 223, 224, 257, 259, 269–79, 289; Schreiner, *Kleinchroniken*, vol. I, 32/23; vol. II, pp. 384–5.

CHAPTER 10

The final years of the Byzantine Morea
(1407–1460)

When Theodore I died, he was succeeded by his nephew, Theodore II Palaiologos (r. 1407–43), the minor son of the Emperor Manuel II. This was undoubtedly welcomed as an opportune moment by the landowning aristocrats of the Byzantine Morea, who had endured obstacles, limited and only partially successful to be sure, but nevertheless threatening enough, to their quest for freedom and autonomy under the government of Theodore I. In a letter written probably from the Morea in the summer–fall of 1408, Manuel II highlights the unstable situation in the province, drawing attention to the traditional social disorders that were all too pervasive in the course of the young Despot's first year in power:

It seems that of old the land of Pelops was destined to look on its inhabitants' fighting with one another as preferable to peace. And nobody is so simple that in the absence of an occasion provided by his neighbor he cannot fabricate or invent one by himself. Everyone wishes to indulge his nature by making use of arms. If only those people had made use of them where they should, things would have been much better for them.[1]

It may be inferred from this passage that the power-vacuum that ensued upon Theodore I's death provided an occasion for the aristocratic families of the Morea to apply their energies against each other with even greater vigor than before. Manuel II was fully aware of the dangerous consequences of this fighting between the inhabitants of the region, whom he would rather have seen using their weapons against the real enemy, the Ottomans.

For the protection of the Despotate against Ottoman attacks, in 1415 Manuel II undertook the restoration of the wall across the Isthmus of Corinth, known as the Hexamilion, traveling to the Peloponnese in order to oversee the project himself. This was the Emperor's second visit to the

---

[1] Dennis, *Letters of Manuel II*, no. 51, pp. 146–7.

province since the accession of Theodore II,[2] which reveals his grave concern with the state of affairs in the Despotate under the direction of his young son. The active role Manuel II assumed in the Morea during this period consequently drove the region's quarrelsome landlords, who were temporarily relieved upon Theodore I's death, to redirect their customary resistance to their despots against the Emperor himself. A major manifestation of this was their opposition to the rebuilding of the Hexamilion.[3] Manuel II has left us his own analysis of this opposition and its causes:

> But then, there was another category, people yielding in rank to no one among the highest, but certainly inferior in their judgement, who neither intended nor did anything at all befitting their station and reputation of long standing, and who in their madness left no stone unturned in their efforts to destroy our undertaking. Although these were few in number, they managed to spread their contagion to a large number of the more unsophisticated, not to say more stupid . . . Everything can be attributed to one cause, their desire not to be within those walls, those on the Isthmus, I mean. For this was a veritable noose around their necks, inasmuch as it completely prevented them from continuing to perpetrate their former outrages and from manifesting their loyalty to the despot, not by deeds, but by the mere claim to be well disposed towards him. It forced them into the position of having to confirm by their actions that they were, in fact, what they only professed to be. The wall, of course, would tilt the scale in favor of the despot and enable him to compel them to act according to their profession . . . As a result, those people did not recognize their real enemies [i.e. the Ottomans] . . . ; thus they practically called down on themselves their own destruction.[4]

The Emperor's testimony is not the only evidence that links the resistance to the restoration of the Hexamilion with the fear of the local aristocracy that this would strengthen and stabilize the central government's control over themselves. Mazaris' *Journey to Hades*, written around the same time, gives almost a duplicate version of Manuel II's observations regarding the "stubbornness," "ingratitude," "plotting and deceit" of people from the aristocratic segment of Peloponnesian society who had no concern for the common good:

> However, even before this illustrious work [i.e. reconstruction of the Hexamilion] had been completed, the local barons, that turbulent, subversive crowd, who spend all their lives upsetting the peace in the Peloponnese, men delighting in battles, riots

---

[2] On his first visit, probably in the summer of 1408, on which occasion he may have written the letter quoted above, see Barker, *Manuel II*, pp. 275–6 (n. 132).

[3] On this event, see the detailed analysis in Barker, *Manuel II*, pp. 301–20 and J. W. Barker, "On the chronology of the activities of Manuel II Palaeologus in the Peloponnesus in 1415," *BZ* 55 (1962), 39–55. See also Zakythinos, *Despotat*, vol. 1, pp. 170–5.

[4] Dennis, *Letters of Manuel II*, no. 68, pp. 212–15.

and bloodshed, always full of deceit, treachery and falsehood, arrogant barbarians, fickle, perjured and forever disloyal to their Emperors and Despots . . . had the insolence, the impudence, to rise against their benefactor and savior, each of them planning to usurp power on his own behalf, and they conspired and schemed with each other, hatching plots against his Majesty; they also threatened the workmen, to get them to destroy the wall that was built for their protection and that of their fellow citizens; and as for their benefactor, leader and patron . . . they boasted that they would do away with this invincible and noble ruler, either by assassination, or in pitched battle.[5]

Similarly, Chalkokondyles, referring to the same event, relates the Emperor's conflict with "the Peloponnesian *archontes*, who, being in control of the land for a long time, by no means wish to obey the rulers of the Greeks, unless something seems to be of advantage to themselves."[6] Thus, Chalkokondyles attributes the audacity and firmness with which the local magnates resisted the Emperor to their more or less autonomous, long-term control over the territories which they held. In a panegyric composed for Manuel II, Demetrios Chrysoloras states, moreover, that some of those who resisted the reconstruction of the Hexamilion attacked and occupied several fortresses, hence testifying to the efforts of Peloponnesian magnates to extend their independent control to new territories.[7] Mazaris adds, on the other hand, that the Emperor recaptured some of these fortresses from the rebels.[8] Probably alluding to such achievements of the Emperor, Isidore of Kiev maintains that Manuel II, during his stay in the Morea, established order and "relieved certain people who had been seized by tyrannical power."[9]

Beneath their reproachful language reserved for the local aristocracy, these sources convey one of the principal underlying causes for the strong opposition shown to the rebuilding of the Hexamilion. From the point of view of some high-ranking inhabitants of the Morea,[10] Manuel II's project, which was primarily intended to strengthen the security of the region

---

[5] *Mazaris' Journey to Hades*, pp. 82–5.

[6] Chalkok.–Darkó, vol. I, p. 173, lines 14–18. Chronologically mistaken, Chalkokondyles places this event under the rule of Theodore I.

[7] Demetrios Chrysoloras, "Σύγκρισις παλαιῶν ἀρχόντων καὶ νέου, τοῦ νῦν αὐτοκράτορος," ed. Sp. Lampros, in *PP*, vol. III, p. 243.

[8] *Mazaris' Journey to Hades*, p. 84. See also *Cronaca dei Tocco di Cefalonia di anonimo*, ed. and trans. G. Schirò (Rome, 1975), p. 380, vv. 2148–51.

[9] Published as "'Ανωνύμου πανηγυρικὸς εἰς Μανουὴλ καὶ Ἰωάννην Η' τοὺς Παλαιολόγους," ed. Sp. Lampros, in *PP*, vol. III, p. 166, lines 2–3.

[10] Manuel II emphasizes that not all Peloponnesians were opposed to the restoration undertaking: Dennis, *Letters of Manuel II*, no. 68, p. 211, line 93. He divides the population (comprising officials, priests and monks, natives and foreigners) into three groups on the basis of their attitude towards the project: those who approved of it and participated in its accomplishment, including the Albanians;

before the Ottomans, had the potential of turning into an instrument of internal control. It is quite pertinent in this respect that, for over a decade since the time of Bayezid I's defeat in the battle of Ankara, Ottoman armies had been virtually absent from the Morea. Consequently, given the lack of an immediate Ottoman threat, the *archontes* of the Morea seem to have construed the rebuilding of the Hexamilion as a measure designed against themselves, more so than a precaution against future enemy attacks.

There was yet another basis for the opposition to the Emperor's undertaking, for which both Chrysoloras and Chalkokondyles provide partial evidence. The former, in his panegyric for Manuel II, vaguely hints that in order to finance the reconstruction work the Emperor imposed extra charges on those who "abounded" in money.[11] Chalkokondyles states more clearly that the Emperor demanded from the Peloponnesians money for the repairs, but that the *archontes* refused to comply with his demand.[12] Venetian documents supplement the information contained in these Byzantine sources, confirming, first, that it was not only the rich who were obliged to pay the special charges as Chrysoloras implies, and revealing, secondly, that there were others besides the *archontes* who avoided paying them. In 1415 Manuel II sent ambassadors to Venice, requesting, among other things, the return of Byzantine subjects from the Morea who had fled to Venetian territories in order to escape the charges. The ambassadors indicated that among the fugitives there were many sailors. On September 23, 1415 the Venetian Senate consented to arrange the return only of the sailors.[13] It can be deduced from the importance placed on the sailors in the course of these negotiations that considerable numbers of them had taken flight, leaving the naval protection of the Despotate under high risk. This would surely account for the Emperor's insistence on their return more than anyone else's. Moreover, the haste with which the above-mentioned fugitives left the Despotate, within about five months or even less from the time of the Emperor's arrival and the beginning of the reconstruction work, gives some idea about how burdensome the new charges must have

those who had strong doubts about its feasibility, yet still cooperated with the Emperor; and those who were completely against it: ibid., pp. 211–17, lines 100–202.

[11] D. Chrysoloras, "Σύγκρισις," in *PP*, vol. III, p. 243. This may be a reference to the *phloriatikon*, a new tax created apparently for the repair and upkeep of the Hexamilion, which we encounter in Byzantine documents only from 1427 onwards. On this and other special taxes for the defense needs of the Morea, see Zakythinos, *Despotat*, vol. II, pp. 237–9; S. Trojanos, "Καστροκτισία. Einige Bemerkungen über die finanziellen Grundlagen des Festungsbaues im byzantinischen Reich," *Βυζαντινά* 1 (1969), 54–5; Vranoussi, "Notes sur quelques institutions du Péloponnèse," 82–8; Bartusis, *Late Byzantine Army*, pp. 288–90.

[12] Chalkok.–Darkó, vol. I, p. 173. Cf. *Χρονικὸν περὶ τῶν τούρκων σουλτάνων*, ed. Zoras, p. 51.

[13] Thiriet, *Régestes*, vol. II, no. 1592; Iorga, *Notes*, vol. I, pp. 238–9.

been.[14] Almost three years later, a representative of Emperor John VIII and of Despot Theodore II demanded from Venice the return of Moreote peasants who had taken refuge in Venetian territories in order to avoid the *angariae* intended to meet the expenses for the Hexamilion.[15] While it is most likely that these *angariae* were established at a later date for the upkeep of the restored fortifications, this information, seen especially in conjunction with the evidence from the document of 1415, indicates how hard the lower classes were hit by Manuel II's impositions. We know from the testimonies of Manuel II himself and of Chrysoloras that the aristocratic leaders of the opposition to the rebuilding of the Hexamilion, who were relatively few in number, had enlisted the common people to their cause.[16] The documents from the Venetian archives suggest that the Emperor's heavy impositions, which gradually drove many of the Despotate's poor inhabitants to flight, must have been a major factor that incited the lower classes to join the rebellious aristocrats in the first place. The latter, on the other hand, also resented the financial burdens brought down upon themselves by the reconstruction work even though they undoubtedly could afford them. Recalling Theodore I's earlier efforts to constrain the aristocracy to pay their regular taxes as well as the role later played by the evasion of taxes in the final Ottoman conquest of the Morea,[17] the protest of the *archontes* against Manuel II's extra exactions for the Hexamilion in 1415 is hardly surprising.

In the course of the fifteenth century many high-ranking Peloponnesians chose instead to secure part of their movable wealth by depositing money and jewels in neighboring Venetian territories. In 1418, and later in 1430, Greek envoys sent from the Morea to Venice demanded the restitution of a sum of money belonging to a certain Sophianos, which had been confiscated by the Venetian authorities of Modon and Coron.[18] In 1429 a Peloponnesian magnate identified as "*Manoli Magaducha, dictus protostrator*" decided to place his property under Venetian custody in Coron, "*videns malum dominium quod fit per grecos.*"[19] Two officials belonging to the Eudaimonoioannes family, one *megas stratopedarches* and one

---

[14] Manuel II arrived in the Morea on March 29 or 30, 1415; the reconstruction was begun on April 8 and finished by May 2: see Barker, "On the chronology," 42–3.

[15] Sathas, *Documents*, vol. III, no. 731 (June 11, 1418), p. 177; Thiriet, *Régestes*, vol. II, no. 1697.

[16] Dennis, *Letters of Manuel II*, no. 68, p. 213; Chrysoloras, "Σύγκρισις," in *PP*, vol. III, p. 243.

[17] See above, ch. 9, pp. 253–4.

[18] Sathas, *Documents*, vol. III, nos. 731 (June 11, 1418) and 953 (Jan. 1, 1430), pp. 178, 366.

[19] Ibid., no. 937 (May 30, 1429), pp. 350–1; Thiriet, *Régestes*, vol. II, no. 2140. Some scholars have dubiously identified the person mentioned in this document as Manuel Phrankopoulos: see *PLP*, no. 30139 and ch. 9 above, note 69.

protostrator, followed suit, entrusting their money and jewels to the Italians of the peninsula.[20] What is even more significant for present purposes is that some of these individuals or members of their families, besides simply seeing greater prospects for their economic security among the Italians, politically upheld pro-Latin sympathies. For example, the *megas stratopedarches* Nicholas Eudaimonoioannes played a consistent role in negotiations with western powers during the first quarter of the fifteenth century. Early in 1416 he went on an embassy to Venice and then, in 1416–17, attended the Council of Constance, where he made proposals concerning a project for the union of the Greek and Latin Churches.[21] In 1419–20 he was back in Italy, this time to arrange for the marriage of two Latin princesses, respectively with the Despot Theodore II and his brother John VIII.[22] During his stay in Venice in the course of this trip, Nicholas Eudaimonoioannes appealed to the Venetian Senate and acquired permission to export 400 planks of timber from Crete to the Morea, for the construction of a church.[23] Eudaomonoioannes' name appears again in a Venetian document of 1422 which shows him to be the leading figure in the Moreote government's negotiations with Venice.[24] Later during the same year the Senate of Venice discussed a proposal concerning the grant of fiefs to Nicholas Eudaimonoioannes and his sons in the Venetian-held territories of the Morea.[25] Furthermore, it may be recalled that at the time of the Frankish conquest in the thirteenth century a Eudaimonoioannes and a Sophianos were among the *archontes* from Monemvasia who submitted to Prince William II Villehardouin.[26] This suggests that these two families maintained a firm pro-Latin stance over several generations, unlike most other aristocratic families of the Morea, whose political attitudes towards foreign powers showed a tendency to vacillate. Finally, it is worth remembering that in Constantinople, too, there were some Sophianoi who had strong connections with Italy,[27] which indicates that different branches

---

[20] Iorga, *Notes*, vol. III, pp. 21–2 (1437), 255–6 (Sept. 12, 1450); Thiriet, *Régestes*, vol. III, no. 2835.

[21] Dölger, *Reg.*, vol. V, nos. 3345, 3354, 3355; Syropoulos, *"Mémoires,"* pp. 104–10, 116. Cf. Gill, *Council of Florence*, pp. 20–2. On Nicholas Eudaimonoioannes, see also Kalligas, *Byzantine Monemvasia*, pp. 162–7; *PLP*, no. 6223.

[22] Dölger, *Reg.*, vol. V, nos. 3369, 3372; Thiriet, *Régestes*, vol. II, nos. 1757, 1782, 1791. Cf. Gill, *Council of Florence*, pp. 23–4. On marriage connections of the Palaiologan dynasty with Latins in general, see S. Origone, "Marriage connections between Byzantium and the West in the age of the Palaiologoi," in *Intercultural Contacts in the Medieval Mediterranean: Studies in Honour of David Jacoby*, ed. B. Arbel (London, 1996), pp. 226–41.

[23] Thiriet, *Régestes*, vol. II, no. 1734 (April 2, 1419). [24] Ibid., no. 1833 (Feb. 26, 1422).

[25] Sathas, *Documents*, vol. I, no. 78 (July 22, 1422), pp. 117–18. The proposal was not accepted.

[26] See above, ch. 9, p. 248 and note 61.

[27] See above, ch. 8, pp. 192, 197–8 and Appendix III below; Oikonomidès, *Hommes d'affaires*, pp. 66–8, 121.

of certain families dispersed throughout various regions of the empire did sometimes share similar economic interests and political attitudes. In addition to the above-mentioned individuals belonging to the most illustrious archontic families of the Morea, occasionally other less renowned or unnamed Greeks from the Despotate with money deposits in Venetian territories are attested in documents of the period.[28]

The family names of two aristocrats who challenged the rebuilding of the Hexamilion in 1415 prove helpful in bringing to light concrete information about the leaders of the rebellion against Manuel II, whom the sources in general collectively call *"toparchai"* or *"archontes,"* or simply describe as Peloponnesians of high rank. According to the Satire of Mazaris, the Emperor's rivals included two men by the names of "Krokodeilos" and "Helleabourkos," the scimitar-bearer.[29] The latter is also mentioned as an opponent of the Emperor in the Cephalonian *Chronicle of the Tocco*, which renders his name as "Eliabourkos" and ascribes to him the title *"megas Tzasi* of the Morea."* This chronicle also adds that Eliabourkos held lands and fortresses, one of which was the castle of Mantena (Mandinia) in Messenia.[30] A sixteenth-century manuscript which contains a theological work by an author bearing the name Thomas Eliabourkos Notaras indicates, moreover, that the Eliabourkoi at some point established marriage ties with the Notarades.[31]

As to the other rebel named by Mazaris, he probably belongs to the family of a Greek magnate who handed over his two sons and surrendered the fortress of Hagios Georgios to Mehmed II in 1460. Sphrantzes identifies this magnate as "Krokondylos," adding that it would be more appropriate to call him "Krokodeilos."[32] Hence, it is very likely that the *archon* who resisted Manuel II in 1415 was the father or grandfather of the Peloponnesian

---

[28] Thiriet, *Régestes*, vol. III, nos. 2810 (Aug. 12, 1449), 3010 (Jan. 17, 1456).

[29] *Mazaris' Journey to Hades*, p. 84; see also the commentary on pp. 118–19. Cf. *PLP*, nos. 13822 and 6018. It has been suggested that Helleabourkos' epithet (δρεπανηφόρος) may be a pun on the name Nikephoros: R.-J. Loenertz, "Épître de Manuel II Paléologue aux moines David et Damien 1416," *Studi bizantini e neoellenici* 9 (1957), 295, n. 6. A rebel from the Morea called "Lamburcho" (Lampoudios?), who, after having escaped from prison, was found in Coron in 1418, may have been one of Manuel II's rivals too: Sathas, *Documents*, vol. III, no. 731 (June 11, 1418), p. 176.

[30] *Cronaca dei Tocco*, ed. Schirò, p. 380, vv. 2148–51; see also pp. 480, 68, 86, 533, 580. The verses referring to Eliabourkos are also published and commented upon by Schirò in his "Manuele II Paleologo incorona Carlo Tocco Despota di Gianina," *B* 29–30 (1959–60), 209–30. For an English translation and further comments on these verses, see Barker, "On the chronology," where Barker refutes Schirò's chronological reinterpretation of the events of 1415.

[31] Loenertz, "Épître," 295, n. 6. The manuscript is *cod. Mosquen. 244* (Vladimir), fos. 13–28.

[32] Sphrantzes–Grecu, XL.9, p. 120. Although Krokodeilos could be regarded as a variant of the name Krokondylos, it appears from Sphrantzes' usage that it is a play on the word "crocodile." See *Mazaris' Journey to Hades*, pp. 118–19. Cf. *PLP*, no. 13823.

who forty-five years later surrendered Hagios Georgios to the Ottomans. The connection of this family with the fortress can be traced back indeed all the way to the end of the thirteenth century. According to the French version of the *Chronicle of the Morea*, in 1296 a Greek silk merchant from Great Arachova called "Corcondille" captured Hagios Georgios with the help of his son-in-law Aninos, who was the storekeeper of the fortress. At that date the fortress was under the control of Florent of Hainault, the Latin Prince of Achaia (r. 1289–97). In order to accomplish this deed, besides the cooperation of his son-in-law, Corcondille relied on a band of one hundred Turkish mercenaries under the command of a Greek general called Leo Mauropapas. Although the *Chronicle* states that Corcondille intended to give the fortress to the Byzantine Emperor, the fact that in 1460 it was in the hands of one of his descendants suggests that either he never gave it to the Emperor, or that the Emperor rewarded his undertaking by allowing him to keep Hagios Georgios.[33] Later, in 1375, some members of the same family donated to the monastery of Brontochion in Mistra several fields situated in the village of Terkova, a fact which reveals other holdings in the possession of this archontic family.[34]

Viewed in the light of the texts quoted earlier, our information on this particular family has wider implications. It is clear that the Krokondyloi, in accordance with Chalkokondyles' general observation about the *archontes* of the Morea cited above,[35] derived their strength from the fortress of Hagios Georgios which, by 1415, had been under their control for almost 120 years. Since the fortress had been captured from the Latins through the individual action of a member of the family, we may presume that thereafter the Krokondyloi held it independently from the government of the Greek Despotate. However, their autonomy was threatened by Manuel II's close supervision of Morean affairs, his presence there in 1415, and especially his refortification of the Isthmus of Corinth, which, by reducing the external threat to the security of the Peloponnese, had the potential to

---

[33] *Livre de la conqueste de la princée de l'Amorée. Chronique de Morée (1204–1305)*, ed. J. Longnon (Paris, 1911), §§ 802–16, 823, 826–7, pp. 319–24, 326–7. Cf. Zakythinos, *Despotat*, vol. ι, p. 65; vol. ιι, pp. 253–4.

[34] N. A. Bees, "Διορθώσεις καὶ παρατηρήσεις εἰς ἀφιερωτήριον τοῦ 1375 ἔτους πρὸς τὴν ἐν Μυστρᾷ Μονὴν τῆς Παναγίας τοῦ Βροντοχίου," *Νέα Σιών* 5 (1907), 241–8. The names and titles of the five donors that appear in the donation contract are as follows: "Οἱ δοῦλοι τοῦ ἁγίου ἡμῶν αὐθέντου Τσαούσιος καὶ στρατοπεδάρχης οἱ Ἀκροκόνδυλοι, κοντόσταυλος ὁ Ἀκροκόνδυλος κοντόσταυλος ὁ Γεωργιτζόπουλος, Σταμάτιος ὁ Ἀκροκόνδυλος καὶ Ἀνδρόνικος ὁ Ἀκροκόνδυλος" (p. 248). Cf. *PLP*, nos. 511–14, 516. For a Krokondylos, βασιλικὸς ἱκέτης, who founded the Theotokos Church in Karytaina (mid fifteenth century), see G. A. Stamires, "Ἡ ἐπιγραφὴ τοῦ Κροκόντυλου," *Πελοποννησιακά* 3–4 (1958–9), 84–6. The latter has been identified with the above-mentioned commander of Hagios Georgios: see *PLP*, no. 13823.

[35] See p. 261 and note 6 above.

create greater opportunity for the government to focus on internal matters. These, then, must have been the factors underlying the opposition of the *archon* "Krokodeilos" to the Emperor. We do not know how Eliabourkos, who also had fortresses under his control, and the other unnamed *archontes* happened to acquire their holdings. But whether or not they occupied their fortresses and lands by the same means as the Krokondylos family, they no doubt rebelled against Manuel II for identical reasons. Finally, seen against the background of the determination with which a member of the Krokondylos family opposed the Byzantine Emperor in 1415, the eventual surrender of the family's fortress of Hagios Georgios to the Ottoman Sultan without apparently much resistance in 1460 is indicative not only of the indisputable power exercised by the Ottomans at this later date, but also of the great impact of the Islamic-Ottoman policy of offering the enemy a choice between conquest by force and surrender with privileges. The reward that Krokondylos received for his submission to Mehmed II was Loi, a place located in the south-western Peloponnese.[36]

To crush the rebellion of the Peloponnesian *archontes*, Manuel II decided in the end to counterattack with an armed force, and on July 15, 1415 he defeated some, at least, of his opponents.[37] The Emperor is known to have received military assistance from Count Leonardo Tocco, who participated with his men in the siege of Eliabourkos' castle.[38] Chalkokondyles additionally relates that Manuel II arrested the disobedient *archontes* and deported them to Constantinople.[39] Yet, by whichever means the Emperor disciplined the magnates of the Morea, as in the time of his brother Theodore I, the internal order that was thus restored to the Despotate was limited and temporary. According to Mazaris, Manuel II's military encounters were accompanied with or followed by "treaties," "embassies," and "favors to the ungrateful," implying that in some cases the Emperor may have been obliged to make concessions to the rebels in order to pacify them.[40]

---

[36] Sphrantzes–Grecu, XL.9, p. 120. On Loi, see above, ch. 9, p. 252. For another branch of the Krokondylos family which intermarried with the Kladades and fought against the Ottomans under Venetian service in the 1460s, see Sathas, *Documents*, vol. v, pp. 31–2 (Nov. 28, 1465), 33 (Dec. 20, 1465). These people were *"Pifani Concordili Clada primarii nobilis Amoree, domini castri Verdogne in Brachio Maine,"* his four brothers, and his nephew Thomas. A Kladas Corcondile, who instigated a rebellion against the Ottomans in 1480 despite the objection of his Venetian overlords, is unlikely to be the same person as the commander of Hagios Georgios in 1460, as has been proposed in *PLP*, no. 13823.

[37] Schreiner, *Kleinchroniken*, vol. i, Chr. 33/27, p. 247; vol. ii, pp. 403–4.

[38] *Cronaca dei Tocco*, ed. Schirò, p. 380, vv. 2145–54.   [39] Chalkok.–Darkó, vol. i, pp. 173, 203.

[40] *Mazaris' Journey to Hades*, p. 84. It may be that Manuel II also turned to Genoa for assistance because a Venetian document records rumors concerning a possible intervention of the Genoese in the Morea at the outset of 1416: Thiriet, *Régestes*, vol. ii, no. 1597 (Jan. 14 and 25, 1416).

Even more significant in terms of confirming the persistence of similar internal conflicts that endangered the security of the Morea before the Ottomans are the efforts of Despot Theodore II in 1422–3 to cede the care and defense of the Isthmian fortifications to Venice and the issues raised by the Venetian Senate in the course of the final negotiations concerning this matter on February 18, 1423.[41] On that day the members of the Senate indicated that they would consider the Despot's proposal on certain conditions, two of which are very revealing. First, the Venetians stressed that everyone, and particularly the landowning segment of the population, would have to contribute to the defense of the Hexamilion, each in accordance with his means. So as to determine the proper amount of contribution from each household and to guarantee its payment, the Senate proposed to carry out an assessment of the inhabitants' resources.[42] It must have been inevitable that the Venetians, who were so accustomed to receiving from the Byzantines of the Morea deposits of money and valuables in their own colonies of Coron and Modon, would realize the importance of compelling the inhabitants with financial means to channel part of their funds to the war effort. The other condition upon which the Senate insisted was the maintenance of peace between the lords and magnates of the Despotate. If the Venetians were to assume the defense of the Hexamilion, those who possessed or held control over the lands, fortresses, and districts of the Despotate would have to put an end to the hostilities against one another. In the event of a disagreeement, moreover, they were to submit the matter to the care of the Senate instead of trying to resolve it among themselves by armed conflict.[43] It is clear that the Venetians perceived the critical internal weaknesses of the Despotate of the Morea that hindered, and would indeed continue to hinder in the future, the successful defense of the province against Ottoman attacks. It is also evident from the persisting reluctance of the rich to make financial contributions and from the ongoing strife for possessions among members of the local aristocracy that, because of inherent elements in the social structure of the Morea, Manuel II's achievements in 1415 did not have long-term influence.

In later years, therefore, Theodore II as well as other despots of the imperial house of the Palaiologoi were compelled to carry on the struggle against the unruly landlords of the Morea. A measure increasingly applied by the despots in the course of this struggle was to reward or entice their

---

[41] Sathas, *Documents*, vol. I, nos. 78 (July 22, 1422) and 83 (wrongly dated Feb. 24, instead of Feb. 18, 1423), pp. 115–19, 126–7; Iorga, *Notes*, vol. I, pp. 322–3; Thiriet, *Régestes*, vol. II, nos. 1849, 1870.

[42] Sathas, *Documents*, vol. I, no. 83, p. 126, lines 19–24.   [43] Ibid., p. 126, lines 24–30.

trusted officials from among the aristocracy with grants of property and privileges. Yet, given the extended history of conflicts between the despots and the *archontes*, this was a dangerous policy from a long-term perspective. It reflects, moreover, the growing weakness of central authority in the Morea. From a series of documents dated between 1427 and 1450, we know for instance that Theodore II ceded to George Gemistos Plethon and his two sons, Demetrios and Andronikos, in hereditary fashion, the control of the fortress of Phanarion and of the village of Brysis, with nearly all their revenues and taxes.[44] Through these grants, Theodore II thus raised an entire family to an indisputable position of power as governors and simultaneously lords of the above-mentioned areas. It is also revealing that whereas Theodore expressly denied the Gemistoi the right to collect from the inhabitants of Phanarion and Brysis one particular tax, the *phloriatikon*, which was reserved for the state, some years after the Despot's death, in 1449, the sons of Gemistos obtained from Emperor Constantine XI a chrysobull which granted them even this tax that was so crucial for fortification maintenance.[45] Constantine, when he himself ruled as Despot of the Morea (1428–48), tried to win or maintain the loyalty of certain aristocrats by similar means. In February 1444 he granted to Demetrios Mamonas Gregoras, in return for his services, a house and tower in Helos, as well as the village of Prinikon together with its inhabitants and revenues.[46] At an unknown date, Demetrios Palaiologos Dermokaïtes and John Rhosatas received from him a garden near Patras.[47] Since in 1429 John Rhosatas had participated in a successful attack led by the Despot Constantine against Patras, which was then in the possession of Venice, this grant may have been a reward for the services he and presumably Dermokaïtes rendered at that time.[48] Constantine even managed to attract

---

[44] *PP*, vol. IV, pp. 104–5 (Nov. 1427); *PP*, vol. III, pp. 331–3 (Oct. 1428); *PP*, vol. IV, pp. 106–9 (Sept. 1433), 19–22 (Feb. 1449) (= S. Kougeas, "Χρυσόβουλλον Κωνσταντίνου τοῦ Παλαιολόγου πρωτόγραφον καὶ ἀνέκδοτον," Ἑλληνικά 1 [1928], 373–5), 192–5 (July 1450). Cf. Ostrogorskij, *Pour l'histoire de la féodalité*, pp. 180–6.

[45] *PP*, vol. IV, pp. 20, 21. On the *phloriatikon*, see note 11 above.

[46] *PP*, vol. IV, pp. 17–18. Cf. Zakythinos, *Despotat*, vol. I, pp. 228–9; vol. II, pp. 123–4; *PLP*, no. 4440.

[47] This may be deduced from an argyrobull of Thomas Palaiologos, which confirms an earlier grant made by his brother, the Emperor, who was then Despot in the Morea: *PP*, vol. IV, pp. 231–2 (= MM, vol. III, p. 258). The date of this document is disputed, and based on the different dates assigned to it (1440, 1445, 1450) the former Despot and present Emperor who made the original grant has been alternatively identified as John VIII or Constantine XI. In my preference for the latter, I have followed Lampros' argument making a case for redating the argyrobull from October 1440 (the date given in MM) to October 1450: see *PP*, vol. IV, p. 232 (I take it that the date 1445, which appears in the title of the document in Lampros' edition, is a printing error). Cf. D. M. Nicol, "The Byzantine family of Dermokaites, circa 940–1453," *BS* 35 (1974), 9, no. 21; *PLP*, nos. 5207 and 24552.

[48] Sphrantzes–Grecu, XIX.4, p. 38.

by such grants Venetian subjects residing in the territories he recovered from the republic. One method that he applied with success was to recognize the prior rights and privileges of certain individuals established at the time of Latin domination.[49] Despot Thomas Palaiologos (r. 1428/30–60), too, recognized previous arrangements made by Latins in certain areas that later came under the control of the Despotate of the Morea.[50] And he, too, offered grants to Byzantines in his entourage, including one John Basilikos and one Thomas Pyropoulos, who received from him the tax revenues of the village of Potamia in the region of Lankada.[51] As we approach the final years of the Despotate, we have evidence of another grant, made this time by Demetrios Palaiologos (r. 1449–60), to two brothers, Michael and Demetrios, the sons of a certain Phrankopoulina and "nephews" of the Despot. In 1456 these two brothers acquired from the Despot the privilege of collecting on their inherited estates certain revenues and tax incomes that were normally received by the state and many of which were designated for the defense needs of the Morea.[52]

As a further measure aimed at reducing the power of the local aristocracy, the Despot Constantine also engaged in a reorganization of the administrative system of the Morea. In September 1446 he granted the control (τὸ κεφαλατίκιον) of Mistra, including the surrounding districts and all their income, to George Sphrantzes with the following instructions:

I want Mistra to be an entity, like Corinth held by John Kantakouzenos, and Patras held by Alexios Laskaris. Know it well: no one else will be an intermediary (μεσάζων) here, except my intermediary Eudaimonoioannes. I do not want to stay here at all times, as I wish to tour my territories pursuing advantageous situations. When I am at Corinth I will take care of my affairs and those of the land through Kantakouzenos and Eudaimonoioannes. At Patras I will proceed through Laskaris and Eudaimonoioannes, while Kantakouzenos will remain in his province. I propose to do the same when I am at Mistra through you and

---

[49] Sathas, *Documents*, vol. III, no. 938 (wrongly dated July 2, instead of June 2, 1429 = see Thiriet, *Régestes*, vol. II, no. 2141), p. 351: "*Intelleximus, quod aliqui ex Subditis nostris querunt habere in pheudum a Despoto Grecorum seu a dragassi de locis jurisditionum nostri dominii usurpatis et ablatis per grecos, que per ipsos grecos presentialiter possidentur . . .*"; E. Gerland, *Neue Quellen zur Geschichte des lateinischen Erzbistums Patras* (Leipzig, 1903), pp. 83–4, 218–20, 222–4. Cf. D. Jacoby, *La féodalité en Grèce médiévale. Les "Assises de Romanie": sources, application et diffusion* (Paris, 1971), pp. 182–3.

[50] Gerland, *Neue Quellen*, p. 125; *PP*, vol. IV, pp. 236–7.

[51] *PP*, vol. IV, p. 14. On these two men, see *PLP*, nos. 2465 and 23920; Matschke, "Zum Anteil der Byzantiner an der Bergbauentwicklung," 67–71; Matschke, "Some merchant families," 227–34; Matschke, "Leonhard von Chios, Gennadios Scholarios, und die 'Collegae' Thomas Pyropulos und Johannes Basilikos vor, während und nach der Eroberung von Konstantinopel durch die Türken," Βυζαντινά 21 (2000), 227–36.

[52] Vranoussi, "Ἕνας ἀνέκδοτος ἀργυρόβουλλος," 347–59; Vranoussi, "Notes sur quelques institutions du Péloponnèse," 81, 86, 87–8. Cf. *PLP*, no. 30078.

Eudaimonoioannes . . . You are to stay here and govern your command well. You are to put an end to the many instances of injustice and reduce the power of the numerous local lords. Make it clear to everybody here that you alone are in charge and that I am the only lord.[53]

This passage indicates, however, that all Constantine actually did in his attempt to reassert central control over the unruly magnates of the Morea was to appoint his own men to govern the most important strongholds of the province. The rights that he ceded to John (Palaiologos) Kantakouzenos,[54] Alexios Laskaris (Philanthropenos?),[55] and George Sphrantzes are in effect comparable to the rights Theodore II had granted in 1427–8 to Plethon and his elder son Demetrios over the fortress of Phanarion and its countryside. Constantine thus perpetuated the old administrative system which in the first place had given rise to the abuses of the local aristocracy, even though in the short run he may have been able to gain some power through his trusted officials. Down to the very last days of the Despotate, the Peloponnesian magnates did not cease from their struggle for the actual possession of the areas they had been assigned to administer. Sphrantzes writes of several *archontes* who in 1459 seized the fortresses they had been governing in the name of the Despot Demetrios, treating them henceforth "as supreme lords rather than as governors."[56]

Nonetheless, circumstances in the Morea remained relatively stable during the years of respite from Ottoman invasions between 1402 and 1423, and there may have been even some improvement in economic conditions. Contemporary documents occasionally refer to abundant food supplies in both the Greek and the Venetian territories of the peninsula. In 1418, for instance, surplus wheat was grown in the Despotate.[57] The year before that Venetian authorities in Coron reported the existence of surplus meat.[58] Similarly, at Venetian Patras oversupplies of wheat and barley are attested in 1411.[59] The extra security and protection provided by the rebuilding of the Hexamilion in 1415, despite the internal dissensions it gave rise to, seems also to have helped the agrarian economy of the Despotate. The following passage from one of Manuel II's letters describes, though perhaps with some degree of exaggeration, the positive consequences of the reconstruction work:

[53] Sphrantzes–Grecu, XXVII.1–6, pp. 68–70. This is a slightly modified version of the translation by M. Philippides, *The Fall of the Byzantine Empire: A Chronicle by George Sphrantzes, 1401–1477* (Amherst, 1980), pp. 55–6.
[54] See *PLP*, no. 10974.   [55] See *PLP*, no. 29753.
[56] Sphrantzes–Grecu, XXXIX.2, p. 112: "ὡς αὐθένται αὐτῶν, οὐχ ὡς κεφαλάδες." See below, pp. 277–8 and 282f.
[57] Sathas, *Documents*, vol. III, p. 178.   [58] Ibid., p. 163.   [59] Ibid., vol. II, p. 263.

For they could now till the fields without fear, reclaim woodlands and sow where trees had once stood, and look with pleasure upon the billowing crops and with still greater pleasure reap them, attend to plants that had been neglected, replant the vineyard that had been left dry and plant new crops besides . . . What is more they were able to sell their surplus at a high price if they wished. Even better, or by no means worse, they were able to fatten herds of cattle and flocks of sheep and their other livestock. For since they no longer lived in fear of barbarian incursions, nothing hindered them from making use even of the outlying borders, cultivating them as they wanted, be it in the plains or in formerly inaccessible places.[60]

But the years of external peace came to an abrupt end in 1423, and, during the period that followed, successive attacks by the Ottomans, combined with the civil discords that permeated the upper echelons of Moreote society, had disastrous effects on the rest of the population, generating in their midst a widespread unwillingness to fight against the Ottomans.[61] In May 1423, before the above-mentioned negotiations between Theodore II and Venice yielded any concrete results, an Ottoman army under the command of Turahan Beg marched to the Morea and destroyed the Hexamilion. According to Chalkokondyles, this disaster took place because the wall was completely deserted.[62] A letter written by a Venetian official in the Morea explains further that the Turks found the Hexamilion unguarded because the people in charge of its defense had abandoned their posts as soon as they saw the approaching enemy.[63] Manuel II's experiences in the Morea had already made it clear that without people to defend the fortifications the restoration of the Hexamilion could not by itself ensure the protection of the peninsula. Therefore, in 1418 the Emperor and Theodore II had asked Pope Martin V to grant indulgences to westerners who would participate in its defense even though at that time there was no immediate danger from the Ottomans other than perhaps some small-scale skirmishing activity.[64] About two decades later, the destroyed fortifications which were repaired again by the efforts of the Despot Constantine suffered the same fate. Gennadios Scholarios informs us that Constantine, who had constrained the Peloponnesians to rebuild the Hexamilion, had not been so successful in obliging them to stand in its defense. Hence, in Scholarios' opinion, the

---

[60] Dennis, *Letters of Manuel II*, no. 68, pp. 208–9.

[61] For a discussion of the political crisis that gave rise to the cessation of peaceful relations with the Ottomans in 1423, see above, ch. 2, pp. 34f.

[62] Chalkok.–Darkó, vol. II, p. 58.

[63] Iorga, *Notes*, vol. I, p. 335. Cf. Zakythinos, *Despotat*, vol. I, pp. 196–8; Barker, *Manuel II*, p. 371, n. 127.

[64] Syropoulos, *"Mémoires,"* II.6, pp. 106–9; *Annales ecclesiastici*, ed. Raynaldus and Baronius, vol. XXVII, p. 475 (1418, no. 17). Cf. Barker, *Manuel II*, pp. 316, 325–6, n. 49. The Pope accepted the request in 1418, but the indulgences apparently did not create much interest among westerners.

wall was destroyed one more time in December 1446 "by the treachery and folly of its defenders."[65] Scholarios' words are echoed in a short chronicle notice which makes an explicit reference to the betrayal of the Hexamilion to Sultan Murad II and Turahan Beg during the attack of 1446, while other sources are in agreement about the flight of its defenders.[66] Following this last disaster, the inhabitants of Sikyon surrendered to Murad II, while those of Patras fled to Venetian territories.[67] All this evidence is indicative of the defeatist attitude that had taken over the population of the Morea and manifested itself in the form of a declining spirit of opposition against the Ottomans.

In a letter to Constantine Palaiologos, written sometime between 1444 and 1446, Cardinal Bessarion has left us perhaps the most perceptive analysis of the problems afflicting the Despotate at that time which help to explain why the defense of the newly repaired fortifications collapsed before the Ottomans so easily shortly thereafter:

> I know that the presentday Peloponnesians have noble and prudent souls and strong bodies, but they are stripped of weapons and lack military training, on the one hand because of the cruelty of their oppressive overlords and the harsh exactions, and on the other hand out of the softness and laziness which has prevailed over the race.[68]

These words reflect the military deficiency and apathy of the population of the Morea which was weighed down under the double burden of government taxes and the excesses of the *archontes*, the "oppressive overlords." In Bessarion's opinion, the sumptuous and decadent lifestyle of the upper classes played a major role in the readiness of the population to surrender to the Ottomans without putting up a fight. He, therefore, counselled the Despot Constantine to restrain the wasteful luxuries of the rich, which included jewelry in gold and silver, expensive clothing made of silk or interwoven with gold, fancy military equipment, costly houses filled with abundant servants, and extravagant feasts, wedding receptions, burials or

---

[65] Scholarios, "Ἐπιτάφιος ἐπὶ τῷ μακαρίτῃ καὶ ἀοιδίμῳ δεσπότῃ κῦρ Θεοδώρῳ Παλαιολόγῳ τῷ πορφυρογεννήτῳ," in *PP*, vol. II, p. 7. Cf. Zakythinos, *Despotat*, vol. I, pp. 234–5.

[66] Schreiner, *Kleinchroniken*, vol. I, Chr. 33/50, 47/9; vol. II, pp. 467–9; Chalkok.–Darkó, vol. II, p. 116. See also Doukas (XXXII.7), who accuses the Albanians of having betrayed the Despots Constantine and Thomas on this occasion. By contrast, in 1423 the Albanians, unlike the rest of the population, had resisted the Ottoman army and lost their lives in the course of their opposition: see Barker, *Manuel II*, p. 371, n. 127.

[67] Chalkok.–Darkó, vol. II, pp. 118–19.

[68] Bessarion, in *PP*, vol. IV, pp. 34–5. Cf. Zakythinos, *Despotat*, vol. II, p. 143; A. E. Vacalopoulos, *Origins of the Greek Nation. The Byzantine Period, 1204–1461*, trans. I. Moles, revised by the author (New Brunswick, NJ, 1970), pp. 169–78, esp. 174; L. Mavromatis, "Ὁ καρδηνάλιος Βησσαρίων καὶ ὁ ἐκσυγχρονισμὸς τῆς Πελοποννήσου," *Σύμμεικτα* 9/2 (1994), 41–50.

funerals.[69] For the improvement of the Despotate's military organization, Bessarion also suggested the division of the population into two distinct groups, one of which was to be strictly occupied with military matters (τὸ στρατιωτικόν), while the other was to engage only in agricultural production (τὸ γεωργικόν).[70]

Bessarion was not the first person to propose a social reorganization of this sort as a remedy for the military problems of the Morea. His teacher George Gemistos Plethon, observing the poor defense system of the Despotate and its underlying social and economic causes, had already expressed similar opinions in his works addressed to Emperor Manuel II and to Despot Theodore II between about 1415 and about 1418.[71] Plethon noted that the use of mercenary troops and the imposition of extra taxes during military emergencies had proven to be an inefficient and inadequate method of protecting the province. He, therefore, emphasized the necessity for a regular army composed of native soldiers who, he suggested, ought to be exempt from taxes and whose livelihood and military needs should be met with the revenues the government was to collect from its taxpaying subjects. This, in Plethon's opinion, would guarantee the proper defense of the Morea as soldiers would not have to worry about their material needs. The taxpayers, on the other hand, comprised the agricultural workers whose occupation and tax liability would discharge them from military service according to Plethon's scheme.[72] Moreover, the tax collection system itself would have to undergo changes, its main drawbacks being that there were numerous taxes, each one small in amount, but collected frequently, by a large number of agents, and mostly in money. Plethon proposed instead that there should be a single lump-sum tax, payable to a single collector, in kind, and of an amount that ought to be just and easy to bear.[73] Finally, Plethon criticized the luxurious lifestyle of the Moreote aristocracy, arguing

[69] Bessarion, in *PP*, vol. IV, p. 38.   [70] Ibid., p. 35.
[71] For these texts, see *PP*, vol. III, pp. 246–65 (Address to Manuel II on Affairs in the Peloponnese), 309–12 (Letter to the Emperor [Manuel II, wrongly identified by Lampros as John VIII]); *PP*, vol. IV, pp. 113–35 (Address to Despot Theodore II on the Peloponnese). Detailed summaries of all three texts are given in C. M. Woodhouse, *George Gemistos Plethon; The Last of the Hellenes* (Oxford, 1986), pp. 92–109. On Plethon and the measures he proposed, see also F. Masai, *Pléthon et le platonisme de Mistra* (Paris, 1956); Ch. P. Baloglou, *Georgios Gemistos-Plethon: Ökonomisches Denken in der spätbyzantinischen Geisteswelt* (Athens, 1998); A. E. Laiou, "Economic thought and ideology," in *EHB*, vol. III, pp. 1139–44.
[72] Plethon, in *PP*, vol. III, pp. 251–7, 310–12; Plethon, in *PP*, vol. IV, pp. 121–2. Cf. Zakythinos, *Despotat*, vol. I, pp. 175–80, 226–8; vol. II, pp. 138–9, 349–58 (= Zakythinos, *Crise monétaire et crise économique*, pp. 131ff.); Woodhouse, *George Gemistos Plethon*, pp. 92, 94, 97, 100–1, 103–5; Bartusis, *Late Byzantine Army*, pp. 217–21; Baloglou, *Georgios Gemistos-Plethon*, pp. 60–2, 94–101.
[73] Plethon, in *PP*, vol. III, pp. 251, 254. Cf. Woodhouse, *George Gemistos Plethon*, pp. 103, 104; Baloglou, *Georgios Gemistos-Plethon*, pp. 83–7.

that the ruling elite should devote its funds to military expenditures rather than to luxuries.[74] He also noted with disdain the self-interested behavior of the officials serving under Despot Theodore II, most of whom "refuse to give advice except for their own financial advantage."[75]

Besides the similarity between these ideas and Bessarion's, attention must be drawn to a striking resemblance with contemporary Ottoman practices insofar as the separation of the population into soldiers and taxpayers is concerned, without, however, overlooking the fact that Plethon's source of inspiration lay in the writings of Plato.[76] Following a dual social system, the Ottomans divided their population into a military class which did not engage in production and paid no taxes ("*askerî*"), and a class of producers who were also the taxpayers ("*reaya*"). While it was possible on rare occasions for a person of "*reaya*" status to enter into the military class by a special decree from the Sultan, normally everyone was expected to remain in his own class for the harmonious functioning of the state and the society.[77] Whatever impact Islamic/Ottoman principles and institutions may have had on Plethon, though, this Byzantine intellectual formulated his ideas with the conviction that the salvation of the Morea could be achieved only through internal reform. He argued on one occasion, in an entirely different context, that so long as the Byzantines remained as they were, neither the help of the Latins nor any other human help could save their land from destruction.[78]

As an additional point concerning agrarian issues, Plethon held that all lands of the Despotate ought to be communal. Although he may have partly foreseen this as a means for the government of the Morea to re-establish its authority over the landlords of the peninsula, he defended his idea on the grounds that it would lead to increased agricultural production and eliminate the existence of uncultivated fields.[79] By referring to the low level

---

[74] Plethon, in *PP*, vol. IV, p. 124. Cf. Woodhouse, *George Gemistos Plethon*, p. 95.

[75] Plethon, in *PP*, vol. III, p. 312. Cf. Woodhouse, *George Gemistos Plethon*, p. 101.

[76] For two occasions in which Plethon specifically pointed to the successful internal organization of the Ottomans as an example, see *PP*, vol. III, p. 310 and *PP*, vol. IV, p. 118. Among contemporaries, Gennadios Scholarios observed the similarity between Plethon's ideas and Ottoman practices: Scholarios, *Œuvres*, vol. IV, pp. 170–1.

[77] İnalcık, *Ottoman Empire: The Classical Age*, pp. 68–9; İnalcık, "Ottoman methods of conquest," 112–13. For two different views regarding Islamic/Ottoman influences on Plethon's ideas, see F. Taeschner, "Georgios Gemistos Plethon. Ein Beitrag zur Frage der Übertragung von islamischem Geistesgut nach dem Abendlande," *Der Islam* 18 (1929), 236–43; F. Taeschner, "Plethon. Ein Vermittler zwischen Morgenland und Abendland," *Byzantinisch-neugriechische Jahrbücher* 8 (1929–30), 110–13; M. V. Anastos, "Pletho's calendar and liturgy," Part II: "Pletho and Islam," *DOP* 4 (1948), 270–305.

[78] Plethon, in *PG* 160, col. 980.

[79] Plethon, in *PP*, vol. III, pp. 260–1. Cf. Zakythinos, *Despotat*, vol. II, p. 354; Woodhouse, *George Gemistos Plethon*, p. 105; Baloglou, *Georgios Gemistos-Plethon*, pp. 75–9.

of production and untilled lands, Plethon thus drew attention to one of the most serious problems of the Despotate during this period, namely the depopulation of the countryside, which resulted in a shortage of agricultural workers. In his aforementioned letter to the Despot Constantine, Bessarion, also concerned with the same problem, offered suggestions aimed at increasing the rural labor force.[80] Some scattered references to the flight of the Despotate's inhabitants to Venetian territories have already been made in the preceding pages. In addition to massive deportations to Ottoman lands carried out by Turkish conquerors,[81] the loss of Greeks to neighboring regions under Venetian rule, frequently attested in the fourteenth and fifteenth centuries, must have contributed largely to the depopulation of the Despotate.[82] While some of these fugitives were directly running away from Ottoman attacks, others were trying to escape the taxes demanded by the government at Mistra, as will be recalled from the examples of sailors and peasants who took flight during and after Manuel II's reconstruction of the Hexamilion.[83] Contrary to their expectations, however, these people did not always find more favorable conditions under Venetian domination. In 1437 the *castellanus* of Modon and Coron reported to the Senate of Venice that many Greek families from the Morea who had settled inside Coron and Modon, as well as peasants inhabiting the countryside, were taking leave because of an annual payment of 27 *soldi* and some other charges imposed on them.[84] Similarly, in 1449 Greeks who had moved to Lepanto were aggrieved about the amount of taxes they were asked to pay there.[85] On the other hand, Greek soldiers who entered Venetian service were treated with extreme distrust; they were frequently discharged and received lower salaries than Latin soldiers.[86] There may have been other reasons besides economic ones for the disgruntlement of the Greeks who went over to Venetian-dominated areas, as suggested by some additional signs of tensions. In 1436, for instance, the Greek bishop of Coron was

---

[80] Bessarion, in *PP*, vol. IV, p. 34.

[81] E.g. fourteen thousand or thirty thousand people from Argos deported to Anatolia in 1397: see above, ch. 9, p. 241 and note 25.

[82] Thiriet, *Régestes*, vol. II, nos. 1592 (1415), 1697 (1418); vol. III, nos. 2446 (1437), 2791 (1449); Marino Sanuto, *Vite dei duchi di Venezia*, ed. Muratori, cols. 970, 978; Chalkok.–Darkó, vol. II, p. 119; Kritob.–Reinsch, III.5,2, p. 123; Sphrantzes–Grecu, XL.8, p. 120; etc.

[83] See above, pp. 262–3.

[84] Sathas, *Documents*, vol. III, no. 1031 (June 12, 1437), p. 437; Thiriet, *Régestes*, vol. III, no. 2446.

[85] Thiriet, *Régestes*, vol. III, no. 2791 (Jan. 23, 1449).

[86] Ibid., vol. I, no. 945 (1398); vol. II, nos. 1034 (1401), 1578 (1415), 2182 (1430); vol. III, nos. 2641 (1444), 2642 (1444), etc. In 1430 Greek soldiers in Modon were paid 8 *libri* per month, whereas Latins received 12 *libri*: Sathas, *Documents*, vol. III, no. 958 (March 2, 1430), pp. 370–1; Thiriet, *Régestes*, vol. II, no. 2182.

asked by the Senate of Venice to leave the city and to take up residence at a certain distance outside it. This was an old regulation, going back to at least 1318, which had fallen into disuse. The Venetians decided to reinstate it in 1436, fearing that the numerous gatherings of the Greek community around their religious leader at this time might lead to an insurrection inside the city of Coron.[87] Several years later, a similar regulation was put into effect by the Senate, this time banning the meetings of the Greek confraternity (*fratalea*) in Modon.[88] Such measures that restrained the religious and social freedom of the Orthodox community may have further disillusioned the inhabitants of the Despotate who had emigrated to Venetian territories of the Peloponnese, expecting their conditions to improve thereby. On a different level, moreover, religious restrictions that were applied to the Greeks living under Latin rule, and which often extended into the social domain too, might well account for the betrayal of places such as Salona (in 1393–4) and Argos (in 1463) to the Ottomans by Orthodox priests.[89]

A new stage in the context of both internal and external events began in 1449 with the arrival of Demetrios Palaiologos as Despot of the Morea to rule parts of the province jointly with his younger brother, the Despot Thomas Palaiologos. Given that from 1428 onwards the government of the Byzantine Morea had been shared by two or three despots at a time, all sons of the Emperor Manuel II, there was in itself nothing unusual about Demetrios' installation there. Yet the different orientations of the two brothers in the arena of foreign politics – Thomas generally leaning towards cooperation with the Latins and Demetrios towards accommodation with the Ottomans[90] – produced a new opportunity for the dissident elements within the local aristocracy who were, as we have seen, habitually inclined towards creating confusion and disorder by cooperating with the external enemies of the Despotate. The unruly magnates of the Morea henceforth capitalized on this major point of disagreement between Thomas and Demetrios, using it to stir up further hostilities and rivalries between the Despot brothers from which they themselves were to benefit. For instance, in 1459 a group of *archontes* who had been governing Karytaina, Bordonia,

---

[87] Iorga, *Notes*, vol. III, p. 10 (Nov. 28, 1436); Thomas and Predelli, *Diplomatarium Veneto-Levantinum*, vol. I, pp. 105–7 (1318).

[88] Fedalto, *Chiesa latina*, vol. III, no. 609 (April 23, 1444), p. 237; Iorga, *Notes*, vol. III, p. 164; Thiriet, *Régestes*, vol. III, no. 2642.

[89] Chalkok.–Darkó, vol. I, pp. 62–3; vol. II, p. 289; Χρονικὸν ἀνέκδοτον Γαλαξειδίου, ed. K. N. Sathas (Athens, 1914), pp. 84–8, 206, 211–12. On the betrayal of Salona to Bayezid I, see also Nicol, *Family of Kantakouzenos*, pp. 160–3; W. Miller, *The Latins in the Levant. A History of Frankish Greece (1204–1566)* (London, 1908; repr. 1964), pp. 346–7.

[90] See above, p. 233 and note 3 of the Introduction to Part IV.

and Kastritzi in the service of Demetrios succeeded in taking possession of these fortresses in the midst of a quarrel they instigated by persuading Thomas to rise up against his brother.[91] It will be instructive, therefore, to conduct an investigation of the partisans of Thomas and Demetrios so as to distinguish between those who genuinely agreed with the respective pro-Latin or pro-Ottoman views of each Despot and those who were merely interested in generating civil discord by switching their loyalty from one Despot to the other.

Demetrios Palaiologos, long before his arrival in the Morea as Despot, had on several occasions already made his pro-Ottoman stance quite clear. In 1423 he had fled from Constantinople to Galata, from where, according to Sphrantzes, he intended to go over to the Turks.[92] In 1442, disappointed by Emperor John VIII's preference for his other brother Constantine as successor to the imperial throne, and denied certain territories which the Emperor had promised him, Demetrios went over to Sultan Murad II and, receiving military help from the Ottomans, led an attack on Constantinople.[93] At the time of the Council of Florence, John VIII had taken Demetrios with him to Italy because he suspected that in his absence the latter might betray Constantinople, presumably to the Ottomans.[94] Demetrios Katadoukinos, in his funeral oration for John VIII (d. 1448), also alludes to Demetrios Palaiologos' cooperation with the Ottomans against the Emperor.[95]

Hence, in 1449, when Demetrios came to the Morea to share the government of the Despotate with Thomas, he had a well established record vis-à-vis the Ottomans. During the same year, Thomas initiated hostilities against Demetrios by capturing Skorta, which was one of the districts under the latter's control. Demetrios immediately responded by seeking the intervention of Murad II through his envoy and brother-in-law Matthew Asanes, about whom more will be said below. Shortly afterwards, Turahan Beg, the Ottoman governor of Thessaly who had not ceased from terrorizing the Morea since his first destruction of the Hexamilion in 1423, came to Demetrios' help with an army and forced Thomas to compensate

[91] Sphrantzes–Grecu, XXXIX.2, p. 112.

[92] Sphrantzes–Grecu, XII.2, p. 16; Schreiner, *Kleinchroniken*, vol. I, Chr. 13/8–9, vol. II, pp. 420–1; Syropoulos, *"Mémoires,"* II.11, p. 112. Demetrios was accompanied by Hilario Doria and the latter's son-in-law George Izaoul. But instead of going over to the Turks, a few days later Demetrios set out for Hungary.

[93] Sphrantzes–Grecu, XXV.1,3, p. 64; Chalkok.–Darkó, vol. II, p. 80; Schreiner, *Kleinchroniken*, vol. I, Chr.29/11, 62/10; vol. II, p. 461. Cf. Scholarios, *Œuvres*, vol. III, p. 118 (= *PP*, vol. II, p. 53); Thiriet, *Régestes*, vol. III, nos. 2583, 2584.

[94] Schreiner, *Kleinchroniken*, vol. I, Chr. 22/43. Cf. Syropoulos, *"Mémoires,"* III.30, pp. 190–1, n. 5.

[95] "Comédie de Katablattas," ed. Canivet and Oikonomidès, 85.

for the seizure of the region of Skorta by ceding the city of Kalamata to Demetrios.[96]

The association of Demetrios Palaiologos with the Asanes family, like his cooperation with the Ottomans, dates back to his days in Constantinople.[97] In 1423, following Demetrios' flight to Galata mentioned above, Emperor Manuel II and Empress Helena had sent Matthew Asanes and other *archontes* from Constantinople to accompany Demetrios to Hungary.[98] In 1441 the two families were united through the marriage of Demetrios with Matthew Asanes' sister Theodora. According to a short chronicle entry, the Empress-mother Helena and Emperor John VIII were opposed to this marriage, while both Sphrantzes and Syropoulos note that Theodora Asanina and her father Paul Asanes fled from Constantinople to Mesembria, where Demetrios was based at this time and where the marriage took place.[99] Paul Asanes, who thus became Demetrios Palaiologos' father-in-law in 1441, was a very important man in the political scene of Constantinople. In 1437 he was sent on an embassy to Murad II to inform the Sultan about John VIII's plan to attend the Council of Union with the Latin Church.[100] During the Council itself, Paul Asanes held the post of governor (κεφαλή) of the capital.[101] In the course of these years, however, somehow dissatisfied with serving the imperial government, he decided in 1441 to associate himself with the Emperor's rebellious younger brother, who one year later blockaded Constantinople with the help of Ottoman troops. According to Syropoulos, Demetrios Palaiologos' efforts against Church union, combined with Paul Asanes' desertion to him, played a crucial role in the general resistance to the Union of Florence.[102] Perhaps Paul Asanes had gradually come to agree with the Ottoman viziers who had told him during his embassy to Murad II that for Byzantium the

---

[96] Chalkok.–Darkó, vol. II, pp. 141, 144–5; Plethon, in *PP*, vol. IV, pp. 207–10. Venetian documents reveal that Demetrios also asked Venice for help, but the Senate declined his request, desiring to remain neutral in the conflict between the brothers: Iorga, *Notes*, vol. III, p. 256; Thiriet, *Régestes*, vol. III, no. 2835 (Sept. 12, 1450).

[97] On the Asanes family in general, see B. Krekić, "Contribution à l'étude des Asanès à Byzance," *TM* 5 (1973), 347–55; Trapp, "Beiträge zur Genealogie der Asanen," 163–77; I. Božilov, "La famille des Asen (1186–1460). Généalogie et prosopographie," *Bulgarian Historical Review* 9 (1981), 135–56; I. Božilov, *Asanevci (1186–1460). Genealogija i prosopografija* (Sofia, 1985). For Matthew and Paul Asanes discussed below, see *PLP*, nos. 1508 and 1518.

[98] Syropoulos, *"Mémoires,"* II.11, p. 112.

[99] Schreiner, *Kleinchroniken*, vol. I, Chr. 22/44; Sphrantzes–Grecu, XXIV.9, p. 64; Syropoulos, *"Mémoires,"* XII.17, p. 570.

[100] Syropoulos, *"Mémoires,"* III.21, p. 182. According to Sphrantzes, however, the envoy sent to the Ottoman court was Andronikos Iagros: Sphrantzes–Grecu, XXIII.8, p. 60. Cf. Dölger, *Reg.*, vol. V, no. 3475.

[101] Syropoulos, *"Mémoires,"* XI.23, p. 544.   [102] Ibid., XII.17, pp. 568–70.

friendship of the Sultan would be more advantageous than that of the Latins.[103]

In the years that followed, Paul's son Matthew Asanes was to be frequently seen at the Ottoman court as Despot Demetrios' envoy. His visit to Murad II in 1449 has been mentioned above. In 1459, when conflicts between Thomas and Demetrios reached another peak, Matthew again rushed to the Ottomans for military assistance for his brother-in-law and to negotiate the marriage of his niece Helena (i.e. the daughter of Demetrios and Theodora) with Sultan Mehmed II.[104] In the year before that he and Nikephoros Loukanes had surrendered Corinth to the Sultan.[105] When Demetrios submitted to Mehmed II in 1460, Matthew remained in the Despot's service and fought on his behalf in the Sultan's campaigns against Mistra, Ainos, and Bosnia. Following Matthew's death in 1467, Sphrantzes reports that Demetrios Palaiologos declined the income (πρόσοδος) he had been receiving from the Sultan in order to be relieved of the military service that was required of him in return for it.[106]

While Demetrios found loyal partisans among the Asanes, gathered around Thomas Palaiologos were several members of the Rhaoul/Rhalles family, some of whom particularly distinguished themselves in their opposition to the Despot's brother and his Ottoman allies. In 1459 the brothers George and Thomas Rhalles, together with the Despot Thomas, stirred up the local population in Ottoman-occupied areas of the Morea and organized an uprising against the Turks, using the Blachernai Monastery in Clarentza as their base.[107] Michael Rhalles Ises, whom Sphrantzes describes as "ὁ πρῶτος ἄρχων τοῦ ὁσπιτίου" of Thomas Palaiologos in the year 1436, lost his life during an unsuccessful Veneto-Greek attack on Patras in

---

[103] Ibid., III.21, p. 182. Cf. Sphrantzes–Grecu, XXIII.8, p. 60.

[104] Chalkok.–Darkó, vol. II, pp. 224–6; Sphrantzes–Grecu, XXXIX.1, pp. 110–12; Kritob.–Reinsch, III.19, p. 142. Cf. Schreiner, *Kleinchroniken*, vol. I, Chr. 38/6.

[105] Sphrantzes–Grecu, XXXVIII.2, p. 110; Kritob.–Reinsch, III.7, pp. 126–7; Chalkok.–Darkó, vol. II, pp. 209–10.

[106] Sphrantzes–Grecu, XLIV.2, p. 134. Cf. A. E. Vacalopoulos, "The flight of the inhabitants of Greece to the Aegean islands, Crete, and Mane, during the Turkish invasions (fourteenth and fifteenth centuries)," in *Charanis Studies*, ed. A. E. Laiou-Thomadakis (New Brunswick, NJ, 1980), p. 280. On Demetrios' income, see Stavrides, *Sultan of Vezirs*, pp. 131–2; İnalcık, "Ottoman state," p. 211. For a Michael Asanes in the service of Despot Demetrios, see *PLP*, no. 91375.

[107] Schreiner, *Kleinchroniken*, vol. I, Chr. 34/24; vol. II, pp. 493–4. For a Thomas Rhaoul who was on the side of Thomas Palaiologos during a conflict that the latter had with the Despot Constantine over the fortress of Chalandritza in 1429, see Sphrantzes–Grecu, XIX.9, p. 42. For a George Rhaoul, *archon*, who left the Despot Thomas and moved to Modon sometime before December 1458, see Sphrantzes–Grecu, XXXIX.10, p. 114. Cf. Fassoulakis, *Family of Raoul-Ral(l)es*, nos. 57, 59, pp. 69–72; *PLP*, nos. 24061, 24115, 24119.

1466 that was aimed at recovering the city from the hands of the Ottomans. It appears that after the Despot Thomas' flight from the Morea in 1460, Michael stayed behind and joined forces with the Venetians against the Ottomans.[108] Following Mehmed II's conquest of the peninsula, various members of the Rhalles family remained in the Morea and, like Michael Rhalles Ises, associated themselves with the Venetians. The names of some of these aristocrats have been preserved in Venetian documents dating from the 1460s, which reconfirm the possessions and privileges they were previously granted by the Despot(s) of the Morea.[109]

However, families such as the Asanes and Rhalles who maintained their loyalty respectively to Demetrios and Thomas Palaiologos, while consistently sharing the political attitudes represented by each Despot towards the Ottomans and the Latins, were exceptions at this time in the Morea. The majority of the local magnates behaved quite differently according to the fifteenth-century Byzantine chroniclers. Kritoboulos, for instance, describes the role they played in the conflict that erupted between the Despots in 1459 as follows:

> That same winter, the Despots of the Peloponnesus quarreled, to their own damage, and made war with each other for the following reason: the grandees who were under them, men who had domains and large revenues and were over cities and fortresses, were not content with these but, grasping in thought and malicious in act, were always aspiring for more. They sought revolution and were rebellious against each other, made war, and filled all those parts with disorder and uproar. They even drew the Despots into the confusion, by attacking and disturbing each other, for first they would come secretly and accuse the opposite party, as if they were revealing some unspeakable mystery, and so by lies and slanders against each other they tried to stir them up against one another and to arm them. Then later, openly and unashamed, they deserted the one side and went over to the other, enticing with them their towns and fortresses.[110]

Among these shifty aristocrats of the Morea, an *archon* called Nikephoros Loukanes takes up the first place. It will be recalled that in August 1458 this man, together with Matthew Asanes, had surrendered Corinth to

[108] Sphrantzes–Grecu, XXII.8, XLIII.4–9, pp. 54, 132–4; Schreiner, *Kleinchroniken*, vol. I, Chr. 34/32; Sathas, *Documents*, vol. I, nos. 161 (March 17, 1464) and 175 (Sept. 7, 1466), pp. 241, 258–9; Spandugnino, *De la origine*, in Sathas, *Documents*, vol. IX, p. 161. Cf. Fassoulakis, *Family of Raoul-Ral(l)es*, no. 64, pp. 77–9; *PLP*, no. 24136.

[109] Sathas, *Documents*, vol. V, pp. 30 (Sept. 9, 1465 – Michael Rhallis Drimys, "*gubernator in Brachio Mayne*"), 35–6 (Dec. 29, 1468 – Matthew Rallis Melikis). For other members of the Morean branch of the family, see Fassoulakis, *Family of Raoul-Ral(l)es*.

[110] Kritob.–Reinsch, III.19, p. 141; trans. by C. T. Riggs, *History of Mehmed the Conqueror, by Kritovoulos* (Princeton, 1954), pp. 149–50.

Mehmed II.[111] According to Sphrantzes, in January 1459 Loukanes, who was considered to be one of Demetrios Palaiologos' most outstanding and trusted men, persuaded Thomas to rise up against his brother and the Sultan. Sphrantzes adds that Loukanes was supported by Albanians and the people of the Morea.[112] Chalkokondyles provides further evidence for the complicated and unpredictable nature of Loukanes' political career, by writing about his involvement in the Albanian uprising of 1453; his cooperation with John Asen Zaccaria against the Despot Thomas, who arrested and imprisoned both of them; and his conflicts with Matthew Asanes before the surrender of Corinth.[113]

Other local magnates who played a role in the rivalries of the Despots include Palaiologos Sgouromalles, the brother of Nikephoros Loukanes' wife, who surrendered Karytaina to Mehmed II in 1460; a certain Proinokokokas, who was one of the leading men in Kastritzi; the *protostrator* Nicholas Sebastopoulos, who was Demetrios Palaiologos' *mesazon* and brother-in-law; a certain Kydonides, also known as Tzamplakon, who was the uncle of Despot Thomas' wife; George Palaiologos, who was Thomas' *mesazon* and cousin; and Manuel Bochales, the son-in-law of George Palaiologos.[114] A closer look at the political career and family ties of George Palaiologos will confirm what has been said about the unreliable and fluctuating nature of the attachments these aristocrats had. George started out as a partisan of the Despot Thomas in Leontarion. Although under Thomas he held the high post of *mesazon*, at an unknown date he left Leontarion with his son-in-law Manuel Bochales and entered the service of Demetrios in Mistra.[115] George was then captured by Thomas' men during a fight and taken back to his former lord who had him confined; but he managed to escape and join the Despot Demetrios. In 1459 Demetrios seized the environs of Leontarion and Pidema from his brother through the agency of George and his son-in-law. A year later, when Mehmed II conquered Leontarion and Gardiki, all the inhabitants of these places were put to death except for George Palaiologos, Manuel Bochales, and the latter's family. They owed their lives to the kinship ties

---

[111] See note 105 above. For Loukanes, cf. *PLP*, no. 15089.

[112] Sphrantzes–Grecu, XXXVIII.2, XXXIX.1, pp. 110, 112.

[113] Chalkok.–Darkó, vol. II, pp. 170–6, 203, 209–11, 214. Cf. Zakythinos, *Despotat*, vol. I, p. 249, for an interpretation of the Albanian revolt of 1453 as part of the historical conflict between the landowning aristocracy and the central government of the Morea.

[114] Sphrantzes–Grecu, XXXIX.2–7, XL.5,11, pp. 112–14, 118, 120. On these individuals, see *PLP*, nos. 24996, 23815, 25084, 27758, 21447, 19805.

[115] In 1456 George Palaiologos was still in the service of Thomas, who received a safe-conduct for him from the Venetian Senate: Thiriet, *Régestes*, vol. III, no. 3010 (Jan. 17, 1456).

of George Palaiologos with the Sultan's grand vizier Mahmud Paşa, who was a former Christian of Byzantine aristocratic descent.[116] If, however, one is prepared to view George's entry into the service of Demetrios and his connections with the Ottoman court as signs of a pro-Turkish orientation on his part, the inaccuracy of such a conclusion is revealed through the information that after his desertion to the Despot Demetrios, George spent a lot of time in Venetian Nauplia where his wife and children had taken refuge.[117] His son-in-law Bochales, on the other hand, ended up killing Mahmud Paşa's men assigned to escort him and his family out of Gardiki and fled to the Venetian-held island of Corfu.[118] Bochales later returned to the Morea and lost his life fighting against the Ottomans on the side of the Venetians.[119]

The same picture emerges when we examine a document which lists the names of a group of *archontes* from the Morea who were invited by Mehmed II to submit to Ottoman sovereignty at the end of 1454.[120] The individuals or families to whom the Sultan promised the security of their lives and property, and even greater prosperity, in return for their submission to him are the following: Sph(r)antzes, Manuel Rhaoul, Sophianos, Demetrios Laskaris, the families of Diplobatatzes, Philanthropenos, Kabakes, (Pe)pagomenos, Phrankopoulos, Sgouromalles, Mauropapas, and the Albanian chief Petro-Bua. It will be noticed that this list does not include names such as Mamonas or Asanes, whose connections with the Ottomans have been demonstrated in the present chapter and in the preceding one. The only family with a former record of association with Turks is that of Mauropapas, if we are to recall that in 1296 "Corcondille" had captured the fortress of Hagios Georgios from the Latins with the assistance of one Leo Mauropapas, who commanded a band of one hundred Turkish mercenaries.[121] By contrast, several of the *archontes* listed in the document of 1454 bear the names of families which are known to have had ties with Italians or a prior record of resistance to the Ottomans, such as Rhaoul, Sophianos, and Kabakes. It appears that during the year and a half that elapsed following the fall of Constantinople, these Moreotes, convinced of the permanence of Ottoman power and concerned as always with their

[116] Sphrantzes–Grecu, XXXIX.6–7, XL.6–8, pp. 112–14, 118–20. According to Sphrantzes, Mahmud Paşa's mother and George Palaiologos were first cousins, and the latter's daughter (i.e. Bochales' wife) was hence second cousin to the grand vizier. On Mahmud Paşa's origins and family, see Stavrides, *Sultan of Vezirs*, pp. 73–106.

[117] Sphrantzes–Grecu, XL.8, p. 120.   [118] Ibid., XL.7, p. 120.

[119] Stavrides, *Sultan of Vezirs*, p. 79 n. 27.   [120] MM, vol. III, p. 290 (Dec. 26, 1454).

[121] See above, p. 266 and note 33. The only two members of this Moreote family listed in *PLP* are nos. 17473 (Theodore Mauropapas) and 17474 (Nicholas Mauropapas).

material interests, adapted their political outlook to the contemporary situation, recognizing that an affiliation with Sultan Mehmed II would serve their interests best. After all, people like Sophianos may well have been familiar with the benefits their ancestors had reaped through an accommodation with the Frankish conquerors of the Peloponnese in the thirteenth century.

In his chapter on the Latins of Greece in *The Cambridge Medieval History*, Setton wrote that in the Morea,

> Greeks and Latins had grown accustomed to each other during the many years that followed the [Latin] conquest . . . [T]he lapse of time and the advent of the Turk tended to bring the Greeks and Latins more closely together . . . Since there was less theological rancour in continental Greece and the Morea than in Constantinople, the turban was not often preferred to the Latin tiara.[122]

It has been seen, however, that other factors besides "theological rancour" determined the choice people made between the "turban" and the "tiara." The sociopolitical and socioeconomic structure of the Despotate of the Morea, which gave occasion to persistent rivalries between the local aristocracy and the central government, played a prominent role in the political choices people made with respect to foreign powers. It has perhaps been difficult to discover many Moreote families with consistent and steady political orientations, yet when it came to guarding their material interests they all proved their consistency and steadfastness.

---

[122] Setton, "Latins in Greece," pp. 48–9.

Conclusion

Having examined and analyzed the effects of Ottoman pressures between about 1370 and 1460 in three major areas of the Byzantine Empire in terms of the political attitudes that emerged among various groups or individuals, we can detect certain patterns that recur in Thessalonike and Constantinople, and to some degree in the Morea as well. First, it has been seen that variations in the political orientation of different groups within the empire's population towards foreign powers were closely intertwined with the social tensions that existed in Byzantium during this period, which resulted in marked differences between the attitudes of people belonging to the upper and the lower segments of Byzantine society. In the two largest urban centers of the empire represented by Constantinople and Thessalonike, generally speaking, an opinion in favor of cooperation with western Christian powers against the Ottomans prevailed among the aristocracy. Included within the ranks of this urban aristocracy were the ruling and intellectual elite of the cities named above, as well as rich merchants and businessmen who had strong economic ties with Italian maritime republics. In the rural areas, too, represented by the countryside of Thessalonike and the Morea, the landowning aristocrats on the whole seem to have shared the western political orientation of their urban counterparts. We have seen, however, that some landowners, responding to the conciliatory policy the Ottomans pursued with regard to the Christians who submitted to their authority, adopted an accommodationist attitude towards the enemy in return for which they won the right to retain their estates, acquired new ones, or were granted other comparable privileges.

The lower-class citizens of Thessalonike and Constantinople, on the other hand, exhibited a generally unfavorable attitude towards the Latins, whether they regarded the Latins as specific powers with a political or economic presence, as in the case of the Venetians and the Genoese, or judged them from a religious and ideological standpoint as Catholics. During times of intense Ottoman pressure, moreover, when faced with what seemed to be an inevitable choice between Latin or Ottoman domination, the common people often showed a preference for the latter and particularly in Thessalonike led several demonstrations in favor of peaceful surrender to the Ottomans as a means of relief from the dangers and hardships they were undergoing. Unfortunately, our information concerning the political attitudes of the common people in the Morea is rather limited and does not conform to much of a pattern. As parallels to the tendencies noted above in reference to the Byzantine capital and Thessalonike, we know of one case in which the inhabitants of Mistra all together stood in opposition to the takeover of their city by the Hospitallers of St. John in 1400, and one case in which the inhabitants of Sikyon surrendered to Murad II following the destruction of the Hexamilion by the Sultan's forces in 1446. But we also know that on the very same occasion the inhabitants of Patras fled to Venetian-dominated areas, and that in 1460 those of Monemvasia sought and acquired the protection of the papacy shortly after their ruler, the Despot Demetrios Palaiologos, surrendered on terms to Mehmed II.[1] The Monemvasiots, it should be noted, had previously made an unsuccessful attempt to place themselves under Venetian sovereignty when Theodore I ceded their town to Bayezid I in 1394.[2] Furthermore, several examples of the flight of Greek peasants from the Despotate of the Morea to the neighboring Venetian territories of the peninsula have been documented in the last two chapters, whereas analogous references to their flight to the Ottomans have not been encountered.

Before attempting to provide an explanation for the divergences and inconsistencies that have emerged in the context of the Morea, we must first complete this outline of the recurring attitudes that can be traced in the three areas under examination. This brings us to the third element within Byzantine society, namely the members of the empire's ecclesiastical and monastic establishments, whose political tendencies as a group show some signs of regularity across the regions. We have seen that religious considerations pushed the majority of the members of this group away from a cooperation with westerners, who often demanded the union of the Byzantine Church with the Latin Church in return for their assistance

[1] On Monemvasia, see B. Krekić, "Monemvasie sous la protection papale," *ZRVI* 6 (1960), 129–35; Kalligas, *Byzantine Monemvasia*, pp. 191–3. For Mistra, Sikyon, and Patras, see above, ch. 9, p. 258 and note 95; ch. 10, p. 273 and note 67.
[2] See above, ch. 9, note 90.

against the Ottomans. A number of people from within the religious circles were in turn driven closer to the Ottomans, whose tolerant religious policy and conciliatory attitude with regard to conquered Christian peoples proved to be very effective in this respect. Nonetheless, there always was a segment within the religious hierarchy that remained strongly attached to an anti-Latin/anti-Ottoman position.

Turning now to the differences noted in connection with the Morea, we can add another major point of departure exhibited by the inhabitants of the province, specifically by its landowning aristocracy, that contrasts with the motives and behavior of the inhabitants of Constantinople and Thessalonike. As pointed out earlier, a desire for the establishment of peace with the Ottomans was what everyone in the last two places, regardless of their rank or social status, wanted even though they differed over the means by which they wished to implement this peace, some siding with the Latins, some with the Ottomans, and others maintaining an anti-Latin/anti-Ottoman stance. In the Morea, on the other hand, there was no great desire for the establishment of peace. To the contrary, the unruly landowners of the province consistently favored the disruption of peace in their quest for independence from central authority, and in this process they welcomed the interference sometimes of the Navarrese mercenaries from the neighboring principality of Achaia and sometimes of Ottoman or other Turkish forces.

These differences stem in large part from the distinct political history of the Despotate of the Morea, dictated particularly by the nature of the Ottoman presence there. For nearly three-quarters of a century before the final conquest of the province by Mehmed II in 1460, Ottoman attacks against the Morea were generally carried out without the aim of conquest or settlement, and the Despotate enjoyed moreover long stretches of peaceful relations with the Ottomans both prior to the last decade of the fourteenth century and during 1402–23. Although the region was by no means free from military and political instability, the Ottomans were for the most part not the ones who were responsible for it, as they were in Thessalonike or in Constantinople. Therefore, in the absence of an imminent threat of conquest and settlement by Ottoman forces, the landowners of the Morea appear to have seen no great risk involved in deterring the establishment of peace for their own ends through the methods they employed. The same historical circumstances also help to explain the inconsistent and often contradictory attitudes of people from the lower ranks of Moreote society with regard to the Ottomans and the Latins. Whereas in Thessalonike and Constantinople many poorer people adopted, for the sake of peace, a position in favor of surrender to the Ottomans whose intention was to conquer these cities together with the lands surrounding them, in the Morea such an option did not really exist when Ottoman armies for a long time went there only for plundering raids, and when unstable and insecure conditions were generated mostly by native landowners or by inhabitants of the small Latin principalities in the vicinity. As to the discontented Greek peasants who fled to the Venetian territories of the peninsula, their choice seems to have been determined primarily by geographical factors, since the Venetians were settled just outside the borders of the Despotate, quite unlike the countryside of Thessalonike which in the late fourteenth and early fifteenth centuries had become almost like an island surrounded by an Ottoman sea. Finally, in discussing the case of the Morea it must be borne in mind that we are dealing with an entire province, rather than a single city with its outlying districts, which makes it all the more likely for variations to exist.

Another point that must be stressed in connection with these concluding remarks and that applies to all three areas of the Byzantine Empire examined in this study is that the question of the political attitudes which different people or groups in Byzantium adopted should not be approached as if this were an either/or issue for them. First, contrary to the impression given by most contemporary Byzantine and Latin authors, and oftentimes accepted at face value by modern historians, the pro-Ottoman disposition that began to emerge among certain sectors of the Byzantine population after the middle of the fourteenth century was not necessarily or solely a result of anti-Latin feelings.[3] We have seen that many other factors besides an antagonism they nurtured for the Latins played a role in driving certain individuals or groups towards an accommodation with the Ottomans. These factors included in the first place the religious policy of the Ottomans and the methods of conquest they employed; expectations of prosperity, high posts, and other opportunities or material benefits in the service of

---

[3] Such a schematic presentation is provided, for instance, by Doukas in the passage quoted in note 1 of ch. 8. Among western authors Bertrandon de la Broquière, who visited Constantinople in 1432, wrote the following words about the city's native inhabitants: "... ilz cuiderent que je fusse Turc et me firent de l'onneur beaucoup ... car en cestuy temps, ilz heoient fort les Crestiens ..." (*Voyage d'Outremer de B. de la Broquière*, pp. 148–9). Similarly, Jean Gerson, the chancellor of the University of Paris, stated to King Charles VI of France in 1409 that the Greeks preferred the Turks to the Latins, attributing the pro-Turkish attitude of the Byzantines to their dislike of the Latins: "... des Grecs qui sur tous autres haissent et mesprisent tous les Latins et les jugent hérétiques et scismatiques et pis encores et se tourneront auant aux Turcs que aux Latins" (A. Galitzin, *Sermon inédit de Jean Gerson sur le retour des Grecs à l'unité* (Paris, 1859), p. 29). In recent years M. Balivet has also questioned whether the pro-Ottoman attitude encountered among the Byzantines was necessarily a manifestation of their anti-Latinism: see his "Personnnage du 'turcophile'," 111–29.

Ottoman sultans; a desire for the re-establishment of internal peace in Byzantium and the conviction that this could be achieved only through the establishment of external peace with the Ottomans. Secondly, we have encountered several examples of Byzantine families or individuals who simultaneously associated with the Ottomans and the Latins, which illustrates another dimension of the caution against an either/or approach. To these must be added the existence of overlaps within the attitudes of people from varying social backgrounds, and the pieces of evidence concerning members of the same family who embraced different views at a given time or changed their position over time through successive generations. Argued differently, the political attitudes that have been presented in this study were by no means constant phenomena that conformed to one rigid pattern, and I hope to have demonstrated that the complex process of their formation can only be interpreted within their proper contextual and historical framework.

Appendices

Archontes of Thessalonike
(fourteenth–fifteenth centuries)

Unless marked with *, the persons listed below are specifically designated as archon *in the documents.*

Date	Name	Other title or occupation	Document[i]	PLP no.
1314–24	Manuel Kampanaropoulos	–	*Ivir.*, vol. III, 73, 78, 81	10825
1314–26	Theodore Chalazas	*myrepsos, depotatos*	*Ivir.*, vol. III, 73, 78, 81, 84	30363
c. 1320	Constantine Kokalas*	fiscal official, *oikeios*	*Ivir.*, vol. III, 76	–
c. 1320	Michael Stavrakios*	*oikeios*	*Ivir*, vol. III, 76	26710
1320	Theodore Brachnos	*exarchos ton myrepson*	*Ivir.*, vol. III, 78	3205
1327	Demetrios Sgouros	*megalyperochos*	*Zogr.*, 25	25051
1327	George Allelouias	*megalyperochos*	*Zogr.*, 25	676
1327	Athanasios Kabakes	*megalyperochos, chrysepilektes*	*Zogr.*, 25, 28	10015
1333–6	Alexios Hyaleas*	*megas adnoumiastes, eparchos, oikeios, doulos*	*Chilan.*(P), 123; *Reg. Patr.*, vol. II, III	29470
1336	George Kokalas*	*megas adnoumiastes, oikeios*	*Reg. Patr.*, vol. II, III	92485
1341	Manuel Phaxenos (brother-in-law of Agape Angelina Sphratzaina Palaiologina)	–	*Lavra*, vol. III, 156, app. XII	29609
1341	Theodore Doukas Spartenos (brother of Agape Angelina Sphratzaina Palaiologina)	*oikeios*	*Lavra*, vol. III, app. XII	26498

(cont.)

Date	Name	Other title or occupation	Document[i]	PLP no.
1348–61	George Kyprianos	–	*Xénophon*, 30; *Dochei.*, 36, 38	92473
1356–66	Manuel Ko(u)llourakes	*oikeios, doulos*	*Dochei.*, 36, 38; *Maked.* 5 (1963): p. 137	92439
1361–6	Symeon Choniates	–	*Dochei.*, 36, 38	31244
1366	Demetrios Phakrases	*megas primikerios, doulos*	*Dochei.*, 38	29576
1366	Demetrios Glabas [Komes?]	*megas droungarios, doulos*	*Dochei.*, 38	91685
1366	Nicholas Prebezianos	–	*Dochei.*, 38	23700
1366	Petros Prebezianos	–	*Dochei.*, 38	23703
1366–78	Manuel Tarchaneiotes	*oikeios, doulos*	*Dochei.*, 38; *Zogr.*, 44; *Lavra*, vol. III, 149	27499 & 27501
1373	Laskaris Kephalas*	*doulos*	*Dochei.*, 41	11677
1373–6	Laskaris Metochites*	*megas chartoularios, doulos, apographeus*	*Dochei.*, 41, 42; *Chilan.*(P), 154; *Vatop.*, vol. II, 147, 148	17983
1373–81	George Doukas Tzykandyles*	judge, *doulos*	*Dochei.*, 41, 48	28126
1379	John Pezos	–	*Gr. Pal.* 6 (1922): p. 283	22245
1379–84	Demetrios Phoberes	*apographeus*	*Gr. Pal.* 6 (1922): p. 283; *Dochei.*, 49	29998
1379–84	John Maroules	*apographeus*	*Gr. Pal.* 6 (1922): p. 283; *Dochei.*, 49	17153
c. 1381	. . . . tos Palaiologos*	*doulos*	*Dochei.*, 48	21410
c. 1381	Andronikos Doukas Tzykandyles*	*doulos*	*Dochei.*, 48	28125
c. 1381	Demetrios Talapas*	*kastrophylax, doulos*	*Dochei.*, 48	27416
1381	Manuel Deblitzenos	*doulos, oikeios*	*Dochei.*, 47, 48, 49	91757
1381	Manuel Kasandrenos	–	*Dochei.*, 47	11316
1381	George Angelos	–	*Dochei.*, 47	91034
1404	Constantine Ibankos*	judge, *doulos*	*Dochei.*, 51	7973
1404–19	Bartholomaios Komes (son-in-law of Manuel Deblitzenos)	–	*Dochei.*, 51, 57, 58	92399

Date	Name	Other title or occupation	Document[i]	PLP no.
1406–9	Paul Gazes	*apographeus, doulos*	*Gr. Pal.* 3 (1919): p. 337; *Xéropot.*, 29; *Dochei.*, 53; *Diony.*, 11; *Lavra*, vol. III, 161	3452
1406–9	Michael Ka. . . . . tes	*apographeus*	*Gr. Pal.* 3 (1919): p. 337; *Xéropot.*, 29	–
1407–9	George Prinkips	*apographeus, doulos*	*Xéropot.*, 29; *Dochei.*, 53; *Diony.*, 11; *Lavra*, vol. III, 161	23746
1409(?)	John Aprenos*	–	*Esphigm.*, 31	1209
1414	John Kantakouzenos*	–	*Dochei.*, 54	92318
1414	Theodore Doukas Kyprianos*	–	*Dochei.*, 54	92474
1415	John Douk(a)s Melachrinos*	*doulos*	*Diony.*, 14	17665
1415–21	Stephanos Doukas Rhadenos	*apographeus, kephale* of Kassandreia, *doulos*	*Gr. Pal.* 3 (1919): pp. 335–6; *Gr. Pal.* 6 (1922): pp. 86–7; *Dochei.*, 56; *St.-Pantél.*, 18; *Lavra*, vol. III, 165; *Diony.*, 20; *Athena* 26 (1914): p. 274	23999
1415–21	John Rhadenos	*apographeus, doulos*	*Gr. Pal.* 3 (1919): p. 336; *Dochei.*, 56; *Lavra*, vol. III, 165; *Diony.*, 20	23991
1418–21	Constantine Palaiologos Oinaiotes	*apographeus, doulos*	*Gr. Pal.* 6 (1922): pp. 86–7; *Dochei.*, 56; *Lavra*, vol. III, 165; *Diony.*, 20	21028

(*cont.*)

Appendix I

Date	Name	Other title or occupation	Document[i]	PLP no.
1421	Demetrios Hidromenos	*apographeus, doulos*	*Diony.*, 20; *Gr. Pal.* 6 (1922): pp. 86–7	8077
1421	John Angelos Philanthropenos	*archon tes synkletou, oikeios*	*Ivir.*, vol. IV, 97	29767
1421	Thomas Chrysoloras	*archon tes synkletou, oikeios*	*Ivir.*, vol. IV, 97	31158
1421	Demetrios Palaiologos Prinkips	*archon tes synkletou, oikeios*	*Ivir.*, vol. IV, 97	23747
1421	Michael Palaiologos Krybitziotes	*archon tes synkletou, oikeios*	*Ivir.*, vol. IV, 97	13840
1421	Andronikos Metochites	*archon tes synkletou, oikeios*	*Ivir.*, vol. IV, 97	17978
1421	Michael Angelos Trypommates	*archon tes synkletou, oikeios*	*Ivir.*, vol. IV, 97	29382
1421	Theodore Diagoupes	*archon tes synkletou, oikeios*	*Ivir.*, vol. IV, 97	7822

[i] Except when indicated otherwise, the references are to document numbers. Below is a list of the abbreviations used:

Chilan.(P)	*Actes de Chilandar*, vol. I: *Actes grecs*, ed. L. Petit, in *VV* 17 (1911)
Diony.	*Actes de Dionysiou*, ed. N. Oikonomidès (Paris, 1968)
Dochei.	*Actes de Docheiariou*, ed. N. Oikonomidès (Paris, 1984)
Esphigm.	*Actes d'Esphigménou*, ed. J. Lefort (Paris, 1973)
Gr. Pal.	Γρηγόριος ὁ Παλαμᾶς
Ivir., vols. III–IV	*Actes d'Iviron*, vols. III–IV, ed. J. Lefort, N. Oikonomidès, D. Papachryssanthou, and V. Kravari, with the collaboration of H. Métrévéli (Paris, 1994–5)
Lavra, vol. III	*Actes de Lavra*, vol. III, ed. P. Lemerle, A. Guillou, N. Svoronos, and D. Papachryssanthou (Paris, 1979)
Maked.	Μακεδονικά
Reg. Patr., vol. II	*Das Register des Patriarchats von Konstantinopel*, vol. II, ed. H. Hunger, O. Kresten, E. Kislinger, and C. Cupane (Vienna, 1995)
St.-Pantél.	*Actes de Saint-Pantéléèmôn*, ed. P. Lemerle, G. Dagron, and S. Ćirković (Paris, 1982)
Vatop., vol. II	*Actes de Vatopédi*, vol. II, ed. J. Lefort, V. Kravari, Ch. Giros, and K. Smyrlis (Paris, 2006)
Xénophon	*Actes de Xénophon*, ed. D. Papachryssanthou (Paris, 1986)
Xéropot.	*Actes de Xéropotamou*, ed. J. Bompaire (Paris, 1964)
Zogr.	*Actes de Zographou*, ed. W. Regel, E. Kurtz, and B. Korablev, in *VV* 13 (1907)

"Nobles" and "small nobles" of Thessalonike (1425)

(From Venetian document of July 7, 1425 reproduced in Mertzios, Μνημεῖα, following p. 48: pl. 2$^{\alpha}$–3$^{\alpha}$)

Name	Monthly salary (in *aspra*)
(1) Thomas Alousianos	300
(2) George Hyaleas (*Jalca*)	300
(3) John Rhadenos	300
(4) Thomas Chrysoloras (*Grusulora/Chrussulora*)	300
(5) Michael *Democrati* (Dermokaites?)	300
(6) Michael *Caromaffi*	200
(7) Theodore *Calatola*	150
(8) John *Falca* (= Jalca?, i.e. Hyaleas)	100
(9) Manuel Hyaleas (*Jalca*)	40
(10) Demetrios *Vuironi* (Vryonis?)	80
(11) John Rhamatas	80
(12) George *Aramando* (Amarantos?)	50
(13) Andronikos Amarantos	raised from 80 to 120
(14) John Aliates	same
(15) Doukas *Milca* (= Jalca?, i.e. Hyaleas)	same
(16) Michael Hyaleas (*Jalca*)	same
(17) George *Gassi* (Gazes?)	same
(18) Manuel Melitas	same
(19) *Inavissil Inamissi* (?), brother-in-law of Aliates	same
(20) Simon, son of *chier* Simon	raised from 70 to 100
(21) Manuel *Calamca*	same
(22) George Laskaris *Defala*	same
(23) Demetrios Melachrinos (*Melachino*)	same
(24) Argyropoulos *Mamoli* (Mamales?)	same
(25) Paschales Laskaris	same
(26) Michael *Plomino*	same
(27) Manuel *Mamoli* (Mamales?)	same
(28) Demetrios *Caroleo*	same
(29) Demetrios Laskaris	same

(*cont.*)

Name	Monthly salary (in *aspra*)
(30) John Melachrinos, son of George Argyropoulos	same
(31) Constantine Argyropoulos	same
(32) Doukas Melachrinos	same
(33) George Melachrinos	same
(34) Michael Amarantos	raised by 20 *aspra*
(35) George Makrenos	same
(36) Alexios Melachrinos	same
(37) George Tzamantouras (*Camandora*)	same
(38) Digenes *Senex* (Presbytes?)	same
(39) Loukas *Arimati*	same
(40) Rhalle *Enbiristi*	same
(41) Pachy Masgidas	same
(42) Michael Tarchaneiotes	same
(43) *Braichus* Masgidas	same
(44) Andronikos Digenes	same
(45) Doukas Kabasilas (*Cavassilla*)	same
(46) Alexios Digenes	same
(47) Angelos Theodoros	same
(48) John Grammatikos	same
(49) Basos *Covazi* (?)	same
(50) John Digenes	same
(51) Angelos *Miropuno* (?)	same
(52) Andronikos Machetares	same
(53) Nicholas Chrysaphes (*Crussaffi*)	same
(54) Demetrios Platyskalites (*Placichaliti*)	same
(55) Doukas *Cotiassi*	same
(56) John *Pesso* (Pezos?)	same
(57) John Basilikos (*Vassilico*)	same
(58) Demetrios Argyropoulos	same
(59) George Rhadenos	raised by 40 *aspra*

Constantinopolitan merchants in Badoer's account book (1436–1440)

Name	Occupation, title, etc.	Reference in Badoer (pp.)
Agallianos	–	115, 160, 251
Andreas Argyros (*Argiro/Algiro*) (= Andreas *Ligiro?*)	*botegier de marzarie*	27, 32, 36, 40, 41, 72, 114, 137, 178, 197, 201, 219, 234, 235, 236, 237, 249, 251, 258, 259, 262, 263, 344, 374, 634
Sebasteianos Argyros (= Sebasteianos *Ligiro?*)	*chir, spizier*	197, 219, 259, 260, 261, 344
Stephanos Argyros (= Stephanos *Ligiro?*)	*chir, spizier*	19, 60, 61, 68, 96, 115, 130, 251, 280
Asanes (*Asani*)	*miser, chapetanio*	499
Basilikos (uncle of Andronikos Synadenos)	–	177
Basilikos	*barcaruol*	452
Andronikos Basilikos	*chir*	21, 29, 40, 41, 114, 178
Kaloioannes Basilikos	–	404, 412, 413, 484, 511, 521, 540, 541, 562, 570, 648, 714, 725, 744
Batatzes (father-in-law of Demetrios Palaiologos)	–	265, 282
Constantine Batatzes	*chir*	27, 33, 61, 68, 69
Doukas (*Ducha*)	*sanser*	168, 394
Demetrios Doukas	*botegier*	500, 555
Doukas Rhadenos	*botegier*	6, 97, 257, 323, 372, 373, 500, 646
Gabalas	partner of A. Argyros	114, 235, 417
Antonios Gabalas	*sanser*	105
George Gabalas	*chir, botegier*	259, 301, 350, 402, 403
Michael Gabras	*botegier*	249, 368, 422, 464, 523

(*cont.*)

Name	Occupation, title, etc.	Reference in Badoer (pp.)
Demetrios *Glivani/ Grivani/Grimani*	*chir, drapier*, partner of J. Tzouknidas and (T.) Makrymalles	177, 178, 207, 219, 221, 223, 225, 227, 234, 235, 264, 313, 344, 356, 357, 374, 417, 716, 717, 744, 749, 784, 792
Manuel Goudeles (*Chutela*)	*drapier*	120, 121, 352, 353, 498
Manuel Iagaris	–	783, 784, 785
Palaiologos Iagaris	–	51
Andronikos *Chaloti* (Kalothetos?)	*chir*	632, 641, 652, 658, 659
Kantakouzenos (*Chatachuxino*)	–	74, 129
Michael *Chatafioti* (Kataphygiotes?)	*sartor, drapier, botegier*, partner of J. *Vrachimi*, T. Tzourakes and A. Kinnamos	139, 155, 219, 223, 225, 227, 344, 350, 356, 357, 374, 444, 480, 481, 487, 498, 499, 500, 580, 622, 623, 634, 640, 641, 656, 686, 744
Andreas Kinnamos (*Chinamo*)	*botegier, sartor*, partner of M. *Chatafioti*	429, 487, 509, 580, 622, 623, 634, 640, 641, 656, 744
Constantine *Chondupi*	*chir*	501, 522
Manuel *Chondupi*	*drapier*	135, 295, 344, 350, 374, 405, 714, 730, 731
Kritopoulos	–	93, 152, 179, 204, 444
Andronikos Kritopoulos	–	240
Constantine Kritopoulos (brother of Andronikos Kritopoulos)	*chir, banchier*, owner of a *draparia*	93, 152, 162, 179, 181, 197, 204, 219, 229, 230, 231, 239, 240, 241, 259, 260, 261, 265, 271, 282, 330, 336, 337, 340, 344, 345, 350, 358, 362, 363, 365, 367, 368, 370, 375, 382, 402, 411, 412, 414, 442, 444, 462, 474, 480, 481, 496, 516, 522, 584, 585, 640, 784, 796, 843
George Laskaris	*chir, drapier*, partner of A. Synadenos	176, 177, 178, 180, 219, 227, 236, 239, 242, 243, 464, 500, 504, 523, 580, 618
Laskaris Theologos, son-in-law of *Chomusi* (Koumouses?)	–	360, 634, 646, 647, 745

(*cont.*)

Name	Occupation, title, etc.	Reference in Badoer (pp.)
Andreas *Ligiro* (Argyros?)	*botegier*	177, 229, 358, 362, 402, 404, 408, 444, 500, 558, 570, 571, 646, 714, 715, 716, 739, 744, 784
Sebasteianos *Ligiro* (Argyros?)	*chir*	261, 340, 362, 368, 376, 381, 404, 480, 519, 580, 588
Stephanos *Ligiro* (Argyros?)	–	252
Constantine Makropoulos (*Mancropulo*)	*drapier*, partner of J. and C. Tzouknidas	29, 58, 84, 85, 96, 114, 120, 121, 129, 133, 153, 176, 177, 236, 264, 344, 364, 365, 370, 371, 511, 577, 625
Manuel Makropoulos	*drapier*, partner of C. Tzouknidas	51, 58, 177, 237, 243, 362, 365, 374, 416, 417, 449, 580, 634, 640, 644, 656, 743, 744, 773, 777, 804, 805
Constantine Makrymalles	*chir*	221
(Theodore) Makrymalles	*drapier*, partner of D. *Glivani*, J. and C. Tzouknidas	129, 234, 235, 264, 305, 313, 364, 365, 374, 444, 716
Mamonas	*sanser*	79, 133, 135, 139, 229, 276, 521, 582, 647, 651, 725
Melissenos	*boter*	405, 610
Demetrios Notaras	*chir, chomerchier*, partner of C. Palaiologos	19, 29, 59, 91, 108, 109, 125, 135, 139, 148, 153, 202, 285, 288, 299, 354, 355, 376, 557, 602
Isaak Notaras	–	404, 729
Loukas Notaras (uncle of Nicholas Sophianos)	*chir, mesazon*	135, 229, 410, 411, 480, 784
Theodore Notaras	–	511, 686, 714
Pagomenos	*sanser de lane*	412, 414, 581, 582
Matthew Pagomenos (son of the late Franzela)	*chir*	105, 344, 362, 364, 365, 388, 444, 604, 611
Constantine Palaiologos	*kephale* of Agathopolis, partner of D. Notaras	29, 108, 135, 148, 153
Demetrios Palaiologos	*chir*	265, 282, 338
Jacob Palaiologos	*chir*	105, 178, 264, 362, 367, 651, 656
Philialites	*chir*	6, 32, 84, 85
Antonios Philomates (Cretan, inhabitant of Constantinople)	–	204, 215
Phokas	*chir, bazarioto*	653, 712, 715

(*cont.*)

Name	Occupation, title, etc.	Reference in Badoer (pp.)
Phrankopoulos	*banchier*	153, 178, 371, 656
Phrankopoulos	*botegier*	178, 201, 451, 680
Theodore Phrankopoulos	–	7
Theodore Prodromos	*chir*	653, 712, 713, 714, 715
Theodore Rhalles	*chir*	59, 194, 196, 200, 203, 205, 231, 235, 237, 258, 262, 263, 266, 345, 468, 469, 784, 787
Kaloioannes Sarantenos (*Sarandino/Sardino*)	*banchier*	11, 27, 32, 33, 47, 54, 55, 58, 59, 61, 64, 72, 96
Nicholas Sarantenos	*chir, banchier*	10, 15, 21, 47, 58, 59, 72, 85, 96, 100, 108, 110, 137, 139, 153, 158, 162, 180, 188, 189, 194, 239, 250, 257, 259, 261, 264, 271, 336, 349, 354, 368, 374, 404, 405, 412, 446, 450, 496, 499, 511, 514, 522, 541, 581, 610, 614, 629, 680, 686, 721, 729, 732, 753, 758, 784
Manuel Skoutariotes	–	219, 240, 362
Demetrios Sophianos	–	739, 784
Kaloioannes Sophianos	*banchier*	4, 5, 6, 7, 10, 14, 15, 32, 33, 34, 36, 41, 60, 70, 73, 78, 79, 84, 85, 94, 96, 97, 100, 105, 110, 112, 114, 115, 129, 153, 160, 163, 165, 194, 210, 229, 231, 232, 235, 236, 237, 241, 243, 246, 247, 249, 264, 265, 276, 284, 344, 359, 365, 580
Nicholas Sophianos (nephew of Loukas Notaras)	–	585, 784, 785, 796
Demetrios Stratiopoulos	–	641, 646
Synadenos	–	349, 417
Andronikos Synadenos (nephew of Basilikos)	*drapier*, partner of G. Laskaris	41, 114, 177, 219, 227, 236, 242, 243, 464, 484, 500, 504, 509, 522, 523, 580, 618
Syropoulos	*botegier*	82, 101, 178

(*cont.*)

Name	Occupation, title, etc.	Reference in Badoer (pp.)
John Tzouknidas (*Zuchinida/Cichnida*)	*drapier*, partner of D. Glivani, Makrymalles, C. and M. Makropoulos	58, 114, 120, 121, 129, 133, 152, 153, 171, 178, 221, 234, 235, 236, 264, 284, 312, 344
Constantine Bardas Tzouknidas	*drapier*, partner of D. Glivani, Makrymalles, C. and M. Makropoulos	51, 177, 227, 237, 243, 264, 295, 362, 364, 365, 368, 370, 371, 374, 417, 444, 449, 450, 511, 577, 580, 625, 634, 639, 640, 644, 656, 744
Constantine Tzouknidas	–	79
Theophylaktos Tzourakes (*Surachi*)	shoe-maker, partner of J. *Vrachimi* and M. *Chatafioti*	27, 154, 155, 178, 225, 264, 419, 444, 480, 481, 580
John *Vrachimi*	shoe-maker, partner of T. Tzourakes, A. Kinnamos and M. *Chatafioti*	27, 140, 141, 154, 155, 178, 225, 264, 417, 419, 444, 480, 481, 487, 580, 623, 634, 656, 743
Alexios Vryonis	*chir*	178, 199, 209, 230, 231, 236, 262, 370, 442, 444, 468
Xanthopoulos (*Xatopulo*)	*banchier*	92, 153
George Xanthopoulos	*chir*	382, 383, 656, 744

Members of the Senate of Constantinople cited in the synodal tome of August 1409

(Published in Laurent, "Trisépiscopat," 133–4)

Manuel Agathon
Andreas Asanes
Constantine Asanes, θεῖος of Manuel II
Demetrios Chrysoloras
Demetrios Palaiologos Eirenikos
George Goudeles
Demetrios Palaiologos Goudeles, ἐξάδελφος of Manuel II
Kantakouzenos
Theodore (Palaiologos) Kantakouzenos, θεῖος of Manuel II
Demetrios (Laskaris) Leontares
Manuel Bryennios Leontares
Andronikos (Apokaukos) Melissenos*
Nicholas Notaras
Matthew Laskaris Palaiologos
Manuel Kantakouzenos Phakrases
Andronikos Tarchaniotes Philanthropenos*
Sphrantzes Sebastopoulos
Nicholas Sophianos
Alexios Kaballarios Tzamplakon*

---

* Also cited as Senate member in a patriarchal register of October 1397: MM, vol. II, no. 686, p. 566.

Some Greek refugees in Italian territories after 1453

(A) **Aristocrats who fled from Constantinople on Zorzi Doria's ship (May 29, 1453)** (from documents published by Mertzios, in Γέρας Α. Κεραμοπούλλου, pp. 359–60 and in *Actes du XIIe Congrès international d'études byzantines*, vol. II, pp. 172–3)

John Bardas
Stamati, Manuel, and Leo Bardas
Michael and Jacob Kalaphates (*Calafati*)
John and Demetrios Kantakouzenos
Jacob, John, and George Katallaktes (*Catalacti*)
Constantine and Isaak Komnenos
Theodore and Manuel Laskaris
Sergios, Antonios, and Nicholas Metaxas
Leo and Antonios Mousouros (*Mussuro*)
Biasio and Matthew Notaras
Manuel, Thomas, and Demetrios Palaiologos
Theodore and Andronikos Palaiologos
Andronikos and Manuel Phokas
Markos, Petros, and Nicholas *Siguriani*
Leo and Andreas Thalassenos (*Talassini*)

(B) **Greeks cited in Venetian *deliberazioni* (1453–63)**

Laskaris Kananos, partner of Michael Kantakouzenos (Thiriet, *Assemblées*, vol. II, no. 1488 [1454])
Michael Kantakouzenos, partner of Laskaris Kananos (same as above)
George Sgouros (Thiriet, *Régestes*, vol. III, no. 3009 [1456])
Petros, nephew of George Sgouros (same as above)
John Stavrakes (*Stavrachi*) (Thiriet, *Assemblées*, vol. II, no. 1579 [1461])

(C) **Greeks in Francesco Filelfo's letters (1453–73)**
(from *Cent-dix lettres*, ed. Legrand)
John Argyropoulos (Letter 73 [1466])
Demetrios Asanes (Notes to letter 33 [1455])
George Asanes, *archon* (Letters 68 [1465], 73 [1466])
Michael Asanes (Notes to letter 33 [1455])
Demetrios Chalkokondyles (Letters 104bis, 105, 110 [1477])
(Michael) Dromokates Chrysoloras (Letter 33 [1454] and notes [1455])
John Gabras (Letter 37 [1454])
Theodore Gazes (Letters 68 and 69 [1465], 86 [1469], 94 [1472])
(George) Glykys (Letter 81 and notes [1469])
Alexander Kananos (Notes to letter 37 [1454])
Demetrios Kastrenos (Letter 80 [1469])
Manuel Palaiologos, *archon* (Letter 68 [1465])
Demetrios Sgouropoulos (Letter 98 [1473])
Nicholas Tarchaniotes (Notes to letter 37 [1454])

(D) **Greeks in Venice (1470–71)**
(from Schreiner, *Texte*, no. 4, pp. 108–13)
Baldasaras (§§ 16, 20, 21, 37, 39, 40)
Basilikos (§§ 49, 64)
Branas (§§ 14, 36, 44, 62)
(Katarina) Kantakouzene (§ 65)
Lagoos (§ 20)
Ma(gi)stromatthaios (§§ 1, 10, 49, 67)
Mamonas (§ 7)
Manas(s)es (§ 15)
Jacob Notaras (§§ 16, 35, 40, 46, 50, 52, 54, 58, 61, 62)
Anna (Notaras) Palaiologina (§§ 2, 10, 31, 36, 51, 56, 60, 62, 63)
Olympias (§ 40)
Physina (§ 33)
Tragos(?) (§§ 18, 34)
Tzoutzide (§ 48)

Bibliography

I. SOURCES

A. DOCUMENTS

Actes de Chilandar, vol. I: *Actes grecs*, ed. L. Petit, *VV* 17 (1911; repr. Amsterdam, 1975)

Actes de Chilandar, vol. I: *Des origines à 1319*, ed. M. Živojinović, V. Kravari, and Ch. Giros (Paris, 1998)

Actes de Dionysiou, ed. N. Oikonomidès (Paris, 1968)

Actes de Docheiariou, ed. N. Oikonomidès (Paris, 1984)

Actes d'Esphigménou, ed. J. Lefort (Paris, 1973)

Actes d'Iviron, vols. III–IV, ed. J. Lefort, N. Oikonomidès, D. Papachryssanthou, and V. Kravari, with the collaboration of H. Métrévéli (Paris, 1994–5)

Actes de Lavra, vols. II–IV, ed. P. Lemerle, A. Guillou, N. Svoronos, and D. Papachryssanthou (Paris, 1977–82)

Actes de Saint-Pantéléèmôn, ed. P. Lemerle, G. Dagron, and S. Ćirković (Paris, 1982)

Actes de Vatopédi, vol. II, ed. J. Lefort, V. Kravari, Ch. Giros, and K. Smyrlis (Paris, 2006)

Actes de Xénophon, ed. D. Papachryssanthou (Paris, 1986)

Actes de Xéropotamou, ed. J. Bompaire (Paris, 1964)

Actes de Zographou, ed. W. Regel, E. Kurtz, and B. Korablev, *VV* 13 (1907; repr. Amsterdam, 1969)

Aus den Schatzkammern des Heiligen Berges, ed. F. Dölger (Munich, 1948)

Balard, M. "Péra au XIVe siècle. Documents notariés des archives de Gênes," in *Les Italiens à Byzance. Édition et présentation de documents*, ed. M. Balard, A. E. Laiou, and C. Otten-Froux (Paris, 1987), pp. 9–78

Belgrano, L. T. "Prima serie di documenti riguardanti la colonia di Pera," *ASLSP* 13 (1877), 97–336

"Seconda serie di documenti riguardanti la colonia di Pera," *ASLSP* 17 (1884), 932–1003

Boškov, V. V. "Ein Nišān des Prinzen Orhan, Sohn Süleyman Çelebis, aus dem Jahre 1412 im Athoskloster Sankt Paulus," *WZKM* 71 (1979), 127–52

Byzantine Monastic Foundation Documents, ed. J. Thomas and A. C. Hero, 5 vols. (Washington, DC, 2000)

Cecconi, E. *Studi storici sul Concilio di Firenze*, vol. 1 (Florence, 1869)

Chrysostomides, J. (ed.) *Monumenta Peloponnesiaca. Documents for the History of the Peloponnese in the 14th and 15th Centuries* (Camberley, 1995)

Darrouzès, J. *Les regestes des actes du patriarcat de Constantinople*, vol. 1: *Les actes des patriarches*, fasc. 6: *Les regestes de 1377 à 1410* (Paris, 1979)

Delehaye, H. *Deux typica byzantins de l'époque des Paléologues* (Brussels, 1921)

Delilbaşı, M. and Arıkan, M. (eds.) *Hicrî 859 Tarihli Sûret-i Defter-i Sancak-ı Tırhala*, 2 vols. (Ankara, 2001)

Dennis, G. T. "The Byzantine–Turkish treaty of 1403," *OCP* 33 (1967), 72–88 (reprinted in G. T. Dennis, *Byzantium and the Franks, 1350–1420* [London, 1982], Study VI)

"Official documents of Manuel II Palaeologus," *B* 41 (1971), 45–58 (reprinted in *Byzantium and the Franks*, Study IX)

"Three reports from Crete on the situation in Romania, 1401–1402," *StVen* 12 (1970), 243–65 (reprinted in *Byzantium and the Franks*, Study XVII)

"Two unknown documents of Manuel II Palaeologus," *TM* 3 (1968), 397–404 (reprinted in *Byzantium and the Franks*, Study VIII)

Dölger, F. *Regesten der Kaiserurkunden des oströmischen Reiches*, vol. v: *1341–1453* (Munich and Berlin, 1965)

Dorini, V. and Bertelè, T. *Il libro dei conti di Giacomo Badoer (Costantinopoli 1436–1440)* (Rome, 1956)

Fedalto, G. *La chiesa latina in Oriente*, vol. III: *Documenti veneziani* (Verona, 1978)

Gerland, E. *Neue Quellen zur Geschichte des lateinischen Erzbistums Patras* (Leipzig, 1903)

Harmenopoulos, C. *Manuale Legum sive Hexabiblos*, ed. G. E. Heimbach (Leipzig, 1851)

Hofmann, G. (ed.) *Acta camerae apostolicae et civitatum Venetiarum, Ferrariae, Florentiae, Ianuae, de Concilio Florentino* (Rome, 1950)

Epistolae pontificiae ad Concilium Florentinum spectantes, 3 vols. (Rome, 1940–6)

Hunger, H. "Das Testament des Patriarchen Matthaios I. (1397–1410)," *BZ* 51 (1958), 288–309

"Zu den restlichen Inedita des Konstantinopler Patriarchatsregisters im Cod. Vindob. Hist. Gr. 48," *REB* 24 (1966), 58–68

Hunger, H. and Vogel, K. *Ein byzantinisches Rechenbuch des 15. Jahrhunderts* (Vienna, 1963)

İnalcık, H. *Hicrî 835 Tarihli Sûret-i Defter-i Sancak-i Arvanid* (Ankara, 1954; repr. 1987)

Iorga, N. "Documents concernant les Grecs et les affaires d'Orient tirés des registres de notaires de Crète," *Revue Historique du Sud-Est Européen* 14 (1937), 89–114

Notes et extraits pour servir à l'histoire des Croisades au XVe siècle, 4 vols. (Paris, 1899–1915); also published in *ROL* 4 (1896), 25–118, 226–30, 503–622; 5 (1897), 108–212, 311–88; 6 (1898), 50–143, 370–434; 7 (1899–1900), 38–107, 375–429; 8 (1900–1), 1–115, 267–310

"Veneţia in Mare Neagră," *Analele Academiei Române, Memoriile secţiunii istorice*, ser. 2, 36 (1913–14), 1058–70 ("Appendice": Docs. I–XXI), 1093–118 ("Annexe": Docs. I–LIX)

Konidares, I. M. and Manaphes, K. A. "Ἐπιτελεύτιος βούλησις καὶ διδασκαλία τοῦ οἰκουμενικοῦ πατριάρχου Ματθαίου Α' (1397–1410)," *ΕΕΒΣ* 45 (1981–2), 472–510

Kravari, V. "Nouveaux documents du monastère de Philothéou," *TM* 10 (1987), 261–356

Krekić, B. *Dubrovnik (Raguse) et le Levant au Moyen Âge* (Paris, 1961)

Kugéas, S. "Notizbuch eines Beamten der Metropolis in Thessalonike aus dem Anfang des XV. Jahrhunderts," *BZ* 23 (1914–19), 143–63

Lampros, Sp. "Ἡ ἑλληνικὴ ὡς ἐπίσημος γλῶσσα τῶν σουλτάνων," *NE* 5 (1908), 40–78

Lampros, Sp. (ed.) *Παλαιολόγεια καὶ Πελοποννησιακά*, 4 vols. (Athens, 1912–30; repr. 1972)

Loenertz, R.-J. "Hospitaliers et Navarrais en Grèce (1376–1383). Regestes et documents," *OCP* 22 (1956), 319–60 (reprinted in R.-J. Loenertz, *Byzantina et Franco-Graeca*, vol. 1 [Rome, 1970], pp. 329–69)

Mertzios, K. D. "Περὶ Παλαιολόγων καὶ ἄλλων εὐγενῶν Κωνσταντινουπολίτων," *Γέρας Α. Κεραμοπούλλου* (Athens, 1953), pp. 355–72

"Περὶ τῶν ἐκ Κωνσταντινουπόλεως διαφυγόντων τὸ 1453 Παλαιολόγων καὶ ἀποβιβασθέντων εἰς Κρήτην," *Actes du XIIe Congrès international d'études byzantines*, vol. 11 (Belgrade, 1964), pp. 171–6

Miklosich, F. and Müller, J. *Acta et diplomata graeca medii aevi sacra et profana*, 6 vols. (Vienna, 1860–90)

Musso, G. G. *Navigazione e commercio genovese con il Levante nei documenti dell'Archivio di Stato di Genova (secc. XIV–XV)* (Rome, 1975)

Noiret, H. *Documents inédits pour servir à l'histoire de la domination vénitienne en Crète de 1380 à 1485, tirés des archives de Venise* (Paris, 1892)

Pagano, C. *Delle imprese e del dominio dei Genovesi nella Grecia* (Genoa, 1846)

Raynaldus, O. and Baronius, C. *Annales ecclesiastici*, vols. xxv–xxvii (Bar-le-Duc, 1872–80)

Roccatagliata, A. *Notai genovesi in Oltremare. Atti rogati a Pera e Mitilene*, vol. 1: *Pera, 1408–1490* (Genoa, 1982)

Rubió i Lluch, A. *Diplomatari de l'Orient Català (1301–1409)* (Barcelona, 1947)

Sathas, C. N. *Documents inédits relatifs à l'histoire de la Grèce au Moyen Âge*, 9 vols. (Paris and Venice, 1880–90)

Schreiner, P. "Eine venezianische Kolonie in Philadelpheia (Lydien)," *Quellen und Forschungen aus italienischen Archiven und Bibliotheken* 57 (1977), 339–46

Texte zur spätbyzantinischen Finanz- und Wirtschaftsgeschichte in Handschriften der Bibliotheca Vaticana (Vatican City, 1991)

Tafel, G. L. and Thomas, G. M. *Urkunden zur älteren Handels- und Staatsgeschichte der Republik Venedig mit besonderen Beziehungen auf Byzanz und die Levante*, vol. 111: *1256–1299* (Vienna, 1857; repr. 1964)

Thiriet, F. *Délibérations des assemblées vénitiennes concernant la Romanie*, vol. ii: *1364–1463* (Paris and The Hague, 1971)
Régestes des délibérations du Sénat de Venise concernant la Romanie, 3 vols. (Paris and The Hague, 1958–61)
Thomas, G. M. and Predelli, R. *Diplomatarium Veneto-Levantinum sive acta et diplomata res Venetas, Graecas atque Levantis illustrantia a 1300–1454*, 2 vols. (Venice, 1880, 1889; repr. 1964)
Vasdravelles, I. Ἱστορικὰ Ἀρχεῖα Μακεδονίας, vol. iii: Ἀρχεῖον Μονῆς Βλατ-τάδων, *1466–1839* (Thessalonike, 1955)
Zachariadou, E. A. "Early Ottoman documents of the Prodromos Monastery (Serres)," *SüdostF* 28 (1969), 1–12 (reprinted in E. A. Zachariadou, *Romania and the Turks (c. 1300–c. 1500)* [London, 1985], Study XV)
"Ottoman documents from the archives of Dionysiou (Mount Athos) 1495–1520," *SüdostF* 30 (1971), 1–35 (reprinted in *Romania and the Turks*, Study XVI)
Zepos, I. and Zepos, P. (eds.) *Jus graecoromanum*, 8 vols. (Athens, 1931; repr. Aalen, 1962)

B. LITERARY AND OTHER SOURCES

Anagnostes, John. Ἰωάννου Ἀναγνώστου Διήγησις περὶ τῆς τελευταίας ἁλώσεως τῆς Θεσσαλονίκης, ed. J. Tsaras (Thessalonike, 1958)
(Argyropoulos, John). "[Jean Argyropoulos], La Comédie de Katablattas. Invective byzantine du XVe s.," ed. and trans. P. Canivet and N. Oikonomidès, Δίπτυχα 3 (1982–3), 5–97
Aşıkpaşazade. *Die altosmanische Chronik des Āşıkpaşazāde*, ed. F. Giese (Leipzig, 1929)
Tevârîh-i Âl-i Osmân, in *Osmanlı Tarihleri*, ed. N. Atsız, vol. i (Istanbul, 1949)
Barbaro, Nicolò. *Giornale dell'assedio di Costantinopoli 1453*, ed. E. Cornet (Vienna, 1856). English trans. J. R. Jones, *Diary of the Siege of Constantinople* (New York, 1969)
Bartolomeo di Giano, Fra. "Epistola de crudelitate Turcarum," ed. Migne, *PG* 158, cols. 1055–68
Bessarion. "Κωνσταντίνῳ δεσπότῃ τῷ Παλαιολόγῳ χαίρειν," ed. Lampros, *PP*, vol. iv, pp. 32–45
Broquière, Bertrandon de la. *Le voyage d'Outremer de Bertrandon de la Broquière*, ed. Ch. Schefer (Paris, 1892; repr. 1972)
Bryennios, Joseph. "Ἐκ τῆς βυζαντινῆς Ἐπιστολογραφίας. Ἰωσὴφ μοναχοῦ τοῦ Βρυεννίου Ἐπιστολαὶ Λ΄ καὶ αἱ πρὸς αὐτὸν Γ΄," ed. N. B. Tomadakes, *EEBΣ* 46 (1983–6), 279–364
"Ἰωσὴφ Βρυεννίου Δημηγορία περὶ τοῦ τῆς Πόλεως ἀνακτίσματος (1415 μ.Χ.)," ed. N. B. Tomadakes, *EEBΣ* 36 (1968), 1–15
Ἰωσὴφ μοναχοῦ τοῦ Βρυεννίου τὰ εὑρεθέντα, vols. i–ii, ed. E. Boulgares (Leipzig, 1768); vol. iii: Τὰ παραλειπόμενα, ed. T. Mandakases (Leipzig, 1784)

"Ἰωσὴφ τοῦ Βρυεννίου μετά τινος Ἰσμαηλίτου Διάλεξις," ed. A. Argyriou, *EEBΣ* 35 (1966–7), 141–95

Bulgarische Chronik von 1296–1413, ed. J. Bogdan, in "Ein Beitrag zur bulgarischen und serbischen Geschichtsschreibung," *Archiv für slavische Philologie* 13 (1891), 481–543

Buondelmonti, Christophe. *Description des îles de l'Archipel. Version grecque par un anonyme*, ed. and trans. E. Legrand (Paris, 1897)

Caresini, Raffaino. *Raphayni de Caresinis cancellarii Venetiarum Chronica: aa. 1343–1388*, ed. E. Pastorello, *RIS*, 12/2 (Bologna, 1923)

Chalkokondyles, Laonikos. *Laonici Chalcocandylae Historiarum Demonstrationes*, ed. E. Darkó, 2 vols. (Budapest, 1922–7)

Chinazzo, Daniele di. *Cronica de la guerra da Veneciani a Zenovesi*, ed. V. Lazzarini (Venice, 1958)

Chortasmenos, John. *Johannes Chortasmenos (ca.1370–ca.1436/37), Briefe, Gedichte und kleine Schriften. Einleitung, Regesten, Prosopographie, Text*, ed. H. Hunger (Vienna, 1969)

Chrysoloras, Demetrios. "Action de grâces de Démétrius Chrysoloras à la Théotocos pour l'anniversaire de la bataille d'Ankara (28 Juillet 1403)," ed. P. Gautier, *REB* 19 (1961), 340–57

"Σύγκρισις παλαιῶν ἀρχόντων καὶ νέου, τοῦ νῦν αὐτοκράτορος," ed. Lampros, *PP*, vol. III, pp. 222–45

Clavijo, Ruy González de. *Embajada a Tamorlán*, ed. F. López Estrada (Madrid, 1999). English trans. G. Le Strange, *Embassy to Tamerlane, 1403–1406* (New York and London, 1928)

Cronaca dei Tocco di Cefalonia di anonimo, ed. and trans. G. Schirò (Rome, 1975)

Cyriacus of Ancona's Journeys in the Propontis and the Northern Aegean, 1444–1445, ed. E. W. Bodnar and C. Mitchell (Philadelphia, 1976)

Darrouzès, J. (ed.) "Lettres de 1453," *REB* 22 (1964), 72–127

Dolfin, Zorzi. *Belagerung und Eroberung von Constantinopel im Jahre 1453 aus der Chronik von Zorzi Dolfin*, ed. G. M. Thomas (Munich, 1868). English trans. in Jones, *The Siege of Constantinople*, pp. 125–30

Doukas. *Ducas, Istoria Turco-Bizantină (1341–1462)*, ed. V. Grecu (Bucharest, 1958). English trans. H. J. Magoulias, *Decline and Fall of Byzantium to the Ottoman Turks by Doukas* (Detroit, 1975)

Enveri. *Fatih Devri Kaynaklarından Düstûrnâme-i Enverî: Osmanlı Tarihi Kısmı (1299–1466)*, ed. N. Öztürk (Istanbul, 2003)

Eugenikos, John. "Ἔργα Ἰωάννου τοῦ Εὐγενικοῦ," ed. Lampros, *PP*, vol. I, pp. 47–218, 271–322

Ferîdûn, Ahmed. *Münşeâtü's-Selâtîn*, vol. I, 2nd edn. (Istanbul, 1857–8)

Filelfo, Francesco. *Cent-dix lettres grecques de François Filelfe*, ed E. Legrand (Paris, 1892)

Gabriel of Thessalonike. "Γαβριὴλ Θεσσαλονίκης ὁμιλίαι," ed. B. Laourdas, Ἀθηνᾶ 57 (1953), 141–78

Gautier, P. (ed.) "Un récit inédit sur le siège de Constantinople par les Turcs (1394–1402)," *REB* 23 (1965), 100–17

Gazavât-ı Sultân Murâd b. Mehemmed Hân. İzladi ve Varna Savaşları (1443–1444) Üzerinde Anonim Gazavâtnâme, ed. H. İnalcık and M. Oğuz (Ankara, 1978). English trans. in C. Imber, *The Crusade of Varna, 1443–45* (Aldershot, 2006), pp. 41–106

Gerson, Jean. *Sermon inédit de Jean Gerson sur le retour des Grecs à l'unité,* ed. A. Galitzin (Paris, 1859)

Gregoras, Nikephoros. *Nicephori Gregorae Byzantina Historia,* vol. II, ed. L. Schopen (Bonn, 1830)

Imber, C. (trans.) *The Crusade of Varna, 1443–45* (Aldershot, 2006)

(Isidore of Kiev). "Ἀνωνύμου πανηγυρικὸς εἰς Μανουὴλ καὶ Ἰωάννην Η' τοὺς Παλαιολόγους," ed. Lampros, *PP,* vol. III, pp. 132–99

Isidore of Thessalonike. "Five homilies of Isidore, Archbishop of Thessalonica. Edition, translation and commentary," ed. A. C. Hero, unpublished MA thesis, Columbia University (1965)

"Ἰσιδώρου Ἀρχιεπισκόπου Θεσσαλονίκης ὁμιλία περὶ τῆς ἁρπαγῆς τῶν παίδων καὶ περὶ τῆς μελλούσης κρίσεως," ed. B. Laourdas, Ἑλληνικά 4 (1953), 389–98

Ἰσιδώρου Ἀρχιεπισκόπου Θεσσαλονίκης, Ὁμιλίαι εἰς τὰς ἑορτὰς τοῦ Ἁγίου Δημητρίου, ed. B. Laourdas (Thessalonike, 1954)

Ἰσιδώρου Γλαβᾶ Ἀρχιεπισκόπου Θεσσαλονίκης ὁμιλίες, ed. B. Ch. Christophorides, 2 vols. (Thessalonike, 1992–6)

"Ἰσιδώρου μητροπολίτου Θεσσαλονίκης, Ὀκτὼ ἐπιστολαὶ ἀνέκδοτοι," ed. Sp. Lampros, *NE* 9 (1912), 343–414

"Συμβολὴ εἰς τὴν ἱστορίαν τῆς Θεσσαλονίκης. Δύο ἀνέκδοτοι ὁμιλίαι Ἰσιδώρου ἀρχιεπισκόπου Θεσσαλονίκης," ed. C. N. Tsirpanlis, Θεολογία 42 (1971), 548–81. English trans. C. N. Tsirpanlis, "Two unpublished homilies of Isidore Glabas, Metropolitan of Thessalonica (1342–1396)," *The Patristic and Byzantine Review* 1/2 (1982), 184–210; 2/1 (1983), 65–83

Jones, J. R. Melville (trans.) *The Siege of Constantinople 1453: Seven Contemporary Accounts* (Amsterdam, 1972)

Kabasilas, Nicholas. I. Ševčenko (ed.), "Nicolas Cabasilas' 'Anti-Zealot' discourse: a reinterpretation," *DOP* 11 (1957), 81–171 (reprinted in I. Ševčenko, *Society and Intellectual Life in Late Byzantium* [London, 1981], Study IV)

Kalekas, Manuel. *Correspondance de Manuel Calécas,* ed. R.-J. Loenertz (Vatican City, 1950)

Kananos, John. *Giovanni Cananos, L'assedio di Costantinopoli. Introduzione, testo critico, traduzione, note e lessico,* ed. E. Pinto (Messina, 1977)

Kantakouzenos, John. *Ioannis Cantacuzeni Eximperatoris Historiarum libri IV,* vol. III, ed. B. G. Niebuhr (Bonn, 1832)

Kritoboulos. *Critobuli Imbriotae Historiae,* ed. D. R. Reinsch (Berlin and New York, 1983). English trans. C. T. Riggs, *History of Mehmed the Conqueror by Kritovoulos* (Princeton, 1954); German trans. D. R. Reinsch, *Mehmet II. erobert Konstantinopel* (Graz, Vienna, and Cologne, 1986)

Kydones, Demetrios. "Apologie della propria fede: I. Ai Greci Ortodossi," ed. G. Mercati, in *Notizie di Procoro e Demetrio Cidone, Manuele Caleca e*

Teodoro Meliteniota ed altri appunti per la storia della teologia e della letteratura bizantina del secolo XIV (Vatican City, 1931), pp. 359–403

Démétrius Cydonès Correspondance, ed. R.-J. Loenertz, 2 vols. (Vatican City, 1956–60). German trans. F. Tinnefeld, *Demetrios Kydones Briefe,* 3 vols. (Stuttgart, 1981–99)

"Oratio de admittendo Latinorum subsidio," ed. Migne, *PG* 154, cols. 961–1008

"Oratio de non reddenda Callipoli petente Amurate," ed. Migne, *PG* 154, cols. 1009–36

Leonardo of Chios. "Historia Constantinopolitanae urbis a Mahumete II captae per modum epistolae," ed. Migne, *PG* 159, cols. 923–44. English trans. in Jones, *The Siege of Constantinople,* pp. 11–41

Livre de la conqueste de la princée de l'Amorée. Chronique de Morée (1204–1305), ed. J. Longnon (Paris, 1911)

Le livre des fais du bon messire Jehan le Maingre, dit Boucicquaut, mareschal de France et gouverneur de Jennes, ed. D. Lalande (Geneva, 1985)

Loenertz, R.-J. (ed.) "Fragment d'une lettre de Jean V Paléologue à la commune de Gênes, 1387–1391," *BZ* 51 (1958), 37–40 (reprinted in R.-J. Loenertz, *Byzantina et Franco-Graeca,* vol. 1 [Rome, 1970], pp. 393–7)

"Res gestae Theodori Ioann. F. Palaeologi. Titulus metricus a.d. 1389," *EEBΣ* 25 (1955), 207–10

Makrembolites, Alexios. I. Ševčenko (ed.), "Alexios Makrembolites and his 'Dialogue between the Rich and the Poor'," *ZRVI* 6 (1960), 203–28 (reprinted in I. Ševčenko, *Society and Intellectual Life in Late Byzantium* [London, 1981], Study VII)

Makres, Makarios. *Macaire Makrès et la polémique contre l'Islam. Édition princeps de l'Éloge de Macaire Makrès et de ses deux œuvres anti-islamiques, précédée d'une étude critique,* ed. A. Argyriou (Vatican City, 1986)

Μακαρίου τοῦ Μακρῆ συγγράμματα, ed. A. Argyriou (Thessalonike, 1996)

Manuel II Palaiologos. "Épître de Manuel II Paléologue aux moines David et Damien 416," ed. R.-J. Loenertz, *Studi bizantini e neoellenici* 9 (1957) (= *Silloge bizantina in onore di Silvio Giuseppe Mercati*), 294–304

The Letters of Manuel II Palaeologus. Text, Translation, and Notes, ed. G. T. Dennis (Washington, DC, 1977)

Manuel II Palaeologus, Funeral Oration on his Brother Theodore. Introduction, Text, Translation and Notes, ed. J. Chrysostomides (Thessalonike, 1985)

Manuel II Palaiologos, Dialoge mit einem "Perser," ed. E. Trapp (Vienna, 1966)

Manuel Palaiologos, Dialogue with the Empress-Mother on Marriage. Introduction, Text and Translation, ed. and trans. A. Angelou (Vienna, 1991)

"Ὁ 'συμβουλευτικὸς πρὸς τοὺς Θεσσαλονικεῖς' τοῦ Μανουὴλ Παλαιολόγου," ed. B. Laourdas, *Μακεδονικά* 3 (1955), 290–307

Mazaris' Journey to Hades, or Interviews with Dead Men about Certain Officials of the Imperial Court, ed. and trans. J. N. Barry, M. J. Share, A. Smithies, and L. G. Westerink (Buffalo, NY, 1975)

Mihailović, Konstantin. *Memoirs of a Janissary,* trans. B. Stolz, commentary and notes by S. Soucek (Ann Arbor, 1975)

Millet, G. (ed.) "Les inscriptions byzantines de Mistra," *Bulletin de Correspondance Hellénique* 23 (1899), 97–156

"Inscriptions inédites de Mistra," *Bulletin de Correspondance Hellénique* 30 (1906), 453–66

Mioni, E. (ed.) "Una inedita cronaca bizantina (dal Marc. gr. 595)," *Rivista di studi bizantini e slavi* 1 (1981), 71–87

Nestor-Iskander, *The Tale of Constantinople (Of its Origins and Capture by the Turks in the Year 1453)*, translated and annotated by W. K. Hanak and M. Philippides (New Rochelle, 1998)

Neşrî, Mehmed. *Kitâb-ı Cihan-nümâ – Neşrî Tarihi*, ed. F. R. Unat and M. A. Köymen, 2 vols. (Ankara, 1949–57)

Pertusi, A. (ed.) *La caduta di Costantinopoli*, 2 vols. (Verona, 1976)

Testi inediti e poco noti sulla caduta di Costantinopoli, edizione postuma a cura di A. Carile (Bologna, 1983)

Plethon, George Gemistos. "Εἰς Μανουὴλ Παλαιολόγον περὶ τῶν ἐν Πελοποννήσῳ πραγμάτων," ed. Lampros, *PP*, vol. III, pp. 246–65

"Πρὸς τὸν βασιλέα," ed. Lampros, *PP*, vol. III, pp. 309–12

"Συμβουλευτικὸς πρὸς τὸν δεσπότην Θεόδωρον περὶ τῆς Πελοποννήσου," ed. Lampros, *PP*, vol. IV, pp. 113–35

Potamios, Theodore. "The letters of Theodore Potamios," ed. G. T. Dennis, *Byzantium and the Franks, 1350–1420* (London, 1982), Study XII, pp. 1–40

Pseudo-Phrantzes. *Macarie Melissenos Cronica, 1258–1481*, in *Georgios Sphrantzes, Memorii, 1401–1477*, ed. V. Grecu (Bucharest, 1966), pp. 149ff.

Pusculo, Ubertino. *Ubertini Pusculi Brixiensis Constantinopoleos Libri IV*, in *Analekten der mittel- und neugriechischen Literatur*, ed. A. Ellissen, vol. III (Leipzig, 1857; repr. 1976), pp. 12–83

Russian Travelers to Constantinople in the Fourteenth and Fifteenth Centuries, ed. and trans. G. P. Majeska (Washington, DC, 1984)

Sadeddîn, Hoca Efendi. *Tâcü't-tevârîh*, vol. I (Istanbul, 1863)

Sanuto, Marino. *Vite dei duchi di Venezia*, ed. L. A. Muratori, *RIS*, 22 (Milan, 1733), cols. 405–1252

Sathas, K. N. (ed.) *Χρονικὸν ἀνέκδοτον Γαλαξειδίου* (Athens, 1914)

Schiltberger. *The Bondage and Travels of Johann Schiltberger, 1396–1427*, trans. J. B. Telfer (London, 1879)

Scholarios, George-Gennadios. *Œuvres complètes de Georges (Gennadios) Scholarios*, ed. L. Petit, H. A. Sideridès, and M. Jugie, 8 vols. (Paris, 1928–36)

Schreiner, P. (ed.) *Die byzantinischen Kleinchroniken*, 3 vols. (Vienna, 1975–9)

Sideras, A. (ed.) *24 unedierte byzantinische Grabreden* (Göttingen, 1982)

Spandugnino, Theodoro. *De la origine deli imparatori Ottomani*, ed. Sathas, *Documents*, vol. IX, pp. 134–261. English trans. D. M. Nicol, *Theodore Spandounes, On the Origin of the Ottoman Emperors* (Cambridge, 1997)

Sphrantzes, Georgios. *Memorii, 1401–1477*, ed. V. Grecu (Bucharest, 1966). English trans. M. Philippides, *The Fall of the Byzantine Empire; A Chronicle by George Sphrantzes, 1401–1477* (Amherst, 1980)

Spieser, J.-M. (ed.) "Les inscriptions de Thessalonique," *TM* 5 (1973), 145–80

Stamires, G. A. (ed.) "Ἡ ἐπιγραφὴ τοῦ Κροκόντυλου," *Πελοποννησιακά* 3–4 (1958–9), 84–6

Symeon of Thessalonike. *Ἁγίου Συμεὼν Ἀρχιεπισκόπου Θεσσαλονίκης (1416/17–1429), Ἔργα Θεολογικά*, ed. D. Balfour (Thessalonike, 1981) *Politico-Historical Works of Symeon Archbishop of Thessalonica (1416/17 to 1429)*, ed. D. Balfour (Vienna, 1979)

Συμεὼν ἀρχιεπισκόπου Θεσσαλονίκης. Τὰ λειτουργικὰ συγγράμματα, vol. 1: *Εὐχαὶ καὶ ὕμνοι*, ed. I. M. Phountoules (Thessalonike, 1968)

Syndika-Laourda, L. (ed.) "Ἐγκώμιον εἰς τὸν ἀρχιεπίσκοπον Θεσσαλονίκης Γαβριήλ," *Μακεδονικά* 4 (1955–60), 352–70

Syropoulos, Sylvester. *Les "Mémoires" du Grand Ecclésiarque de l'Église de Constantinople Sylvestre Syropoulos sur le concile de Florence (1438–1439)*, ed. and trans. V. Laurent (Paris, 1971)

Tafur, Pero. *Travels and Adventures, 1435–1439*, trans. M. Letts (London, 1926)

Tedaldi, Jacopo. "Informazioni," in *Thesaurus novus anecdotorum*, ed. E. Martène and U. Durand, vol. 1 (Paris, 1717; repr. New York, 1968), cols. 1819–26. English trans. in Jones, *The Siege of Constantinople*, pp. 1–10

Tsaras, J. (ed. and trans.) *Η τελευταία άλωση της Θεσσαλονίκης (1430). Τα κείμενα μεταφρασμένα με εισαγωγικό σημείωμα και σχόλια* (Thessalonike, 1985)

Turan, O. (ed.) *İstanbul'un Fethinden Önce Yazılmış Tarihî Takvimler* (Ankara, 1954)

Tursun Bey. *Târîh-i Ebü'l-Feth*, ed. A. M. Tulum (Istanbul, 1977). Text published in facsimile with English trans. by H. İnalcık and R. Murphey, *The History of Mehmed the Conqueror by Tursun Beg* (Minneapolis and Chicago, 1978)

Zeno, Iacobus. *Vita Caroli Zeni*, ed. G. Zonta, *RIS*, 19/6 (Bologna, 1940)

Zoras, G. Th. (ed.) *Χρονικὸν περὶ τῶν τούρκων σουλτάνων (κατὰ τὸν Βαρβερινὸν Κώδικα 111)* (Athens, 1958). English trans. M. Philippides, *Byzantium, Europe, and the Early Ottoman Sultans, 1373–1513: An Anonymous Greek Chronicle of the Seventeenth Century (The Barberini Codex 111)* (New Rochelle, 1990)

II. SECONDARY WORKS

Ahrweiler, H. *L'idéologie politique de l'Empire byzantin* (Paris, 1975)
"La région de Philadelphie au XIVe siècle (1290–1390). Dernier bastion de l'Hellénisme en Asie Mineure," *Comptes Rendus de l'Académie des Inscriptions et Belles-Lettres* (1983), 175–97

Alderson, A. D. *The Structure of the Ottoman Dynasty* (Oxford, 1956)

Alexandrescu-Dersca, M. *La campagne de Timur en Anatolie* (1402) (Bucharest, 1942; 2nd edn., London, 1977)

Alexandrescu-Dersca Bulgaru, M. M. "L'action diplomatique et militaire de Venise pour la défense de Constantinople (1452–1453)," *Revue Roumaine d'Histoire* 13 (1974), 247–67

"La politique démographique des sultans à Istanbul (1453–1496)," *RESEE* 28 (1990), 45–56

Amantos, K. "Ἡ ἀναγνώρισις ὑπὸ τῶν μωαμεθανῶν θρησκευτικῶν καὶ πολιτικῶν δικαιωμάτων τῶν χριστιανῶν καὶ ὁ ὁρισμὸς τοῦ Σινὰν Πασᾶ," *Ἠπειρωτικὰ Χρονικὰ* 5 (1930), 197–210

Anastos, M. V. "Pletho's calendar and liturgy," *DOP* 4 (1948), 183–305

Andréadès, A. "De la population de Constantinople sous les empereurs byzantins," *Metron* 1/2 (1920), 68–119

Angelov, D. "Certains aspects de la conquête des peuples balkaniques par les Turcs," *BS* 17 (1956), 220–75

Angold, M. "Archons and dynasts: local aristocracies and the cities of the later Byzantine Empire," in *The Byzantine Aristocracy, IX to XIII Centuries*, ed. M. Angold (Oxford, 1984), pp. 236–53

"The decline of Byzantium seen through the eyes of western travellers," in *Travel in the Byzantine World*, ed. R. Macrides (Aldershot, 2002), pp. 213–32

Antoniadis-Bibicou, H. *Recherches sur les douanes à Byzance* (Paris, 1963)

Arbel, B., Hamilton, B., and Jacoby, D. (eds.) *Latins and Greeks in the Eastern Mediterranean after 1204* (London, 1989)

Ashtor, E. *Levant Trade in the Later Middle Ages* (Princeton, 1983)

Atiya, A. S. *The Crusade of Nicopolis* (London, 1934)

Babinger, F. *Beiträge zur Frühgeschichte der Türkenherrschaft in Rumelien (14.–15. Jahrhundert)* (Munich and Vienna, 1944)

Mehmed the Conqueror and his Time, trans. R. Manheim (Princeton, 1978)

"Nilüfer Khatun," *EI*, vol. VI (Leiden, 1927; repr. 1987), p. 921

"Sawdji," *EI*, vol. VII (Leiden, 1927; repr. 1987), p. 192

"Von Amurath zu Amurath. Vor- und Nachspiel der Schlacht bei Varna (1444)," *Oriens* 3/2 (1950), 229–65

Bakirtzis, Ch. "The urban continuity and size of late Byzantine Thessalonike," *DOP* 57 (2003), 35–64

Balard, M. "Constantinople vue par les témoins du siège de 1453," in *Constantinople and its Hinterland*, ed. C. Mango and G. Dagron (Aldershot, 1995), pp. 169–77

"The Genoese in the Aegean (1204–1566)," in *Latins and Greeks in the Eastern Mediterranean after 1204*, ed. B. Arbel, B. Hamilton, and D. Jacoby (London, 1989), pp. 158–74

"L'organisation des colonies étrangères dans l'Empire byzantin (XIIe–XVe siècle)," in *Hommes et richesses dans l'Empire byzantin*, vol. II, ed. V. Kravari, J. Lefort, and C. Morrisson (Paris, 1991), pp. 261–76

La Romanie génoise (XIIe–début du XVe siècle), 2 vols. (Rome and Genoa, 1978)

"La société pérote aux XIVe–XVe siècles: autour des Demerode et des Draperio," in *Byzantine Constantinople: Monuments, Topography and Everyday Life*, ed. N. Necipoğlu (Leiden, Boston, and Cologne, 2001), pp. 299–311

Balivet, M. "L'expédition de Mehmed Ier contre Thessalonique: convergences et contradictions des sources byzantines et turques," *Comité International d'Études Pré-Ottomanes et Ottomanes: VIth Symposium, Cambridge, 1–4 July*

1984 (Istanbul, Paris, and Leiden, 1987), pp. 31–7 (reprinted in M. Balivet, *Byzantins et Ottomans: relations, interaction, succession* [Istanbul, 1999], pp. 89–95)

"Le personnage du 'turcophile' dans les sources byzantines antérieures au Concile de Florence (1370–1430)," *Travaux et Recherches en Turquie* 2 (1984), 111–29 (reprinted in *Byzantins et Ottomans*, pp. 31–47)

Romanie byzantine et pays de Rûm turc: histoire d'un espace d'imbrication gréco-turque (Istanbul, 1994)

Baloglou, Ch. P. *Georgios Gemistos-Plethon: Ökonomisches Denken in der spätbyzantinischen Geisteswelt* (Athens, 1998)

Barkan, Ö. L. "Essai sur les données statistiques des registres de recensement dans l'Empire Ottoman aux XVe et XVIe siècles," *Journal of Economic and Social History of the Orient* 1 (1957), 9–36

"Osmanlı İmparatorluğunda bir iskân ve kolonizasyon metodu olarak sürgünler," *İstanbul Üniversitesi İktisat Fakültesi Mecmuası* 11 (1949–50), 524–69; 13 (1951–2), 56–79; 15 (1953–4), 209–37

"Osmanlı İmparatorluğunda bir iskân ve kolonizasyon metodu olarak vakıflar ve temlikler," *Vakıflar Dergisi* 2 (1942), 279–386

"Tımar," *İslam Ansiklopedisi*, vol. XII (Istanbul, 1972–3), pp. 286–333

Barker, J. W. "John VII in Genoa: a problem in late Byzantine source confusion," *OCP* 28 (1962), 213–38

"Late Byzantine Thessalonike: a second city's challenges and responses," *DOP* 57 (2003), 5–33

Manuel II Palaeologus (1391–1425). A Study in Late Byzantine Statesmanship (New Brunswick, NJ, 1969)

"Miscellaneous Genoese documents on the Levantine world of the late fourteenth and early fifteenth centuries," *ByzSt* 6 (1979), 49–82

"The 'Monody' of Demetrios Kydones on the Zealot rising of 1345 in Thessaloniki," in *Essays in Memory of Basil Laourdas* (Thessalonike, 1975), pp. 285–300

"On the chronology of the activities of Manuel II Palaeologus in the Peloponnesus in 1415," *BZ* 55 (1962), 39–55

"The problem of appanages in Byzantium during the Palaiologan period," Βυζαντινά 3 (1971), 103–22

"The question of ethnic antagonisms among Balkan states of the fourteenth century," in *Peace and War in Byzantium. Essays in Honor of George T. Dennis, S.J.*, ed. T. S. Miller and J. Nesbitt (Washington, DC, 1995), pp. 165–77

Bartusis, M. C. "The cost of late Byzantine warfare and defense," *BF* 16 (1991), 75–89

Exaleimma: escheat in Byzantium," *DOP* 40 (1986), 55–81

The Late Byzantine Army: Arms and Society, 1204–1453 (Philadelphia, 1992)

Bees, N. A. "Διορθώσεις καὶ παρατηρήσεις εἰς ἀφιερωτήριον τοῦ 1375 ἔτους πρὸς τὴν ἐν Μυστρᾷ Μονὴν τῆς Παναγίας τοῦ Βροντοχίου," *Νέα Σιών* 5 (1907), 241–8

Beldiceanu, N. "Margarid: un timar monastique," *REB* 33 (1975), 227–55 (reprinted in N. Beldiceanu, *Le monde ottoman des Balkans (1402–1566). Institutions, société, économie* [London, 1976], Study XIV)

Le timar dans l'État ottoman (début XIVe–début XVIe siècle) (Wiesbaden, 1980)

Beldiceanu, N. and Beldiceanu-Steinherr, I. "Colonisation et déportation dans l'État ottoman (XIVe–début XVIe siècle)," in *Coloniser au Moyen Âge*, ed. M. Balard and A. Ducellier (Paris, 1995), pp. 172–85

"Un Paléologue inconnu de la région de Serres," *B* 41 (1971), 5–17 (reprinted in N. Beldiceanu, *Le monde ottoman des Balkans*, Study XIII)

Beldiceanu-Steinherr, I. "La conquête d'Andrinople par les Turcs: la pénétration turque en Thrace et la valeur des chroniques ottomanes," *TM* 1 (1965), 439–61

"Un acte concernant la surveillance des Dardanelles," *Institut Français de Damas, Bulletin d'Etudes Orientales* 29 (1977), 17–24

Bendall, S. "A coin of Constantine XI," *The Numismatic Circular* 82/5 (1974), 188–9

"The coinage of Constantine XI," *Revue Numismatique*, 6e série, 33 (1991), 134–42

Bernicolas-Hatzopoulos, D. "The first siege of Constantinople by the Ottomans (1394–1402) and its repercussions on the civilian population of the city," *ByzSt* 10/1 (1983), 39–51

Bertelè, G. (ed.) *Il Libro dei Conti di Giacomo Badoer (Costantinopoli 1436–1440). Complemento e indici* (Padua, 2002)

Bertelè, T. "Il giro d'affari di Giacomo Badoer: precisazioni e deduzioni," *Akten des XI. internationalen Byzantinistenkongresses, München 1958* (Munich, 1960), pp. 48–57

Numismatique byzantine, suivie de deux études inédites sur les monnaies des Paléologues, ed. C. Morrisson (Wetteren, 1978)

Bisaha, N. *Creating East and West: Renaissance Humanists and the Ottoman Turks* (Philadelphia, 2004)

Bon, A. *La Morée franque. Recherches historiques, topographiques et archéologiques sur la principauté d'Achaïe (1205–1430)*, 2 vols. (Paris, 1969)

Božilov, I. "La famille des Asen (1186–1460). Généalogie et prosopographie," *Bulgarian Historical Review* 9 (1981), 135–56

Browning, R. "A note on the capture of Constantinople in 1453," *B* 22 (1952), 379–86

Bryer, A. "Greek historians on the Turks: the case of the first Byzantine–Ottoman marriage," in *The Writing of History in the Middle Ages: Essays Presented to Richard William Southern*, ed. R. H. C. Davis and J. M. Wallace-Hadrill (Oxford, 1981), pp. 471–93 (reprinted in A. Bryer, *Peoples and Settlement in Anatolia and the Caucasus* [London, 1988], Study IV)

"The late Byzantine monastery in town and countryside," in *The Church in Town and Countryside*, ed. D. Baker (= *Studies in Church History* 16) (Oxford, 1979), pp. 219–41

Bryer, A. and Lowry, H. (eds.) *Continuity and Change in Late Byzantine and Early Ottoman Society* (Birmingham and Washington, DC, 1986)

Burke, J. and Scott, R. (eds.) *Byzantine Macedonia: Identity, Image and History. Papers from the Melbourne Conference July 1995* (Melbourne, 2000)

Carroll, M. "Constantine XI Palaeologus: some problems of image," in *Maistor. Classical, Byzantine and Renaissance Studies for Robert Browning*, ed. A. Moffatt (Canberra, 1984), pp. 329–43

Cazacu, M. "Les parentés byzantines et ottomanes de l'historien Laonikos Chalkokondyle (c. 1423–c. 1470)," *Turcica* 16 (1984), 95–114

Charanis, P. "An important short chronicle of the fourteenth century," *B* 13 (1938), 335–62 (reprinted in P. Charanis, *Social, Economic and Political Life in the Byzantine Empire* [London, 1973], Study XVII)

"Internal strife in Byzantium during the fourteenth century," *B* 15 (1941), 208–30 (reprinted in *Social, Economic and Political Life*, Study VI)

"The monastic properties and the state in the Byzantine Empire," *DOP* 4 (1948), 53–118 (reprinted in *Social, Economic and Political Life*, Study I)

"The role of the people in the political life of the Byzantine Empire: the period of the Comneni and the Palaeologi," *ByzSt* 5 (1978), 69–79

"The strife among the Palaeologi and the Ottoman Turks, 1370–1402," *B* 16 (1942–3), 286–314 (reprinted in *Social, Economic and Political Life*, Study XIX)

Chasin, M. "The Crusade of Varna," in *A History of the Crusades*, gen. ed. K. M. Setton, vol. VI: *The Impact of the Crusades in Europe*, ed. H. W. Hazard and N. P. Zacour (Madison, 1989), pp. 276–310

Cheynet, J.-Cl., Malamut, E., and Morrisson, C. "Prix et salaires à Byzance (Xe–XVe siècle)," in *Hommes et richesses dans l'Empire byzantin*, vol. II, ed. V. Kravari, J. Lefort, and C. Morrisson (Paris, 1991), pp. 339–74

Chrysostomides, J. "Corinth 1394–1397: some new facts," Βυζαντινά 7 (1975), 83–110

"Studies on the Chronicle of Caroldo, with special reference to the history of Byzantium from 1370 to 1377," *OCP* 35 (1969), 123–82

"Venetian commercial privileges under the Palaeologi," *StVen* 12 (1970), 267–356

Dalleggio, d'Alessio, E. "Galata et la souveraineté de Byzance," *REB* 19 (1961), 315–27

"Le texte grec du traité conclu par les Génois de Galata avec Mehmet II le 1er Juin 1453," Ἑλληνικά 11 (1939), 115–24

"Traité entre les Génois de Galata et Mehmet II (1er juin 1453). Versions et commentaires," *Echos d'Orient* 39 (1940), 161–75

Delilbaşı, M. "Selânik ve Yanya'da Osmanlı egemenliğinin kurulması," *Belleten* 51 (1987), 75–106

"Selânik'in Venedik idaresine geçmesi ve Osmanlı-Venedik savaşı," *Belleten* 40 (1976), 573–88 (reprinted in M. Delilbaşı, *Johannis Anagnostis, "Selânik (Thessaloniki)'in Son Zaptı Hakkında Bir Tarih" (Sultan II. Murad Dönemine Ait Bir Bizans Kaynağı)* [Ankara, 1989], pp. 1–16)

Dennis, G. T. "The deposition and restoration of Patriarch Matthew I, 1402–1403," *BF* 2 (1967), 100–6 (reprinted in G. T. Dennis, *Byzantium and the Franks, 1350–1420* [London, 1982], Study IV)

"The late Byzantine metropolitans of Thessalonike," *DOP* 57 (2003), 255–64

The Reign of Manuel II Palaeologus in Thessalonica, 1382–1387 (Rome, 1960)

"Rhadenos of Thessalonica, correspondent of Demetrius Cydones," Βυζαντινά 13 (1985), 261–72

"The second Turkish capture of Thessalonica. 1391, 1394 or 1430?," *BZ* 57 (1964), 53–61 (reprinted in *Byzantium and the Franks*, Study V)

De Vries-van der Velden, E. *L'élite byzantine devant l'avance Turque à l'époque de la guerre civile de 1341 à 1354* (Amsterdam, 1989)

Dimitriades, V. "Ottoman Chalkidiki: an area in transition," in *Continuity and Change in Late Byzantine and Early Ottoman Society*, ed. A. Bryer and H. Lowry (Birmingham and Washington, DC, 1986), pp. 39–50

"Φορολογικὲς κατηγορίες τῶν Χωριῶν τῆς Θεσσαλονίκης κατὰ τὴν Τουρκοκρατία," *Μακεδονικά* 20 (1980), 375–462

Djurić, I. *Le crépuscule de Byzance* (Paris, 1996)

Dölger, F. "Johannes VII., Kaiser der Rhomäer 1390–1408," *BZ* 31 (1931), 21–36

"Politische und geistige Strömungen im sterbenden Byzanz," *Jahrbuch der Österreichischen Byzantinischen Gesellschaft* 3 (1954), 3–18

"Zum Aufstand des Andronikos IV. gegen seinen Vater Johannes V. im Mai 1373," *REB* 19 (1961), 328–32

Ducellier, A. "L'Islam et les Musulmans vus de Byzance au XIVe siècle," *Actes du XIVe Congrès international des études byzantines, Bucarest, 1971*, vol. II (Bucharest, 1975), pp. 79–85

Emrich, G. "Michael Kritobulos, der byzantinische Geschichtsschreiber Mehmeds II.," *Materialia Turcica* 1 (1975), 35–43

Failler, A. "Une donation des époux Sanianoi au monastère des Hodègoi," *REB* 34 (1976), 111–17

Fassoulakis, S. *The Byzantine Family of Raoul-Ral(l)es* (Athens, 1973)

Fedalto, G. *Ricerche storiche sulla posizione giuridiche ed ecclesiastica dei Greci a Venezia nei secoli XV e XVI* (Florence, 1967)

Fine, J. V. A. *The Late Medieval Balkans: A Critical Survey from the Late Twelfth Century to the Ottoman Conquest* (Ann Arbor, 1987)

Fleet, K. *European and Islamic Trade in the Early Ottoman State. The Merchants of Genoa and Turkey* (Cambridge, 1999)

"Italian perceptions of the Turks in the fourteenth and fifteenth centuries," *Journal of Mediterranean Studies* 5/2 (1995), 159–72

"The treaty of 1387 between Murad I and the Genoese," *Bulletin of the School of Oriental and African Studies* 56/1 (1993), 13–33

Francès, E. "Constantinople byzantine aux XIVe et XVe siècles. Population, commerce, métiers," *RESEE* 7/2 (1969), 405–12

"La féodalité byzantine et la conquête turque," *Studia et acta orientalia* 4 (1962), 69–90

Ganchou, Th. "Autonomie locale et relations avec les Latins à Byzance au XIVe siècle: Iôannès Limpidarios/Libadarios, Ainos et les Draperio de Péra," in *Chemins d'outre-mer. Études d'histoire sur la Méditerranée médiévale offertes à Michel Balard*, vol. 1 (Paris, 2004), pp. 353–74

"Autour de Jean VII: luttes dynastiques, interventions étrangères et résistance orthodoxe à Byzance (1373–1409)," in *Coloniser au Moyen Âge*, ed. M. Balard and A. Ducellier (Paris, 1995), pp. 367–85

"Le mésazon Démétrius Paléologue Cantacuzène, a-t-il figuré parmi les défenseurs du siège de Constantinople (29 mai 1453)?," *REB* 52 (1994), 245–72

"Le rachat des Notaras après la chute de Constantinople ou les relations 'étrangères' de l'élite byzantine au XVe siècle," in *Migrations et diasporas méditerranéennes (Xe–XVIe siècles)*, ed. M. Balard and A. Ducellier (Paris, 2002), pp. 149–229

"Sur quelques erreurs relatives aux derniers défenseurs grecs de Constantinople en 1453," Θησαυρίσματα 25 (1995), 70–6

Geanakoplos, D. J. *Byzantine East and Latin West: Two Worlds of Christendom in the Middle Ages and Renaissance. Studies in Ecclesiastical and Cultural History* (New York, 1976)

"The Council of Florence (1438–1439) and the problem of union between the Byzantine and Latin churches," in D. J. Geanakoplos, *Constantinople and the West: Essays on the Late Byzantine (Palaeologan) and Italian Renaissances and the Byzantine and Roman Churches* (Madison, WI, 1989), pp. 224–54

Interaction of the "Sibling" Byzantine and Western Cultures in the Middle Ages and Italian Renaissance (330–1600) (New Haven and London, 1976)

Gill, J. "The 'Acta' and the Memoirs of Syropoulos as history," *OCP* 14 (1948), 303–55 (reprinted in J. Gill, *Church Union: Rome and Byzantium (1204–1453)* [London, 1979], Study XII)

Byzantium and the Papacy, 1198–1400 (New Brunswick, NJ, 1979)

The Council of Florence (Cambridge, 1959; repr. with corrigenda, New York, 1982)

"John V Palaeologus at the court of Louis I of Hungary (1366)," *BS* 38 (1977), 31–8 (reprinted in *Church Union*, Study IX)

"John VI Cantacuzenus and the Turks," Βυζαντινά 13 (1985), 55–76

Personalities of the Council of Florence and Other Essays (London, 1964)

"Venice, Genoa and Byzantium," *BF* 10 (1985), 53–73

Gökbilgin, M. T. *Rumeli'de Yürükler, Tatarlar ve Evlâd-ı Fâtihân* (Istanbul, 1957)

Grecu, V. "Georgios Sphrantzes. Leben und Werk. Makarios Melissenos und sein Werk," *BS* 26 (1965), 62–73

"Kritobulos aus Imbros," *BS* 18 (1957), 1–17

"Pour une meilleure connaissance de l'historien Doukas," in *Mémorial Louis Petit* (Paris, 1948), pp. 128–41

Guilland, R. "Les appels de Constantin XI Paléologue à Rome et à Venise pour sauver Constantinople (1452–1453)," *BS* 14 (1953), 226–44

Halecki, O. *The Crusade of Varna. A Discussion of Controversial Problems* (New York, 1943)

Un Empereur de Byzance à Rome. Vingt ans de travail pour l'union des églises et pour la défense de l'Empire d'Orient, 1355–1375 (Warsaw, 1930; repr. London, 1972)

Harris, J. *Greek Emigres in the West, 1400–1520* (Camberley, 1995)

"Laonikos Chalkokondyles and the rise of the Ottoman Turks," *BMGS* 27 (2003), 153–70

Hendy, M. F. *Studies in the Byzantine Monetary Economy, c. 300–1453* (Cambridge, 1985)

Hero, A. C. "The first Byzantine eyewitness account of the Ottoman institution of *devşirme*: the homily of Isidore of Thessalonike concerning the 'Seizure of the Children'," in *TO EΛΛHNIKON. Studies in Honor of Speros Vryonis, Jr.*, vol. I, ed. J. S. Langdon, S. W. Reinert, J. S. Allen, and C. P. Ioannides (New Rochelle, 1993), pp. 135–43

Heyd, W. *Histoire du commerce du Levant au Moyen Âge*, 2 vols. (Leipzig, 1885–6; repr. Amsterdam, 1967)

Hohlweg, A. "Der Kreuzzug des Jahres 1444," in *Die Türkei in Europa*, ed. K.-D. Grothusen (Göttingen, 1979), pp. 20–37

Hopf, K. *Geschichte Griechenlands vom Beginn des Mittelalters bis auf unserer Zeit*, 2 vols., in *Allgemeine Encyklopädie der Wissenschaften und Künste*, ed. J. S. Ersch and J. G. Gruber, vols. LXXXV–LXXXVI (Leipzig, 1867–8)

Hrochová, V. "Le commerce vénitien et les changements dans l'importance des centres de commerce en Grèce du 13e au 15e siècles," *StVen* 9 (1967), 3–34

"Some specific features of Byzantine cities in the 13th till 15th centuries," *BS* 55 (1994), 347–59

Hunger, H. "Zeitgeschichte in der Rhetorik des sterbenden Byzanz," *Wiener Archiv für Geschichte des Slawentums und Osteuropas* 3 (1959), 152–61

Iliescu, O. "Le montant du tribut payé par Byzance à l'Empire Ottoman en 1379 et 1424," *RESEE* 9 (1971), 427–32

Imber, C. *The Ottoman Empire, 1300–1481* (Istanbul, 1990)

İnalcık, H. "Bāyazīd I," *EI*, vol. I, 2nd edn. (Leiden, 1959), pp. 1117–19

"Byzantium and the origins of the crisis of 1444 under the light of Turkish sources," *Actes du XIIe Congrès international d'études byzantines*, vol. II (Belgrade, 1964), pp. 159–63

"The conquest of Edirne (1361)," *Archivum Ottomanicum* 3 (1971), 185–210 (reprinted in H. İnalcık, *The Ottoman Empire: Conquest, Organization and Economy* [London, 1978], Study III)

Fatih Devri Üzerinde Tetkikler ve Vesikalar (Ankara, 1954)

"Gelibolu," *EI*, vol. II, 2nd edn. (Leiden, 1965), pp. 983–7

"Greeks in the Ottoman economy and finances 1453–1500," in *TO EΛΛH-NIKON. Studies in Honor of Speros Vryonis, Jr.*, vol. II, ed. J. S. Allen, C. P. Ioannides, J. S. Langdon, and S. W. Reinert (New Rochelle, 1993), pp. 307–19

"How to read 'Āshık Pasha-zāde's History," in *Studies in Ottoman History in Honour of Professor V. L. Ménage*, ed. C. Heywood and C. Imber (Istanbul, 1994), pp. 139–56

"Istanbul," *EI*, vol. IV, 2nd edn. (Leiden, 1973), pp. 224–48

"Mehmed the Conqueror (1432–1481) and his time," *Speculum* 35 (1960), 408–27

"Notes on N. Beldiceanu's translation of the *Kanūnnāme*, fonds turc ancien 39, Bibliothèque Nationale, Paris," *Der Islam* 43 (1967), 139–57

The Ottoman Empire: The Classical Age 1300–1600 (New York and Washington, 1973)

"Ottoman Galata, 1453–1553," in *Première rencontre internationale sur l'Empire Ottoman et la Turquie moderne*, ed. E. Eldem (Istanbul and Paris, 1991), pp. 17–116

"Ottoman methods of conquest," *Studia Islamica* 2 (1953), 103–29 (reprinted in *Ottoman Empire*, Study I)

"The Ottoman state: economy and society, 1300–1600," in *An Economic and Social History of the Ottoman Empire, 1300–1914*, ed. H. İnalcık and D. Quataert (Cambridge, 1994), pp. 9–409

"The Ottoman Turks and the Crusades, 1329–1451" and "The Ottoman Turks and the Crusades, 1451–1522," in *A History of the Crusades*, gen. ed. K. M. Setton, vol. VI: *The Impact of the Crusades on Europe*, ed. H. W. Hazard and N. P. Zacour (Madison, 1989), pp. 222–75 and 311–53

"An outline of Ottoman–Venetian relations," in *Venezia, centro di mediazione tra Oriente e Occidente (secoli XV–XVI). Aspetti e problemi*, ed. H.-G. Beck, M. Manoussacas, and A. Pertusi, vol. I (Florence, 1977), pp. 83–90

"The policy of Mehmed II toward the Greek population of Istanbul and the Byzantine buildings of the city," *DOP* 23–4 (1969–70), 231–49 (reprinted in *Ottoman Empire*, Study VI)

"The question of the emergence of the Ottoman state," *International Journal of Turkish Studies* 2/2 (1981–2), 71–9 (reprinted in H. İnalcık, *Studies in Ottoman Social and Economic History* [London, 1985], Study I)

Review of J. W. Barker, *Manuel II Palaeologus (1391–1425): A Study in Late Byzantine Statesmanship*, in *Archivum Ottomanicum* 3 (1971), 272–85

"The rise of Ottoman historiography," in *Historians of the Middle East*, ed. B. Lewis and P. M. Holt (London, 1962), pp. 152–67

"The rise of the Turcoman maritime principalities in Anatolia, Byzantium, and the Crusades," *BF* 9 (1985), 179–217 (reprinted in H. İnalcık, *The Middle East and the Balkans under the Ottoman Empire. Essays on Economy and Society* [Bloomington, 1993], pp. 309–41)

"Sources for fifteenth-century Turkish economic and social history," in İnalcık, *Middle East and the Balkans*, pp. 177–93

"The status of the Greek Orthodox patriarch under the Ottomans," *Turcica* 21–3 (1991), 407–36

"Tursun Beg, historian of Mehmed the Conqueror's time," *WZKM* 69 (1977), 55–71

"The Yürüks: their origins, expansion and economic role," in *Oriental Carpets and Textile Studies*, vol. II: *Carpets of the Mediterranean Countries, 1400–1600*, ed. R. Pinner and W. B. Denny (London, 1986), pp. 39–65 (reprinted in *Middle East and the Balkans*, pp. 97–136)

Iorga, N. *Byzance après Byzance* (Paris, 1992)

Izeddin, M. "Notes sur les mariages princiers en Orient au moyen âge," *Journal asiatique* 257 (1969), 139–56

Jacoby, D. "Les archontes grecs et la féodalité en Morée franque," *TM* 2 (1967), 421–81 (reprinted in D. Jacoby, *Société et démographie à Byzance et en Romanie latine (XIIIe–XVe siècle)* [London, 1975], Study VI)

"The encounter of two societies: western conquerors and Byzantines in the Peloponnesus after the Fourth Crusade," *The American Historical Review* 78/4 (1973), 873–906 (reprinted in D. Jacoby, *Recherches sur la Méditerranée orientale du XIIe au XVe siècle. Peuples, sociétés, économies* [London, 1979], Study II)

"Les états latins en Romanie: phénomènes sociaux et économiques (1204–1350 environ)," in *XVe Congrès international d'études byzantines. Rapports et corapports*, vol. 1.3 (Athens, 1976) (reprinted in *Recherches*, Study I)

La féodalité en Grèce médiévale. Les "Assises de Romanie": sources, application et diffusion (Paris and The Hague, 1971)

"Foreigners and the urban economy in Thessalonike, ca. 1150 – ca. 1450," *DOP* 57 (2003), 85–132

"Les Génois dans l'Empire byzantin: citoyens, sujets et protégés (1261–1453)," *La Storia dei Genovesi* 9 (1989), 245–84 (reprinted in D. Jacoby, *Trade, Commodities and Shipping in the Medieval Mediterranean* [Aldershot, 1997], Study III)

"La population de Constantinople à l'époque byzantine: un problème de démographie urbaine," *B* 31 (1961), 81–109 (reprinted in *Société et démographie*, Study I)

"Thessalonique de la domination de Byzance à celle de Venise. Continuité, adaptation ou rupture?," in *Mélanges Gilbert Dagron* (= *TM* 14) (Paris, 2002), pp. 303–18

"Les Vénitiens naturalisés dans l'Empire byzantin: un aspect de l'expansion de Venise en Romanie du XIIIe au milieu du XVe siècle," *TM* 8 (1981), 217–35 (reprinted in D. Jacoby, *Studies on the Crusader States and on Venetian Expansion* [Northampton, 1989], Study IX)

Janin, R. *Constantinople byzantine: développement urbain et répertoire topographique*, 2nd edn. (Paris, 1964)

Les églises et les monastères des grands centres byzantins (Paris, 1975)

La géographie ecclésiastique de l'Empire byzantin. Première partie: Le siège de Constantinople et le patriarcat œcuménique, vol. III: *Les églises et les monastères*, 2nd edn. (Paris, 1969)

Johnson, J. T. and Kelsay, J. (eds.) *Just War and Jihad: Historical and Theoretical Perspectives on War and Peace in Western and Islamic Traditions* (New York, 1991)

Jones, J. R. "Literary evidence for the coinage of Constantine XI," *The Numismatic Circular* 75/4 (1967), 97

Kafadar, C. "A death in Venice (1575): Anatolian Muslim merchants trading in the Serenissima," in *Raiyyet Rüsûmu. Essays presented to Halil İnalcık* (= *Journal of Turkish Studies* 10 [1986]), pp. 191–218

Between Two Worlds: The Construction of the Ottoman State (Berkeley, Los Angeles, and London, 1995)

Kalligas, H. *Byzantine Monemvasia. The Sources* (Monemvasia, 1990)
   "Monemvasia, seventh–fifteenth centuries," in *The Economic History of Byzantium: From the Seventh through the Fifteenth Century*, vol. II, ed. A. E. Laiou (Washington, DC, 2002), pp. 879–97
Karlin-Hayter, P. "La politique religieuse des conquérants ottomans dans un texte hagiographique (c.1437)," *B* 35 (1965), 353–8
Kazhdan, A. "The Italian and late Byzantine city," *DOP* 49 (1995), 1–22
Khadduri, M. *War and Peace in the Law of Islam* (Baltimore, 1955)
Kianka, F. "The *Apology* of Demetrius Cydones: a fourteenth-century autobiographical source," *ByzSt* 7/1 (1980), 57–71
   "Byzantine–Papal diplomacy: the role of Demetrius Cydones," *The International History Review* 7 (1985), 175–213
   "Demetrios Kydones and Italy," *DOP* 49 (1995), 99–110
   "Demetrius Cydones (c.1324 – c.1397): intellectual and diplomatic relations between Byzantium and the West in the fourteenth century," unpublished PhD thesis, Fordham University (1981)
Kioussopoulou, T. (ed.) *1453. Η άλωση της Κωνσταντινούπολης και η μετάβαση από τους μεσαιωνικούς στους νεώτερους χρόνους* (Iraklion, 2005)
Kissling, H. J. "Das Renegatentum in der Glanzzeit des Osmanischen Reiches," *Scientia* 96 (1961), 18–26
Klopf, M. "The army in Constantinople at the accession of Constantine XI," *B* 40 (1970), 385–92
Kolias, G. "Ή ἀνταρσία Ἰωάννου Ζ΄ Παλαιολόγου ἐναντίον Ἰωάννου Ε΄ Παλαιολόγου (1390)," *Ἑλληνικά* 12 (1951), 36–64
Krekić, B. "Contribution à l'étude des Asanès à Byzance," *TM* 5 (1973), 347–55
   "Monemvasie sous la protection papale," *ZRVI* 6 (1960), 129–35
   "A note on the economic activities of some Greeks in the Latin Levant towards the end of the XIVth century," *StVen* 9 (1967), 187–91
Laiou, A. E. "The agrarian economy, thirteenth–fifteenth centuries," in *The Economic History of Byzantium: From the Seventh through the Fifteenth Century*, vol. II, ed. A. E. Laiou (Washington, DC, 2002), pp. 311–75
   "The Byzantine aristocracy in the Palaeologan period: a story of arrested development," *Viator* 4 (1973), 131–51 (reprinted in A. E. Laiou, *Gender, Society and Economic Life in Byzantium* [Aldershot, 1992], Study VI)
   Constantinople and the Latins; The Foreign Policy of Andronicus II, 1282–1328 (Cambridge, MA, 1972)
   "Economic activities of Vatopedi in the fourteenth century," in *Ιερά Μονή Βατοπεδίου. Ιστορία και Τέχνη* (Athens, 1999), pp. 55–72
   "Economic concerns and attitudes of the intellectuals of Thessalonike," *DOP* 57 (2003), 205–23
   "The economy of Byzantine Macedonia in the Palaiologan period," in *Byzantine Macedonia: Identity, Image and History. Papers from the Melbourne Conference July 1995*, ed. J. Burke and R. Scott (Melbourne, 2000), pp. 199–211

"From 'Roman' to 'Hellene'," *The Byzantine Fellowship Lectures* 1 (1974), 13–28

"In search of the Byzantine economy: assumptions, methods and models of social and economic history," in *Bilan et perspectives des études médiévales en Europe. Actes du premier Congrès européen d'Études Médiévales (Spoleto, 27–29 mai 1993)*, ed. J. Hamesse (Louvain-la-Neuve, 1995), pp. 43–64

"In the medieval Balkans: economic pressures and conflicts in the fourteenth century," in *Byzantina kai Metabyzantina*, vol. IV: *Byzantine Studies in Honor of Milton V. Anastos*, ed. Sp. Vryonis, Jr., (Malibu, 1985), pp. 137–62 (reprinted in *Gender, Society and Economic Life*, Study IX)

"Observations on the results of the Fourth Crusade: Greeks and Latins in port and market," *Medievalia et humanistica*, n.s. 12 (1984), 47–60

"The role of women in Byzantine society," *JÖB* 31 (1981), 233–60 (reprinted in *Gender, Society and Economic Life*, Study I)

"Ἡ Θεσσαλονίκη, ἡ ἐνδοχώρα της καί ὁ οἰκονομικός της χῶρος στήν ἐποχή τῶν Παλαιολόγων," in *Διεθνές Συμπόσιο Βυζαντινή Μακεδονία, 324–1430 μ.Χ.* (Thessalonike, 1995), pp. 183–94

Laiou, A. E. (ed.), *Urbs Capta: The Fourth Crusade and its Consequences. La IVe Croisade et ses conséquences* (Paris, 2005)

Laiou-Thomadakis, A. E. "The Byzantine economy in the Mediterranean trade system, thirteenth–fifteenth centuries," *DOP* 34–5 (1982), 177–222 (reprinted in Laiou, *Gender, Society and Economic Life*, Study VII)

"The Greek merchant of the Palaeologan period: a collective portrait," *Πρακτικά τῆς Ἀκαδημίας Ἀθηνῶν* 57 (1982), 96–132 (reprinted in *Gender, Society and Economic Life*, Study VIII)

Peasant Society in the Late Byzantine Empire: A Social and Demographic Study (Princeton, 1977)

Lampros, Sp. "Ὁ βυζαντιακός οἶκος Γουδέλη," *NE* 13 (1916), 211–21

Lane, F. C. *Venice: A Maritime Republic* (Baltimore and London, 1973)

Laourdas, B. "Ὁ Γαβριήλ Θεσσαλονίκης. Βιογραφικά," *Ἀθηνᾶ* 66 (1952), 199–214

Laskaris, M. Th. "Ναοὶ καὶ μοναὶ Θεσσαλονίκης τὸ 1405 εἰς τὸ Ὁδοιπορικὸν τοῦ ἐκ Σμολένσκ Ἰγνατίου," in *Τόμος Κωνσταντίνου Ἀρμενοπούλου* (Thessalonike, 1952), pp. 315–30

"Θεσσαλονίκη καὶ Τάνα," in *Τόμος Κωνσταντίνου Ἀρμενοπούλου* (Thessalonike, 1952), pp. 331–40

Laurent, V. "Alliances et filiations des Cantacuzènes au XVe siècle. Le Vaticanus latinus 4789," *REB* 9 (1952), 47–105

"Le métropolite de Thessalonique Gabriel (1397–1416/19) et le Couvent de la Néa Μονή," *Ἑλληνικά* 13 (1954), 241–55

"Les premiers patriarches de Constantinople sous domination turque (1454–1476)," *REB* 26 (1968), 229–63

"Le trisépiscopat du Patriarche Matthieu Ier (1397–1410). Un grand procès canonique à Byzance au début du XVe siècle," *REB* 30 (1972), 5–166

"Un agent efficace de l'unité de l'église à Florence. Georges Philanthropène," *REB* 17 (1959), 190–5

"Une nouvelle fondation monastique des Choumnos: la *Néa Moni* de Thessalonique," *REB* 13 (1955), 109–27

Lemerle, P. "La domination vénitienne à Thessalonique," in *Miscellanea Giovanni Galbiati*, vol. III (Milan, 1951), pp. 219–25

L'émirat d'Aydin, Byzance et l'Occident (Paris, 1957)

Philippes et la Macédoine orientale à l'époque chrétienne et byzantine (Paris, 1945)

Lock, P. *The Franks in the Aegean, 1204–1500* (London and New York, 1995)

Loenertz, R.-J. "Autour du Chronicon Maius attribué à Georges Phrantzès," in *Miscellanea Giovanni Mercati*, vol. III (Vatican City, 1946), pp. 273–311 (reprinted in R.-J. Loenertz, *Byzantina et Franco-Graeca*, vol. I [Rome, 1970], pp. 3–44)

"Cardinale Morosini et Paul Paléologue Tagaris, patriarches, et Antoine Ballester, vicaire du Pape dans le patriarcat de Constantinople (1332–34 et 1380–87)," *REB* 24 (1966), 224–56 (reprinted in *Byzantina et Franco-Graeca*, vol. I, pp. 573–611)

"Démétrius Cydonès. I: De la naissance à l'année 1373," *OCP* 36 (1970), 47–72; "Démétrius Cydonès. II: De 1373 à 1375," *OCP* 37 (1971), 5–39

"Isidore Glabas, métropolite de Thessalonique (1380–1396)," *REB* 6 (1948), 181–90 (reprinted in *Byzantina et Franco-Graeca*, vol. I, pp. 267–77)

"Jean V Paléologue à Venise (1370–1371)," *REB* 16 (1958), 217–32

"Notes sur le règne de Manuel II à Thessalonique, 1381/82–1387," *BZ* 50 (1957), 390–6

"Pour la chronologie des œuvres de Joseph Bryennios," *REB* 7 (1949), 12–32 (reprinted in *Byzantina et Franco-Graeca*, vol. II [Rome, 1978], pp. 51–75)

"Pour l'histoire du Péloponèse au XIVe siècle (1382–1404)," *Études Byzantines* 1 (1943), 152–96 (reprinted in *Byzantina et Franco-Graeca*, vol. I, pp. 227–65)

"La première insurrection d'Andronic IV Paléologue (1373)," *Echos d'Orient* 38 (1939), 334–45

Longnon, J. *L'Empire latin de Constantinople et la principauté de Morée* (Paris, 1949)

Lowry, H. W. "The fate of Byzantine monastic properties under the Ottomans: examples from Mount Athos, Limnos and Trabzon," *BF* 16 (1990), 275–311 (reprinted in H. W. Lowry, Jr., *Studies in Defterology. Ottoman Society in the Fifteenth and Sixteenth Centuries* [Istanbul, 1992], pp. 247–75)

The Nature of the Early Ottoman State (New York, 2003)

"A note on the population and status of the Athonite monasteries under Ottoman rule (ca. 1520)," *WZKM* 73 (1981), 114–35 (reprinted in *Studies in Defterology*, pp. 229–46)

"The Ottoman *tahrir defterleri* as a source for social and economic history: pitfalls and limitations," in Lowry, *Studies in Defterology*, pp. 3–18

"Portrait of a city: the population and topography of Ottoman Selânik (Thessaloniki) in the year 1478," Δίπτυχα 2 (1980–1), 254–93

"Privilege and property in Ottoman Maçuka in the opening decades of the *Tourkokratia*: 1461–1553," in *Continuity and Change in Late Byzantine and Early Ottoman Society*, ed. A. Bryer and H. Lowry (Birmingham and Washington, DC, 1986), pp. 97–128 (reprinted in *Studies in Defterology*, pp. 131–64)

Luttrell, A. "Appunti sulle compagnie navarresi in Grecia, 1375–1404," *Rivista di studi byzantini e slavi* 3 (1983), 113–27

"Gregory XI and the Turks: 1370–1378," *OCP* 46 (1980), 391–417

"The Latins of Argos and Nauplia: 1311–1394," *Papers of the British School at Rome*, n.s. 21 (1966), 34–55

Macrides, R. "Dowry and inheritance in the late period: some cases from the Patriarchal Register," in *Eherecht und Familiengut in Antike und Mittelalter*, ed. D. Simon (Munich, 1992), pp. 89–98

"Subversion and loyalty in the cult of St. Demetrios," *BS* 51 (1990), 189–97

Magdalino, P. "Some additions and corrections to the list of Byzantine churches and monasteries of Thessalonica," *REB* 35 (1977), 277–85

Makris, G. *Studien zur spätbyzantinischen Schiffahrt* (Genoa, 1988)

Maksimović, Lj. *The Byzantine Provincial Administration under the Palaiologoi* (Amsterdam, 1988)

"Charakter der sozial-wirtschaftlichen Struktur der spätbyzantinischen Stadt (13.–15. Jh.)," *JÖB* 31 (1981), 149–88 (= *XVI. internationaler Byzantin- istenkongress, Akten*, vol. 1/2)

Malamut, E. "Les ambassades du dernier empereur de Byzance," in *Mélanges Gilbert Dagron* (= *TM* 14) (Paris, 2002), pp. 429–48

"Les discours de Démétrius Cydonès comme témoignage de l'idéologie byzan- tine vis-à-vis des peuples de l'Europe orientale dans les années 1360– 1372," in *Byzantium and East Central Europe*, ed. G. Prinzing and M. Salamon (= *Byzantina et Slavica Cracoviensia*, vol. III) (Cracow, 2001), pp. 203–19

Maltezou, C. A. Ὁ Θεσμὸς τοῦ ἐν Κωνσταντινουπόλει Βενετοῦ βαΐλου *(1268–1453)* (Athens, 1970)

"Οἱ ἱστορικὲς περιπέτειες τῆς Κορίνθου στὰ τέλη τοῦ ΙΔ′ αἰῶνα," Σύμμεικτα 3 (1979), 29–51

Mango, C. "Le Diipion. Étude historique et topographique," *REB* 8 (1950), 152–61

Manoussakas, M. "Les derniers défenseurs crétois de Constantinople d'après les documents vénitiens," in *Akten des XI. internationalen Byzantinistenkongresses, München 1958* (Munich, 1960), pp. 331–40

Marinescu, C. "Contribution à l'histoire des relations économiques entre l'Empire byzantin, la Sicile et le royaume de Naples de 1419 à 1453," *Studi bizantini e neoellenici* 5 (1939), 209–19

Masai, F. *Pléthon et le platonisme de Mistra* (Paris, 1956)

Matschke, K.-P. "Chonoxio – Cumicissi – Coumouses – Chomusi – Commussi – Chomus," *Antičnaja drevnost'i srednie veka* 10 (Sverdlovsk, 1973), 181–3

"Commerce, trade, markets, and money: thirteenth–fifteenth centuries," in *The Economic History of Byzantium: From the Seventh through the Fifteenth Century*, ed. A. E. Laiou, vol. II (Washington, DC, 2002), pp. 771–806

"Der Fall von Konstantinopel 1453 in den Rechnungsbüchern der genuesischen Staatschuldenverwaltung," in ΠΟΛΥΠΛΕΥΡΟΣ ΝΟΥΣ. *Miscellanea für Peter Schreiner zu seinem 60. Geburtstag*, ed. C. Scholz and G. Makris (Munich and Leipzig, 2000), pp. 204–20

Fortschritt und Reaktion in Byzanz im 14. Jahrhundert. Konstantinopel in der Bürgerkriegsperiode von 1341 bis 1354 (Berlin, 1971)

"Geldgeschäfte, Handel und Gewerbe in spät-byzantinischen Rechenbüchern und in der spät-byzantinischen Wirklichkeit," *Jahrbuch für Geschichte des Feudalismus* 3 (1979), 181–204

"Griechische Kaufleute im Übergang von der byzantinischen Epoche zur Türkenzeit," in *Bericht über das Kolloquium der Südosteuropa-Kommission, 28.-31. Oktober 1992*, ed. R. Lauer and P. Schreiner (Göttingen, 1996), pp. 73–88

"The late Byzantine urban economy, thirteenth–fifteenth centuries," in *The Economic History of Byzantium: From the Seventh through the Fifteenth Century*, ed. A. E. Laiou, vol. II (Washington, DC, 2002), pp. 463–95

"Leonhard von Chios, Gennadios Scholarios, und die 'Collegae' Thomas Pyropulos und Johannes Basilikos vor, während und nach der Eroberung von Konstantinopel durch die Türken," *Βυζαντινά* 21 (2000), 227–36

"The Notaras family and its Italian connections," *DOP* 49 (1995), 59–72

"Notes on the economic establishment and social order of the late Byzantine *kephalai*," *BF* 19 (1993), 139–43

"Personengeschichte, Familiengeschichte, Sozialgeschichte: Die Notaras im späten Byzanz," in *Oriente e Occidente tra Medioevo ed Età Moderna. Studi in onore di Geo Pistarino a cura di Laura Balletto*, vol. II (Genoa, 1997), pp. 787–812

Die Schlacht bei Ankara und das Schicksal von Byzanz; Studien zur spätbyzantinischen Geschichte zwischen 1402 und 1422 (Weimar, 1981)

"Some merchant families in Constantinople before, during and after the fall of the city 1453," *Balkan Studies* 38/2 (1997), 219–38

"Sozialschichten und Geisteshaltungen," *JÖB* 31 (1981), 189–212 (= XVI. internationaler Byzantinistenkongress, Akten, vol. 1/2)

"Tuchproduktion und Tuchproduzenten in Thessalonike und in anderen Städten und Regionen des späten Byzanz," *Βυζαντιακά* 9 (1989), 47–87

"Von der Diplomatie des Überflusses zur Diplomatie des Mangels. Byzantinische Diplomaten auf der Suche nach westlicher Hilfe gegen die Türken am Vorabend des Falls von Konstantinopel," in *Gesandtschafts- und Botenwesen im spätmittelalterlichen Europa*, ed. R. C. Schwinges and K. Wriedt (Ostfildern, 2003), pp. 87–133

"Zum Anteil der Byzantiner an der Bergbauentwicklung und an den Berg-bauerträgen Südosteuropas im 14. und 15. Jahrhundert," *BZ* 84–5 (1991–2), 49–71

"Zum Charakter des byzantinischen Schwarzmeerhandels im 13. bis 15. Jahrhundert," *Wissenschaftliche Zeitschrift der Karl-Marx-Universität Leipzig, Gesellschafts- und sprachwiss. Reihe* 19/3 (1970), 447–58

Matschke, K.-P. and Tinnefeld, F. *Die Gesellschaft im späten Byzanz: Gruppen, Strukturen und Lebensformen* (Cologne, Weimar, and Vienna, 2001)

Ménage, V. L. "The beginnings of Ottoman historiography," in *Historians of the Middle East*, ed. B. Lewis and P. M. Holt (London, 1962), pp. 168–79

"The Menāqib of Yakhshī Faqīh," *Bulletin of the School of Oriental and African Studies* 26 (1963), 50–4

Neshrī's History of the Ottomans: The Sources and Development of the Text (London, 1964)

Mertzios, K. D. Μνημεῖα μακεδονικῆς ἱστορίας (Thessalonike, 1947)

Meyendorff, J. "Projets de concile oecuménique en 1367: un dialogue inédit entre Jean Cantacuzène et le légat Paul," *DOP* 14 (1960), 147–77 (reprinted in J. Meyendorff, *Byzantine Hesychasm: Historical, Theological and Social Problems* [London, 1974], Study XI)

Miller, W. *Essays on the Latin Orient* (Cambridge, 1921)

"The historians Doukas and Phrantzes," *Journal of Hellenic Studies* 46 (1926), 63–71

"The last Athenian historian: Laonikos Chalkokondyles," *Journal of Hellenic Studies* 42 (1922), 36–49

The Latins in the Levant. A History of Frankish Greece (1204–1566) (London, 1908; repr. 1964)

Moravcsik, G. *Byzantinoturcica. Die byzantinischen Quellen der Geschichte der Türkvölker*, 2 vols., 2nd edn. (Berlin, 1958; repr. Leiden, 1983)

Morgan, G. "The Venetian claims commission of 1278," *BZ* 69 (1976), 411–38

Morrisson, C. and Cheynet, J.-Cl. "Prices and wages in the Byzantine world," in *The Economic History of Byzantium: From the Seventh through the Fifteenth Century*, vol. II, ed. A. E. Laiou (Washington, DC, 2002), pp. 815–78

Moschonas, N. G. "I Greci a Venezia e la loro posizione religiosa nel XVe secolo," Ὁ Ἐρανιστής 5/27–8 (1967), 105–37

Năsturel, P. Ş. and Beldiceanu, N. "Les églises byzantines et la situation économique de Drama, Serrès et Zichna aux XIVe et XVe siècles," *JÖB* 27 (1978), 269–85

Necipoğlu, N. "The aristocracy in late Byzantine Thessalonike: a case study of the city's *archontes* (late 14th and early 15th centuries)," *DOP* 57 (2003), 133–51

"Byzantine monasteries and monastic property in Thessalonike and Constantinople during the period of Ottoman conquests (late fourteenth and early fifteenth centuries)," *Osmanlı Araştırmaları/The Journal of Ottoman Studies* 15 (1995), 123–35

"Byzantines and Italians in fifteenth-century Constantinople: commercial cooperation and conflict," *New Perspectives on Turkey* 12 (spring 1995), 129–43

"Economic conditions in Constantinople during the siege of Bayezid I (1394–1402)," in *Constantinople and its Hinterland*, ed. C. Mango and G. Dagron (Aldershot, 1995), pp. 157–67

"Ottoman merchants in Constantinople during the first half of the fifteenth century," *BMGS* 16 (1992), 158–69

Nicol, D. M. "The Byzantine family of Dermokaites, circa 940–1453," *BS* 35 (1974), 1–11 (reprinted in D. M. Nicol, *Studies in Late Byzantine History and Prosopography* [London, 1986], Study XIII)

The Byzantine Family of Kantakouzenos (Cantacuzenus) ca. 1100–1460. A Genealogical and Prosopographical Study (Washington, DC, 1968)

"The Byzantine family of Kantakouzenos. Some addenda and corrigenda," *DOP* 27 (1973), 309–15

The Byzantine Lady: Ten Portraits, 1250–1500 (Cambridge, 1994)

Byzantium and Venice: A Study in Diplomatic and Cultural Relations (Cambridge, 1988)

Church and Society in the Last Centuries of Byzantium, 1261–1453 (Cambridge, 1979)

The Immortal Emperor: The Life and Legend of Constantine Palaiologos, Last Emperor of the Romans (Cambridge, 1992)

The Last Centuries of Byzantium, 1261–1453, 2nd rev. edn. (Cambridge, 1993)

The Reluctant Emperor: A Biography of John Cantacuzene, Byzantine Emperor and Monk, c. 1295–1383 (Cambridge, 1996)

Obolensky, D. "A Byzantine grand embassy to Russia in 1400," *BMGS* 4 (1978), 123–32

Oikonomidès, N. "A propos des armées des premiers Paléologues et des compagnies de soldats," *TM* 8 (1981), 353–71 (reprinted in N. Oikonomidès, *Society, Culture and Politics in Byzantium*, ed. E. Zachariadou [Aldershot, 2005], Study XVI)

"Byzantine diplomacy, AD 1204–1453: means and ends," in *Byzantine Diplomacy*, ed. J. Shepard and S. Franklin (Aldershot, 1992), pp. 73–88 (reprinted in *Society, Culture and Politics*, Study XXIII)

"Byzantium between East and West (XIII–XV cent.)," *BF* 13 (1988), 319–32 (reprinted in *Society, Culture and Politics*, Study XVII)

"La décomposition de l'Empire byzantin à la veille de 1204 et les origines de l'Empire de Nicée: à propos de la *Partitio Romaniae*," *XVe Congrès international d'études byzantines. Rapports et co-rapports*, vol. 1.1 (Athens, 1976), pp. 3–28 (reprinted in N. Oikonomidès, *Byzantium from the Ninth Century to the Fourth Crusade. Studies, Texts, Monuments* [Aldershot, 1992], Study XX)

"From soldiers of fortune to gazi warriors: the Tzympe affair," in *Studies in Ottoman History in Honour of Professor V. L. Ménage*, ed. C. Heywood and C. Imber (Istanbul, 1994), pp. 239–47 (reprinted in *Society, Culture and Politics*, Study XX)

"Le haradj dans l'Empire byzantin du XVe siècle," *Actes du Ier Congrès International des Études Balkaniques et Sud-Est Européennes*, vol. III (Sofia, 1969), pp. 681–8 (reprinted in N. Oikonomidès, *Documents et études sur les institutions de Byzance (VIIe–XVe s.)* [London, 1976], Study XIX)

Hommes d'affaires grecs et latins à Constantinople (XIIIe–XVe siècles) (Montreal and Paris, 1979)

"Monastères et moines lors de la conquête ottomane," *SüdostF* 35 (1976), 1–10

"Ottoman influence on late Byzantine fiscal practice," *SüdostF* 45 (1986), 1–24

"Pour une typologie des villes 'séparées' sous les Paléologues," in *Geschichte und Kultur der Palaiologenzeit*, ed. W. Seibt (Vienna, 1996), pp. 169–75 (reprinted in *Society, Culture and Politics*, Study XXI)

"The properties of the Deblitzenoi in the fourteenth and fifteenth centuries," in *Charanis Studies; Essays in Honor of Peter Charanis*, ed. A. E. Laiou-Thomadakis (New Brunswick, NJ, 1980), pp. 176–98

Olgiati, G. "Notes on the participation of the Genoese in the defence of Constantinople," *Macedonian Studies*, n.s. 6/2 (1989), 48–58

Origone, S. "Marriage connections between Byzantium and the West in the age of the Palaiologoi," in *Intercultural Contacts in the Medieval Mediterranean: Studies in Honour of David Jacoby*, ed. B. Arbel (London, 1996), pp. 226–41

Ostrogorski, G. "Byzance, état tributaire de l'Empire turc," *ZRVI* 5 (1958), 49–58

Ostrogorskij, G. *Pour l'histoire de la féodalité byzantine* (Brussels, 1954)

"La prise de Serrès par les Turcs," *B* 35 (1965), 302–19

Pall, F. "Encore une fois sur le voyage diplomatique de Jean V Paléologue en 1365–66," *RESEE* 9 (1971), 535–40

Panaite, V. *The Ottoman Law of War and Peace. The Ottoman Empire and Tribute Payers* (Boulder, 2000)

Papadakis, A. "Gennadius II and Mehmed the Conqueror," *B* 42 (1972), 88–106

Papadopulos, A. Th. *Versuch einer Genealogie der Palaiologen, 1259–1453* (Munich, 1938; repr. Amsterdam, 1962)

Papazotos, Th. "The identification of the Church of 'Profitis Elias' in Thessaloniki," *DOP* 45 (1991), 121–7

Patlagean, E. "L'immunité des Thessaloniciens," in *ΕΥΨΥΧΙΑ. Mélanges offerts à Hélène Ahrweiler*, 2 vols. (Paris, 1998), vol. II, pp. 591–601

Pertusi, A. "The Anconitan colony in Constantinople and the report of its consul, Benvenuto, on the fall of the city," in *Charanis Studies; Essays in Honor of Peter Charanis*, ed. A. E. Laiou-Thomadakis (New Brunswick, NJ, 1980), pp. 199–218

Fine di Bisanzio e fine del mondo. Significato e ruolo storico delle profezie sulla caduta di Costantinopoli in oriente e in occidente, ed. R. Morini (Rome, 1988)

Pertusi, A. (ed.) *Venezia e il Levante fino al secolo XV*, 2 vols. (Florence, 1973–4)

Peschlow, U. "Die befestigte Residenz von Mermerkule. Beobachtungen an einem spätbyzantinischen Bau im Verteidigungssystem von Konstantinopel," *JÖB* 51 (2001), 385–403

"Mermerkule – Ein spätbyzantinischer Palast in Konstantinopel," in *Studien zur byzantinischen Kunstgeschichte. Festschrift für Horst Hallensleben zum 65.*

Geburtstag, ed. B. Borkopp, B. Schellewald, and L. Theis (Amsterdam, 1995), pp. 93–7

Philippides, M. "Some prosopographical considerations in Nestor-Iskander's text," *Macedonian Studies* 6 (1989), 35–49

Philippidis-Braat, A. "La captivité de Palamas chez les Turcs: dossier et commentaire," *TM* 7 (1979), 109–221

Pistarino, G. "The Genoese in Pera – Turkish Galata," *Mediterranean Historical Review* 1 (1986), 63–85

Raby, J. "Mehmed the Conqueror's Greek scriptorium," *DOP* 37 (1983), 15–35

Rakintzakis, G. E. "Orthodox–Muslim mixed marriages, ca. 1297–1453," unpublished MA thesis, University of Birmingham (1975)

Rautman, M. L. "Ignatius of Smolensk and the late Byzantine monasteries of Thessaloniki," *REB* 49 (1991), 143–69

Reinert, S. W. "From Niš to Kosovo Polje. Reflections on Murād I's final years," in *The Ottoman Emirate (1300–1389)*, ed. E. Zachariadou (Rethymnon, 1993), pp. 169–211

"Manuel II Palaeologos and his müderris," in *The Twilight of Byzantium. Aspects of Cultural and Religious History in the Late Byzantine Empire*, ed. S. Ćurčić and D. Mouriki (Princeton, 1991), pp. 39–51

"The Muslim presence in Constantinople, 9th–15th centuries: some preliminary observations," in *Studies on the Internal Diaspora of the Byzantine Empire*, ed. H. Ahrweiler and A. E. Laiou (Washington, DC, 1998), pp. 125–50

"The Palaiologoi, Yıldırım Bāyezīd and Constantinople: June 1389–March 1391" in *TO EΛΛHNIKON. Studies in Honor of Speros Vryonis, Jr.*, vol. 1, ed. J. S. Langdon, S. W. Reinert, J. S. Allen, and C. P. Ioannides (New Rochelle, 1993), pp. 289–365

Reinsch, D. R. "Lieber den Turban als was? Bemerkungen zum Dictum des Lukas Notaras," in *ΦΙΛΕΛΛΗΝ. Studies in Honour of Robert Browning*, ed. C. N. Constantinides, N. M. Panagiotakes, E. Jeffreys, and A. D. Angelou (Venice, 1996), pp. 377–89

Roccatagliata, A. "Con un notaio genovese tra Pera e Chio nel 1453–1454," *RESEE* 17 (1979), 219–39

Runciman, S. *The Fall of Constantinople 1453* (Cambridge, 1965)

The Great Church in Captivity. A Study of the Patriarchate of Constantinople from the Eve of the Turkish Conquest to the Greek War of Independence (Cambridge, 1968)

Mistra. Byzantine Capital of the Peloponnese (London, 1980)

Sahillioğlu, H. "Bir mültezim zimem defterine göre XV. yüzyıl sonunda Osmanlı darphane mukataaları," *İstanbul Üniversitesi İktisat Fakültesi Mecmuası* 23 (1962–3), 145–218

Schilbach, E. *Byzantinische Metrologie* (Munich, 1970)

Schirò, G. "Manuele II Paleologo incorona Carlo Tocco Despota di Gianina," *B* 29–30 (1959–60), 209–30

Schneider, A. M. "Die Bevölkerung Konstantinopels im XV. Jahrhundert," *Nachrichten der Akademie der Wissenschaften in Göttingen, Philologisch-historische Klasse* 9 (1949), 233–44

Schreiner, P. "Bizantini e Genovesi a Caffa. Osservazioni a proposito di un documento latino in un manoscritto greco," *Mitteilungen des bulgarischen Forschungsinstitutes in Österreich* 2/6 (1984), 96–100

"I diritti della città di Malvasia nell'epoca tardobizantina," *Miscellanea di studi storici*, vol. ii (Genoa, 1983), 89–98

"Παρατηρήσεις διὰ τὰ προνόμια τῆς Μονεμβασίας," *Πρακτικὰ τοῦ Β' Διεθνοῦς Συνεδρίου Πελοποννησιακῶν Σπουδῶν*, vol. i (Athens, 1981–2), 160–6

"Venezianer und Genuesen während der ersten Hälfte des 15. Jahrhunderts in Konstantinopel (1432–1434)," *StVen* 12 (1970), 357–68

"Zur Geschichte Philadelpheias im 14. Jahrhundert (1293–1390)," *OCP* 35 (1969), 375–431

Seibt, W. (ed.) *Geschichte und Kultur der Palaiologenzeit. Referate des Internationalen Symposions zu Ehren von Herbert Hunger (Wien, 30. November bis 3. Dezember 1994)* (Vienna, 1996)

Setton, K. M. *Catalan Domination of Athens, 1311–1388* (Cambridge, MA, 1948; rev. edn., London, 1975)

"The Latins in Greece and the Aegean from the Fourth Crusade to the end of the Middle Ages," in *The Cambridge Medieval History*, vol. iv/1 (Cambridge, 1966), pp. 388–430

The Papacy and the Levant (1204–1571), vol. i: *The Thirteenth and Fourteenth Centuries*; vol. ii: *The Fifteenth Century* (Philadelphia, 1976–8)

Ševčenko, I. "The decline of Byzantium seen through the eyes of its intellectuals," *DOP* 15 (1961), 169–86 (reprinted in I. Ševčenko, *Society and Intellectual Life in Late Byzantium* [London, 1981], Study II)

"Intellectual repercussions of the Council of Florence," *Church History* 24/4 (1955), 291–323

Sideras, A. "Neue Quellen zum Leben des Despotes Andronikos Palaiologos," *BZ* 80/1 (1987), 3–15

Silberschmidt, M. *Das orientalische Problem zur Zeit der Entstehung des türkischen Reiches nach venezianischen Quellen. Ein Beitrag zur Geschichte der Beziehungen Venedigs zu Sultan Bajezid I., zu Byzanz, Ungarn und Genua und zum Reiche von Kiptschak (1381–1400)* (Leipzig and Berlin, 1923; repr. 1972)

Šitikov, M. M. "Konstantinopolj i Venetsianskaja torgovlja v pervoij polovine XV v. po dannym knigi sčetov Džakomo Badoera, Delovye krugi Konstantinopolja," *VV* 30 (1969), 48–62

Smyrlis, K. *La fortune des grands monastères byzantins (fin du Xe-milieu du XIVe siècle)* (Paris, 2006)

Spremić, M. "Harač soluna u XV veku," *ZRVI* 10 (1967), 187–95 (Greek trans., with supplementary materials, I. A. Papadrianos, "Ὁ κεφαλικὸς φόρος τῆς Θεσσαλονίκης κατὰ τὸν 15ον αἰῶνα," *Μακεδονικά* 9 [1969], 33–47)

"La Serbie entre les Turcs, les Grecs, et les Latins au XVe siècle," *BF* 11 (1987), 433–43

Stavrides, Th. *The Sultan of Vezirs. The Life and Times of the Ottoman Grand Vezir Mahmud Pasha Angelović (1453–1474)* (Leiden, Boston, and Cologne, 2001)

Taeschner, F. "Georgios Gemistos Plethon. Ein Beitrag zur Frage der Übertragung von islamischem Geistesgut nach dem Abendlande," *Der Islam* 18 (1929), 236–43

"Plethon. Ein Vermittler zwischen Morgenland und Abendland," *Byzantinisch-neugriechische Jahrbücher* 8 (1929–30), 110–13

Tafrali, O. *Thessalonique au quatorzième siècle* (Paris, 1913; repr. Thessalonike, 1993)

Taparel, H. "Notes sur quelques réfugiés byzantins en Bourgogne après la chute de Constantinople," *Balkan Studies* 28/1 (1987), 51–8

Thiriet, F. "Les Chroniques vénitiennes de la Marcienne et leur importance pour l'histoire de la Romanie gréco-vénitienne," *Mélanges d'Archéologie et d'Histoire* 66 (1954), 241–92 (reprinted in F. Thiriet, *Études sur la Romanie gréco-vénitienne (Xe–XVe siècles)* [London, 1977], Study III)

La Romanie vénitienne au Moyen Age. Le développement et l'exploitation du domaine colonial vénitien (XIIe–XVe siècles), 2nd edn. (Paris, 1975)

"Venise et l'occupation de Ténédos au XIVe siècle," *Mélanges d'Archéologie et d'Histoire* 65 (1953), 219–45 (reprinted in *Études*, Study II)

"Les Vénitiens à Thessalonique dans la première moitié du XIVe siècle," *B* 22 (1953), 323–32 (reprinted in *Études*, Study I)

Tinnefeld, F. "Freundschaft und ΠΑΙΔΕΙΑ: Die Korrespondenz des Demetrios Kydones mit Rhadenos (1375–1387/8)," *B* 55 (1985), 210–44

"Kaiser Ioannes V. Palaiologos und der Gouverneur von Phokaia 1356–1358: ein Beispiel für den Verfall der byzantinischen Zentralgewalt um die Mitte des 14. Jahrhunderts," *Rivista di studi bizantini e slavi* 1 (1981), 259–82

Topping, P. "Co-existence of Greeks and Latins in Frankish Morea and Venetian Crete," *XVe Congrès international d'études byzantines. Rapports et co-rapports*, vol. 1.3 (Athens, 1976) (reprinted in P. Topping, *Studies on Latin Greece, AD 1205–1715* [London, 1977], Study XI)

Trapp, E. "Beiträge zur Genealogie der Asanen in Byzanz," *JÖB* 25 (1976), 163–77

Trapp, E. *et al.* (eds.) *Prosopographisches Lexikon der Palaiologenzeit* (Vienna, 1976–94)

Tsaras, J. "La fin d'Andronic Paléologue dernier Despote de Thessalonique," *RESEE* 3 (1965), 419–32

Turner, C. J. G. "The career of George-Gennadius Scholarius," *B* 39 (1969), 420–55

"George Gennadius Scholarius and the Union of Florence," *The Journal of Theological Studies* 18 (1967), 83–103

"Pages from late Byzantine philosophy of history," *BZ* 57 (1964), 346–73

Uzunçarşılı, İ. H. *Çandarlı Vezir Ailesi* (Ankara, 1974)

Vacalopoulos, A. E. "The flight of the inhabitants of Greece to the Aegean islands, Crete, and Mane, during the Turkish invasions (fourteenth and fifteenth centuries)," in *Charanis Studies. Essays in Honor of Peter Charanis*, ed. A. E. Laiou-Thomadakis (New Brunswick, NJ, 1980), pp. 272–83

A History of Thessaloniki, trans. T. F. Carney (Thessaloniki, 1972)

"Les limites de l'empire byzantin depuis la fin du XIVe siècle jusqu'à sa chute (1453)," *BZ* 55 (1962), 56–65

Origins of the Greek Nation. The Byzantine Period, 1204–1461, trans. I. Moles, revised by the author (New Brunswick, NJ, 1970)

"Quelques problèmes relatifs à la résistance de Manuel II Paléologue contre les Turcs Ottomans dans la Macédoine grecque (1383–1391)," *Actes du Ier Congrès International des Études Balkaniques et Sud-Est Européennes*, vol. III (Sofia, 1969), pp. 351–5

"Συμβολὴ στὴν ἱστορία τῆς Θεσσαλονίκης ἐπὶ Βενετοκρατίας (1423–1430)," in *Τόμος Κωνσταντίνου Ἀρμενοπούλου* (Thessalonike, 1952), pp. 127–49

"Zur Frage der zweiten Einnahme Thessalonikis durch die Türken, 1391–1394," *BZ* 61 (1968), 285–90

Van Dieten, J.-L. "Der Streit in Byzanz um die Rezeption der Unio Florentina," *Ostkirchliche Studien* 39 (1990), 160–80

Vasiliev, A. "Pero Tafur, a Spanish traveler of the fifteenth century and his visit to Constantinople, Trebizond, and Italy," *B* 7 (1932), 75–122

Vatin, N. "Tursun Beg assista-t-il au siège de Constantinople en 1453 ?," *WZKM* 91 (2001), 317–29

Verpeaux, J. "Les oikeioi. Notes d'histoire institutionnelle et sociale," *REB* 23 (1965), 89–99

Vranoussi, E. L. "'Ενας ἀνέκδοτος ἀργυρόβουλλος ὁρισμὸς τοῦ Δημητρίου Παλαιολόγου καὶ τὰ προβλήματα του," *Βυζαντινά* 10 (1980), 347–59

"Notes sur quelques institutions du Péloponnèse byzantin," *Études Balkaniques* 14/4 (1978), 81–8

Vryonis, Sp., Jr. "Byzantine attitudes toward Islam during the Late Middle Ages," *Greek, Roman and Byzantine Studies* 12 (1971), 263–86 (reprinted in *Byzantina kai Metabyzantina*, vol. II: *Studies on Byzantium, Seljuks, and Ottomans. Reprinted Studies by Speros Vryonis, Jr.* [Malibu, 1981], Study VIII)

"Byzantine cultural self-consciousness in the fifteenth century," in *The Twilight of Byzantium. Aspects of Cultural and Religious History in the Late Byzantine Empire*, ed. S. Ćurčić and D. Mouriki (Princeton, 1991), pp. 5–14

"The Byzantine Patriarchate and Turkish Islam," *BS* 57 (1996), 69–111

"Crises and anxieties in fifteenth century Byzantium: the reassertion of old and the emergence of new cultural forms," in *Islamic and Middle Eastern Societies. A Festschrift in Honor of Professor Wadie Jwaideh*, ed. R. Olson (Brattleboro, 1987), pp. 100–26

"Decisions of the Patriarchal Synod in Constantinople as a source for Ottoman religious policy in the Balkans prior to 1402," *ZRVI* 19 (1980), 283–97 (reprinted in *Byzantina kai Metabyzantina*, vol. II, Study XVI)

The Decline of Medieval Hellenism in Asia Minor and the Process of Islamization from the Eleventh through the Fifteenth Century (Berkeley and Los Angeles, 1971)

"The 'freedom of expression' in fifteenth century Byzantium," in *La notion de liberté au Moyen Âge. Islam, Byzance, Occident*, ed. G. Makdisi, D. Sourdel, and J. Sourdel-Thomine (Paris, 1985), pp. 261–73

"Isidore Glabas and the Turkish *devshirme*," *Speculum* 31/3 (1956), 433–43

"The Ottoman conquest of Thessaloniki in 1430," in *Continuity and Change in Late Byzantine and Early Ottoman Society*, ed. A. Bryer and H. Lowry (Birmingham and Washington, DC, 1986), pp. 281–321

"Religious change and continuity in the Balkans and Anatolia from the fourteenth through the sixteenth century," in *Islam and Cultural Change in the Middle Ages; Fourth Giorgio Levi Della Vida Biennial Conference*, ed. Sp. Vryonis, Jr. (Wiesbaden, 1975), pp. 127–40 (reprinted in *Byzantina kai Metabyzantina*, vol. II, Study XI)

"Religious changes and patterns in the Balkans, 14th–16th centuries," in *Aspects of the Balkans*, ed. H. Birnbaum and Sp. Vryonis, Jr. (The Hague and Paris, 1972), pp. 151–76 (reprinted in *Byzantina kai Metabyzantina*, vol. II, Study X)

Weiss, G. *Joannes Kantakuzenos – Aristokrat, Staatsmann, Kaiser und Mönch – in der Gesellschaftsentwicklung von Byzanz im 14. Jahrhundert* (Wiesbaden, 1969)

Werner, E. "Johannes Kantakuzenos, Umur Paša und Orchan," *BS* 26 (1965), 255–76

Sultan Mehmed der Eroberer und die Epochenwende im 15. Jahrhundert (Berlin, 1982)

Wifstrand, A. *Laonikos Chalkokondyles, der letzte Athener. Ein Vortrag* (Lund, 1972)

Wirth, P. "Die Haltung Kaiser Johannes V. bei den Verhandlungen mit König Ludwig von Ungarn zu Buda im Jahre 1366," *BZ* 56 (1963), 271–2

"Zum Geschichtsbild Kaiser Johannes VII. Palaiologos," *B* 35 (1965), 592–600

Wittek, P. "De la défaite d'Ankara à la prise de Constantinople (un demi-siècle d'histoire ottomane)," *Revue des Études Islamiques* 12 (1938), 1–34 (reprinted in P. Wittek, *La formation de l'Empire ottoman* [London, 1982], Study II)

The Rise of the Ottoman Empire (London, 1938)

Woodhouse, C. M. *George Gemistos Plethon: The Last of the Hellenes* (Oxford, 1986)

Zachariadou, E. A. "The Catalans of Athens and the beginning of the Turkish expansion in the Aegean area," *Studi medievali*, ser. 3, 21 (1980), 821–38 (reprinted in E. A. Zachariadou, *Romania and the Turks (c.1300 – c.1500)* [London, 1985], Study V)

"Ἐφήμερες ἀπόπειρες γιὰ αὐτοδιοίκηση στὶς Ἑλληνικὲς πόλεις κατὰ τὸν ΙΔ' καὶ ΙΕ' αἰῶνα," *Ἀριάδνη* 5 (1989), 345–51

"Histoires et légendes des premiers ottomans," *Turcica* 27 (1995), 45–89

"John VII (alias Andronicus) Palaeologus," *DOP* 31 (1977), 339–42 (reprinted in *Romania and the Turks*, Study X)

"Τὰ λόγια κι ο θάνατος του Λουκά Νοταρά," in *Ροδωνιά. Τιμή στον Μ. Ι. Μανούσακα* (Rethymnon, 1994), vol. I, pp. 136–46

"More on the Turkish methods of conquest," *Eighth Annual Byzantine Studies Conference: Abstracts of Papers* (Chicago, 1982), p. 20

"The neomartyr's message," Δελτίο Κέντρου μικρασιατικῶν σπουδῶν 8 (Athens, 1990–1), 51–63

"Prix et marchés des céréales en Romanie (1343–1405)," *Nuova rivista storica* 61 (1977), 291–305 (reprinted in *Romania and the Turks*, Study IX)

"Religious dialogue between Byzantines and Turks during the Ottoman expansion," in *Religionsgespräche im Mittelalter*, ed. B. Lewis and F. Niewöhner (Wiesbaden, 1992), pp. 289–304

"Süleyman Çelebi in Rumili and the Ottoman chronicles," *Der Islam* 60/2 (1983), 268–96

Trade and Crusade; Venetian Crete and the Emirates of Menteshe and Aydın (1300–1415) (Venice, 1983)

Zakythinos, D. A. "L'attitude de Venise face au déclin et à la chute de Constantinople," in *Venezia, centro di mediazione tra Oriente e Occidente (secoli XV–XVI). Aspetti e problemi*, ed. H.-G. Beck, M. Manoussacas, and A. Pertusi, vol. 1 (Florence, 1977), pp. 61–75

Crise monétaire et crise économique à Byzance du XIIIe au XVe siècle (Athens, 1948)

Le Despotat grec de Morée, 2 vols., rev. edn. by C. Maltezou (London, 1975)

La Grèce et les Balkans (Athens, 1947)

"La prise de Constantinople, tournant dans la politique et l'économie européennes," in *1453–1953. Le cinq-centième anniversaire de la prise de Constantinople* (Athens, 1953), pp. 85–102

Zoras, G. Th. "Orientations idéologiques et politiques avant et après la chute de Constantinople," in *1453–1953. Le cinq-centième anniversaire de la prise de Constantinople* (Athens, 1953), pp. 103–23

Index

Sophianos family, 167, 192, 263–5, 283, App. III
  archon in the Morea (I), 248, 264
  archon in the Morea (II), 283, 284
  banker, 157
  John, banker, 202, App. III
  Nicholas, 175, 197, App. III, App. IV
Spartenos family, 79
  Theodore Doukas, 79, 80n99, App. I
Sphrantzes
  archon in the Morea, 283
  George, historian, 8–9, 141, 222, 246, 252, 265, 270–1, 278–80, 282
  John (son of George, historian), 9
Spitali, 252
Spyridon family, 158, 176–7
Stoudios, fortress, 220
Strymon, 36n48, 88, 89
Süleyman Çelebi, son of Bayezid I, 33–5, 100
Surgat, 204
Symbolon (Cembalo), 158
Symeon of Thessalonike, 13–14, 42–4, 47–50, 52–3, 56, 62, 69–73, 76–9, 83, 87–8, 103–4, 106, 110
Synadene
  Eirene, 168
  Theodora, 176
Synadenos, family, 192, App. III; *see also* Astras, Michael (Synadenos)
Syria, 195
Syropoulos, Sylvester, 14, 279

Tafur, Pero, 15, 195–6
*tahrir defter*s, 17n55, 89, 99, 101n57
Talapas, Demetrios, *kastrophylax*, 80, App. I
Tana, 75, 215
Tarchaneiotes family, 79, 82, App. I, App. II
  Jacob, 165
Taroneites, Manuel, 134
Tatars, 205–6
tavernkeepers, 156, 159, 210
taxes, 26, 64, 98–9, 107–8, 110, 128, 139, 178, 273, 276
  commercial, 68, 223
  evasion of, 42, 253–4, 262, 276
  for defense purposes, 72, 178, 225, 269, 270; *see also angariae*; *phloriatikon*
  Plethon on, 274
Tedaldi, Jacopo, 15
Tenedos, 121, 122, 125–6, 244
Terkova, village (Morea), 266
Thalassene, Kale, 60
Thamar, daughter of George Sphrantzes, historian, 9
Thasos, 10

Theodore I Palaiologos, despot of the Morea, 13, 31, 46, 122, 236–40, 242–5, 247–51, 253–60, 263, 267, 286
Theodore II Palaiologos, despot of the Morea, 14, 252, 259, 260, 263, 264, 268–9, 271, 272, 274, 275
Theodotos, superior of Pantokrator/Blatadon monastery, 96–7
Thermesion, 257
Thessalonike, 11, 13, 19, 22, 24, 33, 117, 160–2, 179, 186, 198, 202, 227, 231, 232, 285–8
  and Bayezid I, 30, 86–7, 89–90, 248
  and Manuel II, 7, 13, 32, 39, 44–7, 130, 238
  and Mehmed I, 56, 73
  and Musa Çelebi, 47, 49, 64, 72–3
  Asomatoi quarter, 62
  Genoese consul in, 68
  Jewish community in, 108
  Ottoman kadi in, 101–2, 104
  privileges of, 44–5
  under Ottoman rule: first Ottoman domination, 25, 26, 84–102, 113, 239, 249; Murad II's siege and capture, 11, 35, 52, 205
  under Venetian rule, 49–51, 82–3, 103–14, 174, 218
  Venetian consulate in, 66–7
  see also churches; monasteries
Thessaly, 25, 31, 37, 39, 90, 249, 251, 256, 278
Thomas Palaiologos, despot in the Morea, 233–4, 254, 270, 277–83
Thrace, 19, 21, 25, 27, 28, 41, 130, 131, 202, 240, 242, 247
timar, 27, 89–90, 100, 102, 248
Timur (Tamerlane), 32, 33, 143, 181, 182, 258
Tocco
  Carlo I, count of Cephalonia, 257
  Leonardo II, count of Cephalonia, 267
treaties
  between Theodore I and Venice (1394), 251, 257
  Byzantine–Genoese (1382), 30, 130
  Byzantine–Ottoman (*c.* 1373), 29–30, 119, 120
  Byzantine–Ottoman (1403), 33–5, 39, 98, 100–1
  Byzantine–Ottoman (1424), 35–6, 190, 199, 208–9
  Byzantine–Venetian (1406), 196, 212
  Byzantine–Venetian (1418 and 1423), 212
  Venetian–Navarrese (1382 and 1387), 238
  Venetian–Ottoman (1426 and 1427), 102
Trebizond, 8, 38n55, 93n29, 150n7
tribute, *see harac*
Turahan Beg, Ottoman commander, 272, 273, 278–9

Made in the USA
Lexington, KY
12 August 2017